SWEET & MAXWELL'S PROPERTY STATUTES

AUSTRALIA
The Law Book Company Ltd.
Sydney : Melbourne : Brisbane

CANADA AND U.S.A.
The Carswell Company Ltd.
Agincourt, Ontario

INDIA
N. M. Tripathi Ltd.
Bombay
and
Eastern Law House Private Ltd.
Calcutta and Delhi
M.P.P. House
Bangalore

ISRAEL
Steimatzky's Agency Ltd.
Jerusalem : Tel Aviv : Haifa

MALAYSIA : SINGAPORE : BRUNEI
Malayan Law Journal (Pte.) Ltd.
Singapore

NEW ZEALAND
Sweet & Maxwell (N.Z.) Ltd.
Auckland

PAKISTAN
Pakistan Law House
Karachi

SWEET & MAXWELL'S

PROPERTY STATUTES

EDITED BY
SWEET & MAXWELL'S
LEGAL EDITORIAL STAFF

and

ROBERT SPICER, M.A., Diploma in Legal Studies

Barrister

ADVISORY EDITOR

J. H. C. MORRIS
Q.C., D.C.L., F.B.A.

FOURTH EDITION

LONDON
SWEET & MAXWELL
1982

First Edition	1968
Second Edition	1972
Second Impression	1974
Third Impression	1975
Third Edition	1977
Second Impression	1979
Fourth Edition	1982

Published by
Sweet & Maxwell Limited of
11 New Fetter Lane, London,
and printed in Great Britain by
Richard Clay (The Chaucer Press) Ltd.,
Bungay, Suffolk

British Library Cataloguing in Publication Data

[Property acts]. Sweet and Maxwell's property
statutes.—4th ed.
1. Property—England
I. Morris, J.H.C.   II. Sweet and Maxwell's
property statutes
344.2064'02632   KD810.A3

ISBN 0-421-28810-8
ISBN 0-421-28820-5 Pbk

©
Sweet & Maxwell Limited
1982

PREFACE

Sweet & Maxwell's Property Statutes—4th Edition

When first published *Sweet & Maxwell's Property Statutes* was the only collection of statutes of its kind designed for students, and the publishers felt it right to interpret "property" fairly widely. With the establishment of *Sweet & Maxwell's Family Law Statutes*, however, it seemed appropriate to try to reduce some of the overlap between the two volumes. In consequence, in this new edition the Matrimonial Homes Act 1967, the Matrimonial Proceedings and Property Act 1970 and the Inheritance (Provision for Family and Dependants) Act 1975 have been omitted, since they do not belong to the basic law of property, but are designed to empower the court to adjust property rights as between husband and wife and other members of the family.

The book is divided into two parts. The first covers general property law, and as in previous editions the Settled Land Act, the Trustee Act, the Law of Property Act and the Administration of Estates Act of 1925 feature prominently. The general requirements relating to land charges contained in the Land Charges Act 1972 are of course included, but the Local Land Charges Act 1975 is omitted as being too detailed for students. Major new legislation includes the relevant sections of the Limitation Act 1980 and the Supreme Court Act 1981.

In the second part of the book, dealing with land registration, the Land Registration Rules 1925 are printed as amended by the Land Registration Rules 1978, and new material includes the Land Registration (Official Searches) Rules 1981.

Statutes are reproduced as amended by subsequent legislation. On occasion a purely amending measure has been incorporated into the original Act rather than printed separately. Footnotes are carefully cross-referenced to assist the student.

The publishers acknowledge with gratitude the advice and help of Dr. J. H. C. Morris in the preparation of this edition. As with previous editions, his guidance as to content and sharp eye for discrepancies at the proof stage were invaluable. To him we extend our sincere thanks.

We are grateful to Robert Spicer for undertaking the editorial compilation of this new edition and for the preparation of the index. Any errors are, however, the sole responsibility of the publishers.

We trust that, like its predecessors, the fourth edition of Sweet & Maxwell's Property Statutes will prove to be a redoubtable ally of all those involved in this area of the law.

CONTENTS

Part A

GENERAL

Prescription Act 1832[1]

(2 & 3 WILL. 4, C. 71)

An Act for shortening the time of prescription in certain cases.

[1st August 1832]

Claims to right of common and other profits à prendre (except titles, etc.) not to be defeated after thirty years' enjoyment by merely showing the commencement of the right. After sixty years' enjoyment the right to be absolute, unless shown to be had by consent or agreement

1.[2] No claim which may be lawfully made at the common law, by custom, prescription, or grant, to any right of common or other profit or benefit to be taken and enjoyed from or upon any land of our sovereign Lord the King, [. . .][3] or any land being parcel of the Duchy of Lancaster or of the Duchy of Cornwall, or of any ecclesiastical or lay person, or body corporate, except such matters and things as are herein specially provided for, and except tithes, rent, and services, shall, where such right, profit, or benefit shall have been actually taken and enjoyed by any person claiming right thereto without interruption for the full period of thirty years, be defeated or destroyed by shewing only that such right, profit, or benefit was first taken or enjoyed at any time prior to such period of thirty years, but nevertheless such claim may be defeated in any other way by which the same is now liable to be defeated; and when such right, profit, or benefit shall have been so taken and enjoyed as aforesaid for the full period of sixty years, the right thereto shall be deemed absolute and indefeasible, unless it shall appear that the same was taken and enjoyed by some consent or agreement expressly made or given for that purpose by deed or writing.

In claims of rights of way or other easements the periods to be twenty years and forty years

2. No claim which may be lawfully made at the common law, by custom, prescription, or grant, to any way or other easement, or to any watercourse, or the use of any water, to be enjoyed or derived upon, over, or from any land or water of our said Lord the King, [. . .][4] or being parcel of the Duchy of Lancaster or of the Duchy of Cornwall, or being the property of any ecclesiastical or lay person, or body corporate, when such way or other matter as herein last before mentioned shall have been actually enjoyed by any person claiming right thereto without interruption for the full period of twenty years, shall be defeated or destroyed by shewing only that such way or other matter was first enjoyed at any time

---

[1] Extended to cover Northern Ireland by the Prescription (Ireland) Act 1858 (21 & 22 Vict. c. 42); saved by the Law of Property Act 1925 (15 & 16 Geo. 5, c. 20), s. 12; extended by the Commons Registration Act 1965 (c. 64), s. 16(1).

[2] Certain interruptions in prescriptive claims to rights of common are disregarded: Commons Registration Act 1965, s. 16(1).

[3] Words repealed by S.L.R. Act 1890 (53 & 54 Vict. c. 33).

[4] Words repealed by S.L.R. Act 1890.

prior to such period of twenty years, but nevertheless such claim may be defeated in any other way by which the same is now liable to be defeated; and where such way or other matter as herein last before mentioned shall have been so enjoyed as aforesaid for the full period of forty years, the right thereto shall be deemed absolute and indefeasible, unless it shall appear that the same was enjoyed by some consent or agreement expressly given or made for that purpose by deed or writing.

Right to the use of light enjoyed for twenty years, indefeasible, unless shown to have been by consent

3.[5] When the access and use of light to and for any dwelling house, workshop, or other building shall have been actually enjoyed therewith for the full period of twenty years[6] without interruption, the right thereto shall be deemed absolute and indefeasible, any local usage or custom to the contrary notwithstanding, unless it shall appear that the same was enjoyed by some consent or agreement expressly made or given for that purpose by deed or writing.

The before-mentioned periods to be deemed those next before a suit or action in which the claim is brought in question. What shall constitute an interruption

4.[7] Each of the respective periods of years hereinbefore mentioned shall be deemed and taken to be the period next before some suit or action wherein the claim or matter to which such period may relate shall have been or shall be brought into question, and no act or other matter shall be deemed to be an interruption, within the meaning of this statute, unless the same shall have been or shall be submitted to or acquiesced in for one year after the party interrupted shall have had or shall have notice thereof, and of the person making or authorising the same to be made.

In actions on the case, etc., the claimant may allege his right generally, as at present. In pleas to trespass and other pleadings where party used to allege his claim from time immemorial, enjoyment during the period mentioned in this Act may be alleged; and exceptions, or other matters must be replied specially.

5. In all actions upon the case and other pleadings, wherein the party claiming may now by law allege his right generally, without averring the existence of such right from time immemorial, such general allegation shall still be deemed sufficient, and if the same shall be denied, all any every the matters in this Act mentioned and provided, which shall be applicable to the case, shall be admissible in evidence to sustain or rebut such allegation; and in all pleadings to actions of trespass, and in all other pleadings wherein before the passing of this Act it would have been necessary to allege the right to have existed from time immemorial, it shall be sufficient to allege the enjoyment thereof as of right by the occupiers of the tenement in respect whereof the same is claimed for and during such of the periods mentioned in this Act as may be applicable to the case, and without claiming in the name or right of the owner of the fee, as is now usually done; and if the other party shall intend to rely on any proviso, exception, incapacity, disability, contract, agreement, or other matter hereinbefore mentioned, or on any cause or matter of fact or of law not inconsistent with

---

[5] Explained in the Rights of Light Act 1959 (7 & 8 Eliz. 2, c. 56), s. 4(3).
[6] The Rights of Light Act 1959, s. 1, which temporarily amended the period to twenty-seven years, was repealed by the Statute Law (Repeals) Act 1974 (c. 22), Sched., Pt. IV.
[7] Extended by the Rights of Light Act 1959, s. 3(6), and explained by the Commons Registration Act 1965 (c. 64), s. 16(2).

the simple fact of enjoyment, the same shall be specially alleged and set forth in answer to the allegation of the party claiming, and shall not be received in evidence on any general traverse or denial of such allegation.

No presumption to be allowed in support of a claim in proof of enjoyment for less than the requisite number of years

6. In the several cases mentioned in and provided for by this Act, no presumption shall be allowed or made in favour or support of any claim, upon proof of the exercise or enjoyment of the right or matter claimed for any less period of time or number of years than for such period or number mentioned in this Act as may be applicable to the case and to the nature of the claim.

Proviso where any person capable of resisting a claim is an infant, etc.

7.[8] Provided also, that the time during which any person otherwise capable of resisting any claim to any of the matters before mentioned shall have been or shall be an infant, idiot, non compos mentis, feme covert, or tenant for life, or during which any action or suit shall have been pending, and which shall have been diligently prosecuted, until abated by the death of any party or parties thereto, shall be excluded in the computation of the periods hereinbefore mentioned, except only in cases where the right or claim is hereby declared to be absolute and indefeasible.

Time to be excluded in certain cases in computing the term of forty years appointed by this Act

8. Provided always, that when any land or water upon, over, or from which any such way or other convenient watercourse or use of water shall have been or shall be enjoyed or derived hath been or shall be held under or by virtue of any term of life, or any term of years exceeding three years from the granting thereof, the time of the enjoyment of any such way or other matter as herein last before mentioned, during the continuance of such terms, shall be excluded in the computation of the said period of forty years, in case the claim shall within three years next after the end or sooner determination of such term be resisted by any person entitled to any reversion expectant on the determination thereof.

Extent of Act

9. This Act shall not extend to Scotland [. . .].[9]

10, 11. [*Repealed by the S.L.R. Act* 1874 (37 & 38 *Vict. c.* 35).]

---

[8] This section does not apply to a woman married since the passing of the Married Women's Property Act 1882 (45 & 46 Vict. c. 75); see also the Law Reform (Married Women and Joint Tortfeasors) Act 1935 (25 & 26 Geo. 5, c. 30).
[9] Words repealed by the S.L.R. Act 1874 (37 & 38 Vict. c. 35).

Wills Act 1837[1]

(7 WILL. 4 & 1 VICT. c. 26)

An Act for the amendment of the laws with respect to wills. [3rd July 1837.]

Meaning of certain words in this Act

1. The words and expressions herein-after mentioned, which in their ordinary signification have a more confined or a different meaning, shall in this Act, except where the nature of the provision or the context of the Act shall exclude such construction, be interpreted as follows; (that is to say,) the word "will" shall extend to a testament, and to a codicil, and to an appointment by will or by writing in the nature of a will in exercise of a power, and also to a disposition by will and testament or devise of the custody and tuition of any child [. . .][2] and to any other testamentary disposition; and the words "real estate" shall extend to manors, advowsons, messuages, lands tithes, rents, and hereditaments, [. . .][2] whether corporeal, incorporeal, or personal, and to any undivided share thereof, and to any estate, right, or interest (other than a chattel interest) therein; and the words "personal estate" shall extend to leasehold estates and other chattels real, and also to monies, shares of government and other funds, securities for money (not being real estates), debts, choses in action, rights, credits, goods, and all other property whatsoever which by law devolves upon the executor or administrator, and to any share or interest therein; and every word importing the singular number only shall extend and be applied to several persons or things as well as one person or thing; and every word importing the masculine gender only shall extend and be applied to a female as well as a male.

2. [*Repealed by the Statute Law Revision Act 1874 (37 & 38 Vict. c. 35).*]

All property may be disposed of by will

3. It shall be lawful for every person to devise, bequeath, or dispose of, by his will executed in manner herein-after required, all real estate and all personal estate which he shall be entitled to, either at law or in equity, at the time of his death, and which if not so devised, bequeathed, or disposed of would devolve [. . .][2] upon his executor or administrator; and the power hereby given shall extend [. . .][2] to all contingent, executory, or other future interests in any real or personal estate, whether the testator may or may not be ascertained as the person or one of the persons in whom the same respectively may become vested, and whether he may be entitled thereto under the instrument by which the same respectively were created or under any disposition thereof by deed or will; and also to all rights of entry for conditions broken, and other rights of entry; and also to such of the same estates, interests, and rights respectively, and other real and personal estate, as the testator may be entitled to at the time of his death, notwithstanding that he may become entitled to the same subsequently to the execution of his will.

4–6. [*Repealed by Statute Law (Repeals) Act 1969 (c. 52), Sched.*]

---

[1] For the effect of the Law of Property Act 1922 (12 & 13 Geo. 5, c. 16), see the Law of Property (Amendment) Act 1924 (15 & 16 Geo. 5, c. 5), s. 9, Sched. 9.
[2] Repealed by the Statute Law (Repeals) Act 1969 (c. 52), s. 1, Sched., Pt. III.

No will of a minor valid

7. No will made by any person under the age of [eighteen years][3] shall be valid.

8. [*Repealed by Statute Law (Repeals) Act* 1969 (*c.* 52), *Sched.*]

Every will to be in writing, and signed or acknowledged by the testator in the presence of two witnesses

9.[4] No will shall be valid unless it shall be in writing and executed in manner herein-after mentioned; (that is to say,) it shall be signed at the foot or end thereof by the testator, or by some other person in his presence and by his direction; and such signature shall be made or acknowledged by the testator in the presence of two or more witnesses present at the same time, and such witnesses shall attest and shall subscribe the will in the presence of the testator, but no form of attestation shall be necessary.

Appointments by will to be executed like other wills and to be valid although other required solemnity not observed

10. No appointment made by will, in exercise of any power, shall be valid, unless the same be executed in manner herein-before required; and every will executed in manner herein-before required shall, so far as respects the execution and attestation thereof, be a valid execution of a power of appointment by will, notwithstanding it shall have been expressly required that a will made in exercise of such power should be executed with some additional or other form of execution or solemnity.

Saving as to wills of soldiers and mariners

11.[5] Provided always, that any soldier being in actual military service, or any mariner or seaman being at sea, may dispose of his personal estate as he might have done before the making of this Act.

12. [*Repealed by the Admiralty, etc., Acts Repeal Act* 1865 (28 & 29 *Vict. c.* 112) *s.* 1.]

Publication of will not requisite

13. Every will executed in manner herein-before required shall be valid without any other publication thereof.

Will not void by incompetency of witness

14. If any person who shall attest the execution of a will shall at the time of the execution thereof or at any time afterwards be incompetent to be admitted a witness to prove the execution thereof, such will shall not on that account be invalid.

Gifts to an attesting witness to be void

15.[6] If any person shall attest the execution of any will to whom or to whose wife or husband any beneficial devise, legacy, estate, interest, gift, or appointment, of or affecting any real or personal estate (other than and except charges and directions for the payment of any debt or debts), shall

---

[3] Words substituted by the Family Law Reform Act 1969 (c. 46), s. 3(1) (*a*).
[4] For provisions as to position of signature, see Wills Act Amendment Act 1852, s. 1, *post*, p. 10.
[5] Explained and extended by the Wills (Soldiers and Sailors) Act 1918, *post*, p. 11.
[6] See the Wills Act 1968, *post*, p. 312.

be thereby given or made, such devise, legacy, estate, interest, gift, or appointment shall, so far only as concerns such person attesting the execution of such will, or the wife or husband of such person, or any person claiming under such person or wife or husband, be utterly null and void, and such person so attesting shall be admitted as a witness to prove the execution of such will, or to prove the validity or invalidity thereof, notwithstanding such devise, legacy, estate, interest, gift, or appointment mentioned in such will.

Creditor attesting to be admitted a witness

16. In case by any will any real or personal estate shall be charged with any debt or debts, and any creditor, or the wife or husband of any creditor, whose debt is so charged, shall attest the execution of such will, such creditor notwithstanding such charge shall be admitted a witness to prove the execution of such will, or to prove the validity or invalidity thereof.

Executor shall be admitted a witness

17. No person shall, on account of his being an executor of a will, be incompetent to be admitted a witness to prove the execution of such will, or a witness to prove the validity or invalidity thereof.

Will to be revoked by marriage

18.[7] Every will made by a man or woman shall be revoked by his or her marriage (except a will made in exercise of a power of appointment, when the real or personal estate thereby appointed would not in default of such appointment pass to his or her heir, customary heir, executor, or administrator, or the person entitled as his or her next of kin, under the Statute of Distributions).

No will to be revoked by presumption

19. No will shall be revoked by any presumption of an intention on the ground of an alteration in circumstances.

In what cases wills may be revoked

20. No will or codicil, or any part thereof, shall be revoked otherwise than as aforesaid, or by another will or codicil, executed in manner herein-before required, or by some writing declaring an intention to revoke the same, and executed in the manner in which a will is herein-before required to be executed, or by the burning, tearing, or otherwise destroying the same by the testator, or by some person in his presence and by his direction, with the intention of revoking the same.

No alteration in a will after execution shall have any effect unless executed as a will

21. No obliteration, interlineation, or other alteration made in any will after the execution thereof shall be valid or have any effect, except so far as the words or effect of the will before such alteration shall not be apparent, unless such alteration shall be executed in like manner as herein-before is required for the execution of the will; but the will, with such alteration as part thereof, shall be deemed to be duly executed if the signature of the testator and the subscription of the witnesses be made in the margin or on

---

[7] For wills expressed to be made in contemplation of marriage, see the Law of Property Act 1925, s. 177, *post*, p. 208. Descent to the heir was abolished by the Administration of Estates Act 1925, s. 45(1), *post*, p. 264. For persons entitled in succession on intestacy, see *ibid*. s. 46, p. 264.

some other part of the will opposite or near to such alteration, or at the foot or end of or opposite to a memorandum referring to such alteration, and written at the end or some other part of the will.

No revoked will shall be revived otherwise than by re-execution or a codicil, etc.

22. No will or codicil, or any part thereof, which shall be in any manner revoked, shall be revived otherwise than by the re-execution thereof, or by a codicil executed in manner herein-before required and showing an intention to revive the same; and when any will or codicil which shall be partly revoked, and afterwards wholly revoked, shall be revived, such revival shall not extend to so much thereof as shall have been revoked before the revocation of the whole thereof, unless an intention to the contrary shall be shown.

Subsequent conveyance or other act not to prevent operation of will

23. No conveyance or other act made or done subsequently to the execution of a will of or relating to any real or personal estate therein comprised, except an act by which such will shall be revoked as aforesaid, shall prevent the operation of the will with respect to such estate or interest in such real or personal estate as the testator shall have power to dispose of by will at the time of his death.

Wills shall be construed, as to the estate comprised to speak from the death of the testator

24.[8] Every will shall be construed, with reference to the real estate and personal estate comprised in it, to speak and take effect as if it had been executed immediately before the death of the testator, unless a contrary intention shall appear by the will.

Residuary devises shall include estates comprised in lapsed and void devises

25. Unless a contrary intention shall appear by the will, such real estate or interest therein as shall be comprised or intended to be comprised in any devise in such will contained, which shall fail or be void by reason of the death of the devisee in the lifetime of the testator, or by reason of such devise being contrary to law, or otherwise incapable of taking effect, shall be included in the residuary devise (if any) contained in such will.

What a general devise shall include

26. A devise of the land of the testator, or of the land of the testator in any place or in the occupation of any person mentioned in his will, or otherwise described in a general manner, and any other general devise which would describe a [. . .][9] leasehold estate if the testator had no freehold estate which could be described by it, shall be construed to include the [. . .][9] leasehold estates of the testator, or his [. . .][9] leasehold estates, or any of them, to which such description shall extend, as the case may be, as well as freehold estates, unless a contrary intention shall appear by the will.

What a general gift shall include

27. A general devise of the real estate of the testator, or of the real estate of the testator in any place or in the occupation of any person

---

[8] Applied by the Married Women's Property Act 1893 (56 & 57 Vict. c. 63), s. 3.
[9] Repealed by the Statute Law (Repeals) Act 1969 (c. 52) , s. 1, Sched., Pt. III.

mentioned in his will, or otherwise described in a general manner, shall be construed to include any real estate, or any real estate to which such description shall extend (as the case may be), which he may have power to appoint in any manner he may think proper, and shall operate as an execution of such power, unless a contrary intention shall appear by the will; and in like manner a bequest of the personal estate of the testator, or any bequest of personal property described in a general manner, shall be construed to include any personal estate, or any personal estate to which such description shall extend (as the case may be), which he may have power to appoint in any manner he may think proper, and shall operate as an execution of such power, unless a contrary intention shall appear by the will.

How a devise without words of limitation shall be construed

28. Where any real estate shall be devised to any person without any words of limitation, such devise shall be construed to pass the fee simple, or other the whole estate or interest which the testator had power to dispose of by will in such real estate, unless a contrary intention shall appear by the will.

How the words "die without issue," or "die without leaving issue," etc., shall be construed

29. In any devise or bequest of real or personal estate the words "die without issue," or "die without leaving issue," or "have no issue," or any other words which may import either a want or failure of issue of any person in his lifetime or at the time of his death, or an indefinite failure of his issue, shall be construed to mean a want or failure of issue in the lifetime or at the time of the death of such person, and not an indefinite failure of his issue, unless a contrary intention shall appear by the will, by reason of such person having a prior estate tail, or of a preceding gift, being, without any implication arising from such words, a limitation of an estate tail to such person or issue, or otherwise: provided that this Act shall not extend to cases where such words as aforesaid import if no issue described in a preceding gift shall be born, or if there shall be no issue who shall live to attain the age or otherwise answer the description required for obtaining a vested estate by a preceding gift to such issue.

Devise of realty to trustees or executors shall pass the fee etc., except in certain cases

30. Where any real estate (other than or not being a presentation to a church) shall be devised to any trustee or executor, such devise shall be construed to pass the fee simple or other the whole estate or interest which the testator had power to dispose of by will in such real estate, unless a definite term of years, absolute or determinable, or an estate of freehold, shall thereby be given to him expressly or by implication.

Trustees under an unlimited devise, etc., to take the fee

31. Where any real estate shall be devised to a trustee, without any express limitation of the estate to be taken by such trustee, and the beneficial interest in such real estate, or in the surplus rents and profits thereof, shall not be given to any person for life, or such beneficial interest shall be given to any person for life, but the purposes of the trust may continue beyond the life of such person, such devise shall be construed to vest in such trustee the fee simple, or other the whole legal estate which the testator had power to dispose of by will in such real estate, and not an estate determinable when the purposes of the trust shall be satisfied.

Devises of estates tail shall not lapse where inheritable issue survives

32. Where any person to whom any real estate shall be devised for an estate tail [or an estate in quasi entail][10] shall die in the lifetime of the testator leaving issue who would be inheritable under such entail, and any such issue shall be living at the time of the death of the testator, such devise shall not lapse, but shall take effect as if the death of such person had happened immediately after the death of the testator, unless a contrary intention shall appear by the will.

Gifts to children or other issue who leave issue living at the testator's death shall not lapse

33.[11] Where any person being a child or other issue of the testator to whom any real or personal estate shall be devised or bequeathed for any estate or interest not determinable at or before the death of such person shall die in the lifetime of the testator leaving issue, and any such issue of such person shall be living at the time of the death of the testator, such devise or bequest shall not lapse, but shall take effect as if the death of such person had happened immediately after the death of the testator, unless a contrary intention shall appear by the will.

. . . . . .

Act not to extend to Scotland

35. This Act shall not extend to Scotland.

36. [*Repealed by the Statute Law Revision Act* 1874 (37 & 38 *Vict. c.* 35).]

---

[10] Words in square brackets repealed for Northern Ireland by S.L.R.(N.I.) 1973 (c. 55).
[11] Excluded by the Finance Act 1958 (6 & 7 Eliz. 2, c. 56), s. 29(2). Any reference in this section to child or other issue shall have effect as if it included a reference to any illegitimate child or other issue: Family Law Reform Act 1969 (c. 46), s. 16.

Wills Act Amendment Act 1852

(15 & 16 VICT. c. 24)

An Act for the amendment of the Wills Act 1837.   [17th June 1852.]

Position of the testator's signature

1.[1] Where by the Wills Act 1837 it is enacted, that no will shall be valid unless it shall be signed at the foot or end thereof by the testator, or by some other person in his presence, and by his direction: every will shall, so far only as regards the position of the signature of the testator, or of the person signing for him as aforesaid, be deemed to be valid within the said enactment, as explained by this Act, if the signature shall be so placed at or after, or following, or under, or beside or opposite to the end of the will, that it shall be apparent on the face of the will that the testator intended to give effect by such his signature to the writing signed as his will, and no such will shall be affected by the circumstance that the signature shall not follow or be immediately after the foot or end of the will, or by the circumstance that a blank space shall intervene between the concluding word of the will and the signature, or by the circumstance that the signature shall be placed among the words of the testimonium clause or of the clause of attestation, or shall follow or be after or under the clause of attestation, either with or without a blank space intervening, or shall follow or be after, or under, or beside the names or one of the names of the subscribing witnesses, or by the circumstance that the signature shall be on a side or page or other portion of the paper or papers containing the will whereon no clause or paragraph or disposing part of the will shall be written above the signature, or by the circumstance that there shall appear to be sufficient space on or at the bottom of the preceding side or page or other portion of the same paper on which the will is written to contain the signature; and the enumeration of the above circumstances shall not restrict the generality of the above enactment; but no signature under the said Act or this Act shall be operative to give effect to any disposition or direction which is underneath or which follows it, nor shall it give effect to any disposition or direction inserted after the signature shall be made.

Act to extend to certain wills already made

2. The provisions of this Act shall extend and be applied to every will already made, where administration or probate has not already been granted or ordered by a court of competent jurisdiction in consequence of the defective execution of such will, or where the property, not being within the jurisdiction of the ecclesiastical courts, has not been possessed or enjoyed by some person or persons claiming to be entitled thereto in consequence of the defective execution of such will, or the right thereto shall not have been decided to be in some other person or persons than the persons claiming under the will, by a court of competent jurisdiction, in consequence of the defective execution of such will.

Interpretation of "will"

3. The word "will" shall in the construction of this Act be interpreted in like manner as the same is directed to be interpreted under the provisions in this behalf contained in the Wills Act 1837.

Short title

4. This Act may be cited as "The Wills Act Amendment Act 1852."

[1] This section amplifies s. 9 of the Wills Act 1837, *ante*, p. 5.

Wills (Soldiers and Sailors) Act 1918

(7 & 8 GEO. 5, c. 58)

An Act to amend the law with respect to testamentary dispositions by soldiers and sailors   [6th February 1918.]

Explanation of s. 11 of 7 Will. 4 & 1 Vict. c. 26

1. In order to remove doubts as to the construction of the Wills Act 1837, it is hereby declared and enacted that section eleven of that Act authorises and always has authorised any soldier being in actual military service, or any mariner or seaman being at sea, to dispose of his personal estate as he might have done before the passing of that Act, though under the age of [eighteen years].[1]

Extension of s. 11 of Wills Act 1837

2. Section eleven of the Wills Act 1837 shall extend to any member of His Majesty's naval or marine forces not only when he is at sea but also when he is so circumstanced that if he were a soldier he would be in actual military service within the meaning of that section.

Validity of testamentary dispositions of real property made by soldiers and sailors

3.—(1) A testamentary disposition of any real estate in England or Ireland made by a person to whom section eleven of the Wills Act 1837 applies, and who dies after the passing of this Act, shall, notwithstanding that the person making the disposition was at the time of making it under [eighteen years][1] of age or that the disposition has not been made in such manner or form as was at the passing of this Act required by law, be valid in any case where the person making the disposition was of such age and the disposition has been made in such manner and form that if the disposition had been a disposition of personal estate made by such a person domiciled in England or Ireland it would have been valid.

(2) [*Repealed by Succession (Scotland) Act* 1964 (*c.* 41), *s.* 34 (2), *Sched.* 3.*]

Power to appoint testamentary guardians

4. Where any person dies after the passing of this Act having made a will which is, or which, if it had been a disposition of property, would have been rendered valid by section eleven of the Wills Act 1837, any appointment contained in that will of any person as guardian of the infant children of the testator shall be of full force and effect.

Short title and interpretation

5.—(1) This Act may be cited as the Wills (Soldiers and Sailors) Act 1918.

(2) For the purposes of section eleven of the Wills Act 1837 and this Act the expression "soldier" includes a member of the Air Force, and references in this Act to the said section eleven include a reference to that section as explained and extended by this Act.

---

[1] Words substituted by the Family Law Reform Act 1969 (c. 46), s. 3(1) (*b*).

Settled Land Act 1925

(15 Geo. 5, c. 18)

Arrangement of Sections

Part I

General Preliminary Provisions

Settlements and Settled Land

Enforcement of Equitable Interests and Powers against Estate Owner and discharge on termination of Settlement

Restrictions on dispositions of Settled Land where Trustees have not been Discharged

Tenants for Life and Persons with Powers of Tenant for Life

Trustees of Settlement

Provisions as to Undivided Shares

Transitional Provisions

Part II

Powers of a Tenant for Life

Sale and Exchange

Leasing Powers

Provisions as to building, mining and forestry leases

Miscellaneous Powers

Provisions as to special classes of property

Dealings as between tenants for life and the estate

Incumbrances

Raising of Money

Conveyance

An Act to consolidate the enactments relating to settled land in England and Wales.   [9th April 1925.]

PART I

GENERAL PRELIMINARY PROVISIONS

Settlements and Settled Land

What constitutes a settlement

1.—(1) Any deed, will, agreement for a settlement or other agreement, Act of Parliament, or other instrument, or any number of instruments, whether made or passed before or after, or partly before and partly after, the commencement of this Act, under or by virtue of which instrument or instruments any land, after the commencement of this Act, stands for the time being—

   (i) limited in trust for any persons by way of succession; or

  (ii) limited in trust for any person in possession—

     (*a*) for an entailed interest whether or not capable of being barred or defeated;

     (*b*) for an estate in fee simple or for a term of years absolute subject to an executory limitation, gift, or disposition over on failure of his issue or in any other event;

     (*c*) for a base or determinable fee or any corresponding interest in leasehold land;

     (*d*) being an infant, for an estate in fee simple or for a term of years absolute; or

  (iii) limited in trust for any person for an estate in fee simple or for a term of years absolute contingently on the happening of any event; or

  (iv) [*Repealed by the Married Women (Restraint upon Anticipation) Act 1949 (12, 13 & 14 Geo. 6, c. 78), s. 1, Sched. 2.*]

   (v) charged, whether voluntarily or in consideration of marriage or by way of family arrangement, and whether immediately or after an interval, with the payment of any rentcharge for the life of any person, or any less period, or of any capital, annual or periodical sums for the portions, advancement, maintenance, or otherwise for the benefit of any persons, with or without any term of years for securing or raising the same;

creates or is for the purposes of this Act a settlement and is in this Act referred to as a settlement, or as the settlement, as the case requires:

Provided that, where land is the subject of a compound settlement, references in this Act to the settlement shall be construed as meaning such compound settlement, unless the context otherwise requires.

(2) Where an infant is beneficially entitled to land for an estate in fee simple or for a term of years absolute and by reason of an intestacy or otherwise there is no instrument under which the interest of the infant arises or is acquired, a settlement shall be deemed to have been made by the intestate, or by the person whose interest the infant has acquired.

(3)[1] An infant shall be deemed to be entitled in possession notwithstanding any subsisting right of dower (not assigned by metes and bounds) affecting the land, and such a right of dower shall be deemed to be an interest comprised in the subject of the settlement and coming to the dowress under or by virtue of the settlement.

Where dower has been assigned by metes and bounds, the letters of administration or probate granted in respect of the estate of the husband of the dowress shall be deemed a settlement made by the husband.

(4) An estate or interest not disposed of by a settlement and remaining in or reverting to the settlor, or any person deriving title under him, is for the purposes of this Act an estate or interest comprised in the subject of the settlement and coming to the settlor or such person under or by virtue of the settlement.

(5) Where—

> (*a*) a settlement creates an entailed interest which is incapable of being barred or defeated, or a base or determinable fee, whether or not the reversion or right of reverter is in the Crown, or any corresponding interest in leasehold land; or
>
> (*b*) the subject of a settlement is an entailed interest, or a base or determinable fee, whether or not the reversion or right of reverter is in the Crown, or any corresponding interest in leasehold land;

the reversion or right of reverter upon the cesser of the interest so created or settled shall be deemed to be an interest comprised in the subject of the settlement, and limited by the settlement.

(6) Subsections (4) and (5) of this section bind the Crown.

[(7) This section does not apply to land held upon trust for sale.][2]

What is settled land

2. Land which is or is deemed to be the subject of a settlement is for the purposes of this Act settled land, and is in relation to the settlement referred to in this Act as the settled land.

Duration of settlements

3. Land [not held upon trust for sale][3] which has been subject to a settlement shall be deemed for the purposes of this Act to remain and be

---

[1] For the abolition with savings of dower, see the Administration of Estates Act 1925, ss. 45(1) (*c*), 51(2), *post*, pp. 264, 271.
[2] Added by the Law of Property (Amendment) Act 1926, *post*, s. 7, Sched.
[3] *Ibid.*

settled land, and the settlement shall be deemed to be a subsisting settlement for the purposes of this Act so long as—

(*a*) any limitation, charge, or power of charging under the settlement subsists, or is capable of being exercised; or

(*b*) the person who, if of full age, would be entitled as beneficial owner to have that land vested in him for a legal estate is an infant.

Authorised method of settling land inter vivos

4.—(1) Every settlement of a legal estate in land inter vivos shall, save as in this Act otherwise provided, be effected by two deeds, namely, a vesting deed and a trust instrument and if effected in any other way shall not operate to transfer or create a legal estate.

(2) By the vesting deed the land shall be conveyed to the tenant for life or statutory owner (and if more than one as joint tenants) for the legal estate the subject of the intended settlement:

Provided that, where such legal estate is already vested in the tenant for life or statutory owner, it shall be sufficient, without any other conveyance, if the vesting deed declares that the land is vested in him for that estate.

(3) The trust instrument shall—

(*a*) declare the trusts affecting the settled land;

(*b*) appoint or constitute trustees of the settlement;

(*c*) contain the power, if any, to appoint new trustees of the settlement;

(*d*) set out, either expressly or by reference, any powers intended to be conferred by the settlement in extension of those conferred by this Act;

(*e*) bear any ad valorem stamp duty which may be payable (whether by virtue of the vesting deed or otherwise) in respect of the settlement.

Contents of vesting deeds

5.—(1) Every vesting deed for giving effect to a settlement or for conveying settled land to a tenant for life or statutory owner during the subsistence of the settlement (in this Act referred to as a "principal vesting deed") shall contain the following statements and particulars, namely:-

(*a*) A description, either specific or general, of the settled land;

(*b*) A statement that the settled land is vested in the person or persons to whom it is conveyed or in whom it is declared to be vested upon the trusts from time to time affecting the settled land;

(*c*) The names of the persons who are the trustees of the settlement;

(*d*) Any additional or larger powers conferred by the trust instrument relating to the settled land which by virtue of this Act operate and are exercisable as if conferred by this Act on a tenant for life;

(*e*) The name of any person for the time being entitled under the trust instrument to appoint new trustees of the settlement.

(2) The statements or particulars required by this section may be incorporated by reference to an existing vesting instrument, and, where there is a settlement subsisting at the commencement of this Act, by reference to that settlement and to any instrument whereby land has been conveyed to the uses or upon the trusts of that settlement, but not (save as last aforesaid) by reference to a trust instrument nor by reference to a disentailing deed.

(3) A principal vesting deed shall not be invalidated by reason only of

any error in any of the statements or particulars by this Act required to be contained therein.

Procedure in the case of settlements by will

6. Where a settlement is created by the will of an estate owner who dies after the commencement of this Act—
- (*a*) the will is for the purposes of this Act a trust instrument; and
- (*b*) the personal representatives of the testator shall hold the settled land on trust, if and when required so to do, to convey it to the person who, under the will, or by virtue of this Act, is the tenant for life or statutory owner, and, if more than one, as joint tenants.

Procedure on change of ownership

7.—(1) If, on the death of a tenant for life or statutory owner, or of the survivor of two or more tenants for life or statutory owners, in whom the settled land was vested, the land remains settled land, his personal representatives shall hold the settled land on trust, if and when required so to do, to convey it to the person who under the trust instrument or by virtue of this Act becomes the tenant for life or statutory owner and, if more than one, as joint tenants.

(2) If a person by reason of attaining full age becomes a tenant for life for the purposes of this Act of settled land, he shall be entitled to require the trustees of the settlement, personal representatives, or other persons in whom the settled land is vested, to convey the land to him.

(3) If a person who, when of full age, will together with another person or other persons constitute the tenant for life for the purposes of this Act of settled land attains that age, he shall be entitled to require the tenant for life, trustees of the settlement, personal representatives or other persons in whom the settled land is vested to convey the land to him and the other person or persons who together with him constitute the tenant for life as joint tenants.

(4) If by reason of forfeiture, surrender, or otherwise the estate owner of any settled land ceases to have the statutory powers of a tenant for life and the land remains settled land, he shall be bound forthwith to convey the settled land to the person who under the trust instrument, or by virtue of this Act, becomes the tenant for life or statutory owner and, if more than one, as joint tenants.

(5) If any person of full age becomes absolutely entitled to the settled land (whether beneficially, or as personal representative, or as trustee for sale, or otherwise) free from all limitations, powers, and charges taking effect under the settlement, he shall be entitled to require the trustees of the settlement, personal representatives, or other persons in whom the settled land is vested, to convey the land to him, and if more persons than one being of full age become so entitled to the settled land they shall be entitled to require such persons as aforesaid to convey the land to them as joint tenants.

Mode and costs of conveyance, and saving of rights of personal representatives and equitable chargees

8.—(1) A conveyance by personal representatives under either of the last two preceding sections may be made by an assent in writing signed by them which shall operate as a conveyance.

(2) Every conveyance under either of the last two preceding sections shall be made at the cost of the trust estate.

(3) The obligations to convey settled land imposed by the last two preceding sections are subject and without prejudice—

(*a*) where the settlement is created by a will, to the rights and powers of the personal representatives for purposes of administration; and

(*b*) in any case, to the person on whom the obligation is imposed being satisfied that provision has been or will be made for the payment of any unpaid death duties in respect of the land or any interest therein for which he is accountable, and any interest and costs in respect of such duties, or that he is otherwise effectually indemnified against such duties, interest and costs.

(4) Where the land is or remains settled land a conveyance under either of the last two preceding sections shall—

(*a*) if by deed, be a principal vesting deed; and

(*b*) if by an assent, be a vesting assent, which shall contain the like statements and particulars as are required by this Act in the case of a principal vesting deed.

(5) Nothing contained in either of the last two preceding sections affects the right of personal representatives to transfer or create such legal estates to take effect in priority to a conveyance under either of those sections as may be required for giving effect to the obligations imposed on them by statute.

(6) A conveyance under either of the last two preceding sections, if made by deed, may contain a reservation to the person conveying of a term of years absolute in the land conveyed, upon trusts for indemnifying him against any unpaid death duties in respect of the land conveyed or any interest therein, and any interest and costs in respect of such duties.

(7) Nothing contained in either of the last two preceding sections affects any right which a person entitled to an equitable charge for securing money actually raised, and affecting the whole estate the subject of the settlement, may have to require effect to be given thereto by a legal mortgage, before the execution of a conveyance under either of those sections.

Procedure in the case of settlements and of instruments deemed to be trust instruments

9.—(1) Each of the following settlements or instruments shall for the purposes of this Act be deemed to be a trust instrument, and any reference to a trust instrument contained in this Act shall apply thereto, namely:—

(i) An instrument executed, or, in case of a will, coming into operation, after the commencement of this Act which by virtue of this Act is deemed to be a settlement;

(ii) A settlement which by virtue of this Act is deemed to have been made by any person after the commencement of this Act;

(iii) An instrument *inter vivos* intended to create a settlement of a legal estate in land which is executed after the commencement of this Act, and does not comply with the requirements of this Act with respect to the method of effecting such a settlement; and

(iv) A settlement made after the commencement of this Act (including a settlement by the will of a person who dies after such commencement) of any of the following interests—

(*a*) an equitable interest in land which is capable, when in possession, of subsisting at law; or

(*b*) an entailed interest; or

(*c*) a base or determinable fee or any corresponding interest in leasehold land,

but only if and when the interest settled takes effect free from all equitable interests and powers under every prior settlement (if any).

(2) As soon as practicable after a settlement, or an instrument which for the purposes of this Act is deemed to be a trust instrument, takes effect as such, the trustees of the settlement may, and on the request of the tenant for life or statutory owner shall, execute a principal vesting deed, containing the proper statements and particulars, declaring that the legal estate in the settled land shall vest or is vested in the person or persons therein named, being the tenant for life or statutory owner, and including themselves if they are the statutory owners, and such deed shall, unless the legal estate is already so vested, operate to convey or vest the legal estate in the settled land to or in the person or persons aforesaid and, if more than one, as joint tenants.

(3) If there are no trustees of the settlement, then (in default of a person able and willing to appoint such trustees) an application under this Act shall be made to the court for the appointment of such trustees.

(4) The provisions of the last preceding section with reference to a conveyance shall apply, so far as they are applicable, to a principal vesting deed under this section.

Procedure on acquisition of land to be made subject to a settlement

10.—(1) Where after the commencement of this Act land is acquired with capital money arising under this Act or in exchange for settled land, or a rentcharge is reserved on a grant of settled land, the land shall be conveyed to, and the rentcharge shall by virtue of this Act become vested in, the tenant for life or statutory owner, and such conveyance or grant is in this Act referred to as a subsidiary vesting deed:

Provided that, where an instrument is subsisting at the commencement of this Act, or is made or comes into operation after such commencement, by virtue of which any money or securities are liable under this Act, or the Acts which it replaces, or under a trust or direction contained in the instrument, to be invested in the purchase of land to be conveyed so as to become settled land, but at the commencement of this Act, or when such instrument is made or comes into operation after such commencement, as the case may be, there is no land in respect of which a principal vesting deed is capable of being executed, the first deed after the commencement of this Act by which any land is acquired as aforesaid shall be a principal vesting deed and shall be framed accordingly.

(2) A subsidiary vesting deed executed on the acquisition of land to be made subject to a settlement shall contain the following statements and particulars namely—

(*a*) particulars of the last or only principal vesting instrument affecting land subject to the settlement;

(*b*) a statement that the land conveyed is to be held upon and subject to the same trusts and powers as the land comprised in such last or only principal vesting instrument;

(*c*) the names of the persons who are the trustees of the settlement;

(*d*) the name of any person for the time being entitled to appoint new trustees of the settlement.

(3) A subsidiary vesting deed reserving a rentcharge on a grant of settled land shall contain the following statements and particulars—

(*a*) a statement that the rentcharge is vested in the grantor and is subject to the settlement which, immediately before the grant, was subsisting with respect to the land out of which it was reserved;

(*b*) particulars of the last or only principal vesting instrument affecting such land.

(4) A subsidiary vesting deed shall not be invalidated by reason only of any error in any of the statements or particulars by this Act required to be contained therein.

(5) The acquisition of the land shall not operate to increase or multiply charges or powers of charging.

As to contracts for the settlement of land

11.—(1) A contract made or other liability created or arising after the commencement of this Act for the settlement of land—
   (i) by or on the part of an estate owner; or
   (ii) by a person entitled to—
      (*a*) an equitable interest which is capable when in possession of subsisting at law; or
      (*b*) an entailed interest; or
      (*c*) a base or determinable fee or any corresponding interest in leasehold land;
shall, but in cases under paragraph (ii) only if and when the interest of the person entitled takes effect free from all equitable interests and powers under every prior settlement, if any, be deemed an estate contract within the meaning of the Land Charges Act 1925[4] and may be registered as a land charge accordingly, and effect shall be given thereto by a vesting deed and a trust instrument in accordance with this Act.

(2) A contract made or other liability created or arising before the commencement of this Act to make a settlement of land shall be deemed to be sufficiently complied with if effect is given thereto by a vesting deed and a trust instrument in accordance with this Act.

Power to make vesting orders as to settled land

12.—(1) If—
      (*a*) any person who is bound under this Part of this Act to execute a conveyance, vesting deed or vesting assent or in whom settled land is wrongly vested refuses or neglects to execute the requisite conveyance, vesting deed or vesting assent within one month after demand in writing; or
      (*b*) any such person is outside the United Kingdom, or cannot be found, or it is not known whether he is alive or dead; or
      (*c*) for any reason the court is satisfied that the conveyance, vesting deed or vesting assent cannot be executed, or cannot be executed without undue delay or expense;
the court may, on the application of any person interested, make an order vesting the settled land in the tenant for life or statutory owner or person, if any, of full age absolutely entitled (whether beneficially or as personal representative or trustee for sale or otherwise), and, if the land remains settled land, the provisions of this Act relating to a principal vesting deed or a subsidiary vesting deed, as the case may be, shall apply to any order so made and every such order shall contain the like statements and particulars.

(2) No stamp duty shall be payable in respect of a vesting order made in place of a vesting or other assent.

Dispositions not to take effect until vesting instrument is made

13. Where a tenant for life or statutory owner has become entitled to have a principal vesting deed or a vesting assent executed in his favour, then until a vesting instrument is executed or made pursuant to this Act in respect of the settled land, any purported disposition thereof inter vivos by any person, other than a personal representative (not being a disposition

---

[4] Now the Land Charges Act 1972 (c. 61), *post*, p. 320.

which he has power to make in right of his equitable interests or powers under a trust instrument), shall not take effect except in favour of a purchaser of a legal estate [without notice of such tenant for life or statutory owner having become so entitled as aforesaid],[5] but, save as aforesaid, shall operate only as a contract for valuable consideration to carry out the transaction after the requisite vesting instrument has been executed or made, and a purchaser of a legal estate shall not be concerned with such disposition unless the contract is registered as a land charge.

[Nothing in this section affects the creation or transfer of a legal estate by virtue of an order of the court or the Minister or other competent authority.][6]

Forfeiture and stamps

14.—(1) Any vesting effected under the powers conferred by this Act in relation to settled land shall not operate as a breach of a covenant or condition against alienation or give rise to a forfeiture.

(2) Nothing in this Act shall operate to impose any stamp duty on a vesting or other assent.

Examples of instruments

15. Examples of instruments framed in accordance with the provisions of this Act are contained in the First Schedule to this Act.

Enforcement of Equitable Interests and Powers against Estate Owner and discharge on termination of Settlement

Enforcement of equitable interests and powers against estate owner

16.—(1) All equitable interests and powers in or over settled land (whether created before or after the date of any vesting instrument affecting the legal estate) shall be enforceable against the estate owner in whom the settled land is vested (but in the case of personal respresenta- tives without prejudice to their rights and powers for purposes of administration) in manner following (that is to say):—

    (i) The estate owner shall stand possessed of the settled land and the income thereof upon such trusts and subject to such powers and provisions as may be requisite for giving effect to the equitable interests and powers affecting the settled land or the income thereof of which he has notice according to their respective priorities;

    (ii) Where any person of full age becomes entitled to require a legal estate in the settled land to be vested in him in priority to the settlement, by reason of a right of reverter, statutory or otherwise, or an equitable right of entry taking effect, or on the ground that his interest ought no longer to be capable of being overreached under the powers of this Act, the estate owner shall be bound, if so requested in writing, to transfer or create such legal estate as may be required for giving legal effect to the rights of the person so entitled;

    (iii) Where—

        (*a*) any principal sum is required to be raised on the security of the settled land, by virtue of any trust, or by reason of the exercise of an equitable power affecting the settled land, or by any person or persons who under the settlement is or are entitled

---

[5] Substituted by the Law of Property (Amendment) Act 1926, *post*, s. 7, Sched.
[6] Added by Law of Property (Amendment) Act, *post*, s. 6, Sched.

or together entitled to or has or have a general power of appointment over the settled land, whether subject to any equitable charges or powers of charging subsisting under the settlement or not; or

(*b*) the settled land is subject to any equitable charge for securing money actually raised and affecting the whole estate the subject of the settlement;

the estate owner shall be bound, if so requested in writing, to create such legal estate or charge by way of legal mortgage as may be required for raising the money or giving legal effect to the equitable charge:

Provided that, so long as the settlement remains subsisting, any legal estate or charge by way of legal mortgage so created shall take effect and shall be expressed to take effect subject to any equitable charges or powers of charging subsisting under the settlement which have priority to the interests or powers of the person or persons by or on behalf of whom the money is required to be raised or legal effect is required to be given to the equitable charge, unless the persons entitled to the prior charges or entitled to exercise the powers consent in writing to the same being postponed, but it shall not be necessary for such consent to be expressed in the instrument creating such legal estate or charge by way of legal mortgage.

(2) Where a mortgage or charge is expressed to be made by an estate owner pursuant to this section, then, in favour of the mortgagee or chargee and persons deriving title under him, the same shall take effect in priority to all the trusts of the settlement and all equitable interests and powers subsisting or to arise under the settlement except those to which it is expressly made subject, and shall so take effect, whether the mortgagee or chargee has notice of any such trusts, interests, or powers, or not, and the mortgagee or chargee shall not be concerned to see that a case had arisen to authorise the mortgage or charge, or that no more money than was wanted was raised.

(3) Nothing contained in paragraph (iii) of subsection (1) of this section affects the power conferred by this Act on a tenant for life of raising money by mortgage or of directing capital money to be applied in discharge of incumbrances.

(4) Effect may be given by means of a legal mortgage to an agreement for a mortgage, or a charge or lien, whether or not arising by operation of law, if the agreement charge or lien ought to have priority over the settlement.

(5) Save as hereinbefore expressly provided, no legal estate shall, so long as the settlement is subsisting, be transferred or created by the estate owner for giving effect to any equitable interest or power under the settlement.

(6) If a question arises or a doubt is entertained whether any and what legal estate ought to be transferred or created pursuant to this section, an application may be made to the court for directions as hereinafter provided.

(7) If an estate owner refuses or neglects for one month after demand in writing to transfer or create any such legal estate, or if by reason of his being outside the United Kingdom, or being unable to be found, or by reason of the dissolution of a corporation, or for any other reason, the court is satisfied that the transaction cannot otherwise be effected, or cannot be effected without undue delay or expense, the court may, on the application of any person interested, make a vesting order transferring or creating the requisite legal estate.

(8) This section does not affect a purchaser of a legal estate taking free from any equitable interest or power.

Deed of discharge on termination of settlement

17.—(1) Where the estate owner of any settled land holds the land free from all equitable interests and powers under a trust instrument, the persons who in the last or only principal vesting instrument or the last or only endorsement on or annex thereto are declared to be the trustees of the settlement or the survivors of them shall, save as hereinafter mentioned, be bound to execute, at the cost of the trust estate, a deed declaring that they are discharged from the trust so far as regards that land:

Provided that, if the trustees have notice of any derivative settlement, trust for sale or equitable charge affecting such land, they shall not execute a deed of discharge until—

(*a*) in the case of a derivative settlement, or trust for sale, a vesting instrument or a conveyance has been executed or made for giving effect thereto; and

(*b*) in the case of an equitable charge, they are satisfied that the charge is or will be secured by a legal mortgage, or is protected by registration as a land charge, or by deposit of the documents of title, or that the owner thereof consents to the execution of the deed of discharge.

Where the land is affected by a derivative settlement or trust for sale, the deed of discharge shall contain a statement that the land is settled land by virtue of such vesting instrument as aforesaid and the trust instrument therein referred to, or is held on trust for sale by virtue of such conveyance as aforesaid, as the case may require.

(2) If, in the circumstances mentioned in subsection (1) of this section and when the conditions therein mentioned have been complied with, the trustees of a settlement on being requested to execute a deed of discharge—

(*a*) by the estate owner; or

(*b*) by a person interested under, or by the trustees of, a derivative settlement; or

(*c*) by the trustees of a conveyance on trust for sale;

refuse to do so, or if for any reason the discharge cannot be effected without undue delay or expense, the estate owner, person interested, or trustees may apply to the court for an order discharging the first mentioned trustees as respects the whole or any part of the settled land, and the court may make such order as it may think fit.

(3) Where a deed or order of discharge contains no statement to the contrary, a purchaser of a legal estate in the land to which the deed or order relates shall be entitled to assume that the land has ceased to be settled land, and is not subject to any trust for sale.

Restrictions on dispositions of Settled Land where Trustees have not been Discharged

Restrictions on dispositions of settled land where trustees have not been discharged

18.—(1) Where land is the subject of a vesting instrument and the trustees of the settlement have not been discharged under this Act, then—

(*a*) any disposition by the tenant for life or statutory owner of the land, other than a disposition authorised by this Act or any other statute, or made in pursuance of any additional or larger powers mentioned in the vesting instrument, shall be void, except for the purpose of conveying or creating such equitable interests as he has power, in right of his equitable interests and powers under the trust instrument, to convey or create; and (*b*) if any capital money is payable in respect of a transaction, a conveyance to a purchaser of the land shall only take effect under this Act if the capital money is paid to or by the direction of the trustees of the settlement or into court; and

(*c*) notwithstanding anything to the contrary in the vesting instrument, or the trust instrument, capital money shall not, except where the trustee is a trust corporation, be paid to or by the direction of fewer persons than two as trustees of the settlement.

(2) The restrictions imposed by this section do not affect—

(*a*) the right of a personal representative in whom the settled land may be vested to convey or deal with the land for the purposes of administration;

(*b*) the right of a person of full age who has become absolutely entitled (whether beneficially or as trustee for sale or personal representative or otherwise) to the settled land, free from all limitations, powers, and charges taking effect under the trust instrument, to require the land to be conveyed to him;

(*c*) the power of the tenant for life, statutory owner, or personal representative in whom the settled land is vested to transfer or create such legal estates, to take effect in priority to the settlement, as may be required for giving effect to any obligations imposed on him by statute, but where any capital money is raised or received in respect of the transaction the money shall be paid to or by the direction of the trustees of the settlement or in accordance with an order of the court.

Tenants for Life and Persons with Powers of Tenant for Life

Who is tenant for life

19.—(1) The person of full age who is for the time being beneficially entitled under a settlement to possession of settled land for his life is for the purposes of this Act the tenant for life of that land and the tenant for life under that settlement.

(2) If in any case there are two or more persons of full age so entitled as joint tenants, they together constitute the tenant for life for the purposes of this Act.

(3) If in any case there are two or more persons so entitled as joint tenants and they are not all of full age, such one or more of them as is or are for the time being of full age is or (if more than one) together constitute the tenant for life for the purposes of this Act, but this subsection does not affect the beneficial interests of such of them as are not for the time being of full age.

(4) A person being tenant for life within the foregoing definitions shall be deemed to be such notwithstanding that, under the settlement or otherwise, the settled land, or his estate or interest therein, is incumbered or charged in any manner or to any extent, and notwithstanding any assignment by operation of law or otherwise of his estate or interest under the settlement, whether before or after it came into possession, other than an assurance which extinguishes that estate or interest.

Other limited owners having powers of tenant for life

20.—(1) Each of the following persons being of full age shall, when his estate or interest is in possession, have the powers of a tenant for life under this Act, (namely):—

(i) A tenant in tail, including a tenant in tail after possibility of issue extinct, and a tenant in tail who is by Act of Parliament restrained from barring or defeating his estate tail, and although the reversion is in the Crown, but not including such a tenant in tail where the land in respect whereof he is so restrained was purchased with money provided by Parliament in consideration of public services;

(ii) A person entitled to land for an estate in fee simple or for a term of years absolute with or subject to, in any of such cases, an executory limitation, gift, or disposition over on failure of his issue or in any other event;

(iii) A person entitled to a base or determinable fee, although the reversion or right of reverter is in the Crown, or to any corresponding interest in leasehold land;

(iv) A tenant for years determinable on life, not holding merely under a lease at a rent;

(v) A tenant for the life of another, not holding merely under a lease at a rent;

(vi) A tenant for his own or any other life, or for years determinable on life, whose estate is liable to cease in any event during that life, whether by expiration of the estate, or by conditional limitation, or otherwise, or to be defeated by an executory limitation, gift, or disposition over, or is subject to a trust for accumulation of income for any purpose;

(vii) [7] A tenant by the curtesy;

(viii) A person entitled to the income of land under a trust or direction for payment thereof to him during his own or any other life, whether or not subject to expenses of management or to a trust for accumulation of income for any purpose, or until sale of the land, or until forfeiture, cesser or determination by any means of his interest therein, unless the land is subject to an immediate binding trust for sale;

(ix) [8] A person beneficially entitled to land for an estate in fee simple or for a term of years absolute subject to any estates, interests, charges, or powers of charging, subsisting or capable of being exercised under a settlement;

(x) [*Repealed by the Married Women (Restraint upon Anticipation) Act 1949 (12, 13 & 14 Geo. 6, c. 78), s. 1, Sched. 2.*]

(2) In every such case as is mentioned in subsection (1) of this section, the provisions of this Act referring to a tenant for life, either as conferring powers on him or otherwise, shall extend to each of the persons aforesaid, and any reference in this Act to death as regards a tenant for life shall, where necessary, be deemed to refer to the determination by death or otherwise of the estate or interest of the person on whom the powers of a tenant for life are conferred by this section.

(3) For the purposes of this Act the estate or interest of a tenant by the curtesy shall be deemed to be an estate or interest arising under a settlement made by his wife.

(4) Where the reversion or right of reverter or other reversionary right is in the Crown, the exercise by a person on whom the powers of a tenant for life are conferred by this section of his powers under this Act, binds the Crown.

---

[7] Curtesy was abolished by the Administration of Estates Act 1925, s. 45(1) (*b*), *post*, p. 264, but may still apply in certain cases: see *ibid.*, ss. 45 (2), 51(2), pp. 264, 271.

[8] The Law of Property (Amendment) Act 1926, s. 1(1), *post*, p. 276, provides as follows:
"Nothing in the Settled Land Act 1925 shall prevent a person on whom the powers of a tenant for life are conferred by paragraph (ix) of subsection (1) of section twenty of that Act from conveying or creating a legal estate subject to a prior interest as if the land had not been settled land."

Absolute owners subject to certain interests to have the powers of tenant for life

21.—(1) Where a person of full age is beneficially entitled in possession to a legal estate subject to any equitable interests or powers, then, for the purpose of overreaching such interests or powers, he may, notwithstanding any stipulation to the contrary, by deed (which shall have effect as a principal vesting deed within the meaning of this Act) declare that the legal estate is vested in him on trust to give effect to all equitable interests and powers affecting the legal estate, and that deed shall be executed by two or more individuals approved or appointed by the court or a trust corporation, who shall be stated to be the trustees of the settlement for the purposes of this Act.

Thereupon so long as any of the equitable interests and powers are subsisting the following provisions shall have effect:—

(a) The person so entitled as aforesaid and each of his successors in title being an estate owner shall have the powers of a tenant for life and the land shall be deemed to be settled land;

(b) The instrument (if any) under which his estate arises or is acquired, and the instrument (if any) under which the equitable interests or powers are subsisting or capable of taking effect shall be deemed to be the trust instrument:

Provided that where there is no such instrument as last aforesaid then a deed (which shall take effect as a trust instrument) shall be executed contemporaneously with the vesting deed, and shall declare the trusts affecting the land;

(c) The persons stated in the principal vesting deed to be the trustees of the settlement for the purposes of this Act shall also be the trustees of the trust instrument for those purposes; and

(d) Capital money arising on any disposition of the land shall be paid to or by the direction of the trustees of the settlement or into court, and shall be applicable towards discharging or providing for payment in due order of any principal money payable in respect of such interests or charges as are overreached by such disposition, and until so applied shall be invested or applied as capital money under the trust instrument, and the income thereof shall be applied as the income of such capital money, and be liable for keeping down in due order any annual or periodical sum which may be overreached by the disposition.

(2) The following equitable interests and powers are excepted from the operation of subsection (1) of this section, namely—

(i) an equitable interest protected by a deposit of documents relating to the legal estate affected;

(ii) the benefit of a covenant or agreement restrictive of the user of land;

(iii) an easement, liberty or privilege over or affecting land and being merely an equitable interest;

(iv) the benefit of a contract to convey or create a legal estate, including a contract conferring either expressly or by statutory implication a valid option of purchase, a right of pre-emption, or any other like right;

(v) any equitable interest protected by registration under the Land Charges Act 1925[9] other than—

(a) an annuity within the meaning of Part II of that Act;

(b) a limited owner's charge or a general equitable charge within the meaning of that Act.

[9] Now the Land Charges Act 1972 (c. 61), *post*, p. 320.

(3) Subject to the powers conferred by this Act on a tenant for life, nothing contained in this section shall deprive an equitable chargee of any of his rights or of his remedies for enforcing those rights.

Provisions applicable where interest in settled land is restored

22.—(1) Where by a disentailing assurance settled land is expressed to be limited (whether subject or not to any estates, interests, charges or powers expressly created or conferred thereby) upon the trusts subsisting with respect thereto immediately before the execution of such disentailing assurance, or any of such trusts, then, for the purposes of this Act and otherwise, a person entitled to any estate or interest in the settled land under any such previously subsisting trust is entitled thereto after the execution of such disentailing assurance as of his former estate or interest.

(2) Where by a resettlement of settled land any estate or interest therein is expressed to be limited to any person (whether subject or not to any estate, interest, charge or power expressly created or conferred by the resettlement) in restoration or confirmation of his estate or interest under a prior settlement, then, for the purposes of this Act and otherwise, that person is entitled to the estate or interest so restored or confirmed as of his former estate or interest, and in addition to the powers exercisable by him in respect of his former estate or interest, he is capable of exercising all such further powers as he could have exercised by virtue of the resettlement, if his estate or interest under the prior settlement had not been so restored or confirmed, but he had been entitled under the resettlement only.

Powers of trustees, &c. when there is no tenant for life

23.—(1) Where under a settlement there is no tenant for life nor, independently of this section, a person having by virtue of this Act the powers of a tenant for life then—

(*a*) any person of full age on whom such powers are by the settlement expressed to be conferred; and

(*b*) in any other case the trustees of the settlement;

shall have the powers of a tenant for life under this Act.

(2) This section applies to trustees of settlements of land purchased with money provided by Parliament in consideration of public services where the tenant in tail is restrained from barring or defeating his estate tail, except that, if the tenant in tail is of full age and capacity, the powers shall not be exercised without his consent, but a purchaser shall not be concerned to see or inquire whether such consent has been given.

As to a tenant for life who has parted with his interest

24.—(1) If it is shown to the satisfaction of the court that a tenant for life, who has by reason of bankruptcy, assignment, incumbrance, or otherwise ceased in the opinion of the court to have a substantial interest in his estate or interest in the settled land or any part thereof, has unreasonably refused to exercise any of the powers conferred on him by this Act, or consents to an order under this section, the court may, on the application of any person interested in the settled land or the part thereof affected, make an order authorising the trustees of the settlement, to exercise, in the name and on behalf of the tenant for life, any of the powers of a tenant for life under this Act, in relation to the settled land or the part thereof affected, either generally and in such manner and for such period as the court may think fit, or in a particular instance, and the court may by the order direct that any documents of title in the possession of the tenant for life relating to the settled land be delivered to the trustees of the settlement.

(2) While any such order is in force, the tenant for life shall not, in relation to the settled land or the part thereof affected, exercise any of the powers thereby authorised to be exercised in his name and on his behalf, but no person dealing with the tenant for life shall be affected by any such order, unless the order is for the time being registered as an order affecting land.

(3) An order may be made under this section at any time after the estate or interest of the tenant for life under the settlement has taken effect in possession, and notwithstanding that he disposed thereof when it was an estate or interest in remainder or reversion.

Married woman, how to be affected

25.[10]—(1) The foregoing provisions of this Act apply to a married woman of full age, whether or not she is entitled to her estate or interest for her separate use or as her separate property, and she, without her husband, may exercise the powers of a tenant for life under this Act.

(2) [*Repealed by the Married Women* (*Restraint upon Anticipation*) *Act* 1949 (12, 13 & 14 *Geo.* 6, *c.* 78), *s.* 1, *Sched.* 2.]

Infants, how to be affected

26.—(1) Where an infant is beneficially entitled in possession to land for an estate in fee simple or for a term of years absolute or would if of full age be a tenant for life of or have the powers of a tenant for life over settled land, then, during the minority of the infant—

(*a*) if the settled land is vested in a personal representative, the personal representative, until a principal vesting instrument has been executed pursuant to the provisions of this Act; and

(*b*) in every other case, the trustees of the settlement;

shall have, in reference to the settled land and capital money, all the powers conferred by this Act and the settlement on a tenant for life, and on the trustees of the settlement.

(2) If the settled land is vested in a personal representative, then, if and when during the minority the infant, if of full age, would have been entitled to have the legal estate in the settled land conveyed to or otherwise vested in him pursuant to the provisions of this Act, a principal vesting instrument shall, if the trustees of the settlement so require, be executed, at the cost of the trust estate, for vesting the legal estate in themselves, and in the meantime the personal representatives shall, during the minority, give effect to the directions of the trustees of the settlement, and shall not be concerned with the propriety of any conveyance directed to be made by those trustees if the conveyance appears to be a proper conveyance under the powers conferred by this Act or by the settlement, and the capital money, if any, arising under the conveyance is paid to or by the direction of the trustees of the settlement or into court, but a purchaser dealing with the personal representative and paying the capital money, if any, to him shall not be concerned to see that the money is paid to trustees of the settlement or into court, or to inquire whether the personal representative is liable to give effect to any such directions, or whether any such directions have been given.

(3) Subsection (2) of this section applies whether the infant becomes entitled before or after the commencement of this Act, and has effect

---

[10] For the right of a married woman to hold property as if she were a *feme sole*, see the Law Reform (Married Women and Tortfeasors) Act 1935 (25 & 26 Geo. 5, c. 30), ss. 1, 4(1) (*a*).

during successive minorities until a person of full age becomes entitled to require the settled land to be vested in him.

(4) This section does not apply where an infant is beneficially entitled in possession to land for an estate in fee simple or for a term of years absolute jointly with a person of full age (for which case provision is made in the Law of Property Act 1925), but it applies to two or more infants entitled as aforesaid jointly, until one of them attains full age.

(5) This section does not apply where an infant would, if of full age, constitute the tenant for life or have the powers of a tenant for life together with another person of full age, but it applies to two or more infants who would, if all of them were of full age, together constitute the tenant for life or have the powers of a tenant for life, until one of them attains full age.

(6) Nothing in this section affects prejudicially any beneficial interest of an infant.

Effect of conveying legal estate to infant

27.—(1) A conveyance of a legal estate in land to an infant alone, or to two or more persons jointly, both or all of whom are infants, for his or their own benefit shall operate only as an agreement for valuable consideration to execute a settlement by means of a principal vesting deed and a trust instrument in favour of the infant or infants, and in the meantime to hold the land in trust for the infant or infants.

(2) Nothing in this Act prevents an equitable interest in settled land being vested in or transferred to an infant.

(3) [Nothing in this Act affects the powers conferred by the Infant Settlements Act 1855, provided that a legal estate in land is not vested in an infant.][11]

28. [*Repealed by the Mental Health Act* 1959 (7 & 8 *Eliz.* 2, *c.* 78), *s.* 149 (2), *Sched.* 8, *Pt.* I.]

Charitable and public trusts

29.—(1) For the purposes of this section, all land vested or to be vested in trustees on or for charitable, ecclesiastical, or public trusts or purposes shall be deemed to be settled land, and the trustees shall, without constituting them statutory owners, have in reference to the land, all the powers which are by this Act conferred on a tenant for life and on the trustees of a settlement.

In connexion only with the exercise of those powers, and not so as to impose any obligation in respect of or to affect—

(a) the mode of creation or the administration of such trusts; or

(b) the appointment or number of trustees of such trusts;

the statute or other instrument creating the trust or under which it is administered shall be deemed the settlement, and the trustees shall be deemed the trustees of the settlement, and, save where the trust is created by a will coming into operation after the commencement of this Act, a separate instrument shall not be necessary for giving effect to the settlement.

Any conveyance of land held on charitable, ecclesiastical or public trusts shall state that the land is held on such trusts, and, where a purchaser has notice that the land is held on charitable, ecclesiastical, or public trusts, he shall be bound to see that any consents or orders requisite for authorising the transaction have been obtained.

(2) The said powers shall be exercisable subject to such consents or orders, if any, being obtained as would, if this Act had not been passed,

---

[11] Repealed by the Family Law Reform Act 1969 (*c.* 46), s. 27 (3), in respect of anything done after the coming into force of that section.

have been requisite if the transaction were being effected under an express power conferred by the instrument creating the trust, and where the land is vested in [. . .]^{12} persons having no powers of management, the said powers shall be exercisable by the managing trustees or committee of management, and the [. . .]^{13} persons aforesaid shall not be liable for giving effect to directions given by the managing trustees or committee of management:

Provided that where—

> (*a*) a disposition or dealing is to be effected for a nominal price or rent, or for less than the best price or rent that can be reasonably obtained or gratuitously; or
>
> (*b*) any interest in land is to be acquired;

the like consent or order (if any) shall be required in reference to the disposition, dealing or acquisition, as would have been requisite if the intended transaction were a sale.

(3) Nothing in this section affects the jurisdiction of the court, Charity Commissioners, Board of Education,^{14} or other competent authority, in regard to the administration of charitable, ecclesiastical, or public trusts.

(4) [*Repealed by the Charities Act* 1960 (8 & 9 *Eliz.* 2, *c.* 58), *s.* 48(2), *Sched.* 7, *Pt.* II.]

(5) Where any trustees or the majority of any set of trustees have power to transfer or create any legal estate, that estate shall be transferred or created by them in the names and on behalf of the persons [. . .]^{15} in whom the legal estate is vested.

(6) This section applies (save as otherwise provided) whether the trust was created before or after the commencement of this Act, but does not apply to land to which the Universities and College Estates Act 1925 applies.

Trustees of Settlement

Who are trustees for purposes of Act

30.—(1) Subject to the provisions of this Act, the following persons are trustees of a settlement for the purposes of this Act, and are in this Act referred to as the "trustees of the settlement" or "trustees of a settlement," namely—

> (i) the persons, if any, who are for the time being under the settlement, trustees with power of sale of the settled land (subject or not to the consent of any person), or with power of consent to or approval of the exercise of such a power of sale, or if there are no such persons; then
>
> (ii) the persons, if any, for the time being, who are by the settlement declared to be trustees thereof for the purposes of the Settled Land Acts 1882 to 1890, or any of them, or this Act, or if there are no such persons; then
>
> (iii) the persons, if any, who are for the time being under the settlement trustees with power of or upon trust for sale of any other land comprised in the settlement and subject to the same limitations as the land to be sold or otherwise dealt with, or with power of consent to or approval of the exercise of such a power of sale, or, if there are no such persons; then
>
> (iv) the persons, if any, who are for the time being under the settlement trustees with future power of sale, or under a future trust for sale of

---

^{12} Words repealed by the Charities Act 1960 (8 & 9 Eliz. 2, c. 58), s. 48 (2), Sched. 7. Pt. I.
^{13} Words repealed by *ibid.*
^{14} Now the Minister of Education: see the Education Act 1944 (7 & 8 Geo. 6, c. 31) s. 2.
^{15} Words repealed by the Charities Act 1960 (8 & 9 Eliz. 2, c. 58) s. 48 (2), Sched. 7, Pt. I.

the settled land, or with power of consent to or approval of the exercise of such a future power of sale, and whether the power or trust takes effect in all events or not, or, if there are no such persons; then

(v) the persons, if any, appointed by deed to be trustees of the settlement by all the persons who at the date of the deed were together able, by virtue of their beneficial interests or by the exercise of an equitable power, to dispose of the settled land in equity for the whole estate the subject of the settlement.

(2) Paragraphs (i) (iii) and (iv) of the last preceding subsection take effect in like manner as if the powers therein referred to had not by this Act been made exercisable by the tenant for life or statutory owner.

(3) Where a settlement is created by will or a settlement has arisen by the effect of an intestacy, and apart from this subsection there would be no trustees for the purposes of this Act of such settlement, then the personal representatives of the deceased shall, until other trustees are appointed, be by virtue of this Act the trustees of the settlement, but where there is a sole personal representative, not being a trust corporation, it shall be obligatory on him to appoint an additional trustee to act with him for the purposes of this Act, and the provisions of the Trustee Act 1925 relating to the appointment of new trustees and the vesting of trust property shall apply accordingly.

As to trustees of compound settlements

31.—(1) Persons who are for the time being trustees for the purposes of this Act of an instrument which is a settlement, or is deemed to be a subsisting settlement for the purposes of this Act, shall be the trustees for the purposes of this Act of any settlement constituted by that instrument and any instruments subsequent in date or operation.

[Where there are trustees for the purposes of this Act of the instrument under which there is a tenant for life or statutory owner but there are no trustees for those purposes of a prior instrument, being one of the instruments by which a compound settlement is constituted, those trustees shall, unless and until trustees are appointed of the prior instrument or of the compound settlement, be the trustees for the purposes of this Act of the compound settlement.][16]

(2) This section applies to instruments coming into operation before as well as after the commencement of this Act, but shall have effect without prejudice to any appointment made by the court before such commencement of trustees of a settlement constituted by more than one instrument, and to the power of the court in any case after such commencement to make any such appointment, and where any such appointment has been made before such commencement or is made thereafter this section shall not apply or shall cease to apply to the settlement consisting of the instruments to which the appointment relates.

As to trustees of referential settlements

32.—(1) Where a settlement takes or has taken effect by reference to another settlement, the trustees for the time being of the settlement to which reference is made shall be the trustees of the settlement by reference, but this section does not apply if the settlement by reference contains an appointment of trustees thereof for the purposes of the Settled Land Acts 1882 to 1890, or any of them, or this Act.

(2) This section applies to instruments coming into operation before as

---

[16] Added by the Law of Property (Amendment) Act 1926, *post*, s. 7, Sched.

well as after the commencement of this Act, but shall have effect without prejudice to any appointment made by the court before such commencement of trustees of a settlement by reference, or of the compound settlement consisting of a settlement and any other settlement or settlements made by reference thereto, and to the power of the court in any case after such commencement to make any such appointment, and where any such appointment has been made before such commencement or is made thereafter this section shall not apply or shall cease to apply.

(3) In this section "a settlement by reference to another settlement" means a settlement of property upon the limitations and subject to the powers and provisions of an existing settlement, with or without variation.

Continuance of trustees in office, and as to certain compound settlements

33.—(1) Where any persons have been appointed or constituted trustees of a settlement, whether by an order of the court or otherwise, or have by reason of any power of sale, or trust for sale, or by reason of a power of consent to, or approval of, the exercise of a power of sale, or by virtue of this Act, or otherwise at any time become trustees of a settlement for the purposes of the Settled Land Acts 1882 to 1890 or this Act, then those persons or their successors in office shall remain and be trustees of the settlement as long as that settlement is subsisting or deemed to be subsisting for the purposes of this Act.

In this subsection "successors in office" means the persons who, by appointment or otherwise, have become trustees for the purposes aforesaid.

(2) Where settled land is or has been expressed to be disposed of under a compound settlement of which trustees were appointed by the court, and the capital money (if any) arising on the disposition is or was paid to the persons who by virtue of the order or any subsequent appointment appear to be or to have been the trustees of that settlement, and where the person by or on whose behalf the disposition is or was made is or was the tenant for life or statutory owner of the land disposed of under an instrument mentioned in the order as constituting part of such compound settlement (in this subsection called "the principal instrument") then the title of the person to whom the disposition is made shall not be impeachable on the ground—

(*a*) that the instruments mentioned in the order did not constitute a compound settlement; or

(*b*) that those instruments were not all the instruments at the date of the order or of the disposition constituting the compound settlement of the land disposed of; or

(*c*) that any of the instruments mentioned in the order did not form part of the settlement of the land disposed of, or had ceased to form part of the settlement at the date of the dispositon;

but nothing in this subsection shall prejudice the rights of any person in respect of any estate, interest or charge under any instrument existing at the date of the order and not mentioned therein which would not have been overreached if the disposition had been made by or on behalf of the tenant for life or statutory owner under the principal instrument as such, and there had been trustees of that instrument for the purposes of the Settled Land Acts 1882 to 1890 or this Act, and the capital money, if any, arising on the disposition had been paid to the trustees.

(3) The foregoing provisions of this section operate to confirm all dispositions made before the commencement of this Act, but not so as to render invalid or prejudice any order of the court, or any title or right acquired before the commencement of this Act, and operates without prejudice to any appointment already made by the court of trustees of a

settlement, and to the power of the court in any case hereafter to make any such appointment.

Appointment of trustees by court

34.—(1) If at any time there are no trustees of a settlement, or where in any other case it is expedient, for the purposes of this Act, that new trustees of a settlement be appointed, the court may, if it thinks fit, on the application of the tenant for life, statutory owner, or of any other person having, under the settlement, an estate, or interest in the settled land, in possession, remainder or otherwise, or, in the case of an infant, of his testamentary or other guardian or next friend, appoint fit persons to be trustees of the settlement.

(2) The persons so appointed, and the survivors and survivor of them, while continuing to be trustees or trustee, and, until the appointment of new trustees, the personal representatives or representative for the time being of the last surviving or continuing trustee, shall become and be the trustees or trustee of the settlement.

Procedure on appointment of new trustees

35.—(1) Whenever a new trustee for the purposes of this Act is appointed of a trust instrument or a trustee thereof for the purposes aforesaid is discharged from the trust without a new trustee being appointed, a deed shall be executed supplemental to the last or only principal vesting instrument containing a declaration that the persons therein named, being the persons who after such appointment or discharge, as the case may be, are the trustees of the trust instrument for the purposes aforesaid, are the trustees of the settlement for those purposes; and a memorandum shall be endorsed on or annexed to the last or only principal vesting instrument in accordance with the Trustee Act 1925.

(2) Every such deed as aforesaid shall, if the trustee was appointed or discharged by the court, be executed by such person as the court may direct, and, in any other case, shall be executed by—

(i) the person, if any, named in the principal vesting instrument as the person for the time being entitled to appoint new trustees of the settlement, or if no person is so named, or the person is dead or unable or unwilling to act, the persons who if the principal vesting instrument had been the only instrument constituting the settlement would have had power to appoint new trustees thereof;

(ii) the persons named in the deed of declaration as the trustees of the settlement; and

(iii) any trustee who is discharged as aforesaid or retires.

(3) A statement contained in any such deed of declaration as is mentioned in this section to the effect that the person named in the principal vesting instrument as the person for the time being entitled to appoint new trustees of the settlement is unable or unwilling to act, or that a trustee has remained outside the United Kingdom for more than twelve months, or refuses or is unfit to act, or is incapable of acting, shall in favour of a purchaser of a legal estate be conclusive evidence of the matter stated.

Provisions as to Undivided Shares

Undivided shares to take effect behind a trust for sale of the land

36.—(1) If and when, after the commencement of this Act, settled land is held in trust for persons entitled in possession under a trust instrument in undivided shares, the trustees of the settlement (if the settled land is not already vested in them) may require the estate owner in whom the settled land is vested (but in the case of a personal representative subject to his rights and powers for purposes of administration), at the cost of the trust estate, to convey the land to them, or assent to the land vesting in them as joint tenants, and in the meantime the land shall be held on the same trusts as would have been applicable thereto if it had been so conveyed to or vested in the trustees.

(2) If and when the settled land so held in trust in undivided shares is or becomes vested in the trustees of the settlement, the land shall be held by them (subject to any incumbrances affecting the settled land which are secured by a legal mortgage, but freed from any incumbrances affecting the undivided shares or not secured as aforesaid, and from any interests, powers and charges subsisting under the trust instrument which have priority to the trust for the persons entitled to the undivided shares) upon the statutory trusts.

(3) If the estate owner refuses or neglects for one month after demand in writing to convey the settled land so held in trust in undivided shares in manner aforesaid, or if by reason of his being outside the United Kingdom or being unable to be found, or by reason of the dissolution of a corporation, or for any other reason, the court is satisfied that the conveyance cannot otherwise be made, or cannot be made without undue delay or expense, the court may, on the application of the trustees of the settlement, make an order vesting the settled land in them on the statutory trusts.

(4) An undivided share in land shall not be capable of being created except under a trust instrument or under the Law of Property Act 1925, and shall then only take effect behind a trust for sale.

(5) Nothing in this section affects the priority inter se of any incumbrances whether affecting the entirety of the land or an undivided share.

(6) For the purposes of this section land held upon the statutory trusts shall be held upon the trusts and subject to the provisions following, namely, upon trust to sell the same, with power to postpone the sale of the whole or any part thereof, and to stand possessed of the net proceeds of sale, after payment of costs, and of the net rents and profits until sale, after payment of rates, taxes, costs of insurance, repairs, and other outgoings, upon such trusts and subject to such powers and provisions as may be requisite for giving effect to the rights of the persons interested in the settled land, [and the right of a person who, if the land had not been made subject to a trust for sale by virtue of this Act, would have been entitled to an entailed interest in an undivided share in the land, shall be deemed to be a right to a corresponding entailed interest in the net proceeds of sale attributable to that share].[17]

(7) The provisions of this section bind the Crown.

Transitional Provisions

Transitional provisions with respect to existing settlements, &c.

37. The transitional provisions set out in the Second Schedule to this Act shall have effect as regards settlements existing at the commencement of this Act.

---

[17] Added by the Law of Property (Entailed Interests) Act 1932, *post*, s. 1(1).

PART II[18]

POWERS OF A TENANT FOR LIFE[19]

Sale and Exchange

Powers of sale and exchange

38. A tenant for life—
    (i) May sell the settled land, or any part thereof, or any easement, right or privilege of any kind over or in relation to the land; and
    (ii) [*This subsection is repealed by the Statute Law (Repeals) Act 1969 (c. 52), s. 1 and Sched., Pt. III.*]
    (iii) May make an exchange of the settled land, or any part thereof, or of any easement, right, or privilege of any kind, whether or not newly created, over or in relation to the settled land, or any part thereof, for other land, or for any easement, right or privilege of any kind, whether or not newly created, over or in relation to other land, including an exchange in consideration of money paid for equality of exchange.

Regulations respecting sales

39.—(1) Save as hereinafter provided every sale shall be made for the best consideration in money that can reasonably be obtained.

(2) A sale may be made in consideration wholly or partially of a perpetual rent, or a terminable rent consisting of principal and interest combined, payable yearly or half yearly to be secured upon the land sold, or the land to which the easement, right or privilege sold is to be annexed in enjoyment or an adequate part thereof.

In the case of a terminable rent, the conveyance shall distinguish the part attributable to principal and that attributable to interest, and the part attributable to principal shall be capital money arising under this Act:

Provided that, unless the part of the terminable rent attributable to interest varies according to the amount of the principal repaid, the trustees of the settlement shall, during the subsistence of the rent, accumulate the income of the said capital money in the way of compound interest by investing it and the resulting income thereof in securities authorised for the investment of capital money and shall add the accumulations to capital.

(3) The rent to be reserved on any such sale shall be the best rent that can reasonably be obtained, regard being had to any money paid as part of the consideration, or laid out, or to be laid out, for the benefit of the settled land, and generally to the circumstances of the case, but a peppercorn rent, or a nominal or other rent less than the rent ultimately payable, may be made payable during any period not exceeding five years from the date of the conveyance.

(4) Where a sale is made in consideration of a rent, the following provisions shall have effect:—
    (i) The conveyance shall contain a covenant by the purchaser for payment of the rent, and [the statutory powers and remedies for the recovery of the rent shall apply][20];

---

[18] For power to enter into forestry dedication covenants see the Forestry Act 1967 (c. 10), s. 5(4), Sched. 2.

[19] The powers of a tenant for life and of the trustees of a settlement under the Settled Land Act 1925 are extended to trustees for sale by the Law of Property Act 1925, ss. 28, 205 (1) (xxvi), (xxix), *post*, pp. 135, 221. The powers of a tenant for life are extended by the Leasehold Reform Act 1967 (c. 88), s. 6.

[20] Substituted by the Law of Property (Amendment) Act 1926, *post*, s. 7, Sched.

(ii) A duplicate of the conveyance shall be executed by the purchaser and delivered to the tenant for life or statutory owner, of which execution and delivery the execution of the conveyance by the tenant for life or statutory owner shall be sufficient evidence;

(iii) A statement, contained in the conveyance or in an indorsement thereon, signed by the tenant for life or statutory owner, respecting any matter of fact or of calculation under this Act in relation to the sale, shall, in favour of the purchaser and of those claiming under him, be sufficient evidence of the matter stated.

(5) The consideration on a sale to any company incorporated by special Act of Parliament or by provisional order confirmed by Parliament or by any other order, scheme or certificate having the force of an Act of Parliament, may, with the consent of the tenant for life, consist, wholly or in part, of fully-paid securities of any description of the company, and such securities shall be vested in the trustees of the settlement and shall be subject to the provisions of this Act relating to securities representing capital money arising under this Act, and may be retained and held by the trustees in like manner as if they had been authorised by this Act for the investment of capital money.

(6) A sale may be made in one lot or in several lots, and either by auction or by private contract, and may be made subject to any stipulations respecting title, or evidence of title, or other things.

(7) On a sale the tenant for life may fix reserve biddings and may buy in at an auction.

Regulations respecting exchanges

40.—(1) Save as in this Part of this Act provided, every exchange shall be made for the best consideration in land or in land and money that can reasonably be obtained.

(2) An exchange may be made subject to any stipulations respecting title, or evidence of title, or other things.

(3) Settled land in England or Wales shall not be given in exchange for land out of England and Wales.

Leasing Powers

Power to lease for ordinary or building or mining or forestry purposes

41. A tenant for life may lease the settled land, or any part thereof, or any easement, right, or privilege of any kind over or in relation to the land, for any purpose whatever, whether involving waste or not, for any term not exceeding—

(i) In case of a building lease, nine hundred and ninety-nine years;

(ii) In case of a mining lease, one hundred years;

(iii) In case of a forestry lease, nine hundred and ninety-nine years;

(iv) In case of any other lease, fifty years.

Regulations respecting leases generally

42.—(1) Save as hereinafter provided, every lease—

(i) shall be by deed, and be made to take effect in possession not later than twelve months after its date, or in reversion after an existing lease having not more than seven years to run at the date of the new lease;

(ii) shall reserve the best rent that can reasonably be obtained, regard being had to any fine taken, and to any money laid out or to be laid out for the benefit of the settled land, and generally to the circumstances of the case;

(iii) shall contain a covenant by the lessee for payment of the rent, and a condition of re-entry on the rent not being paid within a time therein specified not exceeding thirty days.

(2) A counterpart of every lease shall be executed by the lessee and delivered to the tenant for life or statutory owner, of which execution and delivery the execution of the lease by the tenant for life or statutory owner shall be sufficient evidence.

(3) A statement, contained in a lease or in an indorsement thereon, signed by the tenant for life or statutory owner, respecting any matter of fact or of calculation under this Act in relation to the lease, shall, in favour of the lessee and of those claiming under him, be sufficient evidence of the matter stated.

(4) A fine received on the grant of a lease under any power conferred by this Act shall be deemed to be capital money arising under this Act.

(5) A lease at the best rent that can be reasonably obtained without fine, and whereby the lessee is not exempted from punishment for waste, may be made—

(i) Where the term does not exceed twenty-one years—

(*a*) without any notice of an intention to make the lease having been given under this Act; and

(*b*) notwithstanding that there are no trustees of the settlement; and

(ii) Where the term does not extend beyond three years from the date of the writing, by any writing under hand only containing an agreement instead of a covenant by the lessee for payment of rent.

Leasing powers for special objects

43. The leasing power of a tenant for life extends to the making of—

(i) a lease for giving effect (in such manner and so far as the law permits) to a covenant of renewal, performance whereof could be enforced against the owner for the time being of the settled land; and

(ii) a lease for confirming, as far as may be, a previous lease being void or voidable, but so that every lease, as and when confirmed, shall be such a lease as might at the date of the original lease have been lawfully granted under this Act or otherwise, as the case may require.

Provisions as to building, mining and forestry leases

Regulations respecting building leases

44.—(1) Every building lease shall be made partly in consideration of the lessee, or some person by whose direction the lease is granted, or some other person, having erected or agreeing to erect buildings, new or additional, or having improved or repaired or agreeing to improve or repair buildings, or having executed or agreeing to execute on the land leased, an improvement authorised by this Act for or in connexion with building purposes.

(2) A peppercorn rent or a nominal or other rent less than the rent ultimately payable, may be made payable for the first five years or any less part of the term.

(3) Where the land is contracted to be leased in lots, the entire amount of rent to be ultimately payable may be apportioned among the lots in any manner:

Provided that—

    (i) the annual rent reserved by any lease shall not be less than ten shillings; and

    (ii) the total amount of the rents reserved on all leases for the time being granted shall not be less than the total amount of the rents which, in order that the leases may be in conformity with this Act, ought to be reserved in respect of the whole land for the time being leased; and

    (iii) the rent reserved by any lease shall not exceed one-fifth part of the full annual value of the land comprised in that lease with the buildings thereon when completed.

Regulations respecting mining leases

45.—(1) In a mining lease—

    (i) the rent may be made to be ascertainable by or to vary according to the acreage worked, or by or according to the quantities of any mineral or substance gotten, made merchantable, converted, carried away, or disposed of, in or from the settled land, or any other land, or by or according to any facilities given in that behalf; and

    (ii) the rent may also be made to vary according to the price of the minerals or substances gotten, or any of them, and such price may be the saleable value, or the price or value appearing in any trade or market or other price list or return from time to time, or may be the marketable value as ascertained in any manner prescribed by the lease (including a reference to arbitration), or may be an average of any such prices or values taken during a specified period; and

    (iii) a fixed or minimum rent may be made payable, with or without power for the lessee, in case the rent, according to acreage or quantity or otherwise, in any specified period does not produce an amount equal to the fixed or minimum rent, to make up the deficiency in any subsequent specified period, free of rent other than the fixed or minimum rent.

(2) A lease may be made partly in consideration of the lessee having executed, or agreeing to execute, on the land leased an improvement authorised by this Act, for or in connexion with mining purposes.

Variation of building or mining lease according to circumstances of district

46.—(1) Where it is shown to the court with respect to the district in which any settled land is situate, either—

    (i) that it is the custom for land therein to be leased for building or mining purposes for a longer term or on other conditions than the term or conditions specified in that behalf in this Act; or

    (ii) that it is difficult to make leases for building or mining purposes of land therein, except for a longer term or on other conditions than the term and conditions specified in that behalf in this Act;

the court may, if it thinks fit, authorise generally the tenant for life or statutory owner to make from time to time leases of or affecting the settled land in that district, or parts thereof for any term or on any conditions as in the order of the court expressed, or may, if it thinks fit, authorise the tenant for life or statutory owner to make any such lease in any particular case.

(2) Thereupon the tenant for life or statutory owner, and, subject to any direction in the order of the court to the contrary, each of his successors in title being a tenant for life or statutory owner, may make in any case, or in

the particular case, a lease of the settled land, or part thereof, in conformity with the order.

Capitalisation of part of mining rent

47. Under a mining lease, whether the mines or minerals leased are already opened or in work or not, unless a contrary intention is expressed in the settlement, there shall be from time to time set aside, as capital money arising under this Act, part of the rent as follows, namely—where the tenant for life or statutory owner is impeachable for waste in respect of minerals, three fourth parts of the rent, and otherwise one fourth part thereof, and in every such case the residue of the rent shall go as rents and profits.

Regulations respecting forestry leases

48.[21]—(1) In the case of a forestry lease—

    (i) a peppercorn rent or a nominal or other rent less than the rent ultimately payable, may be made payable for the first ten years or any less part of the term;

    (ii) the rent may be made to be ascertainable by, or to vary according to the value of the timber on the land comprised in the lease, or the produce thereof, which may during any year be cut, converted, carried away, or otherwise disposed of;

    (iii) a fixed or minimum rent may be made payable, with or without power for the lessee, in case the rent according to value in any specified period does not produce an amount equal to the fixed or minimum rent, to make up the deficiency in any subsequent specified period, free of rent other than the fixed or minimum rent; and

    (iv) any other provisions may be made for the sharing of the proceeds or profits of the user of the land between the reversioner and the Forestry Commissioners.

(2) In this section the expression "timber" includes all forest products.

Miscellaneous Powers

Power on dispositions to impose restrictions and make reservations and stipulations

49.—(1) On a sale or other disposition or dealing under the powers of this Act—

    (*a*) any easement, right, or privilege of any kind may be reserved or granted over or in relation to the settled land or any part thereof or other land, including the land disposed of, and, in the case of an exchange, the land taken in exchange; and

    (*b*) any restriction with respect to building on or other user of land, or with respect to mines and minerals, or with respect to or for the purpose of the more beneficial working thereof, or with respect to any other thing, may be imposed and made binding, as far as the law permits, by covenant, condition or otherwise, on the tenant for life or statutory owner and the settled land or any part thereof, or on the other party and any land disposed of to him; and

    (*c*) the whole or any part of any capital or annual sum (and in the case of an annual sum whether temporary or perpetual) charged on or payable out of the land disposed of, or any part thereof, and other

---

[21] References in this section to "Forestry Commissioners" are to be construed as references to the appropriate Minister: Forestry Act 1967 (c. 10), Sched. 6, para. 5.

land subject to the settlement, may as between the tenant for life or statutory owner and his successors in title, and the other party and persons deriving title under or in succession to him (but without prejudice to the rights of the person entitled to such capital or annual sum) be charged exclusively on the land disposed of, or any part thereof, or such other land as aforesaid, or any part thereof, in exoneration of the rest of the land on or out of which such capital or annual sum is charged or payable.

(2) A sale of land may be made subject to a stipulation that all or any of the timber and other trees, pollards, tellers, underwood, saplings and plantations on the land sold (in this section referred to as "timber" or any articles attached to the land (in this section referred to as "fixtures") shall be taken by the purchaser at a valuation, and the amount of the valuation shall form part of the price of the land, and shall be capital money accordingly.

(3) Where on a sale the consideration attributable to any timber or fixtures is by mistake paid to a tenant for life or other person not entitled to receive it, then, if such person or the purchaser or the persons deriving title under either of them subsequently pay the aforesaid consideration, with such interest, if any, thereon as the court may direct, to the trustees of the settlement or other persons entitled thereto or into court, the court may, on the application of the purchaser or the persons deriving title under him, declare that the disposition is to take effect as if the whole of the consideration had at the date thereof been duly paid to the trustees of the settlement or other persons entitled to receive the same.

The person not entitled to receive the same, to whom the consideration is paid, and his estate and effects shall remain liable to make good any loss attributable to the mistake.

Separate dealing with surface and minerals, with or without wayleaves, &c.

50. A sale, exchange, lease or other authorised disposition, may be made either of land, with or without an exception or reservation of all or any of the mines and minerals therein, or of any mines and minerals, and in any such case with or without a grant or reservation of powers of working, wayleaves or rights of way, rights of water and drainage, and other powers, easements, rights, and privileges for or incident to or connected with mining purposes, in relation to the settled land, or any part thereof, or any other land.

Power to grant options

51.—(1) A tenant for life may at any time, either with or without consideration, grant by writing an option to purchase or take a lease of the settled land, or any part thereof, or any easement, right, or privilege over or in relation to the same at a price or rent fixed at the time of the granting of the option.

(2) Every such option shall be made exercisable within an agreed number of years not exceeding ten.

(3) The price or rent shall be the best which, having regard to all the circumstances, can reasonably be obtained and either—

(*a*) may be a specified sum of money or rent, or at a specified rate according to the superficial area of the land with respect to which the option is exercised, or the frontage thereof or otherwise; or

(*b*) in the case of an option to purchase contained in a lease or agreement for a lease, may be a stated number of years' purchase of the highest rent reserved by the lease or agreement; or

(*c*) if the option is exercisable as regards part of the land comprised in the lease or agreement, may be a proportionate part of such highest rent;

and any aggregate price or rent may be made to be apportionable in any manner, or according to any system, or by reference to arbitration.

(4) An option to take a mining lease may be coupled with the grant of a licence to search for and prove any mines or minerals under the settled land, or any part thereof, pending the exercise of the option.

(5) The consideration for the grant of the option shall be capital money arising under this Act.

Surrenders and re-grants

52.—(1) A tenant for life may accept, with or without consideration, a surrender of any lease of settled land, whether made under this Act or not, or a regrant of any land granted in fee simple, whether under this Act or not, in respect of the whole land leased or granted, or any part thereof, with or without an exception of all or any of the mines and minerals therein, or in respect of mines and minerals, or any of them, and with or without an exception of any easement, right or privilege of any kind over or in relation to the land surrendered or regranted.

(2) On a surrender of a lease, or a regrant of land granted in fee simple, in respect of part only of the land or mines and minerals leased or granted, the rent or rentcharge may be apportioned.

(3) On a surrender or regrant, the tenant for life may in relation to the land or mines and minerals surrendered or regranted, or of any part thereof, make a new or other lease, or grant in fee simple, or new or other leases, or grants in fee simple, in lots.

(4) A new or other lease, or grant in fee simple, may comprise additional land or mines and minerals, and may reserve any apportioned or other rent or rentcharge.

(5) On a surrender or regrant, and the making of a new or other lease, whether for the same or for any extended or other term, or of a new or other grant in fee simple, and whether or not subject to the same or to any other covenants, provisions, or conditions, the value of the lessee's or grantee's interest in the lease surrendered, or the land regranted, may be taken into account in the determination of the amount of the rent or rentcharge to be reserved, and of any fine or consideration in money to be taken, and of the nature of the covenants, provisions, and conditions to be inserted in the new or other lease, or grant in fee simple.

(6) Every new or other lease, or grant in fee simple, shall be in conformity with this Act.

(7) All money, not being rent or a rentcharge, received on the exercise by the tenant for life of the powers conferred by this section, shall, unless the court, on an application made within six months after the receipt thereof or within such further time as the court may in special circumstances allow, otherwise directs, be capital money arising under this Act.

(8) A regrant shall be made to the tenant for life or statutory owner, and shall be deemed a subsidiary vesting deed, and the statements and particulars required in the case of subsidiary vesting deeds shall be inserted therein.

(9) In this section "land granted in fee simple" means land so granted with or subject to a reservation thereout of a perpetual or terminable rentcharge which is or forms part of the settled land, and "grant in fee simple" has a corresponding meaning.

Acceptance of leases

53.—(1) A tenant for life may accept a lease of any land, or of any mines and minerals or of any easement, right, or privilege, convenient to be held or worked with or annexed in enjoyment to the settled land, or any part thereof, for such period, and upon such terms and conditions, as the tenant for life thinks fit:

Provided that no fine shall be paid out of capital money in respect of such lease.

(2)[22] The lease shall be granted to the tenant for life or statutory owner, and shall be deemed a subsidiary vesting deed, and the statements and particulars required in the case of subsidiary vesting deeds shall either be inserted therein or endorsed thereon.

(3) The lease may contain an option to purchase the reversion expectant on the term thereby granted.

Power to grant water rights to statutory bodies

54.—(1) For the development, improvement, or general benefit of the settled land, or any part thereof, a tenant for life may make a grant in fee simple or absolutely, or a lease for any term of years absolute, for a nominal price or rent, or for less than the best price or rent that can reasonably be obtained, or gratuitously, to any statutory authority, of any water or streams or springs of water in, upon, or under the settled land, and of any rights of taking, using, enjoying and conveying water, and of laying, constructing, maintaining, and repairing mains, pipes, reservoirs, dams, weirs and other works of any kind proper for the supply and distribution of water, and of any part of the settled land required as a site for any of the aforesaid works, and of any easement, right or privilege over or in relation to the settled land or any part thereof in connexion with any of the aforesaid works.

(2) This section does not authorise the creation of any greater rights than could have been created by a person absolutely entitled for his own benefit to the settled land affected.

(3) In this section "statutory authority" means an authority or company for the time being empowered by any Act of Parliament, public general, or local or private, or by any order or certificate having the force of an Act of Parliament, to provide with a supply of water any town, parish or place in which the settled land or any part thereof is situated.

(4) All money, not being rent, received on the exercise of any power conferred by this section shall be capital money arising under this Act.

Power to grant land for public and charitable purposes

55.—(1) For the development, improvement, or general benefit of the settled land, or any part thereof, a tenant for life may make a grant in fee simple, or absolutely, or a lease for any term of years absolute, for a nominal price or rent, or for less than the best price or rent that can reasonably be obtained, or gratuitously, of any part of the settled land, with or without any easement, right or privilege over or in relation to the settled land or any part thereof, for all or any one or more of the following purposes, namely:—

(i) For the site, or the extension of any existing site, of a place of religious worship, residence for a minister of religion, school house, town hall, market house, public library, public baths, museum, hospital, infirmary, or other public building, literary or scientific institution, drill hall, working-men's club, parish room, reading room or village institute, with or without in any case any yard, garden, or other ground to be held with any such building; or

(ii) For the construction, enlargement, or improvement of any railway, canal, road (public or private), dock, sea-wall, embankment, drain, watercourse, or reservoir; or

---

[22] Applied by the Leasehold Reform Act 1967 (c. 88), s. 6(2) (*b*).

(iii) For any other public or charitable purpose in connexion with the settled land, or any part thereof, or tending to the benefit of the persons residing, or for whom dwellings may be erected, on the settled land, or any part thereof.

Not more than one acre shall in any particular case be conveyed for any purpose mentioned in paragraphs (i) and (iii) of this subsection, nor more than five acres for any purpose mentioned in paragraph (ii) of this subsection, unless the full consideration be paid or reserved in respect of the excess.

(2) All money, not being rent, received on the exercise of any power conferred by this section shall be capital money arising under this Act.

Dedication for streets, open spaces, &c.

56.—(1) On or after or in connexion with a sale or grant for building purposes, or a building lease, or the development as a building estate of the settled land, or any part thereof, or at any other reasonable time, the tenant for life, for the general benefit of the residents on the settled land, or on any part thereof—

(i) may cause or require any parts of the settled land to be appropriated and laid out for streets, roads, paths, squares, gardens, or other open spaces, for the use, gratuitously or on payment, of the public or of individuals, with sewers, drains, watercourses, fencing, paving, or other works necessary or proper in connexion therewith; and

(ii) may provide that the parts so appropriated shall be conveyed to or vested in the trustees of the settlement, or other trustees, or any company or public body, on trusts or subject to provisions for securing the continued appropriation thereof to the purposes aforesaid, and the continued repair or maintenance of streets and other places and works aforesaid, with or without provision for appointment of new trustees when required; and

(iii) may execute any general or other deed necessary or proper for giving effect to the provisions of this section (which deed may be inrolled in the Central Office of the Supreme Court), and thereby declare the mode, terms, and conditions of the appropriation, and the manner in which and the persons by whom the benefit thereof is to be enjoyed, and the nature and extent of the privileges and conveniences granted.

(2) In regard to the dedication of land for the public purposes aforesaid, a tenant for life shall be in the same position as if he were an absolute owner.

(3) A tenant for life shall have power—

(*a*) to enter into any agreement for the recompense to be made for any part of the settled land which is required for the widening of a highway under [the Highways Act 1980][23] or otherwise;

(*b*) to consent to the diversion of any highway over the settled land under [the Highways Act 1980][24] or otherwise;

(*c*) [*repealed by the Highways Act* 1959 (7 & 8 *Eliz.* 2, *c.* 25), *s.* 312 (2), *Sched.* 25.]

and any agreement or consent so made or given shall be as valid and effectual, for all purposes, as if made or given by an absolute owner of the settled land.

(4) All money, not being rent, received on the exercise of any power conferred by this section shall be capital money arising under this Act.

[23] Substituted by the Highways Act 1980 (c. 66), Sched. 24.
[24] *Ibid.*

Provision of land for small dwellings, small holdings and dwellings for working classes

57.—(1) Where land is sold, or given in exchange or leased—
  (*a*) for the purpose of the erection on such land of small dwellings; or
  (*b*) to the council of a county or county borough for the purposes of small holdings;
the sale exchange, or lease may, notwithstanding anything contained in this Act, be made for such consideration in money, or land, or in land and money, or may reserve such rent, as having regard to the said purposes and to all the circumstances of the case, is the best that can reasonably be obtained, notwithstanding that a better consideration or rent might have been obtained if the land were sold, exchanged, or leased, for another purpose.

(2) Notwithstanding anything contained in, and in addition to the other powers conferred by this Act, a tenant for life may at any time—
  (*a*) for the purpose of the erection of dwellings for the working classes, or the provision of gardens to be held therewith; or
  (*b*) for the purpose of the Small Holdings and Allotments Acts 1908 to 1919;
make a grant in fee simple or absolutely, or a lease for any term of years absolute of any part of the settled land, with or without any easement, right or privilege of any kind over or in relation to the settled land or any part thereof, for a nominal price or rent, or for less than the best price or rent that can reasonably be obtained or gratuitously:

Provided that, except under an order of the court, not more than two acres in the case of land situate in an urban district, or ten acres in the case of land situate in a rural district, in any one parish shall be granted or leased under the powers conferred by this subsection, unless the full consideration be paid or reserved in respect of the excess.

(3) All money, not being rent, received on the exercise of any power conferred by this section shall be capital money arising under this Act.

Power to compromise claims and release restrictions, &c.

58.—(1) A tenant for life may, with the consent in writing of the trustees of the settlement, either with or without giving or taking any consideration in money or otherwise, compromise, compound, abandon, submit to arbitration or otherwise settle any claim, dispute, or question whatsoever relating to the settled land, or any part thereof, including in particular claims, disputes or questions as to boundaries, the ownership of mines and minerals, rights and powers of working mines and minerals, local laws and customs relative to the working of mines and minerals, and other matters, [. . .][25] easements, and restrictive covenants, and for any of those purposes may enter into, give execute, and do such agreements, assurances, releases, and other things as the tenant for life may, with such consent as aforesaid, think proper.

(2) A tenant for life may, with the consent in writing of the trustees of the settlement, at any time, by deed or writing, either with or without consideration in money or otherwise, release, waive, or modify, or agree to release, waive, or modify, any covenant, agreement, or restriction imposed on any other land for the benefit of the settled land, or any part thereof, or release, or agree to release, any other land from any easement, right or privilege, including a right of pre-emption, affecting the same for the benefit of the settled land, or any part thereof.

(3) A tenant for life may contract that a transaction effected before or

---

[25] These words were repealed by the Statute Law (Repeals) Act 1969 (c. 52), s. 1, and Sched., Pt. III.

after the commencement of this Act, which (whether subject or not to any variation authorised by this subsection) is affected by section seventy-eight of the Railway Clauses Consolidation Act 1845, or by section twenty-two of the Waterworks Clauses Act 1847 (relating to support by minerals) shall take effect as if some other distance than forty yards or the prescribed distance had been mentioned in such sections or had been otherwise prescribed.

In any case where section seventy-eight aforesaid has effect as amended and re-enacted by Part II of the Mines (Working Facilities and Support) Act 1923, a tenant for life may make any agreement authorised by section eighty-five A of the Railway Clauses Consolidation Act 1845, as enacted in the said Part II.

Power to vary leases and grants and to give licences and consents

59.—(1) A tenant for life may, at any time, by deed, either with or without consideration in money or otherwise, vary, release, waive or modify, either absolutely or otherwise, the terms of any lease whenever made of the settled land or any part thereof, or any covenants or conditions contained in any grant in fee simple whenever made of land with or subject to a reservation thereout of a rent which is or forms part of the settled land, and in either case in respect of the whole or any part of the land comprised in any such lease or grant, but so that every such lease or grant shall, after such variation, release, waiver or modification as aforesaid, be such a lease or grant as might then have been lawfully made under this Act if the lease had been surrendered, or the land comprised in the grant had never been so comprised, or had been regranted.

(2) Where land is or has been disposed of subject to any covenant requiring the licence, consent, or approval of the convenantee or his successors in title as to—

(*a*) the user of the land in any manner; or

(*b*) the erection construction or alteration of or addition to buildings or works of any description on the land; or

(*c*) the plans or elevations of any proposed buildings or other works on the land; or

(*d*) any other act, matter, or thing relating to the land, or any buildings or works thereon; or

(*e*) any assignment, under-letting or parting with the possession of all or any part of the property comprised in any lease affecting the settled land;

and the covenant enures for the benefit of settled land (including, where the disposition is a lease, the reversion expectant on the determination thereof), the licence, consent or approval may be given by the tenant for life of the settled land affected.

Power to apportion rents

60.—(1) A tenant for life may, at any time, by deed either with or without consideration in money or otherwise, agree for the apportionment of any rent reserved or created by any such lease or grant as mentioned in the last preceding section, or any rent being or forming part of the settled land, so that the apportioned parts of such rent shall thenceforth be payable exclusively out of or in respect of such respective portions of the land subject thereto as may be thought proper, and also agree that any covenants, agreements, powers, or remedies for securing such rent and any other covenants or agreements by the lessee or grantee and any conditions shall also be apportioned and made applicable exclusively to the respective portions of the land out of or in respect of which the apportioned parts of such rent shall thenceforth be payable.

(2) Where the settled land, or any part thereof, is held or derived under a lease, or under a grant reserving rent, or subject to covenants, agreements or conditions, whether such lease or grant comprises other land or not, the tenant for life may at any time by deed, with or without giving or taking any consideration in money or otherwise, procure the variation, release, waiver, or modification, either absolutely or otherwise, of the terms, covenants, agreements, or conditions contained in such lease or grant, in respect of the whole or any part of the settled land comprised therein, including the apportionment of any rent, covenants, agreements, conditions, and provisions reserved, or created by, or contained in, such lease or grant.

(3) This section applies to leases or grants made either before or after the commencement of this Act.

Provisions as to consideration

61.—(1) All money, not being rent, payable by the tenant for life in respect of any transaction to which any of the three last preceding sections relates shall be paid out of capital money arising under this Act, and all money, not being rent, received on the exercise by the tenant for life of the powers conferred by any of those sections, shall, unless the court, on an application made within six months after the receipt thereof or within such further time as the court may in special circumstances allow, otherwise directs, be capital money arising under this Act.

(2) For the purpose of the three last preceding sections "consideration in money or otherwise" means—

(*a*) a capital sum of money or a rent;

(*b*) land being freehold or leasehold for any term of years whereof not less than sixty years shall be unexpired;

(*c*) any easement, right or privilege over or in relation to the settled land, or any part thereof, or any other land;

(*d*) the benefit of any restrictive covenant or condition; and

(*e*) the release of the settled land, or any part thereof, or any other land, from any easement, right or privilege, including a right of pre-emption, or from the burden of any restrictive covenant or condition affecting the same.

Special provisions as to manorial incidents, &c.

62. [*Subs.* (1) *to* (3) *were repealed by the Statute Law* (*Repeals*) *Act* 1969 (*c.* 52), *s.* 1 *and Sched., Pt.* III, *manorial incidents having been extinguished by the Law of Property Act* 1922 (12 & 13 *Geo.* 5, *c.* 16), *ss.* 128, 138 (1).]

(4) In reference to the conversion of a perpetually renewable lease or underlease into a long term, a tenant for life may enter into such agreements and do such acts and things as the lessor or lessee or under-lessee, as the case may require, is, by any enactment authorised to enter into or do.

Power to complete predecessor's contracts

63.—A tenant for life may make any disposition which is necessary or proper for giving effect to a contract entered into by a predecessor in title, and which if made by that predecessor would have been valid as against his successors in title.

General power for the tenant for life to effect any transaction under an order of the court

64.—(1) Any transaction affecting or concerning the settled land, or any part thereof, or any other land (not being a transaction otherwise authorised by this Act, or by the settlement) which in the opinion of the court would be for the benefit of the settled land, or any part thereof, or the persons interested under the settlement, may, under an order of the court, be effected by a tenant for life, if it is one which could have been validly effected by an absolute owner.

(2) In this section "transaction" includes any sale, [. . .]²⁶ exchange, assurance, grant, lease, surrender, reconveyance, release, reservation, or other disposition, and any purchase or other acquisition, and any covenant, contract, or option, and any application of capital money [. . .],²⁷ and any compromise or other dealing, or arrangement; [. . .]²⁸; and "effected" has the meaning appropriate to the particular transaction; and the references to land include references to restrictions and burdens affecting land.

Provisions as to special classes of property

Power to dispose of mansion

65.—(1) The powers of disposing of settled land conferred by this Act on a tenant for life may be exercised as respects the principal mansion house, if any, on any settled land, and the pleasure grounds and park and lands, if any, usually occupied therewith:

Provided that those powers shall not be exercised without the consent of the trustees of the settlement or an order of the court—

(a) if the settlement is a settlement made or coming into operation before the commencement of this Act and the settlement does not expressly provide to the contrary; or

(b) if the settlement is a settlement made or coming into operation after the commencement of this Act and the settlement expressly provides that these powers or any of them shall not be exercised without such consent or order.

(2) Where a house is usually occupied as a farmhouse, or where the site of any house and the pleasure grounds and park and lands, if any, usually occupied therewith do not together exceed twenty-five acres in extent, the house is not to be deemed a principal mansion house within the meaning of this section, and may accordingly be disposed of in like manner as any other part of the settled land.

Cutting and sale of timber, and capitalisation of part of proceeds

66.—(1) Where a tenant for life is impeachable for waste in respect of timber, and there is on the settled land timber ripe and fit for cutting, the tenant for life, on obtaining the consent of the trustees of the settlement or an order of the court, may cut and sell that timber, or any part thereof.

(2)²⁹ Three fourth parts of the net proceeds of the sale shall be set aside as and be capital money arising under this Act, and the other fourth part shall go as rents and profits.

Sale and purchase of heirlooms under order of court

67.—(1) Where personal chattels are settled so as to devolve with settled land, or to devolve therewith as nearly as may be in accordance with the law or practice in force at the date of the settlement, or are settled together with land, or upon trusts declared by reference to the trusts

---

²⁶ These words were repealed by the Statute Law (Repeals) Act 1969 (c. 52), s. 1 and Sched., Pt III.

²⁷ These words were repealed by the Settled Land and Trustees Acts (Court's General Powers) Act 1943, s. 2.

²⁸ *Ibid.*

²⁹ Applied by the Forestry Act 1967 (c. 10), s. 29 (3).

affecting land, a tenant for life of the land may sell the chattels or any of them.

(2) The money arising by the sale shall be capital money arising under this Act, and shall be paid, invested, or applied and otherwise dealt with in like manner in all respects as by this Act directed with respect to other capital money arising under this Act, or may be invested in the purchase of other chattels of the same or any other nature, which, when purchased, shall be settled and held on the same trusts, and shall devolve in the same manner as the chattels sold.

(3) A sale or purchase of chattels under this section shall not be made without an order of the court.

(4) Any reference in any enactment to personal chattels settled as heirlooms shall extend to any chattels to which this section applies.

Dealings as between tenants for life and the estate

Provision enabling dealings with tenant for life

68.—(1) In the manner mentioned and subject to the provisions contained in this section—

- (*a*) a sale, grant, lease, mortgage, charge or other disposition of settled land, or of any easement, right, or privilege over the same may be made to the tenant for life; or
- (*b*) capital money may be advanced on mortgage to him; or
- (*c*) a purchase may be made from him of land to be made subject to the limitations of the settlement; or
- (*d*) an exchange may be made with him of settled land for other land; and
- (*e*) any such disposition, advance, purchase, or exchange as aforesaid may be made to, from, or with any persons of whom the tenant for life is one.

(2) In every such case the trustees of the settlement shall, in addition to their powers as trustees, have all the powers of a tenant for life in reference to negotiating and completing the transaction, and shall have power to enforce any covenants by the tenant for life, or, where the tenant for life is himself one of the trustees, then the other or others of them shall have such power, and the said powers of a tenant for life may be exercised by the trustees of the settlement in the name and on behalf of the tenant for life.

(3) This section applies, notwithstanding that the tenant for life is one of the trustees of the settlement, or that an order has been made authorising the trustees to act on his behalf, or that he is [suffering from mental disorder][30] but does not apply to dealings with any body of persons which includes a trustee of the settlement, not being the tenant for life, unless the transaction is either previously or subsequently approved by the court.

Incumbrances

Shifting of incumbrances

69. Where there is an incumbrance affecting any part of the settled land (whether capable of being overreached on the exercise by the tenant for life of his powers under this Act or not), the tenant for life, with the consent of the incumbrancer, may charge that incumbrance on any other part of the settled land, or on all or any part of the capital money or securities representing capital money subject or to become subject to the settlement, whether already charged therewith or not, in exoneration of

---

[30] Substitued by the Mental Health Act 1959 (7 & 8 Eliz. 2, c. 72), s. 149 (1), Sched. 7, Pt. I.

the first mentioned part, and, by a legal mortgage, or otherwise, make provision accordingly.

Power to vary provisions of an incumbrance and to charge by way of additional security

70.—(1) Where an incumbrance affects any part of the settled land, the tenant for life may, with the consent of the incumbrancer, vary the rate of interest charged and any of the other provisions of the instrument, if any, creating the incumbrance, and with the like consent charge that incumbrance on any part of the settled land, whether already charged therewith or not, or on all or any part of the capital money or securities representing capital money subject or to become subject to the settlement, by way of additional security, or of consolidation of securities, and by a legal mortgage or otherwise, make provision accordingly.

(2) "Incumbrance" in this section includes any annual sum payable during a life or lives or during a term of years absolute or determinable, but in any such case an additional security shall be effected so as only to create a charge or security similar to the original charge or security.

Raising of Money

Power to raise money by mortgage

71.[31]—(1) Where money is required for any of the following purposes namely:—

(i) Discharging an incumbrance on the settled land or part thereof;
(ii) Paying for any improvement authorised by this Act or by the settlement;
(iii) Equality of exchange;
(iv) $\begin{bmatrix} \dots \end{bmatrix}$[32].
(v) $\begin{bmatrix} \dots \end{bmatrix}$[32];
(vi) Redeeming a compensation rentcharge in respect of the extinguishment of manorial incidents and affecting the settled land;
(vii) Commuting any additional rent made payable on the conversion of a perpetually renewable leasehold interest into a long term;
(viii) Satisfying any claims for compensation on the conversion of a perpetually renewable leasehold interest into a long term by any officer, solicitor, or other agent of the lessor in respect of fees or remuneration which would have been payable by the lessee or under-lessee on any renewal;
(ix) Payment of the costs of any transaction authorised by this section or either of the two last preceding sections;

the tenant for life may raise the money so required, on the security of the settled land, or of any part thereof, by a legal mortgage, and the money so raised shall be capital money for that purpose, and may be paid or applied accordingly.

(2) "Incumbrance" in this section does not include any annual sum payable only during a life or lives or during a term of years absolute or determinable.

---

[31] The purposes authorised by this section have been extended by the Landlord and Tenant Act 1927 (17 & 18 Geo. 5, c. 36), s. 13(1); the Agricultural Credits Act 1932 (22 & 23 Geo. 5, c. 35), s. 3; the War Damage Act 1943 (6 & 7 Geo. 6, c. 21), s. 66(2); the Town and Country Planning Act 1947 (10 & 11 Geo. 6, c. 51), s. 71(4); the Coast Protection Act 1949 (12, 13 & 14 Geo. 6, c. 74), s. 11(2) (*a*); the Landlord and Tenant Act 1954 (2 & 3 Eliz. 2, c. 56), s. 8(5), Sched. 2, para. 6; the Coal-Mining (Subsidence) Act 1957 (5 & 6 Eliz. 2, c. 59), s. 11(7); the Land Commission Act 1967 (c. 1), s. 92; the Leasehold Reform Act 1967 (c. 88), s. 6(5), Sched. 2, para. 9; the Mines and Quarries (Tips) Act 1969 (c. 10), s. 32(2) (*b*); and the Town and Country Planning Act 1971 (c. 78), s. 275.
[32] Repealed by the Statute Law (Repeals) Act 1969 (c. 52), s. 1 and Sched., Pt. III.

(3) The restrictions imposed by this Part of this Act on the leasing powers of a tenant for life do not apply in relation to a mortgage term created under this Act.

Conveyance

Completion of transactions by conveyance

72.[33]—(1) On a sale, exchange, lease, mortgage, charge, or other disposition, the tenant for life may, as regards land sold, given in exchange, leased, mortgaged, charged, or otherwise disposed of, or intended so to be, or as regards easements or other rights or privileges sold, given in exchange, leased, mortgaged, or otherwise disposed of, or intended so to be, effect the transaction by deed to the extent of the estate or interest vested or declared to be vested in him by the last or only vesting instrument affecting the settled land or any less estate or interest, in the manner requisite for giving effect to the sale, exchange, lease, mortgage, charge, or other disposition, but so that a mortgage shall be effected by the creation of a term of years absolute in the settled land or by charge by way of legal mortgage, and not otherwise.

(2) Such a deed, to the extent and in the manner to and in which it is expressed or intended to operate and can operate under this Act, is effectual to pass the land conveyed, or the easements, rights, privileges or other interests created, discharged from all the limitations, powers, and provisions of the settlement, and from all estates, interests, and charges subsisting or to arise thereunder, but subject to and with the exception of—

(i) all legal estates and charges by way of legal mortgage having priority to the settlement; and

(ii) all legal estates and charges by way of legal mortgage which have been conveyed or created for securing money actually raised at the date of the deed; and

(iii) all leases and grants at fee-farm rents or otherwise, and all grants of easements, rights of common, or other rights or privileges which—

(*a*) were before the date of the deed granted or made for value in money or money's worth, or agreed so to be, by the tenant for life or statutory owner, or by any of his predecessors in title, or any trustees for them, under the settlement, or under any statutory power, or are at that date otherwise binding on the successors in title of the tenant for life or statutory owner; and

(*b*) are at the date of the deed protected by registration under the Land Charges Act 1925[34] if capable of registration thereunder.

(3) Notwithstanding registration under the Land Charges Act 1925 of—

(*a*) an annuity within the meaning of Part II of that Act;

(*b*) a limited owner's charge or a general equitable charge within the meaning of that Act;

a disposition under this Act operates to overreach such annuity or charge which shall, according to its priority, take effect as if limited by the settlement.

(4) Where a lease is by this Act authorised to be made by writing under hand only, such writing shall have the same operation under this section as if it had been a deed.

---

[33] Entering into a forestry dedication covenant is to be treated as a disposition: Forestry Act 1967 (c. 10), Sched. 2, para. 1(2). It may be entered into either for consideration or gratuitously: *ibid*. para. 1(1) (2).

[34] Now the Land Charges Act 1972 (c. 61), *post*, p. 320.

Part III

Investment or other application of Capital Money

Modes of investment or application

73.[35]—(1) Capital money arising under this Act, subject to payment of claims properly payable thereout and to the application thereof for any special authorised object for which the capital money was raised, shall, when received, be invested or otherwise applied wholly in one, or partly in one and partly in another or others, of the following modes (namely):—

(i) In investment in Government securities, or in other securities in which the trustees of the settlement are by the settlement or by law authorised to invest trust money of the settlement, with power to vary the investment into or for any other such securities;

(ii) In discharge, purchase, or redemption or incumbrances affecting the whole estate the subject of the settlement, or of [. . .],[36] rentcharge in lieu of tithe,[37] Crown rent, chief rent, or quit rent, charged on or payable out of the settled land, or of any charge in respect of an improvement created on a holding under the Agricultural Holdings Act 1923,[38] or any similar previous enactment[39];

(iii) In payment for any improvement authorised by this Act;

(iv) In payment as for an improvement authorised by this Act of any money expended and costs incurred by a landlord under or in pursuance of the Agricultural Holdings Act 1923,[40] or any similar previous enactment, or under custom or agreement or otherwise, in or about the execution of any improvement comprised in Part I or Part II of the First Schedule on the said Agricultural Holdings Act[40];

(v) In payment for equality of exchange of settled land;

(vi) [. . .][41];

(vii) [. . .][42];

(viii) In redemption of any compensation rentcharge created in respect of the extinguishment of manorial incidents, and affecting the settled land;

(ix) In commuting any additional rent made payable on the conversion of a perpetually renewable leasehold interest into a long term, and in satisfying any claim for compensation on such conversion by any officer, solicitor, or other agent of the lessor in respect of fees or remuneration which would have been payable by the lessee or under-lessee on any renewal;

---

[35] The purposes authorised by this section for the application of capital moneys have been extended by the Landlord and Tenant Act 1927 (17 & 18 Geo. 5, c. 36), s. 13(1); the Agricultural Credits Act 1932 (22 & 23 Geo. 5, c. 35), s. 3; the War Damage Act 1943 (6 & 7 Geo. 6, c. 21), s. 66(2); the Coast Protection Act 1949 (12 & 13 Geo. 6, c. 74), s. 11(2) (*a*); the Landlord and Tenant Act 1954 (2 & 3 Eliz. 2, c. 56), s. 8(5), Sched. 2, para. 6; the Coal-Mining (Subsidence) Act 1957 (5 & 6 Eliz. 2, c. 59), s. 11(7); the Land Commission Act 1967 (c. 1), s. 92; the Leasehold Reform Act 1967 (c. 88), s. 6(5), Sched. 2, para. 9; the Town and Country Planning Act 1971 (c. 78), s. 275; and the Housing Act 1974 (c. 44), s. 77(3).

[36] Words repealed by the Finance Act 1963 (c. 25), s. 73 (8) (*b*), Sched. 14, Pt. VI.

[37] All tithe rentcharge has been extinguished, with savings: see the the Act 1936 (26 Geo. 5 & 1 Edw. 8, c. 43), s. 1.

[38] The Agricultural Holdings Act 1923 has been repealed and replaced by the Agricultural Holdings Act 1948 (11 & 12 Geo. 6, c. 63).

[39] Applied by the Land Tax (Redemption) Regulations 1950 (S.I. 1950, No. 268), reg. 18, Sched., to the compulsory redemption of land tax under Part V of the Finance Act 1949 (12, 13 & 14 Geo. 6, c. 47).

[40] Now the Agricultural Holdings Act 1948 (11 & 12 Geo. 6, c. 63), Sched. 2, Pts. I, II.

[41] Repealed by the Statute Law (Repeals) Act 1969 (c. 52), s. 1 and Sched., Pt. III.

[42] *Ibid.*

(x) In purchase of the freehold reversion in fee of any part of the settled land, being leasehold land held for years;

(xi) In purchase of land in fee simple, or of leasehold land held for sixty years or more unexpired at the time of purchase, subject or not to any exception or reservation of or in respect of mines or minerals therein, or of or in respect of rights or powers relative to the working of mines or minerals therein, or in other land;

(xii) In purchase either in fee simple, or for a term of sixty years or more, of mines and minerals convenient to be held or worked with the settled land, or of any easement, right, or privilege convenient to be held with the settled land for mining or other purposes;

(xiii)[43] In redemption of an improvement rentcharge, that is to say, a rentcharge (temporary or permanent) created, whether before or after the commencement of this Act, in pursuance of any Act of Parliament, with the object of paying off any money advanced for defraying the expenses of an improvement of any kind authorised by Part I of the Third Schedule to this Act;

(xiv) In the purchase, with the leave of the court, of any leasehold interest where the immediate reversion is settled land, so as to merge the leasehold interest (unless the court otherwise directs) in the reversion, and notwithstanding that the leasehold interest may have less than sixty years to run;

(xv) In payment of the costs and expenses of all plans, surveys, and schemes, including schemes under the Town Planning Act 1925, or any similar previous enactment, made with a view to, or in connexion with the improvement or development of the settled land, or any part thereof, or the exercise of any statutory powers, and of all negotiations entered into by the tenant for life with a view to the exercise of any of the said powers, notwithstanding that such negotiations may prove abortive, and in payment of the costs and expenses of opposing any such proposed scheme as aforesaid affecting the settled land, whether or not the scheme is made;

(xvi)[44] In the purchase of an annuity charged under section four of the Tithe Act 1918, on the settled land or any part thereof, or in the discharge of such part of any such annuity as does not represent interest;

(xvii) In payment to a local or other authority of such sum as may be agreed in consideration of such authority taking over and becoming liable to repair a private road on the settled land or a road for the maintenance whereof a tenant for life is liable ratione tenurae;

(xviii) In financing any person who may have agreed to take a lease or grant for building purposes of the settled land, or any part thereof, by making advances to him in the usual manner on the security of an equitable mortgage of his building agreement;

(xix) In payment to any person becoming absolutely entitled or empowered to give an absolute discharge;

(xx) In payment of costs, charges, and expenses of or incidental to the exercise of any of the powers, or the execution of any of the provisions of this Act including the costs and expenses incidental to any of the matters referred to in this section;

(xxi) In any other mode authorised by the settlement with respect to money produced by the sale of the settled land.

---

[43] In certain cases the reference to redemption shall include a reference to discharging as it falls due so much of any periodical payment as represents repayment of capital: Agriculture Act 1967 (c. 22), s. 68.

[44] Tithe rentcharge was extinguished, with savings, by the Tithe Act 1936 (26 Geo. 5 & 1 Edw. 8, c. 43), ss. 1, 30; see the Corn Rents Act 1963 (c. 14).

(2) Notwithstanding anything in this section capital money arising under this Act from settled land in England or Wales shall not be applied in the purchase of land out of England and Wales, unless the settlement expressly authorises the same.

Power to acquire land subject to certain incumbrances

74.—(1) Land may be acquired on a purchase or exchange to be made subject to a settlement, notwithstanding that the land is subject to any Crown rent, quit rent, chief rent, or other incident of tenure, or to any easement, right or privilege, or to any restrictive covenant, or to any liability to maintain or repair walls, fences, sea-walls, river banks, dykes, roads, streets, sewers, or drains, or to any improvement rentcharge which is capable under this Act of being redeemed out of capital money.

(2) The acquisition on a purchase or exchange before the commencement of this Act of any land subject to any such burden as aforesaid is hereby confirmed.

Regulations respecting investment, devolution, and income of securities, &c.

75.—(1) Capital money arising under this Act shall, in order to its being invested or applied as aforesaid, be paid either to the trustees of the settlement or into court at the option of the tenant for life, and shall be invested or applied by the trustees, or under the direction of the court, as the case may be, accordingly.

(2) The investment or other application by the trustees shall be made according to the direction of the tenant for life, and in default thereof according to the discretion of the trustees, but in the last-mentioned case subject to any consent required or direction given by the settlement with respect to the investment or other application by the trustees of trust money of the settlement, and any investment shall be in the names or under the control of the trustees.

(3) The investment or other application under the direction of the court shall be made on the application of the tenant for life, or of the trustees.

(4) Any investment or other application shall not during the subsistence of the beneficial interest of the tenant for life be altered without his consent.

(5) Capital money arising under this Act while remaining uninvested or unapplied, and securities on which an investment of any such capital money is made shall for all purposes of disposition, transmission and devolution be treated as land, and shall be held for and go to the same persons successively, in the same manner and for and on the same estates, interests, and trusts, as the land wherefrom the money arises would, if not disposed of, have been held and have gone under the settlement.

(6) The income of those securities shall be paid or applied as the income of that land, if not disposed of, would have been payable or applicable under the settlement.

(7) Those securities may be converted into money, which shall be capital money arising under this Act.

(8) All or any part of any capital money paid into court may, if the court thinks fit, be at any time paid out to the trustees of the settlement.

Application of money in court under Land Clauses and other Acts

76. Where, under an Act, or an order or scheme confirmed by or having the force of an Act of Parliament, incorporating or applying, wholly or in part, the Lands Clauses Acts, or under any Act, public general or local or private, money is at the commencement of this Act in court, or is afterwards paid into court, and is liable to be laid out in the purchase of land to be made subject to a settlement, then, in addition to any mode of dealing therewith authorised by the Act under which the money is in court, that money may be invested or applied as capital money arising under this Act, on the like terms, if any, respecting costs and other things, as nearly as circumstances admit, and notwithstanding anything in this Act according to the same procedure, as if the modes of investment or application authorised by this Act were authorised by the Act under which the money is in court.

Application of money in hands of trustees under powers of settlement

77. Where—
  - (*a*) under any instrument coming into operation either before or after the commencement of this Act money is in the hands of trustees, and is liable to be laid out in the purchase of land to be made subject to the trusts declared by that instrument; or
  - (*b*) under any instrument coming into operation after the commencement of this Act money or securities or the proceeds of sale of any property is or are held by trustees on trusts creating entailed interests therein;

then, in addition to such powers of dealing therewith as the trustees have independently of this Act, they may, at the option of the tenant for life, invest or apply the money securities or proceeds as if they were capital money arising under this Act.

Provision as to personal estate settled by reference to capital money, or on trusts corresponding with the limitations of land

78.—(1) Where money or securities or the proceeds of sale of any property is or are by any instrument coming into operation either before or after the commencement of this Act directed to be held on trusts declared by reference to capital money arising under this Act from land settled by that instrument or any other instrument, the money securities or proceeds shall be held on the like trusts as if the same had been or represented money which had actually arisen under this Act from the settled land.

[This subsection operates without prejudice to the rights of any person claiming under a disposition for valuable consideration of any such money securities or proceeds, made before the commencement of this Act.][45]

(2) Where money or securities or the proceeds of sale of any property is or are by any instrument coming into operation after the commencement of this Act directed to be held on the same trusts as, or on trusts corresponding as nearly as may be with the limitations of land settled by that instrument or any other instrument, the money, securities or proceeds shall be held on the like trusts as if the same had been or represented capital money arising under this Act from the settled land.

(3) Such money, securities, or proceeds of sale shall be paid or transferred to or retained by the trustees of the settlement of the settled land, or paid or transferred into court, and invested or applied accordingly.

(4) Where the settled land includes freehold land, the money, securities, or proceeds of sale aforesaid shall be held on the like trusts as if the same had been or represented capital money arising from the freehold land.

(5) This section has effect notwithstanding any direction in the instrument creating the trust that the trust property is not to vest absolutely in any tenant in tail or in tail male or in tail female under the limitations of the settled land who dies under a specified age, or before the happening of

---

[45] Added by the Law of Property (Amendment) Act 1926, *post*, s. 7, Sched.

a specified event, but, save as aforesaid, has effect with any variations and subject to any contrary intention expressed in the instrument creating the trust.

Application of money paid for lease or reversion

79. Where capital money arising under this Act is purchase-money paid in respect of—

(a) a lease for years; or

(b) any other estate or interest in land less than the fee simple; or

(c) a reversion dependent on any such lease, estate, or interest;

the trustees of the settlement or the court, as the case may be, and in the case of the court on the application of any party interested in that money, may, notwithstanding anything in this Act, require and cause the same to be laid out, invested, accumulated, and paid in such manner as, in the judgment of the trustees or of the court, as the case may be, will give to the parties interested in that money the like benefit therefrom as they might lawfully have had from the lease, estate, interest, or reversion in respect whereof the money was paid, or as near thereto as may be.

As to money received by way of damages for breach of covenant

80.—(1) Money, not being rent, received by way of damages or compensation for breach of any covenant by a lessee or grantee contained in any lease or grant of settled land shall, unless in any case the court on the application of the tenant for life or the trustees of the settlement otherwise directs, be deemed to be capital money arising under this Act, and shall be paid to or retained by the trustees of the settlement, or paid into court, and invested or applied, accordingly.

(2) In addition to the other modes in which capital money may be applied under this Act or the settlement, money so received as aforesaid or any part thereof may, if the circumstances permit, be applied at any time within twelve months after such receipt, or such extended period as the court may allow, in or towards payment of the costs of making good in whole or in part the breach of covenant in respect of which it was so received, or the consequences thereof, and the trustees of the settlement, if they think fit, may require any money so received or any part thereof to be so applied.

(3) In the application of any such money in or towards payment of the cost of making good any such breach or the consequences of any such breach as aforesaid, the work required to be done for the purpose shall be deemed to be an improvement authorised by Part I of the Third Schedule to this Act.

(4) This section does not apply to money received by way of damages or compensation for the breach of a covenant to repay to the lessor or grantor money laid out or expended by him, or to any case in which if the money received were applied in making good the breach of covenant or the consequences thereof such application would not enure for the benefit of the settled land, or any buildings thereon.

(5) This section does not apply to money received by way of damages or compensation before the commencement of this Act, but it applies whether the lease or grant was made before or after the commencement of this Act, and whether under the powers conferred by the Settled Land Acts 1882 to 1890 or this Act or not.

(6) The provisions of this section apply only if and as far as a contrary intention is not expressed in the settlement, and have effect subject to the terms of the settlement, and to any provisions therein contained, but a contrary intention shall not be deemed to be expressed merely by words negativing impeachment for waste.

As to capital arising otherwise than under the Act

81. Any money which after the commencement of this Act arises from settled land otherwise than under this Act, as well as any money or securities in the names or under the control of the tenant for life or the trustees of the settlement, being or representing money which had arisen before the commencement of this Act from the settled land otherwise than under the Settled Land Acts 1882 to 1890, and which ought, as between the persons interested in the settled land, to be or to have been treated as capital, shall (without prejudice to any other statutory provisions affecting the same) be deemed to be or to represent capital money arising under this Act, and shall be paid or transferred to or retained by the trustees of the settlement, or paid or transferred into court, and invested or applied, accordingly.

Land acquired may be made a substituted security for released charges

82.—(1) Land acquired by purchase or in exchange or otherwise under the powers of this Act, may be made a substituted security for any charge from which the settled land or any part thereof has theretofore been released on the occasion and in order to the completion of a sale, exchange or other disposition:

Provided that, where a charge does not affect the whole of the settled land, the land acquired shall not be subjected thereto, unless the land is acquired either by purchase with money arising from sale of land which was before the sale subject to the charge, or by an exchange of land which was before the exchange subject to the charge.

(2) On land being so acquired, any person who, by the direction of the tenant for life, so conveys the land as to subject it to any legal estate or charge by way of legal mortgage, is not concerned to inquire whether or not it is proper that the land should be subjected to such legal estate or charge.

Part IV

Improvements

Improvements with Capital Money

Description of improvements authorised by Act

83.[46] Improvements authorised by this Act are the making or execution on, or in connexion with, and for the benefit of settled land, of any of the works mentioned in the Third Schedule to this Act, or of any works for any of the purposes mentioned in that Schedule, and any operation incident to or necessary or proper in the execution of any of those works, or necessary or proper for carrying into effect any of those purposes, or for securing the full benefit of any of those works or purposes.

Mode of application of capital money

84.—(1) Capital money arising under this Act may be applied in or towards payment for any improvement authorised by this Act or by the settlement, without any scheme for the execution of the improvement being first submitted for approval to, or approved by, the trustees of the settlement or the court.

---

[46] The provision of an air-raid shelter is an improvement authorised by this Act: Civil Defence Act 1939 (2 & 3 Geo. 6, c. 31), s. 66(1). Supplementary provisions as to improvements may be made under the Agriculture Act 1967 (c. 22), s. 36(5).

(2) Where the capital money to be expended is in the hands of the trustees of the settlement, they may apply that money in or towards payment for the whole or any part of any work or operation comprised in the improvement, on—

(i) a certificate to be furnished by a competent engineer or able practical surveyor employed independently of the tenant for life, certifying that the work or operation comprised in the improvement or some specific part thereof, has been properly executed, and what amount is properly payable in respect thereof, which certificate shall be conclusive in favour of the trustees as an authority and discharge for any payment made by them in pursuance thereof; or

(ii) an order of the court directing or authorising the trustees so to apply a specified portion of the capital money:

Provided that—

(a) In the case of improvements not authorised by Part I of the Third Schedule to this Act or by the settlement, the trustees may, if they think fit, and shall if so directed by the court, before they make any such application of capital money require that that money, or any part thereof, shall be repaid to them out of the income of the settled land by not more than fifty half-yearly instalments, the first of such instalments to be paid or to be deemed to have become payable at the expiration of six months from the date when the work or operation, in payment for which the money is to be applied, was completed;

(b) No capital money shall be applied by the trustees in payment for improvements not authorised by Parts I and II of the Third Schedule to this Act, or by the settlement, except subject to provision for the repayment thereof being made in manner mentioned in the preceding paragraph of this proviso.

(3) Where the capital money to be expended is in court, the court may, if it thinks fit, on a report or certificate of the Minister, or of a competent engineer or able practical surveyor approved by the court, or on such other evidence as the court may think sufficient, make such order and give such directions as it thinks fit for the application of the money, or any part thereof, in or towards payment for the whole or any part of any work or operation comprised in the improvement.

(4) Where the court authorises capital money to be applied in payment for any improvement or intended improvement not authorised by Part I of the Third Schedule to this Act or by the settlement, the court, as a condition of making the order, may in any case require that the capital money or any part thereof, and shall as respects an improvement mentioned in Part III of that Schedule (unless the improvement is authorised by the settlement), require that the whole of the capital money shall be repaid to the trustees of the settlement out of the income of the settled land by a fixed number of periodical instalments to be paid at the times appointed by the court, and may require that any incumbrancer of the estate or interest of the tenant for life shall be served with notice of the proceedings.

(5) All money received by the trustees of the settlement in respect of any instalments under this section shall be held by them as capital money arising from freehold land under the settlement, unless the court otherwise directs.

Creation of rentcharges to discharge instalments

85.—(1) When the tenant for life is required by the trustees to repay by instalments the capital money expended, or any part thereof, the tenant for life is by this section authorised to create out of the settled land, or any part thereof, a yearly rentcharge in favour of the trustees of the settlement sufficient in amount to discharge the said half-yearly instalments.

(2) Where an order is made requiring repayment by instalments, the settled land shall stand charged with the payment to the trustees of the settlement of a yearly rentcharge sufficient in amount to discharge the periodical instalments, and the rentcharge shall accrue from day to day, and be payable at the times appointed for payment of the periodical instalments, and shall have effect as if limited by the settlement prior to the estate of the tenant for life, and the trustees of the settlement shall have all statutory and other powers for recovery thereof.

(3) A rentcharge created by or under this section shall not be redeemed out of capital money, but may be overreached in like manner as if the same were limited by the settlement, and shall cease if and when the land affected by the improvement ceases to be settled or is sold or exchanged, but if part of the land so affected remains subject to the settlement the rentcharge shall remain in force in regard to the settled land.

Sundry Provisions as to Improvements

Concurrence in improvements

86. The tenant for life may join or concur with any other person interested in executing any improvement authorised by this Act, or in contributing to the cost thereof.

Court may order payment for improvements executed

87. The court may, in any case where it appears proper, make an order directing or authorising capital money to be applied in or towards payment for any improvement authorised by the Settled Land Acts 1882 to 1890 or this Act, notwithstanding that a scheme was not, before the execution of the improvement, submitted for approval, as required by the Settled Land Act 1882 to the trustees of the settlement or to the court, and notwithstanding that no capital money is immediately available for the purpose.

Obligation on tenant for life and successors to maintain, insure, &c.

88.[47]—(1) The tenant for life, and each of his successors in title having under the trust instrument a limited estate or interest only in the settled land, shall, during such period, if any, as the Minister by certificate in any case prescribes, maintain and repair, at his own expense, every improvement executed under the foregoing provisions of this Act or the enactments replaced thereby, and where a building or work in its nature insurable against damage by fire is comprised in the improvement, shall at his own expense insure and keep insured the improvement in such amount, if any, as the Minister by certificate in any case prescribes.

(2) The tenant for life, or any of his successors as aforesaid, shall not cut down or knowingly permit to be cut down, except in proper thinning, any trees planted as an improvement under the foregoing provisions of this Act, or under the enactments replaced by those provisions.

(3) The tenant for life, and each of his successors as aforesaid, shall from time to time, if required by the Minister on or without the application of any person having under the trust instrument any estate or interest in the settled land in possession, remainder, or otherwise, report to the Minister the state of every improvement executed under this Act, and the fact and particulars of fire insurance, if any.

---

[47] The repayment of a loan made for defraying the expenses of an authorised improvement is, for the purposes of this section, to be regarded as an improvement rentcharge: Agricultural Credits Act 1932 (22 & 23 Geo. 5, c. 35), s. 3.

(4) The Minister may vary any certificate made by him under this section in such manner or to such extent as circumstances appear to him to require, but not so as to increase the liabilities of the tenant for life, or any of his successors as aforesaid.

(5) If the tenant for life, or any of his successors as aforesaid, fails in any respect to comply with the requisitions of this section, or does any act in contravention thereof, any person having, under the trust instrument, any estate or interest in the settled land in possession, remainder, or reversion, shall have a right of action, in respect of that default or act, against the tenant for life; and the estate of the tenant for life, after his death, shall be liable to make good to the persons entitled under the trust instrument any damages occasioned by that default or act.

(6) Where in connexion with any improvement an improvement rentcharge, as hereinbefore defined, has been created, and that rentcharge has been redeemed out of capital money, this section shall apply to the improvement as if it had been an improvement executed under this Act.

Protection as regards waste in execution and repair of improvements

89. The tenant for life, and each of his successors in title having, under the trust instrument, a limited estate or interest only in the settled land, and all persons employed by or under contract with the tenant for life or any such successor, may from time to time enter on the settled land, and, without impeachment of waste by any remainderman or reversioner, thereon execute any improvement authorised by this Act, or inspect, maintain, and repair the same, and for the purposes thereof do, make, and use on the settled land, all acts, works, and conveniences proper for the execution, maintenance, repair, and use thereof, and get and work freestone, limestone, clay, sand, and other substances, and make tramways and other ways, and burn and make bricks, tiles, and other things, and cut down and use timber and other trees not planted or left standing for shelter or ornament.

PART V

MISCELLANEOUS PROVISIONS

Power for tenant for life to enter into contracts

90.—(1) A tenant for life—

    (i) may contract to make any sale, exchange, mortgage, charge or other disposition authorised by this Act; and

    (ii) may vary or rescind, with or without consideration, the contract in the like cases and manner in which, if he were absolute owner of the settled land, he might lawfully vary or rescind the same, but so that the contract as varied be in conformity with this Act; and

    (iii) may contract to make any lease, and in making the lease may vary the terms, with or without consideration, but so that the lease be in conformity with this Act; and

    (iv) may accept a surrender of a contract for a lease or a grant in fee simple at a rent, in like manner and on the like terms in and on which he might accept a surrender of a lease or a regrant, and thereupon may make a new or other contract for or relative to a lease or leases, or a grant or grants in fee simple at a rent, in like manner and on the like terms in and on which he might make a new or other lease or grant, or new or other leases or grants, where a lease or a grant in fee simple at a rent had been executed; and

  (v) may enter into a contract for or relating to the execution of any improvement authorised by this Act, and may vary or rescind any such contract; and

 (vi) may, in any other case, enter into a contract to do any act for carrying into effect any of the purposes of this Act, and may vary or rescind any such contract.

(2) Every contract, including a contract arising by reason of the exercise of an option, shall be binding on and shall enure for the benefit of the settled land, and shall be enforceable against and by every successor in title for the time being of the tenant for life, or statutory owner, and may be carried into effect by any such successor, but so that it may be varied or rescinded by any such successor, in the like case and manner, if any, as if it had been made by himself.

(3) The court may, on the application of the tenant for life, or statutory owner, or of any such successor as aforesaid, or of any person interested in any contract, give directions respecting the enforcing, carrying into effect, varying, or rescinding thereof.

(4) A preliminary contract under this Act for or relating to a lease, and a contract conferring an option, shall not form part of the title or evidence of the title of any person to the lease, or to the benefit thereof, or to the land the subject of the option.

(5) All money, not being rent, received on the exercise by the tenant for life or statutory owner of the powers conferred by subsection (1) of this section, shall, unless the court on an application made within six months after the receipt of the money, or within such further time as the court may in special circumstances allow, otherwise directs, be capital money arising under this Act.

Provisions as to different estates settled upon the same limitations

91.—(1) Where estates are settled by different settlements upon the same limitations, whether by reference or otherwise, the following provisions shall have effect:—

  (i) The estates or any two or more of them, as the case may require, may be treated as one aggregate estate, in which case the aggregate estate shall be the settled land for all the purposes of this Act;

 (ii) Where the trustees for the purposes of this Act of the two or several settlements are the same persons they shall be the trustees of the settlement of the aggregate estate for all the purposes of this Act, and all or any part of the capital money arising from one of the estates may be applied by the direction of the tenant for life or statutory owner as if the same had arisen from any other of the estates;

(iii) Where the trustees for the purposes of this Act of the settlements or of any two or more of them are not the same persons—

    (a) any notice required to be given by this Act to the trustees of the settlement and to the solicitor of such trustees shall be given to the trustees of every settlement which comprises any part of the land to which such notice relates and to the solicitor of such trustees;

    (b) any capital money arising on any sale, exchange, lease, mortgage, charge, or other disposition of land comprised in more than one settlement, shall be apportioned between the trustees of the different settlements in such manner as the tenant for life or statutory owner may think fit;

(c) all or any part of the capital money arising from the land comprised in one of the settlements may be paid by the trustees of that settlement, by such direction as aforesaid, to the trustees of any of the other settlements, to be applied by such last-mentioned trustees as if the same had arisen from land comprised in that other settlement:

(iv) For the purposes of this subsection, money liable to be laid out in the purchase of land to be settled upon the same limitations as other land may be applied and dealt with in like manner in all respects as if land had been purchased and settled, and the money were capital money arising therefrom.

(2) Estates shall be deemed to be settled upon the same limitations, notwithstanding that any of them may be subject to incumbrances, charges, or powers of charging to which the other or others of them may not be subject:

Provided that, in any such case as last aforesaid, the powers of this section relating to the payment or application of capital money shall not, unless the settlement under which the capital money is held otherwise provides, be exercisable without an order of the court.

(3) This section has effect without prejudice to any appointment made by the court before the commencement of this Act of trustees of the settlement of an aggregate estate, and to the power of the court in any case after such commencement to make any such appointment, and where any such appointment has been made before such commencement, or is made thereafter, this section has effect as if the trustees so appointed and their successors in office were the trustees for the purposes of this Act of each of the settlements constituting the settlement of the aggregate estate, and there were no other trustees thereof for the purposes of this Act.

(4) In this section "estate" means the land, capital money, and securities representing capital money for the time being subject to a particular settlement.

Proceedings for protection or recovery of land settled or claimed as settled

92. The court may, if it thinks fit, approve of any action, defence, petition to Parliament, parliamentary opposition, or other proceeding taken or proposed to be taken for the protection of settled land, or of any action or proceeding taken or proposed to be taken for the recovery of land being or alleged to be subject to a settlement, and may direct that any costs, charges, or expenses incurred or to be incurred in relation thereto, or any part thereof, be paid out of property subject to the settlement.

Reference of questions to court

93. If a question arises or a doubt is entertained—

(a) respecting the exercise or intended exercise of any of the powers conferred by this Act, or any enactment replaced by this Act, or the settlement, or any matter relating thereto; or

(b) as to the person in whose favour a vesting deed or assent ought to be executed, or as to the contents thereof; or

(c) otherwise in relation to property subject to a settlement;

the tenant for life or statutory owner, or the trustees of the settlement, or any other person interested under the settlement, may apply to the court for its decision or directions thereon, or for the sanction of the court to any conditional contract, and the court may make such order or give such directions respecting the matter as the court thinks fit.

Part VI

General Provisions as to Trustees

Number of trustees to act

94.—(1) Notwithstanding anything in this Act, capital money arising under this Act shall not be paid to fewer than two persons as trustees of a settlement, unless the trustee is a trust corporation.

(2) Subject as aforesaid the provisions of this Act referring to the trustees of a settlement apply to the surviving or continuing trustees or trustee of the settlement for the time being.

Trustees' receipts

95. The receipt or direction in writing of or by the trustees of the settlement, or where a sole trustee is a trust corporation, of or by that trustee, or of or by the personal representatives of the last surviving or continuing trustee, for or relating to any money or securities, paid or transferred to or by the direction of the trustees, trustee, or representatives, as the case may be, effectually discharges the payer or transferor therefrom, and from being bound to see to the application or being answerable for any loss or misapplication thereof, and, in case of a mortgagee or other person advancing money, from being concerned to see that any money advanced by him is wanted for any purpose of this Act, or that no more than is wanted is raised.

Protection of each trustee individually

96. Each person who is for the time being a trustee of a settlement is answerable for what he actually receives only, notwithstanding his signing any receipt for conformity, and in respect of his own acts, receipts, and defaults only, and is not answerable in respect of those of any other trustee, or of any banker, broker, or other person, or for the insufficiency or deficiency of any securities, or for any loss not happening through his own wilful default.

Protection of trustees generally

97. The trustees of a settlement, or any of them—

   (*a*) are not liable for giving any consent, or for not making, bringing, taking, or doing any such application, action, proceeding, or thing, as they might make, bring, take, or do; and

   (*b*) in case of a purchase of land with capital money arising under this Act, or of an exchange, lease, or other disposition, are not liable for adopting any contract made by the tenant for life or statutory owner, or bound to inquire as to the propriety of the purchase, exchange, lease, or other disposition, or answerable as regards any price, consideration, or fine; and

   (*c*) are not liable to see to or answerable for the investigation of the title, or answerable for a conveyance of land, if the conveyance purports to convey the land in the proper mode; and

   (*d*) are not liable in respect of purchase-money paid by them by the direction of the tenant for life or statutory owner to any person joining in the conveyance as a conveying party, or as giving a receipt for the purchase-money, or in any other character, or in respect of any other money paid by them by the direction of the tenant for life or statutory owner on the purchase, exchange, lease, or other disposition.

Protection of trustees in particular cases

98.—(1) Where the tenant for life or statutory owner directs capital money to be invested on any authorised security or investment, the trustees of the settlement shall not be liable for the acts of any agent employed by the tenant for life or statutory owner in connexion with the transaction, or for not employing a separate agent in or about the valuation of the subject of the security or the investigation of the title thereto, or for the form of the security or of any deed conveying the subject thereof to the trustees.

(2) The trustees of the settlement shall not be liable for paying or applying any capital money by the direction of the tenant for life or statutory owner for any authorised purpose.

(3) The trustees of the settlement shall not be liable in any way on account of any vesting instrument or other documents of title relating to the settled land, other than securities for capital money, being placed in the possession of the tenant for life or statutory owner:

Provided that where, if the settlement were not disclosed, it would appear that the tenant for life had a general power of appointment over, or was absolutely and beneficially entitled to the settled land, the trustees of the settlement shall, before they deliver the documents to him, require that notice of the last or only principal vesting instrument be written on one of the documents under which the tenant for life acquired his title, and may, if the documents are not in their possession, require such notice to be written as aforesaid, but, in the latter case, they shall not be liable in any way for not requiring the notice to be written.

(4) This section applies to dealings and matters effected before as well as after the commencement of this Act.

Indemnities to personal representatives and others

99. Personal representatives, trustees, or other persons who have in good faith, pursuant to this Act, executed a vesting deed, assent, or other conveyance of the settled land, or a deed of discharge of trustees, shall be absolutely discharged from all liability in respect of the equitable interests and powers taking effect under the settlement, and shall be entitled to be kept indemnified at the cost of the trust estate from all liabilities affecting the settled land, but the person to whom the settled land is conveyed (not being a purchaser taking free therefrom) shall hold the settled land upon the trusts, if any, affecting the same.

Trustees' reimbursements

100. The trustees of a settlement may reimburse themselves or pay and discharge out of the trust property all expenses properly incurred by them.

Notice to trustees

101.—(1) Save as otherwise expressly provided by this Act, a tenant for life or statutory owner, when intending to make a sale, exchange, lease, mortgage, or charge or to grant an option—

(*a*) shall give notice of his intention in that behalf to each of the trustees of the settlement, by posting registered letters, containing the notice, addressed to the trustees severally, each at his usual or last known place of abode in the United Kingdom; and

(*b*) shall give a like notice to the solicitor for the trustees, if any such solicitor is known to the tenant for life or statutory owner, by posting a registered letter, containing the notice, addressed to the solicitor at his place of business in the United Kingdom;

every letter under this section being posted not less than one month before the making or granting by the tenant for life or statutory owner of the sale, exchange, lease, mortgage, charge, or option, or of a contract for the same:

Provided that a notice under this section shall not be valid unless at the date thereof the trustee is a trust corporation, or the number of trustees is not less than two.

(2) The notice required by this section of intention to make a sale, exchange, or lease, or to grant an option, may be notice of a general intention in that behalf.

(3) The tenant for life or statutory owner is, upon request by a trustee of the settlement, to furnish to him such particulars and information as may reasonably be required by him from time to time with reference to sales, exchanges, or leases effected, or in progress, or immediately intended.

(4) Any trustee, by writing under his hand, may waive notice either in any particular case, or generally, and may accept less than one month's notice.

(5) A person dealing in good faith with the tenant for life is not concerned to inquire respecting the giving of any such notice as is required by this section.

Management of land during minority or pending contingency

102.—(1) If and as long as any person who is entitled to a beneficial interest in possession affecting land is an infant, the trustees appointed for this purpose by the settlement, or if there are none so appointed, then the trustees of the settlement, unless the settlement or the order of the court whereby they or their predecessors in office were appointed to be such trustees expressly provides to the contrary, or if there are none, then any persons appointed as trustees for this purpose by the court on the application of a guardian or next friend of the infant, may enter into and continue in possession of the land on behalf of the infant, and in every such case the subsequent provisions of this section shall apply.

(2) The trustees shall manage or superintend the management of the land, with full power—

(*a*) to fell timber or cut underwood from time to time in the usual course for sale, or for repairs or otherwise; and

(*b*) to erect, pull down, rebuild, and repair houses, and other buildings and erections; and

(*c*) to continue the working of mines, minerals, and quarries which have usually been worked; and

(*d*) to drain or otherwise improve the land or any part thereof; and

(*e*) to insure against loss by fire; and

(*f*) to make allowances to and arrangements with tenants and others; and

(*g*) to determine tenancies, and to accept surrenders of leases and tenancies; and

(*h*) generally to deal with the land in a proper and due course of management;

but so that, where the infant is impeachable for waste, the trustees shall not commit waste, and shall cut timber on the same terms only, and subject to the same restrictions, on and subject to which the infant could, if of full age, cut the same.

(3) The trustees may from time to time, out of the income of the land, including the produce of the sale of timber and underwood, pay the expenses incurred in the management, or in the exercise of any power conferred by this section, or otherwise in relation to the land, and all

outgoings not payable by any tenant or other person, and shall keep down any annual sum, and the interest of any principal sum, charged on the land.

(4) This section has effect subject to an express appointment by the settlement, or the court, of trustees for the purposes of this section or of any enactment replaced by this section.

(5) Where any person is contingently entitled to land, this section shall, subject to any prior interests or charges affecting that land, apply until his interest vests, or, if his interest vests during his minority, until he attains the age of [eighteen years].[48]

This subsection applies only where a person becomes contingently entitled under an instrument coming into operation after the commencement of this Act.

(6) This section applies only if and as far as a contrary intention is not expressed in the instrument, if any, under which the interest of the infant or person contingently entitled as aforesaid arises, and has effect subject to the terms of that instrument and to the provisions therein contained.

PART VII

RESTRICTIONS, SAVINGS, AND PROTECTION OF PURCHASERS

Legal estate in settled land not to vest in trustee in bankruptcy of estate owner

103. The legal estate in settled land shall not vest in the trustee in bankruptcy of an estate owner unless and until the estate owner becomes absolutely and beneficially entitled to the settled land free from all limitations, powers, and charges taking effect under the settlement.

Powers not assignable, and contract not to exercise powers void

104.—(1) The powers under this Act of a tenant for life are not capable of assignment or release, and do not pass to a person as being, by operation of law or otherwise, an assignee of a tenant for life, and remain exercisable by the tenant for life after and notwithstanding any assignment, by operation of law or otherwise, of his estate or interest under the settlement.

This subsection applies notwithstanding that the estate or interest of the tenant for life under the settlement was not in possession when the assignment was made or took effect by operation of law.

(2) A contract by a tenant for life not to exercise his powers under this Act or any of them shall be void.

(3) Where an assignment for value of the estate or interest of the tenant for life was made before the commencement of this Act, this section shall operate without prejudice to the rights of the assignee, and in that case the assignee's rights shall not be affected without his consent, except that—

(*a*) unless the assignee is actually in possession of the settled land or the part thereof affected, his consent shall not be requisite for the making of leases thereof by the tenant for life or statutory owner, provided the leases are made at the best rent that can reasonably be obtained, without fine, and in other respects are in conformity with this Act; and

(*b*) the consent of the assignee shall not be required to an investment of capital money for the time being affected by the assignment in securities authorised by statute for the investment of trust money.

---

[48] These words were substituted by the Family Law Reform Act 1969 (c. 46), s. 1(3) and Sched. 1, Pt. I.

(4) Where such an assignment for value is made or comes into operation after the commencement of this Act, the consent of the assignee shall not be requisite for the exercise by the tenant for life of any of the powers conferred by this Act:

Provided that—

(*a*) the assignee shall be entitled to the same or the like estate or interest in or charge on the land, money, or securities for the time being representing the land, money, or securities comprised in the assignment, as he had by virtue of the assignment in the last-mentioned land, money, or securities; and

(*b*) if the assignment so provides, or if it takes effect by operation of the law of bankruptcy, and after notice thereof to the trustees of the settlement, no investment or application of capital money for the time being affected by the assignment shall be made without the consent of the assignee, except an investment in securities authorised by statute for the investment of trust money; and

(*c*) notice of the intended transaction shall, unless the assignment otherwise provides, be given to the assignee, but a purchaser shall not be concerned to see or inquire whether such notice has been given.

(5) Where such an assignment for value was made before the commencement of this Act, then on the exercise by the tenant for life after such commencement of any of the powers conferred by this Act—

(*a*) a purchaser shall not be concerned to see or inquire whether the consent of the assignee has been obtained; and

(*b*) the provisions of paragraph (*a*)of the last subsection shall apply for the benefit of the assignee.

(6) A trustee or personal representative who is an assignee for value shall have power to consent to the exercise by the tenant for life of his powers under this Act, or to any such investment or application of capital money as aforesaid, and to bind by such consent all persons interested in the trust estate, or the estate of the testator or intestate.

(7) If by the original assignment, or by any subsequent disposition, the estate or interest assigned or created by the original assignment, or any part thereof, or any derivative interest is settled on persons in succession, whether subject to any prior charge or not, and there is no trustee or personal representative in whom the entirety of the estate or interest so settled is vested, then the person for the time being entitled in possession under the limitations of that settlement, whether as trustee or beneficiary, or who would, if of full age, be so entitled, and notwithstanding any charge or incumbrance subsisting or to arise under such settlement, shall have power to consent to the exercise by the tenant for life of his powers under this Act, or to any such investment or application of capital money as aforesaid, and to bind by such consent all persons interested or to become interested under such settlement.

(8) Where an assignee for value, or any person who has power to consent as aforesaid under this section, is an infant, the consent may be given on his behalf by his parents or parent or testamentary or other guardian in the order named.

(9) The court shall have power to authorise any person interested under any assignment to consent to the exercise by the tenant for life of his powers under this Act, or to any such investment or application of capital money as aforesaid, on behalf of himself and all other persons interested, or who may become interested under such assignment.

(10) An assignment by operation of the law of bankruptcy, where the assignment comes into operation after the commencement of this Act,

shall be deemed to be an assignment for value for the purposes of this section.

(11) An instrument whereby a tenant for life, in consideration of marriage or as part or by way of any family arrangement, not being a security for payment of money advanced, makes an assignment of or creates a charge upon his estate or interest under the settlement is to be deemed one of the instruments creating the settlement, and not an assignment for value for the purposes of this section:

Provided that this subsection shall not have effect with respect to any disposition made before the eighteenth day of August, eighteen hundred and ninety, if inconsistent with the nature or terms of the disposition.

(12) This section extends to assignments made or coming into operation before or after the commencement of this Act, and in this section "assignment" includes assignment by way of mortgage, and any partial or qualified assignment, and any charge or incumbrance, "assignee" has a corresponding meaning, and "assignee for value" includes persons deriving title under the original assignee.

Effect of surrender of life estate to the next remainderman

105.—(1) Where the estate or interest of a tenant for life under the settlement has been or is absolutely assured with intent to extinguish the same, either before or after the commencement of this Act, to the person next entitled in remainder or reversion under the settlement, then, [. . .]49 the statutory powers of the tenant for life under this Act shall, in reference to the property affected by the assurance, and notwithstanding the provisions of the last preceding section, cease to be exercisable by him, and the statutory powers shall thenceforth become exercisable as if he were dead, but without prejudice to any incumbrance affecting the estate or interest assured, and to the rights to which any incumbrancer would have been entitled if those powers had remained exercisable by the tenant for life.

This subsection applies whether or not any term of years or charge intervenes, or the estate of the remainderman or reversioner is liable to be defeated, and whether or not the estate or interest of the tenant for life under the settlement was in possession at the date of the assurance.

This subsection does not prejudice anything done by the tenant for life before the commencement of this Act, in exercise of any power operating under the Settled Land Acts 1882 to 1890, or, unless the assurance provides to the contrary, operate to accelerate any such intervening term of years or charge as aforesaid.

(2) In this section "assurance" means any surrender, conveyance, assignment or appointment under a power (whether vested in any person solely, or jointly in two or more persons) which operates in equity to extinguish the estate or interest of the tenant for life, and "assured" has a corresponding meaning.

Prohibition or limitation against exercise of powers void, and provision against forfeiture

106.—(1) If in a settlement, will, assurance, or other instrument executed or made before or after, or partly before and partly after, the commencement of this Act a provision is inserted—

  (*a*) purporting or attempting, by way of direction, declaration, or otherwise, to forbid a tenant for life or statutory owner to exercise any power under this Act, or his right to require the settled land to be vested in him; or

---

49 Words omitted by the Law of Property (Amendment) Act 1926, *post*, Sched.

(*b*) attempting, or tending, or intended, by a limitation, gift, or disposition over of settled land, or by a limitation, gift, or disposition of other real or any personal property, or by the imposition of any condition, or by forfeiture, or in any other manner whatever, to prohibit or prevent him from exercising, or to induce him to abstain from exercising, or to put him into a position inconsistent with his exercising, any power under this Act, or his right to require the settled land to be vested in him;

that provision, as far as it purports, or attempts, or tends, or is intended to have, or would or might have, the operation aforesaid, shall be deemed to be void.

(2) For the purposes of this section an estate or interest limited to continue so long only as a person abstains from exercising any such power or right as aforesaid shall be and take effect as an estate or interest to continue for the period for which it would continue if that person were to abstain from exercising the power or right, discharged from liability to determination or cesser by or on his exercising the same.

(3) Notwithstanding anything in a settlement, the exercise by the tenant for life or statutory owner of any power under this Act shall not occasion a forfeiture.

Tenant for life trustee for all parties interested

107.—(1) A tenant for life or statutory owner shall, in exercising any power under this Act, have regard to the interests of all parties entitled under the settlement, and shall, in relation to the exercise thereof by him, be deemed to be in the position and to have the duties and liabilities of a trustee for those parties.

(2) The provision by a tenant for life or statutory owner, at his own expense, of dwellings available for the working classes on any settled land shall not be deemed to be an injury to any interest in reversion or remainder in that land, but such provision shall not be made by a tenant for life or statutory owner without the previous approval in writing of the trustees of the settlement.

Saving for and exercise of other powers

108.—(1) Nothing in this Act shall take away, abridge, or prejudicially affect any power for the time being subsisting under a settlement, or by statute or otherwise, exercisable by a tenant for life, or (save as hereinafter provided) by trustees with his consent, or on his request, or by his direction, or otherwise, and the powers given by this Act are cumulative.

(2) In case of conflict between the provisions of a settlement and the provisions of this Act, relative to any matter in respect whereof the tenant for life or statutory owner exercises or contracts or intends to exercise any power under this Act, the provisions of this Act shall prevail; and, notwithstanding anything in the settlement, any power (not being merely a power of revocation or appointment) relating to the settled land thereby conferred on the trustees of the settlement or other persons exercisable for any purpose, whether or not provided for in this Act, shall, after the commencement of this Act, be exercisable by the tenant for life or statutory owner as if it were an additional power conferred on the tenant for life within the next following section of this Act and not otherwise.

(3) If a question arises or a doubt is entertained respecting any matter within this section, the tenant for life or statutory owner, or the trustees of the settlement, or any other person interested, under the settlement may apply to the court for its decision thereon, and the court may make such order respecting the matter as the court thinks fit.

Saving for additional or larger powers under settlement

109.—(1) Nothing in this Act precludes a settlor from conferring on the tenant for life, or (save as provided by the last preceding section) on the trustees of the settlement, any powers additional to or larger than those conferred by this Act.

(2) Any additional or larger powers so conferred shall, as far as may be, notwithstanding anything in this Act, operate and be exercisable in the like manner, and with all the like incidents, effects, and consequences, as if they were conferred by this Act, and, if relating to the settled land, as if they were conferred by this Act on a tenant for life.

Protection of purchasers, &c.

110.—(1) On a sale, exchange, lease, mortgage, charge, or other disposition, a purchaser dealing in good faith with a tenant for life or statutory owner shall, as against all parties entitled under the settlement, be conclusively taken to have given the best price, consideration, or rent, as the case may require, that could reasonably be obtained by the tenant for life or statutory owner, and to have complied with all the requisitions of this Act.

(2) A purchaser of a legal estate in settled land shall not, except as hereby expressly provided, be bound or entitled to call for the production of the trust instrument or any information concerning that instrument or any *ad valorem* stamp duty thereon, and whether or not he has notice of its contents he shall, save as hereinafter provided, be bound and entitled if the last or only principal vesting instrument contains the statements and particulars required by this Act to assume that—

(a) the person in whom the land is by the said instrument vested or declared to be vested is the tenant for life or statutory owner and has all the powers of a tenant for life under this Act, including such additional or larger powers, if any, as are therein mentioned;

(b) the persons by the said instrument stated to be the trustees of the settlement, or their successors appearing to be duly appointed, are the properly constituted trustees of the settlement;

(c) the statements and particulars required by this Act and contained (expressly or by reference) in the said instrument were correct at the date thereof;

(d) the statements contained in any deed executed in accordance with this Act declaring who are the trustees of the settlement for the purposes of this Act are correct;

(e) the statements contained in any deed of discharge, executed in accordance with this Act, are correct:

Provided that, as regards the first vesting instrument executed for the purpose of giving effect to—

(a) a settlement subsisting at the commencement of this Act; or

(b) an instrument which by virtue of this Act is deemed to be a settlement; or

(c) a settlement which by virtue of this Act is deemed to have been made by any person after the commencement of this Act; or

(d) an instrument inter vivos intended to create a settlement of a legal estate in land which is executed after the commencement of this Act and does not comply with the requirements of this Act with respect to the method of effecting such a settlement;

a purchaser shall be concerned to see—

(i) that the land disposed of to him is comprised in such settlement or instrument;

(ii) that the person in whom the settled land is by such vesting instrument vested, or declared to be vested, is the person in whom it ought to be vested as tenant for life or statutory owner;

(iii) that the persons thereby stated to be the trustees of the settlement are the properly constituted trustees of the settlement.

(3) A purchaser of a legal estate in settled land from a personal representative shall be entitled to act on the following assumptions:—

(i) if the capital money, if any, payable in respect of the transaction is paid to the personal representative, that such representative is acting under his statutory or other powers and requires the money for purposes of administration;

(ii) If such capital money is, by the direction of the personal representative, paid to persons who are stated to be the trustees of a settlement, that such persons are the duly constituted trustees of the settlement for the purposes of this Act, and that the personal representative is acting under his statutory powers during a minority;

(iii) In any other case, that the personal representative is acting under his statutory or other powers.

(4) Where no capital money arises under a transaction, a disposition by a tenant for life or statutory owner shall, in favour of a purchaser of a legal estate, have effect under this Act notwithstanding that at the date of the transaction there are no trustees of the settlement.

(5) If a conveyance of or an assent relating to land formerly subject to a vesting instrument does not state who are the trustees of the settlement for the purposes of this Act, a purchaser of a legal estate shall be bound and entitled to act on the assumption that the person in whom the land was thereby vested was entitled to the land free from all limitations, powers, and charges taking effect under that settlement, absolutely and beneficially, or, if so expressed in the conveyance or assent, as personal representative, or trustee for sale or otherwise, and that every statement of fact in such conveyance or assent is correct.

Purchaser of beneficial interest of tenant for life to have remedies of a legal owner

111. Where—

(*a*) at the commencement of this Act the legal beneficial interest of a tenant for life under a settlement is vested in a purchaser; or

(*b*) after the commencement of this Act a tenant for life conveys or deals with his beneficial interest in possession in favour of a purchaser, and the interest so conveyed or created would, but for the restrictions imposed by statute on the creation of legal estates, have been a legal interest;

the purchaser shall (without prejudice to the powers conferred by this Act on the tenant for life) have and may exercise all the same rights and remedies as he would have had or have been entitled to exercise if the interest had remained or been a legal interest and the reversion, if any, on any leases or tenancies derived out of the settled land had been vested in him:

Provided that, where the conveyance or dealing is effected after the commencement of this Act, the purchaser shall not be entitled to the possession of the documents of title relating to the settled land, but shall have the same rights with respect thereto as if the tenant for life had given to him a statutory acknowledgment of his right to production and delivery of copies thereof, and a statutory undertaking for the safe custody thereof.

The tenant for life shall not deliver any such documents to a purchaser of his beneficial interest, who is not also a purchaser of the whole of the settled land to which such documents relate.

Exercise of powers; limitation of provisions, &c.

112.—(1) Where a power of sale, exchange, leasing, mortgaging, charging, or other power is exercised by a tenant for life, or statutory owner or by the trustees of a settlement, he and they may respectively execute, make, and do all deeds, instruments, and things necessary or proper in that behalf.

(2) Where any provision in this Act refers to sale, purchase, exchange, mortgaging, charging, leasing, or other disposition or dealing, or to any power, consent, payment, receipt, deed, assurance, contract, expenses, act, or transaction, it shall (unless the contrary appears) be construed as extending only to sales, purchases, exchanges, mortgages, charges, leases, dispositions, dealings, powers, consents, payments, receipts, deeds, assurances, contracts, expenses, acts, and transactions under this Act.

PART VIII

COURT, MINISTRY OF AGRICULTURE AND FISHERIES,[50] PROCEDURE

Jurisdiction and procedure

113.—(1) All matters within the jurisdiction of the court under this Act shall, subject to the enactments for the time being in force with respect to the procedure of the Supreme Court of Judicature, be assigned to the Chancery Division of the High Court.

(2) [*This subsection is repealed by the Courts Act 1971 (c. 23), s. 56 (4) and Sched. 11, Pt. II.*]

(3)[51] The powers of the court may, as regards land not exceeding in capital value [£15,000],[52] or in [net annual value for rating][53] [£900],[54] and, as regards capital money arising under this Act, and securities in which the same is invested, not exceeding in amount or value [£15,000],[53] and as regards personal chattels settled or to be settled, as in this Act mentioned, not exceeding in value [£15,000],[56] be exercised by any county court [. . .].[57]

(4) Payment of money into court effectually exonerates therefrom the person making the payment.

(5) Every application to the court under this Act shall, subject to any rules of court to the contrary, be by summons at Chambers.

(6) On an application by the trustees of a settlement notice shall be served in the first instance on the tenant for life.

(7) On any application notice shall be served on such persons, if any, as the court thinks fit.

(8) The court shall have full power and discretion to make such order as it thinks fit respecting the costs, charges, or expenses of all or any of the parties to any application, and may, if it thinks fit, order that all or any of

---

[50] Now the Ministry of Agriculture, Fisheries and Food. See Transfer of Functions (Ministry of Food) Order 1955 (no. 554).

[51] As to conferring jurisdiction on county courts by agreement, see the County Courts Act 1959 (7 & 8 Eliz. 2, c. 22), s. 53.

[52] Substituted by the County Courts Jurisdiction Order 1977 (No. 600).

[53] Words substituted by County Courts Act 1959 s 202, Sched. 2, para. 1(1). Para. 1(2) provides that s. 200 of that Act (construction of references to net annual value for rating) shall apply to this section.

[54] Substituted by the County Courts Jurisdiction Order 1977 (No. 600).

[55] *Ibid.*

[56] *Ibid.*

[57] These words were repealed by the County Courts (Amendment) Act 1934 (24 & 25 Geo. 5, c. 17), Sched. 5.

those costs, charges, or expenses be paid out of property subject to the settlement.

(9) The provisions of the Trustee Act 1925 relating to vesting orders and orders appointing a person to convey shall apply to all vesting orders authorised to be made by this Act.

Payment of costs out of settled property

114. Where the court directs that any costs, charges, or expenses be paid out of property subject to a settlement, the same shall, subject and according to the directions of the court, be raised and paid—

  (*a*) out of capital money arising under this Act, or other money liable to be laid out in the purchase of land to be made subject to the settlement; or

  (*b*) out of securities representing such money, or out of income of any such money or securities; or

  (*c*) out of any accumulation of income of land, money, or securities; or

  (*d*) by means of a sale of part of the settled land in respect whereof the costs, charges, or expenses are incurred, or of other settled land comprised in the same settlement and subject to the same limitations; or

  (*e*) by means of a legal mortgage of the settled land or any part thereof to be made by such person as the court directs;

or partly in one of those modes and partly in another or others, or in any such mode as the court thinks fit.

Powers of the Minister of Agriculture

115.—(1) The Minister shall, by virtue of this Act, have for the purposes of any Act, public general or local or private, making provision for the execution of improvements on settled land, all such powers and authorities as he has for the purposes of the Improvement of Land Act 1864.

(2) The provisions of the last-mentioned Act relating to proceedings and inquiries, and to authentication of instruments, and to declarations, statements, notices, applications, forms, security for expenses, inspections and examinations, shall extend and apply, as far as the nature and circumstances of the case admit, to acts and proceedings done or taken by or in relation to the Minister under any Act making provision as last aforesaid.

(3) The provisions of any Act relating [. . .][58] to security for costs to be taken in respect of the business transacted under the Acts administered by the Minister as successor of the Land Commissioners for England shall extend and apply to the business transacted by or under the direction of the Minister under any Act, public general or local or private, by which any power or duty is conferred or imposed on him as such successor.

Filing of certificates, &c. at the Ministry of Agriculture

116.—(1) Every certificate and report approved and made by the Minister under this Act shall be filed in the office of the Minister of Agriculture and Fisheries.[59]

(2) An office copy of any certificate or report so filed shall be delivered out of such office to any person requiring the same, on payment of the proper fee, and shall be sufficient evidence of the certificate or report whereof it purports to be a copy.

---

[58] Words repealed by the Agriculture (Miscellaneous Provisions) Act 1963 (c. 11), s. 28, Sched., Pt. II.

[59] Now the Minister of Agriculture, Fisheries and Food: see Transfer of Functions (Ministry of Food) Order 1955 (No. 554).

PART IX

SUPPLEMENTARY PROVISIONS

Definitions

117.—(1) In this Act, unless the context otherwise requires, the following expressions have the meanings hereby assigned to them respectively, that is to say:—

(i) "Building purposes" include the erecting and the improving of, and the adding to, and the repairing of buildings; and a "building lease" is a lease for any building purposes or purposes connected therewith;

(ii) "Capital money arising under this Act" means capital money arising under the powers and provisions of this Act or the Acts replaced by this Act, and receivable for the trusts and purposes of the settlement and includes securities representing capital money;

(iii) "Death duty" means estate duty, *succession duty, legacy duty,*[60] and every other duty leviable or payable on death;

(iv) "Determinable fee" means a fee determinable whether by limitation or condition;

(v) "Disposition" and "conveyance" include a mortgage, charge by way of legal mortgage, lease, assent, vesting declaration, vesting instrument, disclaimer, release and every other assurance of property or of an interest therein by any instrument, except a will, and "dispose of" and "convey" have corresponding meanings;

(vi) "Dower" includes "freebench";

(vii) "Hereditaments" means real property which on an intestacy might before the commencement of this Act have devolved on an heir;

(viii) "Instrument" does not include a statute unless the statute creates a settlement;

(ix) "Land" includes land of any tenure, and mines and minerals whether or not held apart from the surface, buildings or parts of buildings (whether the division is horizontal, vertical or made in any other way) and other corporeal hereditaments; also a manor, an advowson, and a rent and other incorporeal hereditaments, and an easement, right, privilege, or benefit in, over, or derived from land, and any estate or interest in land not being an undivided share in land;

(x)[61] "Lease" includes an agreement for a lease, and "forestry lease" means a lease to the Forestry Commissioners for any purpose for which they are authorised to acquire land by the Forestry Act 1919;

(xi) "Legal mortgage" means a mortgage by demise or subdemise or a charge by way of legal mortgage, and "legal mortgagee" has a corresponding meaning; "legal estate" means an estate interest or charge in or over land (subsisting or created at law) which is by statute authorised to subsist or to be created at law; and "equitable interests" mean all other interests and charges in or over land or in the proceeds of sale thereof; an equitable interest "capable of subsisting at law" means such an equitable interest as could validly subsist at law, if clothed with the legal estate; and "estate owner" means the owner of a legal estate;

(xii) "Limitation" includes a trust, and "trust" includes an implied or constructive trust;

---

[60] Words repealed by the Finance Act 1949 (12 & 13 Geo. 6, c. 47), s. 52, Sched. 11. Part IV, subject to the saving contained there.

[61] The reference to Forestry Commissioners is to be construed as a reference to the appropriate Minister: Forestry Act 1967 (c. 10), Sched. 6, para. 5.

(xiii) [*Repealed by the Mental Health Act* 1959 (7 & 8 *Eliz.* 2, *c.* 72), *Sched.* 8, *Pt.* I.]

(xiv) "Manor" includes lordship, and reputed manor or lordship; and "manorial incident" has the same meaning as in the Law of Property Act 1922[62];

(xv) "Mines and minerals" mean mines and minerals whether already opened or in work or not, and include all minerals and substances in, on, or under the land, obtainable by underground or by surface working; and "mining purposes" include the sinking and searching for, winning, working, getting, making merchantable, smelting or otherwise converting or working for the purposes of any manufacture, carrying away, and disposing of mines and minerals, in or under the settled land, or any other land, and the erection of buildings, and the execution of engineering and other works suitable for those purposes; and a "mining lease" is a lease for any mining purposes or purposes connected therewith, and includes a grant or licence for any mining purposes;

(xvi) "Minister" means the Minister of Agriculture and Fisheries[63];

(xvii) "Notice" includes constructive notice;

(xviii) "Personal representative" means the executor, original or by representation, or administrator, for the time being of a deceased person, and where there are special personal representatives for the purposes of settled land means those personal representatives;

(xix) "Possession" includes receipt of rents and profits, or the right to receive the same, if any; and "income" includes rents and profits;

(xx) "Property" includes any thing in action, and any interest in real or personal property;

(xxi) "Purchaser" means a purchaser in good faith for value, and includes a lessee, mortgagee or other person who in good faith acquires an interest in settled land for value; and in reference o a legal estate includes a chargee by way of legal mortgage;

(xxii) "Rent" includes yearly or other rent, and toll, duty, royalty, or other reservation, by the acre, or the ton, or otherwise; and, in relation to rent, "payment" includes delivery; and "fine" includes premium or fore-gift, and any payment, consideration, or benefit in the nature of a fine, premium, or fore-gift;

(xxiii) "Securities" include stocks, funds, and shares;

(xxiv) "Settled land"[64] includes land which is deemed to be settled land; "settlement" includes an instrument or instruments which under this Act or the Acts which it replaces is or are deemed to be or which together constitute a settlement, and a settlement which is deemed to have been made by any person or to be subsisting for the purposes of this Act; "a settlement subsisting at the commencement of this Act" includes a settlement created by virtue of this Act immediately on the commencement thereof; and "trustees of the settlement" mean the trustees thereof for the purposes of this Act howsoever appointed or constituted;

(xxv) "Small dwellings" mean dwelling-houses of a rateable value not exceeding one hundred pounds per annum;

---

[62] All manorial incidents have now been extinguished: Law of Property Act 1922 (12 & 13 Geo. 5, c. 16).

[63] Now the Minister of Agriculture, Fisheries and Food: see Transfer of Functions (Ministry of Food) Order 1955 (No. 554).

[64] By the Land Compensation Act 1973 (c. 26), s. 10(3), compensation in respect of an interest in such land "shall be treated as capital money (see, *ante*, p. 74) arising under [the 1925 Act]." S. 52(7) provides that any advance payments of such compensation "shall be made to the persons entitled to give a discharge for capital money and shall be treated as capital money arising under [the 1925] Act."

(xxvi) "Statutory owner" means the trustees of the settlement or other persons who, during a minority, or at any other time when there is no tenant for life, have the powers of a tenant for life under this Act, but does not include the trustees of the settlement, where by virtue of an order of the court or otherwise the trustees have power to convey the settled land in the name of the tenant for life;

(xxvii) "Steward" includes deputy steward, or other proper officer, of a manor;

(xxviii) "Tenant for life" includes a person (not being a statutory owner) who has the powers of a tenant for life under this Act, and also (where the context requires) one of two or more persons who together constitute the tenant for life, or have the powers of a tenant for life; and "tenant in tail" includes a person entitled to an entailed interest in any property; and "entailed interest" has the same meaning as in the Law of Property Act 1925;

(xxix) A "term of years absolute" means a term of years, taking effect either in possession or in reversion, with or without impeachment for waste, whether at a rent or not and whether subject or not to another legal estate, and whether certain or liable to determination by notice, re-entry, operation of law, or by a provision for cesser on redemption, or in any other event (other than the dropping of a life, or the determination of a determinable life interest), but does not include any term of years determinable with life or lives or with the cesser of a determinable life interest, nor, if created after the commencement of this Act, a term of years which is not expressed to take effect in possession within twenty-one years after the creation thereof where required by statute to take effect within that period; and in this definition the expression "term of years" includes a term for less than a year, or for a year or years and a fraction of a year or from year to year;

(xxx) "Trust corporation"[65] means the Public Trustee or a corporation either appointed by the court in any particular case to be a trustee or entitled by rules made under subsection (3) of section four of the Public Trustee Act 1906, to act as custodian trustee, and "trust for sale" "trustees for sale" and "power to postpone a sale" have the same meanings as in the Law of Property Act 1925;

(xxxi) In relation to settled land "vesting deed" or "vesting order" means the instrument whereby settled land is conveyed to or vested or declared to be vested in a tenant for life or statutory owner; "vesting assent" means the instrument whereby a personal representative, after the death of a tenant for life or statutory owner, or the survivor of two or more tenants for life or statutory owners, vests settled land in a person entitled as tenant for life or statutory owner; "vesting instrument" means a vesting deed, a vesting assent or, where the land affected remains settled land, a vesting order; "principal vesting instrument" includes any vesting instrument other than a subsidiary vesting deed; and "trust instrument" means the instrument whereby the trusts of the settled land are declared, and includes any two or more such instruments and a settlement or instrument which is deemed to be a trust instrument;

(xxxii) "United Kingdom" means Great Britain and Northern Ireland;

(xxxiii) "Will" includes codicil.

[(1A) Any references in this Act to money, securities or proceeds of sale being paid or transferred into court shall be construed as referring to the money, securities or proceeds being paid or transferred into the Supreme

---

[65] For the definition of "trust corporation," see Law of Property (Amendment) Act 1926, s. 3, *post*, p. 276.

Court or any other court that has jurisdiction, and any reference in this Act to the court, in a context referring to the investment or application of money, securities or proceeds of sale paid or transferred into court, shall be construed, in the case of money, securities or proceeds paid or transferred into the Supreme Court, as referring to the High Court and, in the case of money, securities or proceeds paid or transferred into another court, as referring to that other court.][66]

(2) Where an equitable interest in or power over property arises by statute or operation of law, references to the "creation" of an interest or power include any interest or power so arising.

(3) References to registration under the Land Charges Act 1925 apply to any registration made under any statute which is by the Land Charges Act 1925[67] to have effect as if the registration had been made under that Act.

Retrospective amendment of certain provisions of Settled Land Acts

118. For the purpose of removing certain doubts as to the construction and operation of the Settled Land Acts 1882 to 1890, and validating past transactions, the provisions contained in the Fourth Schedule to this Act shall have effect.

Subject as aforesaid, this Act does not affect the validity of anything done or any order made or directions given by the court before the commencement of this Act.

Repeals, savings, and construction

119.—(1) [*Repealed by S.L.R. Act* 1950 (14 *Geo.* 6, *c.* 6)] without prejudice to the provisions of section thirty-eight of the Interpretation Act 1889:—

(*a*) Nothing in this repeal shall affect the validity or legality of any dealing in land or other transaction completed before the commencement of this Act, or any title or right acquired or appointment made before the commencement of this Act, but, subject as aforesaid, this Act shall, except where otherwise expressly provided, apply to and in respect of settlements and other instruments whether made or coming into operation before or after the commencement of this Act;

(*b*) Nothing in this repeal shall affect any rules, orders, or other instruments made under any enactment so repealed, but all such rules, orders and instruments shall continue in force as if made under the corresponding enactment in this Act;

(*c*) References in any document to any enactment repealed by this Act shall be construed as references to this Act or the corresponding enactment in this Act.

(2) References in any statute to the Settled Estates Act 1877 and to any enactment which it replaced shall be construed as references to this Act.

(3) This Act, as respects registered land, takes effect subject to the provisions of the Land Registration Act 1925.

Short title, commencement and extent

120.—(1) This Act may be cited as the Settled Land Act 1925.

(2) [*Repealed by S.L.R. Act* 1950 (14 *Geo.* 6, *c.* 6).]

(3) This Act extends to England and Wales only.

---

[66] Added by the Administration of Justice Act 1965 (c. 2), Sched. 1.
[67] Now the Land Charges Act 1972 (c. 61), *post*, p. 320.

SCHEDULES

FIRST SCHEDULE

FORMS OF INSTRUMENTS

FORM NO. 1.

VESTING DEED FOR GIVING EFFECT TO A SETTLEMENT SUBSISTING AT THE COMMENCEMENT OF THIS ACT

This Vesting Deed is made [&c.] between *X.* of [&c.] and *Y.* of [&c.] (hereinafter called the trustees) of the one part and *T.L.* of [&c.] of the other part.

[*Recite the Settlement under which T.L. is a tenant for life of full age in possession of the freeholds and leaseholds respectively described in the First and Second Schedules and has power to appoint new trustees, and the trustees are trustees for the purposes of the Settled Land Act 1925, also the request by T.L. that the trustees should execute the requisite vesting deed.*]

Now for giving effect to the requirements of the Settled Land Act 1925 this deed witnesseth as follows:—
1. The trustees as Trustees hereby declare that—
All and singular the hereditaments and premises respectively mentioned in the First and Second Schedules hereto and all other (if any) the premises capable of being vested by this declaration which are now by any means subject to the limitations of the recited settlement are vested in the said *T.L.* as to the freehold hereditaments mentioned in the First Schedule hereto in fee simple, and as to the leasehold hereditaments mentioned in the Second Schedule hereto, for all the residue of the terms of years for which the same are respectively held.
2. The said *T.L.* shall stand possessed of the premises upon the trusts and subject to the powers and provisions upon and subject to which under the recited settlement or otherwise the same ought to be held from time to time.
3. The trustees are the trustees of the settlement for the purposes of the Settled Land Act 1925.
4. The following additional or larger powers are conferred by the said settlement in relation to the settled land, and by virtue of the Settled Land Act 1925 operate and are exercisable as if conferred by that Act on a tenant for life [*Here insert the additional powers*].
5. [*Add the usual covenant by T.L. with the trustees to pay the rent in respect of leasehold hereditaments, observe the lessee's covenants and keep the trustees indemnified.*]
6. The power to appoint a new trustee or new trustees of the settlement is vested in the said *T.L.* during his life.
In witness [&c.].
[NOTE.—Add the schedules. In the first part of the First Schedule give particulars of the manors, advowsons and other incorporeal hereditaments. In the second part give particulars of the freehold land referring, if practicable, to annexed plans, so that the vesting deed may ultimately become a convenient root of title. Unless this is done the deeds referred to will for purposes of the parcels remain part of the title. In the Second Schedule give particulars of the dates of and parties to the leases of the leasehold hereditaments, and short particulars of the properties demised, the terms and the rents. If there are any mortgages having priority to the settlement, these should be mentioned in another schedule and referred to in the recitals.]

———

FORM NO. 2

VESTING DEED ON THE SETTLEMENT OF LAND

This Vesting Deed made [&c.] between *John H.* of [&c.] of the first part, *Jane W.* of [&c.] of the second part, and *X.* of [&c.], *Y.* of [&c.], and *Z.* of [&c.] (hereinafter called the trustees) of the third part.
Witnesseth and it is hereby declared as follows:—
1. In consideration of the intended marriage between *John H.* and *Jane W* the said *John H.* as Settlor hereby declares that
All that (*setting out the parcels by reference to a schedule or otherwise*) are vested in *John H.* in fee simple (*or in the case of leaseholds refer to the terms*).
Upon the trusts declared concerning the same by a Trust Instrument bearing even date with but intended to be executed comtemporaneously with these presents and made between the

same parties and in the same order as these presents or upon such other trusts as the same ought to be held from time to time.

2. The trustees are the trustees of the settlement for the purposes of the Settled Land Act 1925.

3. The following additional or larger powers are conferred by the said trust instrument in relation to the settled land and by virtue of the Settled Land Act 1925 operate and are exercisable as if conferred by that Act on a tenant for life. [*Here insert the additional powers.*]

4. The power of appointing a new trustee or new trustees of the settlement is vested in the said [*John H.*] during his life.

In witness [&c.].

Form No. 3.

Trust Instrument on the Settlement of Land

This Trust Instrument is made [&c.] between *John H.* of [&c.] (hereinafter called the Settlor) of the first part, *Jane W.* of [&c.] of the second part, and *X.* of [&c.], *Y* of [&c.], and *Z.* of [&c.] (hereinafter called the trustees) of the third part.

Whereas by a deed (hereinafter called the Vesting Deed) bearing even date with but executed contemporaneously with these presents, and made between the same parties and in the same order as these presents, certain hereditaments situated at   in the county of   were vested in the Settlor Upon the trusts declared concerning the same by a trust instrument of even date therein referred to (meaning these presents).

Now in consideration of the intended marriage between the Settlor and *Jane W.*, this Deed witnesseth as follows:—

1. The Settlor hereby agrees that he will hold the hereditaments and property comprised in the Vesting Deed In trust for himself until the solemnisation of the said marriage and thereafter Upon the trusts following, that is to say:—

2. Upon trust for the Settlor during his life without impeachment of waste with remainder Upon trust if *Jane W.* survives him that she shall receive out of the premises during the residue of her life a yearly jointure rentcharge of [&c.] and subject thereto Upon trust for the trustees for a term of 800 years from the date of the death of the Settlor without impeachment of waste Upon the trusts hereinafter declared concerning the same. And subject to the said term and the trusts thereof Upon trust for the first and other sons of the said intended marriage successively according to seniority in tail male with remainder [&c.] *with an ultimate remainder in trust for the Settlor in fee simple.*

[*Here add the requisite trusts of the portions term, and any other proper provisions including the appointment of the trustees to be trustees of the settlement for the purposes of the Settled Land Act 1925, extension of Settled Land Act powers, and a power for the tenant for life for the time being of full age to appoint new trustees of the settlement.*]

In witness [&c.].

[Note—The Vesting Deed and the Trust Instrument can be executed as escrows till the marriage.]

Form No. 4

Subsidiary Vesting Deed on Sale when the Land is Purchased with Capital Money

This Subsidiary Vesting Deed is made [&c.] between *Henry V.* of [&c.] (hereinafter called the Vendor) of the first part, *X.* of [&c.], *Y.* of [&c.], and *Z.* of [&c.] (hereinafter called the trustees) of the second part, and *John H.* [&c.] (hereinafter called the Purchaser) of the third part.

Whereas the Vendor is entitled for an estate in fee simple in possession free from incumbrances to the hereditaments hereinafter conveyed and has agreed to sell the same to the Purchaser at the price of   pounds.

And whereas by a principal vesting deed (hereinafter called the principal deed) dated [&c.], and made [&c.] [*Form No. 2*], certain hereditaments were vested in the Purchaser Upon the trusts of a trust instrument of even date therewith, and by [endorsements on] the principal deed the trustees were stated to be the trustees of the settlement for the purposes of the Settled Land Act 1925.

Now this Deed witnesseth as follows:—

1. In consideration of the sum of   pounds now paid to the Vendor by the trustees by the direction of the Purchaser (the receipt of which sum the Vendor hereby acknowledges) the Vendor as Beneficial Owner hereby conveys unto the Purchaser All those [&c.].

To hold unto the Purchaser [in fee simple] upon and subject to the same trusts and powers as are declared by the principal deed by reference as aforesaid with respect to the hereditaments therein comprised.

2 and 3. [*Same as* 2 *and* 4 *in Form No.* 2.].

In witness [&c.].

NOTE.—On a purchase of a term of years absolute out of capital money, the term must be conveyed to the tenant for life, if any, of full age, instead of to the trustees of the settlement. If there is a minority the land will be conveyed to the personal representatives or to the Settled Land Act trustees.

FORM NO. 5

VESTING ASSENT BY PERSONAL REPRESENTATIVE

1. *E.F. of* [&c.] and *G.H. of* [&c.] as the personal representatives of *X.Y.*, late of [&c.] deceased, do this   day of   19   hereby, As Personal Representatives, assent to the vesting in *C.D.* of [&c.] of [All that farm &c.] *or* [All the property described in the Schedule hereto] for all the estate or interest of the said *X.Y.* at the time of his death [*or,* for an estate in fee simple].

2. The premises are vested in the said *C.D.* upon the trusts declared concerning the same by [&c.].

3. The said *E.F.* and *G.H.* are the trustees of the settlement for the purposes of the Settled Land Act 1925.

4 and 5. [*Same as* 3 *and* 4 *in Form No.* 2.]

As witness, &c.

NOTE.—The expression "conveyance" includes an assent, but an assent will relate back to the death unless a contrary intention appears.

An assent will not be properly postponed merely because death duty remains to be paid. The representatives have only to be satisfied (*e.g.,* where the tenant for life has directed payment out of capital money or has executed a mortgage for raising the money as and when an instalment becomes due) that the duty will be paid.

Section 37   SECOND SCHEDULE

TRANSITIONAL PROVISIONS AFFECTING EXISTING SETTLEMENTS

Paragraph 1

PROVISIONS FOR VESTING LEGAL ESTATE IN TENANT FOR LIFE OR STATUTORY OWNER

1.—(1) A settlement subsisting at the commencement of this Act is, for the purposes of this Act, a trust instrument.

(2) As soon as practicable after the commencement of this Act, the trustees for the purposes of this Act of every settlement of land subsisting at the commencement of this Act (whether or not the settled land is already vested in them), may and on the request of the tenant for life or statutory owner, shall at the cost of the trust estate, execute a principal vesting deed (containing the proper statements and particulars) declaring that the legal estate in the settled land shall vest or is vested in the person or persons therein named (being the tenant for life or statutory owner, and including themselves if they are the statutory owners), and such deed shall (unless the legal estate is already so vested) operate to convey or vest the legal estate in the settled land to or in the person or persons aforesaid and, if more than one, as joint tenants.

(3) If there are no trustees of the settlement then (in default of a person able and willing to appoint such trustees), an application shall be made to the court by the tenant for life or statutory owner, or by any other person interested, for the appointment of such trustees.

(4) If default is made in the execution of any such principal vesting deed, the provisions of this Act relating to vesting orders of settled land shall apply in like manner as if the trustees of the settlement were persons in whom the settled land is wrongly vested.

(5) This paragraph does not apply where, at the commencement of this Act, settled land is held at law or in equity in undivided shares vested in possession.

(6) In the case of settlements subsisting at the commencement of this Act, all the estates, interests and powers thereby limited which are not by statute otherwise converted into equitable interests or powers, shall, as from the date of the principal vesting deed or the vesting order, take effect only in equity.

[This sub-paragraph shall not apply to any legal estate or interest vested in a mortgagee or other purchaser for money or money's worth .][68]

(7) This paragraph does not apply where settled land is vested in personal representatives at the commencement of this Act, or where settled land becomes vested in personal representatives before a principal vesting deed has been executed pursuant to this paragraph.

(8) No ad valorem stamp duty shall be payable in respect of a vesting deed or order made for giving effect to an existing settlement.

Paragraph 2

PROVISIONS WHERE SETTLED LAND IS AT COMMENCEMENT OF ACT VESTED IN PERSONAL REPRESENTATIVES

2.—(1) Where settled land remains at the commencement of this Act vested in the personal representatives of a person who dies before such commencement, or becomes vested in personal representatives before a principal vesting deed has been executed pursuant to the last preceding paragraph, the personal representatives shall hold the settled land on trust, if and when required so to do, to convey the same to the person who, under the trust instrument, or by virtue of this Act, is the tenant for life or statutory owner and, if more than one, as joint tenants.

(2) A conveyance under this paragraph shall be made at the cost of the trust estate and may be made by an assent in writing signed by the personal representatives which shall operate as a conveyance. No stamp duty is payable in respect of a vesting assent.

(3) The obligation to convey settled land imposed on the personal representatives by this paragraph is subject and without prejudice—

(*a*) to their rights and powers for purposes of administration, and

(*b*) to their being satisfied that provision has been or will be made for the payment of any unpaid death duties in respect of the land or any interest therein for which they are accountable, and any interest and costs in respect of such duties, or that they are otherwise effectually indemnified against such duties, interest and costs.

(4) A conveyance under this paragraph shall—

(*a*) if by deed, be a principal vesting deed, and

(*b*) if by an assent, be a vesting assent, which shall contain the like statements and particulars as are required by this Act in the case of a principal vesting deed.

(5) Nothing contained in this paragraph affects the rights of personal representatives to transfer or create such legal estates to take effect in priority to a conveyance under this paragraph as may be required for giving effect to the obligations imposed on them by statute.

(6) A conveyance by personal representatives under this paragraph, if made by deed, may contain a reservation to themselves of a term of years absolute in the land conveyed upon trusts for indemnifying them against any unpaid death duties in respect of the land conveyed or any interest therein, and any interest and costs in respect of such duties.

(7) Nothing contained in this paragraph affects any right which a person entitled to an equitable charge for securing money actually raised, and affecting the whole estate the subject of the settlement, may have to require effect to be given thereto by a legal mortgage, before the execution of a conveyance under this section.

Paragraph 3

PROVISIONS AS TO INFANTS

3.—(1) Where, at the commencement of this Act, an infant is beneficially entitled to land in possession for an estate in fee simple or for a term of years absolute, or would, if of full age, be a tenant for life or have the powers of a tenant for life, the settled land shall, by virtue of this Act, vest in the trustees (if any) of the settlement upon such trusts as may be requisite for giving effect to the rights of the infant and other persons (if any) interested:

Provided that, if there are no such trustees, then—

(i) Pending their appointment, the settled land shall, by virtue of this Act, vest in the Public Trustee upon the trusts aforesaid:

(ii) The Public Trustee shall not be entitled to act in the trust, or charge any fee, or be liable in any manner unless and until requested in writing to act on behalf of the infant by his parents or parent or testamentary or other guardian in the order named:

---

[68] Added by the Law of Property (Amendment) Act 1926, *post*, s. 7, Sched.

(iii) After the Public Trustee has been so requested to act, and has accepted the trust, he shall become the trustee of the settlement, and no trustee shall (except by an order of the court) be appointed in his place without his consent:

(iv) If there is no other person able and willing to appoint trustees the parents or parent or testamentary or other guardian of the infant, if respectively able and willing to act, shall (in the order named) have power by deed to appoint trustees of the settlement in place of the Public Trustee in like manner as if the Public Trustee had refused to act in the trust, and to vest the settled land in them on the trusts aforesaid, and the provisions of the Trustee Act 1925, relating to the appointment of new trustees, and the vesting of trust property shall apply as if the persons aforesaid (in the order named) had been nominated by the settlement for the purpose of appointing new trustees thereof; and in default of any such appointment the infant by his next friend, may, at any time during the minority, apply to the court for the appointment of trustees of the settlement, and the court may make such order as it thinks fit, and if thereby trustees of the settlement are appointed, the settled land shall, by virtue of this Act, vest in the trustees as joint tenants upon the trusts aforesaid:

Provided that in favour of a purchaser a statement in the deed of appointment that the father or mother or both are dead or are unable or unwilling to make the appointment shall be conclusive evidence of the fact stated.

(v) If land to which an infant is beneficially entitled in possession for an estate in fee simple or for a term of years absolute vests in the Public Trustee, but the Public Trustee does not become the trustee of the settlement, and trustees of the settlement are not appointed in his place, then, if and when the infant attains the age of twenty-one years, the land shall vest in him.

(2) The provisions of this paragraph shall extend to the legal estate in the settled land, except where such legal estate is, at or immediately after the commencement of this Act, vested in personal representatives, in which case this paragraph shall have effect without prejudice to the provisions of paragraph two of this Schedule.

(3) Where, at the commencement of this Act, any persons appointed under section sixty of the Settled Land Act 1882 have power to act generally or for any specific purpose on behalf of an infant, then those persons shall, by virtue of this Act, become and be the trustees of the settlement.

(4) Notwithstanding that the settled land is by virtue of this paragraph vested in the trustees of the settlement, they shall, at the cost of the trust estate, in accordance with this Act, execute a principal vesting deed declaring that the settled land is vested in them.

(5) This paragraph does not apply where an infant is beneficially entitled in possession to land for an estate in fee simple or for a term of years absolute jointly with a person of full age (for which case provision is made in the Law of Property Act 1925), but it applies to two or more infants entitled as aforesaid jointly.

(6) This paragraph does not apply where an infant would, if of full age, constitute the tenant for life or have the powers of a tenant for life together with another person of full age, but it applies to two or more infants who would, if all of them were of full age, together constitute the tenant for life or have the powers of a tenant for life.

Section 83   THIRD SCHEDULE[69]

PART I[70]

IMPROVEMENTS, THE COSTS OF WHICH ARE NOT LIABLE TO BE REPLACED BY INSTALMENTS

(i) Drainage, including the straightening, widening, or deepening of drains, streams and watercourses:

(ii) Bridges:

(iii) Irrigation; warping:

(iv) Drains, pipes, and machinery for supply and distribution of sewage as manure:

(v) Embanking or weiring from a river or lake, or from the sea, or a tidal water:

(vi) Groynes; sea walls; defences against water:

---

[69] Power to extend the scope of this Schedule was granted by the Agriculture Act 1970 (c. 40), s. 30(1).

[70] As to war damage see the Landlord and Tenant (War Damage) Act 1939 (2 & 3 Geo. 6, c. 72), s. 3.

Part I of this Schedule is extended by the Hill Farming Act 1946 (9 & 10 Geo. 6, c. 73), s. 11; the Agricultural Holdings Act 1948 (11 & 12 Geo. 6, c. 63), s. 81(1); the Livestock Rearing Act 1951 (14 & 15 Geo. 6, c. 18), s. 1; the Hill Farming Improvements (Settled Land and Trusts for Sale) Regulations 1951 (No. 1816), art. 3, and the Agriculture Act 1967 (c. 22), s. 36(5).

(vii) Inclosing; straightening of fences; re-division of fields:

(viii) Reclamation; dry warping:

(ix) Farm roads; private roads; roads or streets in villages or towns:

(x) Clearing; trenching; planting:

(xi) Cottages for labourers, farm-servants, and artisans, employed on the settled land or not:

(xii) Farmhouses, offices, and outbuildings, and other buildings for farm purposes:

(xiii) Saw-mills, scutch-mills, and other mills, water-wheels, engine-houses, and kilns, which will increase the value of the settled land for agricultural purposes or as woodland or otherwise:

(xiv) Reservoirs, tanks, conduits, watercourses, pipes, wells, ponds, shafts, dams, weirs, sluices, and other works and machinery for supply and distribution of water for agricultural, manufacturing, or other purposes, or for domestic or other consumption:

(xv) Tramways; railways; canals; docks:

(xvi) Jetties, piers, and landing places on rivers, lakes, the sea, or tidal waters, for facilitating transport of persons and of agricultural stock and produce, and of manure and other things required for agricultural purposes, and of minerals, and of things required for mining purposes:

(xvii) Markets and market-places;

(xviii) Streets, roads, paths, squares, gardens, or other open spaces for the use, gratuitously or on payment, of the public or of individuals, or for dedication to the public, the same being necessary or proper in connexion with the conversion of land into building land:

(xix) Sewers, drains, watercourses, pipe-making, fencing, paving, brick-making, tile-making, and other works necessary or proper in connexion with any of the objects aforesaid:

(xx) Trial pits for mines, and other preliminary works necessary or proper in connexion with development of mines:

(xxi) Reconstruction, enlargement, or improvement of any of those works:

(xxii) The provision of small dwellings, either by means of building new buildings or by means of the reconstruction, enlargement, or improvement of existing buildings, if that provision of small dwellings is, in the opinion of the court, not injurious to the settled land or is agreed to by the tenant for life and the trustees of the settlement:

(xxiii) Additions to or alterations in buildings reasonably necessary or proper to enable the same to be let:

(xxiv) Erection of buildings in substitution for buildings within an urban sanitary district taken by a local or other public authority, or for buildings taken under compulsory powers, but so that no more money be expended than the amount received for the buildings taken and the site thereof:

(xxv) The rebuilding of the principal mansion house on the settled land:

Provided that the sum to be applied under this head shall not exceed one-half of the annual rental of the settled land.

PART II[71]

IMPROVEMENTS, THE COSTS OF WHICH THE TRUSTEES OF THE SETTLEMENT OR THE COURT MAY REQUIRE TO BE REPLACED BY INSTALMENTS

(i) Residential houses for land or mineral agents, managers, clerks, bailiffs, woodmen, gamekeepers and other persons employed on the settled land, or in connexion with the management or development thereof:

(ii) Any offices, workshops and other buildings of a permanent nature required in connexion with the management or development of the settled land or any part thereof:

(iii) The erection and building of dwelling houses, shops, buildings for religious, educational, literary, scientific, or public purposes, market places, market houses, places of amusement and entertainment, gasworks, electric light or power works, or any other works necessary or proper in connexion with the development of the settled land, or any part thereof as a building estate:

(iv) Restoration or reconstruction of buildings damaged or destroyed by dry rot:

(v) Structural additions to or alterations in buildings reasonably required, whether the buildings are intended to be let or not, or are already let:

(vi) Boring for water and other preliminary works in connexion therewith.

---

[71] Part II of this Schedule is extended by the Civil Defence Act 1939 (2 & 3 Geo. 6, c. 31), s. 66(1), the Agriculture Act 1967 (c. 22), s. 36(5), and the Town and Country Planning Act 1971 (c. 78), s. 275(2).

IMPROVEMENTS, THE COSTS OF WHICH THE TRUSTEES OF THE SETTLEMENT AND THE COURT MUST REQUIRE TO BE REPLACED BY INSTALMENTS

(i) Heating, hydraulic or electric power apparatus for buildings, and engines, pumps, lifts, rams, boilers, flues, and other works required or used in connexion therewith:

(ii) Engine houses, engines, gasometers, dynamos, accumulators, cables, pipes, wiring, switchboards, plant and other works required for the installation of electric, gas, or other artificial light, in connexion with any principal mansion house, or other house or buildings; but not electric lamps, gas fittings, or decorative fittings required in any such house or building:

(iii) Steam rollers, traction engines, motor lorries and moveable machinery for farming or other purposes.

Section 118   FOURTH SCHEDULE

RETROSPECTIVE AMENDMENTS OF THE SETTLED LAND ACTS 1882 TO 1890

Shifting of incumbrances

1. The power conferred by section five of the Settled Land Act 1882 of shifting incumbrances on a sale, exchange, or partition, shall be deemed always to have authorised a charge on all or any part of the capital money or securities representing capital money arising from the transaction or otherwise subject to the settlement, and incumbrance in section five aforesaid shall be deemed always to have included any incumbrance, whether capable of being overreached on the exercise by the tenant for life of the powers conferred by the Settled Land Acts 1882 to 1890 or not.

Rate of interest on incumbrances

2. In the case of an incumbrance affecting the settled land, or any part thereof, the tenant for life shall be deemed always to have had power, with the consent of the incumbrancer, to vary the rate of interest charged, and any of the other provisions of the instrument (if any) creating the incumbrance.

Dedication for streets, open spaces, &c.

3.—(1) Section sixteen of the Settled Land Act 1882 shall be deemed always to have had effect, as if the words "after or" had been inserted after the words "On or," and the words "or the development of the settled land, or any part thereof, as a building estate, or at any other reasonable time" had been inserted after the words "building lease."

(2) A tenant for life shall be deemed always to have had power—
   (*a*) to enter into any agreement for the recompense to be made for any part of the settled land required for the widening of a highway under section eighty-two of the Highway Act 1835 or otherwise;
   (*b*) to consent to the diversion of any highway over the settled land under section eighty-five of that Act or otherwise; and
   (*c*) to consent to any such road as is mentioned in section thirty-six of the Highway Act 1862 being declared a public highway;
and any agreement or consent so made or given shall be deemed to have been as valid and effectual, for all purposes, as if made or given by an absolute owner of the settled land, provided that any money received or receivable in respect of such agreement or consent was or is paid to the trustees of the settlement or into court as capital money.

Separate dealings with surface and minerals

4. Subsection (1) of section seventeen of the Settled Land Act 1882 shall be deemed always to have had effect, as if the words "or mining" had not been contained therein, and the words "or other authorised disposition" had been inserted therein after the word "lease."

Powers on sale, &c.

5. On a sale or other disposition made before the commencement of this Act under the powers of the Settled Land Acts 1882 to 1890, the powers conferred by subsection (1) of section forty-nine of this Act shall be deemed to have been exercisable.

---

[72] Part III of this Schedule is extended by the Agriculture Act 1970 (c. 40), s. 30(1).

Sale of timber and fixtures at a valuation

6. In favour of a purchaser, a sale made before the commencement of this Act shall not be deemed to have been invalidated by reason only of any such stipulation as mentioned in subsection (2) of section forty-nine of this Act, provided that the amount of the valuation was paid to the trustees of the settlement or into court.

Raising of money

7. Where under the Settled Land Acts 1882 to 1890 power was given to raise money for any purpose, the power shall be deemed always to have included power to raise the money properly required for the payment of the costs of the transaction.

Provision where interest in settled land is restored

8. A person entitled to an estate or interest, whether legal or equitable, in settled land shall in the circumstances mentioned in section twenty-two of this Act be deemed always to have been entitled to such estate and interest and to exercise such powers as is in that section mentioned.

Referential settlements

9. Where a settlement has before the commencement of this Act taken effect by reference to another settlement, the trustees who would by virtue of section thirty-two of this Act be the trustees of the settlement by reference shall be deemed always to have been the trustees of such settlement.

Application of capital money

10.—(1) Capital money arising under the Settled Land Acts 1882 to 1890 shall be deemed always to have been capable of being applied in paying any increment value duty which a tenant for life had power to charge on the settled land under section thirty-nine of the Finance (1909–10) Act 1910, and any reversion duty, and any costs and expenditure incurred by the tenant for life, or the trustees of the settlement, in connexion with any valuation under the said Act, or with the assessment and ascertainment of the amount of any increment value duty which a tenant for life had power to charge as aforesaid, or any reversion duty.

(2) Capital money arising under the Settled Land Acts 1882 to 1890 shall be deemed always to have been capable of being applied in any of the modes mentioned in paragraphs (xiii) to (xvi) inclusive of subsection (1) of section seventy-three of this Act as well as in the modes authorised by section twenty-one of the Settled Land Act 1882.

As to capital arising otherwise than under the Settled Land Acts

11. Where before the commencement of this Act any money arising from settled land, otherwise than under the Settled Land Acts 1882 to 1890, which ought, as between the persons interested in the settled land, to have been treated as capital, has been invested, applied, or otherwise dealt with as if it had been capital money arising under those Acts, such investment, application, or other dealing shall be deemed to have been valid.

Power for Public Trustee to give receipts and accept notices

12. Where the Public Trustee or any other trust corporation was sole trustee of a settlement, the corporation shall, notwithstanding anything to the contrary contained in sections thirty-nine and forty-five of the Settled Land Act 1882 or the settlement, be deemed always to have had power to give receipts, accept notices, and otherwise act alone as trustee of the settlement for all the purposes of the Settled Land Acts 1882 to 1890.

Assignments of tenant for life's interest

13.—(1) Section fifty of the Settled Land Act 1882 shall be deemed always to have applied, notwithstanding that the estate or interest of the tenant for life under the settlement was not in possession when the assignment was made, or took effect by operation of law.

(2) The expression "assignee for value" in subsection (3) of section fifty of the Settled Land Act 1882 shall be deemed always to have included persons deriving title under the original assignee.

(3) A trustee or personal representative who is an assignee for value shall be deemed always to have had power to consent to the exercise by the tenant for life of his powers under the Settled Land Acts 1882 to 1890.

(4) A person for the time being entitled in possession under the limitations of such settlement as is mentioned in subsection (7) of section one hundred and four of this Act shall in the circumstances in that subsection mentioned, be deemed always to have had power to

consent to the exercise by the tenant for life of his powers under the Settled Land Acts 1882 to 1890, and to bind by such consent all persons interested or to become interested under the settlement.

As to base fees

14. It shall be deemed always to have been sufficient to enable the fee simple to be disposed of or dealt with under the Settled Land Acts 1882 to 1890 by the owner of a base fee as defined by the Fines and Recoveries Act 1833, or fee determinable whether by limitation or condition, or the tenant for life thereof, if there were at the time of the transaction trustees for the purposes of those Acts or any of them of the settlement consisting of the instrument whereby the estate tail or determinable fee was created, and the capital money (if any) arising on such disposition or dealing was or is paid to such trustees or into court.

Amendment of s. 58(1) (ix) of the Act of 1882

15. Paragraph (ix) of subsection (1) of section fifty-eight of the Settled Land Act 1882 shall be deemed always to have had effect as if in that paragraph—
    (*a*) "trust" included an implied or constructive trust;
    (*b*) "forfeiture" included cesser or determination by any means:
    (*c*) after the words "expenses of management" there had been inserted the words "or to a trust for accumulation of income for any purpose";
but not so as to render invalid or prejudice any title or right acquired before the commencement of this Act.

Married woman, infant, &c.

16. Sections fifty-nine and sixty of the Settled Land Act 1882 shall be deemed always to have applied, although the infant was a married woman; and section fifty-nine aforesaid shall be deemed always to have extended to any leasehold interest whether at a rent or not.

FIFTH SCHEDULE

[*Repealed by S.L.R. Act* 1950 (14 *Geo.* 6, *c.* 6).]

Trustee Act 1925

(15 Geo. 5, c. 19)

Arrangement of Sections

Part I

Investments

Part II

General Powers of Trustees and Personal Representatives

General Powers

Indemnities

Maintenance, Advancement and Protective Trusts

Part III

Appointment and Discharge of Trustees

An Act to consolidate certain enactments relating to trustees in England and Wales.[1]   [9th April 1925.]

---

[1] Applied to vesting orders under the Settled Land Act 1925, s. 113(9), *ante*, p. 73, the Law of Property Act 1925, s. 9(3), *post*, p. 131 and the Administration of Estates Act 1925, s. 43(2), *post*, p. 263. Applied generally to registered land by Land Registration Act 1925 (15 & 16 Geo. 5, c. 21), ss. 47(1), 111(6). Extended by the Local Government Act 1972 (c. 70), s. 146(1) (c) and by the Solicitors Act 1974 (c. 47), s. 38, Sched. 1. para. 11(2).

PART I

INVESTMENTS

1. [*Repealed by the Trustee Investments Act* 1961, *post, Sched.* 5.][2]

Purchase at a premium of redeemable stocks; change of character of investment

2.—(1) A trustee may under the powers of this Act invest in any of the securities mentioned or referred to in section one of this Act, notwithstanding that the same may be redeemable, and that the price exceeds the redemption value.

[*Proviso repealed by the Trustee Investments Act* 1961, *Sched.* 5, *post.*]

(2) A trustee may retain until redemption any redeemable stock, fund, or security which may have been purchased in accordance with the powers of this Act, or any statute replaced by this Act.

Discretion of trustees

3. Every power conferred by the preceding sections shall be exercised according to the discretion of the trustee, but subject to any consent or direction required by the instrument, if any, creating the trust or by statute with respect to the investment of the trust funds.

Power to retain investment which has ceased to be authorised

4.[3] A trustee shall not be liable for breach of trust by reason only of his continuing to hold an investment which has ceased to be an investment authorised by the trust instrument or by the general law.

Enlargement of powers of investment

5.—(1) A trustee having power to invest in real securities may invest and shall be deemed always to have had power to invest—

   (a) [*Repealed by the Trustee Investments Act* 1961, *Sched.* 5.]
   (b) on any charge, or upon mortgage of any charge, made under the Improvement of Land Act 1864.

(2) A trustee having power to invest in real securities may accept the security in the form of a charge by way of legal mortgage, and may, in exercise of the statutory power, convert an existing mortgage into a charge by way of legal mortgage.

(3) A trustee having power to invest in the mortgages or bonds of any railway company or of any other description of company may invest in the debenture stock of a railway company or such other company as aforesaid.

(4), (5) and (6) [*Repealed by the Trustee Investments Act* 1961, *Sched.* 5, *post.*]

Power to invest in land subject to drainage charges

6. A trustee having power to invest in the purchase of land or on mortgage of land may invest in the purchase or on mortgage of any land

---

[2] References in this Act, except in s. 69(2), to s. 1 of this Act are to be construed as references to s. 1 of the Trustee Investments Act 1961, *post*, p. 289; see *ibid.* Sched. 4, para. 1(1), p. 301.

[3] s. 4 is excluded in respect of certain investments by the Trustee Investments Act 1961, Sched. 3, para. 2, *post*, p. 301.

notwithstanding the same is charged with a rent under the powers of [. . .][4] the Landed Property Improvement (Ireland) Act 1847, or by an absolute order made under the Improvement of Land Act 1864, unless the terms of the trust expressly provide that the land to be purchased or taken in mortgage shall not be subject to any such prior charge.

Investment in bearer securities

7.—(1) A trustee may, unless expressly prohibited by the instrument creating the trust, retain or invest in securities payable to bearer which, if not so payable, would have been authorised investments:

Provided that securities to bearer retained or taken as an investment by a trustee (not being a trust corporation) shall, until sold, be deposited by him for safe custody and collection of income with a banker or banking company.

A direction that investments shall be retained or made in the name of a trustee shall not, for the purposes of this subsection, be deemed to be such an express prohibition as aforesaid.

(2) A trustee shall not be responsible for any loss incurred by reason of such deposit, and any sum payable in respect of such deposit and collection shall be paid out of the income of the trust property.

Loans and investments by trustees not chargeable as breaches of trust

8.—(1) A trustee lending money on the security of any property on which he can properly lend shall not be chargeable with breach of trust by reason only of the proportion borne by the amount of the loan to the value of the property at the time when the loan was made, if it appears to the court—

(*a*) that in making the loan the trustee was acting upon a report as to the value of the property made by a person whom he reasonably believed to be an able practical surveyor or valuer instructed and employed independently of any owner of the property, whether such surveyor or valuer carried on business in the locality where the property is situate or elsewhere; and

(*b*) that the amount of the loan does not exceed two third parts of the value of the property as stated in the report; and

(*c*) that the loan was made under the advice of the surveyor or valuer expressed in the report.

(2) A trustee lending money on the security of any leasehold property shall not be chargeable with breach of trust only upon the ground that in making such loan he dispensed either wholly or partly with the production or investigation of the lessor's title.

(3) A trustee shall not be chargeable with breach of trust only upon the ground that in effecting the purchase, or in lending money upon the security, of any property he has accepted a shorter title than the title which a purchaser is, in the absence of a special contract, entitled to require, if in the opinion of the court the title accepted be such as a person acting with prudence and caution would have accepted.

(4) This section applies to transfers of existing securities as well as to new securities and to investments made before as well as after the commencement of this Act.

Liability for loss by reason of improper investment

9.—(1) Where a trustee improperly advances trust money on a mortgage security which would at the time of the investment be a proper investment in all respects for a smaller sum than is actually advanced thereon, the security shall be deemed an authorised investment for the

---

[4] These words are repealed by the Statute Law Revision Act 1963 (c. 30).

smaller sum, and the trustee shall only be liable to make good the sum advanced in excess thereof with interest.

(2) This section applies to investments made before as well as after the commencement of this Act.

Powers supplementary to powers of investment

10.—(1) Trustees lending money on the security of any property on which they can lawfully lend may contract that such money shall not be called in during any period not exceeding seven years from the time when the loan was made, provided interest be paid within a specified time not exceeding thirty days after every half-yearly or other day on which it becomes due, and provided there be no breach of any covenant by the mortgagor contained in the instrument of mortgage or charge for the maintenance and protection of the property.

(2) On a sale of land for an estate in fee simple or for a term having at least five hundred years to run by trustees or by a tenant for life or statutory owner, the trustees, or the tenant for life or statutory owner on behalf of the trustees of the settlement, may, where the proceeds are liable to be invested, contract that the payment of any part, not exceeding two-thirds, of the purchase money shall be secured by a charge by way of legal mortgage or a mortgage by demise or subdemise for a term of at least five hundred years (less a nominal reversion when by sub-demise), of the land sold, with or without the security of any other property, such charge or mortgage, if any buildings are comprised in the mortgage, to contain a covenant by the mortgagor to keep them insured against loss or damage by fire to the full value thereof.

The trustees shall not be bound to obtain any report as to the value of the land or other property to be comprised in such charge or mortgage, or any advice as to the making of the loan, and shall not be liable for any loss which may be incurred by reason only of the security being insufficient at the date of the charge or mortgage; and the trustees of the settlement shall be bound to give effect to such contract made by the tenant for life or statutory owner.

(3) Where any securities of a company are subject to a trust, the trustees may concur in any scheme or arrangement—

    (*a*) for the reconstruction of the company;

    (*b*) for the sale of all or any part of the property and undertaking of the company to another company;

[(*bb*) for the acquisition of the securities of the company, or of control thereof, by another company[5]

    (*c*) for the amalgamation of the company with another company;

    (*d*) for the release, modification, or variation of any rights, privileges or liabilities attached to the securities or any of them;

in like manner as if they were entitled to such securities beneficially, with power to accept any securities of any denomination or description of the reconstructed or purchasing or new company in lieu of or in exchange for all or any of the first-mentioned securities; and the trustees shall not be responsible for any loss occasioned by any act or thing so done in good faith, and may retain any securities so accepted as aforesaid for any period for which they could have properly retained the original securities.

(4)[6] If any conditional or preferential right to subscribe for any securities in any company is offered to trustees in respect of any holding in such company, they may as to all or any such securities, either exercise such right and apply capital money subject to the trust in payment of the consideration, or renounce such right, or assign for the best consideration

---

[5] These words are added by the Trustee Investments Act 1961, s. 9(1), *post*, p. 294.
[6] Explained by *ibid.* s. 9(2).

that can be reasonably obtained the benefit of such right or the title thereto to any person, including any beneficiary under the trust, without being responsible for any loss occasioned by any act or thing so done by them in good faith:

Provided that the consideration for any such assignment shall be held as capital money of the trust.

(5) The powers conferred by this section shall be exercisable subject to the consent of any person whose consent to a change of investment is required by law or by the instrument, if any, creating the trust.

(6) Where the loan referred to in subsection (1), or the sale referred to in subsection (2), of this section is made under the order of the court, the powers conferred by those subsections respectively shall apply only if and as far as the court may by order direct.

Power to deposit money at bank and to pay calls

11.—(1) Trustees may, pending the negotiation and preparation of any mortgage or charge, or during any other time while an investment is being sought for, pay any trust money into a bank to a deposit or other account, and all interest, if any, payable in respect thereof shall be applied as income.

(2) Trustees may apply capital money subject to a trust in payment of the calls on any shares subject to the same trust.

Part II

General Powers of Trustees and Personal Representatives

General Powers

Power of trustees for sale to sell by auction, &c.

12.—(1) Where a trust for sale or a power of sale of property is vested in a trustee, he may sell or concur with any other person in selling all or any part of the property, either subject to prior charges or not, and either together or in lots, by public auction or by private contract, subject to any such conditions respecting title or evidence of title or other matter as the trustee thinks fit, with power to vary any contract for sale, and to buy in at any auction, or to rescind any contract for sale and to re-sell, without being answerable for any loss.

(2) A trust or power to sell or dispose of land includes a trust or power to sell or dispose of part thereof, whether the division is horizontal, vertical, or made in any other way.

(3) This section does not enable an express power to sell settled land to be exercised where the power is not vested in the tenant for life or statutory owner.

Power to sell subject to depreciatory conditions

13.—(1) No sale made by a trustee shall be impeached by any beneficiary upon the ground that any of the conditions subject to which the sale was made may have been unnecessarily depreciatory, unless it also appears that the consideration for the sale was thereby rendered inadequate.

(2) No sale made by a trustee shall, after the execution of the conveyance, be impeached as against the purchaser upon the ground that any of the conditions subject to which the sale was made may have been unnecessarily depreciatory, unless it appears that the purchaser was acting

in collusion with the trustee at the time when the contract for sale was made.

(3) No purchaser, upon any sale made by a trustee, shall be at liberty to make any objection against the title upon any of the grounds aforesaid.

(4) This section applies to sales made before or after the commencement of this Act.

Power of trustees to give receipts

14.—(1) The receipt in writing of a trustee for any money, securities, or other personal property or effects payable, transferable, or deliverable to him under any trust or power shall be a sufficient discharge to the person paying, transferring, or delivering the same and shall effectually exonerate him from seeing to the application of being answerable for any loss or misapplication thereof.

(2) This section does not, except where the trustee is a trust corporation, enable a sole trustee to give a valid receipt for—

(a) the proceeds of sale or other capital money arising under a [. . .]⁷ trust for sale of land;

(b) capital money arising under the Settled Land Act 1925.

(3) This section applies notwithstanding anything to the contrary in the instrument, if any, creating the trust.

Power to compound liabilities

15. A personal representative, or two or more trustees acting together, or, subject to the restrictions imposed in regard to receipts by a sole trustee not being a trust corporation, a sole acting trustee where by the instrument, if any, creating the trust, or by statute, a sole trustee is authorised to execute the trusts and powers reposed in him, may if and as he or they think fit—

(a) accept any property, real or personal, before the time at which it is made transferable or payable; or

(b) sever and apportion any blended trust funds or property; or

(c) pay or allow any debt or claim on any evidence that he or they think sufficient; or

(d) accept any composition or any security, real or personal, for any debt or for any property, real or personal, claimed; or

(e) allow any time of payment of any debt; or

(f) compromise, compound, abandon, submit to arbitration, or otherwise settle any debt, account, claim, or thing whatever relating to the testator's or intestate's estate or to the trust;

and for any of those purposes may enter into, give, execute, and do such agreements, instruments of composition or arrangement, releases, and other things as to him or them seem expedient, without being responsible for any loss occasioned by any act or thing so done by him or them in good faith.

Power to raise money by sale, mortgage, &c.

16.—(1) Where trustees are authorised by the instrument, if any, creating the trust or by law to pay or apply capital money subject to the trust for any purpose or in any manner, they shall have and shall be

---

⁷ These words were repealed retrospectively by the Law of Property (Amendment) Act 1926, *post,* Sched.

deemed always to have had power to raise the money required by sale, conversion, calling in, or mortgage of all or any part of the trust property for the time being in possession.

(2) This section applies notwithstanding anything to the contrary contained in the instrument, if any, creating the trust, but does not apply to trustees of property held for charitable purposes, or to trustees of a settlement for the purposes of the Settled Land Act 1925, not being also the statutory owners.

Protection to purchasers and mortgagees dealing with trustees

17. No purchaser or mortgagee, paying or advancing money on a sale or mortgage purporting to be made under any trust or power vested in trustees, shall be concerned to see that such money is wanted, or that no more than is wanted is raised, or otherwise as to the application thereof.

Devolution of powers or trusts

18.—(1) Where a power or trust is given to or imposed on two or more trustees jointly, the same may be exercised or performed by the survivors or survivor of them for the time being.

(2) Until the appointment of new trustees, the personal representatives or representative for the time being of a sole trustee, or, where there were two or more trustees of the last surviving or continuing trustee, shall be capable of exercising or performing any power or trust which was given to, or capable of being exercised by, the sole or last surviving or continuing trustee, or other the trustees or trustee for the time being of the trust.

(3) This section takes effect subject to the restrictions imposed in regard to receipts by a sole trustee, not being a trust corporation.

(4) In this section "personal representative" does not include an executor who has renounced or has not proved.

Power to insure

19.—(1) A trustee may insure against loss or damage by fire any building or other insurable property to any amount, including the amount of any insurance already on foot, not exceeding three fourth parts of the full value of the building or property, and pay the premiums for such insurance out of the income thereof or out of the income of any other property subject to the same trusts without obtaining the consent of any person who may be entitled wholly or partly to such income.

(2) This section does not apply to any building or property which a trustee is bound forthwith to convey absolutely to any beneficiary upon being requested to do so.

Application of insurance money where policy kept up under any trust, power or obligation

20.—(1) Money receivable by trustees or any beneficiary under a policy of insurance against the loss or damage of any property subject to a trust or to a settlement within the meaning of the Settled Land Act 1925, whether by fire or otherwise, shall, where the policy has been kept up under any trust in that behalf or under any power statutory or otherwise, or in performance of any covenant or of any obligation statutory or otherwise, or by a tenant for life impeachable for waste, be capital money for the purposes of the trust or settlement, as the case may be.

(2) If any such money is receivable by any person, other than the trustees of the trust or settlement, that person shall use his best endeavours to recover and receive the money, and shall pay the net residue thereof, after discharging any costs of recovering and receiving it, to the trustees of the trust or settlement, or, if there are no trustees capable of giving a discharge therefor, into court.

(3) Any such money—

    (*a*) if it was receivable in respect of settled land within the meaning of the Settled Land Act 1925, or any building or works thereon, shall be deemed to be capital money arising under that Act from the settled land, and shall be invested or applied by the trustees, or, if in court, under the direction of the court, accordingly;

    (*b*) if it was receivable in respect of personal chattels settled as heirlooms within the meaning of the Settled Land Act 1925, shall be deemed to be capital money arising under that Act, and shall be applicable by the trustees, or, if in court, under the direction of the court, in like manner as provided by that Act with respect to money arising by a sale of chattels settled as heirlooms as aforesaid;

    (*c*) if it was receivable in respect of property held upon trust for sale, shall be held upon the trusts and subject to the powers and provisions applicable to money arising by a sale under such trust;

    (*d*) in any other case, shall be held upon trusts corresponding as nearly as may be with the trusts affecting the property in respect of which it was payable.

(4) Such money, or any part thereof, may also be applied by the trustees, or, if in court, under the direction of the court, in rebuilding, reinstating, replacing, or repairing the property lost or damaged, but any such application by the trustees shall be subject to the consent of any person whose consent is required by the instrument, if any, creating the trust to the investment of money subject to the trust, and, in the case of money which is deemed to be capital money arising under the Settled Land Act 1925, be subject to the provisions of that Act with respect to the application of capital money by the trustees of the settlement.

(5) Nothing contained in this section prejudices or affects the right of any person to require any such money or any part thereof to be applied in rebuilding, reinstating, or repairing the property lost or damaged, or the rights of any mortgagee, lessor, or lessee, whether under any statute or otherwise.

(6) This section applies to policies effected either before or after the commencement of this Act, but only to money received after such commencement.

Deposit of documents for safe custody

21. Trustees may deposit any documents held by them relating to the trust, or to the trust property, with any banker or banking company or any other company whose business includes the undertaking of the safe custody of documents, and any sum payable in respect of such deposit shall be paid out of the income of the trust property.

Reversionary interests, valuations, and audit

22.—(1) Where trust property includes any share or interest in property not vested in the trustees, or the proceeds of the sale of any such property, or any other thing in action, the trustees on the same falling into possession, or becoming payable or transferable may—

(*a*) agree or ascertain the amount or value thereof or any part thereof in such manner as they may think fit;

(*b*) accept in or towards satisfaction thereof, at the market or current value, or upon any valuation or estimate of value which they may think fit, any authorised investments;

(*c*) allow any deductions for duties, costs, charges and expenses which they may think proper or reasonable;

(*d*) execute any release in respect of the premises so as effectually to discharge all accountable parties from all liability in respect of any matters coming within the scope of such release;

without being responsible in any such case for any loss occasioned by any act or thing so done by them in good faith.

(2) The trustees shall not be under any obligation and shall not be chargeable with any breach of trust by reason of any ommission—

(*a*) to place any distringas notice or apply for any stop or other like order upon any securities or other property out of or on which such share or interest or other thing in action as aforesaid is derived, payable or charged; or

(*b*) to take any proceedings on account of any act, default, or neglect on the part of the persons in whom such securities or other property or any of them or any part thereof are for the time being, or had at any time been, vested;

unless and until required in writing so to do by some person, or the guardian of some person, beneficially interested under the trust, and unless also due provision is made to their satisfaction for payment of the costs of any proceedings required to be taken:

Provided that nothing in this subsection shall relieve the trustees of the obligation to get in and obtain payment or transfer of such share or interest or other thing in action on the same falling into possession.

(3) Trustees may, for the purpose of giving effect to the trust, or any of the provisions of the instrument, if any, creating the trust or of any statute, from time to time (by duly qualified agents) ascertain and fix the value of any trust property in such manner as they think proper, and any valuation so made in good faith shall be binding upon all persons interested under the trust.

(4) Trustees may, in their absolute discretion, from time to time, but not more than once in every three years unless the nature of the trust or any special dealings with the trust property make a more frequent exercise of the right reasonable, cause the accounts of the trust property to be examined or audited by an independent accountant, and shall, for that purpose, produce such vouchers and give such information to him as he may require; and the costs of such examination or audit, including the fee of the auditor, shall be paid out of the capital or income of the trust property, or partly in one way and partly in the other, as the trustees, in their absolute discretion, think fit, but in default of any direction by the trustees to the contrary in any special case, costs attributable to capital shall be borne by capital and those attributable to income by income.

Power to employ agents

23.—(1) Trustees or personal representatives may, instead of acting personally, employ and pay an agent, whether a solicitor, banker, stockbroker, or other person, to transact any business or do any act required to be transacted or done in the execution of the trust, or the administration of the testator's or intestate's estate, including the receipt and payment of money, and shall be entitled to be allowed and paid all charges and expenses so incurred, and shall not be responsible for the default of any such agent if employed in good faith.

(2) Trustees or personal representatives may appoint any person to act as their agent or attorney for the purpose of selling, converting, collecting, getting in, and executing and perfecting insurances of, or managing or cultivating, or otherwise administering any property, real or personal, moveable or immoveable, subject to the trust or forming part of the testator's or intestate's estate, in any place outside the United Kingdom or executing or exercising any discretion or trust or power vested in them in relation to any such property, with such ancillary powers, and with and subject to such provisions and restrictions as they may think fit, including a power to appoint substitutes, and shall not, by reason only of their having made such appointment, be responsible for any loss arising thereby.

(3) Without prejudice to such general power of appointing agents as aforesaid—

(*a*) A trustee may appoint a solicitor to be his agent to receive and give a discharge for any money or valuable consideration or property receivable by the trustee under the trust, by permitting the solicitor to have the custody of, and to produce, a deed having in the body thereof or endorsed thereon a receipt for such money or valuable consideration or property, the deed being executed, or the endorsed receipt being signed, by the person entitled to give a receipt for that consideration;

(*b*) A trustee shall not be chargeable with breach of trust by reason only of his having made or concurred in making any such appointment; and the production of any such deed by the solicitor shall have the same statutory validity and effect as if the person appointing the solicitor had not been a trustee;

(*c*) A trustee may appoint a banker or solicitor to be his agent to receive and give a discharge for any money payable to the trustee under or by virtue of a policy of insurance, by permitting the banker or solicitor to have the custody of and to produce the policy of insurance with a receipt signed by the trustee, and a trustee shall not be chargeable with a breach of trust by reason only of his having made or concurred in making any such appointment:

Provided that nothing in this subsection shall exempt a trustee from any liability which he would have incurred if this Act and any enactment replaced by this Act had not been passed, in case he permits any such money, valuable consideration, or property to remain in the hands or under the control of the banker or solicitor for a period longer than is reasonably necessary to enable the banker or solicitor, as the case may be, to pay or transfer the same to the trustee.

This subsection applies whether the money or valuable consideration or property was or is received before or after the commencement of this Act.

Power to concur with others

24. Where an undivided share in the proceeds of sale of land directed to be sold, or in any other property, is subject to a trust, or forms part of the estate of a testator or intestate, the trustees or personal representatives may (without prejudice to the trust for sale affecting the entirety of the land and the powers of the trustees for sale in reference thereto) execute or exercise any trust or power vested in them in relation to such share in conjunction with the persons entitled to or having power in that behalf over the other share or shares, and notwithstanding that any one or more of the trustees or personal representatives may be entitled to or interested in any such other share, either in his or their own right or in a fiduciary capacity.

Power to delegate trusts during absence abroad

25.[8]—[(1) Notwithstanding any rule of law or equity to the contrary, a trustee may, by power of attorney, delegate for a period not exceeding twelve months the execution or exercise of all or any of the trusts, powers and discretions vested in him as trustee either alone or jointly with any other person or persons.

(2) The persons who may be donees of a power of attorney under this section include a trust corporation but not (unless a trust corporation) the only other co-trustee of the donor of the power.

(3) An instrument creating a power of attorney under this section shall be attested by at least one witness.

(4) Before or within seven days after giving a power of attorney under this section the donor shall give written notice thereof (specifying the date on which the power comes into operation and its duration, the donee of the power, the reason why the power is given and, where some only are delegated, the trusts, powers and discretions delegated) to—

(*a*) each person (other than himself) if any, who under any instrument creating the trust has power (whether alone or jointly) to appoint a new trustee; and

(*b*) each of the other trustees, if any;

but failure to comply with this subsection shall not, in favour of a person dealing with the donee of the powers, invalidate any act done or instrument executed by the donee.

(5) The donor of a power of attorney given under this section shall be liable for the acts or defaults of the donee in the same manner as if they were the acts or defaults of the donor.][9]

[(6)][10] For the purpose of executing or exercising the trusts or powers delegated to him, the donee may exercise any of the powers conferred on the donor as trustee by statute or by the instrument creating the trust, including power, for the purpose of the transfer of any inscribed stock, himself to delegate to an attorney power to transfer but not including the power of delegation conferred by this section.

[(7)][10] The fact that it appears from any power of attorney given under this section, or from any evidence required for the purposes of any such power of attorney or otherwise, that in dealing with any stock the donee of the power is acting in the execution of a trust shall not be deemed for any purpose to affect any person in whose books the stock is inscribed or registered with any notice of the trust.

[(8) This section applies to a personal representative, tenant for life and statutory owner as it applies to a trustee except that subsection (4) shall apply as if it required the notice there mentioned to be given—

(*a*) in the case of a personal representative, to each of the other personal representatives, if any, except any executor who has renounced probate;

(*b*) in the case of a tenant for life, to the trustees of the settlement and to each person, if any, who together with the person giving the notice constitutes the tenant for life;

---

[8] By the Powers of Attorney Act 1971 (*c*. 27), s. 2, no instrument creating a power of attorney, and no copy of any such instrument shall be deposited or filed at the central office of the Supreme Court or at the Land Registry under this section, although any right to search for, inspect, copy, or obtain an office copy of, any such document deposited or filed before October 1, 1971, remains unaffected. Similarly, s. 9 applies whenever the trusts, powers or discretions in question arose but does not invalidate anything done by virtue of this section.

[9] These subsections were substituted for the former subss. (1) to (8) by the Powers of Attorney Act 1971 (c. 27), s. 9(1) and (2).

[10] The former subss. (9) and (10) now stand as subss. (6) and (7): *ibid*. s. 9(1) and (3).

(*c*) in the case of a statutory owner, to each of the persons, if any, who together with the person giving the notice constitute the statutory owner and, in the case of a statutory owner by virtue of section 23 (1) (*a*) of the Settled Land Act 1925, to the trustees of the settlement.][11]

Indemnities

Protection against liability in respect of rents and covenants

26.—(1) Where a personal representative or trustee liable as such for—

(*a*) any rent, covenant, or agreement reserved by or contained in any lease; or

(*b*) any rent, covenant or agreement payable under or contained in any grant made in consideration of a rentcharge; or

(*c*) any indemnity given in respect of any rent, covenant or agreement referred to in either of the foregoing paragraphs;

satisfies all liabilities under the lease or grant [which may have accrued and been claimed][12] up to the date of the conveyance hereinafter mentioned, and, where necessary, sets apart a sufficient fund to answer any future claim that may be made in respect of any fixed and ascertained sum which the lessee or grantee agreed to lay out on the property demised or granted, although the period for laying out the same may not have arrived, then and in any such case the personal representative or trustee may convey the property demised or granted to a purchaser, legatee, devisee, or other person entitled to call for a conveyance thereof and thereafter—

(i) he may distribute the residuary real and personal estate of the deceased testator or intestate, or, as the case may be, the trust estate (other than the fund, if any, set apart as aforesaid) to or amongst the persons entitled thereto, without appropriating any part, or any further part, as the case may be, of the estate of the deceased or of the trust estate to meet any future liability under the said lease or grant;

(ii) notwithstanding such distribution, he shall not be personally liable in respect of any subsequent claim under the said lease or grant.

(2) This section operates without prejudice to the right of the lessor or grantor, or the persons deriving title under the lessor or grantor, to follow the assets of the deceased or the trust property into the hands of the persons amongst whom the same may have been respectively distributed, and applies notwithstanding anything to the contrary in the will or other instrument, if any, creating the trust.

(3) In this section "lease" includes an underlease and an agreement for a lease or underlease and any instrument giving any such indemnity as aforesaid or varying the liabilities under the lease; "grant" applies to a grant whether the rent is created by limitation, grant, reservation, or otherwise, and includes an agreement for a grant and any instrument giving any such indemnity as aforesaid or varying the liabilities under the grant; "lessee" and "grantee" include persons respectively deriving title under them.

Protection by means of advertisements

27.[13]—(1) With a view to the conveyance to or distribution among the persons entitled to any real or personal property, the trustees of a

---

[11] This subsection was substituted for the former subs. (11): *ibid.*
[12] These words are substituted by the Law of Property (Amendment) Act 1926, *post*, Sched.
[13] The provisions of this section are excluded in respect of certain claims by the Land Commission; Land Commission Act 1967 (c. 1). Sched. 12, para. 9(4).

settlement or of a disposition on trust for sale or personal representatives, may give notice by advertisement in the Gazette, and [in a newspaper circulating in the district in which the land is situated][14] and such other like notices, including notices elsewhere than in England and Wales, as would, in any special case, have been directed by a court of competent jurisdiction in an action for administration, of their intention to make such conveyance or distribution as aforesaid, and requiring any person interested to send to the trustees or personal representatives within the time, not being less than two months, fixed in the notice or, where more than one notice is given, in the last of the notices, particulars of his claim in respect of the property of any part thereof to which the notice relates.

(2) At the expiration of the time fixed by the notice the trustees or personal representatives may convey or distribute the property or any part thereof to which the notice relates, to or among the persons entitled thereto, having regard only to the claims, whether formal or not, of which the trustees or personal representatives then had notice and shall not, as respects the property so conveyed or distributed, be liable to any person of whose claim the trustees or personal representatives have not had notice at the time of conveyance or distribution; but nothing in this section—

(a) prejudices the right of any person to follow the property, or any property representing the same, into the hands of any person, other than a purchaser, who may have received it; or

(b) frees the trustees or personal representatives from any obligation to make searches or obtain official certificates of search similar to those which an intending purchaser would be advised to make or obtain.

(3) This section applies notwithstanding anything to the contrary in the will or other instrument, if any, creating the trust.

Protection in regard to notice

28. A trustee or personal representative acting for the purposes of more than one trust or estate shall not, in the absence of fraud, be affected by notice of any instrument, matter, fact or thing in relation to any particular trust or estate if he has obtained notice theeof merely by reason of his acting or having acted for the purposes of another trust or estate.

Exoneration of trustees in respect of certain powers of attorney

29. [*This section was repealed by the Powers of Attorney Act* 1971 (c. 27), s. 11(2), and Sched. 2.]

Implied indemnity of trustees

30.—(1) A trustee shall be chargeable only for money and securities actually received by him notwithstanding his signing any receipt for the sake of conformity, and shall be answerable and accountable only for his own acts, receipts, neglects, or defaults, and not for those of any other trustee, nor for any banker, broker, or other person with whom any trust money or securities may be deposited, nor for the insufficiency or deficiency of any securities, nor for any other loss, unless the same happens through his own wilful default.

(2) A trustee may reimburse himself or pay or discharge out of the trust premises all expenses incurred in or about the execution of the trusts or powers.

[14] These words are substituted by the Law of Property (Amendment) Act 1926, *post*, Sched.

Maintenance, Advancement and Protective Trusts

Power to apply income for maintenance and to accumulate surplus income during a minority

31.—(1) Where any property is held by trustees in trust for any person for any interest whatsoever, whether vested or contingent, then, subject to any prior interests or charges affecting that property—

(i) during the infancy of any such person, if his interest so long continues, the trustees may, at their sole discretion, pay to his parent or guardian, if any, or otherwise apply for or towards his maintenance, education, or benefit, the whole or such part, if any, of the income of that property as may, in all the circumstances, be reasonable, whether or not there is—

    (*a*) any other fund applicable to the same purpose; or

    (*b*) any person bound by law to provide for his maintenance or education; and

(ii) if such person on attaining the age of [eighteen years][15] has not a vested interest in such income, the trustees shall thenceforth pay the income of that property and of any accretion thereto under subsection (2) of this section to him, until he either attains a vested interest therein or dies, or until failure of his interest:

Provided that, in deciding whether the whole or any part of the income of the property is during a minority to be paid or applied for the purposes aforesaid, the trustees shall have regard to the age of the infant and his requirements and generally to the circumstances of the case, and in particular to what other income, if any, is applicable for the same purposes; and where trustees have notice that the income of more than one fund is applicable for those purposes, then, so far as practicable, unless the entire income of the funds is paid or applied as aforesaid or the court otherwise directs, a proportionate part only of the income of each fund shall be so paid or applied.

(2) During the infancy of any such person, if his interest so long continues, the trustees shall accumulate all the residue of that income in the way of compound interest by investing the same and the resulting income thereof from time to time in authorised investments, and shall hold those accumulations as follows:—

(i) If any such person—

    (*a*) attains the age of [eighteen years],[15] or marries under that age, and his interest in such income during his infancy or until his marriage is a vested interest; or

    (*b*) on attaining the age of [eighteen years][15] or on marriage under that age becomes entitled to the property from which such income arose in fee simple, absolute or determinable, or absolutely, or for an entailed interest;

the trustees shall hold the accumulations in trust for such person absolutely, but without prejudice to any provision with respect thereto contained in any settlement by him made under any statutory powers during his infancy, and so that the receipt of such person after marriage, and though still an infant, shall be a good discharge; and

(ii) In any other case the trustees shall, notwithstanding that such person had a vested interest in such income, hold the accumulations as an accretion to the capital of the property from which such accumulations arose, and as one fund with such capital for all

---

[15] These words were substituted by the Family Law Reform Act 1969 (c. 46), s. 1(3) and Sched. 1, Pt. I.

purposes, and so that, if such property is settled land, such accumulations shall be held upon the same trusts as if the same were capital money arising therefrom;
but the trustees may, at any time during the infancy of such person if his interest so long continues, apply those accumulations, or any part thereof, as if they were income arising in the then current year.

(3) This section applies in the case of a contingent interest only if the limitation or trust carries the intermediate income of the property, but it applies to a future or contingent legacy by the parent of, or a person standing in loco parentis to, the legatee, if and for such period as, under the general law, the legacy carries interest for the maintenance of the legatee, and in any such case as last aforesaid the rate of interest shall (if the income available is sufficient, and subject to any rules of court to the contrary) be five pounds per centum per annum.

(4) This section applies to a vested annuity in like manner as if the annuity were the income of property held by trustees in trust to pay the income thereof to the annuitant for the same period for which the annuity is payable, save that in any case accumulations made during the infancy of the annuitant shall be held in trust for the annuitant or his personal representatives absolutely.

(5) This section does not apply where the instrument, if any, under which the interest arises came into operation before the commencement of this Act.

Power of advancement

32.—(1) Trustees may at any time or times pay or apply any capital money subject to a trust, for the advancement or benefit, in such manner as they may, in their absolute discretion, think fit, of any person entitled to the capital of the trust property or of any share thereof, whether absolutely or contingently on his attaining any specified age or on the occurrence of any other event, or subject to a gift over on his death under any specified age or on the occurrence of any other event, and whether in possession or in remainder or reversion, and such payment or application may be made notwithstanding that the interest of such person is liable to be defeated by the exercise of a power of appointment or revocation, or to be diminished by the increase of the class to which he belongs:
Provided that—
    (*a*) the money so paid or applied for the advancement or benefit of any person shall not exceed altogether in amount one-half of the presumptive or vested share or interest of that person in the trust property; and
    (*b*) if that person is or becomes absolutely and indefeasibly entitled to a share in the trust property the money so paid or applied shall be brought into account as part of such share; and
    (*c*) no such payment or application shall be made so as to prejudice any person entitled to any prior life or other interest, whether vested or contingent, in the money paid or applied unless such person is in existence and of full age and consents in writing to such payment or application.

(2) This section applies only where the trust property consists of money or securities or of property held upon trust for sale calling in and conversion, and such money or securities, or the proceeds of such sale calling in and conversion are not by statute or in equity considered as land, or applicable as capital money for the purposes of the Settled Land Act 1925.

(3) This section does not apply to trusts constituted or created before the commencement of this Act.

Protective trusts

33.[16]—(1) Where any income, including an annuity or other periodical income payment, is directed to be held on protective trusts for the benefit of any person (in this section called "the principal beneficiary") for the period of his life or for any less period, then, during that period (in this section called the "trust period") the said income shall, without prejudice to any prior interest, be held on the following trusts, namely:—

(i) Upon trust for the principal beneficiary during the trust period or until he, whether before or after the termination of any prior interest, does or attempts to do or suffers any act or thing, or until any event happens, other than an advance under any statutory or express power, whereby, if the said income were payable during the trust period to the principal beneficiary absolutely during that period, he would be deprived of the right to receive the same or any part thereof, in any of which cases, as well as on the termination of the trust period, whichever first happens, this trust of the said income shall fail or determine;

(ii) If the trust aforesaid fails or determines during the subsistence of the trust period, then, during the residue of that period, the said income shall be held upon trust for the application thereof for the maintenance or support, or otherwise for the benefit, of all or any one or more exclusively of the other or others of the following persons (that is to say)—

(*a*) the principal beneficiary and his or her wife or husband, if any, and his or her children or more remote issue, if any; or

(*b*) if there is no wife or husband or issue of the principal beneficiary in existence, the principal beneficiary and the persons who would, if he were actually dead, be entitled to the trust property or the income thereof or the annuity fund, if any, or arrears of the annuity, as the case may be;

as the trustees in their absolute discretion, without being liable to account for the exercise of such discretion, think fit.

(2) This section does not apply to trusts coming into operation before the commencement of this Act, and has effect subject to any variation of the implied trusts aforesaid contained in the instrument creating the trust.

(3) Nothing in this section operates to validate any trust which would, if contained in the instrument creating the trust, be liable to be set aside.

Part III

Appointment and Discharge of Trustees

Limitation of the number of trustees

34.[17]—(1) Where, at the commencement of this Act, there are more than four trustees of a settlement of land, or more than four trustees

---

[16] By the Family Law Reform Act 1969, s. 15(3), this section shall have effect, in relation to any disposition made after its coming into force, as if (a) the reference to children or more remote issue of the principal beneficiary included a reference to any illegitimate child of the principal beneficiary and to anyone who would rank as such issue if he, or some other person through whom he is descended from the principal beneficiary, had been born legitimate; and (b) the reference to the issue of the principal beneficiary included a reference to anyone who would rank as such issue if he, or some other person through whom he is descended from the principal beneficiary, had been born legitimate.

[17] The restrictions affecting the number of persons entitled to hold land on trust for sale and the number of trustees of a settlement apply to registered land: Land Registration Act 1925 (15 & 16 Geo. 5, c. 21), s. 95. *post*, p. 393.

holding land on trust for sale, no new trustees shall (except where as a result of the appointment the number is reduced to four or less) be capable of being appointed until the number is reduced to less than four, and thereafter the number shall not be increased beyond four.

(2) In the case of settlements and dispositions on trust for sale of land made or coming into operation after the commencement of this Act—

(*a*) the number of trustees thereof shall not in any case exceed four, and where more than four persons are named as such trustees, the four first named (who are able and willing to act) shall alone be the trustees, and the other persons named shall not be trustees unless appointed on the occurrence of a vacancy;

(*b*) the number of the trustees shall not be increased beyond four.

(3) This section only applies to settlements and dispositions of land, and the restrictions imposed on the number of trustees do not apply—

(*a*) in the case of land vested in trustees for charitable, ecclesiastical, or public purposes; or

(*b*) where the net proceeds of the sale of the land are held for like purposes; or

(*c*) to the trustees of a term of years absolute limited by a settlement on trusts for raising money, or of a like term created under the statutory remedies relating to annual sums charged on land.

Appointments of trustees of settlements and dispositions on trust for sale of land

35.—(1) Appointments of new trustees of conveyances on trust for sale on the one hand and of the settlement of the proceeds of sale on the other hand, shall, subject to any order of the court, be effected by separate instruments, but in such manner as to secure that the same persons shall become the trustees of the conveyance on trust for sale as become the trustees of the settlement of the proceeds of sale.

(2) Where new trustees of a settlement are appointed, a memorandum of the names and addresses of the persons who are for the time being the trustees thereof for the purposes of the Settled Land Act 1925 shall be endorsed on or annexed to the last or only principal vesting instrument by or on behalf of the trustees of the settlement, and such vesting instrument shall, for that purpose, be produced by the person having the possession thereof to the trustees of the settlement when so required.

(3) Where new trustees of a conveyance on trust for sale relating to a legal estate are appointed, a memorandum of the persons who are for the time being the trustees for sale shall be endorsed on or annexed thereto by or on behalf of the trustees of the settlement of the proceeds of sale, and the conveyance shall, for that purpose, be produced by the person having the possession thereof to the last-mentioned trustees when so required.

(4) This section applies only to settlements and dispositions of land.

Power of appointing new or additional trustees

36.—(1) Where a trustee, either original or substituted, and whether appointed by a court or otherwise, is dead, or remains out of the United Kingdom for more than twelve months, or desires to be discharged from all or any of the trusts or powers reposed in or conferred on him, or refuses or is unfit to act therein, or is incapable of acting therein, or is an infant, then, subject to the restrictions imposed by this Act on the number of trustees,—

(*a*) the person or persons nominated for the purpose of appointing new trustees by the instrument, if any, creating the trust; or

(*b*) if there is no such person, or no such person able and willing to act, then the surviving or continuing trustees or trustee for the time being, or the personal representatives of the last surviving or continuing trustee;

may, by writing, appoint one or more other person (whether or not being the persons exercising the power) to be a trustee or trustees in the place of the trustee so deceased remaining out of the United Kingdom, desiring to be discharged, refusing, or being unfit or being incapable, or being an infant, as aforesaid.

(2) Where a trustee has been removed under a power contained in the instrument creating the trust, a new trustee or new trustees may be appointed in the place of the trustee who is removed, as if he were dead, or, in the case of a corporation, as if the corporation desired to be discharged from the trust, and the provisions of this section shall apply accordingly, but subject to the restrictions imposed by this Act on the number of trustees.

(3) Where a corporation being a trustee is or has been dissolved, either before or after the commencement of this Act, then, for the purposes of this section and of any enactment replaced thereby, the corporation shall be deemed to be and to have been from the date of the dissolution incapable of acting in the trusts or powers reposed in or conferred on the corporation.

(4) The power of appointment given by subsection (1) of this section or any similar previous enactment to the personal representatives of a last surviving or continuing trustee shall be and shall be deemed always to have been exercisable by the executors for the time being (whether original or by representation) of such surviving or continuing trustee who have proved the will of their testator or by the administrators for the time being of such trustee without the concurrence of any executor who has renounced or has not proved.

(5) But a sole or last surviving executor intending to renounce, or all the executors where they all intend to renounce, shall have and shall be deemed always to have had power, at any time before renouncing probate, to exercise the power of appointment given by this section, or by any similar previous enactment, if willing to act for that purpose and without thereby accepting the office of executor.

(6) Where a sole trustee, other than a trust corporation, is or has been originally appointed to act in a trust, or where, in the case of any trust, there are not more than three trustees (none of them being a trust corporation) either original or substituted and whether appointed by the court or otherwise, then and in any such case—

(*a*) the person or persons nominated for the purpose of appointing new trustees by the instrument, if any, creating the trust; or

(*b*) if there is no such person, or no such person able and willing to act, then the trustee or trustees for the time being;

may, by writing, appoint another person or other persons to be an additional trustee or additional trustees, but it shall not be obligatory to appoint any additional trustee, unless the instrument, if any, creating the trust, or any statutory enactment provides to the contrary, nor shall the number of trustees be increased beyond four by virtue of any such appointment.

(7) Every new trustee appointed under this section as well before as after all the trust property becomes by law, or by assurance, or otherwise, vested in him, shall have the same powers, authorities, and discretions, and may in all respects act as if he had been originally appointed a trustee by the instrument, if any, creating the trust.

(8) The provisions of this section relating to a trustee who is dead include the case of a person nominated trustee in a will but dying before the testator, and those relative to a continuing trustee include a refusing or

retiring trustee, if willing to act in the execution of the provisions of this section.

(9) [Where a trustee is incapable, by reason of mental disorder within the meaning of the Mental Health Act 1959, of exercising his functions as trustee and is also entitled in possession to some beneficial interest in the trust property, no appointment of a new trustee in his place shall be made by virtue of paragraph (*b*) of subsection (1) of this section unless leave to make the appointment has been given by the authority having jurisdiction under Part VIII of the Mental Health Act 1959.][18]

Supplemental provisions as to appointment of trustees

37.—(1) On the appointment of a trustee for the whole or any part of trust property—

(*a*) the number of trustees may, subject to the restrictions imposed by this Act on the number of trustees, be increased; and

(*b*) a separate set of trustees, not exceeding four, may be appointed for any part of the trust property held on trusts distinct from those relating to any other part or parts of the trust property, notwithstanding that no new trustees or trustee are or is to be appointed for other parts of the trust property, and any existing trustee may be appointed or remain one of such separate set of trustees, or, if only one trustee was originally appointed, then, save as hereinafter provided, one separate trustee may be so appointed; and

(*c*) it shall not be obligatory, save as hereinafter provided, to appoint more than one new trustee where only one trustee was originally appointed, or to fill up the original number of trustees where more than two trustees were originally appointed, but, except where only one trustee was originally appointed, and a sole trustee when appointed will be able to give valid receipts for all capital money, a trustee shall not be discharged from his trust unless there will be either a trust corporation or at least two individuals to act as trustees to perform the trust; and

(*d*) any assurance or thing requisite for vesting the trust property, or any part thereof, in a sole trustee, or jointly in the persons who are the trustees, shall be executed or done.

(2) Nothing in this Act shall authorise the appointment of a sole trustee, not being a trust corporation, where the trustee, when appointed, would not be able to give valid receipts for all capital money arising under the trust.

Evidence as to a vacancy in a trust

38.—(1) A statement, contained in any instrument coming into operation after the commencement of this Act by which a new trustee is appointed for any purpose connected with land, to the effect that a trustee has remained out of the United Kingdom for more than twelve months or refuses or is unfit to act, or is incapable of acting, or that he is not entitled to a beneficial interest in the trust property in possession, shall, in favour of a purchaser of a legal estate, be conclusive evidence of the matter stated.

(2) In favour of such purchaser any appointment of a new trustee depending on that statement, and any vesting declaration, express or implied, consequent on the appointment, shall be valid.

Retirement of trustee without a new appointment

39.—(1) Where a trustee is desirous of being discharged from the trust, and after his discharge there will be either a trust corporation or at least

---

[18] Words substituted by the Mental Health Act 1959 (7 & 8 Eliz. 2, c. 72), Sched. 7.

two individuals to act as trustees to perform the trust, then, if such trustee as aforesaid by deed declares that he is desirous of being discharged from the trust, and if his co-trustees and such other person, if any, as is empowered to appoint trustees, by deed consent to the discharge of the trustee, and to the vesting in the co-trustees alone of the trust property, the trustee desirous of being discharged shall be deemed to have retired from the trust, and shall, by the deed, be discharged therefrom under this Act, without any new trustee being appointed in his place.

(2) Any assurance or thing requisite for vesting the trust property in the continuing trustees alone shall be executed or done.

Vesting of trust property in new or continuing trustees

40.[19]—(1) Where by a deed a new trustee is appointed to perform any trust, then—

  (*a*) if the deed contains a declaration by the appointor to the effect that any estate or interest in any land subject to the trust, or in any chattel so subject, or the right to recover or receive any debt or other thing in action so subject, shall vest in the persons who by virtue of the deed become or are the trustees for performing the trust, the deed shall operate, without any conveyance or assignment, to vest in those persons as joint tenants and for the purposes of the trust the estate interest or right to which the declaration relates; and

  (*b*)[20] if the deed is made after the commencement of this Act and does not contain such a declaration, the deed shall, subject to any express provision to the contrary therein contained, operate as if it had contained such a declaration by the appointor extending to all the estates interests and rights with respect to which a declaration could have been made.

(2) Where by a deed a retiring trustee is discharged under the statutory power without a new trustee being appointed, then—

  (*a*) if the deed contains such a declaration as aforesaid by the retiring and continuing trustees, and by the other person, if any, empowered to appoint trustees, the deed shall, without any conveyance or assignment, operate to vest in the continuing trustees alone, as joint tenants, and for the purposes of the trust, the estate, interest, or right to which the declaration relates; and

  (*b*) if the deed is made after the commencement of this Act and does not contain such a declaration, the deed shall, subject to any express provision to the contrary therein contained, operate as if it had contained such a declaration by such persons as aforesaid extending to all the estates, interests and rights with respect to which a declaration could have been made.

(3) An express vesting declaration, whether made before or after the commencement of this Act, shall, notwithstanding that the estate, interest or right to be vested is not expressly referred to, and provided that the other statutory requirements were or are complied with, operate and be deemed always to have operated (but without prejudice to any express provision to the contrary contained in the deed of appointment or discharge) to vest in the persons respectively referred to in subsections (1) and (2) of this section, as the case may require, such estates, interests and rights as are capable of being and ought to be vested in those persons.

---

[19] A memorandum evidencing the appointment or discharge of a trustee, if executed as a deed, shall operate as if the appointment or discharge were effected by the deed: Charities Act 1960 (8 & 9 Eliz. 2, c. 58), s. 35(2).

[20] Applied by the Incumbents and Churchwardens (Trust) Measure 1964 (No. 2), s. 3(3).

(4) This section does not extend—

    (*a*) to land conveyed by way of mortgage for securing money subject to the trust, except land conveyed on trust for securing debentures or debenture stock;

    (*b*) to land held under a lease which contains any covenant, condition or agreement against assignment or disposing of the land without licence or consent, unless, prior to the execution of the deed containing expressly or impliedly the vesting declaration, the requisite licence or consent has been obtained, or unless, by virtue of any statute or rule of law, the vesting declaration, express or implied, would not operate as a breach of covenant or give rise to a forfeiture;

    (*c*) to any share, stock, annuity or property which is only transferable in books kept by a company or other body, or in manner directed by or under an Act of Parliament.

In this subsection "lease" includes an underlease and an agreement for a lease or underlease.

(5) For purposes of registration of the deed in any registry, the person or persons making the declaration expressly or impliedly, shall be deemed the conveying party or parties, and the conveyance shall be deemed to be made by him or them under a power conferred by this Act.

(6) This section applies to deeds of appointment or discharge executed on or after the first day of January, eighteen hundred and eighty-two.

PART IV

POWERS OF THE COURT

Appointment of new Trustees

Power of court to appoint new trustees

41.—(1)[21] The court may, whenever it is expedient to appoint a new trustee or new trustees, and it is found inexpedient difficult or impracticable so to do without the assistance of the court, make an order appointing a new trustee or new trustees either in substitution for or in addition to any existing trustee or trustees, or although there is no existing trustee.

In particular and without prejudice to the generality of the foregoing provision, the court may make an order appointing a new trustee in substitution for a trustee who [. . .][22] is [incapable, by reason of mental disorder within the meaning of the Mental Health Act 1959, of exercising his functions as trustee][23] or is a bankrupt, or is a corporation which is in liquidation or has been dissolved.

(2) The power conferred by this section may, in the case of a deed of arrangement within the meaning of the Deeds of Arrangement Act 1914, be exercised either by the High Court or by the court having jurisdiction in bankruptcy in the district in which the debtor resided or carried on business at the date of the execution of the deed.

(3) An order under this section, and any consequential vesting order or conveyance, shall not operate further or otherwise as a discharge to any former or continuing trustee than an appointment of new trustees under

---

[21] The county court shall have jurisdiction in a case where the trust interest or fund to be dealt with does not exceed £5,000: see the County Courts Act 1959 (7 & 8 Eliz. 2, c. 22), s. 52(3), Sched. 1, as amended by the Administration of Justice Act 1969 (c. 58), s. 5.

[22] Words repealed by the Criminal Law Act 1967 (c. 58), Sched. 3.

[23] Words substituted by the Mental Health Act 1959 (7 & 8 Eliz. 2, c. 72), s. 149(1), Sched. 7, Pt. I.

any power for that purpose contained in any instrument would have operated.

(4) Nothing in this section gives power to appoint an executor or administrator.

Power to authorise remuneration

42.[24] Where the court appoints a corporation, other than the Public Trustee, to be a trustee either solely or jointly with another person, the court may authorise the corporation to charge such remuneration for its services as trustee as the court may think fit.

Powers of new trustee appointed by the court

43. Every trustee appointed by a court of competent jurisdiction shall, as well before as after the trust property becomes by law, or by assurance, or otherwise, vested in him, have the same powers, authorities, and discretions, and may in all respects act as if he had been originally appointed a trustee by the instrument, if any, creating the trust.

Vesting Orders

Vesting orders of land

44.[25] In any of the following cases, namely:—

    (i) Where the court appoints or has appointed a trustee, or where a trustee has been appointed out of court under any statutory or express power;

    (ii) Where a trustee entitled to or possessed of any land or interest therein, whether by way of mortgage or otherwise, or entitled to a contingent right therein, either solely or jointly with any other person—

        (*a*) is under disability; or

        (*b*) is out of the jurisdiction of the High Court; or

        (*c*) cannot be found, or, being a corporation, has been dissolved;

    (iii) Where it is uncertain who was the survivor of two or more trustees jointly entitled to or possessed of any interest in land;

    (iv) Where it is uncertain whether the last trustee known to have been entitled to or possessed of any interest in land is living or dead;

    (v) Where there is no personal representative of a deceased trustee who was entitled to or possessed of any interest in land, or where it is uncertain who is the personal representative of a deceased trustee who was entitled to or possessed of any interest in land;

    (vi) Where a trustee jointly or solely entitled to or possessed of any interest in land, or entitled to a contingent right therein, has been required, by or on behalf of a person entitled to require a conveyance of the land or interest or a release of the right, to convey the land or interest or to release the right, and has wilfully refused or neglected to convey the land or interest or

---

[24] The county court shall have jurisdiction in a case where the trust interest or fund to be dealt with does not exceed £5,000: see the County Courts Act 1959 (7 & 8 Eliz. 2, c. 22), s.52(3), Sched. 1, as amended by the Administration of Justice Act 1969 (c. 58), s. 5.

[25] The county court shall have jurisdiction in a case where the land or the interest or contingent right in the land to be dealt with forms part of a trust estate which does not exceed £5,000: see the County Courts Act 1959 (7 & 8 Eliz. 2, c. 22), s. 52(3), Sched. 1, as amended by the Administration of Justice Act 1969 (c. 58), s. 5.

release the right for twenty-eight days after the date of the requirement;

(vii) Where land or any interest therein is vested in a trustee whether by way of mortgage or otherwise, and it appears to the court to be expedient;

the court may make an order (in this Act called a vesting order) vesting the land or interest therein in any such person in any such manner and for any such estate or interest as the court may direct, or releasing or disposing of the contingent right to such person as the court may direct:

Provided that—

(*a*) Where the order is consequential on the appointment of a trustee the land or interest therein shall be vested for such estate as the court may direct in the persons who on the appointment are the trustees; and

(*b*) Where the order relates to a trustee entitled or formerly entitled jointly with another person, and such trustee is under disability or out of the jurisdiction of the High Court or cannot be found, or being a corporation has been dissolved, the land interest or right shall be vested in such other person who remains entitled, either alone or with any other person the court may appoint.

Orders as to contingent rights of unborn persons

45.[26] Where any interest in land is subject to a contingent right in an unborn person or class of unborn persons who, on coming into existence would, in respect thereof, become entitled to or possessed of that interest on any trust, the court may make an order releasing the land or interest therein from the contingent right, or may make an order vesting in any person the estate or interest to or of which the unborn person or class of unborn persons would, on coming into existence, be entitled or possessed in the land.

Vesting order in place of conveyance by infant mortgagee

46.[27] Where any person entitled to or possessed of any interest in land, or entitled to a contingent right in land, by way of security for money, is an infant, the court may make an order vesting or releasing or disposing of the interest in the land or the right in like manner as in the case of a trustee under disability.

Vesting order consequential on order for sale or mortgage of land

47.[28] Where any court gives a judgment or makes an order directing the sale or mortgage of any land, every person who is entitled to or possessed of any interest in the land, or entitled to a contingent right therein, and is a party to the action or proceeding in which the judgment or order is given or made or is otherwise bound by the judgment or order, shall be deemed to be so entitled or possessed, as the case may be, as a trustee for the purposes of this Act, and the court may, if it thinks expedient, make an order vesting the land or any part thereof for such estate or interest as that court thinks fit in the purchaser or mortgagee or in any other person:

Provided that, in the case of a legal mortgage, the estate to be vested in the mortgagee shall be a term of years absolute.

---

[26] *Ibid.*
[27] *Ibid.*
[28] The county court shall have jurisdiction: see the County Courts Act 1959 (7 & 8 Eliz. 2, c. 22), s. 52(3), Sched. 1.

Vesting order consequential on judgment for specific performance, &c.

48.[29] Where a judgment is given for the specific performance of a contract concerning any interest in land, or for sale or exchange of any interest in land, or generally where any judgment is given for the conveyance of any interest in land either in cases arising out of the doctrine of election or otherwise, the court may declare—

  (*a*) that any of the parties to the action are trustees of any interest in the land or any part thereof within the meaning of this Act; or

  (*b*) that the interests of unborn persons who might claim under any party to the action, or under the will or voluntary settlement of any deceased person who was during his lifetime a party to the contract or transaction concerning which the judgment is given, are the interests of persons who, on coming into existence, would be trustees within the meaning of this Act;

and thereupon the court may make a vesting order relating to the rights of those persons, born and unborn, as if they had been trustees.

Effect of vesting order

49. A vesting order under any of the foregoing provisions shall in the case of a vesting order consequential on the appointment of a trustee, have the same effect—

  (*a*) as if the persons who before the appointment were the trustees, if any, had duly executed all proper conveyances of the land for such estate or interest as the court directs; or

  (*b*) if there is no such person, or no such person of full capacity, as if such person had existed and been of full capacity and had duly executed all proper conveyances of the land for such estate or interest as the court directs;

and shall in every other case have the same effect as if the trustee or other person or description or class of persons to whose rights or supposed rights the said provisions respectively relate had been an ascertained and existing person of full capacity, and had executed a conveyance or release to the effect intended by the order.

Power to appoint person to convey

50.[30] In all cases where a vesting order can be made under any of the foregoing provisions, the court may, if it is more convenient, appoint a person to convey the land or any interest therein or release the contingent right, and a conveyance or release by that person in conformity with the order shall have the same effect as an order under the appropriate provision.

Vesting orders as to stock and things in action

51.[31]—(1) In any of the following cases, namely:—

  (i) Where the court appoints or has appointed a trustee, or where a trustee has been appointed out of court under any statutory or express power;

  (ii) Where a trustee entitled, whether by way of mortgage or otherwise, alone or jointly with another person to stock or to a thing in action—

    (*a*) is under disability; or

---

[29] *Ibid.*

[30] *Ibid.*

[31] The county court shall have jurisdiction in a case where the trust estate or fund to be dealt with by the court does not exceed £5,000: *ibid.* as amended by the Administration of Justice Act 1969 (c. 58) s. 5.

(*b*) is out of the jurisdiction of the High Court; or

(*c*) cannot be found, or, being a corporation, has been dissolved; or

(*d*) neglects or refuses to transfer stock or receive the dividends or income thereof, or to sue for or recover a thing in action, according to the direction of the person absolutely entitled thereto for twenty-eight days next after a request in writing has been made to him by the person so entitled; or

(*e*) neglects or refuses to transfer stock or receive the dividends or income thereof, or to sue for or recover a thing in action for twenty-eight days next after an order of the court for that purpose has been served on him;

(iii) Where it is uncertain whether a trustee entitled alone or jointly with another person to stock or to a thing in action is alive or dead;

(iv) Where stock is standing in the name of a deceased person whose personal representative is under disability;

(v) Where stock or a thing in action is vested in a trustee whether by way of mortgage or otherwise and it appears to the court to be expedient;

the court may make an order vesting the right to transfer or call for a transfer of stock, or to receive the dividends or income thereof, or to sue for or recover the thing in action, in any such person as the court may appoint:

Provided that—

(*a*) Where the order is consequential on the appointment of a trustee, the right shall be vested in the persons who, on the appointment, are the trustees; and

(*b*) where the person whose right is dealt with by the order was entitled jointly with another person, the right shall be vested in that last-mentioned person either alone or jointly with any other person whom the court may appoint.

(2) In all cases where a vesting order can be made under this section, the court may, if it is more convenient, appoint some proper person to make or join in making the transfer:

Provided that the person appointed to make or join in making a transfer of stock shall be some proper officer of the bank, or the company or society whose stock is to be transferred.

(3) The person in whom the right to transfer or call for the transfer of any stock is vested by an order of the court under this Act, may transfer the stock to himself or any other person, according to the order, and the Bank of England and all other companies shall obey every order under this section according to its tenor.

(4) After notice in writing of an order under this section it shall not be lawful for the Bank of England or any other company to transfer any stock to which the order relates or to pay any dividends thereon except in accordance with the order.

(5) The court may make declarations and give directions concerning the manner in which the right to transfer any stock or thing in action vested under the provisions of this Act is to be exercised.

(6) The provisions of this Act as to vesting orders shall apply to shares in ships registered under the Acts relating to merchant shipping as if they were stock.

Vesting orders of charity property

52. The powers conferred by this Act as to vesting orders may be exercised for vesting any interest in land, stock, or thing in action in any trustee of a charity or society over which the court would have jurisdiction upon action duly instituted, whether the appointment of the trustee was made by instrument under a power or by the court under its general or statutory jurisdiction.

Vesting orders in relation to infant's beneficial interests

53.[32] Where an infant is beneficially entitled to any property the court may, with a view to the application of the capital or income thereof for the maintenance, education, or benefit of the infant, make an order—

(*a*) appointing a person to convey such property; or

(*b*) in the case of stock, or a thing in action, vesting in any person the right to transfer or call for a transfer of such stock, or to receive the dividends or incomes thereof, or to sue for and recover such thing in action, upon such terms as the court may think fit.

Jurisdiction of the High Court in regard to lunatics

54.—[(1) Subject to the provisions of this section, the authority having jurisdiction under Part VIII of the Mental Health Act 1959 shall not have power to make any order, or give any direction or authority, in relation to a patient who is a trustee if the High Court has power under this Act to make an order to the like effect.

(2) Where a patient is a trustee and a receiver appointed by the said authority is acting for him or an application for the appointment of a receiver has been made but not determined, then, except as respects a trust which is subject to an order for administration made by the High Court, the said authority shall have concurrent jurisdiction with the High Court in relation to—

(*a*) mortgaged property of which the patient has become a trustee merely by reason of the mortgage having been paid off;

(*b*) matters consequent on the making of provision by the said authority for the exercise of a power of appointing trustees or retiring from a trust;

(*c*) matters consequent on the making of provision by the said authority for the carrying out of any contract entered into by the patient;

(*d*) property to some interest in which the patient is beneficially entitled but which, or some interest in which, is held by the patient under an express, implied or constructive trust.

The Lord Chancellor may make rules with respect to the exercise of the jurisdiction referred to in this subsection.

(3) In this section "patient" means a patient as defined by section one hundred and one of the Mental Health Act 1959, or a person as to whom powers are exercisable and have been exercised under section one hundred and four of that Act.][33]

Orders made upon certain allegations to be conclusive evidence

55. Where a vesting order is made as to any land under this Act or under *the Lunacy Act 1890,*[34] as amended by any subsequent enactment, or under

---

[32] The county court shall have jurisdiction in a case where the amount or value of the property to be dealt with in the court does not exceed £5,000: County Courts Act 1959 (7 & 8 Eliz. 2, c. 22), s. 52(3), Sched. 1, as amended by the Administration of Justice Act 1969 (c. 58), s. 5.

[33] Substituted by the Mental Health Act 1959 (7 & 8 Eliz. 2, c. 72), Sched. 7, Pt. I.

[34] The words "Part VIII of the Mental Health Act 1959," are substituted for the italicised words except in so far as the section applies to vesting orders made before the commencement of the Mental Health Act 1959.

any Act relating to lunacy in Northern Ireland, founded on an allegation of any of the following matters namely—

(*a*) the personal incapacity of a trustee or mortgagee; or

(*b*) that a trustee or mortgagee or the personal representative of or other person deriving title under a trustee or mortgagee is out of the jurisdiction of the High Court or cannot be found, or being a corporation has been dissolved; or

(*c*) that it is uncertain which of two or more trustees, or which of two or more persons interested in a mortgage, was the survivor; or

(*d*) that it is uncertain whether the last trustee or the personal representative of or other person deriving title under a trustee or mortgagee, or the last surviving person interested in a mortgage is living or dead; or

(*e*) that any trustee or mortgagee has died intestate without leaving a person beneficially interested under the intestacy or has died and it is not known who is his personal representative or the person interested;

the fact that the order has been so made shall be conclusive evidence of the matter so alleged in any court upon any question as to the validity of the order; but this section does not prevent the court from directing a reconveyance or surrender or the payment of costs occasioned by any such order if improperly obtained.

Application of vesting order to property out of England

56.[35] The powers of the court to make vesting orders under this Act shall extend to all property in any part of His Majesty's dominions except Scotland.

Jurisdiction to make other Orders

Power of court to authorise dealings with trust property

57.[36]—(1) Where in the management or administration of any property vested in trustees, any sale, lease, mortgage, surrender, release, or other disposition, or any purchase, investment, acquisition, expenditure, or other transaction, is in the opinion of the court expedient, but the same cannot be effected by reason of the absence of any power for that purpose vested in the trustees by the trust instrument, if any, or by law, the court may by order confer upon the trustees, either generally or in any particular instance, the necessary power for the purpose, on such terms, and subject to such provisions and conditions, if any, as the court may think fit and may direct in what manner any money authorised to be expended, and the costs of any transaction, are to be paid or borne as between capital and income.

(2) The court may, from time to time, rescind or vary any order made under this section, or may make any new or further order.

(3) An application to the court under this section may be made by the trustees, or by any of them, or by any person beneficially interested under the trust.

(4) This section does not apply to trustees of a settlement for the purposes of the Settled Land Act 1925.

---

[35] The county court shall have jurisdiction under this section: County Courts Act 1959 (7 & 8 Eliz. 2, c. 22), s. 52(3), Sched. 1.

[36] The powers of the court are extended by the Settled Land and Trustee Acts (Court's General Powers) Act 1943, s. 1, and the Emergency Laws (Miscellaneous Provisions) Act 1953 (1 & 2 Eliz. 2, c. 47), Sched. 3. The county court shall have jurisdiction in a case where the trust estate or fund to be dealt with in the court does not exceed £5,000: County Courts Act 1959 (7 & 8 Eliz. 2, c. 22), s. 52(3), Sched. 1, as amended by the Administration of Justice Act 1969 (c. 58), s. 5.

Persons entitled to apply for orders

58.—(1) An order under this Act for the appointment of a new trustee or concerning any interest in land, stock, or thing in action subject to a trust, may be made on the application of any person beneficially interested in the land, stock, or thing in action, whether under disability or not, or on the application of any person duly appointed trustee thereof.

(2) An order under this Act concerning any interest in land, stock, or thing in action subject to a mortgage may be made on the application of any person beneficially interested in the equity of redemption, whether under disability or not, or of any person interested in the money secured by the mortgage.

Power to give judgment in absence of a trustee

59.[37] Where in any action the court is satisfied that diligent search has been made for any person who, in the character of trustee, is made a defendant in any action, to serve him with a process of the court, and that he cannot be found, the court may hear and determine the action and give judgment therein against that person in his character of a trustee as if he had been duly served, or had entered an appearance in the action, and had also appeared by his counsel and solicitor at the hearing, but without prejudice to any interest he may have in the matters in question in the action in any other character.

Power to charge costs on trust estate

60.[38] The court may order the costs and expenses of and incident to any application for an order appointing a new trustee, or for a vesting order, or of and incident to any such order, or any conveyance or transfer in pursuance thereof, to be raised and paid out of the property in respect whereof the same is made, or out of the income thereof, or to be borne and paid in such manner and by such persons as to the court may seem just.

Power to relieve trustee from personal liability

61.[39] If it appears to the court that a trustee, whether appointed by the court or otherwise, is or may be personally liable for any breach of trust, whether the transaction alleged to be a breach of trust occurred before or after the commencement of this Act, but has acted honestly and reasonably, and ought fairly to be excused for the breach of trust and for omitting to obtain the directions of the court in the matter in which he committed such breach, then the court may relieve him either wholly or partly from personal liability for the same.

Power to make beneficiary indemnify for breach of trust

62.[40]—(1) Where a trustee commits a breach of trust at the instigation or request or with the consent in writing of a beneficiary, the court may, if it thinks fit, [. . .][41] make such order as to the court seems just, for

---

[37] The county court shall have jurisdiction: the County Courts Act 1959 (7 & 8 Eliz. 2, c. 22), s. 52(3), Sched. 1.

[38] The county court shall have jurisdiction in a case where the trust estate or fund to be dealt with in the court does not exceed £5,000: see *ibid.* as amended by the Administration of Justice Act 1969 (c. 58), s. 5.

[39] *Ibid.*

[40] The county court shall have jurisdiction in a case where the trust estate or fund to be dealt with in the court does not exceed £5,000: see *ibid.* as amended by the Administration of Justice Act 1969 (c. 58), s. 5.

[41] These words were repealed by the Married Women (Restraint upon Anticipation) Act 1949 (12, 13 & 14 Geo. 6, c. 78), s. 1, Sched. 2.

impounding all or any part of the interest of the beneficiary in the trust estate by way of indemnity to the trustee or persons claiming through him.

(2) This section applies to breaches of trust committed as well before as after the commencement of this Act.

Payment into Court

Payment into court by trustees

63.[42]—(1) Trustees, or the majority of trustees, having in their hands or under their control money or securities belonging to a trust, may pay the same into court; [. . .].[43]

(2) The receipt or certificate of the proper officer shall be a sufficient discharge to trustees for the money or securities so paid into court.

(3) Where money or securities are vested in any persons as trustees, and the majority are desirous of paying the same into court, but the concurrence of the other or others cannot be obtained, the court may order the payment into court to be made by the majority without the concurrence of the other or others.

(4) Where any such money or securities are deposited with any banker, broker, or other depositary, the court may order payment or delivery of the money or securities to the majority of the trustees for the purpose of payment into court.

(5) Every transfer payment and delivery made in pursuance of any such order shall be valid and take effect as if the same had been made on the authority or by the act of all the persons entitled to the money and securities so transferred, paid, or delivered.

PART V

GENERAL PROVISIONS

Application of Act to Settled Land Act Trustees

64.—(1) All the powers and provisions contained in this Act with reference to the appointment of new trustees, and the discharge and retirement of trustees, apply to and include trustees for the purposes of the Settled Land Act 1925 and trustees for the purpose of the management of land during a minority, whether such trustees are appointed by the court or by the settlement, or under provisions contained in any instrument.

(2) Where, either before or after the commencement of this Act, trustees of a settlement have been appointed by the court for the purposes of the Settled Land Acts 1882 to 1890 or of the Settled Land Act 1925, then, after the commencement of this Act—

    (a) the person or persons nominated for the purpose of appointing new trustees by the instrument, if any, creating the settlement, though no trustees for the purposes of the said Acts were thereby appointed; or

    (b) if there is no such person, or no such person able and willing to act, the surviving or continuing trustees or trustee for the time being for

---

[42] This section is applied by the London Passenger Transport Act 1933 (23 & 24 Geo. 5, c. 14), s. 98 (4) (b) and the Housing Act 1957 (5 & 6 Eliz. 2, c. 56), s. 23 (3) (4).

    The county court has jurisdiction where the money or securities to be paid into court do not exceed £5,000: County Courts Act 1959, s. 52 (3), Sched. 1, as amended by the Administration of Justice Act 1969 (c. 58), s. 5.

[43] These words were repealed by the Administration of Justice Act 1965 (c. 2), s. 36(4), Sched. 3.

the purposes of the said Acts or the personal representatives of the last surviving or continuing trustee for those purposes, shall have the powers conferred by this Act to appoint new or additional trustees of the settlement for the purposes of the said Acts.

(3) Appointments of new trustees for the purposes of the said Acts made or expressed to be made before the commencement of this Act by the trustees or trustee or personal representatives referred to in paragraph (*b*) of the last preceding subsection or by the persons referred to in paragraph (*a*) of that subsection are, without prejudice to any order of the court made before such commencement, hereby confirmed.

65. [*Repealed by the Criminal Law Act* 1967 (*c.* 58), *Sched.* 3, *Pt.* I.]

Indemnity to banks, &c.

66. This Act, and every order purporting to be made under this Act, shall be a complete indemnity to the Bank of England, and to all persons for any acts done pursuant thereto, and it shall not be necessary for the Bank or for any person to inquire concerning the propriety of the order, or whether the court by which the order was made had jurisdiction to make it.

Jurisdiction of the "court"

67.—(1) In this Act "the court" means the High Court, [. . .],[44] or the county court, where those courts respectively have jurisdiction.

(2) The procedure under this Act in [. . .][44] county courts shall be in accordance with the Acts and rules regulating the procedure of those courts.

Definitions

68. In this Act, unless the context otherwise requires, the following expressions having the meanings hereby assigned to them respectively, that is to say:—

(1) "Authorised investments" mean investments authorised by the instrument, if any, creating the trust for the investment of money subject to the trust, or by law;

(2) "Contingent right" as applied to land includes a contingent or executory interest, a possibility coupled with an interest, whether the object of the gift or limitation of the interest, or possibility is or is not ascertained, also a right of entry, whether immediate or future, and whether vested or contingent;

(3) "Convey" and "conveyance" as applied to any person include the execution by that person of every necessary or suitable assurance (including an assent) for conveying, assigning, appointing, surrendering, or otherwise transferring or disposing of land whereof he is seised or possessed, or wherein he is entitled to a contingent right, either for his whole estate or for any less estate, together with the performance of all formalities required by law for the validity of the conveyance; "sale" includes an exchange;

(4) "Gazette" means the London Gazette;

(5) "Instrument" includes Act of Parliament;

(6) "Land" includes land of any tenure, and mines and minerals, whether or not severed from the surface, buildings or parts of buildings, whether the division is horizontal, vertical or made in any other way, and other corporeal hereditaments; also a manor, an

---

[44] These words were repealed by the Courts Act 1971 (c. 58), s. 56 (4) and Sched. 11, Pt. II.

advowson, and a rent and other incorporeal hereditaments, and an easement, right, privilege, or benefit in, over, or derived from land, but not an undivided share in land; and in this definition "mines and minerals" include any strata or seam of minerals or substances in or under any land, and powers of working and getting the same, but not an undivided share thereof; and "hereditaments" mean real property which under an intestacy occurring before the commencement of this Act might have devolved on an heir;

(7) "Mortgage" and "mortgagee" include a charge or chargee by way of legal mortgage, and relate to every estate and interest regarded in equity as merely a security for money, and every person deriving title under the original mortgagee;

(8) [*Repealed by the Administration of Justice Act* 1965 (*c.* 2), *ss.* 17(1), 18, *Sched.* 1.]

(9) "Personal representative" means the executor, original or by representation, or administrator for the time being of a deceased person;

(10) "Possession" includes receipt of rent and profits or the right to receive the same, if any; "income" includes rents and profits; and "possessed" applies to receipt of income of and to any vested estate less than a life interest in possession or in expectancy in any land;

(11) "Property" includes real and personal property, and any estate share and interest in any property, real or personal, and any debt, and any thing in action, and any other right or interest, whether in possession or not;

(12) "Rights" include estates and interests;

(13) "Securities" include stocks, funds, and shares; [. . .]⁴⁵ and "securities payable to bearer" include securities transferable by delivery or by delivery and endorsement;

(14) "Stock" includes fully paid up shares, and so far as relates to vesting orders made by the court under this Act, includes any fund, annuity, or security, transferable in books kept by any company or society, or by instrument of transfer either alone or accompanied by other formalities, and any share or interest therein;

(15) "Tenant for life," "statutory owner," "settled land," "settlement," "trust instrument," "trustees of the settlement" [. . .],⁴⁶ "term of years absolute" and "vesting instrument" have the same meanings as in the Settled Land Act 1925, and "entailed interest" has the same meaning as in the Law of Property Act 1925;

(16) "Transfer" in relation to stock or securities, includes the performance and execution of every deed, power of attorney, act, and thing on the part of the transferor to effect and complete the title in the transferee;

(17) "Trust" does not include the duties incident to an estate conveyed by way of mortgage, but with this exception the expressions "trust" and "trustee" extend to implied and constructive trusts, and to cases where the trustee has a beneficial interest in the trust property, and to the duties incident to the office of a personal representative, and "trustee" where the context admits, includes a personal representative, and "new trustee" includes an additional trustee;

(18) ⁴⁷"Trust corporation" means the Public Trustee or a corporation

---

⁴⁵ These words were repealed by the Administration of Justice Act 1965 (c. 2), ss. 17 (1), 18, Sched. 1.

⁴⁶ These words were repealed by the Mental Health Act 1959 (7 & 8 Eliz. 2, c. 72), s. 149(2), Sched. 8, Pt. I.

⁴⁷ For the extension of the meaning of "trust corporation" see the Law of Property (Amendment) Act 1926, s. 3, *post*, p. 276: the Japanese Treaty of Peace Order 1952 (No. 862), art. 5 (2); and the Clergy Pensions Measure 1961 (9 & 10 Eliz. 2, No. 3), s. 31.

either appointed by the court in any particular case to be a trustee, or entitled by rules made under subsection (3) of section four of the Public Trustee Act 1906 to act as custodian trustee;

(19) "Trust for sale" in relation to land means an immediate binding trust for sale, whether or not exercisable at the request or with the consent of any person, and with or without power at discretion to postpone the sale; "trustees for sale" mean the persons (including a personal representative) holding land on trust for sale;

(20) "United Kingdom" means Great Britain and Northern Ireland.

[(2) Any reference in this Act to paying money or securities into court shall be construed as referring to paying the money or transferring or depositing the securities into or in the Supreme Court or into or in any other court that has jurisdiction, and any reference in this Act to payment of money or securities into court shall be construed—

(*a*) with reference to an order of the High Court, as referring to payment of the money or transfer or deposit of the securities into or in the Supreme Court; and

(*b*) with reference to an order of any other court, as referring to payment of the money or transfer or deposit of the securities into or in that court.]⁴⁸

Application of Act

69.—(1) This Act, except where otherwise expressly provided, applies to trusts including, so far as this Act applies thereto, executorships and administratorships constituted or created either before or after the commencement of this Act.

(2) The powers conferred by this Act on trustees are in addition to the powers conferred by the instrument, if any, creating the trust, but those powers, unless otherwise stated, apply if and so far only as a contrary intention is not expressed in the instrument, if any, creating the trust, and have effect subject to the terms of that instrument.

(3) [*This subsection was repealed by the Statute Law (Repeals) Act* 1978 (*c.* 45), *Sched.* 1.]

Enactments repealed

70. [*Words repealed by S.L.R.* 1950 (14 *Geo.* 6, *c.* 6)] without prejudice to the provisions of section thirty-eight of the Interpretation Act 1889:

(*a*) Nothing in this repeal shall affect any vesting order or appointment made or other thing done under any enactment so repealed, and any order or appointment so made may be revoked or varied in like manner as if it had been made under this Act;

(*b*) References in any document to any enactment repealed by this Act shall be construed as references to this Act or to the corresponding enactment in this Act.

Short title, commencement, extent

71.—(1) This Act may be cited as the Trustee Act 1925.

(2) [*Repealed by S.L.R.* 1950 (14 *Geo.* 6, *c.* 6).]

(3) This Act, except where otherwise expressly provided, extends to England and Wales only.

(4) The provisions of this Act bind the Crown.

---

⁴⁸ Added by the Administration of Justice Act 1965 (c. 2), ss. 17(1), 18, Sched. 1.

SCHEDULES

FIRST SCHEDULE

RETROSPECTIVE AMENDMENTS

[*Repealed by S.L.R.* 1978 (*c.* 45)]

SECOND SCHEDULE

[*Repealed by S.L.R.* 1950 (14 *Geo.* 6, *c.* 6).]

Law of Property Act 1925

(15 Geo. 5, c. 20)

ARRANGEMENT OF SECTIONS

PART I

GENERAL PRINCIPLES AS TO LEGAL ESTATES, EQUITABLE INTERESTS AND POWERS

PART II

CONTRACTS, CONVEYANCES AND OTHER INSTRUMENTS

Contracts

PART III

MORTGAGES, RENTCHARGES AND POWERS OF ATTORNEY

Mortgages

An Act to consolidate the enactments relating to conveyancing and the law
    of property in England and Wales.[1]   [9th April 1925.]

PART I

GENERAL PRINCIPLES AS TO LEGAL ESTATES, EQUITABLE INTERESTS AND
POWERS

Legal estates and equitable interests

1.—(1) The only estates in land which are capable of subsisting or of
being conveyed or created at law are—
    (*a*) An estate in fee simple absolute in possession;
    (*b*) A term of years absolute.
(2) The only interests or charges in or over land which are capable of
subsisting or of being conveyed or created at law are—
    (*a*) An easement, right, or privilege in or over land for an interest
        equivalent to an estate in fee simple absolute in possession or a term
        of years absolute;
    (*b*) [2] A rentcharge in possession issuing out of or charged on land being
        either perpetual or for a term of years absolute;
    (*c*) A charge by way of legal mortgage;

---

[1] This Act is applied by the Land Registration Act 1925 (15 & 16 Geo. 5, c. 21), ss. 36, 38, 69
(3); Civil Defence Act 1939 (2 & 3 Geo. 6, c. 31), ss. 18 (4), 19 (1); Agriculture
(Miscellaneous Provisions) Act 1941 (4 & 5 Geo. 6, c. 50), s. 8 (4); Finance Act 1949 (12 &
13 Geo. 6, c. 47), s. 40 (4) (*b*); (except London) Highways Act 1959 (7 & 8 Eliz. 2, c. 25), s.
181 (3); and the Housing Act 1964 (c. 56), ss. 29 (4), 80 (5); and extended by the Public
Health Act 1936 (26 Geo. 5 & 1 Edw. 8, c. 49), s. 291 (4).
[2] The meaning of "rentcharge" is explained in the Law of Property (Entailed Interests) Act
1932, *post*, p. 279.

(d) [...]³ and any other similar charge on land which is not created by an instrument;

(e) Rights of entry exercisable over or in respect of a legal term of years absolute, or annexed, for any purpose, to a legal rentcharge.

(3) All other estates, interests, and charges in or over land take effect as equitable interests.

(4) The estates, interests, and charges which under this section are authorised to subsist or to be conveyed or created at law are (when subsisting or conveyed or created at law) in this Act referred to as "legal estates," and have the same incidents as legal estates subsisting at the commencement of this Act; and the owner of a legal estate is referred to as "an estate owner" and his legal estate is referred to as his estate.

(5) A legal estate may subsist concurrently with or subject to any other legal estate in the same land in like manner as it could have done before the commencement of this Act.

(6) A legal estate is not capable of subsisting or of being created in an undivided share in land or of being held by an infant.

(7) Every power of appointment over, or power to convey or charge land or any interest therein, whether created by a statute or other instrument or implied by law, and whether created before or after the commencement of this Act (not being a power vested in a legal mortgagee or an estate owner in right of his estate and exercisable by him or by another person in his name and on his behalf), operates only in equity.

(8) Estates, interests, and charges in or over land which are not legal estates are in this Act referred to as "equitable interests," and powers which by this Act are to operate in equity only are in this Act referred to as "equitable powers."

(9) The provisions in any statute or other instrument requiring land to be conveyed to uses shall take effect as directions that the land shall (subject to creating or reserving thereout any legal estate authorised by this Act which may be required) be conveyed to a person of full age upon the requisite trusts.

(10) The repeal of the Statute of Uses (as amended) does not affect the operation thereof in regard to dealings taking effect before the commencement of this Act.

Conveyances overreaching certain equitable interests and powers

2.—(1)⁴ A conveyance to a purchaser of a legal estate in land shall overreach any equitable interest or power affecting that estate, whether or not he has notice thereof, if—

(i) the conveyance is made under the powers conferred by the Settled Land Act 1925, or any additional powers conferred by a settlement, and the equitable interest or power is capable of being overreached thereby, and the statutory requirements respecting the payment of capital money arising under the settlement are complied with;

(ii) the conveyance is made by trustees for sale and the equitable interest or power is at the date of the conveyance capable of being overreached by such trustees under the provisions of subsection (2) of this section or independently of that subsection, and the statutory requirements respecting the payment of capital money arising under a disposition upon trust for sale are complied with;

(iii) the conveyance is made by a mortgagee or personal representative in the exercise of his paramount powers, and the equitable interest

---

³ These words were repealed by the Tithe Act 1936 (26 Geo. 5 & 1 Edw. 8, c. 43), Sched. 9, and the Finance Act 1963 (c. 25), Sched. 14, Pt. VI.
⁴ Applied by the Leasehold Reform Act 1967 (c.88), s.8(4) (a).

or power is capable of being overreached by such conveyance, and any capital money arising from the transaction is paid to the mortgagee or personal representative;

(iv) the conveyance is made under an order of the court and the equitable interest or power is bound by such order, and any capital money arising from the transaction is paid into, or in accordance with the order of, the court.

(2) [Where the legal estate affected is subject to a trust for sale, then if at the date of a conveyance made after the commencement of this Act under the trust for sale or the powers conferred on the trustees for sale, the trustees (whether original or substituted) are either—]⁵

(*a*) two or more individuals approved or appointed by the court or the successors in office of the individuals so approved or appointed; or

(*b*) a trust corporation,

[any equitable interest or power having priority to the trust for sale]⁶ shall, notwithstanding any stipulation to the contrary, be overreached by the conveyance, and shall, according to its priority, take effect as if created or arising by means of a primary trust affecting the proceeds of sale and the income of the land until sale.

(3) The following equitable interests and powers are excepted from the operation of subsection (2) of this section, namely—

(i) Any equitable interest protected by a deposit of documents relating to the legal estate affected;

(ii) The benefit of any covenant or agreement restrictive of the user of land;

(iii) Any easement, liberty, or privilege over or affecting land and being merely an equitable interest (in this Act referred to as an "equitable easement");

(iv) The benefit of any contract (in this Act referred to as an "estate contract") to convey or create a legal estate, including a contract conferring either expressly or by statutory implication a valid option to purchase, a right of pre-emption, or any other like right;

(v) Any equitable interest protected by registration under the Land Charges Act 1925⁷ other than—

(*a*) an annuity within the meaning of Part II of that Act;

(*b*) a limited owner's charge or a general equitable charge within the meaning of that Act.

(4) Subject to the protection afforded by this section to the purchaser of a legal estate, nothing contained in this section shall deprive a person entitled to an equitable charge of any of his rights or remedies for enforcing the same.

(5) So far as regards the following interests, created before the commencement of this Act (which accordingly are not within the provisions of the Land Charges Act 1925⁷), namely—

(*a*) the benefit of any covenant or agreement restrictive of the user of the land;

(*b*) any equitable easement;

(*c*) the interest under a puisne mortgage within the meaning of the Land Charges Act 1925,⁷ unless and until acquired under a transfer made after the commencement of this Act;

(*d*) the benefit of an estate contract, unless and until the same is acquired under a conveyance made after the commencement of this Act;

a purchaser of a legal estate shall only take subject thereto if he has notice

---

⁵ Substituted by the Law of Property (Amendment) Act 1926, *post,* Sched.
⁶ Substituted by *ibid.*
⁷ Now the Land Charges Act 1972 (c. 61), *post,* p. 320.

thereof, and the same are not overreached under the provisions contained or in the manner referred to in this section.

Manner of giving effect to equitable interests and powers

3.——(1) All equitable interests and powers in or over land shall be enforceable against the estate owner of the legal estate affected in manner following (that is to say):—

(*a*) Where the legal estate affected is settled land, the tenant for life or statutory owner shall be bound to give effect to the equitable interests and powers in manner provided by the Settled Land Act 1925;

(*b*) Where the legal estate affected is vested in trustees for sale—

(i) The trustees shall stand possessed of the net proceeds of sale after payment of costs and of the net rents and profits of the land until sale after payment of rates, taxes, costs of insurance, repairs, and other outgoings, upon such trusts and subject to such powers and provisions as may be requisite for giving effect to the equitable interests and powers affecting the same respectively, of which they have notice, and whether created before or after the disposition upon trust for sale, according to their respective priorities:

(ii) Where, by reason of the exercise of any equitable power or under any trust affecting the proceeds of sale, any principal sum is required to be raised, or any person of full age becomes entitled to require a legal estate in the land to be vested in him in priority to the trust for sale, then, unless the claim is satisfied out of the net proceeds of sale, the trustees for sale shall (if so requested in writing) be bound to transfer or create such legal estates, to take effect in priority to the trust for sale, as may be required for raising the money by way of legal mortgage or for giving legal effect to the rights of the person so entitled:

Provided that, if the proceeds of sale are held in trust for persons of full age in undivided shares absolutely free from incumbrances affecting undivided shares, those persons cannot require the land to be conveyed to them in undivided shares, but may (subject to effect being given by way of legal mortgage to incumbrances affecting the entirety) require the same to be vested in any of them (not exceeding four) as joint tenants on trust for sale; and if the conveyance purports to transfer the land to any of them in undivided shares or to more than four such persons, it shall operate only as a transfer to them or (if more than four) to the four first named therein as joint tenants on trust for sale:

(*c*) Where the legal estate affected is neither settled land nor vested in trustees for sale, the estate owner shall be bound to give effect to the equitable interests and powers affecting his estate of which he has notice according to their respective priorities. This provision does not affect the priority or powers of a legal mortgagee, or the powers of personal representatives for purposes of administration.

(2) Effect may be given by means of a legal mortgage to an agreement for a mortgage, charge or lien (whether or not arising by operation of law) if the agreement, charge or lien ought to have priority over the trust for sale.

(3) Where, by reason of a statutory or other right of reverter, or of an equitable right of entry taking effect, or for any other reason, a person becomes entitled to require a legal estate to be vested in him, then and in any such case the estate owner whose estate is affected shall be bound to convey or create such legal estate as the case may require.

(4)[8] If any question arises whether any and what legal estate ought to be transferred or created as aforesaid, any person interested may apply to the court for directions in the manner provided by this Act.

(5)[9] If the trustees for sale or other estate owners refuse or neglect for one month after demand to transfer or create any such legal estate, or if by reason of their being out of the United Kingdom or being unable to be found, or by reason of the dissolution of a corporation, or for any other reason, the court is satisfied that the transaction cannot otherwise be effected, or cannot be effected without undue delay or expense, the court may, on the application of any person interested, make a vesting order transferring or creating a legal estate in the manner provided by this Act.

(6) This section does not affect a purchaser of a legal estate taking free from an equitable interest or power.

Creation and disposition of equitable interests

4.—(1) Interests in land validly created or arising after the commencement of this Act, which are not capable of subsisting as legal estates, shall take effect as equitable interests, and, save as otherwise expressly provided by statute, interests in land which under the Statute of Uses or otherwise could before the commencement of this Act have been created as legal interests, shall be capable of being created as equitable interests:

Provided that, after the commencment of this Act (and save as hereinafter expressly enacted), an equitable interest in land shall only be capable of being validly created in any case in which an equivalent equitable interest in property real or personal could have been validly created before such commencement.

(2) All rights and interests in land may be disposed of, including—

    (*a*) a contingent, executory or future equitable interest in any land, or a possibility coupled with an interest in any land, whether or not the object of the gift or limitation of such interest or possibility be ascertained;

    (*b*) a right of entry, into or upon land whether immediate or future, and whether vested or contingent.

(3) All rights of entry affecting a legal estate which are exercisable on condition broken or for any other reason may after the commencement of this Act, be made exercisable by any person and the persons deriving title under him, but, in regard to an estate in fee simple (not being a rentcharge held for a legal estate) only within the period authorised by the rule relating to perpetuities.

Satisfied terms, whether created out of freehold or leasehold land to cease

5.—(1) Where the purposes of a term of years created or limited at any time out of freehold land, become satisfied either before or after the commencement of this Act (whether or not that term either by express declaration or by construction of law becomes attendant upon the freehold reversion) it shall merge in the reversion expectant thereon and shall cease accordingly.

(2) Where the purposes of a term of years created or limited, at any time, out of leasehold land, become satisfied after the commencement of this Act, that term shall merge in the reversion expectant thereon and shall cease accordingly.

---

[8] The county court shall have jurisdiction in a case where the land which is to be dealt with does not exceed in capital value £5,000 or in net annual value for rating £300: County Courts Act 1959 (7 & 8 Eliz. 2, c. 22), Sched. I, as amended by the Administration of Justice Act 1969 (c. 58), s. 5.

[9] *Ibid.*

(3) Where the purposes are satisfied only as respects part of the land comprised in a term, this section shall have effect as if a separate term had been created in regard to that part of the land.

Saving of lessors' and lessees' covenants

6.—(1) Nothing in this Part of this Act affects prejudicially the right to enforce any lessor's or lessee's covenants, agreements or conditions (including a valid option to purchase or right of pre-emption over the reversion), contained in any such instrument as is in this section mentioned, the benefit or burden of which runs with the reversion or the term.

(2) This section applies where the covenant, agreement or condition is contained in any instrument—

(*a*) creating a term of years absolute, or

(*b*) varying the rights of the lessor or lessee under the instrument creating the term.

Saving of certain legal estates and statutory powers

7.—(1) A fee simple which, by virtue of the Lands Clauses Acts, the School Sites Acts, or any similar statute, is liable to be divested, is for the purposes of this Act a fee simple absolute, and remains liable to be divested as if this Act had not been passed [and a fee simple subject to a legal or equitable right of entry or re-entry is for the purposes of this Act a fee simple absolute.][10]

(2) A fee simple vested in a corporation which is liable to determine by reason of the dissolution of the corporation is, for the purposes of this Act, a fee simple absolute.

(3) The provisions of—

(*a*) [*Repealed by the Criminal Justice Act* 1948 (11 & 12 *Geo.* 6, *c.*58), *Sched.* 10.]

(*b*) the Friendly Societies Act 1896 in regard to land to which that Act applies;

(*c*) any other statutes conferring special facilities or prescribing special modes (whether by way of registered memorial or otherwise) for disposing of or acquiring land, or providing for the vesting (by conveyance or otherwise) of the land in trustees or any person, or the holder for the time being of an office or any corporation sole or aggregate (including the Crown);

shall remain in full force.

This subsection does not authorise an entailed interest to take effect otherwise than as an equitable interest.

(4) Where any such power for disposing of or creating a legal estate is exercisable by a person who is not the estate owner, the power shall, when practicable, be exercised in the name and on behalf of the estate owner.

Saving of certain legal powers to lease

8.—(1) All leases or tenancies at a rent for a term of years absolute authorised to be granted by a mortgagor or mortgagee or by the Settled Land Act 1925 or any other statute (whether or not extended by any instrument) may be granted in the name and on behalf of the estate owner by the person empowered to grant the same, whether being an estate

---

[10] Added by the Law of Property (Amendment) Act 1926, *post*, Sched.

owner or not, with the same effect and priority as if this Part of this Act had not been passed; but this section does not (except as respects the usual qualified covenant for quiet enjoyment) authorise any person granting a lease in the name of an estate owner to impose any personal liability on him.

(2) Where a rentcharge is held for a legal estate, the owner thereof may under the statutory power or under any corresponding power, create a legal term of years absolute for securing or compelling payment of the same; but in other cases terms created under any such power shall, unless and until the estate owner of the land charged gives legal effect to the transaction, take effect only as equitable interests.

Vesting orders and dispositions of legal estates operating as conveyances by an estate owner

9.—(1) Every such order, declaration, or conveyance as is hereinafter mentioned, namely—
  (*a*) every vesting order made by any court or other competent authority[11];
  (*b*) every vesting declaration (express or implied) under any statutory power;
  (*c*) every vesting instrument made by the trustees of a settlement or other persons under the provisions of the Settled Land Act 1925;
  (*d*) every conveyance by a person appointed for the purpose under an order of the court or authorised under any statutory power to convey in the name or on behalf of an estate owner;
  (*e*) every conveyance made under any power reserved or conferred by this Act,
which is made or executed for the purpose of vesting, conveying, or creating a legal estate, shall operate to convey or create the legal estate disposed of in like manner as if the same had been a conveyance executed by the estate owner of the legal estate to which the order, declaration, vesting instrument, or conveyance relates.

(2) Where the order, declaration, or conveyance is made in favour of a purchaser, the provisions of this Act relating to a conveyance of a legal estate to a purchaser shall apply thereto.

(3) The provisions of the Trustee Act 1925 relating to vesting orders and orders appointing a person to convey shall apply to all vesting orders authorised to be made by this Part of this Act.

Title to be shown to legal estates

10.—(1) Where title is shown to a legal estate in land, it shall be deemed not necessary or proper to include in the abstract of title an instrument relating only to interests or powers which will be over-reached by the conveyance of the estate to which title is being shown; but nothing in this Part of this Act affects the liability of any person to disclose an equitable interest or power which will not be so over-reached, or to furnish an abstract of any instrument creating or affecting the same.

(2) A solicitor delivering an abstract framed in accordance with this Part of this Act shall not incur any liability on account of an omission to include therein an instrument which, under this section, is to be deemed not necessary or proper to be included, nor shall any liability be implied by reason of the inclusion of any such instrument.

---

[11] Meaning of "competent authority" extended by the Land Drainage Act 1930 (20 & 21 Geo. 5, c. 44), s. 76 (6).

Registration in Middlesex and Yorkshire as respects legal estates

11.[12]—(1) It shall not be necessary to register a memorial of any instrument made after the commencement of this Act in any local deeds registry unless the instrument operates to transfer or create a legal estate, or to create a charge thereon by way of legal mortgage; nor shall the registration of a memorial of any instrument not required to be registered affect any priority.

(2) Probates and letters of administration shall be treated as instruments capable of transferring a legal estate to personal representatives.

(3) Memorials of all instruments capable of transferring or creating a legal estate or charge by way of legal mortgage, may, when so operating, be registered.

Limitation and Prescription Acts

12.   Nothing in this Part of this Act affects the operation of any statute, or of the general law for the limitation of actions or proceedings relating to land or with reference to the acquisition of easements or rights over or in respect of land.

Effect of possession of documents

13.   This Act shall not prejudicially affect the right or interest of any person arising out of or consequent on the possession by him of any documents relating to a legal estate in land, nor affect any question arising out of or consequent upon any omission to obtain or any other absence of possession by any person of any documents relating to a legal estate in land.

Interests of persons in possession

14.   This Part of this Act shall not prejudicially affect the interest of any person in possession or in actual occupation of land to which he may be entitled in right of such possession or occupation.

Presumption that parties are of full age

15.   The persons expressed to be parties to any conveyance shall, until the contrary is proved, be presumed to be of full age at the date thereof.

16—18.—[*Repealed by the Finance Act* 1975 (*c.* 7), *Sched.* 13.]

Infants and Lunatics

Effect of conveyances of legal estates to infants

19.—(1) A conveyance of a legal estate in land to an infant alone or to two or more persons jointly both or all of whom are infants, shall have such operation as is provided for in the Settled Land Act 1925.

(2) A conveyance of a legal estate in land to an infant, jointly with one or more other persons of full age, shall operate to vest the legal estate in the other person or persons on the statutory trusts, but not so as to sever any joint tenancy in the net proceeds of sale or in the rents and profits until sale, or affect the right of a tenant for life or statutory owner to have settled land vested in him.

---

[12] This section will be repealed, in respect of any Yorkshire deeds register, registry and the area which was within its jurisdiction, with effect from the expiration of two years beginning with the date on which compulsory registration of title under the Land Registration Act 1925 (15 & 16 Geo. 5, c. 21) is extended to any part of the area of the registry, unless the Lord Chancellor specifies an earlier date at the request of the County Council of the Riding: Law of Property Act 1969 (c. 59), s.16(2) and Sched. 2, Pt. I.

(3) The foregoing provisions of this section do not apply to conveyances on trust or by way of mortgage.

(4) A conveyance of a legal estate to an infant alone or to two or more persons jointly, both or all of whom are infants, on any trusts, shall operate as a declaration of trust and shall not be effectual to pass any legal estate.

(5) A conveyance of a legal estate in land to an infant jointly with one or more other persons of full age on any trusts shall operate as if the infant had not been named therein, but without prejudice to any beneficial interest in the land intended to be thereby provided for the infant.

(6) A grant or transfer of a legal mortgage of land to an infant shall operate only as an agreement for valuable consideration to execute a proper conveyance when the infant attains full age, and in the meantime to hold any beneficial interest in the mortgage debt in trust for the persons for whose benefit the conveyance was intended to be made:

Provided that, if the conveyance is made to the infant and another person or other persons of full age, it shall operate as if the infant had not been named therein, but without prejudice to any beneficial interest in the mortgage debt itended to be thereby provided for the infant.

Infants not to be appointed trustees

20.   The appointment of an infant to be a trustee in relation to any settlement or trust shall be void, but without prejudice to the power to appoint a new trustee to fill the vacancy.

Receipts by married infants

21.   A married infant shall have power to give valid receipts for all income (including statutory accumulations of income made during the minority) to which the infant may be entitled in like manner as if the infant were of full age.

Conveyances on behalf of persons suffering from mental disorder and as to land held by them on trust for sale

22.—(1) [Where a legal estate in land (whether settled or not) is vested in a person suffering from mental disorder, either solely or jointly with any other person or persons, his receiver or (if no receiver is acting for him) any person authorised in that behalf shall, under an order of the authority having jurisdiction under Part VIII of the Mental Health Act 1959 or of the court, or under any statutory power, make or concur in making all requisite dispositions for conveying or creating a legal estate in his name and on his behalf.

(2) If land held on trust for sale is vested, either solely or jointly with any other person or persons, in a person who is incapable, by reason of mental disorder, of exercising his functions as trustee, a new trustee shall be appointed in the place of that person, or he shall be otherwise discharged from the trust, before the legal estate is dealt with under the trust for sale or under the powers vested in the trustees for sale.][13]

Dispositions on Trust for Sale

Duration of trusts for sale

23.   Where land has, either before or after the commencement of this Act, become subject to an express or implied trust for sale, such trust shall, so far as regards the safety and protection of any purchaser thereunder, be deemed to be subsisting until the land has been conveyed to or under the direction of the persons interested in the proceeds of sale.

---

[13] Substituted by the Mental Health Act 1959 (7 & 8 Eliz. 2, c. 72), Sched. 7, Pt. I.

This section applies to sales whether made before or after the commencement of this Act, but operates without prejudice to an order of any court restraining a sale.

Appointment of trustees of dispositions on trust for sale

24.—(1) The persons having power to appoint new trustees of a conveyance of land on trust for sale shall be bound to appoint the same persons (if any) who are for the time being trustees of the settlement of the proceeds of sale, but a purchaser shall not be concerned to see whether the proper persons are appointed to be trustees of the conveyance of the land.

(2) This section applies whether the settlement of the proceeds of sale or the conveyance on trust for sale comes into operation before or after the commencement of this Act.

Power to postpone sale

25.—(1) A power to postpone sale shall, in the case of every trust for sale of land, be implied unless a contrary intention appears.

(2) Where there is a power to postpone the sale, then (subject to any express direction to the contrary in the instrument, if any, creating the trust for sale) the trustees for sale shall not be liable in any way for postponing the sale, in the exercise of their discretion, for any indefinite period; nor shall a purchaser of a legal estate be concerned in any case with any directions respecting the postponement of a sale.

(3) The foregoing provisions of this section apply whether the trust for sale is created before or after the commencement or by virtue of this Act.

(4) Where a disposition or settlement coming into operation after the commencement of this Act contains a trust either to retain or sell land the same shall be construed as a trust to sell the land with power to postpone the sale.

Consents to the execution of a trust for sale

26.—(1) If the consent of more than two persons is by the disposition made requisite to the execution of a trust for sale of land, then, in favour of a purchaser, the consent of any two of such persons to the execution of the trust or to the exercise of any statutory or other powers vested in the trustees for sale shall be deemed sufficient.

(2) Where the person whose consent to the execution of any such trust or power is expressed to be required in a disposition is not sui juris or becomes subject to disability, his consent shall not, in favour of a purchaser, be deemed to be requisite to the execution of the trust or the exercise of the power; but the trustees shall, in any such case, obtain the separate consent of the parent or testamentary or other guardian of an infant or of the [. . .][14] receiver (if any) of a [person suffering from mental disorder].[15]

(3) [Trustees for sale shall so far as practicable consult the persons of full age for the time being beneficially interested in possession in the rents and profits of the land until sale, and shall, so far as consistent with the general interest of the trust, give effect to the wishes of such persons, or, in the case of dispute, of the majority (according to the value of their combined interests) of such persons, but a purchaser shall not be concerned to see that the provisions of this subsection have been complied with.

In the case of a trust for sale, not being a trust for sale created by or in pursuance of the powers conferred by this or any other Act, this subsection

[14] Words repealed by the Mental Health Act 1959 (7 & 8 Eliz. 2, c. 72). Sched. 7, Pt. I.
[15] Substituted by *ibid.*

shall not apply unless the contrary intention appears in the disposition creating the trust.][16]

(4) This section applies whether the trust for sale is created before or after the commencement or by virtue of this Act.

Purchaser not to be concerned with the trusts of the proceeds of sale which are to be paid to two or more trustees or to a trust corporation

27.—(1) A purchaser of a legal estate from trustees for sale shall not be concerned with the trusts affecting the proceeds of sale of land subject to a trust for sale (whether made to attach to such proceeds by virtue of this Act or otherwise), or affecting the rents and profits of the land until sale, whether or not those trusts are declared by the same instrument by which the trust for sale is created.

(2) [Notwithstanding anything to the contrary in the instrument (if any) creating a trust for sale of land or in the settlement of the net proceeds, the proceeds of sale or other capital money shall not be paid to or applied by the direction of fewer than two persons as trustees for sale, except where the trustee is a trust corporation, but this subsection does not affect the right of a sole personal representative as such to give valid receipts for, or direct the application of, proceeds of sale or other capital money, nor, except where capital money arises on the transaction, render it necessary to have more than one trustee.][17]

Powers of management, &c. conferred on trustees for sale

28.[18]—(1) Trustees for sale shall, in relation to land or to manorial incidents and to the proceeds of sale, have all the powers of a tenant for life and the trustees of a settlement under the Settled Land Act 1925, including in relation to the land the powers of management conferred by that Act during a minority [and where by statute settled land is or becomes vested in the trustees of the settlement upon the statutory trusts, such trustees and their successors in office shall also have all the additional or larger powers (if any) conferred by the settlement on the tenant for life, statutory owner, or trustees of the settlement][19]: and (subject to any express trust to the contrary) all capital money arising under the said powers shall, unless paid or applied for any purpose authorised by the Settled Land Act 1925, be applicable in the same manner as if the money represented proceeds of sale arising under the trust for sale.

All land acquired under this subsection shall be conveyed to the trustees on trust for sale.

The powers conferred by this subsection shall be exercised with such consents (if any) as would have been required on a sale under the trust for sale, and when exercised shall operate to overreach any equitable interests or powers which are by virtue of this Act or otherwise made to attach to the net proceeds of sale as if created by a trust affecting those proceeds.

(2) Subject to any direction to the contrary in the disposition on trust for sale or in the settlement of the proceeds of sale, the net rents and profits of the land until sale, after keeping down costs of repairs and insurance and

---

[16] Substituted by the Law of Property (Amendment) Act 1926, *post,* Sched.

[17] *Ibid.*

[18] Extended by the Landlord and Tenant Act 1927 (17 & 18 Geo. 5, c. 36), s.13(1); the War Damage Act 1943 (6 & 7 Geo. 6, c. 21), s.66(2); the Hill Farming Act 1946 (9 & 10 Geo. 6, c. 73), s.11(2); the Coast Protection Act 1949 (12 & 13 Geo. 6, c. 74), s.11(2) (*a*); the Coal Mining (Subsidence) Act 1957 (5 & 6 Eliz. 2, c. 59), s.11(2) (*a*); the Land Commission Act 1967 (c. 1), s.92; the Forestry Act 1967 (c. 10), Sched. 2, para. 1 (4); the Agriculture Act 1967 (c. 22), s.36(5); the Leasehold Reform Act 1967 (c. 88), s.6(5), Sched. 2, para. 9: the Town and Country Planning Act 1971 (c. 78), s.275; and the Housing Act 1974 (c. 44), s.77(3).

[19] Added by the Law of Property (Amendment) Act 1926, *post,* Sched.

other outgoings shall be paid or applied, except so far as any part thereof may be liable to be set aside as capital money under the Settled Land Act 1925, in like manner as the income of investments representing the purchase money would be payable or applicable if a sale had been made and the proceeds had been duly invested.

(3) Where the net proceeds of sale have under the trusts affecting the same become absolutely vested in persons of full age in undivided shares (whether or not such shares may be subject to a derivative trust) the trustees for sale may, with the consent of the persons, if any, of full age, not being annuitants, interested in possession in the net rents and profits of the land until sale:—

(*a*) partition the land remaining unsold or any part thereof; and

(*b*) provide (by way of mortgage or otherwise) for the payment of any equality money;

and, upon such partition being arranged, the trustees for sale shall give effect thereto by conveying the land so partitioned in severalty (subject or not to any legal mortgage created for raising equality money) to persons of full age and either absolutely or on trust for sale or, where any part of the land becomes settled land, by a vesting deed, or partly in one way and partly in another in accordance with the rights of the persons interested under the partition, but a purchaser shall not be concerned to see or inquire whether any such consent as aforesaid has been given:

Provided that—

(i) If a share in the net proceeds belongs to a [person suffering from mental disorder][20] the consent of his [. . .][21] receiver shall be sufficient to protect the trustees for sale:

(ii) If a share in the net proceeds is affected by an incumbrance the trustees for sale may either give effect thereto or provide for the discharge thereof by means of the property allotted in respect of such share, as they may consider expedient.

(4) If a share in the net proceeds is absolutely vested in an infant, the trustees for sale may act on his behalf and retain land (to be held on trust for sale) or other property to represent his share, but in other respects the foregoing power shall apply as if the infant had been of full age.

(5) This section applies to dispositions on trust for sale coming into operation either before or after the commencement or by virtue of this Act.

Delegation of powers of management by trustees for sale

29.—(1) The powers of and incidental to leasing, accepting surrenders of leases and management, conferred on trustees for sale whether by this Act or otherwise, may, until sale of the land, be revocably delegated from time to time, by writing, signed by them, to any person of full age (not being merely an annuitant) for the time being beneficially entitled in possession to the net rents and profits of the land during his life or for any less period: and in favour of a lessee such writing shall, unless the contrary appears, be sufficient evidence that the person named therein is a person to whom the powers may be delegated, and the production of such writing shall, unless the contrary appears, be sufficient evidence that the delegation has not been revoked.

(2) Any power so delegated shall be exercised only in the names and on behalf of the trustees delegating the power.

(3) The persons delegating any power under this section shall not, in relation to the exercise or purported exercise of the power, be liable for the acts or defaults of the person to whom the power is delegated, but that

---

[20] Substituted by the Mental Health Act 1959 (7 & 8 Eliz. 2, c. 72), Sched 7, Pt. I.
[21] Repealed by *ibid.*

person shall, in relation to the exercise of the power by him, be deemed to be in the position and to have the duties and liabilities of a trustee.

(4) Where, at the commencement of this Act, an order made under section seven of the Settled Land Act 1884 is in force, the person on whom any power is thereby conferred shall, while the order remains in force, exercise such power in the names and on behalf of the trustees for sale in like manner as if the power had been delegated to him under this section.

Powers of court where trustees for sale refuse to exercise powers

30.[22] If the trustees for sale refuse to sell or to exercise any of the powers conferred by either of the last two sections, or any requisite consent cannot be obtained, any person interested may apply to the court for a vesting or other order for giving effect to the proposed transaction or for an order directing the trustees for sale to give effect thereto, and the court may make such order as it thinks fit.

Trust for sale of mortgaged property where right of redemption is barred

31.—(1) Where any property, vested in trustees by way of security, becomes, by virtue of the statutes of limitation, or of an order for foreclosure or otherwise, discharged from the right of redemption, it shall be held by them on trust for sale.

(2) The net proceeds of sale, after payment of costs and expenses, shall be applied in like manner as the mortgage debt, if received, would have been applicable, and the income of the property until sale shall be applied in like manner as the interest, if received, would have been applicable; but this subsection operates without prejudice to any rule of law relating to the apportionment of capital and income between tenant for life and remainderman.

(3) This section does not affect the right of any person to require that, instead of a sale, the property shall be conveyed to him or in accordance with his directions.

(4) Where the mortgage money is capital money for the purposes of the Settled Land Act 1925, the trustees shall, if the tenant for life or statutory owner so requires, instead of selling any land forming the whole or part of such property, execute such subsidiary vesting deed with respect thereto as would have been required if the land had been acquired on a purchase with capital money.

(5) This section applies whether the right of redemption was discharged before or after the first day of January, nineteen hundred and twelve, but has effect without prejudice to any dealings or arrangements made before that date.

Implied trust for sale in personalty settlements

32.—(1) Where a settlement of personal property or of land held upon trust for sale contains a power to invest money in the purchase of land, such land shall, unless the settlement otherwise provides, be held by the trustees on trust for sale; and the net rents and profits until sale, after keeping down costs of repairs and insurance and other outgoings, shall be paid or applied in like manner as the income of investments representing the purchase-money would be payable or applicable if a sale had been made and the proceeds had been duly invested in personal estate.

---

[22] The county court has jurisdiction in a case where the land to be dealt with does not exceed in capital value £5,000 or in net annual value for rating £300: County Courts Act 1959 (7 & 8 Eliz. 2, c. 22), Sched. 1, as amended by the Administration of Justice Act 1969 (c. 58), s.5.

(2) This section applies to settlements (including wills) coming into operation after the thirty-first day of December, nineteen hundred and eleven, and does not apply to capital money arising under the Settled Land Act 1925, or money liable to be treated as such.

Application of Part I to personal representatives

33.   The provisions of this Part of this Act relating to trustees for sale apply to personal representatives holding on trust for sale, but without prejudice to their rights and powers for purposes of administration.

Undivided Shares and Joint Ownership

Effect of future dispositions to tenants in common

34.[23]—(1) An undivided share in land shall not be capable of being created except as provided by the Settled Land Act 1925, or as hereinafter mentioned.

(2) Where, after the commencement of this Act, land is expressed to be conveyed to any persons in undivided shares and those persons are of full age, the conveyance shall (notwithstanding anything to the contrary in this Act) operate as if the land had been expressed to be conveyed to the grantees, or, if there are more than four grantees, to the four first named in the conveyance, as joint tenants upon the statutory trusts hereinafter mentioned and so as to give effect to the rights of the persons who would have been entitled to the shares had the conveyance operated to create those shares:

Provided that, where the conveyance is made by way of mortgage the land shall vest in the grantees or such four of them as aforesaid for a term of years absolute (as provided by this Act) as joint tenants subject to cesser on redemption in like manner as if the mortgage money had belonged to them on a joint account, but without prejudice to the beneficial interests in the mortgage money and interest.

(3) A devise bequest or testamentary appointment, coming into operation after the commencement of this Act, of land to two or more persons in undivided shares shall operate as a devise bequest or appointment of the land to the trustees (if any) of the will for the purposes of the Settled Land Act 1925, or, if there are no such trustees, then to the personal representatives of the testator, and in each case (but without prejudice to the rights and powers of the personal representatives for purposes of administration) upon the statutory trusts hereinafter mentioned.

(4) Any disposition purporting to make a settlement of an undivided share in land shall only operate as a settlement of a corresponding share of the net proceeds of sale and of the rents and profits until sale of the entirety of the land.

Meaning of the statutory trusts

35.[24]   For the purposes of this Act land held upon the "statutory trusts" shall be held upon the trusts and subject to the provisions following, namely, upon trust to sell the same and to stand possessed of the net proceeds of sale, after payment of costs, and of the net rents and profits until sale after payment of rates, taxes, costs of insurance, repairs, and other outgoings, upon such trusts, and subject to such powers and provisions, as may be requisite for giving effect to the rights of the persons

---

[23] Applied by the Leasehold Reform Act 1967 (c. 88), s.6(1).
[24] Applied by the Leasehold Reform Act 1967 (c. 88), s.6(1).

(including an incumbrancer of a former undivided share or whose incumbrance is not secured by a legal mortgage) interested in the land [and the right of a person who, if the land had not been made subject to a trust for sale by virtue of this Act, would have been entitled to an entailed interest in an undivided share in the land, shall be deemed to be a right to a corresponding entailed interest in the net proceeds of sale attributable to that share].[25]

[Where—
    (*a*) an undivided share was subject to a settlement, and
    (*b*) the settlement remains subsisting in respect of other property, and
    (*c*) the trustees thereof are not the same persons as the trustees for sale,

then the statutory trusts include a trust for the trustees for sale to pay the proper proportion of the net proceeds of sale or other capital money attributable to the share to the trustees of the settlement to be held by them as capital money arising under the Settled Land Act 1925.][26]

Joint tenancies

36.[27]—(1) Where a legal estate (not being settled land) is beneficially limited to or held in trust for any persons as joint tenants, the same shall be held on trust for sale, in like manner as if the persons beneficially entitled were tenants in common, but not so as to sever their joint tenancy in equity.

(2)[28] No severance of a joint tenancy of a legal estate, so as to create a tenancy in common in land, shall be permissible, whether by operation of law or otherwise, but this subsection does not affect the right of a joint tenant to release his interest to the other joint tenants, or the right to sever a joint tenancy in an equitable interest whether or not the legal estate is vested in the joint tenants:

Provided that, where a legal estate (not being settled land) is vested in joint tenants beneficially, and any tenant desires to sever the joint tenancy in equity, he shall give to the other joint tenants a notice in writing of such desire or do such other acts or things as would, in the case of personal estate, have been effectual to sever the tenancy in equity, and thereupon under the trust for sale affecting the land the net proceeds of sale, and the net rents and profits until sale, shall be held upon the trusts which would have been requisite for giving effect to the beneficial interests if there had been an actual severance. [Nothing in this Act affects the right of a survivor of joint tenants, who is solely and beneficially interested, to deal with his legal estate as if it were not held on trust for sale.][29]

(3) Without prejudice to the right of a joint tenant to release his interest to the other joint tenants no severance of a mortgage term or trust estate, so as to create a tenancy in common, shall be permissible.

Rights of husband and wife

37. A husband and wife shall, for all purposes of acquisition of any interest in property, under a disposition made or coming into operation after the commencement of this Act, be treated as two persons.

---

[25] Added by the Law of Property (Entailed Interests) Act 1932, *post,* s.1(1).
[26] Added by the Law of Property (Amendment) Act 1926, *post,* Sched.
[27] Applied by the Leasehold Reform Act 1967 (c. 88), s.6(1).
[28] Extended retrospectively with regard to assumptions on the sale of land by the survivor of joint tenants: see the Law of Property (Joint Tenants) Act 1964, ss. 1, 2, *post.* p. 311.
[29] Added by the Law of Property (Amendment) Act 1926, *post,* Sched.

Party structures

38.—(1) Where under a disposition or other arrangement which, if a holding in undivided shares had been permissible, would have created a tenancy in common, a wall or other structure is or is expressed to be made a party wall or structure, that structure shall be and remain severed vertically as between the respective owners, and the owner of each part shall have such rights to support and user over the rest of the structure as may be requisite for conferring rights corresponding to those which would have subsisted if a valid tenancy in common had been created.

(2) Any person interested may, in case of dispute, apply to the court for an order declaring the rights and interests under this section of the persons interested in any such party structure, and the court may make such order as it thinks fit.

Transitional Provisions

Transitional provisions in First Schedule

39. For the purpose of effecting the transition from the law existing prior to the commencement of the Law of Property Act 1922 to the law enacted by that Act (as amended), the provisions set out in the First Schedule to this Act shall have effect—

(1) for converting existing legal estates, interests and charges not capable under the said Act of taking effect as legal interests into equitable interests;

(2) for discharging, getting in or vesting outstanding legal estates;

(3) for making provision with respect to legal estates vested in infants;

(4) for subjecting land held in undivided shares to trusts for sale;

(5) for dealing with party structures and open spaces held in common;

(6) for converting tenancies by entireties into joint tenancies;

(7) for converting existing freehold mortgages into mortgages by demise;

(8) for converting existing leasehold mortgages into mortgages by sub-demise.

PART II

CONTRACTS, CONVEYANCES AND OTHER INSTRUMENTS

Contracts

Contracts for sale, &c., of land to be in writing

40.—(1) No action may be brought upon any contract for the sale or other disposition of land or any interest in land, unless the agreement upon which such action is brought, or some memorandum or note thereof, is in writing, and signed by the party to be charged or by some other person thereunto by him lawfully authorised.

(2) This section applies to contracts whether made before or after the commencement of this Act and does not affect the law relating to past performance, or sales by the court.

Stipulations not of the essence of a contract

41. Stipulations in a contract, as to time or otherwise, which according to rules of equity are not deemed to be or to have become of the essence of the contract, are also construed and have effect at law in accordance with the same rules.

Provisions as to contracts

42.—(1) A stipulation that a purchaser of a legal estate in land shall accept a title made with the concurrence of any person entitled to an equitable interest shall be void, if a title can be made discharged from the equitable interest without such concurrence—

(*a*) under a trust for sale; or

(*b*) under this Act, or the Settled Land Act 1925, or any other statute.

(2) A stipulation that a purchaser of a legal estate in land shall pay or contribute towards the costs of or incidental to—

(*a*) obtaining a vesting order, or the appointment of trustees of a settlement, or the appointment of trustees of a conveyance on trust for sale; or

(*b*) the preparation stamping or execution of a conveyance on trust for sale, or of a vesting instrument for bringing into force the provisions of the Settled Land Act 1925;

shall be void.

(3) A stipulation contained in any contract for sale or exchange of land made after the commencement of this Act, to the effect that an outstanding legal estate is to be traced or got in by or at the expense of a purchaser or that no objection is to be taken on account of an outstanding legal estate, shall be void.

(4) If the subject matter of any contract for the sale or exchange of land—

(i) is a mortgage term and the vendor has power to convey the fee simple in the land, or, in the case of a mortgage of a term of years absolute, the leasehold reversion affected by the mortgage, the contract shall be deemed to extend to the fee simple in the land or such leasehold reversion;

(ii) is an equitable interest capable of subsisting as a legal estate, and the vendor has power to vest such legal estate in himself or in the purchaser or to require the same to be so vested, the contract shall be deemed to extend to such legal estate;

(iii) is an entailed interest in possession and the vendor has power to vest in himself or in the purchaser the fee simple in the land, (or, if the entailed interest is an interest in a term of years absolute, such term) or to require the same to be so vested, the contract shall be deemed to extend to the fee simple in the land or the term of years absolute.

(5) This section does not affect the right of a mortgagee of leasehold land to sell his mortgage term only if he is unable to convey or vest the leasehold reversion expectant thereon.

(6) Any contract to convey an undivided share in land made before or after the commencement of this Act, shall be deemed to be sufficiently complied with by the conveyance of a corresponding share in the proceeds of sale of the land in like manner as if the contract had been to convey that corresponding share.

(7) Where a purchaser has power to acquire land compulsorily, and a contract, whether by virtue of a notice to treat or otherwise, is subsisting under which title can be made without payment of the compensation money into court, title shall be made in that way unless the purchaser, to avoid expense or delay or for any special reason, considers it expedient that the money should be paid into court.

(8) A vendor shall not have any power to rescind a contract by reason only of the enforcement of any right under this section.

(9) This section only applies in favour of a purchaser for money or money's worth.

Rights protected by registration

43.—(1) Where a purchaser of a legal estate is entitled to acquire the same discharged from an equitable interest which is protected by registration as a pending action, annuity, writ, order, deed of arrangement or land charge, and which will not be over-reached by the conveyance to him, he may notwithstanding any stipulation to the contrary, require—

(*a*) that the registration shall be cancelled; or

(*b*) that the person entitled to the equitable interest shall concur in the conveyance;

and in either case free of expense to the purchaser.

(2) Where the registration cannot be cancelled or the person entitled to the equitable interest refuses to concur in the conveyance, this section does not affect the right of any person to rescind the contract.

Statutory commencement of title

44.—(1) After the commencement of this Act thirty years shall be substituted for forty years as the period of commencement of title which a purchaser of land may require; nevertheless earlier title than thirty years may be required in cases similar to those in which earlier title than forty years might immediately before the commencement of this Act be required.[30]

(2) Under a contract to grant or assign a term of years, whether derived or to be derived out of freehold or leasehold land, the intended lessee or assign shall not be entitled to call for the title to the freehold.

(3) Under a contract to sell and assign a term of years derived out of a leasehold interest in land, the intended assign shall not have the right to call for the title to the leasehold reversion.

(4) On a contract to grant a lease for a term of years to be derived out of a leasehold interest, with a leasehold reversion, the intended lessee shall not have the right to call for the title to that reversion.

(5) Where by reason of any of the three last preceding subsections, an intending lessee or assign is not entitled to call for the title to the freehold or to a leasehold reversion, as the case may be, he shall not, where the contract is made after the commencement of this Act, be deemed to be affected with notice of any matter or thing of which, if he had contracted that such title should be furnished, he might have had notice.

(6) Where land of copyhold or customary tenure has been converted into freehold by enfranchisement, then, under a contract to sell and convey the freehold, the purchaser shall not have the right to call for the title to make the enfranchisement.

(7) Where the manorial incidents formerly affecting any land have been extinguished, then, under a contract to sell and convey the freehold, the purchaser shall not have the right to call for the title of the person entering into any compensation agreement or giving a receipt for the compensation money to enter into such agreement or to give such receipt, and shall not be deemed to be affected with notice of any matter or thing of which, if he had contracted that such title should be furnished, he might have had notice.

(8) A purchaser shall not be deemed to be or ever to have been affected with notice of any matter or thing of which, if he had investigated the title or made enquiries in regard to matters prior to the period of commencement of title fixed by this Act, or by any other statute, or by any rule of law, he might have had notice, unless he actually makes such investigation or enquiries.

[30] This section shall have effect, in its application to contracts made after January 1, 1970, as if it specified fifteen years instead of thirty years as the period of commencement of title which may be required. See the Law of Property Act 1969, s.23, *post*, p. 314.

(9) Where a lease whether made before or after the commencement of this Act, is made under a power contained in a settlement, will, Act of Parliament, or other instrument, any preliminary contract for or relating to the lease shall not, for the purpose of the deduction of title to an intended assign, form part of the title, or evidence of the title, to the lease.

(10) This section, save where otherwise expressly provided, applies to contracts for sale whether made before or after the commencement of this Act, and applies to contracts for exchange in like manner as to contracts for sale, save that it applies only to contracts for exchange made after such commencement.

(11) This section applies only if and so far as a contrary intention is not expressed in the contract.

Other statutory conditions of sale

45.—(1) A purchaser of any property shall not—

> (*a*) require the production, or any abstract or copy, of any deed, will, or other document, dated or made before the time prescribed by law, or stipulated, for the commencement of the title, even though the same creates a power subsequently exercised by an instrument abstracted in the abstract furnished to the purchaser; or
>
> (*b*) require any information, or make any requisition, objection, or inquiry, with respect to any such deed, will, or document, or the title prior to that time, notwithstanding that any such deed, will, or other document, or that prior title, is recited, agreed to be produced, or noticed;

and he shall assume, unless the contrary appears, that the recitals, contained in the abstracted instruments, of any deed, will, or other document, forming part of that prior title, are correct, and give all the material contents of the deed, will, or other document so recited, and that every document so recited was duly executed by all necessary parties, and perfected, if and as required, by fine, recovery, acknowledgment, inrolment, or otherwise:

Provided that this subsection shall not deprive a purchaser of the right to require the production, or an abstract or copy of—

> (i) any power of attorney under which any abstracted document is executed; or
>
> (ii) any document creating or disposing of an interest, power or obligation which is not shown to have ceased or expired, and subject to which any part of the property is disposed of by an abstracted document; or
>
> (iii) any document creating any limitation or trust by reference to which any part of the property is disposed of by an abstracted document.

(2) Where land sold is held by lease (other than an under-lease), the purchaser shall assume, unless the contrary appears, that the lease was duly granted; and, on production of the receipt for the last payment due for rent under the lease before the date of actual completion of the purchase, he shall assume, unless the contrary appears, that all the covenants and provisions of the lease have been duly performed and observed up to the date of actual completion of the purchase.

(3) Where land sold is held by under-lease, the purchaser shall assume, unless the contrary appears, that the under-lease and every superior lease were duly granted; and, on production of the receipt for the last payment due for rent under the under-lease before the date of actual completion of the purchase, he shall assume, unless the contrary appears, that all the covenants and provisions of the under-lease have been duly performed and observed up to the date of actual completion of the purchase, and further

that all rent due under every superior lease, and all the covenants and provisions of every superior lease, have been paid and duly performed and observed up to that date.

(4) On a sale of any property, the following expenses shall be borne by the purchaser where he requires them to be incurred for the purpose of verifying the abstract or any other purpose, that is to say—

(*a*) the expenses of the production and inspection of all Acts of Parliament, inclosure awards, records, proceedings of courts, court rolls, deeds, wills, probates, letters of administration, and other documents, not in the possession of the vendor or his mortgagee or trustee, and the expenses of all journeys incidental to such production or inspection; and

(*b*) the expenses of searching for, procuring, making, verifying, and producing all certificates, declarations, evidences, and information not in the possession of the vendor or his mortgagee or trustee, and all attested, stamped, office, or other copies or abstracts of, or extracts from, any Acts of Parliament or other documents aforesaid, not in the possession of the vendor or his mortgagee or trustee;

and where the vendor or his mortgagee or trustee retains possession of any document, the expenses of making any copy thereof, attested or unattested, which a purchaser requires to be delivered to him, shall be borne by that purchaser.

(5) On a sale of any property in lots, a purchaser of two or more lots, held wholly or partly under the same title, shall not have a right to more than one abstract of the common title, except at his own expense.

(6)[31] Recitals, statements, and descriptions of facts, matters, and parties contained in deeds, instruments, Acts of Parliament, or statutory declarations, twenty years old at the date of the contract, shall, unless and except so far as they may be proved to be inaccurate, be taken to be sufficient evidence of the truth of such facts, matters, and descriptions.

(7) The inability of a vendor to furnish a purchaser with an acknowledgment of his right to production and delivery of copies of documents of title or with a legal covenant to produce and furnish copies of documents of title shall not be an objection to title in case the purchaser will, on the completion of the contract, have an equitable right to the production of such documents.

(8) Such acknowledgments of the right of production or covenants for production and such undertakings or covenants for safe custody of documents as the purchaser can and does require shall be furnished or made at his expense, and the vendor shall bear the expense of perusal and execution on behalf of and by himself, and on behalf of and by necessary parties other than the purchaser.

(9) A vendor shall be entitled to retain documents of title where—

(*a*) he retains any part of the land to which the documents relate; or

(*b*) the document consists of a trust instrument or other instrument creating a trust which is still subsisting, or an instrument relating to the appointment or discharge of a trustee of a subsisting trust.

(10) This section applies to contracts for sale made before or after the commencement of this Act, and applies to contracts for exchange in like manner as to contracts for sale, except that it applies only to contracts for exchange made after such commencement:

Provided that this section shall apply subject to any stipulation or contrary intention expressed in the contract.

(11) Nothing in this section shall be construed as binding a purchaser to

---

[31] Extended by the Welsh Church (Burial Grounds) Act 1945 (8 & 9 Geo. 6, c. 27), s.1(4) (*b*).

complete his purchase in any case where, on a contract made independently of this section, and containing stipulations similar to the provisions of this section, or any of them, specific performance of the contract would not be enforced against him by the court.

Forms of contracts and conditions of sale

46.[32]   The Lord Chancellor may from time to time prescribe and publish forms of contracts and conditions of sale of land, and the forms so prescribed shall, subject to any modification, or any stipulation or intention to the contrary, expressed in the correspondence, apply to contracts by correspondence, and may, but only by express reference thereto, be made to apply to any other cases for which the forms are made available.

Application of insurance money on completion of a sale or exchange

47.—(1) Where after the date of any contract for sale or exchange of property, money becomes payable under any policy of insurance maintained by the vendor in respect of any damage to or destruction of property included in the contract, the money shall, on completion of the contract, be held or receivable by the vendor on behalf of the purchaser and paid by the vendor to the purchaser on completion of the sale or exchange, or so soon thereafter as the same shall be received by the vendor.

(2) This section applies only to contracts made after the commencement of this Act, and has effect subject to—

(*a*) any stipulation to the contrary contained in the contract,

(*b*) any requisite consents of the insurers,

(*c*) the payment by the purchaser of the proportionate part of the premium from the date of the contract.

(3) This section applies to a sale or exchange by an order of the court, as if—

(*a*) for references to the "vendor" there were substituted references to the "person bound by the order";

(*b*) for the reference to the completion of the contract there were substituted a reference to the payment of the purchase or equality money (if any) into court;

(*c*) for the reference to the date of the contract there were substituted a reference to the time when the contract becomes binding.

Stipulations preventing a purchaser, lessee or underlessee from employing his own solicitor to be void

48.—(1) Any stipulation made on the sale of any interest in land after the commencement of this Act to the effect that the conveyance to, or the registration of the title of, the purchaser shall be prepared or carried out at the expense of the purchaser by a solicitor appointed by or acting for the vendor, and any stipulation which migh restrict a purchaser in the selection of a solicitor to act on his behalf in relation to any interest in land agreed to be purchased, shall be void; and, if a sale is effected by demise or subdemise, then, for the purposes of this subsection, the instrument required for giving effect to the transaction shall be deemed to be a conveyance:

Provided that nothing in this subsection shall affect any right reserved to a vendor to furnish a form of conveyance to a purchaser from which the draft can be prepared, or to charge a reasonable fee therefor, or, where a perpetual rentcharge is to be reserved as the only consideration in money or money's worth, the right of a vendor to stipulate that the draft

[32] Restricted by the Leasehold Reform Act 1967 (c.88), s.22(4).

conveyance is to be prepared by his solicitor at the expense of the purchaser.

(2) Any covenant or stipulation contained in, or entered into with reference to any lease or underlease made before or after the commencement of this Act—

(*a*) whereby the right of preparing, at the expense of a purchaser, any conveyance of the estate or interest of the lessee or underlessee in the demised premises or in any part thereof, or of otherwise carrying out, at the expense of the purchaser, any dealing with such estate or interest, is expressed to be reserved to or vested in the lessor or underlessor or his solicitor; or

(*b*) which in any way restricts the right of the purchaser to have such conveyance carried out on his behalf by a solicitor appointed by him;

shall be void:

Provided that, where any covenant or stipulation is rendered void by this subsection, there shall be implied in lieu thereof a covenant or stipulation that the lessee or underlessee shall register with the lessor or his solicitor within six months from the date thereof, or as soon after the expiration of that period as may be practicable, all conveyances and devolutions (including probates or letters of administration) affecting the lease or underlease and pay a fee of one guinea in respect of each registration, and the power of entry (if any) on breach of any covenant contained in the lease or underlease shall apply and extend to the breach of any covenant so to be implied.

(3) Save where a sale is effected by demise or subdemise, this section does not affect the law relating to the preparation of a lease or underlease or the draft thereof.

(4) In this section "lease" and "underlease" include any agreement therefor or other tenancy, and "lessee" and "underlessee" and "lessor" and "underlessor" have corresponding meanings.

Applications to the court by vendor and purchaser

49.[33]—(1) A vendor or purchaser of any interest in land, or their representatives respectively, may apply in a summary way to the court, in respect of any requisitions or objections, or any claim for compensation, or any other question arising out of or connected with the contract (not being a question affecting the existence or validity of the contract), and the court may make such order upon the application as to the court may appear just, and may order how and by whom all or any of the costs of and incident to the application are to be bo ne and paid.

(2) Where the court refuse s to grant specific performance of a contract, or in any action for the return o a deposit, the court may, if it thinks fit, order the repayment of any deposit.

(3) This section applies to a contract for the sale or exchange of any interest in land.

Discharge of incumbrances by the court on sales or exchanges

50.—(1) Where land subject to any incumbrance, whether immediately realisable or payable or not, is sold or exchanged by the court, or out of court, the court may, if it thinks fit, on the application of any party to the

---

[33] The county court has jurisdiction in a case in which the land to be dealt with does not exceed in capital value £5,000 or in net annual value for rating £300: County Courts Act 1959 (7 & 8 Eliz. 2, c. 22), Sched. 1, as amended by the Administration of Justice Act 1969 (c. 58), s.5).

This section is applied by the Leasehold Reform Act 1967 (c. 88), s.22(4).

sale or exchange, direct or allow payment into court of such sum as is hereinafter mentioned, that is to say—

(*a*) in the case of an annual sum charged on the land, or of a capital sum charged on a determinable interest in the land, the sum to be paid into court shall be of such amount as, when invested in Government securities, the court considers will be sufficient, by means of the dividends thereof, to keep down or otherwise provide for that charge; and

(*b*) in any other case of capital money charged on the land, the sum to be paid into court shall be of an amount sufficient to meet the incumbrance and any interest due thereon;

but in either case there shall also be paid into court such additional amount as the court considers will be sufficient to meet the contingency of further costs, expenses and interest, and any other contingency, except depreciation of investments, not exceeding one-tenth part of the original amount to be paid in, unless the court for special reason thinks fit to require a larger additional amount.

(2) Thereupon, the court may, if it thinks fit, and either after or without any notice to the incumbrancer, as the court thinks fit, declare the land to be freed from the incumbrance, and make any order for conveyance, or vesting order, proper for giving effect to the sale or exchange, and give directions for the retention and investment of the money in court and for the payment or application of the income thereof.

(3) The court may declare all other land, if any, affected by the incumbrance (besides the land sold or exchanged) to be freed from the incumbrance, and this power may be exercised either after or without notice to the incumbrancer, and notwithstanding that on a previous occasion an order, relating to the same incumbrance, has been made by the court which was confined to the land then sold or exchanged.

(4) On any application under this section the court may, if it thinks fit, as respects any vendor or purchaser, dispense with the service of any notice which would otherwise be required to be served on the vendor or purchaser.

(5) After notice served on the persons interested in or entitled to the money or fund in court, the court may direct payment or transfer thereof to the persons entitled to receive or give a discharge for the same, and generally may give directions respecting the application or distribution of the capital or income thereof.

(6) This section applies to sales or exchanges whether made before or after the commencement of this Act, and to incumbrances whether created by statute or otherwise.

Conveyances and other Instruments

Lands lie in grant only

51.—(1) All lands and all interests therein lie in grant and are incapable of being conveyed by livery or livery and seisin, or by feoffment, or by bargain and sale; and a conveyance of an interest in land may operate to pass the possession or right to possession thereof, without actual entry, but subject to all prior rights thereto.

(2) The use of the word grant is not necessary to convey land or to create any interest therein.

Conveyances to be by deed

52.—(1) All conveyances of land or of any interest therein are void for the purpose of conveying or creating a legal estate unless made by deed.

(2) This section does not apply to—
- (*a*) assents by a personal representative;
- (*b*) disclaimers made in accordance with section fifty-four of the Bankruptcy Act 1914, or not required to be evidenced in writing;
- (*c*) surrenders by operation of law, including surrenders which may, by law, be effected without writing;
- (*d*) leases or tenancies or other assurances not required by law to be made in writing;
- (*e*) receipts not required by law to be under seal;
- (*f*) vesting orders of the court or other competent authority;
- (*g*) conveyances taking effect by operation of law.

Instruments required to be in writing

53.—(1) Subject to the provisions hereinafter contained with respect to the creation of interests in land by parol—
- (*a*) no interest in land can be created or disposed of except by writing signed by the person creating or conveying the same, or by his agent thereunto lawfully authorised in writing, or by will, or by operation of law;
- (*b*) a declaration of trust respecting any land or any interest therein must be manifested and proved by some writing signed by some person who is able to declare such trust or by his will;
- (*c*) a disposition of an equitable interest or trust subsisting at the time of the disposition, must be in writing signed by the person disposing of the same, or by his agent thereunto lawfully authorised in writing or by will.

(2) This section does not affect the creation or operation of resulting, implied or constructive trusts.

Creation of interests in land by parol

54.—(1) All interests in land created by parol and not put in writing and signed by the persons so creating the same, or by their agents thereunto lawfully authorised in writing, have, notwithstanding any consideration having been given for the same, the force and effect of interests at will only.

(2) Nothing in the foregoing provisions of this Part of this Act shall affect the creation by parol of leases taking effect in possession for a term not exceeding three years (whether or not the lessee is given power to extend the term) at the best rent which can be reasonably obtained without taking a fine.

Savings in regard to last two sections

55. Nothing in the last two foregoing sections shall—
- (*a*) invalidate dispositions by will; or
- (*b*) affect any interest validly created before the commencement of this Act; or
- (*c*) affect the right to acquire an interest in land by virtue of taking possession; or
- (*d*) affect the operation of the law relating to part performance.

Persons taking who are not parties and as to indentures

56.—(1) A person may take an immediate or other interest in land or other property, or the benefit of any condition, right of entry, covenant or agreement over or respecting land or other property, although he may not be named as a party to the conveyance or other instrument.

(2) A deed between parties, to effect its objects, has the effect of an indenture though not indented or expressed to be an indenture.

Description of deeds

57. Any deed, whether or not being an indenture, may be described (at the commencement thereof or otherwise) as a deed simply, or as a conveyance, deed of exchange, vesting deed, trust instrument, settlement, mortgage, charge, transfer of mortgage, appointment, lease or otherwise according to the nature of the transaction intended to be effected.

Provisions as to supplemental instruments

58. Any instrument (whether executed before or after the commencement of this Act) expressed to be supplemental to a previous instrument, shall, as far as may be, be read and have effect as if the supplemental instrument contained a full recital of the previous instrument, but this section does not operate to give any right to an abstract or production of any such previous instrument, and a purchaser may accept the same evidence that the previous instrument does not affect the title as if it had merely been mentioned in the supplemental instrument.

Conditions and certain covenants not implied

59.—(1) An exchange or other conveyance of land made by deed after the first day of October, eighteen hundred and forty-five, does not imply any condition in law.

(2) The word "give" or "grant" does not, in a deed made after the date last aforesaid, imply any covenant in law, save where otherwise provided by statute.

Abolition of technicalities in regard to conveyances and deeds

60.—(1) A conveyance of freehold land to any person without words of limitation, or any equivalent expression, shall pass to the grantee the fee simple or other the whole interest which the grantor had power to convey in such land, unless a contrary intention appears in the conveyance.

(2) A conveyance of freehold land to a corporation sole by his corporate designation without the word "successors" shall pass to the corporation the fee simple or other the whole interest which the grantor had power to convey in such land, unless a contrary intention appears in the conveyance.

(3) In a voluntary conveyance a resulting trust for the grantor shall not be implied merely by reason that the property is not expressed to be conveyed for the use or benefit of the grantee.

(4) The foregoing provisions of this section apply only to conveyances and deeds executed after the commencement of this Act:

Provided that in a deed executed after the thirty-first day of December, eighteen hundred and eighty-one, it is sufficient—

    (*a*) In the limitation of an estate in fee simple, to use the words "in fee simple," without the word "heirs";

    (*b*) In the limitation of an estate tail, to use the words "in tail" without the words "heirs of the body"; and

    (*c*) In the limitation of an estate in tail male or in tail female, to use the words "in tail male" or "in tail female," as the case requires, without the words "heirs male of the body," or "heirs female of the body."

Construction of expressions used in deeds and other instruments

61. In all deeds, contracts, wills, orders and other instruments executed, made or coming into operation after the commencement of this Act, unless the context otherwise requires—

(*a*) "Month" means calendar month;
(*b*) "Person" includes a corporation;
(*c*) The singular includes the plural and vice versâ;
(*d*) The masculine includes the feminine and vice versâ.

General words implied in conveyances

62.[34]—(1) A conveyance of land shall be deemed to include and shall by virtue of this Act operate to convey, with the land, all buildings, erections, fixtures, commons, hedges, ditches, fences, ways, waters, watercourses, liberties, privileges, easements, rights, and advantages whatsoever, appertaining or reputed to appertain to the land or any part thereof, or, at the time of conveyance, demised, occupied, or enjoyed with, or reputed or known as part or parcel of or appurtenant to the land or any part thereof.

(2) A conveyance of land, having houses or other buildings thereon, shall be deemed to include and shall by virtue of this Act operate to convey, with the land, houses, or other buildings, all outhouses, erections, fixtures, cellars, areas, courts, courtyards, cisterns, sewers, gutters, drains, ways, passages, lights, watercourses, liberties, privileges, easements, rights, and advantages whatsoever, appertaining or reputed to appertain to the land, houses, or other buildings conveyed, or any of them, or any part thereof, or, at the time of conveyance, demised, occupied, or enjoyed with, or reputed or known as part or parcel of or appurtenant to, the land, houses, or other buildings conveyed, or any of them, or any part thereof.

(3) A conveyance of a manor shall be deemed to include and shall by virtue of this Act operate to convey, with the manor, all pastures, feedings, wastes, warrens, commons, mines, minerals, quarries, furzes, trees, woods, underwoods, coppices, and the ground and soil thereof, fishings, fisheries, fowlings, courts leet, courts baron, and other courts, view of frankpledge and all that to view of frankpledge doth belong, mills, mulctures, customs, tolls, duties, reliefs, heriots, fines, sums of money, amerciaments, waifs, estrays, chief-rents, quitrents, rentscharge, rents seck, rents of assize, fee farm rents, services, royalties jurisdictions, franchises, liberties, privileges, easements, profits, advantages, rights, emoluments, and hereditaments whatsoever, to the manor appertaining or reputed to appertain, or, at the time of conveyance, demised, occupied, or enjoyed with the same, or reputed or known as part, parcel, or member thereof.

For the purposes of this subsection the right to compensation for manorial incidents on the extinguishment thereof shall be deemed to be a right appertaining to the manor.

(4) This section applies only if and as far as a contrary intention is not expressed in the conveyance, and has effect subject to the terms of the conveyance and to the provisions therein contained.

(5) This section shall not be construed as giving to any person a better title to any property, right, or thing in this section mentioned than the title which the conveyance gives to him to the land or manor expressed to be conveyed, or as conveying to him any property, right, or thing in this section mentioned, further or otherwise than as the same could have been conveyed to him by the conveying parties.

---

[34] Applied by the Land Registration Act 1925 (15 & 16 Geo. 5, c. 21), ss. 19 (3), 22 (3), *post,* pp. 362, 364. Saved in relation to s.8 of the Leasehold Reform Act 1967 (c. 88) by s.10(1) of that Act.

(6) This section applies to conveyances made after the thirty-first day of December, eighteen hundred and eighty-one.

All estate clause implied

63.[35]—(1) Every conveyance is effectual to pass all the estate, right, title, interest, claim, and demand which the conveying parties respectively have, in, to, or on the property conveyed, or expressed or intended so to be, or which they respectively have power to convey in, to, or on the same.

(2) This section applies only if and as far as a contrary intention is not expressed in the conveyance, and has effect subject to the terms of the conveyance and to the provisions therein contained.

(3) This section applies to conveyances made after the thirty-first day of December, eighteen hundred and eighty-one.

Production and safe custody of documents

64.[36]—(1) Where a person retains possession of documents, and gives to another an acknowledgment in writing of the right of that order to production of those documents, and to delivery of copies thereof (in this section called an acknowledgment), that acknowledgment shall have effect as in this section provided.

(2) An acknowledgment shall bind the documents to which it relates in the possession or under the control of the person who retains them, and in the possession or under the control of every other person having possession or control thereof from time to time, but shall bind each individual possessor or person as long only as he has possession or control thereof; and every person so having possession or control from time to time shall be bound specifically to peform the obligations imposed under this section by an acknowledgment, unless prevented from so doing by fire or other inevitable accident.

(3) The obligations imposed under this section by an acknowledgment are to be performed from time to time at the request in writing of the person to whom an acknowledgment is given, or of any person, not being a lessee at a rent, having or claiming any estate, interest, or right through or under that person, or otherwise becoming through or under that person interested in or affected by the terms of any document to which the acknowledgment relates.

(4) The obligations imposed under this section by an acknowledgment are—

   (i) An obligation to produce the documents or any of them at all reasonable times for the purpose of inspection, and of comparison with abstracts or copies thereof, by the person entitled to request production or by any person by him authorised in writing; and

   (ii) An obligation to produce the documents or any of them at any trial, hearing, or examination in any court, or in the execution of any commission, or elsewhere in the United Kingdom, on any occasion on which production may properly be required, for proving or supporting the title or claim of the person entitled to request

---

[35] Saved in relation to s.8 of the Leasehold Reform Act 1967 (c. 88) by s.10(1) of that Act: see note 34 to s.62, *supra.*

[36] Extended by the Coal Act 1938 (1 & 2 Geo. 6, c. 52), s.14(3); the New Towns Act 1965 (c. 59), s.16(1), Sched. 7, para. 13; the Transport Act 1968 (c. 73), Sched. 4, para. 3; the (L.T.E.) Transport (London) Act 1969 (c. 35), s.16(3), Sched. 2, para. 14, and the Airports Authority Act 1975 (c. 78), s.1(6), Sched. 4, para. 1. Applied by the Land Commission Act 1967 (c. 1), Sched 3, para. 19; the Leasehold Reform Act 1967 (c. 88), s.10(6); the Land Commission (Dissolution) Act 1971 (c. 18), Sched. 2, para. 18, and the Civil Aviation Act 1971 (c. 75), Sched. 2, para. 10 (3).

production, or for any other purpose relative to that title or claim; and

(iii) An obligation to deliver to the person entitled to request the same true copies or extracts, attested or unattested, of or from the documents or any of them.

(5) All costs and expenses of or incidental to the specific performance of any obligation imposed under this section by an acknowledgment shall be paid by the person requesting performance.

(6) An acknowledgment shall not confer any right to damages for loss or destruction of, or injury to, the documents to which it relates, from whatever cause arising.

(7) Any person claiming to be entitled to the benefit of an acknowledgment may apply to the court for an order directing the production of the documents to which it relates, or any of them, or the delivery of copies of or extracts from those documents or any of them to him, or some person on his behalf; and the court may, if it thinks fit, order production, or production and delivery, accordingly, and may give directions respecting the time, place, terms, and mode of production or delivery, and may make such order as it thinks fit respecting the costs of the application, or any other matter connected with the application.

(8) An acknowledgment shall by virtue of this Act satisfy any liability to give a covenant for production and delivery of copies of or extracts from documents.

(9) Where a person retains possession of documents and gives to another an undertaking in writing for safe custody thereof, that undertaking shall impose on the person giving it, and on every person having possession or control of the documents from time to time, but on each individual possessor or person as long only as he has possession or control thereof, an obligation to keep the documents safe, whole, uncancelled, and undefaced, unless prevented from so doing by fire or other inevitable accident.

(10) Any person claiming to be entitled to the benefit of such an undertaking may apply to the court to assess damages for any loss or destruction of, or injury to, the documents or any of them, and the court may, if it thinks fit, direct an inquiry respecting the amount of damages, and order payment thereof by the person liable, and may make such order as it thinks fit respecting the costs of the application, or any other matter connected with the application.

(11) An undertaking for safe custody of documents shall by virtue of this Act satisfy any liability to give a covenant for safe custody of documents.

(12) The rights conferred by an acknowledgment or an undertaking under this section shall be in addition to all such other rights relative to the production, or inspection, or the obtaining of copies of documents, as are not, by virtue of this Act, satisfied by the giving of the acknowledgment or undertaking, and shall have effect subject to the terms of the acknowledgment or undertaking, and to any provisions therein contained.

(13) This section applies only if and as far as a contrary intention is not expressed in the acknowledgment or undertaking.

(14) This section applies to an acknowledgment or undertaking given, or a liability respecting documents incurred, after the thirty-first day of December, eighteen hundred and eighty-one.

Reservation of legal estates

65.—(1) A reservation of a legal estate shall operate at law without any execution of the conveyance by the grantee of the legal estate out of which the reservation is made, or any regrant by him, so as to create the legal estate reserved, and so as to vest the same in possession in the person (whether being the grantor or not) for whose benefit the reservation is made.

(2) A conveyance of a legal estate expressed to be made subject to another legal estate not in existence immediately before the date of the conveyance, shall operate as a reservation, unless a contrary intention appears.

(3) This section applies only to reservations made after the commencement of this Act.

Confirmation of past transactions

66.[37]—(1) A deed containing a declaration by the estate owner that his estate shall go and devolve in such a manner as may be requisite for confirming any interests intended to affect his estate and capable under this Act of subsisting as legal estates which, at some prior date, were expressed to have been transferred or created, and any dealings therewith which would have been legal if those interests had been legally and validly transferred or created, shall, to the extent of the estate of the estate owner, but without prejudice to the restrictions imposed by this Act in the case of mortgages, operate to give legal effect to the interests so expressed to have been transferred or created and to the subsequent dealings aforesaid.

(2) The powers conferred by this section may be exercised by a tenant for life or statutory owner, trustee for sale or a personal representative (being in each case an estate owner) as well as by an absolute owner, but if exercised by any person, other than an absolute owner, only with the leave of the court.

(3) This section applies only to deeds containing such a declaration as aforesaid if executed after the commencement of this Act.

Receipt in deed sufficient

67.—(1) A receipt for consideration money or securities in the body of a deed shall be a sufficient discharge for the same to the person paying or delivering the same, without any further receipt for the same being indorsed on the deed.

(2) This section applies to deeds executed after the thirty-first day of December, eighteen hundred and eighty-one.

Receipt in deed or indorsed evidence

68.—(1) A receipt for consideration money or other consideration in the body of a deed or indorsed thereon shall, in favour of a subsequent purchaser, not having notice that the money or other consideration thereby acknowledged to be received was not in fact paid or given, wholly or in part, be sufficient evidence of the payment or giving of the whole amount thereof.

(2) This section applies to deeds executed after the thirty-first day of December, eighteen hundred and eighty-one.

Receipt in deed or indorsed authority for payment to solicitor

69.—(1) Where a solicitor produces a deed, having in the body thereof or indorsed thereon a receipt for consideration money or other consideration, the deed being executed, or the indorsed receipt being signed, by the person entitled to give a receipt for that consideration, the deed shall be a sufficient authority to the person liable to pay or give the same for his paying or giving the same to the solicitor, without the solicitor producing

[37] The county court has jurisdiction in a case where the land which is to be dealt with does not exceed in capital value £5,000 or in net annual value for rating £300: County Courts Act 1959 (7 & 8 Eliz. 2, c. 22), Sched. 1, as amended by the Administration of Justice Act 1969 (c. 58), s. 5.

any separate or other direction or authority in that behalf from the person who executed or signed the deed or receipt.

(2) This section applies whether the consideration was paid or given before or after the commencement of this Act.

Partial release of security from rentcharge

70.—(1) A release from a rentcharge of part of the land charged therewith does not extinguish the whole rentcharge, but operates only to bar the right to recover any part of the rentcharge out of the land released, without prejudice to the rights of any persons interested in the land remaining unreleased, and not concurring in or confirming the release.

(2) This section applies to releases made after the twelfth day of August, eighteen hundred and fifty-nine.

Release of part of land affected from a judgment

71.—(1) A release from a judgment (including any writ or order imposing a charge) of part of any land charged therewith does not effect the validity of the judgment as respects any land not specifically released.

(2) This section operates without prejudice to the rights of any persons interested in the property remaining unreleased and not concurring in or confirming the release.

(3) This section applies to releases made after the twelfth day of August, eighteen hundred and fifty-nine.

Conveyances by a person to himself, &c.

72.—(1) In conveyances made after the twelfth day of August, eighteen hundred and fifty-nine, personal property, including chattels real, may be conveyed by a person to himself jointly with another person by the like means by which it might be conveyed by him to another person.

(2) In conveyances made after the thirty-first day of December, eighteen hundred and eighty-one, freehold land, or a thing in action, may be conveyed by a person to himself jointly with another person, by the like means by which it might be conveyed by him to another person; and may, in like manner, be conveyed by a husband to his wife, and by a wife to her husband, alone or jointly with another person.

(3) After the commencement of this Act a person may convey land to or vest land in himself.

(4) Two or more persons (whether or not being trustees or personal representatives) may convey, and shall be deemed always to have been capable of conveying, any property vested in them to any one or more of themselves in like manner as they could have conveyed such property to a third party; provided that if the persons in whose favour the conveyance is made are, by reason of any fiduciary relationship or otherwise, precluded from validly carrying out the transaction, the conveyance shall be liable to be set aside.

Execution of deeds by an individual

73.—(1) Where an individual executes a deed, he shall either sign or place his mark upon the same and sealing alone shall not be deemed sufficient.

(2) This section applies only to deeds executed after the commencement of this Act.

Execution of instruments by or on behalf of corporations

74.—(1) In favour of a purchaser a deed shall be deemed to have been duly executed by a corporation aggregate if its seal be affixed thereto in the presence of and attested by its clerk, secretary or other permanent officer or his deputy, and a member of the board of directors, council or other governing body of the corporation, and where a seal purporting to be the seal of a corporation has been affixed to a deed, attested by persons purporting to be persons holding such offices as aforesaid, the deed shall be deemed to have been executed in accordance with the requirements of this section, and to have taken effect accordingly.

(2) The board of directors, council or other governing body of a corporation aggregate may, by resolution or otherwise, appoint an agent either generally or in any particular case, to execute on behalf of the corporation any agreement or other instrument not under seal in relation to any matter within the powers of the corporation.

(3)[38] Where a person is authorised under a power of attorney or under any statutory or other power to convey any interest in property in the name or on behalf of a corporation sole or aggregate, he may as attorney execute the conveyance by signing the name of the corporation in the presence of at least one witness, and in the case of a deed by affixing his own seal, and such execution shall take effect and be valid in like manner as if the corporation had executed the conveyance.

(4) Where a corporation aggregate is authorised under a power of attorney or under any statutory or other power to convey any interest in property in the name or on behalf of any other person (including another corporation), an officer appointed for that purpose by the board of directors, council or other governing body of the corporation by resolution or otherwise, may execute the deed or other instrument in the name of such other person; and where an instrument appears to executed by an officer so appointed, then in favour of a purchaser the instrument shall be deemed to have been executed by an officer duly authorised.

(5) The foregoing provisions of this section apply to transactions wherever. effected, but only to deeds and instruments executed after the commencement of this Act, except that, in the case of powers of appointments of an agent or officer, they apply whether the power was conferred or the appointment was made before or after the commencement of this Act or by this Act.

(6) Notwithstanding anything contained in this section, any mode of execution or attestation authorised by law or by practice or by the statute, charter, memorandum or articles, deed of settlement or other instrument constituting the corporation or regulating the affairs thereof, shall (in addition to the modes authorised by this section) be as effectual as if this section had not been passed.

Rights of purchaser as to execution

75.—(1) On a sale, the purchaser shall not be entitled to require that the conveyance to him be executed in his presence, or in that of his solicitor, as such; but shall be entitled to have, at his own cost, the execution of the conveyance attested by some person appointed by him, who may, if he thinks fit, be his solicitor.

(2) This section applies to sales made after the thirty-first day of December, eighteen hundred and eighty-one.

---

[38] An instrument to which either of these subsections applies may be executed either as provided thereby or as provided in the Powers of Attorney Act 1971 (c.27), s.7, whenever the power of attorney was created, but without prejudice to any statutory direction requiring an instrument to be executed in the name of an estate owner within the meaning of this Act: Powers of Attorney Act 1971 (c. 27), s.7(2)–(4).

Covenants

Covenants for title

76.—(1) In a conveyance there shall, in the several cases in this section mentioned, be deemed to be included, and there shall in those several cases, by virtue of this Act, be implied, a covenant to the effect in this section stated, by the person or by each person who conveys, as far as regards the subject matter or share of subject-matter expressed to be conveyed by him, with the person, if one, to whom the conveyance is made, or with the persons jointly, if more than one, to whom the conveyance is made as joint tenants, or with each of the persons, if more than one, to whom the conveyance is (when the law permits) made as tenants in common, that is to say:

(A) In a conveyance for valuable consideration, other than a mortgage, a covenant by a person who conveys and is expressed to convey as beneficial owner in the terms set out in Part I of the Second Schedule to this Act;

(B) In a conveyance of leasehold property for valuable consideration, other than a mortgage, a further covenant by a person who conveys and is expressed to convey as beneficial owner in the terms set out in Part II of the Second Schedule to this Act;

(c) In a conveyance by way of mortgage (including a charge) a covenant by a person who conveys or charges and is expressed to convey or charge as beneficial owner in the terms set out in Part III of the Second Schedule to this Act;

(D) In a conveyance by way of mortgage (including a charge) of freehold property subject to a rent or of leasehold property, a further covenant by a person who conveys or charges and is expressed to convey or charge as beneficial owner in the terms set out in Part IV of the Second Schedule to this Act;

(E) In a conveyance by way of settlement, a covenant by a person who conveys and is expressed to convey as settlor in the terms set out in Part V of the Second Schedule to this Act;

(F)[39] In any conveyance, a covenant by every person who conveys and is expressed to convey as trustee or mortgagee, or as personal representative of a deceased person, [. . .],[40] or under an order of the court, in the terms set out in Part VI of the Second Schedule to this Act, which covenant shall be deemed to extend to every such person's own acts only, and may be implied in an assent by a personal representative in like manner as in a coveyance by deed.

(2) Where in a conveyance it is expressed that by direction of a person expressed to direct as beneficial owner another person conveys, then, for the purposes of this section, the person giving the direction, whether he conveys and is expressed to convey as beneficial owner or not, shall be deemed to convey and to be expressed to convey as beneficial owner the subject-matter so conveyed by his direction; and a covenant on his part shall be implied accordingly.

(3) Where a wife conveys and is expressed to convey as beneficial owner, and the husband also conveys and is expressed to convey as beneficial owner, then, for the purposes of this section, the wife shall be deemed to convey and to be expressed to convey by direction of the husband, as beneficial owner; and, in addition to the covenant implied on the part of the husband as the person giving that direction, and secondly, a covenant

---

[39] Applied in relation to enfranchisement of leaseholds: see the Leasehold Reform Act 1967 (c. 88), s. 10(1).
[40] Words repealed by the Mental Heath Act 1959 (7 & 8 Eliz. 2, c. 72), Sched. 8, Pt. I.

on the part of the husband in the same terms as the covenant implied on the part of the wife.

(4) Where in a conveyance a person conveying is not expressed to convey as beneficial owner, or as settlor, or as trustee, or as mortgagee, or as personal representative of a deceased person, [. . .],[41] or under an order of the court, or by direction of a person as beneficial owner, no covenant on the part of the person conveying shall be, by virtue of this section, implied in the conveyance.

(5) In this section a conveyance does not include a demise by way of lease at a rent, but does include a charge and "convey" has a corresponding meaning.

(6) The benefit of a covenant implied as aforesaid shall be annexed and incident to, and shall go with, the estate or interest of the implied covenantee, and shall be capable of being enforced by every person in whom that estate or interest is, for the whole or any part thereof, from time to time vested.

(7) A covenant implied as aforesaid may be varied or extended by a deed or an assent, and, as so varied or extended, shall, as far as may be, operate in the like manner, and with all the like incidents, effects, and consequences, as if such variations or extensions were directed in this section to be implied.

(8) This section applies to conveyances made after the thirty-first day of December, eighteen hundred and eighty-one, but only to assents by a personal representative made after the commencement of this Act.

Implied covenants in conveyances subject to rents

77.—(1) In addition to the covenants implied under the last preceding section, there shall in the several cases in this section mentioned, be deemed to be included and implied, a covenant to the effect in this section stated, by and with such persons as are hereinafter mentioned, that is to say:—

(A) In a conveyance for valuable consideration, other than a mortgage, of the entirety of the land affected by a rentcharge, a covenant by the grantee or joint and several covenants by the grantees, if more than one, with the conveying parties and with each of them, if more than one in the terms set out in Part VII of the Second Schedule to this Act. Where a rentcharge has been apportioned in respect of any land, with the consent of the owner of the rentcharge, the covenants in this paragraph shall be implied in the conveyance of that land in like manner as if the apportioned rentcharge were the rentcharge referred to, and the document creating the rentcharge related solely to that land:

(B) In a conveyance for valuable consideration, other than a mortgage, of part of land affected by rentcharge, subject to a part of that rentcharge which has been or is by that conveyance apportioned (but in either case without the consent of the owner of the rentcharge) in respect of the land conveyed:—

(i) A covenant by the grantee of the land or joint and several covenants by the grantees, if more than one, with the conveying parties and with each of them, if more than one, in the terms set out in paragraph (i) of Part VIII of the Second Schedule to this Act;

(ii) A covenant by a person who conveys or is expressed to convey as beneficial owner, or joint and several covenants by the persons who so convey or are expressed to so convey, if at the date of the conveyance any part of the land affected by such

---

[41] Words repealed by *ibid.*

rentcharge is retained, with the grantees of the land and with each of them (if more than one) in the terms set out in paragraph (ii) of Part VIII of the Second Schedule to this Act:

(c) In a conveyance for valuable consideration, other than a mortgage, of the entirety of the land comprised in a lease, for the residue of the term or interest created by the lease, a covenant by the assignee or joint and several covenants by the assignees (if more than one) with the conveying parties and with each of them (if more than one) in the terms set out in Part IX of the Second Schedule to this Act. Where a rent has been apportioned in respect of any land, with the consent of the lessor, the covenants in this paragraph shall be implied in the conveyance of that land in like manner as if the apportioned rent were the original rent reserved, and the lease related solely to that land:

(D) In a conveyance for valuable consideration, other than a mortgage, of part of the land comprised in a lease, for the residue of the term or interest created by the lease, subject to a part of the rent which has been or is by the coveyance apportioned (but in either case without the consent of the lessor) in respect of the land conveyed:—

(i) A covenant by the assignee of the land, or joint and several covenants by the assignees, if more than one, with the coveying parties and with each of them, if more than one, in the terms set out in paragraph (i) of Part X of the Second Schedule to this Act;

(ii) A covenant by a person who conveys or is expressed to convey as beneficial owner, or joint and several covenants by the persons who so convey or are expressed to so convey, if at the date of the conveyance any part of the land comprised in the lease is retained, with the assignees of the land and with each of them (if more than one) in the terms set out in paragraph (ii) of Part X of the Second Schedule to this Act.

(2) Where in a conveyance for valuable consideration, other than a mortgage, part of land affected by a rentcharge, or part of land comprised in a lease is, without the consent of the owner of the rentcharge or of the lessor, as the case may be, expressed to be conveyed—

(i) subject to or charged with the entire rent—

then paragraph (B) (I) OR (D) (i) of the last subsection, as the case may require, shall have effect as if the entire rent were the apportioned rent; or

(ii) discharged or exonerated from the entire rent—

then paragraph (B) (ii) or (D) (ii) of the last subsection, as the case may require, shall have effect as if the entire rent were the balance of the rent, and the words "other than the covenant to pay the entire rent" had been omitted.

(3) In this section "conveyance" does not include a demise by way of lease at a rent.

(4) Any covenant which would be implied under this section by reason of a person conveying or being expressed to convey as beneficial owner may, by express reference to this section, be implied, with or without variation, in a conveyance, whether or not for valuable consideration, by a person who conveys or is expressed to convey as settlor, or as trustee, or as mortgagee, or as personal representative of a deceased person, [. . .][42] or under an order of the court.

(5) The benefit of a covenant implied as aforesaid shall be annexed and incident to, and shall go with, the estate or interest of the implied covenantee, and shall be capable of being enforced by every person in whom that estate or interest is, for the whole or any part thereof, from time to time vested.

[42] Words repealed by the Mental Heath Act 1959 (7 & 8 Eliz. 2, c. 72), Sched. 8, Pt. I.

(6) A covenant implied as aforesaid may be varied or extended by deed, and, as so varied or extended, shall, as far as may be, operate in the like manner, and with all the like incidents, effects and consequences, as if such variations or extensions were directed in this section to be implied.

(7) In particular any covenant implied under this section may be extended by providing that—

(*a*) the land conveyed; or

(*b*) the part of the land affected by the rentcharge which remains vested in the convenantor; or

(*c*) the part of the land demised which remains vested in the covenantor;

shall, as the case may require, stand charged with the payment of all money which may become payable under the implied covenant.

(8) This section applies only to conveyances made after the commencement of this Act.

Benefit of covenants relating to land

78.—(1) A covenant relating to any land of the covenantee shall be deemed to be made with the convenantee and his successors in title and the persons deriving title under him or them, and shall have effect as if such successors and other persons were expressed.

For the purposes of this subsection in connection with covenants restrictive of the user of land "successors in title" shall be deemed to include the owners and occupiers for the time being of the land of the covenantee intended to be benefited.

(2) This section applies to covenants made after the commencement of this Act, but the repeal of section fifty-eight of the Conveyancing Act 1881 does not affect the operation of covenants to which that section applied.

Burden of covenants relating to land

79.[43]—(1) A convenant relating to any land of a covenantor or capable of being bound by him, shall, unless a contrary intention is expressed, be deemed to be made by the covenantor on behalf of himself his successors in title and the persons deriving title under him or them, and, subject as aforesaid, shall have effect as if such successors and other persons were expressed.

This subsection extends to a covenant to do some act relating to the land, notwithstanding that the subject-matter may not be in existence when the covenant is made.

(2) For the purpose of this section in connection with covenants restrictive of the user of land "successors in title" shall be deemed to include the owners and occupiers for the time being of such land.

(3) This section applies only to covenants made after the commencement of this Act.

Covenants binding land

80.—(1) A covenant and a bond and an obligation or contract under seal made after the thirty-first day of December, eighteen hundred and eighty-one, binds the real estate as well as the personal estate of the person making the same if and so far as a contrary intention is not expressed in the covenant, bond, obligation, or contract.

This subsection extends to a covenant implied by virtue of this Act.

(2) Every covenant running with the land, whether entered into before

---

[43] Extended by the Coal Act 1938 (1 & 2 Geo. 6, c. 52), s. 19(3); applied by the Forestry Act 1967 (c. 10), s. 5(1)(*a*), and, modified, by the Countryside Act 1968 (c. 41), s. 15(4).

or after the commencement of this Act, shall take effect in accordance with any statutory enactment affecting the devolution of the land, and accordingly the benefit or burden of every such covenant shall vest in or bind the persons who by virtue of any such enactment or otherwise succeed to the title of the covenantee or the covenantor, as the case may be.

(3) The benefit of a covenant relating to land entered into after the commencement of this Act may be made to run with the land without the use of any technical expression if the covenant is of such a nature that the benefit could have been made to run with the land before the commencement of this Act.

(4) For the purposes of this section, a covenant runs with the land when the benefit or burden of it, whether at law or in equity, passes to the successors in title of the covenantee or the covenantor, as the case may be.

Effect of convenant with two or more jointly

81.—(1) A covenant, and a contract under seal, and a bond or obligation under seal, made with two or more jointly, to pay money or to make a conveyance, or to do any other act, to them or for their benefit, shall be deemed to include, and shall, by virtue of this Act, imply, an obligation to do the act to, or for the benefit of, the survivor or survivors of them, and to, or for the benefit of, any other person to whom the right to sue on the covenant, contract, bond, or obligation devolves, and where made after the commencement of this Act shall be construed as being also made with each of them.

(2) This section extends to a covenant implied by virtue of this Act.

(3) This section applies only if and as far as a contrary intention is not expressed in the covenant, contract, bond, or obligation, and has effect subject to the covenant, contract, bond, or obligation, and to the provisions therein contained.

(4) Except as otherwise expressly provided, this section applies to a covenant, contract, bond or obligation made or implied after the thirty-first day of December, eighteen hundred and eighty-one.

Covenants and agreements entered into by a person with himself and another or others

82.—(1) Any covenant, whether express or implied, or agreement entered into by a person with himself and one or more other persons shall be construed and be capable of being enforced in like manner as if the covenant or agreement had been entered into with the other person or persons alone.

(2) This section applies to covenants or agreements entered into before or after the commencement of this Act, and to covenants implied by statute in the case of a person who conveys or is expressed to convey to himself and one or more other persons, but without prejudice to any order of the court made before such commencement.

Construction of implied covenants

83. In the construction of a covenant or proviso, or other provision, implied in a deed or assent by virtue of this Act, words importing the singular or plural number, or the masculine gender, shall be read as also importing the plural or singular number, or as extending to females, as the case may require.

Power to discharge or modify restrictive covenants affecting land

84.[44]—(1)[45] [The Lands Tribunal][46] shall (without prejudice to any concurrent jurisdiction of the court) have power from time to time, on the application of any person interested in any freehold land affected by any restriction arising under covenant or otherwise as to the user thereof or the building thereon, by order wholly or partially to discharge or modify any such restriction [. . .][47] on being satisfied—

(a) that by reason of changes in the character of the property or the neighbourhood or other circumstances of the case which the [Lands Tribunal][48] may deem material, the restriction ought to be deemed obsolete; or

(aa) that [in a case falling within subsection (1A) below][49] the continued existence thereof would impede [some reasonable user][50] of the land for public or private purposes [. . .][51] or, as the case may be, would unless modified so impede such user; or

(b) that the persons of full age and capacity for the time being or from time to time entitled to the benefit of the restriction, whether in respect of estates in fee simple or any lesser estates or interests in the property to which the benefit of the restriction is annexed, have agreed, either expressly or by implication, by their acts or omissions, to the same being discharged or modified; or

(c) that the proposed discharge or modification will not injure the persons entitled to the benefit of the restriction:
[. . .][52]

[and an order discharging or modifying a restriction under this subsection may direct the applicant to pay to any person entitled to the benefit of the restriction such sum by way of consideration as the Tribunal may think it just to award under one, but not both, of the following heads, that is to say, either—

(i) a sum to make up for any loss or disadvantage suffered by that person in consequence of the discharge or modification; or

(ii) a sum to make up for any effect which the restriction had, at the time when it was imposed, in reducing the consideration then received for the land affected by it].[53]

[(1A) Subsection (1) (aa) above authorises the discharge or modification of a restriction by reference to its impeding some reasonable user of land in any case in which the Lands Tribunal is satisfied that the restriction, in impeding that user, either—

(a) does not secure to persons entitled to the benefit of it any practical benefits of substantial value or advantage to them; or

(b) is contrary to the public interest;

and that money will be an adequate compensation for loss or disadvantage (if any) which any such person will suffer from the discharge or modification.

---

[44] For the jurisdiction of the Lands Tribunal under this section, see the Lands Tribunal Act 1949 (12 & 13 Geo. 6, c. 42), s. 1(4)(a). See also the Lands Tribunal Rules 1975 (No. 299).
   This section is applied by the Landlord and Tenant (War Damage) Act 1939 (2 & 3 Geo. 6, c. 72), s. 18; and restricted by the Requisitioned Land and War Works Act 1945 (8 & 9 Geo. 6, c. 43), s. 38(3); the Land Commission Act 1967 (c. 1), s. 19(6); the Forestry Act 1967 (c. 10), s. 5(2)(b); the Leasehold Reform Act 1967 (c. 88), Sched. 4, para. 1 (5); and the Countryside Act 1968 (c. 41), s. 15(4).
[45] Applied by the Land Commission Act 1967 (c. 1), Sched. 4, para. 42 (d).
[46] Words substituted by the Law of Property Act 1969 (c. 59), s. 28.
[47] Words repealed by ibid.
[48] See above, note 46.
[49] Words added by ibid.
[50] See above, note 48.
[51] See above, note 47.
[52] Ibid.
[53] See above, n. 49.

(1B) In determining whether a case is one falling within subsection (1A) above, and in determining whether (in any such case or otherwise) a restriction ought to be discharged or modified, the Lands Tribunal shall take into account the development plan and any declared or ascertainable pattern for the grant or refusal of planning permission in the relevant areas, as well as the period at which the context in which the restriction was created or imposed and any other material circumstances.

(1C) It is hereby declared that the power conferred by this section to modify a restriction includes power to add such further provisions restricting the user of or the building on the land affected as appear to the Lands Tribunal to be reasonable in view of the relaxation of the existing provisions, and as may be accepted by the applicant; and the Lands Tribunal may accordingly refuse to modify a restriction without some such addition.][53]

(2) The court shall have power on the application of any person interested—

    (*a*) To declare whether or not in any particular case any freehold land is [or would in any given event be][53] affected by a restriction imposed by any instrument; or

    (*b*) to declare what, upon the true construction of any instrument purporting to impose a restriction, is the nature and extent of the restriction thereby imposed and whether the same is [or would in any given event be][53] enforceable and if so by whom.

[Neither subsections (7) and (11) of this section nor, unless the contrary is expressed, any later enactment providing for this section not to apply to any restrictions shall affect the operation of this subsection or the operation for the purposes of this subsection of any other provisions of this section.][53]

(3) The [Lands Tribunal][54] shall, before making any order under this section, direct such enquiries, if any, to be made of any [Government department or][54] local authority, and such notices, if any, whether by way of advertisement or otherwise, to be given to such of the persons who appear to be entitled to the benefit of the restriction intended to be discharged, modified, or dealt with as, having regard to any enquiries notices or other proceedings previously made, given or taken, the [Lands Tribunal][54] may think fit.

[(3A) On an application to the Lands Tribunal under this section the Lands Tribunal shall given any necessary directions as to the persons who are or are not to be admitted (as appearing to be entitled to the benefit of the restriction) to oppose the application, and no appeal shall lie against any such direction; but rules under the Lands Tribunal Act 1949 shall make provision whereby, in cases in which there arises on such application (whether or not in connection with the admission of persons to oppose) any such question as is referred to in subsection (2) (*a*) or (*b*) of this section, the proceedings on the application can and, if the rules so provide, shall be suspended to enable the decision of the court to be obtained on that question by an application under the subsection, or by means of a case stated by the Lands Tribunal, or otherwise, as may be provided by those rules or by the rules of court.][55]

(4) [*Repealed by the Lands Tribunal Act* 1949 (12 & 13 *Geo.* 6, *c.* 42), *Sched.* 2.]

(5) Any order made under this section shall be binding on all persons, whether ascertained or of full age or capacity or not, then entitled or thereafter capable of becoming entitled to the benefit of any restriction, which is thereby discharged, modified, or dealt with, and whether such

[54] Substituted by the Law of Property Act 1969 (c. 59), s.28.
[55] Added by the Law of Property Act 1969 (c. 59), s.28.

persons are parties to the proceedings or have been served with notice or not [. . .].[56]

(6) An order may be made under this section notwithstanding that any instrument which is alleged to impose the restriction intended to be discharged, modified, or dealt with, may not have been produced to the court or the [Lands Tribunal],[57] and the court or the [Lands Tribunal][57] may act on such evidence of that instrument as it may think sufficient.

(7) This section applies to restrictions whether subsisting at the commencement of this Act or imposed thereafter, but this section does not apply where the restriction was imposed on the occasion of a disposition made gratuitously or for a nominal consideration or public purposes.

(8) This section applies whether the land affected by the restrictions is registered or not, but, in the case of registered land, the Land Registrar shall give effect on the register to any order under this section [in accordance with the Land Registration Act 1925].[57]

(9) Where any proceedings by action or otherwise are taken to enforce a restrictive covenant, any person against whom the proceedings are taken, may in such proceedings apply to the court for an order giving leave to apply to the [Lands Tribunal][57] under this section, and staying the proceedings in the meantime.

(10) [*Words repealed by the Lands Tribunal Act* 1949 (12 & 13 *Geo.* 6, *c.* 42), *Sched.* 2.]

(11)[58] This section does not apply to restrictions imposed by the Commissioners of Works[59] under any statutory power for the protection of any Royal Park or Garden or to restrictions of a like character imposed upon the occasion of any enfranchisement effected before the commencement of this Act in any manor vested in His Majesty in right of the Crown or the Duchy of Lancaster, nor [subject to subsection (11A) below] to restrictions created or imposed—

(*a*) for Naval, Military or Air Force purposes,

(*b*) for civil aviation purposes under the powers of the Air Navigation Act 1920 [or of section 19 or 23 of the Civil Aviation Act 1949].

(11A) Subsection (11) of this section—

(*a*) shall exclude the application of this section to a restriction falling within subsection (11) (*a*), and not created or imposed in connection with the use of any land as an aerodrome, only so long as the restriction is enforceable by or on behalf of the Crown; and

(*b*) shall exclude the application of this section to a restriction falling within subsection (11) (*b*), or created or imposed in connection with the use of any land as an aerodrome, only so long as the restriction is enforceable by or on behalf of the Crown or any public or international authority.

(12) Where a term of more than [forty][60] years is created in land (whether before or after the commencement of this Act) this section shall after the expiration of [twenty-five][60] years of the term, apply to restrictions affecting such leasehold land in like manner as it would have applied had the land been freehold:

Provided that this subsection shall not apply to mining leases.

(13) [*This subsection was added by the Administration of Justice Act* 1932 (22 & 23 *Geo.* 5, *c.* 55), *s.*6, *which section was later repealed by the Lands Tribunal Act* 1949 (12 & 13 *Geo.* 6, *c.* 42), *Sched.* 2.]

[56] Words repealed by the Lands Tribunal Act 1949 (12 & 13 Geo. 6, c. 42), Sched. 2.
[57] See p. 161, n. 46.
[58] Saved from the operation of the Requisitioned Land and War Works Act 1945 (8 & 9 Geo. 6, c. 43), s. 38(3).
[59] Now Secretary of State for the Environment: the Secretary of State for the Environment Order 1970 (No. 1681).
[60] These words are substituted by the Landlord and Tenant Act 1954 (2 & 3 Eliz. 2, c. 56), s. s. 52(1).

PART III

MORTGAGES, RENTCHARGES, AND POWERS OF ATTORNEY[61]

Mortgages

Mode of mortgaging freeholds

85.—(1) A mortgage of an estate in fee simple shall only be capable of being effected at law either by a demise for a term of years absolute, subject to a provision for cesser on redemption, or by a charge by deed expressed to be by way of legal mortgage:

Provided that a first mortgagee shall have the same right to the possession of documents as if his security included the fee simple.

(2) Any purported conveyance of an estate in fee simple by way of mortgage made after the commencement of this Act shall (to the extent of the estate of the mortgagor) operate as a demise of the land to the mortgagee for a term of years absolute, without impeachment for waste, but subject to cesser on redemption, in manner following, namely:—

(*a*) A first or only mortgagee shall take a term of three thousand years from the date of the mortgage:

(*b*) A second or subsequent mortgagee shall take a term (commencing from the date of the mortgage) one day longer than the term vested in the first or other mortgagee whose security ranks immediately before that of such second or subsequent mortgagee:

and, in this subsection, any such purported conveyance as aforesaid includes an absolute conveyance with a deed of defeasance and any other assurance which, but for this subsection, would operate in effect to vest the fee simple in a mortgagee subject to redemption.

(3) This section applies whether or not the land is registered under the Land Registration Act 1925, or the mortgage is expressed to be made by way of trust for sale or otherwise.

(4) Without prejudice to the provisions of this Act respecting legal and equitable powers, every power to mortgage or to lend money on mortgage of an estate in fee simple shall be construed as a power to mortgage the estate for a term of years absolute, without impeachment for waste, or by a charge by way of legal mortgage or to lend on such security.

Mode of mortgaging leaseholds

86.—(1) A mortgage of a term of years absolute shall only be capable of being effected at law either by a subdemise for a term of years absolute, less by one day at least than the term vested in the mortgagor, and subject to a provision for cesser on redemption, or by a charge by deed expressed to be by way of legal mortgage; and where a licence to subdemise by way of mortgage is required, such licence shall not be unreasonably refused:

Provided that a first mortgagee shall have the same right to the possession of documents as if his security had been effected by assignment.

(2) Any purported assignment of a term of years absolute by way of mortgage made after the commencement of this Act shall (to the extent of the estate of the mortgagor) operate as a subdemise of the leasehold land to the mortgagee for a term of years absolute but subject to cesser on redemption, in manner following, namely:—

(*a*) The term to be taken by a first or only mortgagee shall be ten days less than the term expressed to be assigned:

(*b*) The term to be taken by a second or subsequent mortgagee shall be one day longer than the term vested in the first or other mortgagee

---

[61] Applied by the Housing Act 1957 (5 & 6 Eliz. 2, c. 56), s. 10(7); and the Weeds Act 1959 (7 & 8 Eliz. 2, c. 54), s. 3(4).

whose security ranks immediately before that of the second or subsequent mortgagee, if the length of the last mentioned term permits, and in any case for a term less by one day at least than the term expressed to be assigned:

and, in this subsection, any such purported assignment as aforesaid includes an absolute assignment with a deed of defeasance and any other assurance which, but for this subsection, would operate in effect to vest the term of the mortgagor in a mortgagee subject to redemption.

(3) This section applies whether or not the land is registered under the Land Registration Act 1925, or the mortgage is made by way of sub-mortgage of a term of years absolute, or is expressed to be by way of trust for sale or otherwise.

(4) Without prejudice to the provisions of this Act respecting legal and equitable powers, every power to mortgage for or to lend money on mortgage of a term of years absolute by way of assignment shall be construed as a power to mortgage the term by subdemise for a term of years absolute or by a charge by way of legal mortgage, or to lend on such security.

Charges by way of legal mortgage

87.—(1) Where a legal mortgage of land is created by a charge by deed expressed to be by way of legal mortgage, the mortgagee shall have the same protection, powers and remedies (including the right to take proceedings to obtain possession from the occupiers and the persons in receipt of rents and profits, or any of them) as if—

(*a*) where the mortgage is a mortgage of an estate in fee simple, a mortgage term for three thousand years without impeachment of waste had been thereby created in favour of the mortgagee; and

(*b*) where the mortgage is a mortgage of a term of years absolute, a sub-term less by one day than the term vested in the mortgagor had been thereby created in favour of the mortgagee.

(2) Where an estate vested in a mortgagee immediately before the commencement of this Act has by virtue of this Act been converted into a term of years absolute or sub-term, the mortgagee may, by a declaration in writing to that effect signed by him, convert the mortgage into a charge by way of legal mortgage, and in that case the mortgage term shall be extinguished in the inheritance or in the head term as the case may be, and the mortgagee shall have the same protection, powers and remedies (including the right to take proceedings to obtain possession from the occupiers and the persons in receipt of rents and profits or any of them) as if the mortgage term or sub-term had remained subsisting.

The power conferred by this subsection may be exercised by a mortgagee notwithstanding that he is a trustee or personal representative.

(3) Such declaration shall not affect the priority of the mortgagee or his right to retain possession of documents, nor affect his title to or right over any fixtures or chattels personal comprised in the mortgage.

Realisation of freehold mortgages

88.—(1) Where an estate in fee simple has been mortgaged by the creation of a term of years absolute limited thereout or by a charge by way of legal mortgage and the mortgage sells under his statutory or express power of sale—

(*a*) the conveyance by him shall operate to vest in the purchaser the fee simple in the land conveyed subject to any legal mortgage having priority to the mortgage in right of which the sale is made and to any money thereby secured and thereupon;

(*b*) the mortgage term or the charge by way of legal mortgage and any subsequent mortgage term or charges shall merge or be extinguished as respects the land conveyed;

and such conveyance may, as respects the fee simple, be made in the name of the estate owner in whom it is vested.

(2) Where any such mortgagee obtains an order for foreclosure absolute, the order shall operate to vest the fee simple in him (subject to any legal mortgage having priority to the mortgage in right of which the foreclosure is obtained and to any money thereby secured), and thereupon the mortgage term, if any, shall thereby be merged in the fee simple, and any subsequent mortgage term or charge by way of legal mortgage bound by the order shall thereupon be extinguished.

(3) Where any such mortgagee acquires a title under the Limitation Acts, he, or the persons deriving title under him, may enlarge the mortgage term into a fee simple under the statutory power for that purpose discharged from any legal mortgage affected by the title so acquired, or in the case of a chargee by way of legal mortgage may by deed declare that the fee simple is vested in him discharged as aforesaid, and the same shall vest accordingly.

(4) Where the mortgage includes fixtures or chattels personal any statutory power of sale and any right to foreclosure or take possession shall extend to the absolute or other interest therein affected by the charge.

(5) In the case of a sub-mortgage by subdemise of a long term (less a nominal period) itself limited out of an estate in fee simple, the foregoing provisions of this section shall operate as if the derivative term, if any, created by the sub-mortgage had been limited out of the fee simple, and so as to enlarge the principal term and extinguish the derivative term created by the sub-mortgage as aforesaid, and to enable the sub-mortgagee to convey the fee simple or acquire it by foreclosure, enlargement, or otherwise as aforesaid.

(6) This section applies to a mortgage whether created before or after the commencement of this Act, and to a mortgage term created by this Act, but does not operate to confer a better title to the fee simple than would have been acquired if the same had been conveyed by the mortgage (being a valid mortgage) and the restrictions imposed by this Act in regard to the effect of mortgages were not in force, and all prior mortgages (if any) not being merely equitable charges had been created by demise or by charge by way of legal mortgage.

Realisation of leasehold mortgages

89.—(1)[62] Where a term of years absolute has been mortgaged by the creation of another term of years absolute limited thereout or by a charge by way of legal mortgage and the mortgagee sells under his statutory or express power of sale,—

(*a*) the conveyance by him shall operate to convey to the purchaser not only the mortgage term, if any, but also (unless expressly excepted with the leave of the court) the leasehold reversion affected by the mortgage, subject to any legal mortgage having priority to the mortgage in right of which the sale is made and to any money thereby secured, and thereupon

(*b*) the mortgage term, or the charge by way of legal mortgage and any subsequent mortgage term or charge, shall merge in such leasehold reversion or be extinguished unless excepted as aforesaid;

[62] The county court will have jurisdiction in a case where the amount owing in respect of the mortgage or charge at the date of the commencement of the proceedings does not exceed £5,000: County Courts Act 1959 (7 & 8 Eliz. 2, c. 22), Sched. 1, as amended by the Administration of Justice Act 1969 (c. 58), s. 5.

and such conveyance may, as respects the leasehold reversion, be made in the name of the estate owner in whom it is vested.

Where a licence to assign is required on a sale by a mortgagee, such licence shall not be unreasonably refused.

(2) Where any such mortgagee obtains an order for foreclosure absolute, the order shall, unless it otherwise provides, operate (without giving rise to a forfeiture for want of a licence to assign) to vest the leasehold reversion affected by the mortgage and any subsequent mortgage term in him, subject to any legal mortgage having priority to the mortgage in right of which the foreclosure is obtained and to any money thereby secured, and thereupon the mortgage term and any subsequent mortgage term or charge by way of legal mortgage bound by the order shall, subject to any express provision to the contrary contained in the order, merge in such leasehold reversion or be extinguished.

(3) Where any such mortgagee acquires a title under the Limitation Acts, he, or the persons deriving title under him, may by deed declare that the leasehold reversion affected shall vest in him, free from any right of redemption which is barred, and the same shall (without giving rise to a forfeiture for want of a licence to assign) vest accordingly, and thereupon the mortgage term, if any, and any other mortgage term or charge by way of legal mortgage affected by the title so acquired shall, subject to any express provision to the contrary contained in the deed, merge in such leasehold reversion or be extinguished.

(4) Where the mortgage includes fixtures or chattels personal, any statutory power of sale and any right to foreclosure or take possession shall extend to the absolute or other interest therein affected by the charge.

(5) In the case of a sub-mortgage by subdemise of a term (less a nominal period) itself limited out of a leasehold reversion, the foregoing provisions of this section shall operate as if the derivative term created by the sub-mortgage had been limited out of the leasehold reversion, and so as (subject as aforesaid) to merge the principal mortgage term therein as well as the derivative term created by the sub-mortgage and to enable the sub-mortgagee to convey the leasehold reversion or acquire it by foreclosure, vesting, or otherwise as aforesaid.

(6) This section takes effect without prejudice to any incumbrance or trust affecting the leasehold reversion which has priority over the mortgage in right of which the sale, foreclosure, or title is made or acquired, and applies to a mortgage whether executed before or after the commencement of this Act, and to a mortgage term created by this Act, but does not apply where the mortgage term does not comprise the whole of the land included in the leasehold reversion unless the rent (if any) payable in respect of that reversion has been apportioned as respects the land affected, or the rent is of no money value or no rent is reserved, and unless the lessee's covenants and conditions (if any) have been apportioned, either expressly or by implication, as respects the land affected.

[In this subsection references to an apportionment include an equitable apportionment made without the consent of the lessor.][63]

Realisation of equitable charges by the court

90.—(1)[64] Where an order for sale is made by the court in reference to an equitable mortgage on land (not secured by a legal term of years absolute or by a charge by way of legal mortgage) the court may, in favour

---

[63] Added by the Law of Property (Amendment) Act 1926, *post,* Sched.

[64] The county court will have jurisdiction in a case where the land which is to be dealt with does not exceed in capital value £5,000 or in net annual value for rating £300: County Courts Act 1959 (7 & 8 Eliz. 2, c. 22), Sched. 1, as amended by the Administration of Justice Act 1969 (c. 58), s. 5.

of a purchaser, make a vesting order conveying the land or may appoint a person to convey the land or create and vest in the mortgagee a legal term of years absolute to enable him to carry out the sale, as the case may require, in like manner as if the mortgage had been created by deed by way of legal mortgage pursuant to this Act, but without prejudice to any incumbrance having priority to the equitable mortgage unless the incumbrancer consents to the sale.

(2) This section applies to equitable mortgages made or arising before or after the commencement of this Act, but not to a mortgage which has been over-reached under the powers conferred by this Act or otherwise.

Sale of mortgaged property in action for redemption or foreclosure

91.[64]—(1) Any person entitled to redeem mortgaged property may have a judgment or order for sale instead of for redemption in an action brought by him either for redemption alone, or for sale alone, or for sale or redemption in the alternative.

(2) In any action, whether for foreclosure, or for redemption, or for sale, or for the raising and payment in any manner of mortgage money, the court, on the request of the mortgagee, or of any person interested either in the mortgage money or in the right of redemption, and, notwithstanding that—

(*a*) any other person dissents; or
(*b*) the mortgagee or any person so interested does not appear in the action;

and without allowing any time for redemption or for payment of any mortgage money, may direct a sale of the mortgaged property, on such terms as it thinks fit, including the deposit in court of a reasonable sum fixed by the court to meet the expenses of sale and to secure performance of the terms.

(3) But, in an action brought by a person interested in the right of redemption and seeking a sale, the court may, on the application of any defendant, direct the plaintiff to give such security for costs as the court thinks fit, and may give the conduct of the sale to any defendant, and may give such directions as it thinks fit respecting the costs of the defendants or any of them.

(4) In any case within this section the court may, if it thinks fit, direct a sale without previously determining the priorities of incumbrancers.

(5) This section applies to actions brought either before or after the commencement of this Act.

(6) In this section "mortgaged property" includes the estate or interest which a mortgagee would have had power to convey if the statutory power of sale were applicable.

(7) For the purpose of this section the court may, in favour of a purchaser, make a vesting order conveying the mortgaged property, or appoint a person to do so, subject or not to any incumbrance, as the court may think fit; or, in the case of an equitable mortgage, may create and vest a mortgage term in the mortgagee to enable him to carry out the sale as if the mortgage had been made by deed by way of legal mortgage.

Power to authorise land and minerals to be dealt with separately

92.[64] Where a mortgagee's power of sale in regard to land has become exercisable but does not extend to the purposes mentioned in this section, the court may, on his application, authorise him and the persons delivering title under him to dispose—

(*a*) of the land, with an exception or reservation of all or any mines and minerals, and with or without rights and powers of or incidental to the working, getting or carrying away of minerals; or

(b) of all or any mines and minerals, with or without the said rights or powers separately from the land;

and thenceforth the powers so conferred shall have effect as if the same were contained in the mortgage.

Restriction on consolidation of mortgages

93.—(1) A mortgagor seeking to redeem any one mortgage is entitled to do so without paying any money due under any separate mortgage made by him, or by any person through whom he claims, solely on property other than that comprised in the mortgage which he seeks to redeem.

This subsection applies only if and as far as a contrary intention is not expressed in the mortgage deeds or one of them.

(2) This section does not apply where all the mortgages were made before the first day of January, eighteen hundred and eighty-two.

(3) Save as aforesaid, nothing in this Act, in reference to mortgages, affects any right of consolidation or renders inoperative a stipulation in relation to any mortgage made before or after the commencement of this Act reserving a right to consolidate.

Tacking and further advances

94.[65]—(1) After the commencement of this Act, a prior mortgagee shall have a right to make further advances to rank in priority to subsequent mortgages (whether legal or equitable)—

(a) if an arrangement has been made to that effect with the subsequent mortgagees; or

(b) if he had no notice of such subsequent mortgages at the time when the further advance was made by him; or

(c) whether or not he had such notice as aforesaid, where the mortgage imposes an obligation on him to make such further advances.

This subsection applies whether or not the prior mortgage was made expressly for securing further advances.

(2) In relation to the making of further advances after the commencement of this Act a mortgagee shall not be deemed to have notice of a mortgage merely by reason that it was registered as a land charge *or in a local deeds registry*,[66] if it was not so registered at the [time when the original mortgage was created][67] or when the last search (if any) by or on behalf of the mortgagee was made, whichever last happened.

This subsection only applies where the prior mortgage was made expressly for securing a current account or other further advances.

(3) Save in regard to the making of further advances as aforesaid, the right to tack is hereby abolished:

Provided that nothing in this Act shall affect any priority acquired before the commencement of this Act by tacking, or in respect of further advances made without notice of a subsequent incumbrance or by arrangement with the subsequent incumbrancer.

(4) This section applies to mortgages of land made before or after the commencement of this Act, but not to charges registered under the Land Registration Act 1925, or any enactment replaced by that Act.

---

[65] For the effect of the statutory right of occupation as a charge on a matrimonial dwelling-house, see the Matrimonial Homes Act 1967 (c. 75), s. 2(8).

[66] Words in italics will be repealed, in respect of any Yorkshire deeds register, registry and the area which was within its jurisdiction, with effect from the expiration of two years beginning with the date on which compulsory registration of title under the Land Regisration Act 1925 (15 & 16 Geo. 5, c. 21) is extended to any part of the area of the registry, unless the Lord Chancellor specifies an earlier date at the request of the County Council of the Riding: Law of Property Act 1969 (c. 59), s. 16(2) and Sched. 2, Pt. I.

[67] Substituted by the Law of Property (Amendment) Act 1926, *post,* Sched.

Obligation to transfer instead of reconveying and as to right to take possession

95.—(1) Where a mortgagor is entitled to redeem, then subject to compliance with the terms on compliance with which he would be entitled to require a reconveyance or surrender, he shall be entitled to require the mortgagee, instead of reconveying or surrendering, to assign the mortgage debt and convey the mortgaged property to any third person, as the mortgagor directs; and the mortgagee shall be bound to assign and convey accordingly.

(2) The rights conferred by this section belong to and are capable of being enforced by each incumbrancer, or by the mortgagor, notwithstanding any immediate incumbrance; but a requisition of an incumbrancer prevails over a requisition of the mortgagor, and, as between incumbrancers, a requisition of a prior incumbrancer prevails over a requisition of a subsequent incumbrancer.

(3) The foregoing provisions of this section do not apply in the case of a mortgagee being or having been in possession.

(4) Nothing in this Act affects prejudicially the right of a mortgagee of land whether or not his charge is secured by a legal term of years absolute to take possession of the land, but the taking of possession by the mortgagee does not convert any legal estate of the mortgagor into an equitable interest.

(5) This section applies to mortgages made either before or after the commencement of this Act, and takes effect notwithstanding any stipulation to the contrary.

Regulations respecting inspection, production and delivery of documents, and priorities

96.—(1) A mortgagor, as long as his right to redeem subsists, shall be entitled from time to time, at reasonable times, on his request, and at his own cost, and on payment of the mortgagee's costs and expenses in this behalf, to inspect and make copies or abstracts of or extracts from the documents of title relating to the mortgaged property in the custody or power of the mortgagee.

This subsection applies to mortgages made after the thirty-first day of December, eighteen hundred and eighty-one, and takes effect notwithstanding any stipulation to the contrary.

(2) A mortgagee, whose mortgage is surrendered or otherwise extinguished, shall not be liable on account of delivering documents of title in his possession to the person not having the best right thereto, unless he has notice of the right or claim of a person having a better right, whether by virtue of a right to require a surrender or re-conveyance or otherwise.

[In this subsection notice does not include notice implied by reason of registration under the Land Charges Act 1925[68] *or in a local deeds register.*[69]][70]

Priorities as between puisne mortgages

97.[71] Every mortgage affecting a legal estate in land made after the commencement of this Act, whether legal or equitable (not being a mortgage protected by the deposit of documents relating to the legal estate affected) shall rank according to its date of registration as a land charge pursuant to the Land Charges Act 1925.[72]

[68] Now the Land Charges Act 1972 (c. 61), *post,* p. 320.
[69] See p. 169, n. 66.
[70] Added by the Law of Property (Amendment) Act 1926, *post,* Sched.
[71] Extended by the Middlesex Deeds Act 1940 (3 & 4 Geo. 6, c. 34), s. 2(3).
[72] See above, note 68.

This section does not apply [to mortgages or charges to which the Land Charges Act 1972 does not apply by virtue of section 14(3) of that Act (which excludes certain land charges created by instrument necessitating registration under the Land Registration Act 1925), or][73] to mortgages or charges of registered land [or of land within the jurisdiction of a local deeds registry].[74]

Actions for possession by mortgagors

98.—(1) A mortgagor for the time being entitled to the possession or receipt of the rents and profits of any land, as to which the mortgagee has not given notice of his intention to take possession or to enter into the receipt of the rents and profits thereof, may sue for such possession, or for the recovery of such rents or profits, or to prevent or recover damages in respect of any trespass or other wrong relative thereto, in his own name only, unless the cause of action arises upon a lease or other contract made by him jointly with any other person.

(2) This section does not prejudice the power of a mortgagor independently of this section to take proceedings in his own name only, either in right of any legal estate vested in him or otherwise.

(3) This section applies whether the mortgage was made before or after the commencement of this Act.

Leasing powers of mortgagor and mortgagee in possession

99.[75]—(1) A mortgagor of land while in possession shall, as against every incumbrancer, have power to make from time to time any such lease of the mortgaged land, or any part thereof, as is by this section authorised.

(2) A mortagee of land while in possession shall, as against all prior incumbrancers, if any, and as against the mortgagor, have power to make from time to time any such lease as aforesaid.

(3) The leases which this section authorises are—
- (i) agricultural or occupation leases for any term not exceeding twenty-one years, or, in the case of a mortgage made after the commencement of this Act, fifty years; and
- (ii) building leases for any term not exceeding ninety-nine years, or, in the case of a mortgage made after the commencement of this Act, nine hundred and ninety-nine years.

(4) Every person making a lease under this section may execute and do all assurances and things necessary or proper in that behalf.

(5) Every such lease shall be made to take effect in possession not later than twelve months after its date.

(6) Every such lease shall reserve the best rent that can reasonably be obtained, regard being had to the circumstances of the case, but without any fine being taken.

(7) Every such lease shall contain a covenant by the lessee for payment of the rent, and a condition of re-entry on the rent not being paid within a time therein specified not exceeding thirty days.

(8) A counterpart of every such lease shall be executed by the lessee and delivered to the lessor, of which execution and delivery the execution of the lease by the lessor shall, in favour of the lessee and all persons deriving title under him, be sufficient evidence.

(9) Every such building lease shall be made in consideration of the

---

[73] Inserted by the Land Charges Act 1972 (c. 61), Sched. 3.
[74] These words will be repealed with effect from the same date as in note 66, *supra*. See Law of Property Act 1969 (c. 59), ss. 16 (2), 17 (1) and Sched. 2, Pt. II.
[75] This section is extended by the Reserve and Auxiliary Forces (Protection of Civil Interests) Act 1951 (14 & 15 Geo. 6, c. 65), s. 30(6), and the Landlord and Tenant Act 1954 (2 & 3 Eliz. 2, c. 56), s. 36(4), and applied by the Housing Act 1961 (9 & 10 Eliz. 2, c. 65), s. 18(5).

lessee, or some person by whose direction the lease is granted, having erected, or agreeing to erect within not more than five years from the date of the lease, buildings, new or additional, or having improved or repaired buildings, or agreeing to improve or repair buildings within that time, or having executed, or agreeing to execute within that time, on the land leased, an improvement for or in connection with building purposes.

(10) In any such building lease a peppercorn rent, or a nominal or other rent less than the rent ultimately payable, may be made payable for the first five years, or any less part of the term.

(11) In case of a lease by the mortgagor, he shall, within one month after making the lease, deliver to the mortgagee, or, where there are more than one, to the mortgagee first in priority, a counterpart of the lease duly executed by the lessee, but the lessee shall not be concerned to see that this provision is complied with.

(12) A contract to make or accept a lease under this section may be enforced by or against every person on whom the lease if granted would be binding.

(13)[76] This section applies only if and as far as a contrary intention is not expressed by the mortgagor and mortgagee in the mortgage deed, or otherwise in writing, and has effect subject to the terms of the mortgage deed or of any such writing and to the provisions therein contained.

(14) The mortgagor and mortgagee may, by agreement in writing, whether or not contained in the mortgage deed, reserve to or confer on the mortgagor or the mortgagee, or both, any further or other powers of leasing or having reference to leasing; and any further or other powers so reserved or conferred shall be exercisable, as far as may be, as if they were conferred by this Act, and with all the like incidents, effects, and consequences:

Provided that the powers so reserved or conferred shall not prejudicially affect the rights of any mortgagee interested under any other mortgage subsisting at the date of the agreement, unless that mortgagee joins in or adopts the agreement.

(15) Nothing in this Act shall be construed to enable a mortgagor or mortgagee to make a lease for any longer term or on any other conditions than such as could have been granted or imposed by the mortgagor, with the concurrence of all the incumbrancers, if this Act and the enactments replaced by this section had not been passed:

Provided that, in the case of a mortgage of leasehold land, a lease granted under this section shall reserve a reversion of not less than one day.

(16) Subject as aforesaid, this section applies to any mortgage made after the thirty-first day of December, eighteen hundred and eighty-one, but the provisions thereof, or any of them, may, by agreement in writing made after that date between mortgagor and mortgagee, be applied to a mortgage made before that date, so nevertheless that any such agreement shall not prejudicially effect any right or interest of any mortgagee not joining in or adopting the agreement.

(17) The provisions of this section referring to a lease shall be construed to extend and apply, as far as circumstances admit, to any letting, and to an agreement, whether in writing or not, for leasing or letting.

(18) For the purposes of this section "mortgagor" does not include an incumbrancer deriving title under the original mortgagor.

(19) The powers of leasing conferred by this section shall, after a receiver of the income of the mortgaged property or any part thereof has

---

[76] This subsection shall not have effect in relation to a mortgage made after March 1, 1948, of agricultural land within the meaning of the Agriculture Act 1947 (10 & 11 Geo. 6, c. 48): see the Agricultural Holdings Act 1948 (11 & 12 Geo. 6, c. 63), and Tenant Act 1954 (2 & 3 Eliz. 2, c. 56): see *ibid.* s. 36(4).

been appointed by a mortgagee under his statutory power, and so long as the receiver acts, be exercisable by such mortgagee instead of by the mortgagor, as respects any land affected by the receivership, in like manner as if such mortgagee were in possession of the land, and the mortgagee may, by writing, delegate any of such powers to the receiver.

Powers of mortgagor and mortgagee in possession to accept surrenders of leases

100.[77]—(1) For the purpose only of enabling a lease authorised under the last preceding section, or under any agreement made pursuant to that section, or by the mortgage deed (in this section referred to as an authorised lease) to be granted, a mortgagor of land while in possession shall, as against every incumbrancer, have, by virtue of this Act, power to accept from time to time a surrender of any lease of the mortgaged land or any part thereof comprised in the lease, with or without an exception of or in respect of all or any of the mines and minerals therein, and, on a surrender of the lease so far as it comprises part only of the land or mines and minerals leased, the rent may be apportioned.

(2) For the same purpose, a mortgagee of land while in possession shall, as against all prior or other incumbrancers, if any, and as against the mortgagor, have, by virtue of this Act, power to accept from time to time any such surrender as aforesaid.

(3) On a surrender of part only of the land or mines and minerals leased, the original lease may be varied, provided that the lease when varied would have been valid as an authorised lease if granted by the person accepting the surrender; and, on a surrender and the making of a new or other lease, whether for the same or for any extended or other term, and whether subject or not to the same or to any other covenants, provisions, or conditions, the value of the lessee's interest in the lease surrendered may, subject to the provisions of this section, be taken into account in the determination of the amount of the rent to be reserved, and of the nature of the covenants, provisions, and conditions to be inserted in the new or other lease.

(4) Where any consideration for the surrender, other than an agreement to accept an authorised lease, is given by or on behalf of the lessee to or on behalf of the person accepting the surrender, nothing in this section authorises a surrender to a mortgagor without the consent of the incumbrancers, or authorises a surrender to a second or subsequent incumbrancer without the consent of every prior incumbrancer.

(5) No surrender shall, by virtue of this section, be rendered valid unless:—

(*a*) An authorised lease is granted of the whole of the land or mines and minerals comprised in the surrender to take effect in possession immediately or within one month after the date of the surrender; and

(*b*) The term certain or other interest granted by the new lease is not less in duration than the unexpired term or interest which would have been subsisting under the original lease if that lease had not been surrendered; and

(*c*) Where the whole of the land mines and minerals originally leased has been surrendered, the rent reserved by the new lease is not less than the rent which would have been payable under the original lease if it had not been surrendered; or where part only of the land or mines and minerals has been surrendered, the aggregate rents respectively remaining payable or reserved under the original lease and new lease are not less than the rent which would have been

[77] Applied by the Housing Act 1961 (9 & 10 Eliz. 2, c. 65), s. 18(5).

payable under the original lease if no partial surrender had been accepted.

(6) A contract to make or accept a surrender under this section may be enforced by or against every person on whom the surrender, if completed, would be binding.

(7) This section applies only if and as far as a contrary intention is not expressed by the mortgagor and mortgagee in the mortgage deed, or otherwise in writing, and shall have effect subject to the terms of the mortgage deed or of any such writing and to the provisions therein contained.

(8) This section applies to a mortgage made after the thirty-first day of December, nineteen hundred and eleven, but the provisions of this section, or any of them, may, by agreement in writing made after that date, between mortgagor and mortgagee, be applied to a mortgage made before that date, so nevertheless that any such agreement shall not prejudicially affect any right or interest of any mortgagee not joining in or adopting the agreement.

(9) The provisions of this section referring to a lease shall be construed to extend and apply, as far as circumstances admit, to any letting, and to any agreement, whether in writing or not, for leasing or letting.

(10) The mortgagor and mortgagee may, by agreement in writing, whether or not contained in the mortgage deed, reserve or confer on the mortgagor or mortgagee, or both, any further or other powers relating to the surrender of leases; and any further or other powers so conferred or reserved shall be exercisable, as far as may be, as if they were conferred by this Act, and with all the like incidents, effects and consequences:

Provided that the powers so reserved or conferred shall not prejudicially affect the rights of any mortgagee interested under any other mortgage subsisting at the date of the agreement, unless that mortgagee joins in or adopts the agreement.

(11) Nothing in this section operates to enable a mortgagor or mortgagee to accept a surrender which could not have been accepted by the mortgagor with the concurrence of all the incumbrancers if this Act and the enactments replaced by this section had not been passed.

(12) For the purposes of this section "mortgagor" does not include an incumbrancer deriving title under the original mortgagor.

(13) The powers of accepting surrenders conferred by this section shall, after a receiver of the income of the mortgaged property or any part thereof has been appointed by the mortgagee, under the statutory power, and so long as the receiver acts, be exercisable by such mortgagee instead of by the mortgagor, as respects any land affected by the receivership, in like manner as if such mortgagee were in possession of the land; and the mortgagee may, by writing, delegate any of such powers to the receiver.

Powers incident to estate or interest of mortgagee

101.[78]—(1) A mortgagee, where the mortgage is made by deed, shall, by virtue of this Act, have the following powers, to the like extent as if they had been in terms conferred by the mortgage deed, but not further (namely):

(i) A power, when the mortgage money has become due, to sell, or to concur with any other person in selling, the mortgaged property, or any part thereof, either subject to prior charges or not, and either together or in lots, by public auction or by private contract, subject to such conditions respecting title, or evidence of title, or other

---

[78] Applied by the Agriculture (Miscellaneous Provisions) Act 1941 (4 & 5 Geo. 6, c. 50), s. 8(4); the Housing Act 1961 (9 & 10 Eliz. 2, c. 65), s. 18(5); and Leasehold Reform Act 1967 (c. 88), s. 19(8).

matter, as the mortgagee thinks fit, with power to vary any contract for sale, and to buy in at an auction, or to rescind any contract for sale, and to re-sell, without being answerable for any loss occasioned thereby; and

(ii) A power, at any time after the date of the mortgage deed, to insure and keep insured against loss or damage by fire any building, or any effects or property of an insurable nature, whether affixed to the freehold or not, being or forming part of the property which or an estate or interest wherein is mortgaged, and the premiums paid for any such insurance shall be a charge on the mortgaged property or estate or interest, in addition to the mortgage money, and with the same priority, and with interest at the same rate, as the mortgage money; and

(iii) A power, when the mortgage money has become due, to appoint a receiver of the income of the mortgaged property, or any part thereof; or, if the mortgaged property consists of an interest in income, or of a rentcharge or an annual or other periodical sum, a receiver of that property or any part thereof; and

(iv) A power, while the mortgagee is in possession, to cut and sell timber and other trees ripe for cutting, and not planted or left standing for shelter or ornament, or to contract for any such cutting and sale, to be completed within any time not exceeding twelve months from the making of the contract.

(2) Where the mortgage deed is executed after the thirty-first day of December, nineteen hundred and eleven, the power of sale aforesaid includes the following powers as incident thereto (namely):—

(i) A power to impose or reserve or make binding, as far as the law permits, by covenant, condition, or otherwise, on the unsold part of the mortgaged property or any party thereof, or on the purchaser and any property sold, any restriction or reservation with respect to building on or other user of land, or with respect to mines and minerals, or for the purpose of the more beneficial working thereof, or with respect to any other thing:

(ii) A power to sell the mortgaged property or any part thereof, or all or any mines and minerals apart from the surface:—

(*a*) With or without a grant or reservation of rights of way, rights of water, easements, rights, and privileges, for or connected with building or other purposes in relation to the property remaining in mortgage or any part thereof, or to any property sold: and

(*b*) With or without an exception or reservation of all or any of the mines and minerals in or under the mortgaged property, and with or without a grant or reservation of powers of working, wayleaves, or rights of way, rights of water and drainage and other powers, easements, rights, and privileges for or connected with mining purposes in relation to the property remaining unsold or any part thereof, or to any property sold: and

(*c*) With or without covenants by the purchaser to expend money on the land sold.

(3) The provisions of this Act relating to the foregoing powers, comprised either in this section, or in any other section regulating the exercise of those powers, may be varied or extended by the mortgage deed, and, as so varied or extended, shall, as far as may be, operate in the like manner and with all the like incidents, effects, and consequences, as if such variations or extensions were contained in this Act.

(4) This section applies only if and as far as a contrary intention is not expressed in the mortgage deed, and has effect subject to the terms of the mortgage deed and to the provisions therein contained.

(5) Save as otherwise provided, this section applies where the mortgage deed is executed after the thirty-first day of December, eighteen hundred and eighty-one.

(6) The power of sale conferred by this section includes such power of selling the estate in fee simple or any leasehold reversion as is conferred by the provisions of this Act relating to the realisation of mortgages.

Provision as to mortgages of undivided shares in land

102.—(1) A person who was before the commencement of this Act a mortgagee of an undivided share in land shall have the same power to sell his share in the proceeds of sale of the land and in the rents and profits thereof until sale, as, independently of this Act, he would have had in regard to the share in the land; and shall also have a right to require the trustees for sale in whom the land is vested to account to him for the income attributable to that share or to appoint a receiver to receive the same from such trustees corresponding to the right which, independently of this Act, he would have had to take possession or to appoint a receiver of the rents and profits attributable to the same share.

(2) The powers conferred by this section are exercisable by the persons deriving title under such mortgagee.

Regulation of exercise of power of sale

103. A mortgagee shall not exercise the power of sale conferred by this Act unless and until—
  (i) Notice requiring payment of the mortgage money has been served on the mortgagor or one of two or more mortgagors, and default has been made in payment of the mortgage money, or of part thereof for three months after such service; or
  (ii) Some interest under the mortgage is in arrear and unpaid for two months after becoming due; or
  (iii) There has been a breach of some provision contained in the mortgage deed or in this Act, or in an enactment replaced by this Act, and on the part of the mortgagor, or of some person concurring in making the mortgage, to be observed or performed, other than and besides a covenant for payment of the mortgage money or interest thereon.

Conveyance on sale

104.—(1) A mortgagee exercising the power of sale conferred by this Act shall have power, by deed, to convey the property sold, for such estate and interest therein as he is by this Act authorised to sell or convey or may be the subject of the mortgage, freed from all estates, interests, and rights to which the mortgage has priority, but subject to all estates, interests, and rights which have priority to the mortgage.

(2) Where a conveyance is made in exercise of the power of sale conferred by this Act, or any enactment replaced by this Act, the title of the purchaser shall not be impeachable on the ground—
  (*a*) that no case had arisen to authorise the sale; or
  (*b*) that due notice was not given; or
  (*c*) where the mortgage is made after the commencement of this Act, that leave of the court, when so required, was not obtained; or
  (*d*) whether the mortgage was made before or after such commencement, that the power was otherwise improperly or irregularly exercised;
and a purchaser is not, either before or on conveyance, concerned to see or inquire whether a case has arisen to authorise the sale, or due notice has

been given, or the power is otherwise properly and regularly exercised; but any person damnified by an unauthorised, or improper, or irregular exercise of the power shall have his remedy in damages against the person exercising the power.

(3) A conveyance on sale by a mortgagee, made after the commencement of this Act, shall be deemed to have been made in exercise of the power of sale conferred by this Act unless a contrary intention appears.

Application of proceeds of sale

105. The money which is received by the mortgagee, arising from the sale, after discharge of prior incumbrances to which the sale is not made subject, if any, or after payment into court under this Act of a sum to meet any prior incumbrance, shall be held by him in trust to be applied by him, first, in payment of all costs, charges, and expenses properly incurred by him as incident to the sale or any attempted sale, or otherwise; and secondly, in discharge of the mortgage money, interest, and costs, and other money, if any, due under the mortgage; and the residue of the money so received shall be paid to the person entitled to the mortgaged property, or authorised to give receipts for the proceeds of the sale thereof.

Provisions as to exercise of power of sale

106.—(1) The power of sale conferred by this Act may be exercised by any person for the time being entitled to receive and give a discharge for the mortgage money.

(2) The power of sale conferred by this Act does not affect the right of foreclosure.

(3) The mortgagee shall not be answerable for any involuntary loss happening in or about the exercise or execution of the power of sale conferred by this Act, or of any trust connected therewith, or, where the mortgage is executed after the thirty-first day of December, nineteen hundred and eleven, of any power or provision contained in the mortgage deed.

(4) At any time after the power of sale conferred by this Act has become exercisable, the person entitled to exercise the power may demand and recover from any person, other than a person having in the mortgaged property an estate, interest, or right in priority to the mortgage, all the deeds and documents relating to the property, or to the title thereto, which a purchaser under the power of sale would be entitled to demand and recover from him.

Mortgagee's receipts, discharges, &c.

107.—(1) The receipt in writing of a mortgagee shall be a sufficient discharge for any money arising under the power of sale conferred by this Act, or for any money or securities comprised in his mortgage, or arising thereunder; and a person paying or transferring the same to the mortgagee shall not be concerned to inquire whether any money remains due under the mortgage.

(2) Money received by a mortgagee under his mortgage or from the proceeds of securities comprised in his mortgage shall be applied in like manner as in this Act directed respecting money received by him arising from a sale under the power of sale conferred by this Act, but with this variation, that the costs, charges, and expenses payable shall include the costs, charges, and expenses properly incurred of recovering and receiving the money or securities, and of conversion of securities into money, instead of those incident to sale.

Amount and application of insurance money

108.—(1) The amount of an insurance effected by a mortgagee against loss or damage by fire under the power in that behalf conferred by this Act shall not exceed the amount specified in the mortgage deed, or, if no amount is therein specified, two third parts of the amount that would be required, in case of total destruction, to restore the property insured.

(2) An insurance shall not, under the power conferred by this Act, be effected by a mortgagee in any of the following cases (namely):

   (i) Where there is a declaration in the mortgage deed that no insurance is required:

  (ii) Where an insurance is kept up by or on behalf of the mortgagor in accordance with the mortgage deed:

 (iii) Where the mortgage deed contains no stipulation respecting insurance, and an insurance is kept up by or on behalf of the mortgagor with the consent of the mortgagee to the amount to which the mortgagee is by this Act authorised to insure.

(3) All money received on an insurance or mortgaged property against loss or damage by fire or otherwise effected under this Act, or any enactment replaced by this Act, or on an insurance for the maintenance of which the mortgagor is liable under the mortgage deed, shall, if the mortgagee so requires, be applied by the mortgagor in making good the loss or damage in respect of which the money is received.

(4) Without prejudice to any obligation to the contrary imposed by law, or by special contract, a mortgagee may require that all money received on an insurance of mortgaged property against loss or damage by fire or otherwise effected under this Act, or any enactment replaced by this Act, or on an insurance for the maintenance of which the mortgagor is liable under the mortgage deed, be applied in or towards the discharge of the mortgage money.

Appointment, powers, remuneration and duties of receiver

109.—(1) A mortgagee entitled to appoint a receiver under the power in that behalf conferred by this Act shall not appoint a receiver until he has become entitled to exercise the power of sale conferred by this Act, but may then, by writing under his hand, appoint such person as he thinks fit to be receiver.

(2) A receiver appointed under the powers conferred by this Act or any enactment replaced by this Act, shall be deemed to be the agent of the mortgagor; and the mortgagor shall be solely responsible for the receiver's acts or defaults unless the mortgage deed otherwise provides.

(3) The receiver shall have power to demand and recover all the income of which he is appointed receiver, by action, distress, or otherwise, in the name either of the mortgagor or of the mortgagee, to the full extent of the estate or interest which the mortgagor could dispose of, and to give effectual receipts accordingly for the same, and to exercise any powers which may have been delegated to him by the mortgagee pursuant to this Act.

(4) A person paying money to the receiver shall not be concerned to inquire whether any case has happened to authorise the receiver to act.

(5) The receiver may be removed, and a new receiver may be appointed, from time to time by the mortgagee by writing under his hand.

(6) The receiver shall be entitled to retain out of any money received by him, for his remuneration, and in satisfaction of all costs, charges, and expenses incurred by him as receiver, a commission at such rate, not exceeding five per centum on the gross amount of all money received, as is specified in his appointment, and if no rate is so specified, then at the rate

of five per centum on that gross amount, or at such other rate as the court thinks fit to allow, on application made by him for that purpose.

(7) The receiver shall, if so directed in writing by the mortgagee, insure to the extent, if any, to which the mortgagee might have insured and keep insured against loss or damage by fire, out of the money received by him, any building, effects, or property comprised in the mortgage, whether affixed to the freehold or not, being of an insurable nature.

(8) Subject to the provisions of this Act as to the application of insurance money, the receiver shall apply all money received by him as follows, namely:

- (i) In discharge of all rents, taxes, rates, and outgoings whatever affecting the mortgaged property; and
- (ii) In keeping down all annual sums or other payments, and the interest on all principal sums, having priority to the mortgage in right whereof he is receiver; and
- (iii) In payment of his commission, and of the premiums on fire, life, or other insurances, if any, properly payable under the mortgage deed or under this Act, and the cost of executing necessary or proper repairs directed in writing by the mortgagee; and
- (iv) In payment of the interest accruing due in respect of any principal money due under the mortgage; and
- (v) In or towards discharge of the principal money if so directed in writing by the mortgagee;

and shall pay the residue, if any, of the money received by him to the person who, but for the possession of the receiver, would have been entitled to receive the income of which he is appointed receiver, or who is otherwise entitled to the mortgaged property.

Effect of bankruptcy of the mortgagor on the power to sell or appoint a receiver

110.—(1) Where the statutory or express power for a mortgagee either to sell or to appoint a receiver is made exercisable by reason of the mortgagor committing an act of bankruptcy or being adjudged a bankrupt, such power shall not be exercised only on account of the act of bankruptcy or adjudication, without the leave of the court.

(2) This section applies only where the mortgage deed is executed after the commencement of this Act; and in this section "act of bankruptcy" has the same meaning as in the Bankruptcy Act 1914.

Effect of advance on joint account

111.—(1) Where—

- (*a*) in a mortgage, or an obligation for payment of money, or a transfer of a mortgage or of such an obligation, the sum, or any part of the sum, advanced or owing is expressed to be advanced by or owing to more persons than one out of money, or as money, belonging to them on a joint account; or
- (*b*) a mortgage, or such an obligation, or such a transfer is made to more persons than one, jointly;

the mortgage money, or other money or money's worth, for the time being due to those persons on the mortgage or obligation, shall, as between them and the mortgagor or obligor, be deemed to be and remain money or money's worth belonging to those persons on a joint account; and the receipt in writing of the survivors or last survivor of them, or of the personal representative of the last survivor, shall be a complete discharge for all money or money's worth for the time being due, notwithstanding any notice to the payer of a severance of the joint account.

(2) This section applies if and so far as a contrary intention is not expressed in the mortgage, obligation, or transfer, and has effect subject to the terms of the mortgage, obligation, or transfer, and to the provisions therein contained.

(3) This section applies to any mortgage obligation or transfer made after the thirty-first day of December, eighteen hundred and eighty-one.

Notice of trusts on transfer of mortgage

112.—(1) Where, on the transfer of a mortgage, the stamp duty, if payable according to the amount of the debt transferred, would exceed the sum of ten shillings, a purchaser shall not, by reason only of the transfer bearing a ten-shilling stamp, whether adjudicated or not, be deemed to have or to have had notice of any trust, or that the transfer was made for effectuating the discharge of a trustee or the appointment of a new trustee.

(2) This section applies to transfers made before as well as after the commencement of this Act.

Notice of trusts affecting mortgage debts

113.—(1) A person dealing in good faith with a mortgagee, or with the mortgagor if the mortgage has been discharged, released or postponed as to the whole or any part of the mortgaged property, shall not be concerned with any trust at any time affecting the mortgage money or the income thereof, whether or not he has notice of the trust, and may assume unless the contrary is expressly stated in the instruments relating to the mortgage—

(*a*) that the mortgagees (if more than one) are or were entitled to the mortgage money on a joint account; and

(*b*) that the mortgagee has or had power to give valid receipts for the purchase money or mortgage money and the income thereof (including any arrears of interest) and to release or postpone the priority of the mortgage debt or any part thereof or to deal with the same or the mortgaged property or any part thereof;

without investigating the equitable title to the mortgage debt or the appointment or discharge of trustees in reference thereto.

(2) This section applies to mortgages made before or after the commencement of this Act, but only as respects dealings effected after such commencement.

(3) This section does not affect the liability of any person in whom the mortgage debt is vested for the purposes of any trust to give effect to that trust.

Transfers of mortgages

114.—(1) A deed executed by a mortgagee purporting to transfer his mortgage or the benefit thereof shall, unless a contrary intention is therein expressed, and subject to any provisions therein contained, operate to transfer to the transferee—

(*a*) the right to demand, sue for, recover, and give receipts for, the mortgage money or the unpaid part thereof, and the interest then due, if any, and thenceforth to become due thereon; and

(*b*) the benefit of all securities for the same, and the benefit of and the right to sue on all covenants with the mortgagee, and the right to exercise all powers of the mortgagee; and

(*c*) all the estate and interest in the mortgaged property then vested in the mortgagee subject to redemption or cesser, but as to such estate and interest subject to the right of redemption then subsisting.

(2) In this section "transferee" includes his personal representatives and assigns.

(3) A transfer of mortgage may be made in the form contained in the Third Schedule to this Act with such variations and additions, if any, as the circumstances may require.

(4) This section applies, whether the mortgage transferred was made before or after the commencement of this Act, but applies only to transfers made after the commencement of this Act.

(5) This section does not extend to a transfer of a bill of sale of chattels by way of security.

Reconveyances of mortgages by endorsed receipts

115.—(1)[79] A receipt endorsed on, written at the foot of, or annexed to, a mortgage for all money thereby secured, which states the name of the person who pays the money and is executed by the chargee by way of legal mortgage or the person in whom the mortgaged property is vested and who is legally entitled to give a receipt for the mortgage money, shall operate, without any reconveyance, surrender, or release—

(a) Where a mortgage takes effect by demise or subdemise, as a surrender of the term, so as to determine the term or merge the same in the reversion immediately expectant thereon;

(b) Where the mortgage does not take effect by demise or subdemise, as a reconveyance thereof to the extent of the interest which is the subject matter of the mortgage, to the person who immediately before the execution of the receipt was entitled to the equity of redemption;

and in either case, as a discharge of the mortgaged property from all principal money and interest secured by, and from all claims under the mortgage, but without prejudice to any term or other interest which is paramount to the estate or interest of the mortgagee or other person in whom the mortgaged property was vested.

(2) Provided that, where by the receipt the money appears to have been paid by a person who is not entitled to the immediate equity of redemption, the receipt shall operate as if the benefit of the mortgage had by deed been transferred to him; unless—

(a) it is otherwise expressly provided; or

(b) the mortgage is paid off out of capital money, or other money in the hands of a personal representative or trustee properly applicable for the discharge of the mortgage, and it is not expressly provided that the receipt is to operate as a transfer.

(3)[80] Nothing in this section confers on a mortgagor a right to keep alive a mortgage paid off by him, so as to affect prejudicially any subsequent incumbrancer; and where there is no right to keep the mortgage alive, the receipt does not operate as a transfer.

(4) This section does not affect the right of any person to require a reassignment, surrender, release, or transfer to be executed in lieu of a receipt.

(5) A receipt may be given in the form contained in the Third Schedule to this Act, with such variations and additions, if any, as may be deemed expedient; [. . .].[81]

(6)[82] In a receipt given under this section the same covenants shall be implied as if the person who executes the receipt had by deed been

[79] Applied by the Building Societies Act 1962 (10 & 11 Eliz. 2, c. 37), s. 37(2). Extended by the Industrial and Provident Societies Act 1965 (c. 12), s. 33 and by the Friendly Societies Act 1974 (c. 46), s. 97.
[80] Applied by the Building Societies Act 1962, *ibid*. s. 37(2).
[81] Words repealed by the Finance Act 1971 (c. 68), s. 64 and Sched. 14, Pt. VI.
[82] See above, note 80.

expressed to convey the property as mortgagee, subject to any interest which is paramount to the mortgage.

(7) Where the mortgage consists of a mortgage and a further charge or of more than one deed, it shall be sufficient for the purposes of this section, if the receipt refers either to all the deeds whereby the mortgage money is secured or to the aggregate amount of the mortgage money thereby secured and for the time being owing, and is endorsed on, written at the foot of, or annexed to, one of the mortgage deeds.

(8)[83] This section applies to the discharge of a charge by way of legal mortgage, and to the discharge of a mortgage, whether made by way of statutory mortgage or not, executed before or after the commencement of this Act, but only as respects discharges effected after such commencement.

(9)[84] The provisions of this section relating to the operation of a receipt shall (in substitution for the like statutory provisions relating to receipts given by or on behalf of a building, [. . .][85] [. . .][86] society) apply to the discharge of a mortgage made to any such society, provided that the receipt is executed in the manner required by the statute relating to the society [. . .].[87]

(10) This section does not apply to the discharge of a charge or incumbrance registered under the Land Registration Act 1925.

(11) In this section "mortgaged property" means the property remaining subject to the mortgage at the date of the receipt.

Cesser of mortgage terms

116. Without prejudice to the right of a tenant for life or other person having only a limited interest in the equity of redemption to require a mortgage to be kept alive by transfer or otherwise, a mortgage term shall, when the money secured by the mortgage has been discharged, become a satisfied term and shall cease.

Forms of statutory legal charges

117.—(1) As a special form of charge by way of legal mortgage, a mortgage of freehold or leasehold land may be made by a deed expressed to be made by way of statutory mortgage, being in one of the forms (Nos. 1 or 4) set out in the Fourth Schedule to this Act, with such variations and additions, if any, as circumstances may require, and if so made the provisions of this section shall apply thereto.

(2) There shall be deemed to be included, and there shall by virtue of this Act be implied, in such a mortgage deed—

First, a covenant with the mortgagee by the person therein expressed to charge as mortgagor to the effect following, namely:

That the mortgagor will, on the stated day, pay to the mortgagee the stated mortgage money, with interest thereon in the meantime at the stated rate, and will thereafter, if and as long as the mortgage money or any part thereof remains unpaid, pay to the mortgagee (as well after as before any judgment is obtained under the mortgage) interest thereon, or on the unpaid part thereof, at the stated rate, by equal half-yearly payments the first thereof to be made at the end of six months from the day stated for payment of the mortgage money:

Secondly, a provision to the following effect (namely):

That if the mortgagor on the stated day pays to the mortgagee the

---

[83] See p. 181, n. 80.
[84] Restricted and modified by the Building Societies Act 1962 (10 & 11 Eliz. 2, c. 37), s. 37(3).
[85] This word was repealed by the Friendly Societies Act 1971 (c. 66), s. 14(2) and Sched. 3.
[86] Words repealed by the Industrial and Provident Societies Act 1965 (c. 12), Sched. 5.
[87] Words repealed by the Finance Act 1971 (c. 68), s. 64 and Sched. 14, Pt. VI.

stated mortgage money, with interest thereon in the meantime at the stated rate, the mortgagee at any time thereafter, at the request and cost of the mortgagor, shall discharge the mortgaged property or transfer the benefit of the mortgage as the mortgagor may direct.

This subsection applies to a mortgage deed made under section twenty-six of the Conveyance Act 1881, with a substitution of a reference to "the person therein expressed to convey as mortgagor" for the references in this subsection to "the person therein expressed to charge as mortgagor."

Forms of statutory transfers of legal charges

118.—(1) A transfer of a statutory mortgage may be made by a deed expressed to be made by way of statutory transfer of mortgage, being in such one of the three forms (Nos. 2, 3 or 4) set out in the Fourth Schedule to this Act as may be appropriate to the case with such variations and additions, if any, as circumstances may require, and if so made the provisions of this section shall apply thereto.

(2) In whichever of those three forms the deed of transfer is made, it shall have effect as follows (namely):—

  (i) There shall become vested in the person to whom the benefit of the mortgage is expressed to be transferred (who, with his personal representatives and assigns, is in this section designated the transferee), the right to demand, sue for, recover, and give receipts for the mortgage money, or the unpaid part thereof, and the interest then due, if any, and thenceforth to become due thereon, and the benefit of all securities for the same, and the benefit of and the right to sue on all covenants with the mortgagee, and the right to exercise all powers of the mortgagee:

  (ii) All the term and interest, if any, subject to redemption, of the mortgagee in the mortgaged land shall vest in the transferee, subject to redemption.

(3) If a covenantor joins in the deed of transfer, there shall also be deemed to be included, and there shall by virtue of this Act be implied therein, a covenant with the transferee by the person expressed to join therein as covenantor to the effect following (namely):

That the covenantor will, on the next of the days by the mortgage deed fixed for payment of interest pay to the transferee the stated mortgage money, or so much thereof as then remains unpaid, with interest thereon, or on the unpaid part thereof, in the meantime, at the rate stated in the mortgage deed; and will thereafter, as long as the mortgage money or any part thereof remains unpaid, pay to the transferee interest on that sum, or the unpaid part thereof, at the same rate, on the successive days by the mortgage deed fixed for payment of interest.

(4) If the deed of transfer is made in the Form No. 4, it shall, by virtue of this Act, operate not only as a statutory transfer of mortgage, but also as a statutory mortgage, and the provisions of this section shall have effect in relation thereto accordingly; but it shall not be liable to any increased stamp duty by reason only of it being designated a mortgage.

(5) This section applies to the transfer of a statutory mortgage created under any enactment replaced by this Act.

Implied covenants, joint and several

119. In a deed of statutory mortgage, or of statutory transfer of mortgage, where more persons than one are expressed to convey or charge as mortgagors, or to join as covenantors, the implied covenant on their part shall be deemed to be a joint and several covenant by them; and where there are more mortgagees or more transferees than one, the implied covenant with them shall be deemed to be a covenant with them jointly, unless the amount secured is expressed to be secured to them in shares or distinct sums, in which latter case the implied covenant with them shall be deemed to be a covenant with each severally in respect of the share or distinct sum secured to him.

Form of discharge of statutory mortgage or charge

120. A statutory mortgage may be surrendered or discharged by a receipt in the form (No. 5) set out in the Fourth Schedule to this Act with such variations and additions, if any, as circumstances may require.

Rentcharges

Remedies for the recovery of annual sums charged on land

121.[88]—(1) Where a person is entitled to receive out of any land, or out of the income of any land, any annual sum, payable half-yearly or otherwise, whether charged on the land or on the income of the land, and whether by way of rentcharge or otherwise, not being rent incident to a reversion, then, subject and without prejudice to all estates, interests, and rights having priority to the annual sum, the person entitled to receive the annual sum shall have such remedies for recovering and compelling payment thereof as are described in this section, as far as those remedies might have been conferred by the instrument under which the annual sum arises, but not further.

(2) If at any time the annual sum or any part thereof is unpaid for twenty-one days next after the time appointed for any payment in respect thereof, the person entitled to receive the annual sum may enter into and distrain on the land charged or any part thereof, and dispose according to law of any distress found, to the intent that thereby or otherwise the annual sum and all arrears thereof, and all costs and expenses occasioned by non-payment thereof, may be fully paid.

(3) If at any time the annual sum or any part thereof is unpaid for forty days next after the time appointed for any payment in respect thereof, then, although no legal demand has been made for payment thereof, the person entitled to receive the annual sum may enter into possession of and hold the land charged or any part thereof, and take the income thereof, until thereby or otherwise the annual sum and all arrears thereof due at the time of his entry, or afterwards becoming due during his continuance in possession, and all costs and expenses occasioned by non-payment of the annual sum, are fully paid; and such possession when taken shall be without impeachment of waste.

(4) In the like case the person entitled to the annual sum, whether taking possession or not, may also by deed demise the land charged or any part thereof, to a trustee for a term of years, with or without impeachment of waste, on trust, by all or any of the means hereinafter mentioned, or by any other reasonable means, to raise and pay the annual sum and all arrears thereof due or to become due, and all costs and expenses occasioned by non-payment of the annual sum, or incurred in compelling or obtaining payment thereof, or otherwise relating thereto, including the costs of the preparation and execution of the deed of demise, and the costs of the execution of the trusts of that deed:

Provided that this subsection shall not authorise the creation of a legal

---

[88] This section shall not have effect in relation to an annuity: Tithe Act 1936 (26 Geo. 5 & 1 Edw. 8, c. 43), s. 13(9). It was saved by the Perpetuities and Accumulations Act 1964 (c. 55), s. 11(1), *post*, p. 308 and extended by the Statute Law (Repeals) Act 1969 (c. 52), s. 3.

term of years absolute after the commencement of this Act, save where the annual sum is a rentcharge held for a legal estate.

The surplus, if any, of the money raised, or of the income received, under the trusts of the deed shall be paid to the person for the time being entitled to the land therein comprised in reversion immediately expectant on the term thereby created.

The means by which such annual sum, arrears, costs, and expenses may be raised includes—

(*a*) the creation of a legal mortgage or a sale (effected by assignment or subdemise) of the term created in the land charged or any part thereof,

(*b*) the receipt of the income of the land comprised in the term.

(5) This section applies only if and as far as a contrary intention is not expressed in the instrument under which the annual sum arises, and has effect subject to the terms of that instrument and to the provisions therein contained.

(6) The rule of law relating to perpetuities does not apply to any powers or remedies conferred by this section [. . .][89]

(7) The powers and remedies conferred by this section apply where the instrument creating the annual sum comes into operation after the thirty-first day of December, eighteen hundred and eighty-one, and whether the instrument conferring the power under which the annual sum was authorised to be created came into operation before or after that date, unless the instrument creating the power or under which the annual sum is created otherwise directs.

Creation of rentcharges charged on another rentcharge and remedies for recovery thereof

122.—(1) A rentcharge or other annual sum (not being rent incident to a reversion) payable half yearly or otherwise may be granted, reserved, charged or created out of or on another rentcharge or annual sum (not being rent incident to a reversion) charged on or payable out of land or on or out of the income of land, in like manner as the same could have been made to issue out of land.

(2) If at any time the annual sum so created or any part thereof is unpaid for twenty-one days next after the time appointed for any payment in respect thereof, the person entitled to receive the annual sum shall (without prejudice to any prior interest or charge) have power to appoint a receiver of the annual sum charged or any part thereof, and the provisions of this Act relating to the appointment, powers, remuneration and duties of a receiver, shall apply in like manner as if such person were a mortgagee entitled to exercise the power of sale conferred by this Act, and the annual sum charged were the mortgaged property and the person entitled thereto were the mortgagor.

(3) The power to appoint a receiver conferred by this section shall (where the annual sum is charged on a rentcharge) take effect in substitution for the remedies conferred, in the case of annual sums charged on land, by the last preceding section, by subsection (6) of that section shall apply and have effect as if herein re-enacted and in terms made applicable to the powers conferred by this section.

(4) This section applies to annual sums expressed to be created before as well as after the commencement of this Act, and, but without prejudice to any order of the court made before the commencement of this Act, operates to confirm any annual sum which would have been validly created if this section had been in force.

---

[89] Words repealed by the Perpetuities and Accumulations Act 1964, s. 11(2), *post*, p. 308.

Powers of Attorney

[*Ss.* 123 *and* 124 *were repealed by the Powers of Attorney Act* 1971, (*c.* 27), *s.*11(2) *and Sched.* 2.]

Powers of attorney relating to land to be filed

125.[90]—(1) [*This subsection was repealed by the Powers of Attorney Act* 1971 (*c.* 27), *s.*11(2) *and Sched.* 2.]

(2) Notwithstanding any stipulation to the contrary, a purchaser of any interest in or charge upon land (not being land or a charge registered [under the Land Registration Act 1925])[91] shall be entitled to have any instrument creating a power of attorney which affects his title, or [a copy][92] thereof or of the material portions thereof delivered to him free of expense.

(3) This section only applies to instruments executed after the commencement of this Act, and no right to rescind a contract shall arise by reason of the enforcement of the provisions of this section.

126–128. [*Repealed by the Powers of Attorney Act* 1971 (*c.* 27), *s.*11(2) *and Sched.* 2.]

Power of attorney granted by married woman

129. [*This section was repealed by the Powers of Attorney Act* 1971 (*c.* 27), *s.*8 *and Sched.* 2.]

Part IV

Equitable Interests and Things in Action

Creation of entailed interests in real and personal property

130.—(1) An interest in tail or in tail male or in tail female or in tail special (in this Act referred to as "an entailed interest") may be created by way of trust in any property, real or personal, but only by the like expressions as those by which before the commencement of this Act a similar estate tail could have been created by deed (not being an executory instrument) in freehold land, and with the like results, including the right to bar the entail either absolutely or so as to create an interest equivalent to a base fee, and accordingly all statutory provisions relating to estates tail in real property shall apply to entailed interests in personal property.

Personal estate so entailed (not being chattels settled as heirlooms) may be invested, applied, and otherwise dealt with as if the same were capital money or securities representing capital money arising under the Settled Land Act 1925 from land settled on the like trusts.

(2) Expressions contained in an instrument coming into operation after the commencement of this Act, which, in a will, or executory instrument coming into operation before such commencement, would have created an entailed interest in freehold land, but would not have been effectual for that purpose in a deed not being an executory instrument, shall (save as provided by the next succeeding section) operate in equity, in regard to

---

[90] As from October 1, 1971, no instrument creating a power of attorney, and no copy of any such instrument, shall be deposited or filed at the Central Office of the Supreme Court or at the Land Registry under this section, although any right to search for, inspect or copy or obtain an office copy of any such document which has been deposited or filed before that date, remains unaffected: Powers of Attorney Act (c. 27), s. 2(1) and (2).

[91] Words substituted by the Powers of Attorney Act 1971 (c. 27), s. 11(3).

[92] Substituted by the Law of Property (Amendment) Act 1926, *post*, Sched.

property real or personal, to create absolute, fee simple or other interests corresponding to those which, if the property affected had been personal estate, would have been created therein by similar expressions before the commencement of this Act.

(3) Where personal estate (including the proceeds of sale of land directed to be sold and chattels directed to be held as heirlooms) is, after the commencement of this Act, directed to be enjoyed or held with, or upon trusts corresponding to trusts affecting, land in which, either before or after the commencemenet of this Act an entailed interest has been created, and is subsisting, such direction shall be deemed sufficient to create a corresponding entailed interest in such personal estate.

(4) In default of and subject to the execution of a disentailing assurance or the exercise of the testamentary power conferred by this Act, an entailed interest (to the extent of the property affected) shall devolve as an equitable interest, from time to time, upon the persons who would have been successively entitled thereto as the heirs of the body (either generally or of a particular class) of the tenant in tail or other person, or as tenant by the curtesy, if the entailed interest had, before the commencement of this Act, been limited in respect of freehold land governed by the general law in force immediately before such commencement, and such law had remained unaffected.

(5) Where personal chattels are settled without reference to settled land on trusts creating entailed interests therein, the trustees, with the consent of the usufructuary for the time being if of full age, may sell the chattels or any of them, and the net proceeds of any such sale shall be held for and shall go to the same persons successively, in the same manner and for the same interests, as the chattels sold would have been held and gone if they had not been sold, and the income of investments representing such proceeds of sale shall be applied accordingly.

(6) An entailed interest shall only be capable of being created by a settlement of real or personal property or the proceeds of sale thereof (including the will of a person dying after the commencement of this Act), or by an agreement for a settlement in which the trusts to affect the property are sufficiently declared.

(7) In this Act where the context so admits "entailed interest" includes an estate tail (now made to take effect as an equitable interest) created before the commencement of this Act.

Abolition of the Rule in Shelley's case

131. Where by any instrument coming into operation after the commencement of this Act an interest in any property is expressed to be given to the heir or heirs or issue or any particular heir or any class of the heirs or issue of any person in words which, but for this section would, under the rule of law known as the Rule in Shelley's case, have operated to give that person an interest in fee simple or an entailed interest, such words shall operate in equity as words of purchase and not of limitation, and shall be construed and have effect accordingly, and in the case of an interest in any property expressed to be given to an heir or heirs or any particular heir or class of heirs, the same person or persons shall take as would in the case of freehold land have answered that description under the general law in force before the commencement of this Act.

As to heirs taking by purchase

132.—(1) A limitation of real or personal property in favour of the heir, either general or special, of a deceased person which, if limited in respect of freehold land before the commencement of this Act, would have conferred on the heir an estate in the land by purchase, shall operate to confer a corresponding equitable interest in the property on the person who would, if the general law in force immediately before such commencement had remained unaffected, have answered the description of the heir, either general or special, of the deceased in respect of his freehold land, either at the death of the deceased or at the time named in the limitation, as the case may require.

(2) This section applies whether the deceased person dies before or after the commencement of this Act, but only applies to limitations or trusts created by an instrument coming into operation after such commencement.

Abolition of enrolment of disentailing assurances, &c.

133. [*This section was repealed by the Statute Law (Repeals) Act* 1969 (*c.* 52), *s.* 1 *and Sched., Pt.* III.]

Restriction on executory limitations

134.—(1) Where there is a person entitled to—
  (*a*) an equitable interest in land for an estate in fee simple or for any less interest not being an entailed interest, or
  (*b*) any interest in other property, not being an entailed interest,
with an executory limitation over on default or failure of all or any of his issue, whether within or at any specified period or time or not, that executory limitation shall be or become void and incapable of taking effect, if and as soon as there is living any issue who has atained the age of [eighteen years][93] of the class on default or failure whereof the limitation over was to take effect.

(2) This section applies where the executory limitation is contained in an instrument coming into operation after the thirty-first day of December, eighteen hundred and eighty-two, save that, as regards instruments coming into operation before the commencement of this Act, it only applies to limitations of land for an estate in fee, or for a term of years absolute or determinable on life or for a term of life.

Equitable waste

135. An equitable interest for life without impeachment of waste does not confer upon the tenant for life any right to commit waste of the description known as equitable waste, unless an intention to confer such right expressly appears by the instrument creating such equitable interest.

Legal assignments of things in action

136.—(1) Any absolute assignment by writing under the hand of the assignor (not purporting to be by way of charge only) of any debt or other legal thing in action, of which express notice in writing has been given to the debtor, trustee or other person from whom the assignor would have been entitled to claim such debt or thing in action, is effectual in law (subject to equities having priority over the right of the assignee) to pass and transfer from the date of such notice—
  (*a*) the legal right to such debt or thing in action;
  (*b*) all legal and other remedies for the same; and
  (*c*) the power to give a good discharge for the same without the concurrence of the assignor:

[93] Words substituted by the Family Law Reform Act 1969 (c. 46), s. 1(3) and Sched. , Pt. I.

Provided[94] that, if the debtor, trustee or other person liable in respect of such debt or thing in action has notice—

(*a*) that the assignment is disputed by the assignor or any person claiming under him; or

(*b*) of any other opposing or conflicting claims to such debt or thing in action;

he may, if he thinks fit, either call upon the persons making claim thereto to interplead concerning the same, or pay the debt or other thing in action into court under the provisions of the Trustee Act 1925.

(2) This section does not affect the provisions of the Policies of Assurance Act 1867.

Dealings with life interests, reversions and other equitable interests

137.—(1) The law applicable to dealings with equitable things in action which regulates the priority of competing interests therein, shall, as respects dealings with equitable interests in land, capital money, and securities representing capital money effected after the commencement of this Act, apply to and regulate the priority of competing interests therein.

This subsection applies whether or not the money or securities are in court.

(2) (i) In the case of a dealing with an equitable interest in settled land, capital money or securities representing capital money, the persons to be served with notice of the dealing shall be the trustees of the settlement; and where the equitable interest is created by a derivative or subsidiary settlement, the persons to be served with notice shall be the trustees of that settlement.

(ii) In the case of a dealing with an equitable interest in the proceeds of sale of land or in the rents and profits until sale the persons to be served with notice shall, as heretofore, be the trustees for sale.

(iii) In any other case the person to be served with notice of a dealing with an equitable interest in land shall be the estate owner of the land affected.

The persons on whom notice is served pursuant to this subsection shall be affected thereby in the same manner as if they had been trustees of personal property out of which the equitable interest was created or arose.

This subsection does not apply where the money or securities are in court.

(3) A notice, otherwise than in writing, given to, or received by, a trustee after the commencement of this Act as respects any dealing with an equitable inteest in real or personal property, shall not affect the priority of competing claims of purchasers in that equitable interest.

(4) Where, as respects any dealing with an equitable interest in real or personal property—

(*a*) the trustees are not persons to whom a valid notice of the dealing can be given; or

(*b*) there are no trustees to whom a notice can be given; or

(*c*) for any other reason a valid notice cannot be served, or cannot be served without unreasonable cost or delay;

a purchaser may at his own cost require that—

(i) a memorandum of the dealing be endorsed, written on or permanently annexed to the instrument creating the trust;

---

[94] The county court will have jurisdiction in a case where the amount or value of the debt or thing in action does not exceed £1,000: see the County Courts Act 1959 (7 & 8 Eliz. 2, c. 22), Sched. 1, as amended by the County Courts Jurisdiction Order 1974 (No. 1273), s. 2. For general provisions concerning appeals on questions of fact in proceedings where the amount or value of the money or property claimed or paid into court exceeds £200, see *ibid.* s. 109(2)(*e*).

(ii) the instrument be produced to him by the person having the possession or custody thereof to prove that a sufficient memorandum has been placed thereon or annexed thereto.

Such memorandum shall, as respects priorities, operate in like manner as if notice in writing of the dealing had been given to trustees duly qualified to receive the notice at the time when the memorandum is placed on or annexed to the instrument creating the trust.

(5) Where the property affected is settled land, the memorandum shall be placed on or annexed to the trust instrument and not the vesting instrument.

Where the property affected is land held on trust for sale, the memorandum shall be placed on or annexed to the instrument whereby the equitable interest is created.

(6) Where the trust is created by statute or by operation of law, or in any other case where there is no instrument whereby the trusts are declared, the instrument under which the equitable interest is acquired or which is evidence of the devolution thereof shall, for the purposes of this section, be deemed the instrument creating the trust.

In particular, where the trust arises by reason of an intestacy, the letters of administration or probate in force when the dealing was effected shall be deemed such instrument.

(7) Nothing in this section affects any priority acquired before the commencement of this Act.

(8) Where a notice in writing of a dealing with an equitable interest in real or personal property has been served on a trustee under this section, the trustees from time to time of the property affected shall be entitled to the custody of the notice, and the notice shall be delivered to them by any person who for the time being may have the custody thereof; and subject to the payment of costs, any person interested in the equitable interest may require production of the notice.

(9) The liability of the estate owner of the legal estate affected to produce documents and furnish information to persons entitled to equitable interests therein shall correspond to the liability of a trustee for sale to produce documents and furnish information to persons entitled to equitable interests in the proceeds of sale of the land.

(10) This section does not apply until a trust has been created, and in this section "dealing" includes a disposition by operation of law.

Power to nominate a trust corporation to receive notices

138.—(1) By any settlement or other instrument creating a trust, a trust corporation may be nominated to whom notices of dealings affecting real or personal property may be given, whether or not under the foregoing section, and in default of such nomination the trustees (if any) of the instrument, or the court on the application of any person interested, may make the nomination.

(2) The person having the possession or custody of any instrument on which notices under that section may be endorsed shall cause the name of the trust corporation to whom notices may be given to be endorsed upon that instrument.

(3) Notice given to any trust corporation whose name is so endorsed shall operate in the same way as a notice or endorsement under the foregoing section.

(4) Where a trust corporation is acting for the purposes of this section a notice given to a trustee of the trust instrument of a dealing relating to the trust property shall forthwith be delivered or sent by post by the trustee to the trust corporation, and until received by the corporation shall not affect any priority.

(5) A trust corporation shall not be nominated for the purposes of this section—

(*a*) unless that corporation consents to act; or

(*b*) where that corporation has any beneficial interest in or charge upon the trust property; or

(*c*) where a trust corporation is acting as the trustee or one of the trustees of the instrument creating the trust.

(6) Where a trust corporation acting for the purposes of this section becomes entitled to any beneficial interest in or charge upon the trust property, another trust corporation shall be nominated in its place and all documents relating to notices affecting the trust shall be delivered to the corporation so nominated.

(7) A trust corporation acting for the purposes of this section shall be bound to keep a separate register of notices of dealings in respect of each equitable interest and shall enter therein—

(*a*) the date of the notice;

(*b*) the name of the person giving the notice;

(*c*) short particulars of the equitable interest intended to be affected; and

(*d*) short particulars of the effect of the dealing if mentioned in the notice.

(8) The trust corporation may, before making any entry in the register, require the applicant to pay a fee not exceeding the prescribed fee.

(9) Subject to the payment of a fee not exceeding the prescribed fee, the trust corporation shall permit any person who would, if the corporation had been the trustee of the trust instrument, have been entitled to inspect notices served on the trustee, to inspect and take copies of the register and any notices held by the corporation.

(10) Subject to the payment by the applicant of a fee not exceeding the prescribed fee, the trust corporation shall reply to all inquiries respecting notices received by the corporation in like manner and in the same circumstances as if the corporation had been the trustee of the trust instrument.

(11) In this section "prescribed fee" means the fee prescribed by the Treasury, with the sanction of the Lord Chancellor, in cases where the Public Trustee acts as a trust corporation for the purposes of this section.

PART V

LEASES AND TENANCIES

Effect of extinguishment of reversion

139.—(1)[95] Where a reversion expectant on a lease of land is surrendered or merged, the estate or interest which as against the lessee for the time being confers the next vested right to the land, shall be deemed the reversion for the purpose of preserving the same incidents and obligations as would have affected the original reversion had there been no surrender or merger thereof.

(2) This section applies to surrenders or mergers effected after the first day of October, eighteen hundred and forty-five.

---

[95] In the case of a tenancy continuing by virtue of the Landlord and Tenant Act 1954 (2 & 3 Eliz. 2, c. 56) or of s. 29(4) of the Reserve and Auxiliary Forces (Protection of Civil Interests) Act 1951 (14 & 15 Geo. 6, c. 65), after the coming to an end of the interest in reversion immediately expectant upon the termination thereof this subsection shall apply as if references therein to the surrender or merger of the reversion included references to the determination of the reversion for any reason other than surrender or merger: Landlord and Tenant Act 1954, s. 65(2); Reserve and Auxiliary Forces (Protection of Civil Interests) Act 1951, s. 32(3).

Apportionment of conditions on severance

140.—(1) Notwithstanding the severance by conveyance, surrender, or otherwise of the reversionary estate in any land comprised in a lease, and notwithstanding the avoidance or cesser in any other manner of the term granted by a lease as to part only of the land comprised therein, every condition or right of re-entry, and every other condition contained in the lease, shall be apportioned, and shall remain annexed to the severed parts of the reversionary estate as severed, and shall be in force with respect to the term whereon each severed part is reversionary, or the term in the part of the land as to which the term has not been surrendered, or has not been avoided or has not otherwise ceased, in like manner as if the land comprised in each severed part, or the land as to which the term remains subsisting, as the case may be, had alone originally been comprised in the lease.

(2)[96] In this section "right of re-entry" includes a right to determine the lease by notice to quit or otherwise; but where the notice is served by a person entitled to a severed part of the reversion so that it extends to part only of the land demised, the lessee may within one month determine the lease in regard to the rest of the land by giving to the owner of the reversionary estate therein a counter notice expiring at the same time as the original notice.

(3) This section applies to leases made before or after the commencement of this Act and whether the severance of the reversionary estate or the partial avoidance or cesser of the term was effected before or after such commencement:

Provided that, where the lease was made before the first day of January eighteen hundred and eighty-two nothing in this section shall affect the operation of a severance of the reversionary estate or partial avoidance or cesser of the term which was effected before the commencement of this Act.

Rent and benefit of lessee's covenants to run with the reversion

141.—(1) Rent reserved by a lease, and the benefit of every covenant or provision therein contained, having reference to the subject-matter thereof, and on the lessee's part to be observed or performed, and every condition of re-entry and other condition therein contained, shall be annexed and incident to and shall go with the reversionary estate in the land, or in any part thereof, immediately expectant on the term granted by the lease, notwithstanding severance of that reversionary estate, and without prejudice to any liability affecting a covenantor or his estate.

(2) Any such rent, covenant or provision shall be capable of being recovered, received, enforced, and taken advantage of, by the person from time to time entitled, subject to the term, to the income of the whole or any part, as the case may require, of the land leased.

(3) Where that person becomes entitled by conveyance or otherwise, such rent, covenant or provision may be recovered, received, enforced or taken advantage of by him notwithstanding that he becomes so entitled after the condition of re-entry or forfeiture has become enforceable, but this subsection does not render enforceable any condition of re-entry or other condition waived or released before such person becomes entitled as aforesaid.

(4) This section applies to leases made before or after the commencement of this Act, but does not affect the operation of—

(*a*) any severance of the reversionary estate; or

---

[96] The proviso added to this subsection by the Law of Property (Amendment) Act 1926, *post*, s. 2, was repealed with savings by the Agricultural Holdings Act 1948 (11 & 12 Geo. 6, c. 63), ss. 98–100, Sched. 8.

(*b*) any acquisition by conveyance or otherwise of the right to receive or enforce any rent covenant or provision;

effected before the commencement of this Act.

Obligation of lessor's covenants to run with reversion

142.—(1) The obligation under a condition or of a covenant entered into by a lessor with reference to the subject-matter of the lease shall, if and as far as the lessor has power to bind the reversionary estate immediately expectant on the term granted by the lease, be annexed and incident to and shall go with that reversionary estate, or the several parts thereof, notwithstanding severance of that reversionary estate, and may be taken advantage of and enforced by the person in whom the term is from time to time vested by conveyance, devolution in law, or otherwise; and, if and as far as the lessor has power to bind the person from time to time entitled to that reversionary estate, the obligation aforesaid may be taken advantage of and enforced against any person so entitled.

(2) This section applies to leases made before or after the commencement of this Act, whether the severance of the reversionary estate was effected before or after such commencement:

Provided that, where the lease was made before the first day of January eighteen hundred and eighty-two, nothing in this section shall affect the operation of any severance of the reversionary estate effected before such commencement.

This section takes effect without prejudice to any liability affecting a covenantor or his estate.

Effect of licences granted to lessees

143.—(1) Where a licence is granted to a lessee to do any act, the licence, unless otherwise expressed, extends only—

(*a*) to the permission actually given; or

(*b*) to the specific breach of any provision or covenant referred to; or

(*c*) to any other matter thereby specifically authorised to be done;

and the licence does not prevent any proceeding for any subsequent breach unless otherwise specified in the licence.

(2) Notwithstanding any such licence—

(*a*) All rights under covenants and powers of re-entry contained in the lease remain in full force and are available as against any subsequent breach of covenant, condition or other matter not specifically authorised or waived, in the same manner as if no licence had been granted; and

(*b*) The condition or right of entry remains in force in all respects as if the licence had not been granted, save in respect of the particular matter authorised to be done.

(3) Where in any lease there is a power or condition of re-entry on the lessee assigning, subletting or doing any other specified act without a licence, and a licence is granted—

(*a*) to any one of two or more lessees to do any act, or to deal with his equitable share or interest; or

(*b*) to any lessee, or to any one of two or more lessees to assign or underlet part only of the property, or to do any act in respect of part only of the property;

the licence does not operate to extinguish the right of entry in case of any breach of covenant or condition by the co-lessees of the other shares or interests in the property, or by the lessee or lessees of the rest of the property (as the case may be) in respect of such shares or interests or remaining property, but the right of entry remains in force in respect of the shares interests or property not the subject of the licence.

This subsection does not authorise the grant after the commencement of this Act of a licence to create an undivided share in a legal estate.

(4) This section applies to licences granted after the thirteenth day of August, eighteen hundred and fifty-nine.

No fine to be exacted for licence to assign

144. In all leases containing a covenant, condition, or agreement against assigning, underletting, or parting with the possession, or disposing of the land or property leased without licence or consent, such covenant, condition, or agreement shall, unless the lease contains an express provision to the contrary, be deemed to be subject to a proviso to the effect that no fine or sum of money in the nature of a fine shall be payable for or in respect of such licence or consent; but this proviso does not preclude the right to require the payment of a reasonable sum in respect of any legal or other expense incurred in relation to such licence or consent.

Lessee to give notice of ejectment to lessor

145. Every lessee to whom there is delivered any writ for the recovery of premises demised to or held by him, or to whose knowledge any such writ comes, shall forthwith give notice thereof to his lessor or his bailiff or receiver, and, if he fails so to do, he shall be liable to forfeit to the person of whom he holds the premises an amount equal to the value of three years' improved or rack rent of the premises, to be recovered by action in any court having jurisdiction in respect of claims for such an amount.

Restrictions on and relief against forfeiture of leases and underleases

146.[97]—(1) A right of re-entry or forfeiture under any proviso or stipulation in a lease for a breach of any covenant or condition in the lease shall not be enforceable, by action or otherwise, unless and until the lessor serves on the lessee a notice—

- (*a*) specifying the particular breach complained of; and
- (*b*) if the breach is capable of remedy, requiring the lessee to remedy the breach; and
- (*c*) in any case, requiring the lessee to make compensation in money for the breach;

and the lessee fails, within a reasonable time thereafter, to remedy the breach, if it is capable of remedy, and to make reasonable compensation in money, to the satisfaction of the lessor, for the breach.

(2) Where a lessor is proceeding, by action or otherwise, to enforce such a right of re-entry or forfeiture, the lessee may, in the lessor's action, if any, or in any action brought by himself, apply to the court for relief, and the court may grant or refuse relief, as the court, having regard to the proceedings and conduct of the parties under the foregoing provisions of this section, and to all the other circumstances, thinks fit; and in case of relief may grant it on such terms, if any, as to costs, expenses, damages, compensation, penalty, or otherwise, including the granting of an

---

[97] For amendments relating to the service of notice see the Landlord and Tenant Act 1927 (17 & 18 Geo. 5, c. 36), s. 18(2), as amended by the Recorded Delivery Service Act 1962 (10 & 11 Eliz. 2, c. 27), s. 1.

For restrictions on the enforcement of repairing covenants in long leases of small houses, see the Leasehold Property (Repairs) Act 1938 (1 & 2 Geo. 6, c. 34), ss. 1–3, 9.

The county court shall have jurisdiction in a case where the lessor is proceeding by action in the court to enforce the right of entry or forfeiture, or, if the lessor is proceeding by action in the court to enforce the right of entry or forfeiture, or, if the lessor is proceeding to enforce the said right otherwise than by action, in a case where the net annual value for rating of the property comprised in the lease is not above the county court limit: see the County Courts Act 1959 (7 & 8 Eliz. 2, c. 22), Sched. 1, as amended by the Administration of Justice Act 1973 (c. 15), Sched. 2, Pt. 1.

injunction to restrain any like breach in the future, as the court, in the circumstances of each case, thinks fit.

(3) A lessor shall be entitled to recover as a debt due to him from a lessee, and in addition to damages (if any), all reasonable costs and expenses properly incurred by the lessor in the employment of a solicitor and surveyor or valuer, or otherwise, in reference to any breach giving rise to a right of re-entry or forfeiture which, at the request of the lessee, is waived by the lessor, or from which the lessee is relieved, under the provisions of this Act.

(4)[98] Where a lessor is proceeding by action or otherwise to enforce a right of re-entry or forfeiture under any covenant, proviso, or stipulation in a lease, or for non-payment of rent, the court may, on application by any person claiming as under-lessee any estate or interest in the property comprised in the lease or any part thereof, either in the lessor's action (if any) or in any action brought by such person for that purpose, make an order vesting, for the whole term of the lease or any less term, the property comprised in the lease or any part thereof in any person entitled as under-lessee to any estate or interest in such property upon such conditions as to execution of any deed or other document, payment of rent, costs, expenses, damages, compensation, giving security, or otherwise, as the court in the circumstances of each case may think fit, but in no case shall any such under-lessee be entitled to require a lease to be granted to him for any longer term than he had his original sub-lease.

(5)[99] For the purposes of this section—

(*a*) "Lease" includes an original or derivative under-lease; also an agreement for a lease where the lessee has become entitled to have his lease granted; also a grant at a fee farm rent, or securing a rent by condition;

(*b*) "Lessee" includes an original or derivative under-lessee, and the persons deriving title under a lessee; also a grantee under any such grant as aforesaid and the persons deriving title under him;

(*c*) "Lessor" includes an original or derivative under-lessor, and the persons deriving title under a lessor; also a person making such grant as aforesaid and the persons deriving title under him;

(*d*) "Under-lease" includes an agreement for an under-lease where the under-lessee has become entitled to have his under-lease granted;

(*e*) "Under-lessee" includes any person deriving title under an under-lessee.

(6) This section applies although the proviso or stipulation under which the right of re-entry or forfeiture accrues is inserted in the lease in pursuance of the directions of any Act of Parliament.

(7) For the purposes of this section a lease limited to continue as long only as the lessee abstains from committing a breach of covenant shall be and take effect as a lease to continue for any longer term for which it could subsist, but determinable by a proviso for re-entry on such a breach.

(8)[1] This section does not extend—

(i) To a covenant or condition against assigning, underletting, parting with the possession, or disposing of the land leased

---

[98] Nothing in subss. (8) (9) or (10) of this section shall affect the provsions of subs. (4) of this section: Law of Property (Amendment) Act 1929 (19 & 20 Geo. 5, c. 9).
    This subsection is saved by the Leasehold Property (Repairs) Act 1938 (1 & 2 Geo. 6, c. 34), s. 7.

[99] For the application of "lessor" and "lessee" see the Leasehold Property (Repairs) Act 1938 (1 & 2 Geo. 6, c. 34), s. 7.

[1] See note 98, *supra.*

where the breach occurred before the commencement of this Act; or

(ii) In the case of a mining lease, to a covenant or condition for allowing the lessor to have access to or inspect books, accounts, records, weighing machines or other things, or to enter or inspect the mine or the workings thereof.

(9)[1] This section does not apply to a condition for forfeiture on the bankruptcy of the lessee or on taking in execution of the lessee's interest if contained in a lease of—

(*a*) Agricultural or pastoral land;
(*b*) Mines or minerals;
(*c*) A house used or intended to be used as a public-house or beer-shop;
(*d*) A house let as a dwelling-house, with the use of any furniture, books, works of art, or other chattels not being in the nature of fixtures;
(*e*) Any property with respect to which the personal qualifications of the tenant are of importance for the preservation of the value or character of the property, or on the ground of neighbourhood to the lessor, or to any person holding under him.

(10)[1] Where a condition of forfeiture on the bankruptcy of the lessee or on taking in execution of the lessee's interest is contained in any lease, other than a lease of any of the classes mentioned in the last subsection, then—

(*a*) if the lessee's interest is sold within one year from the bankruptcy or taking in execution, this section applies to the forfeiture condition aforesaid;
(*b*) if the lessee's interest is not sold before the expiration of that year, this section only applies to the forfeiture condition aforesaid during the first year from the date of the bankruptcy or taking in execution.

(11) This section does not, save as otherwise mentioned, affect the law relating to re-entry or forfeiture or relief in case of non-payment of rent.

(12) This section has effect notwithstanding any stipulation to the contrary.

Relief against notice to effect decorative repairs

147.[2]—(1) After a notice is served on a lessee relating to the internal decorative repairs to a house or other building, he may apply to the court for relief, and if, having regard to all the circumstances of the case (including in particular the length of the lessee's term or interest remaining unexpired), the court is satisfied that the notice is unreasonable, it may, by order, wholly or partially relieve the lessee from liability for such repairs.

(2) This section does not apply:—

(i) where the liability arises under an express covenant or agreement to put the property in a decorative state of repair and the covenant or agreement has never been performed;
(ii) to any matter necessary or proper—
(*a*) for putting or keeping the property in a sanitary condition, or
(*b*) for the maintenance or preservation of the structure;
(iii) to any statutory liability to keep a house in all respects reasonably fit for human habitation;
(iv) to any covenant or stipulation to yield up the house or other building in a specified state of repair at the end of the term.

---

[1] See note 98, *supra*.
[2] The county court shall have jurisdiction in a case where the net annual value for rating of the house or other building is not above the county court limit: the County Courts Act 1959 (7 & 8 Eliz. 2, c. 22), Sched. 1, as amended by the Administration of Justice Act 1973 (c. 15), Sched. 2, Pt. 1.

(3) In this section "lease" includes an underlease and an agreement for a lease, and "lessee" has a corresponding meaning and includes any person liable to effect the repairs.

(4) This section applies whether the notice is served before or after the commencement of this Act, and has effect notwithstanding any stipulation to the contrary.

Waiver of a covenant in a lease

148.—(1) Where any actual waiver by a lessor or the persons deriving title under him of the benefit of any covenant or condition in any lease is proved to have taken place in any particular instance, such waiver shall not be deemed to extend to any instance, or to any breach of covenant or condition save that to which such waiver specially relates, nor operate as a general waiver of the benefit of any such covenant or condition.

(2) This section applies unless a contrary intention appears and extends to waivers effected after the twenty-third day of July, eighteen hundred and sixty.

Abolition of interesse termini, and as to reversionary leases and leases for lives

149.—(1) The doctrine of interesse termini is hereby abolished.

(2) As from the commencement of this Act all terms of years absolute shall, whether the interest is created before or after such commencement, be capable of taking effect at law or in equity, according to the estate interest or powers of the grantor, from the date fixed for commencement of the term, without actual entry.

(3) A term, at a rent or granted in consideration of a fine, limited after the commencement of this Act to take effect more than twenty-one years from the date of the instrument purporting to create it, shall be void, and any contract made after such commencement to create such a term shall likewise be void; but this subsection does not apply to any term taking effect in equity under a settlement, or created out of an equitable interest under a settlement, or under an equitable power for mortgage, indemnity or other like purposes.

(4) Nothing in subsections (1) and (2) of this section prejudicially affects the right of any person to recover any rent or to enforce or take advantage of any covenants or conditions, or, as respects terms or interests created before the commencement of this Act, operates to vary any statutory or other obligations imposed in respect of such terms or interests.

(5) Nothing in this Act affects the rule of law that a legal term, whether or not being a mortgage term, may be created to take effect in reversion expectant on a longer term, which rule is hereby confirmed.

(6)[3] Any lease or underlease, at a rent, or in consideration of a fine, or life or lives or for any term of years determinable with life or lives, or on the marriage of the lessee, or any contract therefor, made before or after the commencement of this Act, or created by virtue of Part V of the Law of Property Act 1922 shall take effect as a lease, underlease or contract therefor, for a term of ninety years determinable after the death or marriage (as the case may be) of the original lessee, or of the survivor of the original lessees, by at least one month's notice in writing given to determine the same on one of the quarter days applicable to the tenancy, either by the lessor or the persons deriving title under him, to the person entitled to the leasehold interest, or if no such person is in existence by affixing the same to the premises, or by the lessee or other persons in

---

[3] For the proportion of liability as between landlords and tenants, see the War Damage Act 1943 (6 & 7 Geo. 6, c. 21), s. 50(6).

whom the leasehold interest is vested to the lessor or the persons deriving title under him:

Provided that—

    (*a*) this subsection shall not apply to any term taking effect in equity under a settlement or created out of an equitable interest under a settlement for mortgage, indemnity, or other like purposes;

    (*b*) the person in whom the leasehold interest is vested by virtue of Part V of the Law of Property Act 1922 shall, for the purposes of this subsection, be deemed an original lessee;

    (*c*) if the lease, underlease, or contract therefor is made determinable on the dropping of the lives of persons other than or besides the lessees, then the notice shall be capable of being served after the death of any person or of the survivor of any persons (whether or not including the lessees) on the cesser of whose life or lives the lease, underlease, or contract is made determinable, instead of after the death of the original lessee or of the survivor of the original lessees;

    (*d*) if there are no quarter days specially applicable to the tenancy, notice may be given to determine the tenancy on one of the usual quarter days.

Surrender of a lease, without prejudice to underleases with a view to the grant of a new lease

150.—(1) A lease may be surrendered with a view to the acceptance of a new lease in place thereof, without a surrender of any under-lease derived thereout.

(2) A new lease may be granted and accepted, in place of any lease so surrendered, without any such surrender of an under-lease as aforesaid, and the new lease operates as if all under-leases derived out of the surrendered lease had been surrendered before the surrender of that lease was effected.

(3) The lessee under the new lease and any person deriving title under him is entitled to the same rights and remedies in respect of the rent reserved by and the covenants, agreements and conditions contained in any under-lease as if the original lease had not been surrendered but was or remained vested in him.

(4) Each under-lessee and any person deriving title under him is entitled to hold and enjoy the land comprised in his under-lease (subject to the payment of any rent reserved by and to the observance of the covenants agreements and conditions contained in the under-lease) as if the lease out of which the under-lease was derived had not been surrendered.

(5) The lessor granting the new lease and any person deriving title under him is entitled to the same remedies, by distress or entry in and upon the land comprised in any such under-lease for rent reserved by or for breach of any covenant, agreement or condition contained in the new lease (so far only as the rents reserved by or the covenants, agreements or conditions contained in the new lease do not exceed or impose greater burdens than those reserved by or contained in the original lease out of which the under-lease is derived) as he would have had—

    (*a*) If the original lease had remained on foot; or

    (*b*) If a new under-lease derived out of the new lease had been granted to the under-lessee or a person deriving title under him; as the case may require.

(6) This section does not affect the powers of the court to give relief against forfeiture.

Provision as to attornments by tenants

151.—(1) Where land is subject to a lease—

(*a*) the conveyance of a reversion in the land expectant on the determination of the lease; or

(*b*) the creation or conveyance of a rentcharge to issue or issuing out of the land;

shall be valid without any attornment of the lessee:

Nothing in this subsection—

(i) affects the validity of any payment of rent by the lessee to the person making the conveyance or grant before notice of the conveyance or grant is given to him by the person entitled thereunder; or

(ii) renders the lessee liable for any breach of covenant to pay rent, on account of his failure to pay rent to the person entitled under the conveyance or grant before such notice is given to the lessee.

(2) An attornment by the lessee in respect of any land to a person claiming to be entitled to the interest in the land of the lessor, if made without the consent of the lessor, shall be void.

This subsection does not apply to an attornment—

(*a*) made pursuant to a judgment of a court of competent jurisdiction; or

(*b*) to a mortgagee, by a lessee holding under a lease from the mortgagor where the right of redemption is barred; or

(*c*) to any other person rightfully deriving title under the lessor.

Leases invalidated by reason of non-compliance with terms of powers under which they are granted

152.—(1) Where in the intended exercise of any power of leasing, whether conferred by an Act of Parliament or any other instrument, a lease (in this section referred to as an invalid lease) is granted, which by reason of any failure to comply with the terms of the power is invalid, then—

(*a*) as against the person entitled after the determination of the interest of the grantor to the reversion; or

(*b*) as against any other person who, subject to any lease properly granted under the power, would have been entitled to the land comprised in the lease;

the lease, if it was made in good faith, and the lessee has entered thereunder, shall take effect in equity as a contract for the grant, at the request of the lessee, of a valid lease under the power, of like effect as the invalid lease, subject to such variations as may be necessary in order to comply with the terms of the power:

Provided that a lessee under an invalid lease shall not, by virtue of any such implied contract, be entitled to obtain a variation of the lease if the other persons who would have been bound by the contract are willing and able to confirm the lease without variation.

(2) Where a lease granted in the intended exercise of such a power is invalid by reason of the grantor not having power to grant the lease at the date thereof, but the grantor's interest in the land comprised therein continues after the time when he might, in the exercise of the power, have properly granted a lease in the like terms, the lease shall take effect as a valid lease in like manner as if it had been granted at that time.

(3) Where during the continuance of the possession taken under an invalid lease the person for the time being entitled, subject to such possession, to the land comprised therein or to the rents and profits thereof, is able to confirm the lease without variation, the lessee, or other person who would have been bound by the lease had it been valid, shall, at

the request of the person so able to confirm the lease, be bound to accept a confirmation thereof, and thereupon the lease shall have effect and be deemed to have had effect as a valid lease from the grant thereof.

Confirmation under this subsection may be by a memorandum in writing signed by or on behalf of the persons respectively confirming and accepting the confirmation of the lease.

(4) Where a receipt or a memorandum in writing confirming an invalid lease is, upon or before the acceptance of rent thereunder, signed by or on behalf of the person accepting the rent, that acceptance shall, as against that person, be deemed to be a confirmation of the lease.

(5) The foregoing provisions of this section do not affect prejudicially—

(*a*) any right of action or other right or remedy to which, but for those provisions or any enactment replaced by those provisions, the lessee named in an invalid lease would or might have been entitled under any covenant on the part of the grantor for title or quiet enjoyment contained therein or implied thereby; or

(*b*) any right of re-entry or other right or remedy to which, but for those provisions or any enactment replaced thereby, the grantor or other person for the time being entitled to the reversion expectant on the termination of the lease, would or might have been entitled by reason of any breach of the covenants, conditions or provisions contained in the lease and binding on the lessee.

(6) Where a valid power of leasing is vested in or may be exercised by a person who grants a lease which, by reason of the determination of the interest of the grantor or otherwise, cannot have effect and continuance according to the terms thereof independently of the power, the lease shall for the purposes of this section be deemed to have been granted in the intended exercise of the power although the power is not referred to in the lease.

(7) This section does not apply to a lease of land held on charitable, ecclesiastical or public trusts.

(8) This section takes effect without prejudice to the provision in this Act for the grant of leases in the name and on behalf of the estate owner of the land affected.

Enlargement of residue of long terms into fee simple estates

153.—(1) Where a residue unexpired of not less than two hundred years of a term, which, as originally created, was for not less than three hundred years, is subsisting in land, whether being the whole land originally comprised in the term, or part only thereof,—

(*a*) without any trust or right or redemption affecting the term in favour of the freeholder, or other person entitled in reversion expectant on the term; and

(*b*) without any rent, or with merely a peppercorn rent or other rent having no money value, incident to the reversion, or having had a rent, not being merely a peppercorn rent or other rent having no money value, originally so incident, which subsequently has been released or has become barred by lapse of time, or has in any other way ceased to be payable;

the term may be enlarged into a fee simple in the manner, and subject to the restrictions in this section provided.

(2) This section applies to and includes every such term as aforesaid whenever created, whether or not having the freehold as the immediate reversion thereon; but does not apply to—

(i) Any term liable to be determined by re-entry for condition broken; or

(ii) Any term created by subdemise out of a superior term, itself incapable of being enlarged into fee simple.

(3) This section extends to mortgage terms, where the right of redemption is barred.

(4) A rent not exceeding the yearly sum of one pound which has not been collected or paid for a continuous period of twenty years or upwards shall, for the purposes of this section, be deemed to have ceased to be payable:

Provided that, of the said period, at least five years must have elapsed after the commencement of this Act.

(5) Where a rent incident to a reversion expectant on a term to which this section applies is deemed to have ceased to be payable for the purposes aforesaid, no claim for such rent or for any arrears thereof shall be capable of being enforced.

(6) Each of the following persons, namely—
- (i) Any person beneficially entitled in right of the term, whether subject to any incumbrance or not, to possession of any land comprised in the term, and, in the case of a married woman without the concurrence of her husband, whether or not she is entitled for her separate use or as her separate property [. . .]⁴;
- (ii) Any person being in receipt of income as trustee, in right of the term, or having the term vested in him in trust for sale, whether subject to any incumbrance or not;
- (iii) Any person in whom, as personal representative of any deceased person, the term is vested, whether subject to any incumbrance or not;

shall, so far as regards the land to which he is entitled, or in which he is interested in right of the term, in any such character as aforesaid, have power by deed to declare to the effect that, from and after the execution of the deed, the term shall be enlarged into a fee simple.

(7) Thereupon, by virtue of the deed and of this Act, the term shall become and be enlarged accordingly, and the person in whom the term was previously vested shall acquire and have in the land a fee simple instead of the term.

(8) The estate in fee simple so acquired by enlargement shall be subject to all the same trusts, powers, executory limitations over, rights, and equities, and to all the same covenants and provisions relating to user and enjoyment, and to all the same obligations of every kind, as the term would have been subject to if it had not been so enlarged.

(9) But where—
- (*a*) any land so held for the residue of a term has been settled in trust by reference to other land, being freehold land, so as to go along with that other land, or, in the case of settlements coming into operation before the commencement of this Act, so as to go along with that other land as far as the law permits; and
- (*b*) at the time of enlargement, the ultimate beneficial interest in the term, whether subject to any subsisting particular estate or not, has not become absolutely and indefeasibly vested in any person, free from charges or powers of charging created by a settlement;

the estate in fee simple acquired as aforesaid shall, without prejudice to any conveyance for value previously made by a person having a contingent or defeasible interest in the term, be liable to be, and shall be, conveyed by means of a subsidiary vesting instrument and settled in like manner as the

---

⁴ Words repealed by the Married Women (Restraint upon Anticipation) Act 1949 (12, 13 & 14 Geo. 6, c. 78), s. 1, Sched. 2.

other land, being freehold land, aforesaid, and until so conveyed and settled shall devolve beneficially as if it had been so conveyed and settled.

(10) The estate in fee simple so acquired shall, whether the term was originally created without impeachment of waste or not, include the fee simple in all mines and minerals which at the time of enlargement have not been severed in right or in fact, or have not been severed or reserved by an inclosure Act or award.

Application of Part V to existing leases

154.[5] This Part of this Act, except where otherwise expressly provided, applies to leases created before or after the commencement of this Act, and "lease" includes an under-lease or other tenancy.

PART VI

POWERS

Release of powers simply collateral

155. A person to whom any power, whether coupled with an interest or not, is given may by deed release, or contract not to exercise, the power.

Disclaimer of powers

156.—(1) A person to whom any power, whether coupled with an interest or not, is given may by deed disclaim the power, and, after disclaimer, shall not be capable of exercising or joining in the exercise of the power.

(2) On such disclaimer, the power may be exercised by the other person or persons or the survivor or survivors of the other persons, to whom the power is given, unless the contrary is expressed in the instrument creating the power.

Protection of purchasers claiming under certain void appointments

157.—(1) An instrument purporting to exercise a power of appointment over property, which, in default of and subject to any appointment, is held in trust for a class or number of persons of whom the appointee is one, shall not (save as hereinafter provided) be void on the ground of fraud on the power as against a purchaser in good faith:

Provided that, if the interest appointed exeeds, in amount or value, the interest in such property to which immediately before the execution of the instrument the appointee was presumptively entitled under the trust in default of appointment, having regard to any advances made in his favour and to any hotchpot provision, the protection afforded by this section to a purchaser shall not extend to such excess.

(2) In this section "a purchaser in good faith" means a person dealing with an appointee of the age of not less than twenty-five years for valuable consideration in money or money's worth, and without notice of the fraud, or of any circumstances from which, if reasonable inquiries had been made, the fraud might have been discovered.

(3) Persons deriving title under any purchaser entitled to the benefit of this section shall be entitled to the like benefit.

(4) This section applies only to dealings effected after the commencement of this Act.

---

[5] Applied by the Leasehold Property (Repairs) Act 1938 (1 & 2 Geo. 6, c. 34), s. 7(1), as amended by the Landlord and Tenant Act 1954 (2 & 3 Eliz. 2, c. 56), s. 51(2)(g).

Validation of appointments where objects are excluded or take illusory shares

158.—(1) No appointment made in exercise of any power to appoint any property among two or more objects shall be invalid on the ground that—

(*a*) an unsubstantial, illusory, or nominal share only is appointed to or left unappointed to devolve upon any one or more of the objects of the power; or

(*b*) any object of the power is thereby altogether excluded;

but every such appointment shall be valid notwithstanding that any one or more of the objects is not thereby, or in default of appointment, to take any share in the property.

(2) This section does not affect any provision in the instrument creating the power which declares the amount of any share from which any object of the power is not to be excluded.

(3) This section applies to appointments made before or after the commencement of this Act.

Execution of powers not testamentary

159.—(1) A deed executed in the presence of and attested by two or more witnesses (in the manner in which deeds are ordinarily executed and attested) is so far as respects the execution and attestation thereof, a valid execution of a power of appointment by deed or by any instrument in writing, not testamentary, notwithstanding that it is expressly required that a deed or instrument in writing, made in exercise of the power, is to be executed or attested with some additional or other form of execution or attestation or solemnity.

(2) This section does not operate to defeat any direction in the instrument creating the power that—

(*a*) the consent of any particular person is to be necessary to a valid execution;

(*b*) in order to give validity to any appointment, any act is to be performed having no relation to the mode of executing and attesting the instrument.

(3) This section does not prevent the donee of a power from executing it in accordance with the power by writing, or otherwise than by an instrument executed and attested as a deed; and where a power is so executed this section does not apply.

(4) This section applies to appointments by deed made after the thirteenth day of August, eighteen hundred and fifty-nine.

Application of Part VI to existing powers

160. This Part of this Act applies to powers created or arising either before or after the commencement of this Act.

PART VII

PERPETUITIES AND ACCUMULATIONS

Perpetuities

Abolition of the double possibility rule

161.—(1) The rule of law prohibiting the limitation, after a life interest to an unborn person, of an interest in land to the unborn child or other issue of an unborn person is hereby abolished, but without prejudice to any other rule relating to perpetuities.

(2) This section only applies to limitations or trusts created by an instrument coming into operation after the commencement of this Act.

Restrictions on the perpetuity rule

162.—(1) For removing doubts, it is hereby declared that the rule of law relating to perpetuities does not apply and shall be deemed never to have applied—

(*a*) To any power to distrain on or to take possession of land or the income thereof given by way of indemnity against a rent, whether charged upon or payable in respect of any part of that land or not; or

(*b*) To any rentcharge created only as an indemnity against another rentcharge, although the indemnity rentcharge may only arise or become payable on breach of a condition or stipulation; or

(*c*) To any power, whether exercisable on breach of a condition or stipulation or not, to retain or withhold payment of any instalment of a rentcharge as an indemnity against another rentcharge; or

(*d*) To any grant, exception, or reservation of any right of entry on, or user of, the surface of land or of any easements, rights, or privileges over or under land for the purpose of—

(i) winning, working, inspecting, measuring, converting, manufacturing, carrying away, and disposing of mines and minerals;

(ii) inspecting, grubbing up, felling and carrying away timber and other trees, and the tops and lops thereof;

(iii) executing repairs, alterations, or additions to any adjoining land, or the buildings and erections thereon;

(iv) constructing, laying down, altering, repairing, renewing, cleansing, and maintaining sewers, watercourses, cesspools, gutters, drains, water-pipes, gas-pipes, electric wires or cables or other like works.

(2) This section applies to instruments coming into operation before or after the commencement of this Act.

Validation of certain gifts void for remoteness

163.—[(1) Where in a will, settlement or other instrument the absolute vesting either of capital or income of property, or the ascertainment of a beneficiary or class of beneficiaries, is made to depend on the attainment by the beneficiary or members of the class of an age exceeding twenty-one years, and thereby the gift to that beneficiary or class or any member thereof, or any gift over, remainder, executory limitation, or trust arising on the total or partial failure of the original gift, is, or but for this section would be, rendered void for remoteness, the will, settlement, or other instrument shall take effect for the purposes of such gift, gift over, remainder, executory limitation, or trust as if the absolute vesting or ascertainment aforesaid had been made to depend on the beneficiary or member of the class attaining the age of twenty-one years, and that age shall be substituted for the age stated in the will, settlement, or other instrument.

(2) This section applies to any instrument executed after the commencement of this Act and to any testamentary appointment (whether made in exercise of a general or special power), devise, or bequest contained in the will of a person dying after such commencement, whether the will is made before or after such commencement.

(3) This section applies without prejudice to any provision whereby the absolute vesting or ascertainment is also made to depend on the marriage

of any person, or any other event which may occur before the age stated in the will, settlement, or other instrument is attained.][6]

Accumulations

General restrictions on accumulation of income

164.[7]—(1) No person may by any instrument or otherwise settle or dispose of any property in such manner that the income thereof shall, save as hereinafter mentioned, be wholly or partially accumulated for any longer period than one of the following, namely:—

(*a*) the life of the grantor or settlor; or

(*b*) a term of twenty-one years from the death of the grantor, settlor or testator; or

(*c*) the duration of the minority or respective minorities of any person or persons living or en ventre sa mere at the death of the grantor, settlor or testator; or

(*d*) the duration of the minority or respective minorities only of any person or persons who under the limitations of the instrument directing the accumulations would, for the time being, if of full age, be entitled to the income directed to be accumulated.

In every case where any accumulation is directed otherwise than as aforesaid, the direction shall (save as hereinafter mentioned) be void; and the income of the property directed to be accumulated shall, so long as the same is directed to be accumulated contrary to this section, go to and be received by the person or persons who would have been entitled thereto if such accumulation had not been directed.

(2) This sections does not extend to any provision—

(i) for payment of the debts of any grantor, settlor, testator or other person;

(ii) for raising portions for—

(*a*) any child, children or remoter issue of any grantor, settlor or testator; or

(*b*) any child, children or remoter issue of a person taking any interest under any settlement or other disposition directing the accumulations or to whom any interest is thereby limited;

(iii) respecting the accumulation of the produce of timber or wood;

and accordingly such provisions may be made as if no statutory restrictions on accumulation of income had been imposed.

(3) The restrictions imposed by this section apply to instruments made on or after the twenty-eighth day of July, eighteen hundred, but in the case of wills only where the testator was living and of testamentary capacity after the end of one year from that date.

Qualification of restrictions on accumulation

165. Where accumulations of surplus income are made during a minority under any statutory power or under the general law, the period for which such accumulations are made is not (whether the trust was created or the accumulations were made before or after the commencement of this Act) to be taken into account in determining the periods for which accumulations are permitted to be made by the last preceding section, and accordingly an express trust for accumulation for any other permitted period shall not be deemed to have been invalidated or become invalid, by

---

[6] Repealed, in respect of instruments taking effect after July 15, 1964, by the Perpetuities and Accumulations Act 1964 (c. 55), ss. 4(6), 15(5), *post*, pp. 307, 310.

[7] For extensions and restrictions relating to the power to accumulate income: see the Perpetuities and Accumulations Act 1964, s. 13, *post*, p. 309.

reason of accumulations also having been made as aforesaid during such minority.

Restriction on accumulation for the purchase of land

166.—(1) No person may settle or dispose of any property in such manner that the income thereof shall be wholly or partially accumulated for the purchase of land only, for any longer period than the duration of the minority or respective minorities of any person or persons who, under the limitations of the instrument directing the accumulation, would for the time being, if of full age, be entitled to the income so directed to be accumulated.

(2) This section does not, nor do the enactments which it replaces, apply to accumulations to be held as capital money for the purposes of the Settled Land Act 1925, or the enactments replaced by that Act, whether or not the accumulations are primarily liable to be laid out in the purchase of land.

(3) This section applies to settlements and dispositions made after the twenty-seventh day of June, eighteen hundred and ninety-two.

PART VIII

[*Repealed by the Mental Health Act* 1959 (7 & 8 *Eliz.* 2, *c.* 72) *s.*149(2), *Sched.* 8, *Pt. I, and the Statute Law (Repeals) Act* 1969 (*c.* 52), *s.*1 *and Sched., Pt.* III.]

PART IX

VOIDABLE DISPOSITIONS

Voluntary conveyances to defraud creditors voidable

172.—(1) Save as provided in this section, every conveyance of property, made whether before or after the commencement of this Act, with intent to defraud creditors, shall be voidable, at the instance of any person thereby prejudiced.

(2) This section does not affect the operation of a disentailing assurance, or the law of bankruptcy for the time being in force.

(3) This section does not extend to any estate or interest in property conveyed for valuable consideration and in good faith or upon good consideration and in good faith to any person not having, at the time of the conveyance, notice of the intent to defraud creditors.

Voluntary disposition of land how far voidable as against purchasers

173.—(1) Every voluntary disposition of land made with intent to defraud a subsequent purchaser is voidable at the instance of that purchaser.

(2) For the purposes of this section, no voluntary disposition, whenever made, shall be deemed to have been made with intent to defraud by reason only that a subsequent conveyance for valuable consideration was made, if such subsequent conveyance was made after the twenty-eighth day of June, eighteen hundred and ninety-three.

Acquisitions of reversions at an under value

174.—(1) No acquisition made in good faith, without fraud or unfair dealing, of any reversionary interest in real or personal property, for money or money's worth, shall be liable to be opened or set aside merely on the ground of under value.

In this subsection "reversionary interest" includes an expectancy or possibility.

(2) This section does not affect the jurisdiction of the court to set aside or modify unconscionable bargains.

PART X

WILLS

Contingent and future testamentary gifts to carry the intermediate income

175.—(1) A contingent or future specific devise or bequest of property, whether real or personal, and a contingent residuary devise of freehold land, and a specific or residuary devise of freehold land to trustees upon trust for persons whose interests are contingent or executory shall, subject to the statutory provisions relating to accumulations, carry the intermediate income of that property from the death of the testator, except so far as such income, or any part thereof, may be otherwise expressly disposed of.

(2) This section applies only to wills coming into operation after the commencement of this Act.

Power for tenant in tail in possession to dispose of property by specific devise or bequest

176.—(1) A tenant in tail of full age shall have power to dispose by will, by means of a devise or bequest referring specifically either to the property or to the instrument under which it was acquired or to entailed property generally—

(*a*) of all property of which he is tenant in tail in possession at his death; and

(*b*) of money (including the proceeds of property directed to be sold) subject to be invested in the purchase of property, of which if it had been so invested he would have been tenant in tail in possession at his death;

in like manner as if, after barring the entail, he had been tenant in fee-simple or absolute owner thereof for an equitable interest at his death, but, subject to and in default of any such disposition by will, such property shall devolve in the same manner as if this section had not been passed.

(2) This section applies to entailed interests authorised to be created by this Act as well as to estates tail created before the commencement of this Act, but does not extend to a tenant in tail who is by statute restrained from barring or defeating his estate tail, whether the land or property in respect whereof he is so restrained was purchased with money provided by Parliament in consideration of public services or not, or to a tenant in tail after possibility of issue extinct, and does not render any interest which is not disposed of by the will of the tenant in tail liable for his debts or other liabilities.

(3) In this section "tenant in tail" includes an owner of a base fee in possession who has power to enlarge the base fee into a fee-simple without the concurrence of any other person.

(4) This section only applies to wills executed after the commencement of this Act, or confirmed or republished by codicil executed after such commencement.

Wills in contemplation of marriage

177.—(1) A will expressed to be made in contemplation of a marriage shall, notwithstanding anything in section eighteen of the Wills Act 1837, or any other statutory provision or rule of law to the contrary, not be revoked by the solemnisation of the marriage contemplated.

(2) This section only applies to wills made after the commencement of this Act.

Power for persons having no issue to dispose of real estate by will

178. [*Repealed by the Statute Law (Repeals) Act* 1969 (*c.* 52), *s.* 1, *Sched., Pt.* III.]

Prescribed forms for reference in wills

179. The Lord Chancellor may from time to time prescribe and publish forms to which a testator may refer in his will, and give directions as to the manner in which they may be referred to, but, unless so referred to, such forms shall not be deemed to be incorporated in a will.

PART XI

MISCELLANEOUS

Miscellaneous

Provisions as to corporations

180.—(1) Where either after or before the commencement of this Act any property or any interest therein is or has been vested in a corporation sole (including the Crown), the same shall, unless and until otherwise disposed of by the corporation, pass and devolve to and vest in and be deemed always to have passed and devolved to or vested in the successors from time to time of such corporation.

(2) Where either after or before the commencement of this Act there is or has been a vacancy in the office of a corporation sole or in the office of the head of a corporation aggregate (in any case in which the vacancy affects the status or powers of the corporation) at the time when, if there had been no vacancy, any interest in or charge on property would have been acquired by the corporation, such interest shall notwithstanding such vacancy vest and be deemed to have vested in the successor to such office on his appointment as a corporation sole, or in the corporation aggregate (as the case may be), but without prejudice to the right of such successor, or of the corporation aggregate after the appointment of its head officer, to disclaim that interest or charge.

(3) Any contract or other transaction expressed or purported to be made with a corporation sole, or any appointment of a corporation sole as a custodian or other trustee or as a personal representative, at a time (either after or before the commencement of this Act) when there was a vacancy in the office, shall on the vacancy being filled take effect and be deemed to have taken effect as if the vacancy had been filled before the contract, transaction or appointment was expressed to be made or was capable of taking effect, and on the appointment of a successor shall be capable of being enforced, accepted, disclaimed or renounced by him.

Dissolution of a corporation

181.[8] Where, by reason of the dissolution of a corporation either before or after the commencement of this Act, a legal estate in any property has determined, the court may by order create a corresponding estate and vest the same in the person who would have been entitled to the estate which determined had it remained a subsisting estate.

Protection of solicitor and trustees adopting Act

182.—(1) The powers given by this Act to any person, and the covenants, provisions, stipulations, and words which under this Act are to be deemed to be included or implied in any instrument, or are by this Act made applicable to any contract for sale or other transaction, are and shall be deemed in law proper powers, covenants, provisions, stipulations, and words, to be given by or to be contained in any such instrument, or to be adopted in connection with, or applied to, any such contract or transaction, and a solicitor shall not be deemed guilty of neglect or breach of duty, or become in any way liable, by reason of his omitting, in good faith, in any such instrument, or in connection with any such contract or transaction, to negative the giving, inclusion, implication, or application of any of those powers, covenants, provisions, stipulations, or words, or to insert or apply any others in place thereof, in any case where the provisions of this Act would allow of his doing so.

(2) But, save as expressly provided by this Act, nothing in this Act shall be taken to imply that the insertion in any such instrument, or the adoption in connection with, or the application to, any contract or transaction, of any further or other powers, covenants, provisions, stipulations, or words is improper.

(3) Where the solicitor is acting for trustees, executors, or other persons in a fiduciary position, those persons shall also be protected in like manner.

(4) Where such persons are acting without a solicitor, they shall also be protected in like manner.

Fraudulent concealment of documents and falsification of pedigrees

183.[9]—(1) Any person disposing of property or any interest therein for money or money's worth to a purchaser, or the solicitor or other agent of such person, who—

(a) conceals from the purchaser any instrument or incumbrance material to the title; or

(b) falsifies any pedigree upon which the title may depend in order to induce the purchaser to accept the title offered or produced;

with intent in any of such cases to defraud, is guilty of a misdemeanour punishable by fine, or by imprisonment for a term not exceeding two years, or by both.

(2) Any such person or his solicitor or agent is also liable to an action for damages by the purchaser or the persons deriving title under him for any loss sustained by reason of—

(a) the concealment of the instrument or incumbrance; or

(b) any claim made by a person under such pedigree whose right was concealed by such falsification as aforesaid.

---

[8] The county court shall have jurisdiction in a case where the amount or value of the property or interest in the property does not exceed £5,000: County Courts Act 1959 (7 & 8 Eliz. 2, c. 22), Sched. 1, as amended by the Administration of Justice Act 1969 (c. 58), s. 5.

[9] An annuity shall be deemed to be an encumbrance for the purpose of this section:Tithe Act 1936 (26 Geo. 5 & 1 Edw. 8, c. 43), s. 13(8).

(3) In estimating damages, where the property or any interest therein is recovered from the purchaser or the persons deriving title under him, regard shall be had to any expenditure by him or them in improvements of any land.

(4) No prosecution for any offence under this section shall be commenced without the leave of the Attorney-General.

(5) Before leave to prosecute is granted there shall be given to the person intended to be prosecuted such notice of the application for leave to prosecute as the Attorney-General may direct.

Presumption of survivorship in regard to claims to property

184.[10] In all cases where, after the commencement of this Act, two or more persons have died in circumstances rendering it uncertain which of them survived the other or others, such deaths shall (subject to any order of the court), for all purposes affecting the title to property, be presumed to have occurred in order of seniority, and accordingly the younger shall be deemed to have survived the elder.

Merger

185. There is no merger by operation of law only of any estate the beneficial interest in which would not be deemed to be merged or extinguished in equity.

Rights of pre-emption capable of release

186. All statutory and other rights of pre-emption affecting a legal estate shall be and be deemed always to have been capable of release, and unless released shall remain in force as equitable interests only.

Legal easements

187.—(1) Where an easement, right or privilege for a legal estate is created, it shall enure for the benefit of the land to which it is intended to be annexed.

(2) Nothing in this Act affects the right of a person to acquire, hold or exercise an easement, right or privilege over or in relation to land for a legal estate in common with any other person, or the power of creating or conveying such an easement right or privilege.

Power to direct division of c attels

188.[11] Where any chattel belong to persons in undivided shares, the persons interested in a moiety or upwards may apply to the court for an order for division of the chattels or any of them, according to a valuation or otherwise, and the court may make such order and give any consequential directions as it thinks fit.

Indemnities against rents

189.—(1) A power of distress given by way of indemnity against a rent or any part thereof in respect of any land, or against the breach of any

---

[10] Excluded in the case of husband and wife by Administration of Estate Act 1925, s. 46(3), *post*, p. 267.

[11] The county court shall have jurisdiction in a case where the amount or value of the property or interest in the property does not exceed £5,000: County Courts Act 1959 (7 & 8 Eliz. c. 22), Sched. 1, as amended by the Administration of Justice Act 1969 (c. 58), s. 5.

covenant or condition in relation to land, is not and shall not be deemed ever to have been a bill of sale within the meaning of the Bills of Sale Acts 1878 and 1882 as amended by any subsequent enactment.

(2) The benefit of all covenants and powers given by way of indemnity against a rent or any part thereof payable in respect of land, or against the breach of any covenant or condition in relation to land, is and shall be deemed always to have been annexed to the land to which the indemnity is intended to relate, and may be enforced by the estate owner for the time being of the whole or any part of that land, notwithstanding that the benefit may not have been expressly apportioned or assigned to him or to any of his predecessors in title.

Redemption and Apportionment of Rents, &c.

Equitable apportionment of rents and remedies for non-payment or breach of covenant

190.—(1)[12] Where in a conveyance for valuable consideration, other than a mortgage, of part of land which is affected by a rentcharge, such rentcharge or a part therof is, without the consent of the owner thereof, expressed to be—

(*a*) charged exclusively on the land conveyed or any part thereof in exoneration of the land retained or other land; or

(*b*) charged exclusively on the land retained or any part thereof in exoneration of the land conveyed or other land; or

(*c*) apportioned between the land conveyed or any part thereof, and the land retained by the grantor or any part thereof;

then, without prejudice to the rights of the owner of the rentcharge, such charge or apportionment shall be binding as between the grantor and the grantee under the conveyance and their respective successors in title.

(2)[13] Where—

(*a*) any default is made in payment of the whole or part of a rentcharge by the person who, by reason of such charge or apportionment as aforesaid, is liable to pay the same; or

(*b*) any breach occurs of any of the covenants (other than in the case of an apportionment the covenant to pay the entire rentcharge) or conditions contained in the deed or other document creating the rentcharge, so far as the same relate to the land retained or conveyed, as the case may be;

the owner for the time being of any other land affected by the entire rentcharge who—

(i) pays or is required to pay the whole or part of the rentcharge which ought to have been paid by the defaulter aforesaid; or

(ii) incurs any costs, damages or expenses by reason of the breach of covenant or condition aforesaid;

may enter into and distrain on the land in respect of which the default or breach is made or occurs, or any part of that land, and dispose according to law of any distress found, and may also take possession of the income of the same land until, by means of such distress and receipt of income or otherwise the whole or part of the rentcharge (charged or apportioned as aforesaid) so unpaid and all costs, damages and expenses incurred by reason of the non-payment thereof or of the breach of the said covenants and conditions, are fully paid or satisfied.

(3) Where in a conveyance for valuable consideration, other than a mortgage, of part of land comprised in a lease, for the residue of the term

[12] Applied by the Leasehold Reform Act 1967 (c. 88), s. 11(1).
[13] Applied by *ibid.* s. 11(2).

or interest created by the lease, the rent reserved by such lease or a part thereof is, without the consent of the lessor, expressed to be—

(*a*) charged exclusively on the land conveyed or any part thereof in exoneration of the land retained by the assignor or other land; or

(*b*) charged exclusively on the land retained by the assignor or any part thereof in exoneration of the land conveyed or other land; or

(*c*) apportioned between the land conveyed or any part thereof and the land retained by the assignor or any part thereof;

then, without prejudice to the rights of the lessor, such charge or apportionment shall be binding as between the assignor and the assignee under the conveyance and their respective successors in title.

(4) Where—

(*a*) any default is made in payment of the whole or part of a rent by the person who, by reason of such charge or apportionment as aforesaid, is liable to pay the same; or

(*b*) any breach occurs of any of the lessee's covenants (other than in the case of an apportionment the covenant to pay the entire rent) or conditions contained in the lease, so far as the same relate to the land retained or conveyed, as the case may be;

the lessee for the time being of any other land comprised in the lease, in whom, as respects that land, the residue of the term or interest created by the lease is vested, who—

(i) pays or is required to pay the whole or part of the rent which ought to have been paid by the defaulter aforesaid; or

(ii) incurs any costs, damages or expenses by reason of the breach of covenant or condition aforesaid;

may enter into and distrain on the land comprised in the lease in respect of which the default or breach is made or occurs, or any part of that land, and dispose according to law of any distress found, and may also take possession of the income of the same land until (so long as the term or interest created by the lease is subsisting) by means of such distress and receipt of income or otherwise, the whole or part of the rent (charged or apportioned as aforesaid) so unpaid and all costs, damages and expenses incurred by reason of the non-payment thereof or of the breach of the said covenants and conditions, are fully paid or satisfied.

(5) The remedies conferred by this section take effect so far only as they might have been conferred by the conveyance whereby the rent or any part thereof is expressed to be charged or apportioned as aforesaid, but a trustee, personal representative, mortgagee or other person in a fiduciary position has, and shall be deemed always to have had, power to confer the same or like remedies.

(6) This section applies only if and so far as a contrary intention is not expressed in the conveyance whereby the rent or any part thereof is expressed to be charged or apportioned as aforesaid, and takes effect subject to the terms of that conveyance and to the provisions therein contained.

(7) The remedies conferred by this section apply only where the conveyance whereby the rent or any part thereof is expressed to be charged or apportioned is made after the commencement of this Act, and do not apply where the rent is charged exclusively as aforesaid or legally apportioned with the consent of the owner or lessor.

(8) The rule of law relating to perpetuities does not affect the powers or remedies conferred by this section or any like powers or remedies expressly conferred, before or after the commencement of this Act, by an instrument.

Redemption and apportionment of rents

191. [*Repealed by the Rentcharges Act* 1977 (*c.* 30), *Sched.* 2.].

Apportionment of charges payable for redemption of tithe rentcharge

192.[14] An order of apportionment of a charge on land by way of annuity for redemption of tithe rentcharge may be made by the Minister under sections ten to fourteen (inclusive) of the Inclosure Act 1854 on the application of any person interested, according to the provisions of the Inclosure Acts 1845 to 1882, in the land charged or any part thereof without the concurrence of any other person:

Provided that the Minister may, in any such case, on the application of any person interested in the annuity, require as a condition of making the order that any apportioned part of the annuity which does not exceed the yearly sum of two pounds shall be redeemed forthwith.

Commons and Waste lands

Rights of the public over commons and waste lands

193.—(1) Members of the public shall, subject as hereinafter provided, have rights of access for air and exercise to any land which is a metropolitan common within the meaning of the Metropolitan Commons Acts 1866 to 1898, or manorial waste, or a common, which is wholly or partly situated within [an area which immediately before April 1, 1974 was][14a] a borough or urban district, and to any land which at the commencement of this Act is subject to rights of common and to which this section may from time to time be applied in manner hereinafter provided: Provided that—

    (*a*) such rights of access shall be subject to any Act, scheme, or provisional order for the regulation of the land, and to any byelaw, regulation or order made thereunder or under any other statutory authority; and

    (*b*) the Minister[15] shall, on the application of any person entitled as lord of the manor or otherwise to the soil of the land, or entitled to any commonable rights affecting the land, impose such limitations on and conditions as to the exercise of the rights of access or as to the extent of the land to be affected as, in the opinion of the Minister, are necessary or desirable for preventing any estate, right or interest of a profitable or beneficial nature in, over, or affecting the land from being injuriously affected, or for protecting any object of historical interest and, where any such limitations or conditions are so imposed, the rights of access shall be subject thereto; and

    (*c*) such rights of access shall not include any right to draw or drive upon the land a carriage, cart, caravan, truck, or other vehicle, or to camp or light any fire thereon; and

    (*d*) the rights of access shall cease to apply—

        (i) to any land over which the commonable rights are extinguished under any statutory provision;

---

[14] This section is excluded in relation to an annuity: Tithe Act 1936 (26 Geo. 5 & 1 Edw. 8, c. 43), s. 13(9)

    In so far as they concern annuities charged on land for the redemption of rentcharges or money payments redeemed under the Tithe Acts 1836 to 1936, the functions of the Minister are transferred to the Commissioners of Inland Revenue: Tithe Act 1951 (14 & 15 Geo. 6, c. 62), s. 10(4) and the Tithe Redemption Commission (Transfer of Functions and Dissolution) Order 1959 (No. 1971).

[14a] Words inserted by the Local Government Act 1972, s. 189(4).

[15] In this and the following sections "Minister" means the Minister of Housing and Local Government on the Secretary of State for Wales: Minister of Land and National Resources (Dissolution) Order 1967 (No. 156).

(ii) to any land over which the commonable rights are otherwise extinguished if the council of the county [. . .]¹⁵ᵃ in which the land is situated by resolution assent to its exclusion from the operation of this section, and the resolution is approved by the Minister.

(2) The lord of the manor or other person entitled to the soil of any land subject to rights of common may by deed, revocable or irrevocable, declare that this section shall apply to the land, and upon such deed being deposited with the Minister the land shall, so long as the deed remains operative, be land to which this section applies.

(3) Where limitations or conditions are imposed by the Minister under this section, they shall be published by such person and in such manner as the Minister may direct.

(4) Any person who, without lawful authority, draws or drives upon any land to which this section applies any carriage, cart, caravan, truck, or other vehicle, or camps or lights any fire thereon, or who fails to observe any limitation or condition imposed by the Minister under this section in respect of any such land, shall be liable on summary conviction to a fine not exceeding [twenty pounds]¹⁶ for each offence.

(5) Nothing in this section shall prejudice or affect the right of any person to get and remove mines or minerals or to let down the surface of the manorial waste or common.

(6) This section does not apply to any common or manorial waste which is for the time being held for Naval, Military or Air Force purposes and in respect of which rights of common have been extinguished or cannot be exercised.

Restrictions on inclosure of commons

194.¹⁷—(1) The erection of any building or fence, or the construction of any other work, whereby access to land to which this section applies is prevented or impeded, shall not be lawful unless the consent of the Minister¹⁸ thereto is obtained, and in giving or withholding his consent the Minister shall have regard to the same considerations and shall, if necessary, hold the same inquiries as are directed by the Commons Act 1876 to be taken into consideration and held by the Minister before forming an opinion whether an application under the Inclosure Acts 1845 to 1882 shall be acceded to or not.

(2)¹⁹ Where any building or fence is erected, or any other work constructed without such consent as is required by this section, the county court within whose jurisdiction the land is situated, shall, on an application being made by the council of any county [. . .]¹⁹ᵃ or district concerned, or by the lord of the manor or any other person interested in the common, have power to make an order for the removal of the work, and the restoration of the land to the condition in which it was before the work was erected or constructed, but any such order shall be subject to the like appeal as an order made under section thirty of the Commons Act 1876.

(3) This section applies to any land which at the commencement of this Act is subject to rights of common:

Provided that this section shall cease to apply—

(a) to any land over which the rights of common are extinguished under any statutory provision;

---

¹⁵ᵃ Words repealed by the Local Government Act 1972, Sched. 30.
¹⁶ Substituted by the Criminal Justice Act 1967 (c. 80), Sched. 3, Pt. I.
¹⁷ Excluded by the New Forest Act 1964 (c. 83), ss. 3 (2) (4) (6), 4 (1).
¹⁸ See note 15, *supra.*
¹⁹ For amendments relating to appeals from county courts see the Administration of Justice (Appeals) Act 1934 (24 & 25 Geo. 5, c. 40), s. 2(1), Sched., Pt. I.
¹⁹ᵃ Words repealed by the Local Government Act 1972, Sched. 30.

(b) to any land over which the rights of common are otherwise extinguished, if the council of the county [. . .]¹⁹ᵃ in which the land is situated by resolution assent to its exclusion from the operation of this section and the resolution is approved by the Minister.

(4) This section does not apply to any building or fence erected or work constructed if specially authorised by Act of Parliament, or in pursuance of an Act of Parliament or Order having the force of an Act, or if lawfully erected or constructed in connection with the taking or working of minerals in or under any land to which the section is otherwise applicable, or to any telegraphic line as defined by the Telegraph Act 1878 of the Postmaster-General.²⁰

Judgments, &c. affecting Land

Equitable charges in right of judgment debt, &c.

195.—(1)–(3) [*Repealed by the Administration of Justice Act* 1956 (4 & 5 *Eliz.* 2, *c.* 46), *ss.* 34 (2), 57 (2), *Sched.* 2.]

(4) A recognisance, on behalf of the Crown or otherwise, whether entered into before or after the commencement of this Act, and an inquisition finding a debt due to the Crown, and any obligation or specially made to or in favour of the Crown whatever may have been its date, shall not operate as a charge on any interest in land, or on the unpaid purchase money for any land, unless or until a writ or order, for the purpose of enforcing it, as registered in the register of writs and orders at the Land Registry.

(5) [*Repealed by the Administration of Justice Act* 1956 (4 & 5 *Eliz.* 2, *c.* 46), *ss.* 34 (2), 57(2), *Sched.* 2.]

Notices

Regulations respecting notices

196.²¹—(1) Any notice required or authorised to be served or given by this Act shall be in writing.

(2) Any notice required or authorised by this Act to be served on a lessee or mortgagor shall be sufficient, although only addressed to the lessee or mortgagor by that designation, without his name, or generally to the persons interested, without any name, and notwithstanding that any person to be affected by the notice is absent, under disability, unborn, or unascertained.

(3) Any notice required or authorised by this Act to be served shall be sufficiently served if it is left at the last-known place or abode or business in the United Kingdom of the lessee, lessor, mortgagee, mortgagor, or other person to be served, or, in case of a notice required or authorised to be served on a lessee or mortgagor, is affixed or left for him on the land or any house or building comprised in the lease or mortgage, or, in case of a mining lease, is left for the lessee at the office or counting-house of the mine.

(4)²² Any notice required or authorised by this Act to be served shall also be sufficiently served, if it is sent by post in a registered letter

---

²⁰ This is to be construed as a reference to the Post Office Act 1969 (c. 48), s. 76 and Sched. 4, para. 26.

²¹ Extended by the Leasehold Property (Repairs) Act 1938 (1 & 2 Geo. 6, c. 34), s. 7(2); applied by the Reserve and Auxiliary Forces (Protection of Civil Interests) Act 1951 (14 & 15 Geo. 6, c. 65), ss. 16 (8), 29 (6).

²² Amended to cover the recorded delivery service: Recorded Delivery Service Act 1962 (10 & 11 Eliz. 2, c. 27), s. 1, Sched.

addressed to the lessee, lessor, mortgagee, mortgagor, or other person to be served, by name, at the aforesaid place of abode or business, office, or counting-house, and if that letter is not returned through the post-office undelivered; and that service shall be deemed to be made at the time at which the registered letter would in the ordinary course be delivered.

(5) The provisions of this section shall extend to notices required to be served by any instrument affecting property executed or coming into operation after the commencement of this Act unless a contrary intention appears.

(6) This section does not apply to notices served in proceedings in the court.

Notice of memorials registered in Middlesex and Yorkshire

197.[23]—[(1) The registration in a local deeds registry of a memorial of any instrument transferring or creating a legal estate or charge by way of legal mortgage, shall be deemed to constitute actual notice of the transfer or creation of the legal estate or charge by way of legal mortgage, to all persons and for all purposes whatsoever, as from the date of registration or other prescribed date, and so long as the registration continues in force.

(2) The registration of a memorial of an instrument not required to be registered does not operate to give notice of such instrument or of the contents thereof.

(3) This section operates without prejudice to the provisions of this Act respecting the making of further advances by a mortgagee, and only applies to land within the jurisdiction of the registry.][24]

Registration under the Land Charges Act 1925 to be notice

198.[25]—(1) The registration of any instrument or matter under the provisions of the Land Charges Act 1925,[26] or any enactment which it replaces, in any register kept at the land registry or elsewhere, shall be deemed to constitute actual notice of such instrument or matter, and of the fact of such registration, to all persons and for all purposes connected with the land affected, as from the date of registration or other prescribed date and so long as the registration continues in force.

(2) This section operates without prejudice to the provisions of this Act respecting the making of further advances by a mortgagee, and applies only to instruments and matters required or authorised to be registered under the Land Charges Act 1925.[27]

Restrictions on constructive notice

199.[28]—(1) A purchaser shall not be prejudicially affected by notice of—
  (i) any instrument or matter capable of registration under the provisions of the Land Charges Act 1925,[29] or any enactment which

---

[23] Restricted by the Middlesex Deeds Act 1940 (3 & 4 Geo. 6, c. 34), s. 1(1)(*b*).

[24] This section will be repealed in respect of any Yorkshire deeds register, registry and the area which was within its jurisdiction, with effect from the expiration of two years beginning with the date on which compulsory registration of title under the Land Registration Act 1925 (15 & 16 Geo. 5, c. 21) is extended to any part of the area of the registry, unless the Lord Chancellor specifies an earlier date at the request of the County Council of the Riding: Law of Property Act 1969 (c. 59), s. 16(2) and Sched. 2, Pt. I.

[25] This section was excluded by the Law of Property Act 1969 (c. 59), ss. 24 (1), 25 (2), *post*, pp. 314, 315.

[26] Now the Land Charges Act 1972 (c. 61), *post*, p. 320.

[27] Now the Land Charges Act 1972 (c. 61), *post*, p. 320.

[28] This section is extended by the Middlesex Deeds Act 1940 (3 & 4 Geo. 6, c. 34), s. 5(2).

[29] See above, note 27.

it replaces, which is void or not enforceable as against him under that Act or enactment, by reason of the non-registration thereof;

(ii) any other instrument or matter or any fact or thing unless—

> (*a*) it is within his own knowledge, or would have come to his knowledge if such inquiries and inspections had been made as ought reasonably to have been made by him; or
>
> (*b*) in the same transaction with respect to which a question of notice to the purchaser arises, it has come to the knowledge of his counsel, as such, or of his solicitor or other agent, as such, or would have come to the knowledge of his solicitor or other agent, as such, if such inquiries and inspections had been made as ought reasonably to have been made by the solicitor or other agent.

(2) Paragraph (ii) of the last subsection shall not exempt a purchaser from any liability under, or any obligation to perform or observe, any covenant, condition, provision, or restriction contained in any instrument under which his title is derived, mediately or immediately; and such liability or obligation may be enforced in the same manner and to the same extent as if that paragraph had not been enacted.

(3) A purchaser shall not by reason of anything in this section be affected by notice in any case where he would not have been so affected if this section had not been enacted.

(4) This section applies to purchases made either before or after the commencement of this Act.

Notice of restrictive covenants and easements

200.—(1) Where land having a common title with other land is disposed of to a purchaser (other than a lessee or a mortgagee) who does not hold or obtain possession of the documents forming the common title, such purchaser, notwithstanding any stipulation to the contrary, may require that a memorandum giving notice of any provision contained in the disposition to him restrictive of user of, or giving rights over, any other land comprised in the common title, shall, where practicable, be written or indorsed on, or, where impracticable, be permanently annexed to some one document selected by the purchaser but retained in the possession or power of the person who makes the disposition, and being or forming part of the common title.

(2) The title of any person omitting to require an indorsement to be made or a memorandum to be annexed shall not, by reason only of this enactment, be prejudiced or affected by the omission.

(3) This section does not apply to dispositions of registered land.

(4) Nothing in this section affects the obligation to register a land charge in respect of—

(*a*) any restrictive covenant or agreement affecting freehold land; or

(*b*) any estate contract; or

(*c*) any equitable easement, liberty or privilege.

PART XII

CONSTRUCTION, JURISDICTION, AND GENERAL PROVISIONS

Provisions of Act to apply to incorporeal hereditaments

201.—(1) The provisions of this Act relating to freehold land apply to manors, reputed manors, lordships, advowsons, [. . .]³⁰ perpetual

---

³⁰ Words repealed by the Tithe Act 1936 (26 Geo. 5 & 1 Edw. 8, c. 43), Sched. 9.

rentcharges, and other incorporeal hereditaments, subject only to the qualifications necessarily arising by reason of the inherent nature of the hereditament affected.

(2) This Act does not affect the special restrictions imposed on dealings with advowsons by the Benefices Act 1898, or any other statute or measure, nor affect the limitation of, or authorise any disposition to be made of, a title or dignity of honour which in its nature is inalienable.

(3) This section takes effect subject to the express provisions of this Act relating to undivided shares.

Provisions as to enfranchisement of copyholds, &c.

202. For giving effect to this Act, the enfranchisement of copyhold land, and the conversion into long terms of perpetually renewable leaseholds, and of leases for lives and of leases for years terminable with life or lives or on marriage, effected by the Law of Property Act 1922 as amended by any subsequent enactment, shall be deemed to have been effected immediately before the commencement of this Act.

Payment into court, jurisdiction and procedure

203.—(1) Payment of money into court effectually exonerates therefrom the person making the payment.

(2) Subject to any rules of court to the contrary—
> (*a*) Every application to the court under this Act shall, save as otherwise expressly provided, be by summons at chambers;
> (*b*) On an application by a purchaser notice shall be served in the first instance on the vendor;
> (*c*) On an application by a vendor notice shall be served in the first instance on the purchaser;
> (*d*) On any application notice shall be served on such persons, if any, as the court thinks fit.

(3) In this Act, unless the contrary intention appears, "the court" means the High Court, [. . .]³¹ or the county court, where those courts respectively have jurisdiction.

(4) All matters within the jurisdiction of the High Court under this Act shall, save as otherwise expressly provided, and subject to the enactments for the time being in force with respect to the Supreme Court of Judicature, be assigned to the Chancery Division of the court.

(5) The court shall have full power and discretion to make such order as it thinks fit respecting the costs, charges and expenses of all or any of the parties to any application.

Orders of court conclusive

204.³²—(1) An order of the court under any statutory or other jurisdiction shall not, as against a purchaser, be invalidated on the ground of want of jurisdiction, or of want of any concurrence, consent, notice, or service, whether the purchaser has notice of any such want or not.

(2) This section has effect with respect to any lease, sale, or other act under the authority of the court, and purporting to be in pursuance of any statutory power notwithstanding any exception in such statute.

(3) This section applies to all orders made before or after the commencement of this Act.

---

³¹ Words repealed by the Courts Act 1971 (c. 23), s. 56 and Sched. 11, Pt. II.
³² For the effect of orders of the court, see the Mental Health Act 1959 (7 & 8 Eliz. 2, c. 72), s. 116(1).

General definitions

205.—(1) In this Act unless the context otherwise requires, the following expressions have the meanings hereby assigned to them respectively, that is to say:—

(i) "Bankruptcy" includes liquidation by arrangement; also in relation to a corporation means the winding up thereof;

(ii) "Conveyance" includes a mortgage, charge, lease, assent, vesting declaration, vesting instrument, disclaimer, release and every other assurance of property or of an interest therein by any instrument, except a will; "convey" has a corresponding meaning; and "disposition" includes a conveyance and also a devise, bequest, or an appointment of property contained in a will; and "dispose of" has a corresponding meaning;

(iii) "Building purposes" include the erecting and improving of, and the adding to, and the repairing of buildings; and a "building lease" is a lease for building purposes or purposes connected therewith;

(iv) "Death duty" means estate duty, *succession duty, legacy duty,*[33] and every other duty leviable or payable on a death;

(v) "Estate owner" means the owner of a legal estate, but an infant is not capable of being an estate owner;

(vi) "Gazette" means the London Gazette;

(vii) "Incumbrance" includes a legal or equitable mortgage and a trust for securing money, and a lien, and a charge of a portion, annuity, or other capital or annual sum; and "incumbrancer" has a meaning corresponding with that of incumbrance, and includes every person entitled to the benefit of an incumbrance, or to require payment or discharge thereof;

(viii) "Instrument" does not include a statute, unless the statute creates a settlement;

(ix) "Land" includes land of any tenure, and mines and minerals, whether or not held apart from the surface, buildings or parts of buildings (whether the division is horizontal vertical or made in any other way) and other corporeal hereditaments; also a manor, an advowson, and a rent and other incorporeal hereditaments, and an easement, right, privilege, or benefit in, over, or derived from land; but not an undivided share in land; and "mines and minerals" include any strata or seam of minerals or substances in or under any land, and powers of working and getting the same but not an undivided share thereof; and "manor" includes a lordship, and reputed manor or lordship; and "hereditament" means any real property which on an intestacy occurring before the commencement of this Act might have devolved upon an heir;

(x) "Legal estates" mean the estates, interests and charges, in or over land (subsisting or created at law) which are by this Act authorised to subsist or to be created as legal estates; "equitable interests" mean all the other interests and charges in or over land or in the proceeds of sale thereof; and equitable interest "capable of subsisting as a legal estate" means such as could validly subsist or be created as a legal estate under this Act;

(xi) "Legal powers" include the powers vested in a chargee by way of legal mortgage or in an estate owner under which a legal estate can be transferred or created; and "equitable powers"

---

[33] The italicised words were repealed with saving by the Finance Act 1949 (12 & 13 Geo. 6, c. 47), Sched. 11, Pt. IV.

mean all the powers in or over land under which equitable interests or powers only can be transferred or created;

(xii) "Limitation Acts" mean the Real Property Limitation Acts 1833, 1837 and 1874 and "limitation" includes a trust;

(xiii) ["Mental disorder" has the meaning assigned to it by section four of the Mental Health Act 1959 and "receiver," in relation to a person suffering from mental disorder, means a receiver appointed for that person under Part VIII of that Act][34];

(xiv) A "mining lease" means a lease for mining purposes, that is, the searching for, winning, working, getting, making merchantable, carrying away, or disposing of mines and minerals, or purposes connected therewith, and includes a grant or licence for mining purposes;

(xv) "Minister" means the Minister of Agriculture and Fisheries;

(xvi) "Mortgage" includes any charge or lien on any property for securing money or money's worth; "legal mortgage" means a mortgage by demise or subdemise or a charge by way of legal mortgage and "legal mortgagee" has a corresponding meaning; "mortgage money" means money or money's worth secured by a mortgage; "mortgagor" includes any person from time to time deriving title under the original mortgagor or entitled to redeem a mortgage according to his estate interest or right in the mortgaged property; "mortgagee" includes a chargee by way of legal mortgage and any person from time to time deriving title under the original mortgagee; and "mortgagee in possession" is, for the purposes of this Act, a mortgagee who, in right of the mortgage, has entered into and is in possession of the mortgaged property; and "right of redemption" includes an option to repurchase only if the option in effect creates a right of redemption;

(xvii) "Notice" includes constructive notice;

(xviii) "Personal representative" means the executor, original or by representation, or administrator for the time being of a deceased person, and as regards any liability for the payment of death duties includes any person who takes possession of or intermeddles with the property of a deceased person without the authority of the personal representatives or the court;

(xix) "Possession" includes receipt of rents and profits or the right to receive the same, if any; and "income" includes rents and profits;

(xx) "Property" includes any thing in action, and any interest in real or personal property;

(xxi) "Purchaser" means a purchaser in good faith for valuable consideration and includes a lessee, mortgagee or other person who for valuable consideration acquires an interest in property except that in Part I of this Act and elsewhere where so expressly provided "purchaser" only means a person who acquires an interest in or charge on property for money or money's worth; and in reference to a legal estate includes a chargee by way of legal mortgage; and where the context so requires "purchaser" includes an intending purchaser; "purchase" has a meaning corresponding with that of "purchaser"; and "valuable consideration" includes marriage but does not include a nominal consideration" in money;

(xxii) "Registered land" has the same meaning as in the Land

---

[34] Substituted by the Mental Health Act 1959 (7 & 8 Eliz. 2, c. 72), Sched. 7, Pt. I.

Registration Act 1925 and "Land Registrar" means the Chief Land Registrar under that Act;

(xxiii) "Rent" includes a rent service or a rentcharge, or other rent, toll, duty, royalty, or annual or periodical payment in money or money's worth, reserved or issuing out of or charged upon land, but does not include mortgage interest; "rentcharge" includes a fee farm rent; "fine" includes a premium or foregift and any payment, consideration, or benefit in the nature of a fine, premium or foregift; "lessor" includes an underlessor and a person deriving title under a lessor or underlessor; and "lessee" includes an underlessee and a person deriving title under a lessee or under-lessee, and "lease" includes an underlease or other tenancy;

(xxiv) "Sale" includes an extinguishment of manorial incidents, but in other respects means a sale properly so called;

(xxv) "Securities" include stocks, funds and shares;

(xxvi) "Tenant for life," "statutory owner," "settled land," "settlement," "vesting deed," "subsidiary vesting deed," "vesting order," "vesting instrument," "trust instrument," "capital money," and "trustees of the settlement" have the same meanings as in the Settled Land Act 1925;

(xxvii) "Term of years absolute" means a term of years (taking effect either in possession or in reversion whether or not at a rent) with or without impeachment for waste, subject or not to another legal estate, and either certain or liable to determination by notice, re-entry, operation of law, or by a provision for cesser on redemption, or in any other event (other than the dropping of a life, or the determination of a determinable life interest); but does not include any term of years determinable with life or lives or with the cesser of a determinable life interest, nor, if created after the commencement of this Act, a term of years which is not expressed to take effect in possession within twenty-one years after the creation thereof where required by this Act to take effect within that period; and in this definition the expression "term of years" includes a term for less than a year, or for a year or years and a fraction of a year or from year to year;

(xxviii)[35] "Trust Corporation" means the Public Trustee or a corporation either appointed by the court in any particular case to be a trustee or entiled by rules made under subsection (3) of section four of the Public Trustee Act 1906 to act as custodian trustee;

(xxix) "Trust for sale," in relation to land, means an immediate binding trust for sale, whether or not exercisable at the request or with the consent of any person, and with or without a power at discretion to postpone the sale; "trustees for sale" mean the persons (including a personal representative) holding land on trust for sale; and "power to postpone a sale" means power to postpone in the exercise of a discretion;

(xxx) "United Kingdom" means Great Britain and Northern Ireland;

(xxxi) "Will" includes codicil.

[(1A) Any reference in this Act to money being paid into court shall be construed as referring to the money being paid into the Supreme Court or any other court that has jurisdiction, and any reference in this Act to the court, in a context referring to the investment or application of money paid

---

[35] For extension of "Trust Corporation" see the Law of Property (Amendment) Act 1926, s. 3, *post*, p. 276; Japanese Treaty of Peace Order 1952 (No. 862), art. 5 (2); the Clergy Pensions Measure 1961 (9 & 10 Eliz. 2, No. 3), s. 31.

into court, shall be construed, in the case of money paid into the Supreme Court, as referring to the High Court, and in the case of money paid into another court, as referring to that other court.][36]

(2) Where an equitable interest in or power over property arises by statute or operation of law, references to the creation of an interest or power include references to any interest or power so arising.

(3) References to registration under the Land Charges Act 1925[37] apply to any registration made under any other statute which is by the Land Charges Act 1925 to have effect as if the registration had been made under that Act.

Forms of instruments and examples of abstracts

206.—(1) Instruments in the form of, and using the expressions in the forms given in the Fifth Schedule to this Act, or in the like form or using expressions to the like effect, shall, in regard to form and expression be sufficient.

(2) Examples of abstracts of title framed in accordance with the enactments which will take effect at the commencement of this Act are contained in the Sixth Schedule to this Act.

Repeals as respects England and Wales

207. [*Words repealed by S.L.R.* 1950 (14 *Geo.* 6, *c.* 6).]
Provided that, without prejudice to the provisions of section thirty-eight of the Interpretation Act 1889[38]:—

(*a*) Nothing in this repeal shall affect the validity or legality of any dealing in property or other transaction completed before the commencement of this Act, or any title or right acquired or appointment made before such commencement, but, subject as aforesaid, this Act shall, except where otherwise expressly provided, apply to and in respect of instruments whether made or coming into operation before or after such commencement:

(*b*) Nothing in this repeal shall affect any rules, orders, or other instruments made under any enactment so repealed, but all such rules, orders and instruments shall continue in force as if made under the corresponding enactment in this Act:

(*c*) References in any document to any enactment repealed by this Act shall be construed as references to this Act or to the corresponding enactment in this Act.

Application to the Crown

208.—(1) Nothing in this Act shall be construed as rendering any property of the Crown subject to distress, or liable to be taken or disposed of by means of any distress.

(2) This Act shall not in any manner (save as otherwise expressly provided and except so far as it relates to undivided shares, joint ownership, leases for lives or leases for years terminable with life or marriage) affect or alter the descent, devolution or tenure or the nature of the estates and interests of or in any land for the time being vested in His Majesty either in right of the Crown or of the Duchy of Lancaster or of or in any land for the time being belonging to the Duchy of Cornwall and held in right or in respect of the said Duchy, but so nevertheless that, after the commencement of this Act, no estates, interests or charges in or over any such lands as aforesaid shall be conveyed or created, except such estates,

---

[36] Added by the Administration of Justice Act 1965 (c. 2), Sched. 1.
[37] Now the Land Charges Act 1972 (c. 61), *post*, p. 320.
[38] Now ss. 16(1) and 17(2) of the Interpretation Act 1978 (c. 30).

interests or charges as are capable under this Act of subsisting or of being conveyed or created.

(3) Subject as aforesaid the provisions of this Act bind the Crown.

Short title, commencement, extent

209.—(1) This Act may be cited as the Law of Property Act 1925.

(2) [*Repealed by S.L.R.* 1950 (14 *Geo.* 6, *c.* 6).]

(3) This Act extends to England and Wales only.

SCHEDULES

Section 39   FIRST SCHEDULE

TRANSITIONAL PROVISIONS

PART I

CONVERSION OF CERTAIN EXISTING LEGAL ESTATES INTO EQUITABLE INTERESTS

All estates, interests and charges in or over land, including fees determinable whether by limitation or condition, which immediately before the commencement of this Act were estates, interests or charges, subsisting at law, or capable of taking effect as such, but which by virtue of Part I of this Act are not capable of taking effect as legal estates, shall as from the commencement of this Act be converted into equitable interests, and shall not fail by reason of being so converted into equitable interests either in the land or in the proceeds of sale thereof, nor shall the priority of any such estate, charge or interest over other equitable interests be affected.

PART II

VESTING OF LEGAL ESTATES

1. Where the purposes of a term of years, created or limited out of leasehold land, are satisfied at the commencement of this Act, that term shall merge in the reversion expectant thereon and shall cease accordingly; but where the term was vested in the owner of the reversion, the merger and cesser shall take effect without prejudice to any protection which would have been afforded to the owner for the time being of that reversion had the term remained subsisting.

Where the purposes are satisfied only as respects part of the land comprised in a term, this provision has effect as if a separate term had been created in regard to that part of the land.

2. Where immediately after the commencement of this Act any owner of a legal estate is entitled, subject or not to the payment of the costs of tracing the title and of conveyance, to require any other legal estate in the same land to be surrendered, released or conveyed to him so as to merge or be extinguished, the last-mentioned estate shall by virtue of this Part of this Schedule be extinguished, but without prejudice to any protection which would have been afforded to him had that estate remained subsisting.

3. Where immediately after the commencement of this Act any person is entitled, subject or not to the payment of the costs of tracing the title and of conveyance, to require any legal estate (not vested in trustees for sale) to be conveyed to or otherwise vested in him, such legal estate shall, by virtue of this Part of this Schedule, vest in manner hereinafter provided. [The divesting of a legal estate by virtue of this paragraph shall not, where the person from whom the estate is so divested was a trustee, operate to prevent the legal estate being conveyed, or a legal estate being created, by him in favour of a purchaser for money or money's worth, if the purchaser has no notice of the trust and if the documents of title relating to the estate divested are produced by the trustee or by persons deriving title under him.][39]

This paragraph shall (without prejudice to any claim, in respect of fines, fees, and other customary payments) apply to a person who, under a surrender or any disposition having the effect of a surrender, or under a covenant to surrender or otherwise, was, immediately before the commencement of this Act, entitled to require a legal customary estate of inheritance to

---

[39] Added by the Law of Property (Amendment) Act 1926, *post,* Sched.

be vested in him, or who, immediately after such commencement becomes entitled to enfranchised land.

4. Any person who, immediately after the commencement of this Act, is entitled to an equitable interest capable of subsisting as a legal estate which has priority over any legal estate in the same land, shall be deemed to be entitled for the foregoing purposes to require a legal estate to be vested in him for an interest of a like nature not exceeding in extent or duration the equitable interest:

Provided that this paragraph shall not—

 (*a*) apply where the equitable interest is capable of being over-reached by virtue of a subsisting trust for sale or a settlement;

 (*b*) operate to prevent such person from acquiring any other legal estate under this Part of this Schedule to which he may be entitled.

5. For the purposes of this Part of this Schedule, a tenant for life, statutory owner or personal representative, shall be deemed to be entitled to require to be vested in him any legal estate in settled land (whether or not vested in the Crown) which he is, by the Settled Land Act 1925, given power to convey.

6. Under the provisions of this Part of this Schedule, the legal estate affected (namely, any estate which a person is entitled to require to be vested in him as aforesaid) shall vest as follows:—

 (*a*) Where at the commencement of this Act land is subject to a mortgage (not being an equitable charge unsecured by any estate), the legal estate affected shall vest in accordance with the provisions relating to mortgages contained in this Schedule;

 (*b*) Where the land is at the commencement or by virtue of this Act or any Act coming into operation at the same time subject or is by virtue of any statute made subject to a trust for sale, the legal estate affected shall vest in the trustees for sale (including personal representatives holding land on trust for sale) but subject to any mortgage term subsisting or created by this Act;

 (*c*) Where at the commencement of this Act or by virtue of any statute coming into operation at the same time the land is settled land, the legal estate affected shall vest in the tenant for life or statutory owner entitled under the Settled Land Act 1925 to require a vesting deed to be executed in his favour, or in the personal representative, if any, in whom the land may be vested or the Public Trustee, as the case may require but subject to any mortgage term subsisting or created by this Act;

 (*d*) In any case to which the foregoing sub-paragraphs do not apply the legal estate affected shall vest in the person of full age who, immediately after the commencement of this Act, is entitled (subject or not to the payment of costs and any customary payments) to require the legal estate to be vested in him, but subject to any mortgage term subsisting or created by this Act.

7. Nothing in this Part of this Schedule shall operate—

 (*a*) To vest in a mortgagee of a term of years absolute any nominal leasehold reversion which is held in trust for him subject to redemption; or

 (*b*) To vest in a mortgagee any legal estate except a term of years absolute; or

 (*c*) To vest in a person entitled to a leasehold interest, as respects such interest, any legal estate except a term of years absolute; or

 (*d*) To vest in a person entitled to a rentcharge (either perpetual or held for a term of years absolute) as respects such rentcharge, any legal estate except a legal estate in the rentcharge; or

 (*e*) To vest in a person entitled to an easement, right or privilege with reference thereto, any legal estate except a legal estate in the easement, right or privilege; or

 (*f*) To vest any legal estate in a person for an undivided share; or

 (*g*) To vest any legal estate in an infant; or

 (*h*) To affect prejudicially the priority of any mortgage or other incumbrance or interest subsisting at the commencement of this Act; or

 (*i*) To render invalid any limitation or trust which would have been capable of taking effect as an equitable limitation or trust; or

 (*j*) To vest in a purchaser or his personal representatives any legal estate which he has contracted to acquire and in regard to which a contract, including an agreement to create a legal mortgage, is pending at the commencement of this Act, although the consideration may have been paid or satisfied and the title accepted, or to render unnecessary the conveyance of such estate; or

 (*k*) To vest in the managing trustees or committee of management of a charity any legal estate vested in the Official Trustee of Charity Lands; or

 (*l*) To vest in any person any legal estate which failed to pass to him by reason of his omission to be registered as proprietor under the Land Transfer Acts 1875 and 1897, until brought into operation by virtue of the Land Registration Act 1925.

 [(*m*) To vest in any person any legal estate affected by any rent covenants or conditions if, before any proceedings are commenced in respect of the rent covenants or conditions, and before any conveyance of the legal estate or dealing therewith inter vivos is effected, he or his personal representatives disclaim it in writing signed by him or them.][40]

---

[40] Added by the Law of Property (Amendment) Act 1926, *post,* Sched.

8. Any legal estate acquired by virtue of this Part of this Schedule shall be held upon the trusts and subject to the powers, provisions, rents, covenants, conditions, rights of redemption (as respects terms of years absolute) and other rights, burdens and obligations, if any, upon or subject to which the estate acquired ought to be held.

9. No stamp duty shall become payable by reason only of any vesting surrender or release effected by this Schedule.

Part III

Provisions as to Legal Estate vested in Infant

1. Where immediately before the commencement of this Act a legal estate in land is vested in one or more infants beneficially, or where immediately after the commencement of this Act a legal estate in land would by virtue of this Act have become vested in one or more infants beneficially if he or they had been of full age, the legal estate shall vest in the manner provided by the Settled Land Act 1925.

2. Where immediately before the commencement of this Act a legal estate in land is vested in an infant jointly with one or more other persons of full age beneficially, the legal estate shall by virtue of this Act vest in that other person or those other persons on the statutory trusts, but not so as to sever any joint tenancy in the net proceeds of sale or in the rents and profits until sale:

Provided that, if by virtue of this paragraph the legal estate becomes vested in one person as trustee, then, if no other person is able and willing to do so, the parents or parent testamentary or other guardian of the infant, if respectively able and willing to act, (in the order named) may, and at the request of any person interested shall (subject to the costs being provided for) by writing appoint an additional trustee and thereupon by virtue of this Act the legal estate shall vest in the additional trustee and existing trustee as joint tenants.

3. Where immediately before the commencement of this Act, a legal estate in land is vested solely in an infant as a personal representative, or a trustee of a settlement, or on trust for sale or on any other trust, or by way of mortgage, or where immediately after the commencement of this Act a legal estate in land would by virtue of any provision of this Act or otherwise have been so vested if the infant were of full age, the legal estate and the mortgage debt (if any) and interest thereon shall, by virtue of this Act, vest in the Public Trustee, pending the appointment of trustees as hereinafter provided—

(a) as to the land, upon the trusts, and subject to the equities affecting the same (but in the case of a mortgage estate for a term of years absolute in accordance with this Act); and

(b) as to the mortgage debt and interest, upon such trusts as may be requisite for giving effect to the rights (if any) of the infant or other persons beneficially interested therein:

Provided that—

(i) The Public Trustee shall not be entitled to act in the trust, or charge any fee, or be liable in any manner, unless and until requested in writing to act by or on behalf of the persons interested in the land or the income thereof, or in the mortgage debt or interest thereon (as the case may be), which request may be made on behalf of the infant by his parents or parent, or testamentary or other guardian (in the order named), and those persons may, in the order aforesaid (if no other person is able and willing to do so) appoint new trustees in the place of the Public Trustee, and thereupon by virtue of this Act the land or term and mortgage money shall vest in the trustees so appointed upon the trusts and subject to the equities aforesaid: Provided that the Public Trustee may, before he accepts the trust, but subject to the payment of his costs, convey to a person of full age who becomes entitled;

(ii) After the Public Trustee has been so requested to act, and has accepted the trust, no trustee shall (except by an order of the court) be appointed in his place without his consent;

(iii) [41] Any person interested in the land or the income thereof, or in the mortgage debt or in the interest thereon (as the case may be), may, at any time during the minority, apply to the court for the appointment of trustees of the trust, and the court may make such order as it thinks fit, and if thereby new trustees are appointed the legal estate (but in the case of a mortgage estate only for a term of years absolute as aforesaid) and the mortgage debt (if any) and interest shall, by virtue of this Act, vest in the trustees as joint tenants upon the trusts and subject to the equities aforesaid;

(iv) Neither a purchaser of the land nor a transferee for money or money's worth of the mortgage shall be concerned in any way with the trusts affecting the legal estate or the mortgage debt and interest thereon;

---

[41] The county court shall have jurisdiction in a case where the land to be dealt with does not exceed in capital value £5,000 or in net annual for rating £300: County Courts Act 1959 (7 & 8 Eliz, c. 22), Sched. 1, as amended by the Administration of Justice Act 1969 (c. 58), s. 5.

(v) The vesting in the Public Trustee of a legal estate or a mortgage debt by virtue of this Part of this Schedule shall not affect any directions previously given as to the payment of income or of interest on any mortgage money, but such instructions may, until he accepts the trust, continue to be acted on as if no such vesting had been effected.

4. Where, immediately before the commencement of this Act, a legal estate in land is vested in two or more persons jointly as personal representatives, trustees, or mortgagees, and anyone of them is an infant, or where immediately after the commencement of this Act a legal estate in land would, by virtue of this Act, or otherwise have been so vested if the infant were of full age, the legal estate in the land with the mortgage debt (if any) and the interest thereon shall, by virtue of this Act, vest in the other person or persons of full age—

(*a*) as to the legal estate, upon the trusts and subject to the equities affecting the same (but in the case of a mortgage estate only for a term of years absolute as aforesaid); and

(*b*) as to the mortgage debt and interest, upon such trusts as may be requisite for giving effect to the rights (if any) of the infant or other persons beneficially interested therein; but neither a purchaser of the land nor a transferee for money or money's worth of the mortgage shall be concerned in any way with the trusts affecting the legal estate or the mortgage debt and interest thereon:

Provided that, if, by virtue of this paragraph, the legal estate and mortgage debt, if any, become vested in a sole trustee, then, if no other person is able and willing to do so, the parents or parent, testamentary or other guardian of the infant (in the order named) may, and at the request of any person interested shall, (subject to the costs being provided for) by writing appoint a new trustee in place of the infant, and thereupon by virtue of this Act the legal estate and mortgage money shall vest in the new and continuing trustees upon the trusts and subject to the equities aforesaid.

5. This Part of this Schedule does not affect the estate or powers of an administrator durante minore aetate, nor, where there is a tenant for life or statutory owner of settled land, operate to vest the legal estate therein in the Public Trustee.

PART IV

PROVISIONS SUBJECTING LAND HELD IN UNDIVIDED SHARES TO A TRUST FOR SALE[42]

1. Where, immediately before the commencement of this Act, land is held at law or in equity in undivided shares vested in possession, the following provisions shall have effect:—

(1) If the entirety of the land is vested in trustees or personal representatives (whether subject or not to incumbrances affecting the entirety or an undivided share) in trust for persons entitled in undivided shares, then—

(*a*) if the land is subject to incumbrances affecting undivided shares or to incumbrances affecting the entirety which under this Act or otherwise are not secured by legal terms of years absolute, the entirety of the land shall vest free from such incumbrances in such trustees or personal representatives and be held by them upon the statutory trusts; and

(*b*) in any other case, the land shall be held by such trustees or personal representatives upon the statutory trusts;

subject in the case of personal representatives, to their rights and powers for the purposes of administration.

(2) If the entirety of the land (not being settled land) is vested absolutely and beneficially in not more than four persons of full age entitled thereto in undivided shares free from incumbrances affecting undivided shares, but subject or not to incumbrances affecting the entirety, it shall, by virtue of this Act, vest in them as joint tenants upon the statutory trusts.

(3) If the entirety of the land is settled land (whether subject or not to incumbrances affecting the entirety or an undivided share) held under one and the same settlement, it shall, by virtue of this Act, vest, free from incumbrances affecting undivided shares, and from incumbrances affecting the entirety, which under this Act or otherwise are not secured by a legal [mortgage, and free from any interests, powers and charges subsisting under the settlement, which have priority to the interests of the persons entitled to the undivided shares],[43] in the trustees (if any) of the settlement as joint tenants upon the statutory trusts.

Provided that if there are no such trustees, then—

(i) pending their appointment, the land shall, by virtue of this Act, vest (free as aforesaid) in the Public Trustee upon the statutory trusts;

(ii) the Public Trustee shall not be entitled to act in the trust, or charge any fee, or be liable in any manner, unless and until requested in writing to

---

[42] For the effect of this Part of this Schedule on property under the management of the Commissioners of Crown Lands, see the Crown Estate Act 1961 (9 & 10 Eliz. 2 c. 55), s. 8(2).

[43] Substituted by the Law of Property (Amendment) Act 1926, *post*, Sched.

act by or on behalf of persons interested in more than an undivided half of the land or the income thereof;

(iii) after the Public Trustee has been so requested to act, and has accepted the trust, no trustee shall (except by an order of the court) be appointed in the place of the Public Trustee without his consent;

(iv) if, before the Public Trustee has accepted the trust, trustees of the settlement are appointed, the land shall, by virtue of this Act, vest (free as aforesaid) in them as joint tenants upon the statutory trusts;

(v)[44] if, before the Public Trustee has accepted the trust, the persons having power to appoint new trustees are unable or unwilling to make an appointment, or if the tenant for life having power to apply to the court for the appointment of trustees of the settlement neglects to make the application for at least three months after being requested by any person interested in writing so to do, or if the tenants for life of the undivided shares are unable to agree, any person interested under the settlement may apply to the court for the appointment of such trustees.

(4) In any case to which the foregoing provisions of this Part of this Schedule do not apply, the entirety of the land shall vest (free as aforesaid) in the Public Trustee upon the statutory trusts:

Provided that—

(i) The Public Trustee shall not be entitled to act in the trust, or charge any fee, or be liable in any manner, unless and until requested in writing to act by or on behalf of the persons interested in more than an undivided half of the land or the income thereof;

(ii) After the Public Trustee has been so requested to act, and has accepted the trust, no trustee shall (except by an order of the court) be appointed in the place of the Public Trustee without his consent;

(iii)[44] Subject as aforesaid, any persons interested in more than an undivided half of the land or the income thereof may appoint new trustees in the place of the Public Trustee with the consent of any incumbrancers of undivided shares (but so that a purchaser shall not be concerned to see whether any such consent has been given) and [thereupon the land shall by virtue of this Act vest][45] in the persons so appointed (free as aforesaid) upon the statutory trusts; or such persons may (without such consent as aforesaid), at any time, whether or not the Public Trustee has accepted the trust, apply to the court for the appointment of trustees of the land, and the court may make such order as it thinks fit, and if thereby trustees of the land are appointed, the same shall by virtue of this Act, vest (free as aforesaid) in the trustees as joint tenants upon the statutory trusts;

(iv)[46] If the persons interested in more than an undivided half of the land or the income thereof do not either request the Public Trustee to act, or (whether he refuses to act or has not been requested to act) apply to the court for the appointment of trustees in his place, within three months from the time when they have been requested in writing by any person interested so to do, then and in any such case, any person interested may apply to the court for the appointment of trustees in the place of the Public Trustee, and the court may make such order as it thinks fit, and if thereby trustees of the land are appointed the same shall by virtue of this Act, vest (free as aforesaid) in the trustees upon the statutory trusts.

(5) The vesting in the Public Trustee of land by virtue of this Part of this Schedule shall not affect any directions previously given as to the payment of income or of interest on any mortgage money, but such instructions may, until he accepts the trust, continue to be acted on as if no such vesting had been effected.

(6) The court or the Public Trustee may act on evidence given by affidavit or by statutory declaration as respects the undivided shares without investigating the title to the land.

(7) Where all the undivided shares in the land are vested in the same mortgagees for securing the same mortgage money and the rights of redemption affecting the land are the same as might have been subsisting if the entirety had been mortgaged by an owner before the undivided shares were created, the land shall, by virtue of this Act, vest in the mortgagees as joint tenants for a legal term of years absolute (in accordance with this Act) subject to cesser on redemption by the trustees for sale in whom the right of redemption is vested by this Act, and for the purposes of this Part of this Schedule the mortgage shall be deemed an incumbrance affecting the entirety.

(8) This Part of this Schedule does not (except where otherwise expressly provided) prejudice incumbrancers whose incumbrances affect the entirety of the land at the

---

[44] The county court shall have jurisdiction in cases where the land to be dealt with does not exceed in capital value £5,000 or in net annual value for rating £300; County Courts Act 1959 (7 & 8 Eliz. 2, c. 22), Sched. 1, as amended by the Administration of Justice Act 1969 (c. 58), s. 5.

[45] Substituted by the Law of Property (Amendment) Act 1926, *post,* Sched.

[46] See above, n. 44.

commencement of this Act, but (if the nature of the incumbrance admits) the land shall vest in them for legal terms of years absolute in accordance with this Act but not so as to affect subsisting priorities.

(9) The trust for sale and powers of management vested in persons who hold the entirety of the land on trust for sale shall, save as hereinafter mentioned, not be exercisable without the consent of any incumbrancer, being of full age, affected whose incumbrance is divested by this Part of this Schedule, but a purchaser shall not be concerned to see or inquire whether any such consent has been given, nor, where the incumbrancer is not in possession, shall any such consent be required if, independently of this Part of this Schedule or any enactment replaced thereby the transaction would have been binding on him, had the same been effected by the mortgagor.

(10) This Part of this Schedule does not apply to land in respect of which a subsisting contract for sale (whether made under an order in a partition action or by or on behalf of all the tenants in common or coparceners) is in force at the commencement of this Act if the contract is completed in due course (in which case title may be made in like manner as if this Act, and any enactment thereby replaced, had not been passed), nor to the land in respect of which a partition action is pending at such commencement if an order for a partition or sale is subsequently made in such action [within eighteen months from the commencement of this Act].[47]

(11) The repeal of the enactments relating to partition shall operate without prejudice to any proceedings thereunder commenced before the commencement of this Act, and to the jurisdiction of the court to make any orders in reference thereto, and subject to the following provisions, namely:—

(i) In any such proceedings, and at any stage thereof, any person or persons interested individually or collectively in [one half or upwards][48] of the land to which the proceedings relate, may apply to the court for an order staying such proceedings;

(ii) The court may upon such application make an order staying the proceedings as regards the whole or any part, not being an undivided share, of the land;

(iii) As from the date of such order the said enactments shall cease to apply to the land affected by the order and the provisions of this Part of this Schedule shall apply thereto;

(iv) The court may by such order appoint trustees of the land and the same shall by virtue of this Act vest (free as aforesaid) in the trustees as joint tenants upon the statutory trusts;

(v) The court may order that the costs of the proceedings and of the application shall be raised by the trustees, by legal mortgage of the land or any part thereof, and paid either wholly or partially into court or to the trustees;

(vi) The court may act on such evidence as appears to be sufficient, without investigating the title to the land.

(12) In this Part of this Schedule "incumbrance" does not include [a legal rentcharge affecting the entirety][49] land tax, tithe rentcharge, or any similar charge on the land not created by an instrument.

2. Where undivided shares in land, created before the commencement of this Act, fall into possession after such commencement, and the land is not settled land when the shares fall into possession, the personal representatives (subject to their rights and powers for purposes of administration) or other estate owners in whom the entirety of the land is vested shall, by an assent or a conveyance, give effect to the foregoing provisions of this Part of this Schedule in like manner as if the shares had fallen into possession immediately before the commencement of this Act, and in the meantime the land shall be held on the statutory trusts.

3. This Part of this Schedule shall not save as hereinafter mentioned apply to party structures and open spaces within the meaning of the next succeeding Part of this Schedule.

[4. Where, immediately before the commencement of this Act there are two or more tenants for life of full age entitled under the same settlement in undivided shares, and, after the cesser of all their interests in the income of the settled land, the entirety of the land is limited so as to devolve together (not in undivided shares), their interests shall, but without prejudice to any beneficial interest, be converted into a joint tenancy; and the joint tenants and the survivor of them shall, until the said cesser occurs, constitute the tenant for life for the purposes of the Settled Land Act 1925 and this Act.][50]

PART V

PROVISIONS AS TO PARTY STRUCTURES AND OPEN SPACES

1. Where, immediately before the commencement of this Act, a party wall or other party structure is held in undivided shares, the ownership thereof shall be deemed to be severed

[47] Inserted by the Law of Property (Amendment) Act 1926, *post,* Sched.
[48] Substituted by *ibid.*
[49] Inserted by *ibid.*
[50] Inserted by *ibid.*

vertically as between the respective owners, and the owner of each part shall have such rights to support and of user over the rest of the structure as may be requisite for conferring rights corresponding to those subsisting at the commencement of this Act.

2. Where, immediately before the commencement of this Act, an open space of land (with or without any building used in common for the purposes of any adjoining land) is held in undivided shares, in right whereof each owner has rights of access and user over the open space, the ownership thereof shall vest in the Public Trustee on the statutory trusts which shall be executed only with the leave of the court, and, subject to any order of the court to the contrary, each person who would have been a tenant in common shall, until the open space is conveyed to a purchaser, have rights of access and user over the open space corresponding to those which would have subsisted if the tenancy in common had remained subsisting.

3. Any person interested may apply to the court for an order declaring the rights and interests under this Part of this Schedule, of the persons interested in any such party structure or open space, or generally may apply in relation to the provisions of this Part of this Schedule, and the court may make such order as it thinks fit.

PART VI

CONVERSION OF TENANCIES BY ENTIRETIES INTO JOINT TENANCIES

Every tenancy by entireties existing immediately before the commencement of this Act shall, but without prejudice to any beneficial interest, as from such commencement be converted into a joint tenancy.

PART VII

CONVERSION OF EXISTING FREEHOLD MORTGAGES INTO MORTGAGES BY DEMISE

1. All land, which immediately before the commencement of this Act, was vested in a first or only mortgagee for an estate in fee simple in possession, whether legal or equitable, shall, from and after the commencement of this Act, vest in the first or only mortgagee for a term of three thousand years from such commencement, without impeachment of waste, but subject to a provision for cesser corresponding to the right of redemption which, at such commencement, was subsisting with respect to the fee simple.

2. All land, which immediately before the commencement of this Act, was vested in a second or subsequent mortgagee for an estate in fee simple in possession, whether legal or equitable, shall, from and after the commencement of this Act, vest in the second or subsequent mortgagee for a term one day longer than the term vested in the first or other mortgagee whose security ranks immediately before that of such second or subsequent mortgagee, without impeachment of waste, but subject to the term or terms vested in such first or other prior mortgagee and subject to a provision for cesser corresponding to the right of redemption which, at such commencement, was subsisting with respect to the fee simple.

3. The estate in fee simple which, immediately before the commencement of this Act, was vested in any such mortgagee shall, from and after such commencement, vest in the mortgagor or tenant for life, statutory owner, trustee for sale, personal representative, or other person of full age who, if all money owing on the security of the mortgage and all other mortgages or charges (if any) had been discharged at the commencement of this Act, would have been entitled to have the fee simple conveyed to him, but subject to any mortgage term created by this Part of this Schedule or otherwise and to the money secured by any such mortgage or charge.

4. If a sub-mortgage by conveyance of the fee simple is subsisting immediately before the commencement of this Act, the principal mortgagee shall take the principal term created by paragraphs 1 or 2 of this Part of this Schedule (as the case may require) and the sub-mortgagee shall take a derivative term less by one day than the term so created, without impeachment of waste, subject to a provision for cesser corresponding to the right of redemption subsisting under the sub-mortgage.

5. This Part of this Schedule applies to land enfranchised by statute as well as to land which was freehold before the commencement of this Act, and (save where expressly excepted) whether or not the land is registered under the Land Registration Act 1925, or the mortgage is made by way of trust for sale or otherwise.

6. A mortgage affecting a legal estate made before the commencement of this Act which is not protected, either by a deposit of documents of title relating to the legal estate or by registration as a land charge, shall not, as against a purchaser in good faith without notice thereof, obtain any benefit by reason of being converted into a legal mortgage by this Schedule, but shall, in favour of such purchaser, be deemed to remain an equitable interest.

This paragraph does not apply to mortgages or charges registered or protected under the Land Registration Act 1925, or to mortgages or charges registered in a local deeds register.

7. Nothing in this Part of this Schedule shall affect priorities or the right of any mortgagee to retain possession of documents, nor affect his title to or rights over any fixtures or chattels personal comprised in the mortgage.

8. This Part of this Schedule does not apply unless a right of redemption is subsisting immediately before the commencement of this Act.

Part VIII

Conversion of existing Leasehold Mortgages into Mortgages by subdemise

1. All leasehold land, which immediately before the commencement of this Act, was vested in a first or only mortgagee by way of assignment of a term of years absolute shall, from and after the commencement of this Act, vest in the first or only mortgagee for a term equal to the term assigned by the mortgage, less the last days thereof, but subject to a provision for cesser corresponding to the right of redemption which at such commencement was subsisting with respect to the term assigned.

2. All leasehold land, which immediately before the commencement of this Act, was vested in a second or subsequent mortgagee by way of assignment of a term of years absolute (whether legal or equitable) shall, from and after the commencement of this Act, vest in the second or subsequent mortgagee for a term one day longer than the term vested in the first or other mortgagee whose security ranks immediately before that of such second or subsequent mortgagee if the length of the last-mentioned term permits, and in any case for a term less by one day at least than the term assigned by the mortgage, but subject to the term or terms vested in such first or other prior mortgagee, and subject to a provision for cesser corresponding to the right of redemption which, at the commencement of this Act, was subsisting with respect to the term assigned by the mortgage.

3. The term of years absolute which was assigned by any such mortgage shall, from and after the commencement of this Act, vest in the mortgagor or tenant for life, statutory owner, trustee for sale, personal representative, or other person of full age who, if all the money owing on the security of the mortgage and all other mortgages or charges, if any, had been discharged at the commencement of this Act, would have been entitled to have the term assigned or surrendered to him, but subject to any derivative mortgage term created by this Part of this Schedule or otherwise and to the money secured by any such mortgage or charge.

4. If a sub-mortgage by assignment of a term is subsisting immediately before the commencement of this Act, the principal mortgagee shall take the principal derivative term created by paragraphs 1 or 2 of this Part of this Schedule or the derivative term created by his mortgage (as the case may require), and the sub-mortgagee shall take a derivative term less by one day than the term so vested in the principal mortgagee, subject to a provision for cesser corresponding to the right of redemption subsisting under the sub-mortgage.

5. A mortgage affecting a legal estate made before the commencement of this Act which is not protected, either by a deposit of documents of title relating to the legal estate or by registration as a land charge shall not, as against a purchaser in good faith without notice thereof, obtain any benefit by reason of being converted into a legal mortgage by this Schedule, but shall, in favour of such purchaser, be deemed to remain an equitable interest.

This paragraph does not apply to mortgages or charges registered or protected under the Land Registration Act 1925, or to mortgages or charges registered in a local deeds register.

6. This Part of this Schedule applies to perpetually renewable leaseholds, and to leaseholds for lives, which are by statute converted into long terms, with the following variations, namely:—

    (*a*) The term to be taken by a first or only mortgagee shall be ten days less than the term created by such statute:

    (*b*) The term to be taken by a second or subsequent mortgagee shall be one day longer than the term vested in the first or other mortgagee whose security ranks immediately before that of the second or subsequent mortgagee, if the length of the last-mentioned term permits, and in any case for a term less by one day at least than the term created by such statute:

    (*c*) The term created by such statute shall, from and after the commencement of this Act, vest in the mortgagor or tenant for life, statutory owner, trustee for sale, personal representative, or other person of full age, who if all the money owing on the security of the mortgage and all other mortgages or charges, if any, had been discharged at the commencement of this Act, would have been entitled to have the term assigned or surrendered to him, but subject to any derivative mortgage term created by this Part of this Schedule or otherwise and to the money secured by any such mortgage or charge.

7. This Part of this Schedule applies (save where expressly excepted) whether or not the leasehold land is registered under the Land Registration Act 1925, or the mortgage is made by way of trust for sale or otherwise.

8. Nothing in this Part of this Schedule shall affect priorities or the right of any mortgagee to retain possession of documents, nor affect his title to or rights over any fixtures or chattels personal comprised in the mortgage, but this Part of this Schedule does not apply unless a right of redemption is subsisting at the commencement of this Act.

Sections 76 and 77   SECOND SCHEDULE

IMPLIED COVENANTS

PART I

COVENANT IMPLIED IN A CONVEYANCE FOR VALUABLE CONSIDERATION, OTHER THAN A MORTGAGE, BY A PERSON WHO CONVEYS AND IS EXPRESSED TO CONVEY AS BENEFICIAL OWNER

That, notwithstanding anything by the person who so conveys or any one through whom he derives title otherwise than by purchase for value, made, done, executed, or omitted, or knowingly suffered, the person who so conveys, has, with the concurrence of every other person, if any, conveying by his direction, full power to convey the subject-matter expressed to be conveyed, subject as, if so expressed, and in the manner in which, it is expressed to be conveyed, and that, notwithstanding anything as aforesaid, that subject-matter shall remain to and be quietly entered upon, received, and held, occupied, enjoyed, and taken, by the person to whom the conveyance is expressed to be made, and any person deriving title under him, and the benefit thereof shall be received and taken accordingly, without any lawful interruption or disturbance by the person who so conveys or any person conveying by his direction, or rightfully claiming or to claim by, through, under, or in trust for the person who so conveys, or any person conveying by his direction, or by, through, or under any one (not being a person claiming in respect of an estate or interest subject whereto the conveyance is expressly made), through whom the person who so conveys derives title, otherwise than by purchase for value:

And that, freed and discharged from, or otherwise by the person who so conveys sufficiently indemnified against, all such estates, incumbrances, claims, and demands, other than those subject to which the conveyance is expressly made, as, either before or after the date of the conveyance, have been or shall be made, occasioned, or suffered by that person or by any person conveying by his direction, or by any person rightfully claiming by, through, under, or in trust for the person who so conveys, or by, through, or under any person conveying by his direction, by, through, or under any one through whom the person who so conveys derives title, otherwise than by purchase for value:

And further, that the person who so conveys, and any person conveying by his direction, and every other person having or rightfully claiming any estate or interest in the subject-matter of conveyance, other than an estate or interest subject whereto the conveyance is expressly made, by, through, under, or in trust for the person who so conveys, or by, through, or under any person conveying by his direction, or by, through, or under any one through whom the person who so conveys derives title, otherwise than by purchase for value, will, from time to time and at all times after the date of the conveyance, on the request and at the cost of any person to whom the conveyance is expressed to be made, or of any person deriving title under him, execute and do all such lawful assurances and things for further or more perfectly assuring the subject-matter of the conveyance to the person to whom the conveyance is made, and to those deriving title under him, subject as, if so expressed, and in the manner in which the conveyance is expressed to be made, as by him or them or any of them shall be reasonably required.

In the above covenant a purchase for value shall not be deemed to include a conveyance in consideration of marriage.

PART II

FURTHER COVENANT IMPLIED IN A CONVEYANCE OF LEASEHOLD PROPERTY FOR VALUABLE CONSIDERATION, OTHER THAN A MORTGAGE, BY A PERSON WHO CONVEYS AND IS EXPRESSED TO CONVEY AS BENEFICIAL OWNER

That, notwithstanding anything by the person who so conveys, or any one through whom he derives title, otherwise than by purchase for value, made, done, executed, or omitted, or knowingly suffered, the lease or grant creating the term or estate for which the land is conveyed is, at the time of conveyance, a good, valid, and effectual lease or grant of the property conveyed, and is in full force, unforfeited, unsurrendered, and has in nowise become void or voidable, and that, notwithstanding anything as aforesaid, all the rents reserved by, and all the covenants, conditions, and agreements contained in, the lease or grant, and on the part of the lessee or grantee and the persons deriving title under him to be paid, observed, and performed, have been paid, observed, and performed up to the time of conveyance.

In the above covenant a purchase for value shall not be deemed to include a conveyance in consideration of marriage.

Part III

Covenant implied in a Conveyance by way of Mortgage by a Person who Conveys and is expressed to Convey as Beneficial Owner

That the person who so conveys, has, with the concurrence of every other person, if any, conveying by his direction, full power to convey the subject-matter expressed to be conveyed by him, subject as, if so expressed, and in the manner in which it is expressed to be conveyed:

And also that, if default is made in payment of the money intended to be secured by the conveyance, or any interest thereon, or any part of that money or interest, contrary to any provision in the conveyance, it shall be lawful for the person to whom the conveyance is expressed to be made, and the persons deriving title under him, to enter into and upon, or receive, and thenceforth quietly hold, occupy, and enjoy or take and have, the subject-matter expressed to be conveyed, or any part thereof, without any lawful interruption or disturbance by the person who so conveys, or any person conveying by his direction, or any other person (not being a person claiming in respect of an estate or interest subject whereto the conveyance is expressly made):

And that, freed and discharged from, or otherwise by the person who so conveys sufficiently indemnified against all estates, incumbrances, claims, and demands whatever, other than those subject whereto the conveyance is expressly made:

And further, that the person who so conveys and every person conveying by his direction, and every person deriving title under any of them, and every other person having or rightfully claiming any estate or interest in the subject-matter of conveyance, or any part thereof, other than an estate or interest subject whereto the conveyance is expressly made, will from time to time and at all times, on the request of any person to whom the conveyance is expressed to be made, or of any person deriving title under him, but, as long as any right of redemption exists under the conveyance, at the cost of the person so conveying, or of those deriving title under him, and afterwards at the cost of the person making the request, execute and do all such lawful assurances and things for further or more perfectly assuring the subject-matter of conveyance and every part thereof to the person to whom the conveyance is made, and to those deriving title under him, subject as, if so expressed, and in the manner in which the conveyance is expressed to be made, as by him or them or any of them shall be reasonably required.

The above covenant in the case of a charge shall have effect as if for references to "conveys," "conveyed" and "conveyance" there were substituted respectively references to "charges," "charged" and "charge."

Part IV

Covenant implied in a Conveyance by way of Mortgage of Freehold Property subject to a Rent or of Leasehold Property by a Person who Conveys and is expressed to Convey as Beneficial Owner

That the lease or grant creating the term or estate for which the land is held is, at the time of conveyance, a good, valid, and effectual lease or grant of the land conveyed and is in full force, unforfeited, and unsurrendered and has in nowise become void or voidable, and that all the rents reserved by, and all the covenants, conditions, and agreements contained in, the lease or grant, and on the part of the lessee or grantee and the persons deriving title under him to be paid, observed, and performed, have been paid, observed, and performed up to the time of conveyance:

And also that the person so conveying, or the persons deriving title under him, will at all times, as long as any money remains owing on the security of the conveyance, pay, observe, and perform, or cause to be paid, observed, and performed all the rents reserved by, and all the covenants, conditions, and agreements contained in, the lease or grant, and on the part of the lessee or grantee and the persons deriving title under him to be paid, observed, and performed, and will keep the person to whom the conveyance is made, and those deriving title under him, indemnified against all actions, proceedings, costs, charges, damages, claims and demands, if any, to be incurred or sustained by him or them by reason of the non-payment of such rent or the non-observance or non-performance of such covenants, conditions, and agreements, or any of them.

The above covenant in the case of a charge shall have effect as if for references to "conveys," "conveyed" and "conveyance" there were substituted respectively references to "charges," "charged" and "charge."

Part V

Covenant implied in a Conveyance by way of Settlement, by a Person who Conveys and is expressed to Convey as Settlor

That the person so conveying, and every person deriving title under him by deed or act or operation of law in his lifetime subsequent to that conveyance, or by testamentary disposition or devolution in law, on his death, will, from time to time, and at all times, after the date of that conveyance, at the request and cost of any person deriving title thereunder, execute and do all such lawful assurances and things for further or more perfectly assuring the subject-matter of the conveyance to the persons to whom the conveyance is made and those deriving title under them, as by them or any of them shall be reasonably required, subject as, if so expressed, and in the manner in which the conveyance is expressed to be made.

PART VI

COVENANT IMPLIED IN ANY CONVEYANCE, BY EVERY PERSON WHO CONVEYS AND IS EXPRESSED TO CONVEY AS TRUSTEE OR MORTGAGEE, OR AS PERSONAL REPRESENTATIVE OF A DECEASED PERSON [. . .][51] OR UNDER AN ORDER OF THE COURT

That the person so conveying has not exeuted or done, or knowingly suffered, or been party or privy to, any deed or thing, whereby or by means whereof the subject-matter of the conveyance, or any part thereof, is or may be impeached, charged, affected, or incumbered in title, estate, or otherwise, or whereby or by means whereof the person who so conveys is in anywise hindered from conveying the subject-matter of the conveyance, or any part thereof, in the manner in which it is expressed to be conveyed.

The foregoing covenant may be implied in an assent in like manner as in a conveyance by deed.

PART VII

COVENANT IMPLIED IN A CONVEYANCE FOR VALUABLE CONSIDERATION, OTHER THAN A MORTGAGE, OF THE ENTIRETY OF LAND AFFECTED BY A RENTCHARGE

That the grantees or the persons delivering title under them will at all times, from the date of the conveyance or other date therein stated, duly pay the said rentcharge and observe and perform all the covenants, agreements and conditions contained in the deed or other document creating the rentcharge, and thenceforth on the part of the owner of the land to be observed and performed:

And also will at all times, from the date aforesaid, save harmless and keep indemnified the conveying parties and their respective estates and effects, from and against all proceedings, costs, claims and expenses on account of any omission to pay the said rentcharge or any part thereof, or any breach of any of the said covenants, agreements and conditions.

PART VIII

COVENANTS IMPLIED IN A CONVEYANCE FOR VALUABLE CONSIDERATION, OTHER THAN A MORTGAGE, OF PART OF LAND AFFECTED BY A RENTCHARGE, SUBJECT TO A PART (NOT LEGALLY APPORTIONED) OF THAT RENTCHARGE

(i) That the grantees, or the persons deriving title under them, will at all times, from the date of the conveyance or other date therein stated, pay the apportioned rent and observe and perform all the covenants (other than the covenant to pay the entire rent) and conditions contained in the deed or other document creating the rentcharge, so far as the same relate to the land conveyed:

And also will at all times, from the date aforesaid, save harmless and keep indemnified the conveying parties and their respective estates and effects, from and against all proceedings, costs, claims and expenses on account of any omission to pay the said apportioned rent, or any breach of any of the said covenants and conditions, so far as the same relate as aforesaid.

(ii) That the conveying parties, or the persons deriving title under them, will at all times, from the date of the conveyance or other date therein stated, pay the balance of the rentcharge (after deducting the apportioned rent aforesaid, and any other rents similarly apportioned in respect of land not retained), and observe and perform all the covenants, other than the covenant to pay the entire rent, and conditions contained in the deed or other document creating the rentcharge, so far as the same relate to the land not included in the conveyance and remaining vested in the covenantors:

And also will at all times, from the date aforesaid, save harmless and keep indemnified the grantees and their estates and effects, from and against all proceedings, costs, claims and expenses on account of any omission to pay the aforesaid balance of the rentcharge, or any breach of any of the said covenants and conditions so far as they relate as aforesaid.

---

[51] Words repealed by the Mental Health Act 1959 (7 & 8 Eliz. 2, c. 72), Sched. 8, Pt. I.

Part IX

COVENANT IN A CONVEYANCE FOR VALUABLE CONSIDERATION, OTHER THAN A MORTGAGE, OF THE ENTIRETY OF THE LAND COMPRISED IN A LEASE FOR THE RESIDUE OF THE TERM OR INTEREST CREATED BY THE LEASE

That the assignees, or the persons deriving title under them, will at all times, from the date of the conveyance or other date therein stated, duly pay all rent becoming due under the lease creating the term or interest for which the land is conveyed, and observe and perform all the covenants, agreements and conditions therein contained and thenceforth on the part of the lessees to be observed and performed:

And also will at all times, from the date aforesaid, save harmless and keep indemnified the conveying parties and their estates and effects, from and against all proceedings, costs, claims and expenses on account of any omission to pay the said rent or any breach of any of the said covenants, agreements and conditions.

Part X

COVENANTS IMPLIED IN A CONVEYANCE FOR VALUABLE CONSIDERATION, OTHER THAN A MORTGAGE, OF PART OF THE LAND COMPRISED IN A LEASE, FOR THE RESIDUE OF THE TERM OR INTEREST CREATED BY THE LEASE, SUBJECT TO A PART (NOT LEGALLY APPORTIONED) OF THAT RENT

(i) That the assignees, or the persons deriving title under them, will at all times, from the date of the conveyance or other date therein stated, pay the apportioned rent and observe and perform all the covenants, other than the covenant to pay the entire rent, agreements and conditions contained in the lease creating the term or interest for which the land is conveyed, and thenceforth on the part of the lessees to be observed and performed, so far as the same relate to the land conveyed:

And also will at all times from the date aforesaid save harmless and keep indemnified, the conveying parties and their respective estates and effects, from and against all proceedings, costs, claims and expenses on account of any omission to pay the said apportioned rent or any breach of any of the said covenants, agreements and conditions so far as the same relate as aforesaid.

(ii) That the conveying parties, or the persons deriving title under them, will at all times, from the date of the conveyance, or other date therein stated, pay the balance of the rent (after deducting the apportioned rent aforesaid and any other rents similarly apportioned in respect of land not retained) and observe and perform all the covenants, other than the covenant to pay the entire rent, agreements and conditions contained in the lease and on the part of the lessees to be observed and performed so far as the same relate to the land demised (other than the land comprised in the conveyance) and remaining vested in the convenantors:

And also will at all times, from the date aforesaid, save harmless and keep indemnified, the assignees and their estates and effects, from and against all proceedings, costs, claims and expenses on account of any omission to pay the aforesaid balance of the rent or any breach of any of the said covenants, agreements and conditions so far as they relate as aforesaid.

Sections 114 and 115   THIRD SCHEDULE

FORMS OF TRANSFER AND DISCHARGE OF MORTGAGES

FORM No. 1

FORM OF TRANSFER OF MORTGAGE

This Transfer of Mortgage made the   day of   19   between *M.* of [&c.] of the one part and *T.* of [&c.] of the other part, supplemental to a Mortgage dated [&c.], and made between [&c.], and to a Further Charge dated [&c.], and made between [&c.] affecting &c. (*here state short particulars of the mortgaged property*).

WITNESSETH that in consideration of the sums of £   and £   (for interest) now paid by *T.* to *M.*, being the respective amounts of the mortgage money and interest owing in respect of the said mortgage and further charge (the receipt of which sums *M.* hereby acknowledges) *M.*, as mortgagee, hereby conveys and tranfers to *T.* the benefit of the said mortgage and further charge.

In witness, &c.

FORM NO. 2

FORM OF RECEIPT ON DISCHARGE OF A MORTGAGE

I, *A.B.,* of [&c.] hereby acknowledge that I have this   day
of   19   , received the sum of £   representing the [aggregate]
[balance remaining owing in respect of the] principal money secured by the within [above]
written [annexed] mortgage [and by a further charge dated, &c., *or otherwise as required*]
together with all interest and costs, the payment having been made by *C.D.* of [&c.] and *E.F.*
of [&c.]
As witness, &c.
Note.—If the persons paying are not entitled to the equity of redemption state that they are
paying the money out of a fund applicable to the discharge of the mortgage.

FOURTH SCHEDULE

FORMS RELATING TO STATUTORY CHARGES OR MORTGAGES OF FREEHOLD OR LEASEHOLD LAND

Section 117   FORM NO. 1

STATUTORY CHARGE BY WAY OF LEGAL MORTGAGE

This Legal Charge made by way of Statutory Mortgage the   day
of   19   , between *A.* of [&c.] of the one part and *M.* of [&c.] of the other part
Witnesseth that in consideration of the sum of £   now paid to *A.* by *M.* of which
sum *A.* hereby acknowledges the receipt *A.* As Mortgagor and As Beneficial Owner hereby
charges by way of legal mortgage All That [&c.] with the payment to *M.* on the
day of   19   , of the principal sum of £   as the mortgage money with interest
thereon at the rate of   per centum per annum.
In witness, &c.
Note.—Variations in this and the subsequent forms in this Schedule to be made, if required,
for leasehold land or for giving effect to special arrangements. *M.* will be in the same position
as if the Charge had been effected by a demise of freeholds or a subdemise of leaseholds.

Section 118   FORM NO. 2

STATUTORY TRANSFER, MORTGAGOR NOT JOINING

This Transfer of Mortgage made by way of statutory transfer the   day
of   19   , between *M.* of [&c.] of the one part and *T.* [of &c.] of the other part
supplemental to a legal charge made by way of statutory mortgage dated [&c.] and made
[&c.] Witnesseth that in consideration of the sum of £   now paid to *M.* by *T.* (being the
aggregate amount of £   mortgage money and £   interest due in
respect of the said legal charge of which sum *M.* hereby acknowledges the receipt) *M.* as
Mortgagee hereby conveys and transfers to *T.* the benefit of the said legal charge.
In witness, &c.
Note.—This and the next two forms also apply to a transfer of a statutory mortgage made
before the commencement of this Act, which will then be referred to as a mortgage instead of
a legal charge.

FORM NO. 3

STATUTORY TRANSFER, A COVENANTOR JOINING

This Transfer of Mortgage made by way of statutory transfer the   day
of   19   , between *A.* of [&c.] of the first part *B.* of [&c.] of the second part and
C. of [&c.] of the third part Supplemental to a Legal Charge made by way of statutory

mortgage dated [&c.] and made [&c.] Witnesseth that in consideration of the sum of £   now paid by *A.* to *C.* (being the mortgage money due in respect of the said Legal Charge no interest being now due or payable thereon of which sum *A.* hereby acknowledges the receipt) *A.* as Mortgagee with the concurrence of *B.* who joins herein as covenantor hereby conveys and transfers to *C.* the benefit of the said Legal Charge.

In witness, &c.

Sections 117 and 118   Form No. 4

Statutory Transfer and Mortgage Combined

This Transfer and Legal Charge is made by way of statutory transfer and mortgage the   day of   19   , between *A.* of [&c.] of the first part *B.* of [&c.] of the second part and *C.* of [&c.] of the third part Supplemental to a Legal Charge made by way of statutory mortgage dated [&c.] and made [&c.] Whereas a principal sum of £   only remains due in respect of the said Legal Charge as the mortgage money and no interest is now due thereon And Whereas *B.* is seised in fee simple of the land comprised in the said Legal Charge subject to that Charge.

Now this Deed Witnesseth as follows:—

1. In consideration of the sum of £   now paid to *A.* by *C.* (the receipt and payment of which sum *A.* & *B.* hereby respectively acknowledge) *A.* as mortgagee hereby conveys and transfers to *C.* the benefit of the said Legal Charge.

2. For the consideration aforesaid *B*† as beneficial owner hereby charges by way of legal mortgage All the premises comprised in the said Legal Charge with the payment to *C.* on the   day of   19   of‡ the sum of £   as the mortgage money with interest thereon at the rate of   per centum per annum In Witness &c. [or in the case of a further advance after "acknowledge" at *insert* "and of the further sum of £   now paid by *C.* to *B.* of which sum *B.* hereby acknowledges the receipt" *also at* † *before* "as beneficial owner" *insert* "as mortgagor and" *as well as where B. is not the original mortgagor. And after* "of" *at* ‡ *insert* "the sums of £   and £   making together"].

Note.—Variations to be made, as required, in case of the deed being by indorsement, or in respect of any other thing.

Section 120   Form No. 5

Receipt on Discharge of Statutory Legal Charge or Mortgage

I   *A.B.*   of   [&c.]   hereby   acknowledge   that   I   have   this   day of   19   received the sum of £   representing the [aggregate] [balance remaining owing in respect of the] mortgage money secured by the [annexed] within [above] written statutory legal charge [*or* statutory mortgage] [and by the further statutory charge dated &c. *or otherwise as required*] together with all interest and costs the payment having been made by *C.D.* of [&c.] and *E.F.* of [&c.]

As witness &c.

Note.—If the persons paying are not entitled to the equity of redemption state that they are paying the money out of a fund applicable to the discharge of the statutory legal charge or mortgage.

Section 206   FIFTH SCHEDULE

Forms of Instruments

Form No. 1

Charge by way of Legal Mortgage

This Legal Charge is made [&c.] between *A.* of [&c.] of the one part and *B.* of [&c.] of the other part.

[*Recite the title of A. to the freeholds or leaseholds in the Schedule and agreement for the loan by B.*]

Now in consideration of the sum of   pounds now paid by *B.* to *A.* (the receipt &c.) this Deed witnesseth as follows:—

1. *A.* hereby covenants with *B.* to pay [*Add the requisite covenant to pay principal and interest*].

2. *A.* as Beneficial Owner hereby charges by way of legal mortgage All and Singular the property mentioned in the Schedule hereto with the payment to *B.* of the principal money, interest, and other money hereby covenanted to be paid by *A.*

3. [*Add covenant to insure buildings and any other provisions desired.*]

In witness [&c.] [*Add Schedule*].

Note.—*B.* will be in the same position as if a mortgage had been effected by a demise of freeholds or a subdemise of leaseholds.

Form No. 2

Further Charge by way of Legal Mortgage

This Further Charge made [&c.] between [&c.] [*same parties as foregoing legal charge*] Supplemental to a Legal Charge (hereinafter called the Principal Deed) Dated [&c.] and made between the same parties as are parties hereto and in the same order for securing the sum of £   and interest at   per centum per annum on [freehold] [leasehold] land at [&c.].

Witnesseth as follows:—

1. In consideration of the further sum of £   now paid to *A.* by *B.* [*add receipt and covenant to pay the further advance and interest.*].

2. For the consideration aforesaid *A.* as Beneficial Owner hereby charges by way of legal mortgage the premises comprised in the Principal Deed with the payment to *B.* of the principal money and interest hereinbefore covenanted to be paid as well as the principal money, interest, and other money secured by the Principal Deed.

In witness [&c.].

Form No. 3

Conveyance on Sale, Legal Chargees or Mortgagees concurring

This Conveyance is made [&c.] between *A.* of [&c.] (hereinafter called the Vendor) of the first part *B.* of [&c.] and *C.* of [&c.] (hereinafter called the Mortgagees) of the second part and *D.* of [&c.] (hereinafter called the Purchaser) of the third part [*Recite the Charge by way of legal mortgage, the state of the debt, the agreement for sale and for the mortgagees to concur.*]

Now in the consideration of the sum of £   paid by the Purchaser by the direction of the Vendor to the Mortgagees (*the receipt &c.*) and of the sum of £   paid by the Purchaser to the Vendor (*the receipt &c.*) this Deed witnesseth as follows:—

1. The Vendor As Beneficial Owner hereby conveys and the Mortgagees As Mortgagees hereby [surrender and] release unto the Purchaser All That &c.

To Hold unto the Purchaser [in fee simple] discharged from all claims under the recited Legal Charge [Mortgage and to the intent that the term subsisting thereunder shall as respects the premises conveyed merge and be extinguished.].

2. [*Add any necessary acknowledgments and undertakings with respect to documents not handed over which relate to the title and any other special provisions.*]

In witness &c.

Form No. 4

Conveyance on Sale by Legal Chargees or Mortgagees

This Conveyance is made [&c.] between *A.* of [&c.] and *B.* of [&c.] (hereinafter called the Vendors) of the one part and *C.* of [&c.] (hereinafter called the Purchaser) of the other part [*Recite the Legal Charge or the Mortgage, with or without a deed converting the Mortgage into a legal charge and the agreement for sale*].

Now in consideration of the sum of £   paid by the Purchaser to the Vendors (the receipt &c.) this Deed witnesseth as follows:—

1. The Vendors As Mortgagees in exercise of the power for this purpose conferred on them by the Law of Property Act 1925, and of all other powers hereby convey unto the Purchaser All Those &c.

To Hold unto the Purchaser [in fee simple] discharged from all right of redemption and claims under the recited Legal Charge [Mortgage].

2. [*Add any necessary acknowledgments as to documents retained and any other special provisions.*]

In witness &c.

FORM NO. 5

CONVEYANCE BY PERSONAL REPRESENTATIVES OF A FEE SIMPLE RESERVING THEREOUT A TERM OF YEARS ABSOLUTE FOR GIVING LEGAL EFFECT TO A MORTGAGE

This Conveyance is made [&c.] between *James Cook* of [&c.] and *Harry Cook* of [&c.] of the first part, *L.* of [&c.] and *M.* of [&c.] of the second part, and *Thomas Wilson* of [&c.] of the third part.

Whereas on the first day of October 1927 Letters of Administration to the real and personal estate of *Henry Wilson*, late of [&c.], who died [&c.], were granted by the principal probate registry to *James Cook* and *Harry Cook.*

And whereas *Henry Wilson* was at his death solely entitled to the hereditaments hereinafter conveyed for an estate in fee simple.

Now this Deed witnesseth that *James Cook* and *Harry Cook*, as Personal Representatives of the said *Henry Wilson* deceased, hereby convey unto the said *Thomas Wilson*

All that [&c.]

Reserving out of the premises nevertheless unto *L.* and *M.* a term of eight hundred years, without impeachment of waste, to commence from the date hereof but subject to cesser on redemption by *Thomas Wilson* under a Mortgage dated [&c.] and made between [&c.] on payment of the sum of five thousand pounds, and interest thereon at the rate of five pounds per centum per annum.

To hold the premises subject to the said term unto *Thomas Wilson* [in fee simple].

In witness [&c.]

Note.—The reservation will be valid at law, though the deed may not be executed by *Thomas Wilson.*

FORM NO. 6.

CONVEYANCE ON SALE RESERVING MINERALS AND RIGHT TO WORK AND A PERPETUAL RENTCHARGE

This conveyance made [&c.] between *A.* of [&c.] of the one part and *B.* [&c.] of the other part.

Witnesseth that in consideration of the sum of   pounds now paid by *B.* to *A.* (the receipt, &c.) and of the rentcharge hereinafter reserved *A.* as Beneficial Owner hereby conveys unto *B.*

All those [&c.] except and reserving unto *A.* in fee simple all mines and minerals Together with full power to work [&c.]

To hold (except and reserved as aforesaid) unto *B.* in fee simple reserving out of the premises to *A.* in fee simple a perpetual yearly rentcharge of   pounds, to be for ever charged upon and issuing out of the premises hereby conveyed clear of all deductions (except landlord's property tax), and payable by equal half-yearly payments on [&c.], the first payment to be made on [&c.]

And *B.* hereby covenants with *A.*, and the persons deriving title under him to pay [&c.]

In witness [&c.]

Note.—The reservations will be valid at law even if the deed is not executed by *B.*

FORM NO. 7

DEED FOR CONFIRMING LEGAL ESTATES WHICH HAVE NOT BEEN VALIDLY CREATED

To All to whom this Further Assurance shall come *A.B.* of &c. sends greeting this   day of   19

[Recite the invalid dealings, giving short particulars in schedules of the Conveyances, Grants and Leases which purport to transfer or create legal estates, that A.B. is entitled in fee simple or for a term of years absolute in the land affected and desires to confirm the dealings.]

Now these presents witness and the said *A.B.* hereby declares that his legal estate in the premises affected to which he is entitled as aforesaid shall go and devolve in such manner as may be requisite for legally confirming the interests capable of subsisting as legal estates expressed to have been transferred or created by the documents mentioned in the schedules hereto or any of those documents and any dealings with the interests so confirmed which would have been legal if those interests had in the first instance been validly transferred or created:

Provided always that subject to such confirmation of interests and dealings nothing herein contained shall affect the legal estate of the said *A.B.* in the premises.

In witness, &c. *[Add Schedules.]*

Note.—This form takes the place of a conveyance to uses for confirming past transactions and is applicable to a term of years absolute as well as a fee simple.

FORM No. 8

ASSENT BY PERSONAL RRESENTATIVE IN FAVOUR OF A PERSON ABSOLUTELY ENTITLED FREE FROM INCUMBRANCES

I, *A.B.*, of [&c.] as the personal representative of *X.Y.*, late of [&c.] deceased, do this   day of   19   hereby, As Personal Representative, assent to the vesting in *C.D.* of [&c.] of [All that farm &c.] *or* [All the property described in the Schedule hereto] for all the estate or interest of the said *X.Y.* at the time of his death [*or,* for an estate in fee simple].

As witness, &c.

Note.—The expression "conveyance" includes an assent, but an assent will relate back to the death unless a contrary intention appears. An assent may be properly given though duties remain to be paid if the personal representative is satisfied in regard to the arrangements made for payment.

FORM No.9

ASSENT BY PERSONAL REPRESENTATIVES IN FAVOUR OF TRUSTEES FOR SALE

We, *A.B.*, of [&c.] and *C.D.*, of [&c.] as the Personal Representatives of *X.Y.*, late of [&c.] deceased do this   day of   19   hereby:—

1. As Personal Representatives assent to the vesting in [ourselves *or*] *T.A.* of [&c.] and *T.B.* of [&c.] of All Those &c. To Hold unto [ourselves *or*] the said *T.A.* and *T.B.* in fee simple Upon trust to sell the same or any part thereof with full power to postpone the sale and to stand possessed of the net proceeds of sale and other money applicable as capital and the net rents and profits until sale upon the trusts respectively declared concerning the same [*or* the proceeds of sale and the rents and profits of certain property at   ] by the Will dated [&c.] of [&c.] [*or by the Settlement dated &c. or otherwise as the case may require*].

2. And declare that *F.* of [&c.] and *M.* of [&c.] during their joint lives and the survivor of them during his or her life have or has power to appoint new trustees of this Assent [*or* "that the statutory power to appoint new trustees applies to this Assent" *or otherwise as the case requires to correspond with the power applicable to the Will or Settlement*].

As witness &c.

Section 206   SIXTH SCHEDULE

EPITOMES OF ABSTRACTS OF TITLE

SPECIMEN No. 1

OF THE TITLE OF JOHN WILLIAMS TO BLACKACRE

WHERE THE TITLE COMMENCES BEFORE THE COMMENCEMENT OF THIS ACT

The italics show how the abstract is to be framed and what documents are to be abstracted. After the commencement of this Act, the parts not in italics may be ignored.

10th June 1897

*Will of H. Jones, appointing Maria Jones and W. Jones executors and Settled Land Act
trustees.*
Devises, Blackacre.
*To the use that Maria Jones may receive a yearly rentcharge of five hundred pounds for her life,
and, subject thereto,*
To the use of W. Jones for life with remainder,
To the use of X. and Y., for a term of one thousand years, and subject thereto,
To the use of the first and other sons of W.Jones in tail with remainders over.
Trusts of term of one thousand years declared for raising ten thousand pounds for portions for
younger children of W. Jones, as he shall appoint, and in default equally.
Hotchpot Clause. Power to appoint new trustees.

4th June 1898

Death of H. Jones.

1st August 1898

Will of H. Jones proved.
[*Note.*—After the execution of the Vesting Deed the will only takes effect in equity
and can be withdrawn from the abstract when not required as a root of title.]

20th August 1899

Conveyance by the executors to the uses of the Will.

2nd September 1915

Appointment of R. and S. to be Settled Land Act trustees of the will in place of Maria Jones
and W. Jones who retire.

1st January 1926

The Settled Land and Law of Property Acts 1925 come into operation.
[*Note.*—The legal estate in fee simple will vest in W. Jones in fee simple, but he cannot
deal with it till the vesting deed is executed.]

20th January 1926

*Deed by the Settled Land Act trustees declaring the fee simple is vested in W. Jones on the trusts
of the Will and stating that they are the trustees of the settlement.*

2nd February 1926

Appointment by W. Jones of five thousand pounds, part of the ten thousand pounds, to his
daughter, Ann Jones.

3rd February 1926

Assignment by Ann Jones of her five thousand pounds, part of the ten thousand pounds
raisable for portions, to trustees *F.* and *G.* on her marriage to J. Robinson.

4th February 1926

Will of W. Jones, appointing T. Brooks his executor.

6th March 1926

Death of W. Jones leaving three children, Frederick Jones, his eldest son, and E. Jones and
Ann Robinson.

2nd April 1926

Disentail by Frederick Jones in trust for himself in fee simple.

3rd May 1926

Will of W. Jones proved by R. and S. in regard to the settled land.

6th June 1926

Mortgage by E. Jones of his one-half of the ten thousand pounds to *K.*

1st December 1926

Death of Maria Jones, jointress.

2nd January 1927

Release by *F.* and *G.* on payment to them of the five thousand pounds of Ann Robinson.

Same date

Release by E. Jones and *K.*, his mortgagee, of the five thousand pounds raisable for E. Jones.

3rd January 1927

Assent by R. and S., as personal representatives to Frederick Jones in fee, without nominating Settled Land Act trustees.
    [*Note.*—If the Assent had been made before the family charges had been cleared, the personal representatives would have nominated themselves as being the trustees of the settlement, and a discharge from them would have been required when the charges were cleared.]

6th February 1927

Mortgage either by charge by way of legal mortgage or for a term of one thousand years by Frederick Jones to the Estate Trustees of the C. Assurance Society to secure five thousand pounds and interest.

20th March 1927

Second Mortgage either by charge by way of legal mortgage or for a term of two thousand years by Frederick Jones to *D.*, to secure three thousand pounds and interest.

1st June 1927

Third mortgage either by charge by way of legal mortgage or for a term of three thousand years by Frederick Jones to *E.*, to secure two thousand pounds and interest.

8th August 1927

Conveyance by Frederick Jones on his marriage (subject to above mortgages) to *M.* and *N.* upon trust for sale, the proceeds of sale being settled by a deed of even date.

12th November 1927

Death of *M.*

20th December 1927

Appointment of *F.* as trustee of the conveyance on trust for sale in the place of *M.*, and jointly with *N.*

10th June 1928

Conveyance by the then Estate Trustees of the C. Assurance Society, under their power of sale as first mortgagees, to John Williams in fee.
    [*Note.*—The title being made under the power of sale of the Estate Trustees, the fee simple passes and not merely the mortgage term. They can if desired convey the fee in the names of *M.* and *N.* It is unnecessary to disclose the second and third mortgages or the conveyance on trust for sale. It would have been necessary to disclose them if title had been made by the trustees for sale, as the mortgages and the conveyance all dealt with legal estates. The right to vest the debt and mortgaged property in Estate Trustees by memorial enrolled under a Private Act is preserved.
    No evidence of deaths, births, &c., is required. Probate of the will of H. Jones is conveyancing evidence of his death.]

12th January 1929

John Williams leaves Great Britain and Northern Ireland is believed to be alive but cannot be found.

10th August 1929

Private Act passed authorising the X. Company to acquire Blackacre under compulsory powers.

15th June 1930

Statutory declaration as to facts known with reference to John Williams.

16th June 1930

Deed Poll by X. Company (who by their agent also execute in the name of John William
under section seventy-seven of the Lands Clauses Consolidation Act 1845, vesting the land in
themselves.
[*Note.*—This is an example of an exercise of a power over a legal estate the operation
of which is expressly preserved.]

SPECIMEN NO.2

OF THE TITLE OF THE TRUSTEES OF FRANK SMITHERS TO GREENACRE RELATING TO UNDIVIDED
SHARES

2nd January 1910

Mortgage by James Smith of Greenacre to M. Coy., Ltd. in fee to secure 1,000l. and interest

4th February 1910

Will of James Smith devising Greenacre to his ten children named therein in equal shares an
appointing E. to be his executor.

1st March 1910

Death of James Smith, leaving the ten children surviving.

3rd April 1910

Probate by E.

4th December 1910

Assent by E. to the devise to the ten children.

5th January 1911

Mortgage by one of the sons of his tenth share.

15th April 1911

Conveyance by one of the daughters on her marriage of a tenth share to trustees on trust for
sale, the net proceeds to be held on the trusts of her settlement of even date.

20th May 1911

Settlement by another of the sons of his tenth share and appointing Settled Land Act trustees.

8th June 1913

Will of another daughter devising her tenth to her husband and appointing him executor.

20th June 1913

Death of the testatrix.

4th August 1913

Probate by her husband.

2nd May 1918

Death of another son intestate.

30th July 1918

Letters of administration granted to two of his brothers.

1st January 1926

The Law of Property Act 1925 comes into operation and vests Greenacre, subject only to the
mortgage of 1910 affecting the entirety (which is converted into a mortgage for a term of
three thousand years), in the Public Trustee, pending the appointment of new trustees, on
trust for sale.

4th June 1926

Order of the court (Chancery Division) made on the application of persons entitled to six tenths, appointing M. and N. to be trustees of the trust affecting Greenacre in place of the Public Trustee.

7th May 1927

Conveyance on sale to Walter Robinson by M. and N., the M. Company, Limited, being paid off out of part of the purchase money, and joining to surrender the three thousand years term.
[*Note.*—The balance of the purchase money is available in the hands of the trustees to answer the claims of the mortgagee and other persons interested in undivided shares.]

4th June 1927

Will of Walter Robinson devising and bequeathing Greenacre and his residuary real and personal estate to *X.* and *Y.* upon trust for his son John Robinson for life with remainder upon trust for his first and other sons successively according to seniority in tail male with remainder upon trust for the same sons in tail general with remainder upon trust for all the daughters of John Robinson as tenants in common in tail with cross remainders in tail between them in equal shares. Appointment of *X.* and *Y.* to be executors and Settled Land Act trustees.

1st December 1927

Death of testator.

20th April 1928

Probate by X. and Y.

3rd May 1928

Assent by X. and Y. vesting the settled land in John Robinson upon the trusts of the will of Walter Robinson, and stating that they are the trustees of the settlement.

14th July 1928

Will of John Robinson appointing his daughters Mary Robinson and Jane Robinson his executors.

16th March 1930

Death of John Robinson without having had a son and leaving five daughters.

12th June 1930

Probate by X. and Y. in regard to the settled land.

25th July 1930

Assent by X. and Y. to the vesting of the settled land in themselves on trust for sale, the net proceeds to be held on the trusts of the will of Walter Robinson.

7th January 1931

Conveyance on sale by X. and Y. of Greenacre to Frank Smithers in fee.

8th January 1931

Equitable charge by Frank Smithers to James Montagu by way of indemnity and agreement to vest Greenacre in a trust corporation on trust for sale to raise the money when the amount is ascertained and for other purposes.
[*Note.*—A mere equitable charge not secured by deposit of documents can be overriden when the land is made subject to a trust for sale without joining the chargee.]

9th January 1932

Lease by Frank Smithers of part of Greenacre to his wife for life at a rent.
[*Note.*—A lease for life is made to take effect as a demise for a term of ninety years determinable by notice after the death of the lessee by his representatives or by the lessor.]

23rd June 1933

Conveyance by Frank Smithers, of Greenacre, to a trust corporation on trust for sale subject to the lease. The net proceeds to be held on the trusts of a deed of even date, under which effect is given to the Agreement of 1931.

4th July 1926

Settlement by John Wilson, being a deed declaring that Whiteacre is vested in himself in fee upon the trusts of a deed of even date.
Appointment of R. and S. to be trustees for the purposes of the Settled Land Act 1925.
Provisions extending the powers conferred by the Settled Land Act, so far as they relate to dealings with land, and giving power for John Wilson during his life to appoint new trustees.

Same date

Trust Instrument.
Trusts declared for John Wilson for life, with remainder.
    Upon trust that Elizabeth Wilson, if she survives him shall have a rentcharge of 200*l.* during the residue of her life, and subject thereto.
    Upon trust for *R.* and *S.* for a term of five hundred years to raise five thousand pounds portions for younger children of John Wilson, with remainder.
    Upon trust for Henry Wilson for life, with remainder.
    Upon trust for *H.* and *K.* for a term of one thousand years to raise five thousand pounds portions for younger children of Henry Wilson, with remainder.
    Upon trust for the first and other sons of Henry Wilson successively in tail, with further remainders over. Appointment of *R.* and *S.* to be Settled Land Act trustees. Extension of Settled Land Act powers by reference to the Vesting Deed of even date or otherwise. Power for tenant for life of full age to appoint new trustees.

4th September 1926

Appointment of new trustee of the Trust Instrument and of the five hundred years' term.
Recites that *S.* is incapable of acting. Appointment by John Wilson of *P.* to be trustee of the term of five hundred years and for the purposes of the Trust Deed in the place of *S.* and jointly with *R.* Declaration (express or implied) vesting the equitable term of five hundred years in *R.* and *P.*

Same date

Deed stating that R. and P. are the trustees of the settlement. Memorandum of the deed endorsed on the Vesting Deed.

7th January 1927

Will of John Wilson appointing Issac James and Joseph James executors.

3rd September 1927

Death of John Wilson, leaving younger children and his widow.

4th April 1928

Will of John Wilson proved by R. and P. in regard to the settled land.

1st October 1928

Assignment by *R.* and *P.* to *B.* of term of five hundred years by way of mortgage for securing five thousand pounds and interest.
    [*Note.*—As money has been raised on the term the mortgagee could call on the executors to create a legal term for securing it in priority to the settlement.]

2nd December 1928

Assent by R. and P., as personal representatives, to the vesting of the settled land in Henry Wilson in fee upon the trusts of the Trust Deed.
Statement that R. and P. are the trustees of the settlement. Power for Henry Wilson during his life to appoint new trustees.
The same provisions for extending powers conferred by the Settled Land Act as are contained in the Vesting Deed.
    [*Note.*—These may be inserted either expressly, if short, or by reference to the former Vesting Deed, if long.]

2nd June 1929

Appointment of James Cook and Harry Cook to be trustees of the Trust Deed.

2nd June 1929

Deed stating that they are the trustees of the settlement. Endorsement of notice on the Vesting Deed.

4th November 1929

Transfer of the mortgage for five thousand pounds by *B.* to *C.*

10th July 1930

Death of Henry Wilson, leaving Thomas Wilson, his eldest son, and two younger children.

1st October 1930

Letters of Administration to the settled land of Henry Wilson granted to James Cook and Harry Cook.

3rd November 1930

Disentail by Thomas Wilson.

4th November 1930

Release by *C.* on payment off of his mortgage debt of five thousand pounds and surrender of the equitable term of five hundred years.

10th November 1930

Death of Elizabeth Wilson.
     [*Note.*—Though her jointure took effect in equity only she has power to create a term of years absolute for raising arrears of the jointure, and the estate owner would be bound to give legal effect to a mortgage of the term.]

20th November 1930

Release by two younger children of Henry Wilson of their portions.

Same date

Demise by Thomas Wilson to *L.* and *M.* for an equitable term of eight hundred years, subject to cesser on payment of five thousand pounds and interest.

Same date

Demise by James Cook and Harry Cook to L. and M. for the term of eight hundred years, subject to cesser on redemption or charge by way of legal mortgage.

Same date

Assent by them to the vesting of the settled land, subject to the term or legal charge, in Thomas Wilson in fee, without nominating Settled Land Act trustees.

10th March 1931

Conveyance by Thomas Wilson and L. and M. to R. Horne to fee.

SPECIMEN No. 4

OF THE TITLE OF THE ADMINISTRATORS OF M. CURTIS TO RICH AND MIDDLE FARMS

RELATING TO INFANTS

2nd January 1922

Will of James Wilcox devising Rich Farm and Middle Farm to the use of his elder son John Wilcox (an infant) for his life with remainders over for the issue of John Wilcox which failed with remainder to the use of his younger son Gilbert Wilcox (an infant) for his life with remainders over. Appointment of *X.* and *Y.* to be executors and Settled Land Act trustees.

4th February 1922

Death of testator, leaving his two sons, giving dates of their births.

12th May 1922
Probate by X. and Y.

15th December 1922
Assent to the devise, John Wilcox being still an infant.

1st January 1926
The Settled Land Act 1925 and the Law of Property Act 1925 come into force and vest the settled land in *X.* and *Y.* as Settled Land Act trustees by reason of John Wilcox being an infant.

4th January 1926
Instrument declaring that the settled land is vested in X. and Y.

3rd June 1926
Death of John Wilcox a bachelor and an infant.

29th September 1926
Conveyance on sale of Rich Farm by X. and Y. to M. Curtis.

12th October 1927
Conveyance by X. and Y. vesting Middle Farm in Gilbert Wilcox (who had attained full age) on the trusts of the will of James Wilcox with a statement that they are the trustees of the settlement.

10th November 1927
Conveyance on sale of Middle Farm by Gilbert Wilcox to M. Curtis, X and Y. joining to receive the purchase money.

1st February 1928
Will of M. Curtis purporting to appoint his infant son John Curtis executor.

3rd April 1928
Death of M. Curtis.

5th September 1928
Letters of administration with the will annexed granted to M. and N.
    [*Note.*—Administration will either be granted to a trust Corporation or to not less than two individuals, if there are Settled Land Act trustees, it will, as respects the settled land, be granted to them.]

Specimen No. 5

Of the Title of George Smith to Houses in John Street

Relating to Leasehold Property

25th March 1921
Lease by Charles Robinson to Henry Chubb, of 10 to 16 (even numbers) John Street, in the city of X., for 99 years from date at a yearly rent of 5l. for each house.

26th March 1921
First Mortgage (by subdemise) by Henry Chubb to A. for the residue of the term less 3 days for securing 3,000l. and interest. Declaration by Henry Chubb that he holds the head term in trust for A. subject to redemption.

Same date
Second Mortgage (by subdemise) to B. for the residue of the term less 2 days for securing 1,000l. and interest. Declaration by Henry Chubb that (subject to the First Mortgage) he holds the head term in trust for B. subject to redemption.

Same date

Third Mortgage (by subdemise) to *C.* for residue of term less 1 day for securing 500*l.* and interest.

24th December 1924

Transfer of First Mortgage by A. to T. in trust for Henry Chubb, who pays off the First Mortgage debt.

1st January 1926

The Law of Property Act 1925 comes into operation.

[*Note.*—It extinguishes the first mórtgage term, because Henry Chubb was not entitled to keep it alive to the prejudice of his mesne incumbrancers.]

1st July 1926

Order of Court directing Henry Chubb to hand over the Lease, First Mortgage, and Transfer of that Mortgage to *B.*

20th July 1926

Assignment on sale by B., under his power, to George Smith.

[*Note.*—This conveys the head term created by the Lease and extinguishes all the mortgage terms. The head term may, if desired, be conveyed in the name of Henry Chubb.]

Section 207 SEVENTH SCHEDULE

[*Repealed by S.L.R.* 1950 (14 *Geo.* 6, *c.* 6).]

Administration of Estates Act 1925

(15 & 16 Geo. 5, c. 23)

PART IV

DISTRIBUTION OF RESIDUARY ESTATE

PART V

SUPPLEMENTAL

An Act to consolidate enactments relating to the administration of the estates of deceased persons.   [9th April 1925.]

PART I

DEVOLUTION OF REAL ESTATE

Devolution of real estate on personal representative

1.—(1) Real estate to which a deceased person was entitled for an interest not ceasing on his death shall on his death, and notwithstanding any testamentary disposition thereof, devolve from time to time on the personal representative of the deceased, in like manner as before the commencement of this Act chattels real devolved on the personal representative from time to time of a deceased person.

(2) The personal representatives for the time being of a deceased person are deemed in law his heirs and assigns within the meaning of all trusts and powers.

(3) The personal representatives shall be the representative of the deceased in regard to his real estate to which he was entitled for an interest not ceasing on his death as well as in regard to his personal estate.

Application to real estate of law affecting chattels real.

2.—(1) Subject to the provisions of this Act, all enactments and rules of law, and all jurisdiction of any court with respect to the appointment of administrators or to probate or letters of administration, or to dealings before probate in the case of chattels real, and with respect to costs and other matters in the administration of personal estate, in force before the commencement of this Act, and all powers, duties, rights, equities, obligations, and liabilities of a personal representative in force at the commencement of this Act with respect to chattels real, shall apply and attach to the personal representative and shall have effect with respect to real estate vested in him, and in particular all such powers of disposition and dealing as were before the commencement of this Act exercisable as respects chattels real by the survivor or survivors of two or more personal representatives, as well as by a single personal representative, or by all the personal representatives together, shall be exercisable by the personal representatives or representative of the deceased with respect to his real estate.

(2) Where as respects real estate there are two or more personal representatives, a conveyance of real estate devolving under this Part of this Act shall not, save as otherwise provided as respects trust estates including settled land, be made without the concurrence therein of all such representatives or an order of the court, but where probate is granted to one or some of two or more persons named as executors, whether or not power is reserved to the other or others to prove, any conveyance of the real estate may be made by the proving executor or executors for the time being, without an order of the court, and shall be as effectual as if all the persons named as executors had concurred therein.

(3) Without prejudice to the rights and powers of a personal representative, the appointment of a personal representative in regard to real estate shall not, save as hereinafter provided, affect—

(*a*) any rule as to marshalling or as to administration of assets;
(*b*) the beneficial interest in real estate under any testamentary disposition;
(*c*) any mode of dealing with any beneficial interest in real estate, or the proceeds of sale thereof;
(*d*) the right of any person claiming to be interested in the real estate to take proceedings for the protection or recovery thereof against any person other than the personal representative.

Interpretation of Part I

3.—(1) In this Part of this Act "real estate" includes—

(i) Chattels real, and land in possession, remainder, or reversion, and every interest in or over land to which a deceased person was entitled at the time of his death; and
(ii) Real estate held on trust (including settled land) or by way of mortgage or security, but not money to arise under a trust for sale of land, nor money secured or charged on land.

(2) A testator shall be deemed to have been entitled at his death to any interest in real estate passing under any gift contained in his will which operates as an appointment under a general power to appoint by will, or operates under the testamentary power conferred by statute to dispose of an entailed interest.

(3) An entailed interest of a deceased person shall (unless disposed of under the testamentary power conferred by statute) be deemed an interest ceasing on his death, but any further or other interest of the deceased in the same property in remainder or reversion which is capable of being disposed of by his will shall not be deemed to be an interest so ceasing.

(4) The interest of a deceased person under a joint tenancy where another tenant survives the deceased is an interest ceasing on his death.

(5) On the death of a corporator sole his interest in the corporation's real and personal estate shall be deemed to be an interest ceasing on his death and shall devolve to his successor.

This subsection applies on the demise of the Crown as respects all property, real and personal, vested in the Crown as a corporation sole.

Part II

Executors and Administrators

General Provisions

4. [*Repealed by the Supreme Court of Judicature (Consolidation) Act 1925 (15 & 16 Geo. 5, c. 49), Sched. 6.*]

Cesser of right of executor to prove

5. Where a person appointed executor by a will—
>   (i) survives the testator but dies without having taken out probate of the will; or
>   (ii) is cited to take out probate of the will and does not appear to the citation; or
>   (iii) renounces probate of the will;

his rights in respect of the executorship shall wholly cease, and the representation to the testator and the administration of his real and personal estate shall devolve and be committed in like manner as if that person had not been appointed executor.

Withdrawal of renunciation

6.—(1) Where an executor who has renounced probate has been permitted, whether before or after the commencement of this Act, to withdraw the renunciation and prove the will, the probate shall take effect and be deemed always to have taken effect without prejudice to the previous acts and dealings of and notices to any other personal representative who has previously proved the will or taken out letters of administration, and a memorandum of the subsequent probate shall be endorsed on the original probate or letters of administration.

(2) This section applies whether the testator died before or after the commencement of this Act.

Executor of executor represents original testator

7.[1]—(1) An executor of a sole or last surviving executor of a testator is the executor of that testator.

This provision shall not apply to an executor who does not prove the will of his testator, and, in the case of an executor who on his death leaves surviving him some other executor of his testator who afterwards proves the will of that testator, it shall cease to apply on such probate being granted.

(2) So long as the chain of such representation is unbroken, the last executor in the chain is the executor of every preceding testator.

(3) The chain of such representation is broken by—
>   (*a*) an intestacy; or
>   (*b*) the failure of a testator to appoint an executor; or
>   (*c*) the failure to obtain probate of a will;

but is not broken by a temporary grant of administration if probate is subsequently granted.

(4) Every person in the chain of representation to a testator—:
>   (*a*) has the same rights in respect of the real and personal estate of that testator as the original executor would have had if living; and
>   (*b*) is, to the extent to which the estate whether real or personal of that testator has come to his hands, answerable as if he were an original executor.

[1] Excluded by the Administration of Estates Act 1971 (c. 25), s. 1(3).

Right of proving executors to exercise powers

8.—(1) Where probate is granted to one or some of two or more persons named as executors, whether or not power is reserved to the others or other to prove, all the powers which are by law conferred on the personal representative may be exercised by the proving executor or executors for the time being and shall be as effectual as if all the persons named as executors had concurred therein.

(2) This section applies whether the testator died before or after the commencement of this Act.

Vesting of estate of intestate between death and grant of administration

9.[2] Where a person dies intestate, his real and personal estate, until administration is granted in respect thereof, shall vest in the Probate Judge in the same manner and to the same extent as formerly in the case of personal estate it vested in the ordinary.

10–14. [*Repealed by the Supreme Court of Judicature (Consolidation) Act 1925 (15 & Geo. 5, c. 49, Sched. 6.*]

Executor not to act while administration is in force

15. Where administration has been granted in respect of any real or personal estate of a deceased person, no person shall have power to bring any action or otherwise act as executor of the deceased person in respect of the estate comprised in or affected by the grant until the grant has been recalled or revoked.

16. [*Repealed by the Supreme Court of Judicature (Consolidation) Act 1925 (15 & 16 Geo. 5, c. 49), Sched. 6.*]

Continuance of legal proceedings after revocation of temporary administration

17.[3] If, while any legal proceeding is pending in any court by or against an administrator to whom a temporary administration has been granted, that administration is revoked, that court may order that the proceeding be continued by or against the new personal representative in like manner as if the same had been originally commenced by or against him, but subject to such conditions and variations, if any, as that court directs.

18–20. [*Repealed by the Supreme Court of Judicature (Consolidation) Act 1925 (15 & Geo. 5, c. 49), Sched. 6.*]

Rights and liabilities of administrator

21. Every person to whom administration of the real and personal estate of a deceased person is granted, shall, subject to the limitations contained in the grant, have the same rights and liabilities and be accountable in like manner as if he were the executor of the deceased.

[Debtor who becomes creditor's executor by representation or administrator to account for debt to estate

21A.—(1) Subject to subsection (2) of this section, where a debtor becomes his decreased creditor's executor by representation or administrator—

    (*a*) his debt shall thereupon be extinguished; but

    (*b*) he shall be accountable for the amount of the debt, as part of the creditor's estate in any case where he would be so

---

[2] Excluded by the Companies Act 1967 (c. 81), s. 33(4)(*c*).
[3] The county court shall have jurisdiction: County Courts Act 1959 (7 & 8 Eliz. 2, c. 22), Sched. 1.

accountable if he had been appointed as an executor by the creditor's will.

(2) Subsection (1) of this section does not apply where the debtor's authority to act as executor or administrator is limited to part only of the creditor's estate which does not include the debt; and a debtor whose debt is extinguished by virtue of paragraph (*a*) shall not be accountable for its amount by virtue of paragraph (*b*) of that subsection in any case where the debt was barred by the Limitation Act [1980][4] before he became the creditor's executor or administrator.

(3) In this section 'debt' includes any liability, and 'debtor' and 'creditor' shall be construed accordingly."][5]

Special Provisions as to Settled Land

Special executors as respects settled land

22.[6]—(1) A testator may appoint, and in default of such express appointment shall be deemed to have appointed, as his special executors in regard to settled land, the persons, if any, who are at his death the trustees of the settlement thereof, and probate may be granted to such trustees specially limited to the settled land.

In this subsection "settled land" means land vested in the testator which was settled previously to his death and not by his will.

(2) A testator may appoint other persons either with or without such trustees as aforesaid or any of them to be his general executors in regard to his other property and assets.

Provisions where, as respects settled land, representation is not granted to the trustees of the settlement

23.—(1) Where settled land becomes vested in a personal representative, not being a trustee of the settlement, upon trust to convey the land to or assent to the vesting thereof in the tenant for life or statutory owner in order to give effect to a settlement created before the death of the deceased and not by his will, or would, on the grant of representation to him, have become so vested, such representative may—

(*a*) before representation has been granted, renounce his office in regard only to such settled land without renouncing it in regard to other property;

(*b*) after representation has been granted, apply to the court for revocation of the grant in regard to the settled land without applying in regard to other property.

(2) Whether such renunciation or revocation is made or not, the trustees of the settlement, or any person beneficially interested thereunder, may apply to the High Court for an order appointing a special or additional personal representative, if and when appointed under the order, shall be in the same position as if representation had originally been granted to him alone in place of the original personal representative, if any, or to him jointly with the original personal represenative, as the case may be, limited to the settled land, but without prejudice to the previous acts and dealings, if any, of the personal representative originally constituted or the effect of notices given to such personal representative.

(3) The court may make such order as aforesaid subject to such security, if any, being given by or on behalf of the special or additional personal representative, as the court may direct, and shall, unless the court

---

[4] Substituted by Limitation Act 1980 (c. 58), Sched. 3, para. 2.
[5] This section was added by the Limitation (Amendment) Act 1980 (c. 24), s. 10.
[6] Applied by the Chevening Estate Act 1959 (7 & 8 Eliz. 2, c. 49), s. 1(4).

considers that special considerations apply, appoint such persons as may be necessary to secure that the persons to act as representatives in respect of the settled land shall, if willing to act, be the same persons as are the trustees of the settlement, and an office copy of the order when made shall be furnished to the [principal registry of the Family Division of the High Court][7] for entry, and a memorandum of the order shall be endorsed on the probate or administration.

(4) The person applying for the appointment of a special or additional personal representative shall give notice of the application to the [principal registry of the Family Division of the High Court][7] in the manner prescribed.

(5) Rules of court may be made for prescribing for all matters required for giving effect to the provisions of this section, and in particular—

(a) for notice of any application being given to the proper officer;

(b) for production of orders, probates, and administration to the registry;

(c) for the endorsement on a probate or administration of a memorandum of an order, subject or not to any exceptions;

(d) for the manner in which the costs are to be borne;

(e) for protecting purchasers and trustees and other persons in a fiduciary position, dealing in good faith with or giving notices to a personal representative before notice of any order has been endorsed on the probate or administration or a pending action has been registered in respect of the proceedings.

Power for special personal representatives to dispose of settled land

24. —(1) The special personal representatives may dispose of the settled land without the concurrence of the general personal representatives, who may likewise dispose of the other property and assets of the deceased without the concurrence of the special personal representatives.

(2) In this section the expression "special personal representatives" means the representatives appointed to act for the purposes of settled land and includes any original personal representative who is to act with an additional personal representative for those purposes.

Duties, Rights, and Obligations

[Duty of personal representatives

25. The personal representatives of a deceased person shall be under a duty to—

(a) collect and get in the real and personal estate of the deceased and administer it according to law;

(b) when required to do so by the court, exhibit on oath in the court a full inventory of the estate and when so required render an account of the administration of the estate to the court;

(c) when required to do so by the High Court, deliver up the grant of probate or administration to that court.][8]

Rights of action by and against personal representative

26.—(1) and (2) [*Repealed by the Law Reform (Miscellaneous Provisions) Act* 1934 (24 & 25 *Geo.* 5, *c.* 41), *s.*1(7).]

(3) A personal representative may distrain for arrears of a rentcharge

---

[7] These words were substituted by the Administration of Justice Act 1970 (c. 31), s. 1(6) and Sched. 2, para. 2.

[8] This section was substituted by the Administration of Estates Act 1971 (c. 25), s. 9, restricted by *ibid.* s. 1 and applied by *ibid.* s. 11.

due or accruing to the deceased in his lifetime on the land affected or charged therewith, so long as the land remains in the possession of the person liable to pay the rentcharge or of the persons deriving title under him, and in like manner as the deceased might have done had he been living.

(4) A personal representative may distrain upon land for arrears of rent due or accruing to the deceased in like manner as the deceased might have done had he been living.

Such arrears may be distrained for after the termination of the lease or tenancy as if the term or interest had not determined, if the distress is made—

(*a*) within six months after the termination of the lease or tenancy;

(*b*) during the continuance of the possession of the lessee or tenant from whom the arrears were due.

The statutory enactments relating to distress for rent apply to any distress made pursuant to this subsection.

(5) and (6) [*Repealed by the Law Reform (Miscellaneous Provisions) Act 1934 (24 & 25 Geo. 5, c. 41), s.*1(7).]

Protection of persons acting on probate or administration

27.—(1) Every person making or permitting to be made any payment or disposition in good faith under a representation shall be indemnified and protected in so doing, notwithstanding any defect or circumstance whatsoever affecting the validity of the representation.

(2) Where a representation is revoked, all payments and dispositions made in good faith to a personal representative under the representation before the revocation thereof are a valid discharge to the person making the same; and the personal representative who acted under the revoked representation may retain and reimburse himself in respect of any payments or dispositions made by him which the person to whom representation is afterwards granted might have properly made.

Liability of person fraudulently obtaining or retaining estate of deceased

28. If any person, to the defrauding of creditors or without full valuable consideration, obtains, receives or holds any real or personal estate of a deceased person or effects the release of any debt or liability due to the estate of the deceased, he shall be charged as executor in his own wrong to the extent of the real and personal estate received or coming to his hands, or the debt or liability released, after deducting—

(*a*) any debt for valuable consideration and without fraud due to him from the deceased person at the time of his death; and

(*b*) any payment made by him which might properly be made by a personal representative.

Liability of estate of personal representative

29. Where a person as personal representative of a deceased person (including an executor in his own wrong) wastes or converts to his own use any part of the real or personal estate of the deceased, and dies, his personal representative shall to the extent of the available assets of the defaulter be liable and chargeable in respect of such waste or conversion in the same manner as the defaulter would have been if living.

Provisions applicable where administration granted to nominee of the Crown

30.—(1) Where the administration of the real and personal estate of any deceased person is granted to a nominee of the Crown (whether the

Treasury Solicitor, or a person nominated by the Treasury Solicitor, or any other person), any legal proceeding by or against that nominee for the recovery of the real or personal estate, or any part or share thereof, shall be of the same character, and be instituted and carried on in the same manner, and be subject to the same rules of law and equity (including, except as otherwise provided by this Act, the rules of limitation under the statutes of limitation or otherwise), in all respects as if the administration had been granted to such nominee as one of the persons interested under this Act in the estate of the deceased.

(2) An information or other proceeding on the part of His Majesty shall not be filed or instituted, and a petition of right shall not be presented, in respect of the real or personal estate of any deceased person or any part or share thereof, or any claim thereon, except [. . .][9] subject to the same rules of law and equity within the subject to which a proceeding for the like purposes might be instituted by or against a subject.

(3) The Treasury Solicitor shall not be required, when applying for or obtaining administration of the estate of a deceased person for the use or benefit of His Majesty, to deliver, nor shall [. . .][10] the High Court or the Commissioners of Inland Revenue be entitled to receive in connection with any such application or grant of administration, any affidavit, statutory declaration, account, certificate, or other statement verified on oath; but the Treasury Solicitor shall deliver and the said Division and Commissioners respectively shall accept, in lieu thereof, an account or particulars of the estate of the deceased by or on behalf of the Treasury Solicitor.

(4) References in sections two, four, [. . .][11] and seven of the Treasury Solicitor Act 1876 and in subsection (3) of section three of the Duchy of Lancaster Act 1920 to "personal estate" shall include real estate.

Power to make rules

31. Provision may be made by rules of court for giving effect to the provisions of this Part of this Act so far as relates to real estate and in particular for adapting the procedure and practice on the grant of letters of administration to the case of real estate.

Part III

Administration of Assets

Real and personal estate of deceased are assets for payment of debts

32.—(1) The real and personal estate, whether legal or equitable, of a deceased person, to the extent of his beneficial interest therein, and the real and personal estate of which a deceased person in pursuance of any general power (including the statutory power to dispose of entailed interests) disposes by his will, are assets for payment of his debts (whether by specialty or simple contract) and liabilities, and any disposition by will inconsistent with this enactment is void as against the creditors, and the court shall, if necessary, administer the property for the purpose of the payment of the debts and the liabilities.

This subsection takes effect without prejudice to the rights of incumbrancers.

(2) If any person to whom any such beneficial interest devolves or is given, or in whom any such interest vests, disposes thereof in good faith

---

[9] Words repealed by the Limitation Act 1939, Sched.
[10] Words repealed by the Administration of Justice Act 1970 (c. 31), s. 54(3) and Sched. 11.
[11] Word repealed by Statute Law (Repeals) Act 1981 (c. 19), Sched. 1.

before an action is brought or process is sued out against him, he shall be personally liable for the value of the interest so disposed of by him, but that interest shall not be liable to be taken in execution in the action or under the process.

Trust for sale

33.—(1) On the death of a person intestate as to any real or personal estate, such estate shall be held by his personal representatives—

(*a*) as to the real estate upon trust to sell the same; and

(*b*) as to the personal estate upon trust to call in sell and convert into money such part thereof as may not consist of money,

with power to postpone such sale and conversion for such a period as the personal representative shall pay all such funeral, testamentary and proper, and so that any reversionary interest be not sold until it falls into possession, unless the personal representatives see special reason for sale, and so also that, unless required for purposes of administration owing to want of other assets, personal chattels be not sold except for special reason.

(2) Out of the net money to arise from the sale and conversion of such real and personal estate (after payment of costs), and out of the ready money of the deceased (so far as not disposed of by his will, if any), the personal representative shall pay all such funeral, testamenary and administration expenses, debts and other liabilities as are properly payable thereout having regard to the rules of administration contained in this Part of this Act, and out of the residue of the said money the personal representative shall set aside a fund sufficient to provide for any pecuniary legacies bequeathed by the will (if any) of the deceased.

(3) During the minority of any beneficiary or the subsistence of any life interest and pending the distribution of the whole or any part of the estate of the deceased, the person representatives may invest the residue of the said money, or so much thereof as may not have been distributed, in any investments for the time being authorised by statute for the investment of trust money, with power, at the discretion of the personal representatives, to change such investments for others of a like nature.

(4) The residue of the said money and any investments for the time being representing the same, including (but without prejudice to the trust for sale) any part of the estate of the deceased which may be retained unsold and is not required for the administration purposes aforesaid, is in this Act referred to as "the residuary estate of the intestate."

(5) The income (including net rents and profits of real estate and chattels real after payment of rates, taxes, rent, costs of insurance, repairs and other outgoings properly attributable to income) of so much of the real and personal estate of the deceased as may not be disposed of by his will, if any, or may not be required for the administration purposes aforesaid, may, however such estate is invested, as from the death of the deceased, be treated and applied as income, and for that purpose any necessary apportionment may be made between tenant for life and remainderman.

(6) Nothing in this section affects the rights of any creditor of the deceased or the rights of the Crown in respect of death duties.

(7) Where the deceased leaves a will, this section has effect subject to the provisions contained in the will.

Administration of assets

34.—(1) Where the estate of a deceased person is insolvent, his real and personal estate shall be administered in accordance with the rules set out in Part I of the First Schedule to this Act.

(2) [*This subsection was repealed by the Administration of Estates Act 1971 (c. 25), s.12 and Sched. 2, Pt. II.*]

(3) Where the estate of a deceased person is solvent his real and personal estate shall, subject to rules of court and the provisions hereinafter contained as to charges on property of the deceased, and to the provisions, if any, contained in his will, be applicable towards the discharge of the funeral, testamentary and administration expenses, debts and liabilities payable thereout in the order mentioned in Part II of the First Schedule to this Act.

Charges on property of deceased to be paid primarily out of the property charged

35.—(1) Where a person dies possessed of, or entitled to, or, under a general power of appointment (including the statutory power to dispose of entailed interests) by his will disposes of, an interest in property, which at the time of his death is charged with the payment of money, whether by way of legal mortgage, equitable charge or otherwise (including a lien for unpaid purchase money), and the deceased has not by will deed or other document signified a contrary or other intention, the interest so charged shall, as between the different persons claiming through the deceased, be primarily liable for the payment of the charge; and every part of the said interest, according to its value, shall bear a proportionate part of the charge on the whole thereof.

(2) Such contrary or other intention shall not be deemed to be signified—

(*a*) by a general direction for the payment of debts or of all the debts of the testator out of his personal estate, or his residuary real and personal estate, or his residuary real estate; or

(*b*) by a charge of debts upon any such estate;

unless such intention is further signified by words expressly or by necessary implication referring to all or some part of the charge.

(3) Nothing in this section affects the right of a person entitled to the charge to obtain payment or satisfaction thereof either out of the other assets of the deceased or otherwise.

Effect of assent or conveyance by personal representative

36.—(1) A personal representative may assent to the vesting, in any person who (whether by devise, bequest, devolution, appropriation or otherwise) may be entitled thereto, either beneficially or as a trustee or personal representative, of any estate or interest in real estate to which the testator or intestate was entitled or over which he exercised a general power of appointment by his will, including the statutory power to dispose of entailed interests, and which devolved upon the personal representative.

(2) The assent shall operate to vest in that person the estate or interest to which the assent relates, and, unless a contrary intention appears, the assent shall relate back to the death of the deceased.

(3) The statutory covenants implied by a person being expressed to convey as personal representative, may be implied in an assent in like manner as in a conveyance by deed.

(4) An assent to the vesting of a legal estate shall be in writing, signed by the personal representative, and shall name the person in whose favour it is given and shall operate to vest in that person the legal estate to which it relates; and an assent not in writing or not in favour of a named person shall not be effectual to pass a legal estate.

(5) Any person in whose favour an assent or conveyance of a legal estate is made by a personal representative may require that notice of the assent

or conveyance be written or endorsed on or permanently annexed to the probate or letters of administration, at the cost of the estate of the deceased, and that the probate or letters of administration be produced, at the like cost, to prove that the notice has been placed thereon or annexed thereto.

(6) A statement in writing by a personal representative that he has not given or made an assent or conveyance in respect of a legal estate, shall, in favour of a purchaser, but without prejudice to any previous disposition made in favour of another purchaser deriving title mediately or immediately under the personal representative, be sufficient evidence that an assent or conveyance has not been given or made in respect of the legal estate to which the statement relates, unless notice of a previous assent or conveyance affecting that estate has been placed on or annexed to the probate or administration.

A conveyance by a personal representative of a legal estate to a purchaser accepted on the faith of such a statement shall (without prejudice as aforesaid and unless notice of a previous assent or conveyance affecting that estate has been placed on or annexed to the probate or administration) operate to transfer or create the legal estate expressed to be conveyed in like manner as if no previous assent or conveyance had been made by the personal representative.

A personal representative making a false statement, in regard to any such matter, shall be liable in like manner as if the statement had been contained in a statutory declaration.

(7) An assent or conveyance by a personal representative in respect of a legal estate shall, in favour of a purchaser, unless notice of a previous assent or conveyance affecting that legal estate has been placed on or annexed to the probate or administration, be taken as sufficient evidence that the person in whose favour the assent or conveyance is given or made is the person entitled to have the legal estate conveyed to him, and upon the proper trusts, if any, but shall not otherwise prejudicially affect the claim of any person rightfully entitled to the estate vested or conveyed or any charge thereon.

(8) A conveyance of a legal estate by a personal representative to a purchaser shall not be invalidated by reason only that the purchaser may have notice that all the debts, liabilities, funeral, and testamentary or administration expenses, duties, and legacies of the deceased have been discharged or provided for.

(9) An assent or conveyance given or made by a personal representative shall not, except in favour of a purchaser of a legal estate, prejudice the right of the personal representative or any other person to recover the estate or interest to which the assent or conveyance relates, or to be indemnified out of such estate or interest against any duties, debt, or liability to which such estate or interest would have been subject if there had not been any assent or conveyance.

(10) A personal representative may, as a condition of giving an assent or making a conveyance, require security for the discharge of any such duties, debt, or liability, but shall not be entitled to postpone the giving of an assent merely by reason of the subsistence of any such duties, debt or liability if reasonable arrangements have been made for discharging the same; and an assent may be given subject to any legal estate or charge by way of legal mortgage.

(11) This section shall not operate to impose any stamp duty in respect of an assent, and in this section "purchaser" means a purchaser for money or money's worth.

(12) This section applies to assents and conveyances made after the commencement of this Act, whether the testator or intestate died before or after such commencement.

Validity of conveyance not affected by revocation of representation

37.—(1) All conveyances of any interest in real or personal estate made to a purchaser either before or after the commencement of this Act by a person to whom probate or letters of administration have been granted are valid, notwithstanding any subsequent revocation or variation, either before or after the commencement of this Act, of the probate or administration.

(2) This section takes effect without prejudice to any order of the court made before the commencement of this Act, and applies whether the testator or intestate died before or after such commencement.

Right to follow property and powers of the court in relation thereto

38.—(1) An assent or conveyance by a personal representative to a person other than a purchaser does not prejudice the rights of any person to follow the property to which the assent or conveyance relates, or any property representing the same, into the hands of the person in whom it is vested by the assent or conveyance, or of any other person (not being a purchaser) who may have received the same or in whom it may be vested.

(2)[12] Notwithstanding any such assent or conveyance the court may, on the application of any creditor or other person interested,—

(a) order a sale, exchange, mortgage, charge, lease, payment, transfer or other transaction to be carried out which the court considers requisite for the purpose of giving effect to the rights of the persons interested;

(b) declare that the person, not being a purchaser, in whom the property is vested is a trustee for those purposes;

(c) give directions respecting the preparation and execution of any conveyance or other instrument or as to any other matter required for giving effect to the order;

(d) make any vesting order, or appoint a person to convey in accordance with the provisions of the Trustee Act 1925.

(3) This section does not prejudice the rights of a purchaser or a person deriving title under him, but applies whether the testator or intestate died before or after the commencement of this Act.

Powers of management

39.—(1) In dealing with the real and personal estate of the deceased his personal representatives shall, for purposes of administration, or during a minority of any beneficiary or the subsistence of any life interest, or until the period of distribution arrives, have—

(i) the same powers and discretions, including power to raise money by mortgage or charge (whether or not by deposit of documents), as a personal representative had before the commencement of this Act, with respect to personal estate vested in him, and such power of raising money by mortgage may in the case of land be exercised by way of legal mortgage; and

(ii) all the powers, discretions and duties conferred or imposed by law on trustees holding land upon an effectual trust for sale (including power to overreach equitable interests and powers as if the same affected the proceeds of sale); and

(iii) all the powers conferred by statute on trustees for sale, and so that every contract entered into by a personal representative shall be binding on and be enforceable against and by the personal

---

[12] For cases where the county court shall have jurisdiction, see the County Courts Act 1959 (7 & 8 Eliz. 2, c. 22), Sched. 1 as amended by the Administration of Justice Act 1969 (c. 58), s. 5.

representative for the time being of the deceased, and may be carried into effect, or be varied or rescinded by him, and, in the case of a contract entered into by a predecessor, as if it had been entered into by himself.

(2) Nothing in this section shall affect the right of any person to require an assent or conveyance to be made.

(3) This section applies whether the testator or intestate died before or after the commencement of this Act.

Powers of personal representatives for raising money, &c.

40.—(1) For giving effect to beneficial interests the personal representative may limit or demise land for a term of years absolute, with or without impeachment for waste, to trustees on usual trusts for raising or securing any principal sum and the interest thereon for which the land, or any part thereof, is liable, and may limit or grant a rentcharge for giving effect to any annual or periodical sum for which the land or the income thereof or any part thereof is liable.

(2) This section applies whether the testator or intestate died before or after the commencement of this Act.

Powers of personal representative as to appropriation

41.[13]—(1) The personal representative may appropriate any part of the real or personal estate, including things in action, of the deceased in the actual condition or state of investment thereof at the time of appropriation in or towards satisfaction of any legacy bequeathed by the deceased, or of any other interest or share in his property, whether settled or not, as to the personal representative may seem just and reasonable, according to the respective rights of the persons interested in the property of the deceased:
Provided that—

    (i) an appropriation shall not be made under this section so as to affect prejudicially any specific devise or bequest;

    (ii) [14] an appropriation of property, whether or not being an investment authorised by law or by the will, if any, of the deceased for the investment of money subject to the trust, shall not (save as hereinafter mentioned) be made under this section except with the following consents:—

        (*a*) when made for the benefit of a person absolutely and beneficially entitled in possession, the consent of that person;

        (*b*) when made in respect of any settled legacy share or interest, the consent of either the trustee thereof, if any (not being also the personal representative), or the person who may for the time being be entitled to the income:

    If the person whose consent is so required as aforesaid is an infant or [is incapable, by reason of mental disorder within the meaning of the Mental Health Act 1959 of managing and administering his property and affairs],[15] the consent shall be given on his behalf by his parents or parent, testamentary or other guardian, [. . .][16] or receiver, or if, in the case of an infant, there is no such parent or guardian, by the court on the application of his next friend;

[13] This section is excluded in respect of requirements or consents made under Sched. 2, para. 6 (2) to the Intestates' Estates Act 1952, *post*, p. 282.

[14] For cases where the county court shall have jurisdiction, see the County Courts Act 1959 (7 & 8 Eliz. 2, c. 22), Sched. 1, as amended by the Administration of Justice Act 1969 (c. 58), s. 5.

[15] Substituted by the Mental Health Act 1959 (7 & 8 Eliz. 2, c. 72), Sched. 7, Pt. I.

[16] Word repealed by *ibid.*

      (iii) no consent (save of such trustee as aforesaid) shall be required on behalf of a person who may come into existence after the time of appropriation, or who cannot be found or ascertained at that time;

      (iv) if no [receiver is acting for a person suffering from mental disorder],[17] then, if the appropriation is of an investment authorised by law or by the will, if any, of the deceased for the investment of money subject to the trust, no consent shall be required on behalf of the [said person];[18]

      (v) if, independently of the personal representative, there is no trustee of a settled legacy share or interest, and no person of full age and capacity entitled to the income thereof, no consent shall be required to an appropriation in respect of such legacy share or interest, provided that the appropriation is of an investment authorised as aforesaid.

(2) Any property duly appropriated under the powers conferred by this section shall thereafter be treated as an authorised investment, and may be retained or dealt with accordingly.

(3) For the purposes of such appropriation, the personal representative may ascertain and fix the value of the respective parts of the real and personal estate and the liabilities of the deceased as he may think fit, and shall for that purpose employ a duly qualified valuer in any case where such employment may be necessary; and may make any conveyance (including an assent) which may be requisite for giving effect to the appropriation.

(4) An appropriation made purusant to this section shall bind all persons interested in the property of the deceased whose consent is not hereby made requisite.

(5)[19] The personal representative shall, in making the appropriation, have regard to the rights of any person who may thereafter come into existence, or who cannot be found or ascertained at the time of appropriation, and of any other person whose consent is not reqired by this section.

(6) This section does not prejudice any other power of appropriation conferred by law or by the will (if any) of the deceased, and takes effect with any extended powers conferred by the will (if any) of the deceased, and where an appropriation is made under this section, in respect of a settled legacy, share or interest, the property appropriated shall remain subject to all trusts for sale and powers of leasing, disposition, and management or varying investments which would have been applicable thereto or to the legacy, share or interest in respect of which the appropriation is made, if no such appropriation had been made.

(7) If after any real estate has been appropriated in purported exercise of the powers conferred by this section, the person to whom it was conveyed disposes of it or any interest therein, then, in favour of a purchaser, the appropriation shall be deemed to have been made in accordance with the requirements of this section and after all requisite consents, if any, had been given.

(8) In this section, a settled legacy, share or interest includes any legacy, share or interest to which a person is not absolutely entitled in possession at the date of the appropriation, also an annuity, and "purchaser" means a purchaser for money or money's worth.

(9) This section applies whether the deceased died intestate or not, and whether before or after the commencement of this Act, and extends to

---

[17] Substituted by *ibid.*

[18] *Ibid.*

[19] For the rights of the surviving spouse as respects the matrimonial home, see the Intestates' Estates Act 1952, Sched. 2, para. 1 (3), *post,* p. 280, as amended by the Leasehold Reform Act 1967 (c. 88), s. 7(8).

property over which a testator exercises a general power of appointment, including the statutory power to dispose of entailed interests, and authorises the setting apart of a fund to answer an annuity by means of the income of that fund or otherwise.

Power to appoint trustees of infants' property

42.—(1) Where an infant is absolutely entitled under the will or on the intestacy of a person dying before or after the commencement of this Act (in this subsection called "the deceased") to a devise or legacy, or to the residue of the estate of the deceased, or any share therein, and such devise, legacy, residue or share is not under the will, if any, of the deceased, devised or bequeathed to trustees for the infant, the pesonal representatives of the deceased may appoint a trust corporation or two or more individuals not exceeding four (whether or not including the personal representatives or one or more of the personal representatives), to be the trustee or trustees of such devise, legacy, residue or share for the infant, and to be trustees of any land devised or any land being or forming part of such residue or share for the purposes of the Settled Land Act 1925 and of the statutory provisions relating to the management of land during a minority, and may execute or do any assurance or thing requisite for vesting such devise, legacy, residue or share in the trustee or trustees so appointed.

On such appointment the personal representatives, as such, shall be discharged from all further liability in respect of such devise, legacy, residue, or share, and the same may be retained in its existing condition or state of investment, or may be converted into money, and such money may be invested in any authorised investment.

(2) Where a personal representative has before the commencement of this Act retained or sold any such devise, legacy, residue or share, and invested the same or the proceeds thereof in any investments in which he was authorised to invest money subject to the trust, then, subject to any order of the court made before such commencement, he shall not be deemed to have incurred any liability on that account, or by reason of not having paid or transferred the money or property into court.

Obligations of personal representative as to giving possession of land and powers of the court

43.—(1) A personal representative, before giving an assent or making a conveyance in favour of any person entitled, may permit that person to take possession of the land, and such possession shall not prejudicially affect the right of the personal representative to take or resume possession nor his power to convey the land as if he were in possession thereof, but subject to the interest of any lessee, tenant or occupier in possession or in actual occupation of the land.

(2)[20] Any person who as against the personal representative claims possession of real estate, or the appointment of a receiver thereof or a conveyance thereof, or an assent to the vesting thereof, or to be registered as proprietor thereof under the Land Registration Act 1925 may apply to the court for directions with reference thereto, and the court may make such vesting or other order as may be deemed proper, and the provisions of the Trustee Act 1925, relating to vesting orders and to the appointment of a person to convey, shall apply.

(3) This section applies whether the testator or intestate died before or after the commencement of this Act.

[20] For cases where the county court shall have jurisdiction, see the County Courts Act 1959 (7 & 8 Eliz. 2, c. 22), Sched. 1, as amended by the Administration of Justice Act 1969 (c. 58), s. 5.

Power to postpone distribution

44. Subject to the foregoing provisions of this Act, a personal representative is not bound to distribute the estate of the deceased before the expiration of one year from the death.

PART IV

DISTRIBUTION OF RESIDUARY ESTATE

Abolition of descent to heir, curtesy, dower and escheat

45.—(1) With regard to the real estate and personal inheritance of every person dying after the commencement of this Act, there shall be abolished—

(*a*) All existing modes rules and canons of descent, and of devolution by special occupancy or otherwise, of real estate, or of a personal inheritance, whether operating by the general law or by the custom of gavelkind or borough english or by any other custom of any county, locality, or manor, or otherwise howsoever; and

(*b*) Tenancy by the curtesy and every other estate and interest of a husband in real estate as to which his wife dies intestate, whether arising under the general law or by custom or otherwise; and

(*c*) Dower and freebench and every other estate and interest of a wife in real estate as to which her husband dies intestate, whether arising under the general law or by custom or otherwise: Provided that where a right (if any) to freebench or other like right has attached before the commencement of this Act which cannot be barred by a testamentary or other disposition made by the husband, such right shall, unless released, remain in force as an equitable interest; and

(*d*) Escheat to the Crown or the Duchy of Lancaster or the Duke of Cornwall or to a mesne lord for want of heirs.

(2) Nothing in this section affects the descent or devolution of an entailed interest.

Succession to real and personal estate on intestacy

46.[21]—(1) The residuary estate of an intestate shall be distributed in the manner or be held on the trusts mentioned in this section, namely:—

(i) [If the intestate leaves a husband or wife, then in accordance with the following Table:

TABLE

If the intestate—

(1) leaves—	the residuary estate shall be held in trust for
(*a*) no issue,[22] and	the surviving husband or wife absolutely.
(*b*) no parent,[23] or brother or sister of the whole blood, or issue of a brother or sister of the whole blood	

[21] The amendments to ss. 46–49 have effect as respects a person dying intestate after January 1, 1953.

[22] In this Part of the Act, any reference to the issue of the intestate shall have effect as if it included a reference to any illegitimate child of his or to the issue of any such child: Family Law Reform Act 1969 (c. 46), s. 14(3)(*a*)

[23] In this Part of the Act, any reference to the parent, parents, father or mother of the intestate shall have effect as if it were a reference to his natural parent, parents, mother or father: *ibid.* s. 14(3)(*c*).

(2) leaves issue (whether or not persons mentioned in sub-paragraph (*b*) above also survive)

the surviving husband or wife shall take the personal chattels absolutely and, in addition, the residuary estate of the intestate (other than the personal chattels) shall stand charged with the payment of a [fixed net sum],[24] free of death duties and costs, to the surviving husband or wife with interest thereon from the date of the death at such rate as the Lord Chancellor may specify by order[25] until paid or appropriated, and, subject to providing for that sum and the interest thereon, the residuary estate (other than the personal chattels) shall be held—

(*a*) as to one half upon trust for the surviving husband or wife during his or her life, and, subject to such life interest, on the statutory trusts for the issue of the intestate, and

(*b*) as to the other half, on the statutory trusts for the issue of the intestate.

(3) leaves one or more of the following, that is to say, a parent, a brother or sister of the whole blood, or issue of a brother or sister of the whole blood, but leaves no issue

the surviving husband or wife shall take the personal chattels absolutely and, in addition, the residuary estate of the intestate (other than the personal chattels) shall stand charged with the payment of a [fixed net sum],[26] free of death duties and costs, to the surviving husband or wife with interest thereon from the date of the death at such rate as the Lord Chancellor may specify by order[27] until paid or appropriated, and, subject to providing for that sum and the interest thereon, the residuary estate (other than the personal chattels) shall be held—

(*a*) as to one half in trust for the surviving husband or wife absolutely, and

(*b*) as to the other half—

(i) where the intestate leaves one parent or both parents (whether or not brothers or sisters of the intestate or their issue also survive) in trust for the parent absolutely or, as the case may be, for the two parents in equal shares absolutely

(ii) where the intestate leaves no parent, on the statutory trusts for

[24] Substituted by the Family Provision Act 1966, s. 1(2)(*a*). The sum is £40,000: Family Provision (Intestate Succession) Order 1981 (No. 255).
[25] Substituted by the Administration of Justice Act 1977 (c. 38), s. 28(1). See the Intestate Succession (Interest and Capitalisation) Order 1977 (No. 1491), which provides that the specified rate of interest shall be 7 per cent. per annum.
[26] See note 24, above. The sum if £85,000: Family Provision (Intestate Succession) Order 1981 (No. 255).
[27] See note 25, above.

> the brothers and sisters of the
> whole blood of the intestate.][28]
> [The fixed sums referred to in paragraphs
> (2) and (3) of this Table shall be of the
> amounts provided by or under section 1 of
> the Family Provision Act 1966.][29]

(ii) If the intestate leaves issue but no husband or wife, the residuary estate of the intestate shall be held on the statutory trusts for the issue of the intestate;

(iii) If the intestate leaves [no husband or wife and][30] no issue but both parents, then [. . .][31] the residuary estate of the intestate shall be held in trust for the father and mother in equal shares absolutely;

(iv) If the intestate leaves [no husband or wife][32] no issue but one parent, then [. . .][33] the residuary estate of the intestate shall be held in trust for the surviving father or mother absolutely;

(v) If the intestate leaves no [husband or wife and no issue and no][34] parent, then, [. . .][35] the residuary estate of the intestate shall be held in trust for the following persons living at the death of the intestate, and in the following order and manner, namely:—

> First, on the statutory trusts for the brothers and sisters of the whole blood of the intestate; but if no person takes an absolutely vested interest under such trusts; then
>
> Secondly, on the statutory trusts for the brothers and sisters of the half blood of the intestate; but if no person takes an absolutely vested interest under such trusts; then
>
> Thirdly, for the grandparents of the intestate and, if more than one survive the intestate, in equal shares; but if there is no member of this class; then
>
> Fourthly, on the statutory trusts for the uncles and aunts of the intestate (being brothers or sisters of the whole blood of a parent of the intestate); but if no person takes an absolutely vested interest under such trusts; then
>
> Fifthly, on the statutory trusts for the uncles and aunts of the intestate (being brothers or sisters of the half blood of a parent of the intestate); [. . .][35]

(vi) [36] In default of any person taking an absolute interest under the foregoing provisions, the residuary estate of the intestate shall belong to the Crown or to the Duchy of Lancaster or to the Duke of Cornwall for the time being, as the case may be, as bona vacantia, and in lieu of any right to escheat.

> The Crown or the said Duchy or the said Duke may (without prejudice to the powers reserved by section nine of the Civil List Act 1910, or any other powers), out of the whole or any part of the property devolving on them respectively, provide, in accordance with the existing practice, for dependants, whether kindred or not, of the intestate, and other persons for whom the intestate might reasonably have been expected to make provision.

[(1A) The power to make orders under subsection (1) above shall be exercisable by statutory instrument subject to annulment in pursuance of a

---

[28] S. 46.(1) (i) was substituted by the Intestates' Estates Act 1952, *post,* s. 1(2).
[29] Added by the Family Provision Act 1966, s. 1(2)(*a*).
[30] Added by the Intestates' Estates Act 1952, *post,* s. 1(3).
[31] Repealed by *ibid.*
[32] See above, note 30.
[33] See above, note 31.
[34] Substituted by *ibid.*
[35] See above, note 31.
[36] Restricted by Inheritance (Provision for Family and Dependants) Act 1975, s. 24.

resolution of either House of Parliament; and any such order may be varied or revoked by a subsequent order made under the power.]³⁷

(2) A husband and wife shall for all purposes of distribution or division under the foregoing provisions of this section be treated as two persons.

[(3) Where the intestate and the intestate's husband or wife have died in circumstances rendering it uncertain which of them survived the other and the intestate's husband or wife is by virtue of section one hundred and eighty-four of the Law of Property Act 1925 deemed to have survived the intestate, this section shall, nevertheless, have effect as respects the intestate as if the husband or wife had not survived the intestate.

(4) The interest payable on the [fixed net sum]³⁸ payable to a surviving husband or wife shall be primarily payable out of income.]³⁹

Statutory trusts in favour of issue and other classes of relatives of intestate

47.—(1) Where under this Part of this Act the residuary estate of an intestate, or any part thereof, is directed to be held on the statutory trusts for the issue of the intestate,⁴⁰ the same shall be held upon the following trusts, namely:—

   (i) In trust, in equal shares if more than one, for all or any the children or child of the intestate,⁴¹ living at the death of the intestate, who attain the age of [eighteen years]⁴² or marry under that age, and for all or any of the issue living at the death of the intestate who attains the age [eighteen years]⁴² or marry under that age of any child of the intestate who pre-deceases the intestate, such issue to take through all degrees, according to their stocks, in equal shares if more than one, the share which their parent would have taken if living at the death of the intestate, and so that no issue shall take whose parent is living at the death of the intestate and so capable of taking;

  (ii) The statutory power of advancement, and the statutory provisions which relate to maintenance and accumulation of surplus income, shall apply, but when an infant marries such infant shall be entitled to give valid receipts for the income of the infant's share or interest;

 (iii) Where the property held on the statutory trusts for issue is divisible into shares, then any money or property which, by way of advancement or on the marriage of a child of the intestate, has been paid to such child by the intestate or settled by the intestate for the benefit of such child (including any life or less interest and including property covenanted to be paid or settled) shall, subject to any contrary intention expressed or appearing from the circumstances of the case, be taken as being so paid or settled in or towards satisfaction of the share of such child or the share which such child would have taken if living at the death of the intestate, and shall be brought into account, at a valuation (the value to be reckoned as at the death of the intestate), in accordance with the requirements of the personal representatives;

 (iv) The personal representatives may permit any infant contingently interested to have the use and enjoyment of any personal chattels in

---

³⁷ Subsection added by Administration of Justice Act 1977 (c. 38), s. 28(1).

³⁸ Substituted by the Family Provision Act 1966, s. 1(2)(*b*). The sum is £40,000 if the intestate leaves issue and £85,000 if the intestate leaves no issue: Family Provision (Intestate Succession) Order 1981 (No. 255).

³⁹ Added by the Intestates' Estates Act 1952, s. 1(4).

⁴⁰ See p. 264, n. 22.

⁴¹ In this Part of the Act, any reference to the child or children of the intestate shall have effect as if it included a reference to any illegitimate child or children of his: Family Law Reform Act 1969 (c. 46), s. 14(3) (*b*).

⁴² These words were substituted, in respect of the estate of an intestate dying after January 1, 1970, for the words "twenty-one years" by *ibid.* s. 3(2).

such manner and subject to such conditions (if any) as the personal representatives may consider reasonable, and without being liable to account for any consequential loss.

(2) If the trusts in favour of the issue of the intestate fail by reason of no child or other issue attaining an absolutely vested interest—

(*a*) the residuary estate of the intestate and the income thereof and all statutory accumulations, if any, of the income thereof, or so much thereof as may not have been paid or applied under any power affecting the same, shall go, devolve and be held under the provisions of this Part of this Act as if the intestate had died without leaving issue living at the death of the intestate;

(*b*) References in this Part of this Act to the intestate "leaving no issue" shall be construed as "leaving no issue who attain an absolutely vested interest;"

(*c*) References in this Part of this Act to the intestate "leaving issue" or "leaving a child or other issue" shall be construed as "leaving issue who attain an absolutely vested interest."

(3) Where under this Part of this Act the residuary estate of an intestate or any part thereof is directed to be held on the statutory trusts for any class of relatives of the intestate, other than issue of the intestate, the same shall be held on trusts corresponding to the statutory trusts for the issue of the intestate (other than the provision for bringing any money or property into account) as if such trusts (other than as aforesaid) were repeated with the substitution of references to the members or member of that class for references to the children or child of the intestate.

(4) References in paragraph (i) of subsection (1) of the last foregoing section to the intestate leaving, or not leaving, a member of the class consisting of brothers or sisters of the whole blood of the intestate and issue of brothers or sisters of the whole blood of the intestate shall be construed as references to the intestate leaving, or not leaving, a member of that class who attains an absolutely vested interest.

(5) [*Repealed by the Family Provision Act* 1966, *post*, *s*. 9, *Sched*. 2.]][43]

[**47A.**[44]—(1) Where a surviving husband or wife is entitled to a life interest in part of the residuary estate, and so elects, the personal representative shall purchase or redeem the life interest by paying the capital value thereof to the tenant for life, or the persons deriving title under the tenant for life, and the costs of the transaction; and thereupon the residuary estate of the intestate may be dealt with and distributed free from the life interest.

(2) [*Repealed by the Administration of Justice Act* 1977 (*c*. 38), *s*.28(2).]

(3) An election under this section shall only be exercisable if at the time of the election the whole of the said part of the residuary estate consists of property in possession, but, for the purposes of this section, a life interest in property partly in possession and partly not in possession shall be treated as consisting of two separate life interests in those respective parts of the property.

[(3A) The capital value shall be reckoned in such manner as the Lord Chancellor may by order direct, and an order under this subsection may include transitional provisions.

(3B) The power to make orders under subsection (3A) above shall be exercisable by statutory instrument subject to annulment in pursuance of a resolution of either House of Parliament; and any such order may be varied or revoked by a subsequent order made under the power.][45]

[43] Added by the Intestates' Estates Act 1952, s. 1(3)(*c*).
[44] Added by the Intestates' Estates Act 1952, s. 2(*b*).
[45] Subsections added by the Administration of Justice Act 1977 (c. 38), s. 28(3). See the Intestate Succession (Interest and Capitalisation) Order 1977 (No. 1491).

(4) [*Repealed by the Administration of Justice Act 1977 (c. 38), s.28(2).*]

(5) An election under this section shall be exercisable only within the period of twelve months from the date on which representation with respect to the estate of the intestate is first taken out:

Provided that if the surviving husband or wife satisfies the court that the limitation to the said period of twelve months will operate unfairly—

    (*a*) in consequence of the representation first taken out being probate of a will subsequently revoked on the ground that the will was invalid, or

    (*b*) in consequence of a question whether a person had an interest in the estate, or as to the nature of an interest in the estate, not having been determined at the time when representation was first taken out, or

    (*c*) in consequence of some other circumstances affecting the administration or distribution of the estate.

the court may extend the said period.

(6) An election under this section shall be exercisable, except where the tenant for life is the sole personal representative, by notifying the personal representative (or, where there are two or more personal representatives of whom one is the tenant for life, all of them except the tenant for life) in writing; and a notification in writing under this subsection shall not be revocable except with the consent of the personal representative.

(7) Where the tenant for life is the sole personal representative an election under this section shall not be effective unless written notice thereof is given to the [[Senior Registrar][46] of the Family Division of the High Court][47] within the period within which it must be made; and provision may be made by probate rules for keeping a record of such notices and making that record available to the public.

In this subsection the expression "probate rules" means rules [of court made under section 127 of the Supreme Court Act 1981][48]

(8) An election under this section by a tenant for life who is an infant shall be as valid and binding as it would be if the tenant for life were of age; but the personal representative shall, instead of paying the capital value of the life interest to the tenant for life, deal with it in the same manner as with any other part of the residuary estate to which the tenant for life is absolutely entitled.

(9) In considering for the purposes of the foregoing provisions of this section the question when representation was first taken out, a grant limited to settled land or to trust property shall be left out of account and a grant limited to real estate or to personal estate shall be left out of account unless a grant limited to the remainder of the estate has previously been made or is made at the same time.]

Powers of personal representative in respect of interests of surviving spouse

48.—(1) [*Repealed by the Intestates' Estates Act 1952 (15 & 16 Geo. 6 & 1 Eliz. 2, c. 64), s. 2 (a).*]

(2) The personal representatives may raise—

    (*a*) [the fixed net sum][49] or any part thereof and the interest thereon payable to the surviving husband or wife of the intestate on the security of the whole or any part of the residuary estate of the intestate (other than the personal chattels), so far as that estate may be sufficent for the purpose

---

[46] These words were substituted by the Supreme Court Act 1981 (c. 48), Sched. 5.
[47] These words were substituted by the Administration of Justice Act 1970 (c. 31), s. 1(6) and Sched. 2, para. 4.
[48] These words were substituted by the Supreme Court Act 1981 (c. 48), Sched. 5.
[49] Substituted by the Family Provision Act 1966, s.1 (2) (*b*)

or the said sum and interest may not have been satisfied by an appropriation under the statutory power available in that behalf; and

(*b*) in like manner the capital sum, if any, required for the purchase or redemption of the life interest of the surviving husband or wife of the intestate, or any part thereof not satisfied by the application for that purpose of any part of the residuary estate of the intestate;

and in either case the amount, if any, properly required for the payment of the costs of the transaction.

Application to cases of partial intestacy

49.—(1) Where any person dies leaving a will effectively disposing of part of his property, this Part of this Act shall have effect as respects the part of his property no so disposed of subject to the provisions contained in the will and subject to the following modifications:—

[(*aa*) where the deceased leaves a husband or wife who acquires any beneficial interests under the will of the deceased (other than personal chattels specifically bequeathed) the references in this Part of this Act to the [fixed net sum][50] payable to a surviving husband or wife, and to interest on that sum, shall be taken as references to the said sum diminished by the value at the date of death of the said beneficial interests, and to interest on that sum as so diminished, and, accordingly, where the said value exceeds the said sum, this Part of this Act shall have effect as if references to the said sum, and interest thereon, were omitted.][51]

(*a*) The requirements [of section forty-seven of this Act][52] as to bringing property into account shall apply to any beneficial interests acquired by any issue of the deceased under the will of the deceased, but not to beneficial interests so acquired by any other persons:

(*b*) the personal representative shall, subject to his rights and powers for the purposes of administration, be a trustee for the persons entitled under this Part of this Act in respect of the part of the estate not expressly disposed of unless it appears by the will that the personal representative is intended to take such part beneficially.

[(2) References in the foregoing provisions of this section to beneficial interests acquired under a will shall be construed as including a reference to a beneficial interest acquired by virtue of the exercise by the will of a general power of appointment (including the statutory power to dispose of entailed interests), but not of a special power of appointment.

(3) For the purpose of paragraph (*aa*) in the foregoing provisions of this section the personal representative shall employ a duly qualified valuer in any case where such employment may be necessary.

(4) The references in subsection (3) of section forty-seven A of this Act to property are references to property comprised in the residuary estate and, accordingly, where a will of the deceased creates a life interest in property in possession, and the remaining interest in that property forms part of the residuary estate, the said references are references to that remaining interest (which, until the life interest determines, is property not in possession).][53]

---

[50] Substituted by the Family Provision Act 1966, s. 1 (2) (*b*).
[51] Added by the Intestates' Estates Act 1952, s. 3 (2).
[52] Added by *ibid*.
[53] Added by *ibid*.

Construction of documents

50.—(1)[54] References to any Statutes of Distribution in an instrument *inter vivos* made or in a will coming into operation after the commencement of this Act, shall be construed as references to this Part of this Act; and references in such an instrument or will to statutory next of kin shall be construed, unless the context otherwise requires, as referring to the persons who would take beneficially on an intestacy under the foregoing provisions of this Part of this Act.

(2) Trusts declared in an instrument *inter vivos* made, or in a will coming into operation, before the commencement of this Act by reference to the Statutes of Distribution, shall, unless the contrary thereby appears, be construed as referring to the enactments (other than the Intestates' Estates Act 1890) relating to the distribution of effects of intestates which were in force immediately before the commencement of this Act.

Savings

51.—(1) Nothing in this Part of this Act affects the right of any person to take beneficially, by purchase, as heir either general or special.

(2) The foregoing provisions of this Part of this Act do not apply to any beneficial interest in real estate (not including chattels real) to which a lunatic or defective living and of full age at the commencement of this Act, and unable by reason of his incapacity, to make a will, who thereafter dies intestate in respect of such interest without having recovered his testamentary capacity, was entitled at his death, and any such beneficial interest (not being an interest ceasing on his death) shall, without prejudice to any will of the deceased, devolve in accordance with the general law in force before the commencement of this Act applicable to freehold land, and that law shall, notwithstanding any repeal, apply to the case.

For the purposes of this subsection, a lunatic or defective who dies intestate as respects any beneficial interest in real estate shall not be deemed to have recovered his testamentary capacity unless his [. . .][55] receiver has been discharged.

(3) Where an infant dies after the commencement of this Act without having been married, and independently of this subsection he would, at his death, have been equitably entitled under a settlement (including a will) to a vested estate in fee simple or absolute interest in freehold land, or in any property settled to devolve therewith or as freehold land, such infant shall be deemed to have had an entailed interest, and the settlement shall be construed accordingly.

(4) This Part of this Act does not affect the devolution of an entailed interest as an equitable interest.

Interpretation of Part IV

52. In this Part of this Act "real and personal estate" means every beneficial interest (including rights of entry and reverter) of the intestate in real and personal estate which (otherwise than in right of a power of appointment or of the testamentary power conferred by statute to dispose of entailed interests) he could, if of full age and capacity, have disposed of by his will.

---

[54] Reference to this Part of this Act shall in relation to instruments made or instruments coming into operation after the commencement of the Intestates' Estates Act 1952 (*c.* 64) include references to Part I of that Act: *ibid. s.*6 (2); and after the commencement of the Family Law Reform Act 1969 (c. 46) include references to Part IV of that Act: *ibid. s.* 14 (6).

[55] Words repealed by the Mental Health Act 1959 (7 & 8 Eliz. 2, (c. 72), Sched. 8, Pt.I.

PART V

SUPPLEMENTAL

General savings

53.—(1) Nothing in this Act shall derogate from the powers of the High Court which exist indepently of this Act or alter the distribution of business between the several divisions of the High Court, or operate to transfer any jurisdiction from the High Court to any other court.

(2) Nothing in this Act shall affect any unrepealed enactment in a public general Act dispensing with probate or administration as respects personal estate not including chattels real.

(3) [*Repealed by Finance Act* 1975 (*c.* 7), *Sched.* 13.]

Application of Act

54. Save as otherwise expressly provided, this Act does not apply in any case where the death occurred before the commencement of this Act.

Definitions

55.—(1) In this Act, unless the context otherwise requires, the following expressions have the meanings hereby assigned to them respectively, that is to say:—

(i) "Administration" means, with reference to the real and personal estate of a deceased person, letters of administration, whether general or limited, or with the will annexed or otherwise:

(ii) "Administrator" means a person to whom administration is granted:

(iii) "Conveyance" includes a mortgage, charge by way of legal mortgage, lease, assent, vesting declaration, vesting instrument, disclaimer, release and every other assurance of property or of an interest therein by any instrument, except a will, and "convey" has a corresponding meaning, and "disposition" includes a "conveyance" also a devise bequest and an appointment of property contained in a will, and "dispose of" has a corresponding meaning:

(iv) "the Court" means the High Court, and also the county court, where that court has jurisdiction [. . .][56]

(v) "Income" includes rents and profits:

(vi) "Intestate" includes a person who leaves a will but dies intestate as to some beneficial interest in his real or personal estate:

(vii) "Legal estates" mean the estates charges and interests in or over land (subsisting or created at law) which are by statute authorised to subsist or to be created at law; and "equitable interests" mean all other interests and charges in or over land or in the proceeds of sale thereof:

(viii) "Lunatic" includes a lunatic whether so found or not, and in relation to a lunatic not so found; [*words repealed by the Mental Health Act* 1959 (7 & 8 *Eliz* 2,*c* 72), *Sched.* 8, *Pt.I*] and "defective" includes every person affected by the provisions of section one hundred and sixteen of the Lunacy Act 1890 as extended by section sixty-four of the Mental Deficiency Act 1913 and for whose benefit a receiver has been appointed:

(ix) "Pecuniary legacy" includes an annuity, a general legacy, a demonstrative legacy so far as it is not discharged out of the designated property, and any other general direction by a testator

---

[56] These words were repealed by the Courts Act 1971 (c. 23), s.56 and Sched II, Pt. II.

for the payment of money, including all death duties free from which any devise, bequest, or payment is made to take effect:

(x) "Personal chattels" mean carriages, horses, stable furniture and effects (not used for business purposes), motor cars and accessories (not used for business purposes), garden effects, domestic animals, plate, plated articles, linen, china, glass, books, pictures, prints, furniture, jewellery, articles of household or personal use or ornament, musical and scientific instruments and apparatus, wines, liquors and consumable stores, but do not include any chattels used at the death of the intestate for business purposes nor money or securities for money.

(xi) "Personal representative" means the executor, original or by representation, or administrator for the time being of a deceased person, and as regards any liability for the payment of death duties includes any person who takes possession of or intermeddles with the property of a deceased person without the authority of the personal representatives or the court, and "executor" includes a person deemed to be appointed executor as respects settled land:

(xii) "Possession" includes the receipt of rents and profits or the right to receive the same, if any:

(xiii) "Prescribed" means prescribed by rules of court [. . .]⁵⁷

(xiv) "Probate" means the probate of a will:

(xv) ["Probate judge" means the President of the Family Division of the High Court]⁵⁸

(xvi) [. . .]⁵⁹

(xvii) "Property" includes a thing in action and any interest in real or personal property:

(xviii) "Purchaser" means a lessee, mortagee or other person who in good faith acquires an interest in property for valuable consideration, also an intending purchaser and "valuable consideration" includes marriage, but does not include a nominal consideration in money:

(xix) "Real Estate" save as provided in Part IV of this Act means real estate, including chattels real, which by virtue of Part I of this Act devolves on the personal representative of a deceased person:

(xx) "Representation" means the probate of a will and administration, and the expression "taking out representation" refers to the obtaining of the probate of a will or of the grant of administration:

(xxi) "Rent" includes a rent service or a rent-charge, or other rent, toll, duty, or annual or periodical payment in money or money's worth, issuing out of or charged upon land, but does not include mortgage interest; and "rent charge" includes a fee farm rent:

(xxii) [. . .]⁶⁰

(xxiii) "Securities" include stocks, funds, or shares:

(xxiv) 'Tenant for life," "statutory owner," "land," "settled land," "settlement," "trustees of the settlement," "term of years abso-lute," "death duties," and "legal mortgage" have the same meanings as in the ·Settled Land Act 1925 and "entailed interest" and "charge by way of legal mortgage" have the same meanings as in the Law of Property Act 1925:

(xxv) ⁶¹ "Treasury solicitor" means the solicitor for the affairs of His

---

⁵⁷ Words repealed by Supreme Court Act 1981 (c. 48), Sched. 7.
⁵⁸ These words were substituted by the Administration of Justice Act 1970 (c. 31), s.1 (6) and Sched. 2, para. 5.
⁵⁹ Words repealed by Supreme Court Act 1981 (c. 48), Sched. 7.
⁶⁰ Words repealed by Supreme Court Act 1981 (c. 48), Sched. 7
⁶¹ For the extension of "treasury solicitor," see the Law of Property (Amendment) Act 1926, s. 3(2), *post*, p. 277.

Majesty's Treasury, and includes the solicitor for the affairs of the Duchy of Lancaster:

(xxvi) [62] "Trust corporation" means the public trustee or a corporation either appointed by the court in any particular case to be a trustee or entitled by rules made under sub-section (3) of section four of the Public Trustee Act 1906 to act as custodian trustee:

(xxvii) "Trust for sale" in relation to land, means an immediate binding trust for sale, whether or not exercisable at the request or with the consent of any person, and with or without a power at discretion to postpone the sale; and "power to postpone a sale" means power to postpone in the exercise of a discretion:

(xxviii) "Will" includes codicil:

(2) References to a child or issue living at the death of any person include a child or issue *en ventre sa mere* at the death.

(3) References to the estate of a deceased person include property over which the deceased exercises a general power of appointment (including the statutory power to dispose of entailed interests)by his will.

Repeal

56. The Acts mentioned in the Second Schedule to this Act are hereby repealed to the extent specified in the third column of that Schedule, but as respects the Acts mentioned in Part I of that Schedule only so far as they apply to deaths occurring after the commencement of this Act.

Application to Crown

57.—(1) The provisions of this Act bind the Crown and the Duchy of Lancaster, and the Duke of Cornwall for the time being, as respects the estates of persons dying after the commencement of this Act, but not so as to affect the time within which proceedings for the recovery of real or personal estate vesting in or devolving on His Majesty in right of His Crown, or His Duchy of Lancaster, or on the Duke of Cornwall, may be instituted.

(2) Nothing in this Act in any manner affects or alters the descent or devolution of any property for the time being vested in His Majesty either in right of the Crown or of the Duchy of Lancaster or of any property for the time being belonging to the Duchy of Cornwall.

Short title, commencement and extent

58.—(1)This Act may be cited as the Administration of Estates Act 1925.

(2) [*Repealed by S.L.R. A t 1950 (14 & 15 Geo. 6, c. 6).*]

(3) This Act extends to England and Wales only.

SCHEDULES

Section 34   FIRST SCHEDULE

PART I

RULES AS TO PAYMENT OF DEBTS WHERE THE ESTATE IS INSOLVENT

1. The funeral, testamentary, and administration expenses have priority.

2. Subject as aforesaid, the same rules shall prevail and be observed as to the respective rights of secured and unsecured creditors and as to debts and liabilities provable and as to the

---

[62] For the extension of "trust corporation," see *ibid.* s.3(1); the Japanese Treaty of Peace Order 1952 (No. 862), art. 5 (2); and the Clergy Pensions Measure 1961 (9 & 10 Eliz. 2, No 3), s.31.

valuation of annuities and future and contingent liabilities respectively, and as to the priorities of debts and liabilities as may be in force for the time being under the law of bankruptcy with respect to the assets of persons adjudged bankrupt.

PART II

ORDER OF APPLICATION OF ASSETS WHERE THE ESTATE IS SOLVENT

1. Property of the deceased undisposed of by will, subject to the retention thereout of a fund sufficient to meet any pecuniary legacies.

2. Property of the deceased not specifically devised or bequethed but included (either by a specific or general description) in a residuary gift, subject to the retention out of such property of a fund sufficient to meet any pecuniary legacies, so far as not provided for as aforesaid.

3. Property of the deceased specifically appropriated or devised or bequeathed (either by a specific or general description) for the payment of debts.

4. Property of the deceased charged with, or devised or bequeathed (either by a specific or general description) subject to a charge for the payment of debts.

5. The fund, if any, retained to meet pecuniary legacies.

6. Property specifically devised or bequeathed, rateably according to value.

7. Property appointed by will under a general power, including the statutory power to dispose of entailed interests, rateably according to value.

8. The following provisions shall also apply—
    (*a*) The order of application may be varied by the will of the deceased.
    (*b*) This part of this Schedule does not affect the liability of land to answer the death duty imposed thereon in exoneration of other assets.

Section 56   SECOND SCHEDULE

[*Repealed by S.L.R.Act* 1950 (14 & 15 *Geo* 6, *c*.6).]

Law of Property (Amendment) Act 1926

(16 & 17 GEO. 5, c. 11)

An Act to amend certain enactments relating to the law of property and trustees. [16th June 1926.]

Conveyance of legal estates subject to certain interest

1.—(1) Nothing in the Settled Land Act 1925 shall prevent a person on whom the powers of a tenant for life are conferred by paragraph (ix) of subsection (1) of section twenty of that Act from conveying or creating a legal estate subject to a prior interest as if the land had not been settled land.

(2) In any of the following cases, namely—

(a) where a legal estate has been conveyed or created under subsection one of this section, or under section sixteen of the Settled Land Act 1925, subject to any prior interest, or

(b) where before the first day of January, nineteen hundred and twenty-six, land has been conveyed to a purchaser for money or money's worth subject to any prior interest whether or not on the purchase the land was expressed to be exonerated from, or the grantor agreed to indemnify the purchaser against, such prior interest,

the estate owner for the time being of the land subject to such prior interest may, notwithstanding any provision contained in the Settled Land Act 1925 but without prejudice to any power whereby such prior interest is capable of being overreached, convey or create a legal estate subject to such prior interest as if the instrument creating the prior interest was not an instrument or one of the instruments constituting a settlement of the land.

(3) In this section "interest" means an estate, interest, charge or power of charging subsisting, or capable of arising or of being exercised, under a settlement, and, where a prior interest arises under the exercise of a power, "instrument" includes both the instrument conferring the power and the instrument excercising it.

2. [*Repealed by the Agricultural Holdings Act* 1948 (11 & 12 *Geo.* 6, *c.* 63), *ss.* 98–100, *Sched.* 8.]

Meaning of "trust corporation"

3.—(1) For the purposes of the Law of Property Act 1925, the Settled Land Act 1925, the Administration of Estates Act 1925 and the Supreme Court [Act 1981][1] the expression "Trust Corporation" includes the Treasury Solicitor, the Official Solicitor and any person holding any other official position prescribed by the Lord Chancellor, and, in relation to the property of a bankrupt and property subject to a deed of arrangement, includes the trustee in bankruptcy and the trustee under the deed respectively, and, in relation to charitable ecclesiastical and public trusts, also includes any local or public authority so prescribed, and any other corporation constituted under the laws of the United Kingdom or any part thereof which satisfies the Lord Chancellor that it undertakes the administration of any such trusts without remuneration, or that by its constitution it is required to apply the whole of its net income after payment of outgoings for charitable, ecclesiastical or public purposes, and is prohibited from distributing, directly or indirectly, any part thereof by

[1] Words substituted by Supreme Court Act 1981 (c. 48), Sched. 5.

way of profits amongst any of its members, and is authorised by him to act in relation to such trusts as a trust corporation.

(2) For the purposes of this provision, the expression "Treasury Solicitor" means the solicitor for the affairs of His Majesty's Treasury, and includes the solicitor for the affairs of the Duchy of Lancaster.[2]

4. [*Repealed by the Land Charges Act* 1972 (*c.* 61), *Sched.* 5.]

. . . . . .

[*The remainder of this Act contains amendments to the Settled Land Act 1925 and the Law of Property Act 1925, ante.*]

---

[2] The Church of England Pensions Board and the Administrator of Japanese Property are also to be treated as a trust corporation for the purposes of this Act; see Clergy Pensions Measure 1961 (9 & 10 Eliz. 2, No. 3), s.31, and the Japanese Treaty of Peace Order 1952 (No. 862), art. 5 (2).

Landlord and Tenant Act 1927

(17 & 18 Geo. 5, c. 36)

Part II

General Amendments of the Law of Landlord and Tenant

Provisions as to covenants to repair

18.[1]—(1) Damages for a breach of a covenant or agreement to keep or put premises in repair during the currency of a lease, or to leave or put premises in repair at the termination of a lease, whether such covenant or agreement is expressed or implied, and whether general or specific, shall in no case exceed the amount (if any) by which the value of the reversion (whether immediate or not) in the premises is diminished owing to the breach of such covenant or agreement as aforesaid; and in particular no damage shall be recovered for a breach of any such covenant or agreement to leave or put premises in repair at the termination of a lease, if it is shown that the premises, in whatever state of repair they might be, would at or shortly after the termination of the tenancy have been or be pulled down, or such structural alterations made therein as would render valueless the repairs covered by the covenant or agreement.

(2) A right of re-entry or forfeiture for a breach of any such covenant or agreement as aforesaid shall not be enforceable, by action or otherwise, unless the lessor proves that the fact that such a notice as is required by section one hundred and forty-six of the Law of Property Act 1925 had been served on the lessee was known either—

(a) to the lessee; or

(b) to an under-lessee holding under an under-lease which reserved a nominal reversion only to the lessee; or

(c) to the person who last paid the rent due under the lease either on his own behalf or as agent for the lessee or the under-lessee;

and that a time reasonably sufficient to enable the repairs to be executed had elapsed since the time when the fact of the service of the notice came to the knowledge of any such person.

Where a notice has been sent by registered post[2] addressed to a person at his last known place of abode in the United Kingdom, then, for the purposes of this subsection, that person shall be deemed, unless the contrary is proved, to have had knowledge of the fact that the notice had been served as from the time at which the letter would have been delivered in the ordinary course of post.

This subsection shall be construed as one with section one hundred and forty-six of the Law of Property Act 1925.

(3) This section applies whether the lease was created before or after the commencement of this Act.

. . . . . .

---

[1] This section is to be construed together with s.146 of the Law of Property Act 1925, *ante*, p. 194.

[2] This shall have effect so as to authorise the notice to be sent by registered post or the recorded delivery service: Recorded Delivery Service Act 1962 (10 & 11 Eliz. 2, c. 27), s.1(1).

Law of Property (Entailed Interests) Act 1932

(22 & 23 GEO. 5, c. 27)

An Act to prevent the conversion of entailed interests into absolute interests and the destruction of interests expectant thereon by the statutory trusts for sale, and to define the expression "rent charge in possession." [16th June 1932.]

1. [*Amends s. 36 (6) of the Settled Land Act* 1925, *ante, p.* 35 and *s.* 35 *of the Law of Property Act* 1925, *ante, p.* 138].

Definition of rent charge

2. For removing doubt it is hereby declared that a rent charge (not being a rent charge limited to take effect in remainder after or expectant on the failure or determination of some other interest) is a rent charge in possession within the meaning of paragraph (*b*) of subsection (2) of section one of the Law of Property Act 1925 notwithstanding that the payments in respect therefore are limited to commence or accrue at some time subsequent to its creation.

Short title and construction

3.—(1) This Act may be cited as the Law of Property (Entailed Interests) Act 1932 and so far as it amends any Act shall be construed as one with that Act.

(2) The Law of Property Acts 1925 to 1929 and this Act, so far as it amends those Acts, may be cited together as the Law of Property Acts 1925 to 1932.

Intestates' Estates Act 1952

(15 & 16 Geo. 6 & 1 Eliz. 2, c. 64)

An Act to amend the law of England and Wales about the property of persons dying intestate; and for purposes connected therewith.

[30th October 1952.]

Part I

Amendments of Law of Intestate Succession

1–4. [*These sections amend the Administration of Estates Act 1925, ss. 46–49, ante, pp. 264–270.*]

Rights of surviving spouse as respects the matrimonial home

5. The Second Schedule to this Act shall have effect for enabling the surviving husband or wife or a person dying intestate after the commencement of this Act to acquire the matrimonial home.

Part III

General

Short title and commencement

9.—(1) This Act may be cited as the Intestates' Estates Act 1952.

(2) This Act shall come into operation on the first day of January, nineteen hundred and fifty-three

SCHEDULES

FIRST SCHEDULE

[*This Schedule sets out ss. 46–49 of the Administration of Estates Act 1925, ante, pp. 273-280, as amended by Part I of this Act.*]

Section 5

SECOND SCHEDULE

Rights of Surviving Spouse as respects the Matrimonial Home

1.—(1) Subject to the provisions of this Schedule, where the residuary estate of the intestate comprises an interest in a dwelling-house in which the surviving husband or wife was resident at the time of the intestate's death, the surviving husband or wife may require the personal representative, in exercise of the power conferred by section forty-one of the principal Act (and with due regard to the requirements of that section as to valuation) to appropriate the said interest in the dwelling-house in or towards satisfaction of any absolute interest of the surviving husband or wife in the real and personal estate of the intestate.

(2)[1] The right conferred by this paragraph shall not be exercisable where the interest is—

(*a*) a tenancy which at the date of the death of the intestate was a tenancy which would determine within the period of two years from that date; or

---

[1] This sub-paragraph shall not apply in certain cases: Leasehold Reform Act 1967 (c. 88), s.7(8).

   (*b*) a tenancy which the landlord by notice given after that date could determine within the remainder of that period.

   (3) Nothing in subsection (5) of section forty-one of the principal Act (which requires the personal representative, in making an appropriation to any person under that section, to have regard to the rights of others) shall prevent the personal representative from giving effect to the right conferred by this paragraph.

   (4) The reference in this paragraph to an absolute interest in the real and personal estate of the intestate includes a reference to the capital value of a life interest which the surviving husband or wife has under this Act elected to have redeemed.

   (5) Where part of a building was, at the date of the death of the intestate, occupied as a separate dwelling, that dwelling shall for the purposes of this Schedule be treated as a dwelling-house.

   2. Where—

      (*a*) the dwelling-house forms part of a building and an interest in the whole of the building is comprised in the residuary estate; or

      (*b*) the dwelling-house is held with agricultural land and an interest in the agricultural land is comprised in the residuary estate; or

      (*c*) the whole or part of the dwelling-house was at the time of the intestate's death used as a hotel or lodging house; or

      (*d*) a part of the dwelling-house was at the time of the intestate's death used for purposes other than domestic purposes,

the right conferred by paragraph 1 of this Schedule shall not be exercisable unless the court, on being satisfied that the exercise of that right is not likely to diminish the value of assets in the residuary estate (other than the said interest in the dwelling-house) or make them more difficult to dispose of, so orders.

   3.—(1) The right conferred by paragraph 1 of this Schedule—

      (*a*) shall not be exercisable after the expiration of twelve months from the first taking out of representation with respect to the intestate's estate;

      (*b*) shall not be exercisable after the death of the surviving husband or wife;

      (*c*) shall be exercisable, except where the surviving husband or wife is the sole personal representative (or, where there are two or more personal representatives of whom one is the surviving husband or wife, all of them except the surviving husband or wife) in writing.

   (2) A notification in writing under parapgraph (*c*) of the foregoing sub-paragraph shall not be revocable except with the consent of the personal representative; but the surviving husband or wife may require the personal representative to have the said interest in the dwelling-house valued in accordance with section forty-one of the prinicpal Act and to inform him or her of the result of that valuation before he of she decides whether to exercise the right.

   (3) Subsection (9) of the section forty-seven A added to the principal Act by section two of this Act shall apply for the purposes of the construction of the reference in this paragraph to the first taking out of representation, and the proviso to subsection (5) of that section shall apply for the purpose of enabling the surviving husband or wife to apply for an extension of the period of twelve months mentioned in this paragraph.

   4.—(1) During the period of twelve months mentioned in paragraph 3 of this Schedule the personal representative shall not without the written consent of the surviving husband or wife sell or otherwise dispose of the said interest in the dwelling-house except in the course of administration owing to want of other assets.

   (2) An application to the court under paragraph 2 of this Schedule may be made by the personal representative as well as by the surviving husband or wife, and if, on an application under that paragraph, the court does not order that the right conferred by paragraph 1 of this Schedule shall be exercisable by the surviving husband or wife, the court may authorise the personal representative to dispose of the said interest in the dwelling-house within the said period of twelve months.

   (3) Where the court under sub-paragraph (3) of paragraph 3 of this Schedule extends the said period of twelve months, the court may direct that this paragraph shall apply in relation to the extended period as it applied in relation to the original period of twelve months.

   (4) This paragraph shall not apply where the surviving husband or wife is the sole personal representative or one of two or more personal representatives.

   (5) Nothing in this paragraph shall confer any right on the surviving husband or wife as against a purchaser from the personal representative.

   5.—(1) Where the surviving husband or wife is one of two or more personal representatives, the rule that a trustee may not be a purchaser of trust property shall not prevent the surviving husband or wife from purchasing out of the estate of the intestate an interest in a dwelling-house in which the surviving husband or wife was resident at the time of the intestate's death.

   (2) The power of appropriation under section forty-one of the principal Act shall include power to appropriate an interest in a dwelling-house in which the surviving husband or wife was resident at the time of the intestate's death partly in satisfaction of an interest of the surviving husband or wife in the real and personal estate of the intestate and partly in return for a payment of money by the surviving husband or wife to the personal representative.

   6.—(1) Where the surviving husband or wife is a person of unsound mind or a defective, a requirement or consent under this Schedule may be made or given on his or her behalf by the committee or receiver, if any, or, where there is no committee or receiver, by the court.

(2) A requirement or consent made or given under this Schedule by a surviving husband or wife who is an infant shall be as valid and binding as it would be if he or she were of age; and, as respects an appropriation in pursuance of paragraph 1 of this Schedule, the provisions of section forty-one of the principal Act as to obtaining the consent of the infant's parent or guardian, or of the court on behalf of the infant, shall not apply.

7.—(1) Except where the context otherwise requires, references in this Schedule to a dwelling-house include references to any garden or portion of ground attached to and usually occupied with the dwelling-house or otherwise required for the amenity or convenience of the dwelling-house.

(2) This Schedule shall be construed as one with Part IV of the principal Act.

Variation of Trusts Act 1958

(6 & 7 ELIZ. 2, c.53)

An Act to extend the jurisdiction of courts of law to vary trusts in the interests of beneficiaries and sanction dealings with trust property.

[23rd July, 1958]

Jurisdiction of courts to vary trusts

1.—(1) Where property, whether real or personal, is held on trusts arising, whether before or after the passing of this Act, under any will, settlement or other disposition, the court may if it thinks fit by order approve on behalf of—

(*a*) any person having, directly or indirectly, an interest, whether vested or contingent, under the trusts who by reason of infancy or other incapacity is incapable of assenting, or

(*b*) any person (whether ascertained or not) who may become entitled, directly or indirectly, to an interest under the trusts as being at a future date or on the happening of a future event a person of any specified description or a member of any specified class of persons, so however that this paragraph shall not include any person who would be of that description, or a member of that class, as the case may be, if the said date had fallen or the said event had happened at the date of the application to the court, or

(*c*) any person unborn, or

(*d*) any person in respect of any discretionary interest of his under protective trusts where the interests of the principal beneficiary has not failed or determined,

any arrangement (by whomsoever proposed, and whether or not there is any other person beneficially interested who is capable of assenting thereto) varying or revoking all or any of the trusts, or enlarging the powers of the trustees of managing or administering any of the property subject to the trusts:

Provided that except by virtue of paragraph (*d*) of this subsection the court shall not approve an arrangement on behalf of any person unless the carrying out thereof would be for the benefit of that person.

(2) In the foregoing subsection "protective trusts" means the trusts specified in paragraphs (i) and (ii) of subsection (1) of section thirty-three of the Trustee Act 1925, or any like trusts, "the principal beneficiary" has the same meaning as in the said subsection (1) and "discretionary interest" means an interest arising under the trust specified in paragraph (ii) of the said subsection (1) or any like trust.

(3) [. . .]¹ the jurisdiction conferred by subsection (1) of this section shall be exercisable by the High Court, except that the question whether the carrying out of any arrangement would be for the benefit of a person falling within paragraph (*a*) of the said subsection (1) shall be determined by order of [the authority having jurisdiction under Part VIII of the Mental Health Act 1959, if that person is a patient within the meaning of the said Part VIII].²

(4) [*Repealed by the County Courts Act* 1959 (7 & 8 *Eliz.* 2, *c.* 22), *Sched.* 3.]

(5) Nothing in the foregoing provisions of this section shall apply to trusts affecting property settled by Act of Parliament.

---

¹ Words repealed by the County Court Act 1959 (7 & 8 Eliz. 2, c. 22), Sched. 3.
² Substituted by the Mental Health Act 1959 (7 & 8 Eliz. 2, c.72), Sched. 7, Pt. I.

(6) Nothing in this section shall be taken to limit the powers conferred by section sixty-four of the Settled Land Act 1925, section fifty-seven of the Trustee Act 1925, or [the powers of the authority having jurisdiction under Part VIII of the Mental Health Act 1959].[3]

. . . .

---

[3] Substituted by the Mental Health Act 1959 (7 & 8 Eliz. 2, c.72), Sched. 7, Pt. I.

Rights of Light Act 1959

(7 & 8 ELIZ. 2, c. 56)

An Act to amend the law relating to rights of light, and for purposes connected therewith. [16th July 1959]

1. [*This section was repealed by the Statute Law (Repeals) Act 1974 (c. 22), Sched., Pt.* IV.]

Registration of notice in lieu of obstruction of access of light

2.—(1) For the purpose of preventing the access and use of light from being taken to be enjoyed without interruption, any person who is an owner of land (in this and the next following section referred to as "the servient land") over which light passes to a dwelling-house, workshop or other building (in this and the next following section referred to as "the dominant building") may apply to the local authority in whose area the dominant building is situated for the registration of a notice under this section.

(2) An application for the registration of a notice under this section shall be in the prescribed form and shall—

(*a*) identify the servient land and the dominant building in the prescribed manner, and

(*b*) state that the registration of a notice in pursuance of the application is intended to be equivalent to the obstruction of the access of light to the dominant building across the servient land which would be caused by the erection, in such position on the servient land as may be specified in the application, of an opaque structure of such dimensions (including, if the application so states, unlimited height) as may be so specified.

(3) Any such application shall be accompanied by one or other of the following certificates issued by the Lands Tribunal, that is to say,—

(*a*) a certificate certifying that adequate notice of the proposed application has been given to all persons who, in the circumstances existing at the time when the certificate is issued, appear to the Lands Tribunal to be persons likely to be affected by the registration of a notice in pursuance of the application;

(*b*) a certificate certifying that, in the opinion of the Lands Tribunal, the case is one of exceptional urgency, and that accordingly a notice should be registered forthwith as a temporary notice for such period as may be specified in the certificate.

(4) Where application is duly made to a local authority for the registration of a notice under this section, it shall be the duty of [that authority to register the notice in the appropriate local land charges register, and—

(*a*) any notice so registered under this section shall be a local land charge; but (*b*) section 5 (1) and (2) and section 10 of the Local Land Charges Act 1975 shall not apply in relation thereto.][1]

(5) Provision shall be made by rules under section three of the Lands Tribunal Act 1949 for regulating proceedings before the Lands Tribunal with respect to the issue of certificates for the purposes of this section, and, subject to the approval of the Treasury, the fees chargeable in respect of those proceedings; and, without prejudice to the generality of subsection (6) of that section, any such rules made for the purposes of this section shall include provision—

(*a*) for requiring applicants for certificates under paragraph (*a*) of subsection (3) of this section to give such notices, whether by way of advertisement or otherwise, and to produce such documents and provide such information, as may be determined by or under the rules;

(*b*) for determining the period to be specified in a certificate issued under paragraph (*b*) of subsection (3) of this section; and

(*c*) in connection with any certificate issued under the said paragraph (*b*), for enabling a further certificate to be issued in accordance (subject to the necessary modifications) with paragraph (*a*) of subsection (3) of this section.

Effect of registered notice and proceedings relating thereto

3.—(1) Where, in pursuance of an application made in accordance with the last preceding section, a notice is registered thereunder, then for the purpose of determining whether any person is entitled (by virtue of the Prescription Act 1832, or otherwise) to a right to the access of light to the dominant building across the servient land, the access of light to that building across that land shall be treated as obstructed to the same extent, and with the like consequences, as if an opaque structure, of the dimensions specified in the application,—

(*a*) had, on the date of registration of the notice, been erected in the position on the servient land specified in the application, and had been so erected by the person who made the application, and

(*b*) had remained in that position during the period for which the notice has effect and had been removed at the end of that period.

(2) For the purposes of this section a notice registered under the last preceding section shall be taken to have effect until either—

(*a*) the registration is cancelled, or

(*b*) the period of one year beginning with the date of registration of the notice expires, or

(*c*) in the case of a notice registered in pursuance of an application accompanied by a certificate issued under paragraph (*b*) of subsection (3) of the last preceding section, the period specified in the certificate expires without such a further certificate as is mentioned in paragraph (*c*) of subsection (5) of that section having before the end of that period been lodged with the local authority,

and shall cease to have effect on the occurrence of any one of those events.

(3) Subject to the following provisions of this section, any person who, if such a structure as is mentioned in subsection (1) of this section had been erected as therein mentioned, would have had a right of action in any court in respect of that structure, on the grounds that he was entitled to a right to the access of light to the dominant building across the servient land, and that the said right was infringed by that structure, shall have the like right of action in that court in respect of the registration of a notice under the last preceding section:

[1] The words in brackets were substituted by the Local Land Charges Act 1975 (c. 76), Sched. 1.

Provided that an action shall not be begun by virtue of this subsection after the notice in question has ceased to have effect.

(4) Where, at any time during the period for which a notice registered under the last preceding section has effect, the circumstances are such that, if the access of light to the dominant building had been enjoyed continuously from a date one year earlier than the date on which the enjoyment thereof in fact began, a person would have had a right of action in any court by virtue of the last preceding subsection in respect of the registration of the notice, that person shall have the like right of action in that court by virtue of this subsection in respect of the registration of the notice.

(5) The remedies available to the plaintiff in an action brought by virtue of subsection (3) or subsection (4) of this section (apart from any order as to costs) shall be such declaration as the court may consider appropriate in the circumstances, and an order directing the registration of the notice to be cancelled or varied, as the court may determine.

(6) For the purposes of section four of the Prescriptions Act 1832 (under which a period of enjoyment of any of the rights to which that Act applies is not to be treated as interrupted except by a matter submitted to or acquiesced in for one year after notice thereof)—

(a) as from the date of registration of a notice under the last preceding section, all persons interested in the dominant building or any part thereof shall be deemed to have notice of the registration thereof and of the person on whose application it was registered;

(b) until such time as an action is brought by virtue of subsection (3) or subsection (4) of this section in respect of the registration of a notice under the last preceding section, all persons interested in the dominant building or any part thereof shall be deemed to acquiesce in the obstruction which, in accordance with subsection (1) of this section, is to be treated as resulting from the registration of the notice;

(c) as from the date on which such an action is brought, no person shall be treated as submitting to or acquiescing in that obstruction:

Provided that if, in any such action, the court decides against the claim of the plaintiff, the court may direct that the preceding provisions of this subsection shall apply in relation to the notice as if that action had not been brought.

Application to Crown land

4.—(1) Subject to the next following subsection, this Act shall apply in relation to land in which there is a Crown or Duchy interest as it applies in relation to land in which there is no such interest.

(2) Section three of the Prescription Act 1832 as modified by the preceding provisions of this Act, shall not by virtue of this section be construed as applying to any land to which (by reason that there is a Crown or Duchy interest therein) that section would not apply apart from this Act.

(3) In this section "Crown or Duchy interest" means an interest belonging to Her Majesty in right of the Crown or of the Duchy of Lancaster, or belonging to the Duchy of Cornwall, or belonging to a government department, or held in trust for Her Majesty for the purposes of a government department.

Power to make rules

5.—(1) [*Repealed by the Local Land Charges Act* 1975 (*c.* 76), *Sched.* 2.]
(2) Any rules made [under section 14 of the Local Land Charges Act

1975 for the purposes of section 2 of this Act][2] shall (without prejudice to the inclusion therein of other provisions as to cancelling or varying the registration of notices or agreements) include provision for giving effect to any order of the court under subsection (5) of section three of this Act.

6. [*This section was repealed by the Northern Ireland Constitution Act 1973 (c. 36), Sched. 6.*]

Interpretation

7.—(1) In this Act, except in so far as the context otherwise requires, the following expressions have the meanings hereby assigned to them respectively, that is to say:—

"action" includes a counterclaim, and any reference to the plaintiff in an action shall be construed accordingly;

"local authority," in relation to land in a [district or a London borough, means the council of the district or borough,][3] and, in relation to land in the City of London, means the Common Council of the City;

"owner," in relation to any land, means a person who is the estate owner in respect of the fee simple thereof, or is entitled to a tenancy thereof (within the meaning of the Landlord and Tenant Act 1954) for a term of years certain of which, at the time in question, not less than seven years remain unexpired, or is a mortgagee in possession (within the meaning of the Law of Property Act 1925) where the interest mortgaged is either the fee simple of the land or such a tenancy thereof;

"prescribed" means prescribed by rules made by virtue of subsection (6) of section fifteen of the Land Charges Act 1925[4] as applied by section five of this Act.

(2) References in this Act to any enactment shall, except where the context otherwise requires, be construed as references to that enactment as amended by or under any other enactment.

Short title, commencement and extent

8.—(1) This Act may be cited as the Rights of Light Act 1959.

(2) This Act, except sections one and six thereof, shall come into operation at the end of the period of three months beginning with the day on which it is passed.

(3) This Act shall not extend to Scotland.

(4) This Act, [. . .][5] shall not extend to Northern Ireland.

---

[2] The words in brackets were substituted by the Local Land Charges Act 1975 (c. 76), Sched. 1.

[3] The words in brackets were substituted by the Local Land Charges Act 1975 (c. 76), Sched. 1.

[4] Now s. 14 of the Local Land Charges Act 1975 (c. 76).

[5] Repealed by the Northern Ireland Constitution Act 1973 (c. 36), Sched. 6.

Trustee Investments Act 1961

(9 & 10 Eliz. 2, c. 62)

An Act to make fresh provision with respect to investment by trustees and persons having the investment powers of trustees, and by local authorities, and for purposes connected therewith.

[3rd August 1961]

New powers of investment of trustees

1.[1]—(1) A trustee may invest any property in his hands, whether at the time in a state of investment or not, in any manner specified in Part I or II of the First Schedule to this Act or, subject to the next following section, in any manner specified in Part III of that Schedule, and may also from time to time vary any such investments.

(2) The supplemental provisions contained in Part IV of that Schedule shall have effect for the interpretation and for restricting the operation of the said Parts I to III.

(3) No provisions relating to the powers of the trustee contained in any instrument (not being an enactment or an instrument made under an enactment) made before the passing of this Act shall limit the powers conferred by this section, but those powers are exercisable only in so far as a contrary intention is not expressed in any Act or instrument made under an enactment, whenever passed or made, and so relating or in any other instrument so relating which is made after the passing of this Act.

For the purposes of this subsection any rule of the law of Scotland whereby a testamentary writing may be deemed to be made on a date other than that on which it was actually executed shall be disregarded.

(4) In this Act "narrower-range investment" means an investment falling within Part I or II of the First Schedule to this Act and "wider-range investment" means an investment falling within Part III of that Schedule.

---

[1] Applied by the Cathedrals Measure 1963 (No. 2), s. 21 (1): (London) the London Government Act 1963 (c. 33), s.2 (4), Sched. 2, para. 30 (5); the Cereals Marketing Act 1965 (c. 14), s. 18 (3); the Industrial and Provident Societies Act 1965 (c. 12), s. 31; and the Agriculture Act 1967 (c. 22), s. 18 (3). Extended by the Agriculture Act 1970 (c. 40), s. 17 (3).

289

Restrictions on wider-range investment

2.[2]—(1) A trustee shall not have power by virtue of the foregoing section to make or retain any wider-range investment unless the trust fund has been divided into two parts (hereinafter referred to as the narrower-range part and the wider-range part), the parts being, subject to the provisions of this Act, equal in value at the time of the division; and where such a division has been made no subsequent division of the same fund shall be made for the purposes of this section, and no property shall be transferred from one part of the fund to the other unless either—

(*a*) the transfer is authorised or required by the following provisions of this Act, or

(*b*) a compensating transfer is made at the same time.

In this section "compensating transfer," in relation to any transferred property, means a transfer in the opposite direction of property of equal value.

(2) Property belonging to the narrower-range part of a trust fund shall not by virtue of the foregoing section be invested except in narrower-range investments, and any property invested in any other manner which is or becomes comprised in that part of the trust fund shall either be transferred to the wider-range part of the fund, with a compensating transfer, or be reinvested in narrower-range investments as soon as may be.

(3) Where any property accrues to a trust fund after the fund has been divided in pursuance of subsection (1) of this section, then—

(*a*) if the property accrues to the trustee as owner or former owner of property comprised in either part of the fund, it shall be treated as belonging to that part of the fund;

(*b*) in any other case, the trustee shall secure, by apportionment of the accruing property or the transfer of property from one part of the fund to the other, or both, that the value of each part of the fund is increased by the same amount.

Where a trustee acquires property in consideration of a money payment the acquisition of the property shall be treated for the purposes of this section as investment and not as the accrual of property to the trust fund, notwithstanding that the amount of the consideration is less than the value of the property acquired; and paragraph (*a*) of this subsection shall not include the case of a dividend or interest becoming part of a trust fund.

(4) Where in the exercise of any power or duty of a trustee property falls to be taken out of the trust fund, nothing in this section shall restrict his discretion as to the choice of property to be taken out.

Relationship between Act and other powers of investment

3.[3]—(1) The powers conferred by section one of this Act are in addition to and not in derogation from any power conferred otherwise than by this act of investment or postponing conversion exercisable by a trustee (hereinafter referred to as a "special power").

(2) Any special power (however expressed) to invest property in any investment for the time being authorised by law for the investment of trust property, being a power conferred on a trustee before the passing of this Act or conferred on him under any enactment passed before the passing of

---

[2] Extended by the House of Commons Members' Fund Act 1962 (10 & 11 Eliz. 2, c. 53), s.1 (3); explained by *ibid.* s. 1 (3) (4); applied by (London) the London Government Act 1963 (c. 33), s. 2 (4), Sched. 2, para. 30 (5); Cereals Marketing Act 1965 (c. 14) s. 18 (3); Industrial and Provident Societies Act 1965 (c. 12), s. 31; and the Agriculture Act 1967 (c. 22), s. 18 (3).

[3] Restricted by the House of Commons Members' Fund Act 1962 (10 & 11 Eliz. 2, c. 53), s. 1 (5); applied: (London) London Government Act 1963 (c. 33), s. 2 (4), Sched. 2, para. 30 (5); and the Industrial and Provident Societies Act 1965 (c. 12), s. 31.

this Act, shall have effect as a power to invest property in like manner and subject to the like provisions as under the foregoing provisions of this Act.

(3) In relation to property, including wider-range but not including narrower-range investments,—

    (*a*) which a trustee is authorised to hold apart from—

        (i) the provisions of section one of this Act or any of the provisions of Part I of the Trustee Act 1925, or any of the provisions of the Trusts (Scotland) Act 1921, or

        (ii) any such power to invest in authorised investments as is mentioned in the foregoing subsection, or

    (*b*) which became part of a trust fund in consequence of the exercise by the trustee, as owner of property falling within this subsection, of any power conferred by subsection (3) or (4) of section ten of the Trustee Act 1925, or paragraph (*o*) or (*p*) or subsection (1) of section four of the Trusts (Scotland) Act 1921,

the foregoing section shall have effect subject to the modification set out in the Second Schedule to this Act.

(4) The foregoing subsection shall not apply where the powers of the trustee to invest or postpone conversion have been conferred or varied—

    (*a*) by an order of any court made within the period of ten years ending with the passing of this Act, or

    (*b*) by any enactment passed, or instrument having effect under an enactment made, within that period, being an enactment or instrument relating specifically to the trusts in question; or

    (*c*) by an enactment contained in a local Act of the present Session;

but the provisions of the Third Schedule to this Act shall have effect in a case falling within this subsection.

Interpretation of references to trust property and trust funds

4.[4]—(1) In this Act "property" includes real or personal property of any description, including money and things in action:

Provided that it does not include an interest in expectancy, but the falling into possession of such an interest, or the receipt of proceeds of the sale thereof, shall be treated for the purposes of this Act as an accrual of property to the trust fund.

(2) So much of the property in the hands of a trustee shall for the purposes of this Act constitute one trust fund as is held on trusts which (as respects the beneficiaries or their respective interests or the purposes of the trust or as respects the powers of the trustee) are not identical with those on which any other property in his hands is held.

(3) Where property is taken out of a trust fund by way of appropriation so as to form a separate fund, and at the time of the appropriation the trust fund had (as to the whole or a part thereof) been divided in pursuance of subsection (1) of section two of this Act, or that subsection as modified by the Second Schedule to this Act, then if the separate fund is so divided the narrower-range and wider-range parts of the separate fund may be constituted so as either to be equal, or to bear to each other the same proportion as the two corresponding parts of the fund out of which it was so appropriated (the values of those parts of those funds being ascertained as at the time of appropriation), or some intermediate proportion.

(4) In the application of this section to Scotland the following subsection shall be substituted for subsection (1) thereof:–

"(1) In this Act "property" includes property of any description whether heritable or moveable, corporeal or incorporeal) which is

---

[4] Applied: (London) London Government Act 1963 (c. 33), s. 2 (4), Sched. 2, para. 30 (5); and the Industrial and Provident Societies Act 1965 (c. 12), s. 31.

presently enjoyable, but does not include a future interest, whether vested or contingent."

Certain valuations to be conclusive for purposes of division of trust fund

5.[5]—(1) If for the purposes of section two or four of this Act or the Second Schedule thereto a trustee obtains, from a person reasonably believed by the trustee to be qualified to make it, a valuation in writing of any property, the valuation shall be conclusive in determining whether the division of the trust fund in pursuance of subsection (1) of the said section two, or any transfer or apportionment of property under that section or the said Second Schedule, has been duly made.

(2) The foregoing subsection applies to any such valuation notwithstanding that it is made by a person in the course of his employment as an officer or servant.

Duty of trustees in choosing investments

6.[6]—(1) In the exercise of his powers of investment a trustee shall have regard—

    (*a*) to the need for diversification of investments of the trust, in so far as is appropriate to the circumstances of the trust;

    (*b*) to the suitability to the trust of investments of the description of investment proposed and of the investment proposed as an investment of that description.

(2) Before exercising any power conferred by section one of this Act to invest in a manner specified in Part II or III of the First Schedule to this Act, or before investing in any such manner in the exercise of a power falling within subsection (2) of section three of this Act, a trustee shall obtain and consider proper advice on the question whether the investment is satisfactory having regard to the matters mentioned in paragrahs (*a*) and (*b*) of the foregoing subsection.

(3) A trustee retaining any investment made in the exercise of such a power and in such a manner as aforesaid shall determine at what intervals the circumstances, and in particular the nature of the investment, make it desirable to obtain such advice as aforesaid, and shall obtain and consider such advice accordingly.

(4) For the purposes of the two foregoing subsections, proper advice is the advice of a person who is reasonably believed by the trustee to be qualified by his ability in and practical experience of financial matters; and such advice may be given by a person notwithstanding that he gives it in the course of his employment as an officer or servant.

(5) A trustee shall not be treated as having complied with subsection (2) or (3) of this section unless the advice was given or has been subsequently confirmed in writing.

(6) Subsections (2) and (3) of this section shall not apply to one of two or more trustees where he is the person giving the advice required by this section to his co-trustee or co-trustees, and shall not apply where powers of a trustee are lawfully exercised by an officer or servant competent under subsection (4) of this section to give proper advice.

(7) Without prejudice to section eight of the Trustee Act 1925, or section thirty of the Trusts (Scotland) Act 1921 (which relate to valuation, and the

---

[5] Applied by (London) London Government Act 1963 (c. 33), s. 2 (4), Sched. 2, para. 30 (5); Cereals Marketing Act 1965 (c. 14), s. 18 (3); Industrial and Provident Societies Act 1965 (c. 12), s. 31; and the Agriculture Act 1967 (c. 22), s. 18 (3).
[6] Applied by (London) London Government Act 1963 (c. 33), s. 2 (4), Sched. 2, para. 30 (5); Cereals Marketing Act 1965 (c. 14), s. 18 (3); Industrial and Provident Societies Act 1965 (c. 12), s. 31; and the Agriculture Act 1967 (c. 22), s. 18 (3). Explained by the Cathedrals Measure 1963 (No. 2), s. 21 (5). Extended by the Agriculture Act 1970 (c. 40), s. 17 (3).

proportion of the value to be lent, where a trustee lends on the security of property) the advice required by this section shall not include, in the case of a loan on the security of freehold or leasehold property in England and Wales or Northern Ireland or on heritable security in Scotland, advice on the suitability of the particular loan.

Application of ss. 1–6 to persons, other than trustees, having trustee investment powers

7.—(1) Where any persons, not being trustees, have a statutory power of making investments which is or includes power—

    (*a*) to make the like investments as are authorised by section one of the Trustee Act 1925, or section ten of the Trusts (Scotland) Act 1921, or

    (*b*) to make the like investments as trustees are for the time being by law authorised to make,

however the power is expressed, the foregoing provisions of this Act shall with the necessary modifications apply in relation to them as if they were trustees:

Provided that property belonging to a Consolidated Loans Fund or any other fund applicable wholly or partly for the redemption of debt shall not by virtue of the foregoing provisions of this Act be invested or held invested in any manner specified in paragraph 6 of Part II of the First Schedule to this Act or in wider-range investments.

(2) Where, in the exercise of powers conferred by any enactment, an authority to which paragraph 9 of Part II of the First Schedule to this Act applies uses money belonging to any fund for a purpose for which the authority has power to borrow, the foregoing provisions of this Act, as applied by the foregoing subsection, shall apply as if there were comprised in the fund (in addition to the actual content thereof) property, being narrower-range investments, having a value equal to so much of the said money as for the time being has not been repaid to the fund, and accordingly any repayment of such money to the fund shall not be treated for the said purposes as the accrual of property to the fund:

Provided that nothing in this subsection shall be taken to require compliance with any of the provisions of section six of this Act in relation to the exercise of such powers as aforesaid.

(3) In this section "Consolidated Loans Fund" means a fund established under section fifty-five of the Local Government Act 1958, and includes a loans fund established under section two hundred and seventy-five of the Local Government (Scotland) Act 1947, and "statutory power" means a power conferred by an enactment passed before the passing of this Act or by any instrument made under any such enactment.

Application of ss. 1–6 in special cases

8.—(1) In relation to persons to whom this section applies—

    (*a*) notwithstanding anything in subsection (3) of section one of this Act, no provision of any enactment passed, or instrument having effect under an enactment and made, before the passing of this Act, shall limit the powers conferred by the said section one;

    (*b*) subsection (1) of the foregoing section shall apply where the power of making investments therein mentioned is or includes a power to make some only of the investments mentioned in paragraph (*a*) or (*b*) of that subsection.

(2) This section applies to—

    (*a*) the persons for the time being authorised to invest funds of the Duchy of Lancaster;

(*b*) any persons specified in an order made by the Treasury by statutory instrument, being persons (whether trustees or not) whose power to make investments is conferred by or under any enactment contained in a local or private Act.

(3) An order of the Treasury made under the foregoing subsection may provide that the provisions of sections one to six of this Act (other than the provisions of subsection (3) of section one) shall, in their application to any persons specified therein, have effect subject to such exceptions and modifications as may be specified.

Supplementary provisions as to investments

9.—(1) In subsection (3) of section ten of the Trustee Act 1925, before paragraph (*c*) (which enables trustees to concur in any scheme or arrangement for the amalgamation of a company in which they hold securities with another company, with power to accept securities in the second company) there shall be inserted the following paragraph:–

"(*bb*) for the acquisition of the securities of the company, or of control thereof, by another company."

(2) It is hereby declared that the power to subscribe for securities conferred by subsection (4) of the said section ten includes power to retain them for any period for which the trustee has power to retain the holding in respect of which the right to subscribe for the securities was offered, but subject to any conditions subject to which the trustee has that power.

Powers of Scottish trustees supplementary to powers of investment

10. Section four of the Trusts (Scotland) Act 1921 (which empowers trustees in trusts the execution of which is governed by the law in force in Scotland to do certain acts, where such acts are not at variance with the terms or purposes of the trust) shall have effect as if, in subsection (1) thereof, after paragraph (*n*), there were added the following paragraphs:

"(*o*) to concur, in respect of any securities of a company (being securities comprised in the trust estate), in any scheme or arrangement—

(i) for the reconstruction of the company,

(ii) for the sale of all or any part of the property and undertaking of the company to another company,

(iii) for the acquisition of the securities of the company, or of control thereof, by another company,

(iv) for the amalgamation of the company with another company, or

(v) for the release, modification, or variation of any rights, privileges or liabilities attached to the securities or any of them,

in like manner as if the trustees were entitled to such securities beneficially; to accept any securities of any denomination or description of the reconstructed or purchasing or new company in lieu of, or in exchange for, all or any of the first mentioned securities; and to retain any securities so accepted as aforesaid for any period for which the trustees could have properly retained the original securities;

(*p*) to exercise, to such extent as the trustees think fit, any conditional or preferential right to subscribe for any securities in a company (being a right offered to them in respect of any holding in the company), to apply capital money of the trust estate in payment of the consideration, and to retain any such securities for which they have subscribed for any period for which they have power to retain the holding in respect of which the right to subscribe for the securities was offered (but subject to any conditions subject to which they have that power); to renounce, to such extent as they think fit, any such right; or to assign, to such extent as they think fit and for the best consideration that can reasonably be obtained, the benefit of such right or the title thereto to any person, including any beneficiary under the trust."

Local Authority investment schemes

11.[7]—(1) Without prejudice to powers, conferred by or under any other enactment, any authority to which this section applies may invest property held by the authority in accordance with a scheme submitted to the Treasury by any association of local authorities [. . .][8] and approved by the Treasury as enabling investments to be made collectively without in substance extending the scope of powers of investment.

(2) A scheme under this section may apply to a specified authority or to a specified class of authorities, may make different provisions as respects different authorities or different classes of authorities or as respects different descriptions of property or property held for different purposes, and may impose restrictions on the extent to which the power conferred by the foregoing subsections shall be exercisable.

(3) In approving a scheme under this section, the Treasury may direct that the Prevention of Fraud (Investments) Act 1958, or the Prevention of Fraud (Investments) Act (Northern Ireland) 1940, shall not apply to dealings undertaken or documents issued for the purposes of the scheme, or to such dealings or documents of such descriptions as may be specified in the direction.

(4) The authorities to which this section applies are—

(*a*) in England and Wales, the council of a county, a [. . .][9] borough [. . .][10] a [. . .][11] district or a parish, [a river authority],[12] the Common Council of the City of London [the Greater London Council],[13] and the Council of the Isles of Scilly;

(*b*) in Scotland, a local authority within the meaning of the Local Goverment (Scotland) Act 1947;

(*c*) in any part of Great Britain, a joint board or joint committee constituted to discharge or advise on the discharge of the functions of any two or more of the authorities mentioned in the foregoing paragraphs (including a joint committee established by [those authorities acting in combination in accordance with regulations made under section 7 of the Superannuation Act 1972.][14]

(*d*) in Northern Ireland, the council of a county, a county or other borough, or an urban or rural district, and the Northern Ireland Local Government Officers' Superannuation Committee established under the Local Government (Superannuation) Act (Northern Ireland) 1950.

Power to confer additional powers of investment

12.[15]—(1) Her Majesty may by Order in Council extend the powers of investment conferred by section one of this Act by adding to Part I, Part II or Part III of the First Schedule to this Act any manner of investment specified in the Order.

[7] Excluded by the Companies Act 1967 (c. 81), s. 28 (9).
[8] Words repealed by the London Government Act 1963 (c. 33), Sched. 18, Pt. II.
[9] Words repealed by *ibid.* Pt. I.
[10] Words repealed by the Local Government Act 1972 (c. 70), s. 272 (1), Sched. 30.
[11] Words repealed by *ibid.*
[12] Added by the Water Resources Act 1963 (c. 38), Sched. 13, para. 16.
[13] Added by the London Government Act 1963 (c. 33), Sched. 17, para. 25 (*a*).
[14] The words in brackets were substituted by the Superannuation Act 1972 (c. 11), Sched. 6.
[15] Applied by the Cereals Marketing Act 1965 (c. 14), s. 18 (3), and the Agriculture Act 1967 (c. 22), s. 18 (3). Extended by the Agriculture Act 1970 (c. 40), s. 17 (3).

(2) Any Order under this section shall be subject to annulment in pursuance of a resolution of either House of Parliament.

Power to modify provisions as to division of trust fund

13.[15]—(1) The Treasury may by order made by statutory instrument direct that, subject to subsection (3) of section four of this Act, any division of a trust fund made in pursuance of subsection (1) of section two of this Act during the continuance in force of the order shall be made so that the value of the wider-range part at the time of the division bears to the then value of the narrower-range part such proportion, greater than one but not greater than three to one, as may be prescribed by the order; and in this Act "the prescribed proportion" means the proportion for the time being prescribed under this subsection.

(2) A fund which has been divided in pursuance of subsection (1) of section two of this Act before the coming into operation of an order under the foregoing subsection may notwithstanding anything in that subsection be again divided (once only) in puruance of the said subsection (1) during the continuance in force of the order.

(3) If an order is made under subsection (1) of this section, then as from the coming into operation of the order—

 (a) paragraph (b) of subsection (3) of section two of this Act and sub-paragraph (b) of paragraph 3 of the Second Schedule thereto shall have effect with the substitution, for the words from "each" to the end, of the words "the wider-range part of the fund is increased by an amount which bears the prescribed proportion to the amount by which the value of the narrower-range part of the fund is increased";

 (b) subsection (3) of section four of this Act shall have effect as if for the words "so as either" to "each other" there were substituted the words "so as to bear to each other either the prescribed proportion or."

(4) An order under this section may be revoked by a subsequent order thereunder prescribing a greater proportion.

(5) An order under this section shall not have effect unless approved by a resolution of each House of Parliament.

Amendment of s.27 of Trusts (Scotland) Act 1921

14. So much of section twenty-seven of the Trusts (Scotland) Act 1921 as empowers the Court of Session to approve as investments for trust funds any stocks, funds or securities in addition to those in which trustees are by that Act authorised to invest trust funds shall cease to have effect.

Saving for powers of court

15. The enlargement of the investment powers of trustees by this Act shall not lessen any power of a court to confer wider powers of investment on trustees, or affect the extent to which any such power is to be exercised.

Minor and consequential amendments and repeals

16.—(1) The provisions of the Fourth Schedule to this Act (which contain minor amendments and amendments consequential on the foregoing provisions of this Act) shall have effect.

(2) [*Repealed by the Statute Law (Repeals) Act* 1974 (*c.* 22), *Sched.*, *Pt. XI.*]

Short title, extent and construction

17.—(1) This Act may be cited as the Trustee Investments Act 1961.

(2) Section eleven and sixteen of this Act shall extend to Northern Ireland, but except as aforesaid and except so far as any other provisions of the Act apply by virtue of subsection (1) of section one of the Trustee Act (Northern Ireland) 1958, or any other enactment of the Parliament of Northern Ireland, to trusts the execution of which is governed by the law in force in Northern Ireland, this Act does not apply to such trusts.

(3) So much of section sixteen of this Act as relates to [the National Savings Bank][16] and to trustee savings banks shall extend to the Isle of Man and the Channel Islands.

(4) Except where the context otherwise requires, in this Act, in its application to trusts the execution of which is governed by the law in force in England and Wales, expressions have the same meaning as in the Trustee Act 1925.

(5) Except where the context otherwise requires, in this Act in its application to trusts the execution of which is governed by the law in force in Scotland, expressions have the same meaning as in the Trusts (Scotland) Act 1921.

SCHEDULES

Section 1   FIRST SCHEDULE[17]

MANNER OF INVESTMENT

PART I

NARROWER-RANGE INVESTMENTS NOT REQUIRING ADVICE

1.[18] In Defence Bonds, National Savings Certificates and Ulster Savings Certificates.

2. In deposits in [the National Savings Bank],[19] [. . .][20] and deposits in a bank or department thereof certified under subsection (3) of section nine of the Finance Act 1956.

PART II[21]

NARROWER-RANGE INVESTMENTS REQUIRING ADVICE

1. In securities issued by Her Majesty's Government in the United Kingdom, the Government of Northern Ireland or the Government of the Isle of Man, not being securities falling within Part I of this Schedule and being fixed-interest securities registered in the United Kingdom or the Isle of Man, Treasury Bills or Tax Reserve Certificates [or any variable interest securities issued by Her Majesty's Government in the United Kingdom and registered in the United Kingdom.][22]

2. In any securities the payment of interest on which is guaranteed by Her Majesty's Government in the United Kingdom or the Government of Northern Ireland.

3. In fixed-interest securities issued in the United Kingdom by any public authority or nationalised industry or undertaking in the United Kingdom.

[16] Words substituted by the Post Office Act 1969 (c. 48), s. 94 (2) (*c*) and Sched. 6, Pt. III.

[17] Extended by the Post Office Act 1969 (c. 48), ss. 41, 88 (1), Sched. 2, paras. 4, 15.

[18] The Trustee Investments (Additional Powers) No. 2) Order 1962 (No. 2611) adds Ulster Development Bonds to this para. S.I. 1964 (No. 702) adds National Development Bonds.

[19] See above n. 16.

[20] Words repealed by the Trustee Savings Banks Act 1976 (c. 4), Sched. 6.

[21] This Part is applied by the Post Office Savings Bank Act 1966 (c. 12), s. 4 (1), the Trustee Savings Bank Act 1969 (c. 50), s. 46 (1), the Insolvency Services (Accounting and Investment) Act 1970 (c. 8), s. 2, the Hospital Endowments(Scotland) Act 1971 (c. 8), ss. 3 and 10 as amended by the National Health Service (Scotland) Act 1972 (c. 58), s. 38, Sched. 6, and the National Savings Bank Act 1971 (c. 29), s. 22.

[22] Added by the Trustee Investments (Additional Powers) Order 1977 (No. 831).

4. In fixed-interest securities issued in the United Kingdom by the government of any overseas territory within the Commonwealth or by any public or local authority within such territory, being securities registered in the United Kingdom.

References in this paragraph to an overseas territory or to the government of such a territory shall be construed as if they occurred in the Overseas Services Act 1958.

[4A. In securities issued in the United Kingdom by the government of an overseas territory within the Commonwealth or by any public or local authority within such a territory, being securities registered in the United Kingdom and in respect of which the rate of interest is variable by reference to one or more of the following:—

(*a*) the Bank of England's minimum lending rate;
(*b*) the average rate of discount on allotment on 91-day Treasury bills;
(*c*) a yield on 91-day Treasury bills;
(*d*) a London sterling inter-bank offered rate;
(*e*) a London sterling certificate of deposit rate.

References in this paragraph to an overseas territory or to the government of such a territory shall be construed as if they occurred in the Overseas Service Act 1958.][23]

5. In fixed-interest securities issued in the United Kingdom by the International Bank for Reconstruction and Development, being securities registered in the United Kingdom.

[In fixed-interest securities issued in the United Kingdom by the Inter-American Development Bank.][24]

[In fixed-interest securities issued in the United Kingdom by the European Investment Bank or by the European Coal and Steel Community, being securities registered in the United Kingdom.][25]

[5A. In securities issued in the United Kingdom by
(i) the International Bank for Reconstruction and Development or by the European Investment Bank or by the European Coal and Steel Community, being securities registered in the United Kingdom or
(ii) the Inter-American Development Bank

being securities in respect of which the rate of interest is variable by reference to one or more of the following:—

(*a*) the Bank of England's minimum lending rate;
(*b*) the average rate of discount on allotment on 91-day Treasury bills;
(*c*) a yield on 91-day Treasury bills;
(*d*) a London sterling inter-bank offered rate;
(*e*) a London sterling certificate of deposit rate.][26]

6. In debentures issued in the United Kingdom by a company incorporated in the United Kingdom, being debentures registered in the United Kingdom.

7. In stock of the Bank of Ireland.

[In Bank of Ireland 7 per cent. Loan Stock 1986/91.][27]

8. In debentures issued by the Agricultural Mortgage Corporation Limited or the Scottish Agricultural Securities Corporation Limited.

9.[28] In loans to any authority to which this paragraph applies charged on all or any of the revenues of the authority or on a fund into which all or any of those revenues are payable, in any fixed-interest securities issued in the United Kingdom by any such authority for the purpose of borrowing money so charged, and in deposits with any such authority by way of temporary loan made on the giving of a receipt for the loan by the treasurer or other similar officer of the authority and on the giving of an undertaking by the authority that, if requested to charge the loan as aforesaid, it will either comply with the request or repay the loan.

This paragraph applies to the following authorities, that is to say—

(*a*) any local authority in the United Kingdom;
(*b*) any authority all the members of which are appointed or elected by one or more local authorities in the United Kingdom;
(*c*) any authority the majority of the members of which are appointed or elected by one or more local authorities in the United Kingdom, being an authority which by virtue of any enactment has power to issue a precept to a local authority in England or Wales, or a requisition to a local authority in Scotland, or to the expenses of which, by virtue of any enactment, a local authority in the United Kingdom is or can be required to contribute;
(*d*) the Receiver for the Metropolitan Police District or a combined police authority (within the meaning of the Police Act 1946);
(*e*) the Belfast City and District Water Commissioners.

[9A. In any securities issued in the United Kingdom by any authority to which paragraph 9 applies for the purpose of borrowing money charged on all or any of the revenues of

[23] Added by the Trustee Investments (Additional Powers) (No. 2) Order 1977 (No. 1878).
[24] Added by the Trustee Investments (Additional Powers) (No. 2) Order 1964 (No. 1404).
[25] Added by the Trustee Investments (Additional Powers) Order 1972 (No. 1818).
[26] Added by the Trustee Investments (Additional Powers) (No. 2) Order 1977 (No. 1878).
[27] Added by the Trustee Investments (Additional Powers) Order 1966 (No. 401).
[28] The Trustee Investments (Additional Powers) Order 1962 (No. 658) adds the Great Ouse Water Authority to the list in this para. This para. is modified by the Post Office Savings Bank Act 1966 (c. 12), s. 7 (2), Sched.

the authority or on a fund into which all or any of those revenues are payable and being securities in respect of which the rate of interest is variable by reference to one or more of the following –
  (*a*) the Bank of England's minimum lending rate;
  (*b*) the average rate of discount on allotment on 91-day Treasury bills;
  (*c*) a yield on 91-day Treasury bills;
  (*d*) a London sterling inter-bank offered rate;
  (*e*) a London sterling certificate of deposit rate.][29]

10.[30] In debentures or in the guaranteed or preference stock of any incorporated company, being statutory water undertakers within the meaning of the Water Act 1945, or any corresponding enactment in force in Northern Ireland, and having during each of the ten years immediately preceding the calendar year in which the investment was made paid a dividend of not less than [3½][31] per cent. on its ordinary shares.

11. [. . .][32]

12. In deposits in a building society designated under section one of the House Purchase and Housing Act 1959.

13. In mortgages of freehold property in England and Wales or Northern Ireland and of leasehold property in those countries of which the unexpired term at the time of investment is not less than sixty years, and in loans on heritable security in Scotland.

14. In perpetual rent-charges on land in England and Wales or Northern Ireland and fee-farm rents (not being rent-charges) issuing out of such land, and in feu-duties or ground annuals in Scotland.

PART III

WIDER-RANGE INVESTMENTS

1. In any securities issued in the United Kingdom by a company incorporated in the United Kingdom, being securities registered in the United Kingdom and not being securities falling within Part II of this Schedule.

2. In shares in any building society designated under section one of the House Purchase and Housing Act 1959.

3. In any units, or other shares of the investments subject to the trusts, of a unit trust scheme in the case of which there is in force at the time of investment an order of the Board of Trade under section seventeen of the Prevention of Fraud (Investments) Act 1958, or of the Ministry of Commerce for Northern Ireland under section sixteen of the Prevention of Fraud (Investments) Act (Northern Ireland) 1940.

PART IV

SUPPLEMENTAL

1.[33] The securities mentioned in Parts I to Part III of this Schedule do not include any securities where the holder can be required to accept repayment of the principal, or the payment of any interest, otherwise than in sterling.

2.[34] The securities mentioned in paragraphs 1 to 8 of Part II, other than Treasury Bills or Tax Reserve Certificates issued before the passing of this Act by the Government of the Isle of Man, securities falling within paragraph 4 of the said Part II issued before the passing of this Act or securities falling within paragraph 9 of that Part, and the securities mentioned in paragraph 1 of Part III of this Schedule do not include—
  (*a*) securities the price of which is not quoted on a recognised stock exchange within the meaning of the Prevention of Fraud (Investments) Act 1958, or the Belfast stock exchange;
  (*b*) shares or debenture stock not fully paid up (except shares or debenture stock which by the terms of issue are required to be fully paid up within nine months of the date of issue).

3.[35] The securities mentioned in paragraph 6 of Part II and paragraph 1 of Part III of this Schedule do not include—
  (*a*) shares or debentures of an incorporated company of which the total issued and paid up share capital is less than one million pounds;

[29] Added by the Trustee Investments (Additional Powers) (No. 2) Order 1977 (No. 1878).
[30] The Treasury was given power to amend this section by the Finance Act 1973 (c. 51), s. 58 (1).
[31] Substituted by the Trustee Investments (Water Companies) Order 1973 (No. 1393).
[32] Excluded by the Local Authorities' Mutual Investment Trust Act 1968 (c. 25), s. 1 (2).
[33] Repealed by the Trustee Savings Bank Act 1976 (c. 4), Sched. 6.
[34] Excluded by the Local Authorities' Mutual Investment Trust Act 1968 (c. 25), s. 1(2) and the Trustee Savings Bank Act 1969 (c. 50), s. 46 (2).
[35] Excluded by the Local Authorities' Investment Trust Act 1968 (c.25), s. 1 (2).

(*b*) shares or debentures of an incorporated company which has not in each of the five years immediately preceding the calendar year in which the investment is made paid a dividend on all the shares issued by the company, excluding any shares issued after the dividend was declared and any shares which by their terms of issue did not rank for the dividend for that year.

For the purposes of sub-paragraph (*b*) of this paragraph a company formed—
    (i) to take over the business of another company or other companies, or
   (ii) to acquire the securities of, or control of, another company or other companies,
or for either of those purposes and for other purposes shall be deemed to have paid a dividend as mentioned in that sub-paragraph in any year in which such a dividend has been paid by the other company or all the other companies, as the case may be.

4. In this Schedule, unless the context otherwise requires, the following expressions have the meanings hereby respectively assigned to them, that is to say—
"debenture" includes debenture stock and bonds, whether constituting a charge on assets or not, and loan stock or notes;
"enactment" includes an enactment of the Parliament of Northern Ireland;
"fixed-interest securities" means securities which under their terms of issue bear a fixed rate of interest;
"local authority" in relation to the United Kingdom, means any of the following authorities—
          (*a*) in England and Wales, the council of a county, a county, metropolitan or other borough [. . .],[36] an urban or rural district or a parish, the Common Council of the City of London, [the Greater London Council][37] and the Council of the Isles of Scilly;
          (*b*) in Scotland, a local authority within the meaning of the Local Government (Scotland) Act 1947;
    $\begin{bmatrix} \ldots \,]^{38} \\ \ldots \,]^{39} \end{bmatrix}$
"securities" includes shares, debentures, Treasury Bills and Tax Reserve Certificates;
"share" includes stock;
"Treasury Bills" includes [. . .][40] bills issued by Her Majesty's Government in the United Kingdom and Northern Ireland Treasury Bills.

5. It is hereby declared that in this Schedule "mortgage," in relation to freehold or leasehold property in Northern Ireland, includes a registered charge which, by virtue of subsection (4) of section forty of the Local Registration of Title (Ireland) Act 1891, or any other enactment, operates as a mortgage by deed.

6. References in this Schedule to an incorporated company are references to a company incorporated by or under any enactment and include references to a body of persons established for the purpose of trading for profit and incorporated by Royal Charter.

7. The references in paragraph 12 of Part II and paragraph 2 of Part III of this Schedule to a building society designated under section one of the House Purchase and Housing Act 1959 includes references to a permanent society incorporated under the Building Societies Acts (Northern Ireland) 1874 to 1940 for the time being designated by the Registrar for Northern Ireland under subsection (2) of that section (which enables such a society to be so designated for the purpose of trustees' powers of investment specified in paragraph (a) of subsection (1) of that section).

Section 3
SECOND SCHEDULE[41]

MODIFICATION OF s.2 IN RELATION TO PROPERTY FALLING WITHIN s.3(3)

1. In this Schedule "special-range property" means property falling within subsection (3) of section three of this Act.

2.—(1) Where a trust fund includes special-range property, subsection (1) of section two of this Act shall have effect as if references to the trust fund were references to so much thereof as does not consist of special-range property, and the special range property shall be carried to a separate part of the fund.

(2) Any property which—
          (*a*) being property belonging to the narrower-range or wider-range part of a trust fund, is converted into special-range property, or
          (*b*) being special-range property, accrues to a trust fund after the division of the fund or part thereof in pursuance of subsection (1) of section two of this Act or of that subsection as modified by sub-paragraph (1) of this paragraph,

[36] Words repealed by the Local Government Act 1972 (c. 70), s. 272 (1), Sched. 30.
[37] Added by the London Government Act 1963 (c. 33), Sched. 17, para. 25 (*b*).
[38] Words repealed by Statute Law (Repeals) Act 1981 (c. 19), Sched. 1.
[39] Words repealed by Trustee Savings Banks Act 1976 (c. 4), Sched. 6.
[40] Words repealed by the National Loans Act 1968, (c.13), s. 24 (2) and Sched. 6.
[41] Scheds. 2 and 3 are restricted by the House of Commons Members' Fund Act 1962 (10 & 11 Eliz. 2, c. 53).

shall be carried to such a separate part of the fund as aforesaid; and subsections (2) and (3) of the said section two shall have effect subject to this sub-paragraph.

3. Where property carried to such a separate part as aforesaid is converted into property other than special-range property,—

(a) it shall be transferred to the narrower-range part of the fund or the wider-range part of the fund or apportioned between them, and

(b) any transfer of property from one of those parts to the other shall be made which is necessary to secure that the value of each of those parts of the fund is increased by the same amount.

Section 3   THIRD SCHEDULE[41]

PROVISIONS SUPPLEMENTARY TO S. 3(4)

1. Where in a case falling within subsection (4) of section three of this Act, property belonging to the narrower-range part of a trust fund—

(a) is invested otherwise than in a narrower-range investment, or

(b) being so invested, is retained and not transferred or as soon as may be reinvested as mentioned in subsection (2) of this Act,

then so long as the property continues so invested and comprised in the narrower-range part of the fund, section one of this Act shall not authorise the making or retention of any wider-range investment.

2. Section four of the Trustee Act 1925, or section thirty-three of the Trusts (Scotland Act 1921 (which relieve a trustee from liability for retaining an investment which has ceased to be authorised), shall not apply where an investment ceases to be authorised in consequence of the foregoing paragraph.

Section 16   FOURTH SCHEDULE

MINOR AND CONSEQUENTIAL AMENDMENTS

1.—(1) References in the Trustee Act 1925, except in subsection (2) of section sixty-nine of that Act, to section one of that Act or to provisions which include that section shall be construed respectively as references to section one of this Act and as including references to section one of this Act.

(2) References in the Trusts (Scotland) Act 1921 to section ten or eleven of that Act, or to provisions which include either of those sections, shall be construed respectively as references to section one of this Act and as including references to that section.

2. [*Repealed by the Building Societies Act 1962* (10 & 11 *Eliz.* 2, *c.* 37), *Sched.* 10, *Pt.* I.]

3. The following enactments and instruments, that is to say—

(a) subsection (3) of section seventy-four of the Third Schedule to the Water Act 1945, and any order made under that Act applying the provisions of that subsection;

(b) any local and personal Act which, or any order or other instrument in the nature of any such Act which, modifies paragraph(1) of subsection (1) of section one of the Trustee Act 1925,

shall have effect as if for any reference to the said paragraph (1) there were substituted a reference to paragraph 10 of Part II of the First Schedule to this Act.

4. [*This paragraph was repealed by the Trustee Savings Bank Act 1969* (*c.* 50), *s.* 96 (1) *and Sched.* 3, *Pt.* I, *and the National Savings Bank Act 1971* (*c.* 29), *s.* 28 *and Sched.* 2.]

5. [*This paragraph was repealed by the Trustee Savings Bank Act 1969* (*c.* 50), *s.* 96 (1) *and Sched.* 3, *Pt.* I, *and the National Savings Bank Act 1971* (*c.* 29), *s.* 28 *and Sched.* 2.]

6. For the reference in subsection (2) of section one of the House Purchase and Housing Act 1959 to paragraph (a) of subsection (1) of that section there shall be substituted a reference to paragraph 12 of Part II and paragraph 2 of Part III of the First Schedule to this Act.

Section 16   FIFTH SCHEDULE

[*Repealed by the Statute Law (Repeals) Act 1974* (*c.22*), *Sched., Pt. XI.*]

Wills Act 1963

(1963 c. 44)

An Act to repeal the Wills Act 1861 and make new provision in lieu thereof; and to provide that certain testamentary instruments shall be probative for the purpose of the conveyance of heritable property in Scotland. [31st July 1963]

General rule as to formal validity

1. A will shall be treated as properly executed if its execution conformed to the internal law in force in the territory where it was executed, or in the territory where, at the time of its execution or of the testator's death, he was domiciled or had his habitual residence, or in a state of which, at either of those times, he was a national.

Additional rules

2.—(1) Without prejudice to the preceding section, the following shall be treated as properly executed—

    (*a*) a will executed on board a vessel or aircraft of any description, if the execution of the will conformed to the internal law in force in the territory with which, having regard to its registration (if any) and other relevant circumstances, the vessel or aircraft may be taken to have been most closely connected;

    (*b*) a will so far as it disposes of immovable property, if its execution conformed to the internal law in force in the territory where the property was situated;

    (*c*) a will so far as it revokes a will which under this Act would be treated as properly executed or revokes a provision which under this Act would be treated as comprised in a properly executed will, if the execution of the later will conformed to any law by reference to which the revoked will or provision would be so treated;

    (*d*) a will so far as it exercises a power of appointment, if the execution of the will conformed to the law governing the essential validity of the power.

(2) A will so far as it exercises a power of appointment shall not be treated as improperly executed by reason only that its execution was not in accordance with any formal requirements contained in the instrument creating the power.

Certain requirements to be treated as formal

3. Where (whether in pursuance of this Act or not) a law in force outside the United Kingdom falls to be applied in relation to a will, any requirement of that law whereby special formalities are to be observed by testators answering a particular description, or witnesses to the execution of a will are to possess certain qualifications, shall be treated, notwithstanding any rule of that law to the contrary, as a formal requirement only.

Construction of wills

4. The construction of a will shall not be altered by reason of any change in the testator's domicile after the execution of the will.

5. [*Repealed by the Succession (Scotland) Act* 1964 (*c.* 41), *Sched.* 3.]

Interpretation

6.—(1) In this Act—

"internal law" in relation to any territory or state means the law which would apply in a case where no question of the law in force in any other territory or state arose;

"state" means a territory or group of territories having its own law of nationality;

"will" includes any testamentary instrument or act, and "testator" shall be construed accordingly.

(2) Where under this Act the internal law in force in any territory or state is to be applied in the case of a will, but there are in force in that territory or state two or more systems of internal law relating to the formal validity of wills, the system to be applied shall be ascertained as follows—

(*a*) if there is in force throughout the territory or state a rule indicating which of those systems can properly be applied in the case in question, that rule shall be followed; or

(*b*) if there is no such rule, the system shall be that with which the testator was most closely connected at the relevant time, and for this purpose the relevant time is the time of the testator's death where the matter is to be determined by reference to circumstances prevailing at his death, and the time of execution of the will in any other case.

(3) In determining for the purpose of this Act whether or not the execution of a will conformed to a particular law, regard shall be had to the formal requirements of that law at the time of execution, but this shall not prevent account being taken of an alteration of law affecting wills executed at that time if the alteration enables the will to be treated as properly executed.

Short title, commencement, repeal and extent

7.—(1) This Act may be cited as the Wills Act 1963.

(2) This Act shall come into operation on 1st January 1964.

(3) The Wills Act 1861 is hereby repealed.

(4) This Act shall not apply to a will of a testator who died before the time of the commencement of this Act and shall apply to a will of a testator who dies after that time whether the will was executed before or after that time, but so that the repeal of the Wills Act 1861 shall not invalidate a will executed before that time.

(5) It is hereby declared that this Act extends to Northern Ireland, [. . .][1]

---

[1] Words repealed by the Northern Ireland Constitution Act 1973 (c. 36), Sched. 6, Pt. 1.

Perpetuities and Accumulations Act 1964

(1964 c. 55)

An Act to modify the law of England and Wales relating to the avoidance of future interests in property on grounds of remoteness and governing accumulations of income from property.   [16th July 1964]

Perpetuities

Power to specify perpetuity period

1.—(1) Subject to section 9 (2) of this Act and subsection (2) below, where the instrument by which any disposition is made so provides, the perpetuity period applicable to the disposition under the rule against perpetuities, instead of being of any other duration, shall be of a duration equal to such number of years not exceeding eighty as is specified in that behalf in the instrument.

(2) Subsection (1) above shall not have effect where the disposition is made in exercise of a special power of appointment, but where a period is specified under that subsection in the instrument creating such a power the period shall apply in relation to any disposition under the power as it applies in relation to the power itself.

Presumptions and evidence as to future parenthood

2.—(1) Where in any proceedings there arises on the rule against perpetuities a question which turns on the ability of a person to have a child at some future time, then—

(a) subject to paragraph (b) below, it shall be presumed that a male can have a child at the age of fourteen years or over, but not under that age, and that a female can have a child at the age of twelve years or over, but not under that age or over the age of fifty-five years; but

(b) in the case of a living person evidence may be given to show that he or she will or will not be able to have a child at the time in question.

(2) Where any such question is decided by treating a person as unable to have a child at a particular time, and he or she does so, the High Court may make such order as it thinks fit for placing the persons interested in the property comprised in the disposition, so far as may be just, in the position they would have held if the question had not been so decided.

(3) Subject to subsection (2) above, where any such question is decided in relation to a disposition by treating a person as able or unable to have a child at a particular time, then he or she shall be so treated for the purpose of any question which may arise on the rule against perpetuities in relation to the same disposition in any subsequent proceedings.

(4) In the foregoing provisions of this section references to having a child are references to begetting or giving birth to a child, but those provisions (except subsection (1)(*b*)) shall apply in relation to the possibility that a person will at any time have a child by adoption,[1] legitimation or other means as they apply to his or her ability at that time to beget or give birth to a child.

Uncertainty as to remoteness

3.—(1) Where, apart from the provisions of this section and sections 4 and 5 of this Act, a disposition would be void on the ground that the interest disposed of might not become vested until too remote a time, the disposition shall be treated, until such time (if any) as it becomes established that the vesting must occur, if at all, after the end of the perpetuity period, as if the disposition were not subject to the rule against perpetuities; and its becoming so established shall not affect the validity of anything previously done in relation to the interest disposed of by way of advancement, application of intermediate income or otherwise.

(2) Where, apart from the said provisions, a disposition consisting of the conferring of a general power of appointment would be void on the ground that the power might not become exercisable until too remote a time, the disposition shall be treated, until such time (if any) as it becomes established that the power will not be exercisable within the perpetuity period, as if the disposition were not subject to the rule against perpetuities.

(3) Where, apart from the said provisions, a disposition consisting of the conferring of any power, option or other right would be void on the ground that the right might be exercised at too remote a time, the disposition shall be treated as regards any exercise of the right within the perpetuity period as if it were not subject to the rule against perpetuities and, subject to the said provisions, shall be treated as void for remoteness only if, and so far as, the right is not fully exercised within that period.

(4) Where this section applies to a disposition and the duration of the perpetuity period is not determined by virtue of section 1 or 9 (2) of this Act, it shall be determined as follows:–

(*a*) where any persons falling within subsection (5) below are individuals in being and ascertainable at the commencement of the perpetuity period the duration of the period shall be determined by reference to their lives and no others, but so that the lives of any description of persons falling within paragraph (*b*) or (*c*) of that subsection shall be disregarded if the number of persons of that description is such as to render it impracticable to ascertain the date of death of the survivor;

(*b*) where there are no lives under paragraph (*a*) above the period shall be twenty-one years.

(5) The said persons are as follows:—

(*a*) the person by whom the disposition was made;

---

[1] As to adoption, see the Children Act 1975 (c. 72), Sched. 1, para. 6 (5).

(*b*) a person to whom or in whose favour the disposition was made, that is to say—

    (i) in the case of a disposition to a class of persons, any member or potential member of the class;

    (ii) in the case of an individual disposition to a person taking only on certain conditions being satisfied, any person as to whom some of the conditions are satisfied and the remainder may in time be satisfied;

    (iii) in the case of a special power of appointment exercisable in favour of members of a class, any member or potential member of the class;

    (iv) in the case of a special power of appointment exercisable in favour of one person only, that person or, where the object of the power is ascertainable only on certain conditions being satisfied, any person as to whom some of the conditions are satisfied and the remainder may in time be satisfied;

    (v) in the case of any power, option or other right, the person on whom the right is conferred;

(*c*) a person having a child or grandchild within sub-paragraphs (i) to (iv) of paragraph (*b*) above, or any of whose children or grandchildren, if subsequently born, would by virtue of his or her descent fall within those sub-paragraphs;

(*d*) any person on the failure or determinatin of whose prior interest the disposition is limited to take effect.

Reduction of age and exclusion of class members to avoid remoteness

4.—(1) Where a disposition is limited by reference to the attainment by any person or persons of a specified age exceeding twenty-one years, and it is apparent at the time the disposition is made or becomes apparent at a subsequent time—

(*a*) that the disposition would, apart from this section, be void for remoteness, but

(*b*) that it would not be so void if the specified age had been twenty-one years,

the disposition shall be treated for all purposes as if, instead of being limited by reference to the age in fact specified, it had been limited by reference to the age nearest to that age which would, if specified instead, have prevented the disposition from being so void.

(2) Where in the case of any disposition different ages exceeding twenty-one years are specified in relation to different persons—

(*a*) the reference in paragraph (*b*) of subsection (1) above to the specified age shall be construed as a reference to all the specified ages, and

(*b*) that subsection shall operate to reduce each such age so far as is necessary to save the disposition from being void for remoteness.

(3) Where the inclusion of any persons, being potential members of a class or unborn persons who at birth would become members or potential members of the class, prevents the foregoing provisions of this section from operating to save a disposition from being void for remoteness, those persons shall thenceforth be deemed for all the purposes of the disposition to be excluded from the class, and the said provisions shall thereupon have effect accordingly.

(4) Where, in the case of a disposition to which subsection (3) above does not apply, it is apparent at the time the disposition is made or becomes apparent at a subsequent time that, apart from this subsection, the inclusion of any persons, being potential members of a class or unborn

persons who at birth would become members or potential members of the class, would cause the disposition to be treated as void for remoteness, those persons shall, unless their exclusion would exhaust the class, thenceforth be deemed for all the purposes of the disposition to be excluded from the class.

(5) Where this section has effect in relation to a disposition to which section 3 above applies, the operation of this section shall not affect the validity of anything previously done in relation to the interest disposed of by way of advancement application of intermediate income or otherwise.

(6) Section 163 of the Law of Property Act 1925 (which saves a disposition from remoteness arising out of a condition requiring the attainment of an age exceeding twenty-one years) is hereby repealed.

[(7) For the avoidance of doubt it is hereby declared that a question arising under section 3 of this Act or subsection (1) (a) above of whether a disposition would be void apart from this section is to be determined as if subsection (6) above had been a separate section of this Act.]²

Condition relating to death of surviving spouse

5. Where a disposition is limited by reference to the time of death of the survivor of a person in being at the commencement of the perpetuity period and any spouse of that person, and that time has not arrived at the end of the perpetuity period, the disposition shall be treated for all purposes, where to do so would save it from being void for remoteness, as if it had instead been limited by reference to the time immediately before the end of that period.

Saving and acceleration of expectant interests

6. A disposition shall not be treated as void for remoteness by reason only that the interest disposed of is ulterior to and dependent upon an interest under a disposition which is so void, and the vesting of an interest shall not be prevented from being accelerated on the failure of a prior interest by reason only that the failure arises because of remoteness.

Powers of appointment

7. For the purposes of the rule against perpetuities, a power of appointment shall be treated as a special power unless—
  (*a*) in the instrument creating the power it is expressed to be exercisable by one person only, and
  (*b*) it could, at all times during its currency when that person is of full age and capacity, be exercised by him so as immediately to transfer to himself the whole of the interest governed by the power without the consent of any other person or compliance with any other condition, not being a formal condition relating only to the mode of exercise of the power:

Provided that for the purpose of determining whether a disposition made under a power of appointment exercisable by will only is void for remoteness, the power shall be treated as a general power where it would have fallen to be so treated if exercisable by deed.

Administrative powers of trustees

8.—(1) The rule against perpetuities shall not operate to invalidate a power conferred on trustees or other persons to sell, lease, exchange or otherwise dispose of any property for full consideration, or to do any other act in the administration (as opposed to the distribution) of any property,

---

² Added by the Children Act 1975 (c. 72), Sched. 3.

and shall not prevent the payment to trustees or other persons of reasonable remuneration for their services.

(2) Subsection (1) above shall apply for the purpose of enabling a power to be exercised at any time after the commencement of this Act notwithstanding that the power is conferred by an instrument which took effect before that commencement.

Options relating to land

9.—(1) The rule against perpetuities shall not apply to a disposition consisting of the conferring of an option to acquire for valuable consideration an interest reversionary (whether directly or indirectly) on the term of a lease if—

(*a*) the option is exercisable only by the lessee or his successors in title, and

(*b*) it ceases to be exercisable at or before the expiration of one year following the determination of the lease.

This subsection shall apply in relation to an agreement for a lease as it applies in relation to a lease, and "lessee" shall be construed accordingly.

(2) In the case of a disposition consisting of the conferring of an option to acquire for valuable consideration any interest in land, the perpetuity period under the rule against perpetuities shall be twenty-one years, and section 1 of this Act shall not apply:

Provided that this subsection shall not apply to a right of premption conferred on a public or local authority in respect of land used or to be used for religious purposes where the right becomes exercisable only if the land ceases to be used for such purposes.

Avoidance of contractual and other rights in cases of remoteness

10. Where a disposition *inter vivos* would fall to be treated as void for remoteness if the rights and duties thereunder were capable of transmission to persons other than the original parties and had been so transmitted, it shall be treated as void as between the person by whom it was made and the person to whom or in whose favour it was made or any successor of his, and no remedy shall lie in contract or otherwise for giving effect to it or making restitution for its lack of effect.

Rights for enforcement of rentcharges

11.—(1) The rule against perpetuities shall not apply to any powers or remedies for recovering or compelling the payment of an annual sum to which section 121 or 122 of the Law of Property Act 1925 applies, or otherwise becoming exercisable or enforceable on the breach of any condition or other requirement relating to that sum.

(2) In section 121 (6) of the Law of Property Act 1925 the words from "nor to the same"onwards are hereby repealed.

Possibilities of reverter, conditions subsequent, exceptions and reservations

12.—(1) In the case of—

(*a*) a possibility of reverter on the determination of a determinable fee simple, or

(*b*) a possibility of a resulting trust on the determination of any other determinable interest in property.

the rule against perpetuities shall apply in relation to the provision causing the interest to be determinable as it would apply if that provision were expressed in the form of a condition subsequent giving rise, on breach thereof, to a right of re-entry or an equivalent right in the case of property other than land, and where the provision falls to be treated as void for remoteness the determinable interest shall become an absolute interest.

(2) Where a disposition is subject to any such provision, or to any such condition subsequent, or to any exception or reservation, the disposition shall be treated for the purposes of this Act as including a separate disposition of any rights arising by virtue of the provision, condition subsequent, exception or reservation.

Accumulations

Amendment of s.164 of Law of Property Act 1925

13.—(1) The periods for which accumulations of income under a settlement or other disposition are permitted by section 164 of the Law of Property Act 1925 shall include—

(*a*) a term of twenty-one years from the date of the making of the disposition, and

(*b*) the duration of the minority or respective minorities of any person or persons in being at that date.

(2) It is hereby declared that the restrictions imposed by the said section 164 apply in relation to a power to accumulate income whether or not there is a duty to exercise that power, and that they apply whether or not the power to accumulate extends to income produced by the investment of income previously accumulated.

Right to stop accumulations

14. Section 2 above shall apply to any question as to the right of beneficiaries to put an end to accumulations of income under any disposition as it applies to questions arising on the rule against perpetuities.

Supplemental

Short title, interpretation and extent

15.—(1) This Act may be cited as the Perpetuities and Accumulations Act 1964.

(2) In this Act—

"disposition" includes the conferring of a power of appointment and any other disposition of an interest in or right over property, and references to the interest disposed of shall be construed accordingly;

"in being" means living or en ventre sa mère;

"power of appointment" includes any discretionary power to transfer a beneficial interest in property without the furnishing of valuable consideration;

"will" includes a codicil;

and for the purposes of this Act a disposition contained in a will shall be deemed to be made at the death of the testator.

(3) For the purposes of this Act a person shall be treated as a member of a class if in his case all the conditions identifying a member of the class are satisfied, and shall be treated as a potential member if in his case some only of those conditions are satisfied but there is a possibility that the remainder will in time be satisfied.

(4) Nothing in this Act shall affect the operation of the rule of law rendering void for remoteness certain dispositions under which property is limited to be applied for purposes other than the benefit of any person or class of persons in cases where the property may be so applied after the end of the perpetuity period.

(5) The foregoing sections of this Act shall apply (except as provided in section 8 (2) above) only in relation to instruments taking effect after the commencement of this Act, and in the case of an instrument made in the exercise of a special power of appointment shall apply only where the instrument creating the power takes effect after that commencement:

Provided that section 7 above shall apply in all cases for construing the foregoing reference to a special power of appointment.

(6) This Act shall apply in relation to a disposition made otherwise than by an instrument as if the disposition had been contained in an instrument taking effect when the disposition was made.

(7) This Act binds the Crown.

(8) Except in so far as the contrary intention appears, any enactment of the Parliament of Northern Ireland passed for purposes similar to the purposes of this Act shall bind the Crown.

(9) This Act shall not extend to Scotland or (apart from subsection (8) above) to Northern Ireland.

Law of Property (Joint Tenants) Act 1964

(1964 c. 63)

An Act to amend the law with respect to land vested in joint tenants.

[31st July 1964]

Assumptions on sale of land by survivor of joint tenants

1.—(1) For the purposes of section 36 (2) of the Law of Property Act 1925, as amended by section 7 of and the Schedule to the Law of Property (Amendment) Act 1926, the survivor of two or more joint tenants shall, in favour of a purchaser of the legal estate, be deemed to be solely and beneficially interested if he conveys as beneficial owner or the conveyance includes a statement that he is so interested.

Provided that the foregoing provisions of this subsection shall not apply if, at any time before the date of the conveyance by the survivor—

   (a) a memorandum of severance (that is to say a note or memorandum signed by the joint tenants or one of them and recording that the joint tenancy was severed in equity on a date therein specified) had been endorsed on or annexed to the conveyance by virtue of which the legal estate was vested in the joint tenants; or

   (b) a receiving order in bankruptcy made against any of the joint tenants, or a petition for such an order, had been registered under the Land Charges Act 1925,[1] being an order or petition of which the purchaser has notice, by virtue of the registration, on the date of the conveyance by the survivor.

(2) The foregoing provisions of this section shall apply with the necessary modifications in relation to a conveyance by the personal representatives of the survivor of joint tenants as they apply in relation to a conveyance by such a survivor.

Retrospective and transitional provisions

2. Section 1 of this Act shall be deemed to have come into force on 1st January 1926, and for the purposes of that section in its application to a conveyance executed before the passing of this Act a statement signed by the vendor or by his personal representatives that he was solely and beneficially interested shall be treated as if it had been included in the conveyance.

Exclusion of registered land

3. This Act shall not apply to any land the title of which has been registered under the provisions of the Land Registration Acts 1925 and 1936.

Short title, construction, citation and extent

4.—(1) This Act may be cited as the Law of Property (Joint Tenants) Act 1964, and shall be construed as one with the Law of Property Act 1925.

(2) The Law of Property Acts 1925 to 1932 and this Act, may be cited together as the Law of Property Acts 1925 to 1964.

(3) This Act extends to England and Wales only.

---

[1] Now the Land Charges Act 1972 (c. 61), *post*, p. 320.

Wills Act 1968

(1968 c. 28)

An Act to restrict the operation of section 15 of the Wills Act 1837.

[30th May 1968]

Restriction of operation of Wills Act 1837, s.15

1.—(1) For the purposes of section 15 of the Wills Act 1837 (avoidance of gifts to attesting witnesses and their spouses) the attestation of a will by a person to whom or to whose spouse there is given or made any such disposition as is described in that section shall be disregarded if the will is duly executed without his attestation and without that of any other such person.

(2) This section applies to the will of any person dying after the passing of this Act, whether executed before or after the passing of this Act.

Short title and extent

2.—(1) This Act may be cited as the Wills Act 1968.

(2) This Act does not extend to Scotland or Northern Ireland.

Family Law Reform Act 1969

(1969 c. 46)

An Act to amend the law relating to the age of majority, to persons who have not attained that age and to the time when a particular age is attained; . . . and for connected purposes. [25th July 1969]

PART I

REDUCTION OF AGE OF MAJORITY AND RELATED PROVISIONS

Reduction of age of majority from 21 to 18

1.—(1) As from the date on which this section comes into force a person shall attain full age on attaining the age of eighteen instead of on attaining the age of twenty-one; and a person shall attain full age on that date if he has then already attained the age of eighteen but not the age of 21.

(2) The foregoing subsection applies for the purposes of any rule of law, and, in the absence of a definition or of any indication of a contrary intention, for the construction of "full age," "infant," "infancy," "minor," "minority" and similar expressions in—

(a) any statutory provision, whether passed or made before, on or after the date on which this section comes into force, and

(b) any deed, will or other instrument of whatever nature (not being a statutory provision) made on or after that date.

. . . . . .

Provisions relating to wills and intestacy

3.—(1) [See the Wills Act 1837 (7 Will. 4 & 1 Vict. c.26), s.7,[1] and the Wills (Soldiers and Sailors) Act 1918 (7 & 8 Geo. 5, c.58), ss.1 and 3(1).[2]]

(2) [See the Administration of Estates Act 1925 (15 & 16 Geo. 5, c.23), s.47(1)(i).[3]]

(3) Any will which—

(a) has been made, whether before or after the coming into force of this section, by a person under the age of eighteen; and

(b) is valid by virtue of the provisions of section 11 of the said Act of 1837 and the said Act of 1918,

may be revoked by that person notwithstanding that he is still under that age whether or not the circumstances are then such that he would be entitled to make a valid will under those provisions.

(4) In this section "will" has the same meaning as in the said Act of 1837 and "intestate" has the same meaning as in the said Act of 1925.

. . . . . .

Time at which a person attains a particular age

9.[4]—(1) The time at which a person attains a particular age expressed in years shall be the commencement of the relevant anniversary of the date of his birth.

(2) This section applies only where the relevant anniversary falls on a date after that on which this section comes into force, and in relation to any enactment, deed, will or other instrument, has effect subject to any provision therein.

. . . . . .

[1] *Ante*, p. 3.
[2] *Ante*, p. 11.
[3] *Ante*, p. 267.
[4] Excluded by the Income and Corporation Taxes Act 1970 (c. 10), s. 10 (7).

Law of Property Act 1969

(1969 c. 59)

An Act . . . to amend the law relating to dispositions of estates and interests in land and to land charges; to make further provision as to the powers of the Lands Tribunal and court in relation to restrictive covenants affecting land; and for purposes connected with those matters. [22nd October 1969]

PART III

AMENDMENT OF LAW RELATING TO DISPOSITIONS OF ESTATES AND INTERESTS IN LAND AND TO LAND CHARGES

Reduction of statutory period of title

23. Section 44 (1) of the Law of Property Act 1925 (under which the period of commencement of title which may be required under a contract expressing no contrary intention is thirty years except in certain cases) shall have effect, in its application to contracts made after the commencement of this Act, as if it specified fifteen years instead of thirty years as the period of commencement of title which may be so required.

Contracts for purchase of land affected by land charge, etc.

24.—(1) Where under a contract for the sale or other disposition of any estate or interest in land the title to which is not registered under the Land Registration Act 1925 or any enactment replaced by it any question arises whether the purchaser had knowledge, at the time of entering into the contract, of a registered land charge, that question shall be determined by reference to his actual knowledge and without regard to the provisions of section 198 of the Law of Property Act 1925 (under which registration under the Land Charges Act 1925[1] or any enactment replaced by it is deemed to constitute actual notice).

(2) Where any estate or interest with which such a contract is concerned is affected by a registered land charge and the purchaser, at the time of entering into the contract, had not received notice and did not otherwise actually know that the estate or interest was affected by the charge, any provision of the contract shall be void so far as it purports to exclude the operation of subsection (1) above or to exclude or restrict any right or remedy that might otherwise be exercisable by the purchaser on the ground that the estate or interest is affected by the charge.

(3) In this section—

"purchaser" includes a lessee, mortgagee or other person acquiring or intending to acquire an estate or interest in land; and

"registered land charge" means any instrument or matter registered, otherwise than in a register of local land charges, under the Land Charges Act 1925[1] or any Act replaced by it.

(4) For the purposes of this section any knowledge acquired in the course of a transaction by a person who is acting therein as counsel, or as solicitor or other agent, for another shall be treated as the knowledge of that other.

(5) This section does not apply to contracts made before the commencement of this Act.

---

[1] Now the Land Charges Act 1972 (c. 61), *post*, p. 320.

Compensation in certain cases for loss due to undisclosed land charges

25.—(1) Where a purchaser of any estate or interest in land under a disposition to which this section applies has suffered loss by reason that the estate or interest is affected by a registered land charge, then if—

> (a) the date of completion was after the commencement of this Act; and

> (b) on that date the purchaser had no actual knowledge of the charge; and

> (c) the charge was registered against the name of an owner of an estate in the land who was not as owner of any such estate a party to any transaction, or concerned in any event, comprised in the relevant title;

the purchaser shall be entitled to compensation for the loss.

(2) For the purposes of subsection (1)(b) above, the question whether any person had actual knowledge of a charge shall be determined without regard to the provisions of section 198 of the Law of Property Act 1925 (under which registration under the Land Charges Act 1925[1] or any enactment replaced by it is deemed to constitute actual notice).

(3) Where a transaction comprised in the relevant title was affected or evidenced by a document which expressly provided that it should take effect subject to an interest or obligation capable of registration in any of the relevant registers, the transaction which created that interest or obligation shall be treated for the purposes of subsection (1)(c) above as comprised in the relevant title.

(4) Any compensation for loss under this section shall be paid by the Chief Land Registrar, and where the purchaser of the estate or interest in question has incurred expenditure for the purpose—

> (a) of securing that the estate or interest is no longer affected by the registered land charge or is so affected to a less extent; or

> (b) of obtaining compensation under this section;

the amount of the compensation shall include the amount of the expenditure (so far as it would not otherwise fall to be treated as compensation for loss) reasonably incurred by the purchaser for that purpose.

(5) In the case of an action to recover compensation under this section, the cause of action shall be deemed for the purposes of the Limitation Act [1980][2] to accrue at the time when the registered land charge affecting the estate or interest in question comes to the notice of the purchaser.

(6) Any proceedings for the recovery of compensation under this section shall be commenced in the High Court; and if in such proceedings the High Court dismisses a claim to compensation it shall not order the purchaser to pay the Chief Land Registrar's costs unless it considers that it was unreasonable for the purchaser to commence the proceedings.

(7) [*Repealed by the Land Charges Act* 1972 (*c.*61), *Sched.* 5.]

(8) Where compensation under this section has been paid in a case where the purchaser would have had knowledge of the registered land charge but for the fraud of any person, the Chief Land Registrar, on behalf of the Crown, may recover the amount paid from that person.

(9) This section applies to the following dispositions, that is to say—

> (a) any sale or exchange and, subject to the following provisions of this subsection, any mortgage of an estate or interest in land;

> (b) any grant of a lease for a term of years derived out of a leasehold interest;

---

[2] Substituted by the Limitation Act 1980 (c. 58), Sched. 3, para. 9.

(c) any compulsory purchase, by whatever procedure, of land; and
(d) any conveyance of a fee simple in land under Part I of the Leasehold
Reform Act 1967;

but does not apply to the grant of a term of years derived out of the freehold or the mortgage of such a term by the lessee; and references in this section to a purchaser shall be construed accordingly.

(10) In this section—

"date of completion," in relation to land which vests in the Land Commission or another acquiring authority by virtue of a general vesting declaration under the Land Commission Act 1967 or the Town and Country Planning Act 1968, means the date on which it so vests;

"mortgage" includes any charge;

"registered land charge " means any instrument or matter registered, otherwise than in a register of local land charges, under the Land Charges Act 1925 or any Act replaced by it, except that—

(a) in relation to an assignment of a lease or underlease or a mortgage by an assignee under such an assignment, it does not include any instrument or matter affecting the title to the freehold or to any relevant leasehold reversion; and

(b) in relation to the grant of an underlease or the mortgage by the underlessee of the term of years created by an underlease, it does not include any instrument or matter affecting the title to the freehold or to any leasehold rversion superior to the leasehold interest out of which the term of years is derived;

"relevant registers" means the registers kept under section 1 of the Land Charges Act 1925[3];

"relevant title" means—

(a) in relation to a disposition made under a contract, the title which the purchaser was, apart from any acceptance by him (by agreement or otherwise) of a shorter or an imperfect title, entitled to require; or

(b) in relation to any other disposition, the title which he would have been entitled to require if the disposition had been made under a contract to which section 44 (1) of the Law of Property Act 1925 applied and that contract had been made on the date of completion.

(11) For the purposes of this section any knowledge acquired in the course of a transaction by a person who is acting therein as counsel, or as solicitor or other agent, for another shall be treated as the knowledge of that other.

PART IV

RESTRICTIVE COVENANTS

Powers of Lands Tribunal and court in relation to restrictive covenants affecting land

28. [*See Law of Property Act* 1925 (15 & 16 *Geo.* 5, *c.*20), *s.*84][4]

---

[3] Now the Land Charges Act 1972 (c. 61), *post*, p. 320.
[4] *Ante*, p. 161.

PART V

SUPPLEMENTARY PROVISIONS

. . . . . .

Short title, commencement and extent

31.—(1) This Act may be cited as the Law of Property Act 1969.

(2) This Act, except section 28 (6), shall come into force on 1st January 1970

(3) This Act does not extend to Scotland or Northern Ireland.

. . . . . .

Administration of Justice Act 1970

(1970 c. 31)

An Act . . . to amend the law respecting the enforcement of debt and other liabilities . . . [29th May 1970]

. . . . . .

PART IV

ACTIONS BY MORTGAGEES FOR POSSESSION

Additional powers of court in action by mortgagee for possession of dwelling-house

36.[1]—(1) Where the mortgagee under a mortgage of land which consists of or includes a dwelling-house brings an action in which he claims possession of the mortgaged property, not being an action for foreclosure in which a claim for possession of the mortgaged property is also made, the court may exercise any of the powers conferred on it by subsection (2) below if it appears to the court that in the event of its exercising the power the mortgagor is likely to be able within a reasonable period to pay any sums due under the mortgage or to remedy a default consisting of a breach of any other obligation arising under or by virtue of the mortgage.

(2) The court—

    (*a*) may adjourn the proceedings, or

    (*b*) on giving judgment, or making an order, for delivery of possession of the mortgaged property, or at any time before the execution of such judgment or order, may—

        (i) stay or suspend execution of the judgment or order, or

        (ii) postpone the date for delivery of possession,

for such period or periods as the court thinks reasonable.

(3) Any such adjournment, stay, suspension or postponement as is referred to in subsection (2) above may be made subject to such conditions with regard to payment by the mortgagor of any sum secured by the mortgage or the remedying of any default as the court thinks fit.

(4) The court may from time to time vary or revoke any condition imposed by virtue of this section.

(5) This section shall have effect in relation to such an action as is referred to in subsection (1) above begun before the date on which this section comes into force unless in that action judgment has been given, or an order made, for delivery of possession of the mortgaged property and that judgment or order was executed before that date.

(6) In the application of this section to Northern Ireland, "the court" means a judge of the High Court in Northern Ireland, and in subsection (1) the words from "not being" to "made" shall be omitted.

. . . . . .

Interpretation of Part IV

39.—(1) In this Part of this Act—

    "dwelling-house" includes any building or part thereof which is used as a dwelling;

---

[1] This section was extended, and modified, by the Administration of Justice Act 1973 (c. 15), s. 8, *post* p. 331.

"mortgage" includes a charge and "mortgagor" and "mortgagee" shall be construed accordingly;

"mortgagor" and "mortgagee" includes any person deriving title under the original mortgagor or mortgagee.

(2) The fact that part of the premises comprised in a dwelling-house is used as a shop or office or for business, trade or professional purposes shall not prevent the dwelling-house from being a dwelling-house for the purposes of this Part of this Act.

. . . . . .

Land Charges Act 1972

(1972 c. 61)

. . . . . .

An Act to consolidate certain enactments relating to the registration of land charges and other instruments and matters affecting land.
[9th August 1972]

Preliminary

The registers and the index

1.—(1) The registrar shall continue to keep at the registry in the prescribed manner the following registers, namely—

(*a*) a register of land charges;

(*b*) a register of pending actions;

(*c*) a register of writs and orders affecting land;

(*d*) a register of deeds of arrangement affecting land;

(*e*) a register of annuities,

and shall also continue to keep there an index whereby all entries made in any of those registers can readily be traced.

(2) Every application to register shall be in the prescribed form and shall contain the prescribed particulars.

(3) [Where any charge or other matter is registerable in more than one of the registers kept under this Act, it shall be sufficient if it is registered in one such register, and if it is so registered the person entitled to the benefit

of it shall not be prejudicially affected by any provision of this Act as to the effect of non-registration in any other such register.

(3A) Where any charge or other matter is registrable in a register kept under this Act and was also, before the commencement of the Local Land Charges Act 1975 registrable, in a local land charges register, then, if before the commencement of the said Act it was registered in the appropriate local land charges register, it shall be treated for the purposes of the provisions of this Act as to the effect of non-registration as if it had been registered in the appropriate register under this Act; and any certificate setting out the result of an official search of the appropriate land charges register shall, in relation to it, have effect as if it were a certificate setting out the result of an official search under this Act.]¹

(4) Schedule 1 to this Act shall have effect in relation to the register of annuities.

(5) An office copy of an entry in any register kept under this section shall be admissible in evidence in all proceedings and between all parties to the same extent as the original would be admissible.

(6) Subject to the provisions of this Act, registration may be vacated pursuant to an order of the court.

(7) In this section "index" includes any device or combination of devices serving the purpose of an index.

Registration in register of land charges

The register of land charges

2.—(1) If a charge on or obligation affecting land falls into one of the classes described in this section, it may be registered in the register of land charges as a land charge of that class.

(2) A Class A land charge is—

    (*a*) a rent or annuity or principal money payable by instalments or otherwise, with or without interest, which is not a charge created by deed but is a charge upon land (other than a rate) created pursuant to the application of some person under the provisions of any Act of Parliament, for securing to any person either the money spent by him or the costs, charges and expenses incurred by him under such Act, or the money advanced by him for repaying the money spent or the costs, charges and expenses incurred by another person under the authority of an Act of Parliament; or

    (*b*) a rent or annuity or principal money payable as mentioned in paragraph (*a*) above which is not a charge created by deed but is a charge upon land (other than a rate) created pursuant to the application of some person under any of the enactments mentioned in Schedule 2 to this Act.

(3) A Class B land charge is a charge on land (not being a local land charge [. . .]²) of any of the kinds described in paragraph (*a*) of subsection (2) above, created otherwise than pursuant to the application of any person.

(4) A Class C land charge is any of the following [(not being a local land charge)]³ namely—

    (i) a puisne mortgage;

    (ii) a limited owner's charge;

    (iii) a general equitable charge;

    (iv) an estate contract;

¹ Subs. (3) was substituted, and subs. (3A) was added, by the Local Land Charges Act 1975 (c. 76), s. 17 (1) (*a*).
² Words omitted were repealed by *ibid*. Sched. 2.
³ Added by *ibid*. s.17 (1) (*b*).

and for this purpose—
>   (i) a puisne mortgage is a legal mortgage which is not protected by a deposit of documents relating to the legal estate affected;
>   (ii) a limited owner's charge is an equitable charge acquired by a tenant for life or statutory owner under [Part III of the Finance Act 1975 or under]⁴ any other statute by reason of the discharge by him of any [capital transfer tax]⁵ or other liabilities and to which special priority is given by the statute;
>   (iii) a general equitable charge is any equitable charge which—
>> (*a*) is not secured by a deposit of documents relating to the legal estate affected; and
>> (*b*) does not arise or affect an interest arising under a trust for sale or a settlement; and
>> (*c*) is not a charge given by way of indemnity against rents equitably apportioned or charged exclusively on land in exoneration or other land and against the breach or non-observance of covenants or conditions; and
>> (*d*) is not included in any other class of land charge;
>   (iv) an estate contract is a contract by an estate owner or by a person entitled at the date of the contract to have a legal estate conveyed to him to convey or create a legal estate, including a contract conferring either expressly or by statutory implication a valid option to purchase, a right of pre-emption or any other like right.

(5) A Class D land charge is any of the following, [(not being a local land charge)]⁶ namely—
>   (i) an Inland Revenue charge;
>   (ii) a restrictive covenant;
>   (iii) an equitable easement;

and for this purpose—
>   (i) an Inland Revenue charge is a charge on land, being a charge acquired by the Board under [Part III of the Finance Act 1975 (capital transfer tax)]⁷;
>   (ii) a restrictive covenant is a covenant or agreement (other than a covenant or agreement between a lessor and a lessee) restrictive of the user of land and entered into on or after 1st January 1926;
>   (iii) an equitable easement is an easement, right or privilege over or affecting land created or arising on or after 1st January 1926, and being merely an equitable interest.

(6) A Class E land charge is an annuity created before 1st January 1926 and not registered in the register of annuities.

(7) A Class F land charge is a charge affecting any land by virtue of the Matrimonial Homes Act 1967.

(8) A charge or obligation created before 1st January 1926 can only be registered as a Class B land charge or a Class C land charge if it is acquired under a conveyance made on or after that date.

(9) [. . .]⁸

Registration of land charges

3.—(1) A land charge shall be registered in the name of the estate owner whose estate is intended to be affected.

(2) A land charge registered before 1st January 1926 under any enactment replaced by the Land Charges Act 1925 in the name of a person

---

⁴ Substituted by the Finance Act 1975 (c. 7), Sched. 12
⁵ Substituted by *ibid.*
⁶ Added by the Local Land Charges Act 1976 (c. 76), s.17 (1) (*b*).
⁷ Substituted by the Finance Act 1975 (c. 7), Sched. 12.
⁸ Repealed by the Finance Act 1977 (c. 36), Sched. 9, Part V.

other than the estate owner may remain so registered until it is registered in the name of the estate owner in the prescribed manner.

(3) A puisne mortgage created before 1st January 1926 may be registered as a land charge before any transfer of the mortgage is made.

(4) The expenses incurred by the person entitled to the charge in registering a land charge of Class A, Class B or Class C (other than an estate contract) or by the Board in registering an Inland Revenue charge shall be deemed to form part of the land charge, and shall be recoverable accordingly on the day for payment of any part of the land charge next after such expenses are incurred.

(5) Where a land charge is not created by an instrument, short particulars of the effect of the charge shall be furnished with the application to register the charge.

(6) An application to register an Inland Revenue charge shall state the [tax]⁹ in respect of which the charge is claimed and, so far as possible, shall define the land affected, and such particulars shall be entered or referred to in the register.

(7) In the case of a land charge for securing money created by a company before 1st January 1970 or so created at any time as a floating charge, registration under any of the enactments mentioned in subsection (8) below shall be sufficient in place of registration under this Act, and shall have effect as if the land charge had been registered under this Act.

(8) The enactments referred to in subsection (7) above are section 93 of the Companies (Consolidation) Act 1908, section 79 of the Companies Act 1929 and section 95 of the Companies Act 1948.

Effect of land charges and protection of purchasers

4.—(1) A land charge of Class A (other than a land improvement charge registered after 31st December 1969) or of Class B shall, when registered, take effect as if it had been created by a deed of charge by way of legal mortgage, but without prejudice to the priority of the charge.

(2) A land charge of Class A created after 31st December 1888 shall be void as against a purchaser of the land charged with it or of any interest in such land, unless the land charge is registered in the register of land charges before the completion of the purchase.

(3) After the expiration of one year from the first conveyance occuring on or after 1st January 1889 of a land charge of Class A created before that date the person entitled to the land charge shall not be able to recover the land charge or any part of it as against a purchaser of the land charged with it or of any interest in the land, unless the land charge is registered in the register of land charges before the completion of the purchase.

(4) If a land improvement charge was registered as a land charge of Class A before 1st January 1970, any body corporate which, but for the charge, would have power to advance money on the security of the estate or interest affected by it shall have that power notwithstanding the charge.

(5) A land charge of Class B and a land charge of Class C (other than an estate contract) created or arising on or after 1st January 1926 shall be void as against a purchaser of the land charged with it, or of any interest in such land, unless the land charge is registered in the appropriate register before the completion of the purchase.

(6) An estate contract and a land charge of Class D created or entered into on or after 1st January 1926 shall be void as against a purchaser for money or money's worth [(or, in the case of an Inland Revenue charge, a purchaser within the meaning of Part III of the Finance Act 1975)]¹⁰ of a

⁹ Substituted by the Finance Act 1975 (c. 7), Sched. 12.
¹⁰ Words in square brackets added by the Finance Act 1975 (c. 7), Sched. 12.

legal estate in the land charged with it, unless the land charge is registered in the appropriate register before the completion of the purchase.

(7) After the expiration of one year from the first conveyance occurring on or after 1st January 1926 of a land charge of Class B or Class C created before that date the person entitled to the land charge shall not be able to enforce or recover the land charge or any part of it as against a purchaser of the land charged with it, or of any interest in the land, unless the land charge is registered in the appropriate register before the completion of the purchase.

(8) A land charge of Class F shall be void as against a purchaser of the land charged with it, or of any interest in such land, unless the land charge is registered in the appropriate register before the completion of the purchase.

Registration in registers of pending actions, writs and orders and deeds of arrangement

The register of pending actions

5.—(1) There may be registered in the register of pending actions—
    (*a*) a pending land action;
    (*b*) a petition in bankruptcy filed on or after 1st January 1926.

(2) Subject to general rules under section 16 of this Act, every application for registration under this section shall contain particulars of the title of the proceedings and the name, address and description of the estate owner or other person whose estate or interest is intended to be affected.

(3) An application for registration shall also state—
    (*a*) if it relates to a pending land action, the court in which and the day on which the action was commenced; and
    (*b*) if it relates to a petition in bankruptcy, the court in which and the day on which the petition was filed.

(4) The registrar shall forthwith enter the particulars in the register, in the name of the estate owner or other person whose estate or interest is intended to be affected.

(5) An application to register a petition in bankruptcy against a firm shall state the names and addresses of the partners, and the registration shall be effected against each partner as well as against the firm.

(6) No fee shall be charged for the registration of a petition in bankruptcy if the application for registration is made by the registrar of the court in which the petition is filed.

(7) A pending land action shall not bind a purchaser without express notice of it unless it is for the time being registered under this section.

(8) A petition in bankruptcy shall not bind a purchaser of a legal estate in good faith, for money or money's worth, without notice of an available act of bankruptcy, unless it is for the time being registered under this section.

(9) As respects any transfer or creation of a legal estate, a petition in bankruptcy which is not for the time being registered under this section shall not be notice or evidence of any act of bankruptcy alleged in the petition.

(10) The court, if it thinks fit, may, upon the determination of the proceedings, or during the pendency of the proceedings if satisfied that they are not prosecuted in good faith, make an order vacating a registration under this section, and direct the party on whose behalf it was made to pay all or any of the costs and expenses occasioned by the registration and by its vacation.

The register of writs and orders affecting land

6.—(1) There may be registered in the register of writs and orders affecting land—

(*a*) any writ or order affecting land issued or made by any court for the purpose of enforcing a judgment or recognisance;

(*b*) any order appointing a receiver or sequestrator of land;

(*c*) any receiving order in bankruptcy made on or after 1st January 1926, whether or not it is known to affect land.

(2) Every entry made pursuant to this section shall be made in the name of the estate owner or other person whose land, if any, is affected by the writ or order registered.

(3) No fee shall be charged for the registration of a receiving order in bankruptcy if the application for registration is made by an official receiver.

(4) Except as provided by subsection (5) below and by [section 37(5) of the Supreme Court Act 1981][11] and section 142 (3) of the County Courts Act 1959 (which makes special provision as to receiving orders in respect of land of judgment debtors) every such writ and order as is mentioned in subsection (1) above, and every delivery in execution or other proceeding taken pursuant to any such writ or order, or in obedience to any such writ or order, shall be void as against a purchaser of the land unless the writ or order is for the time being registered under this section.

(5) A receiving order in bankruptcy shall be void as against a purchaser of a legal estate in good faith for money or money's worth, without notice of an available act of bankruptcy, unless it is for the time being registered under this section.

(6) Where a petition in bankruptcy has been registered under section 5 above, the title of the trustee in bankruptcy shall be void as against a purchaser of a legal estate in good faith for money or money's worth without notice of an available act of bankruptcy claiming under a conveyance made after the date of registration, unless at the date of the conveyance either the registration of the petition is in force or a receiving order on the petition is registered under this section.

The register of deeds of arrangement affecting land

7.—(1) A deed of arrangement affecting land may be registered in the register of deeds of arrangement affecting land, in the name of the debtor, on the application of a trustee of the deed or a creditor assenting to or taking the benefit of the deed.

(2) Every deed of arrangement shall be void as against a purchaser of any land comprised in it or affected by it unless it is for the time being registered under this section.

Expiry and renewal of registrations

8. A registration under section 5, section 6 or section 7 of this Act shall cease to have effect at the end of the period of five years from the date on which it is made, but may be renewed from time to time and, if so renewed, shall have effect for five years from the date of renewal.

Searches and official searches

Searches

9.—(1) Any person may search in any register kept under this Act on paying the prescribed fee.

[11] Substituted by the Supreme Court Act 1981 (c. 48), Sched. 5.

(2) Without prejudice to subsection (1) above, the registrar may provide facilities for enabling persons entitled to search in any such register to see photographic or other images or copies of any portion of the register which they may wish to examine.

Official searches

10.—(1) Where any person requires search to be made at the registry for entries of any matters or documents, entries of which are required or allowed to be made in the registry by this Act, he may make a requisition in that behalf to the registrar, which may be either—

    (*a*) a written requisition delivered at or sent by post to the registry; or

    (*b*) a requisition communicated by teleprinter, telephone or other means in such manner as may be prescribed in relation to the means in question, in which case it shall be treated as made to the registrar if, but only if, he accepts it;

and the registrar shall not accept a requisition made in accordance with paragraph (*b*) above unless it is made by a person maintaining a credit account at the registry, and may at his discretion refuse to accept it notwithstanding that it is made by such a person.

(2) The prescribed fee shall be payable in respect of every requisition made under this section; and that fee—

    (*a*) in the case of a requisition made in accordance with subsection (1) (*a*) above, shall be paid in such manner as may be prescribed for the purposes of this paragraph unless the requisition is made by a person maintaining a credit account at the registry and the fee is debited to that account;

    (*b*) in the case of a requisition made in accordance with subsection (1) (*b*) above, shall be debited to the credit account of the person by whom the requisition is made.

(3) Where a requisition is made under subsection (1) above and the fee payable in respect of it is paid or debited in accordance with subsection (2) above, the registrar shall thereupon make the search required and—

    (*a*) shall issue a certificate setting out the result of the search; and

    (*b*) without prejudice to paragraph (*a*) above, may take such other steps as he considers appropriate to communicate that result to the person by whom the requisition was made.

(4) In favour of a purchaser or an intending purchaser, as against persons interested under or in respect of matters or documents entries of which are required or allowed as aforesaid, the certificate, according to its tenor, shall be conclusive, affirmatively or negatively, as the case may be.

(5) If any officer, clerk or person employed in the registry commits, or is party or privy to, any act of fraud or collusion, or is wilfully negligent, in the making of or otherwise in relation to any certificate under this section, he shall be guilty of an offence and shall be liable on conviction on indictment to imprisonment for a term not exceeding two years, or on summary conviction to imprisonment for a term not exceeding three months or to a fine not exceeding £20, or to both such imprisonment and fine.

(6) Without prejudice to subsection (5) above, no officer, clerk or person employed in the registry shall, in the absence of fraud on his part, be liable for any loss which may be suffered—

    (*a*) by reason of any discrepancy between—

        (i) the particulars which are shown in a certificate under this section as being the particulars in respect of which the search for entries was made, and

        (ii) the particulars in respect of which a search for entries was required by the person who made the requisition; or (*b*) by reason of any communication of the result of a search under this section made otherwise than by issuing a certificate under this section.

Miscellaneous and supplementary

Date of effective registration and priority notices

11.—(1) Any person intending to make an application for the registration of any contemplated charge, instrument or other matter in pursuance of this Act or any rule made under this Act may give a priority notice in the prescribed form at least the relevant number of days before the registration is to take effect.

(2) Where a notice is given under subsection (1) above, it shall be entered in the register to which the intended application when made will relate.

(3) If the application is presented within the relevant number of days thereafter and refers in the prescribed manner to the notice, the registration shall take effect as if the registration had been made at the time when the charge, instrument or matter was created, entered into, made or arose, and the date at which the registration so takes effect shall be deemed to be the date of registration.

(4) Where—

    (*a*) any two charges, instruments or matters are contemporaneous; and

    (*b*) one of them (whether or not protected by a priority notice) is subject to or dependent on the other; and

    (*c*) the latter is protected by a priority notice,

the subsequent or dependent charge, instrument or matter shall be deemed to have been created, entered into or made, or to have arisen, after the registration of the other.

(5) Where a purchaser has obtained a certificate under section 10 above, any entry which is made in the register after the date of the certificate and before the completion of the purchase, and is not made pursuant to a priority notice entered on the register on or before the date of the certificate, shall not affect the purchaser if the purchase is completed before the expiration of the relevant number of days after the date of the certificate.

(6) The relevant number of days is—

    (*a*) for the purposes of subsections (1) and (5) above, fifteen;

    (*b*) for the purposes of subsection (3) above, thirty.

or such other number as may be prescribed; but in reckoning the relevant number of days for any of the purposes of this section any days when the registry is not open to the public shall be excluded.

Protection of solicitors, trustees, etc.

12. A solicitor, or a trustee, personal representative, agent or other person in a fiduciary position, shall not be answerable—

    (*a*) in respect of any loss occasioned by reliance on an office copy of an entry in any register kept under this Act;

    (*b*) for any loss that may arise from error in a certificate under section 10 above obtained by him.

Saving for overreaching powers

13.—(1) The registration of any charge, annuity or other interest under this Act shall not prevent the charge, annuity or interest being overreached under any other Act, except where otherwise provided by that other Act.

(2) The registration as a land charge of a puisne mortgage or charge shall not operate to prevent that mortgage or charge being overreached in favour of a prior mortgagee or a person deriving title under him where, by reason of a sale or foreclosure, or otherwise, the right of the puisne mortgagee or subsequent chargee to redeem is barred.

Exclusion of matters affecting registered land or created by instruments necessitating registration of land

14.—(1) This Act shall not apply to instruments or matters required to be registered or re-registered on or after 1st January 1926, if and so far as they affect registered land, and can be protected under the Land Registration Act 1925 by lodging or registering a creditor's notice, restriction, caution, inhibition or other notice.

(2) Nothing in this Act imposes on the registrar any obligation to ascertain whether or not an instrument or matter affects registered land.

(3) Where an instrument executed on or after 27th July 1971 conveys, grants or assigns an estate in land and creates a land charge affecting that estate, this Act shall not apply to the land charge, so far as it affects that estate, if under section 123 of the Land Registration Act 1925 (effect of that Act in areas where registration is compulsory) the instrument will, unless the necessary application for registration under that Act is made within the time allowed by or under that section, become void so far as respects the conveyance, grant or assignment of that estate.

. . . . . .

Interpretation

17.—(1) In this Act, unless the context otherwise requires,—

"annuity" means a rentcharge or an annuity for a life or lives or for any term of years or greater estate determinable on a life or on lives and created after 25th April 1855 and before 1st January 1926, but does not include an annuity created by a marriage settlement or will;

"the Board" means the Commissioners of Inland Revenue;

"conveyance" includes a mortgage, charge, lease, assent, vesting declaration, vesting instrument, release and every other assurance of property, or of an interest in property, by any instrument except a will, and "convey" has a corresponding meaning;

"court" means the High Court, or the county court in a case where that court has jurisdiction;

"deed of arrangement" has the same meaning as in the Deeds of Arrangement Act 1914;

"estate owner," "legal estate," "equitable interest," "trust for sale," "charge by way of legal mortgage," [and "will"][12] have the same meanings as in the Law of Property Act 1925;

"judgment" includes any order or decree having the effect of a judgment;

"land" includes land of any tenure and mines and minerals, whether or not severed from the surface, buildings or parts of buildings (whether the division is horizontal, vertical or made in any other way) and other corporeal hereditaments, also a manor, an advowson and a rent and other incorporeal hereditaments, and an easement, right, privilege or benefit in, over or derived from land, but not an undivided share in land, and "heredita-

---

[12] Substituted by the Finance Act 1975 (c. 7), Sched. 12.

ment" means real property which, on an intestacy occurring before 1st January 1926, might have devolved on an heir;

"land improvement charge" means any charge under the Improvement of Land Act 1864 or under any special improvement Act within the meaning of the Improvement of Land Act 1899;

"pending land action" means any action or proceeding pending in court relating to land or any interest in or charge on land;

"prescribed" means prescribed by rules made pursuant to this Act;

"purchaser" means any person (including a mortgagee or lessee) who, for valuable consideration, takes any interest in land or in a charge on land, and "purchase" has a corresponding meaning;

"registrar" means the Chief Land Registrar, "registry" means Her Majesty's Land Registry, and "registered land" has the same meaning as in the Land Registration Act 1925;

"tenant for life," "statutory owner," "vesting instrument" and "settlement" have the same meanings as in the Settled Land Act 1925.

(2) For the purposes of any provision in this Act requiring or authorising anything to be done at or delivered or sent to the registry, any reference to the registry shall, if the registrar so directs, be read as a reference to such office of the registry (whether in London or elsewhere) as may be specified in the direction.

(3) Any reference in this Act to any enactment is a reference to it as amended by or under any other enactment, including this Act.

.   .   .   .   .   .

Short title, commencement and extent

19.—(1) This Act may be cited as the Land Charges Act 1972.

(2) This Act shall come into force on such day as the Lord Chancellor may by order made by statutory instrument appoint; and different days may be so appointed for different purposes.

(3) This Act extends to England and Wales only.

SCHEDULES

Section 1

FIRST SCHEDULE

ANNUITIES

1. No further entries shall be made in the register of annuities.

2. An entry of an annuity made in the register of annuities before 1st January 1926 may be vacated in the prescribed manner on the prescribed evidence as to satisfaction, cesser or discharge being furnished.

3. The register shall be closed when all the entries in it have been vacated or the prescribed evidence of the satisfaction, cesser or discharge of all the annuities has been furnished.

4. An annuity which before 1st January 1926 was capable of being registered in the register of annuities shall be void as against a creditor or a purchaser of any interest in the land charged with the annuity unless the annuity is for the time being registered in the register of annuities or in the register of land charges.

Section 2

SECOND SCHEDULE

CLASS A LAND CHARGES

1. Charges created pursuant to applications under the enactments mentioned in this Schedule may be registered as land charges of Class A by virtue of paragraph (*b*)) of section 2(2) of this Act:—

Section 2   SECOND SCHEDULE

(*a*) The Tithe Act 1918   Sections 4(2) and 6(1) (charge of consideration money
    (8 & 9 Geo. 5. c. 54)   for redemption of tithe rentcharge).

(*b*) The Tithe Annuities   Section 1 (charge of apportioned part of tithe redemption
    Apportionment Act 1921   annuity).
    (11 & 12 Geo. 5. c. 20)

(*c*) The Landlord and Tenant   Paragraph (7) of Schedule 1 (charge in respect of
    Act 1927   improvements to business premises).
    (17 & 18 Geo. 5. c. 36)

(*d*) The Land Drainage Act   Section [26(6)][15] (charge in respect of sum paid in
    [1970][13]   commutation of certain obligations to repair banks,
    [(c. 70)][14]   water-courses etc.).

(*e*) The Tithe Act 1936   Section 30(1) (charge for redemption of corn rents etc.).
    (26 Geo. 5 & 1 Edw. 8.
    c. 43)

(*f*) The Civil Defence Act   Sections 18(4) and 19(1) (charges in respect of civil
    1939   defence works).
    (2 & 3 Geo. 6. c. 31)

(*g*) The Agricultural Holdings   Sections 72, 73 and 74 (charges in respect of sums due to
    Act 1948   tenant or occupier of agricultural holding).
    (11 & 12 Geo. 6. c. 63)   Section 82 (charge in favour of landlord of agricultural
       holding in respect of compensation for or cost of
       certain improvements).

(*h*) The Corn Rents Act 1963   Section 1(5) (charge under a scheme for the apportion-
    (1963 c. 14)   ment or redemption of corn rents or other payments in
       lieu of tithes).

2. The following provisions of paragraph 1 above shall cease to have effect upon the coming into operation of the first scheme under the Corn Rents Act 1963, that is to say:—
(*a*) in sub-paragraph (*a*), the words "and 6 (1)"; and
(*b*) sub-paragraph (*e*).
The references in paragraph 1 (*g*) above to sections 72, 73, 74 and 82 of the Agricultural Holdings Act 1948 include references to any previous similar enactment.

---

[13] Substituted by the Land Drainage Act 1976 (c. 70), Sched.7.
[14] *Ibid.*
[15] *Ibid.*

Administration of Justice Act 1973

(1973 c. 15)

An Act to amend the law relating to justices of the peace and to make further provision with respect to the administration of justice and matters connected therewith. [18th April 1973]

. . . . . .

Extension of powers of court in action by mortgagee of dwelling-house

8.—(1) Where by a mortgage of land which consists of or includes a dwelling-house, or by any agreement between the mortgagee under such a mortgage and the mortgagor, the mortgagor is entitled or is to be permitted to pay the principal sum secured by instalments or otherwise to defer payment of it in whole or in part, but provision is also made for earlier payment in the event of any default by the mortgagor or of a demand by the mortgagee or otherwise, then for purposes of section 36 of the Administration of Justices Act 1970 (under which a court has power to delay giving a mortgagee possession of the mortgaged property so as to allow the mortgagor a reasonable time to pay any sums due under the mortgage) a court may treat as due under the mortgage on account of the principal sum secured and of interest on it only such amounts as the mortgagor would have expected to be required to pay if there had been no such provision for earlier payment.

(2) A court shall not exercise by virtue of subsection (1) above the powers conferred by section 36 of the Administration of Justice Act 1970 unless it appears to the court not only that the mortgagor is likely to be able within a reasonable period to pay any amounts regarded (in accordance with subsection (1) above) as due on account of the principal sum secured, together with the interest on those amounts, but also that he is likely to be able by the end of that period to pay any further amounts that he would have expected to be required to pay by then on account of that sum and of interest on it if there had been no such provision as is referred to in subsection (1) above for earlier payment.

(3) Where subsection (1) above would apply to an action in which a mortgagee only claimed possession of the mortgaged property, and the mortgagee brings an action for foreclosure (with or without also claiming possession of the property), then section 36 of the Administration of Justice Act 1970 together with subsections (1) and (2) above shall apply as they would apply if it were an action in which the mortgagee only claimed possession of the mortgaged property, except that—

(a) section 36 (2) (b)) shall apply only in relation to any claim for possession; and

(b) section 36 (5) shall not apply.

(4) For purposes of this section the expressions "dwelling-house," "mortgage," "mortgagee" and "mortgagor" shall be construed in the same way as for the purposes of Part IV of the Administration of Justice Act 1970.

(5) This section shall have effect in relation to an action begun before the date on which this section comes into force if before that date judgment has not been given, nor an order made, in that action for delivery of possession of the mortgaged property and, where it is a question of subsection (3) above, an order *nisi* for foreclosure has not been made in that action.

(6) In the application of this section to Northern Ireland, subsection (3) shall be omitted.

. . . . . .

Matrimonial Causes Act 1973

(1973 c. 18)

An Act to consolidate certain enactments relating to matrimonial proceedings, maintenance agreements, and declarations of legitimacy, validity of marriage and British nationality, with amendments to give effect to recommendations of the Law Commission.   [23rd May 1973]

. . . . . .

Effects of judicial separation

18.—(2) If while a decree of judicial separation is in force and the separation is continuing either of the parties to the marriage dies intestate as respects all or any of his or her real or personal property, the property as respects which he or she died intestate shall devolve as if the other party to the marriage had then been dead.

(3) Notwithstanding anything in section 2 (1) (*a*) of the Matrimonial Proceedings (Magistrates' Courts) Act 1960, a provision in force under an order made, or having effect as if made, under that section exempting one party to a marriage from the obligation to cohabit with the other shall not have effect as a decree of judicial separation for the purposes of subsection (2) above.

. . . . . .

Limitation Act 1980

(1980 c. 58)

An Act to consolidate the Limitation Acts 1939 to 1980.

[13th November 1980]

. . . . . .

Actions to recover land and rent

Time limit for actions to recover land

15.—(1) No action shall be brought by any person to recover any land after the expiration of twelve years from the date on which the right of action accrued to him or, if it first accrued to some person through whom he claims, to that person.

(2) Subject to the following provisions of this section, where—

(*a*) the estate or interest claimed was an estate or interest in reversion or remainder or any other future estate or interest and the right of action to recover the land accrued on the date on which the estate or interest fell into possession by the determination of the preceding estate or interest; and

(*b*) the person entitled to the preceding estate or interest (not being a term of years absolute) was not in possession of the land on that date;

no action shall be brought by the person entitled to the succeeding estate or interest after the expiration of twelve years from the date on which the right of action accrued to the person entitled to the preceding estate or interest or six years from the date on which the right of action accrued to the person entitled to the succeeding estate or interest, whichever period last expires.

(3) Subsection (2) above shall not apply to any estate or interest which falls into possession on the determination of an entailed interest and which might have been barred by the person entitled to the entailed interest.

(4) No person shall bring an action to recover any estate or interest in land under an assurance taking effect after the right of action to recover the land had accrued to the person by whom the assurance was made or some person through whom he claimed or some person entitled to a preceding estate or interest, unless the action is brought within the period in which the person by whom the assurance was made could have brought such an action.

(5) Where any person is entitled to any estate or interest in land in possession and, while so entitled, is also entitled to any future estate or interest in that land, and his right to recover the estate or interest in possession is barred under this Act, no action shall be brought by that person, or by any person claiming through him, in respect of the future estate or interest, unless in the meantime possession of the land has been recovered by a person entitled to an intermediate estate or interest.

(6) Part I of Schedule 1 to this Act contains provisions for determining the date of accrual of rights of action to recover land in the cases there mentioned.

(7) Part II of that Schedule contains provisions modifying the provisions of this section in their application to actions brought by, or by a person claiming through, the Crown or any spiritual or eleemosynary corporation sole.

Time limit for redemption actions

16.—When a mortgagee of land has been in possession of any of the mortgaged land for a period of twelve years, no action to redeem the land of which the mortgagee has been so in possession shall be brought after the end of that period by the mortgagor or any person claiming through him.

Extinction of title to land after expiration of time limit

17.—Subject to—
(*a*) section 18 of this Act; and
(*b*) section 75 of the Land Registration Act 1925;
at the expiration of the period prescribed by this Act for any person to bring an action to recover land (including a redemption action) the title of that person to the land shall be extinguished.

Settled land and land held on trust

18.—(1) Subject to section 21 (1) and (2) of this Act, the provisions of this Act shall apply to equitable interests in land, including interests in the proceeds of the sale of land held upon trust for sale, as they apply to legal estates.

Accordingly a right of action to recover the land shall, for the purposes of this Act but not otherwise, be treated as accruing to a person entitled in possession to such an equitable interest in the like manner and circumstances, and on the same date, as it would accrue if his interest were a legal estate in the land (and any relevant provision of Part I of Schedule 1 to this Act shall apply in any such case accordingly).

(2) Where the period prescribed by this Act has expired for the bringing of an action to recover land by a tenant for life or a statutory owner of settled land—

(*a*) his legal estate shall not be extinguished if and so long as the right of action to recover the land of any person entitled to a beneficial interest in the land either has not accrued or has not been barred by this Act; and

(*b*) the legal estate shall accordingly remain vested in the tenant for life or statutory owner and shall devolve in accordance with the Settled Land Act 1925;

but if and when every such right of action has been barred by this Act, his legal estate shall be extinguished.

(3) Where any land is held upon trust (including a trust for sale) and the period prescribed by this Act has expired for the bringing of an action to recover the land by the trustees, the estate of the trustees shall not be extinguished if and so long as the right of action to recover the land of any person entitled to a beneficial interest in the land or in the proceeds of sale either has not accrued or has not been barred by this Act; but if and when every such right of action has been so barred the estate of the trustees shall be extinguished.

(4) Where—

(*a*) any settled land is vested in a statutory owner; or

(*b*) any land is held upon trust (including a trust for sale);

an action to recover the land may be brought by the statutory owner or trustees on behalf of any person entitled to a beneficial interest in possession in the land or in the proceeds of sale whose right of action has not been barred by this Act, notwithstanding that the right of action of the statutory owner or trustees would apart from this provision have been barred by this Act.

Time limit for actions to recover rent

19.—No action shall be brought, or distress made, to recover arrears of rent, or damages in respect of arrears of rent, after the expiration of six years from the date on which the arrears became due.

*Actions to recover money secured by a mortgage or charge or to recover
proceeds of the sale of land*

Time limit for actions to recover money secured by a mortgage or charge or to recover proceeds of the sale of land

20.—(1) No action shall be brought to recover—

(*a*) any principal sum of money secured by a mortgage or other
charge on property (whether real or personal); or

(*b*) proceeds of the sale of land;

after the expiration of twelve years from the date on which the right to
receive the money accrued.

(2) No foreclosure action in respect of mortgaged personal property shall
be brought after the expiration of twelve years from the date on which the
right to foreclose accrued.

But if the mortgagee was in possession of the mortgaged property after
that date, the right to foreclose on the property which was in his possession
shall not be treated as having accrued for the purposes of this subsection
until the date on which his possession discontinued.

(3) The right to receive any principal sum of money secured by a
mortgage or other charge and the right to foreclose on the property subject
to the mortgage or charge shall not be treated as accruing so long as that
property comprises any future interest or any life insurance policy which
has not matured or been determined.

(4) Nothing in this section shall apply to a foreclosure action in respect of
mortgaged land, but the provisions of this Act relating to actions to recover
land shall apply to such an action.

(5) Subject to subsections (6) and (7) below, no action to recover arrears
of interest payable in respect of any sum of money secured by a mortgage
or other charge or payable in respect of proceeds of the sale of land, or to
recover damages in respect of such arrears shall be brought after the
expiration of six years from the date on which the interest became due.

(6) Where—

(*a*) a prior mortgagee or other incumbrancer has been in possession of the property charged; and

(*b*) an action is brought within one year of the discontinuance of
that possession by the subsequent incumbrancer;

the subsequent incumbrancer may recover by that action all the arrears of
interest which fell due during the period of possession by the prior
incumbrancer or damages in respect of those arrears, notwithstanding that
the period exceeded six years.

(7) Where—

(*a*) the property subject to the mortgage or charge comprises any
future interest or life insurance policy; and

(*b*) it is a term of the mortgage or charge that arrears of interest
shall be treated as part of the principal sum of money secured
by the mortgage or charge;

interest shall not be treated as becoming due before the right to recover the
principal sum of money has accrued or is treated as having accrued.

Actions in respect of trust property or the personal estate of deceased persons

Time limits for actions in respect of trust property

21.—(1) No period of limitation prescribed by this Act shall apply to an
action by a beneficiary under a trust, being an action—

(*a*) in respect of any fraud or fraudulent breach of trust to which the
trustee was a party or privy; or

(*b*) to recover from the trustee trust property or the proceeds of trust property in the possession of the trustee, or previously received by the trustee and converted to his use.

(2) Where a trustee who is also a beneficiary under the trust receives or retains trust property or its proceeds as his share on a distribution of trust property under the trust, his liability in any action brought by virtue of subsection (1) (*b*)) above to recover that property or its proceeds after the expiration of the period of limitation prescribed by this Act for bringing an action to recover trust property shall be limited to the excess over his proper share.

This subsection only applies if the trustee acted honestly and reasonably in making the distribution.

(3) Subject to the preceding provisions of this section, an action by a beneficiary to recover trust property or in respect of any breach of trust, not being an action for which a period of limitation is prescribed by any other provision of this Act, shall not be brought after the expiration of six years from the date on which the right of action accrued.

For the purposes of this subsection, the right of action shall not be treated as having accrued to any beneficiary entitled to a future interest in the trust property until the interest fell into possession.

(4) No beneficiary as against whom there would be a good defence under this Act shall derive any greater or other benefit from a judgment or order obtained by any other beneficiary than he could have obtained if he had brought the action and this Act had been pleaded in defence.

Time limit for actions claiming personal estate of a deceased person

22.—Subject to section 21 (1) and (2) of this Act—

    (*a*) no action in respect of any claim to the personal estate of a deceased person or to any share or interest in any such estate (whether under a will or on intestacy) shall be brought after the expiration of twelve years from the date on which the right to receive the share or interest accrued; and

    (*b*) no action to recover arrears of interest in respect of any legacy, or damages in respect of such arrears, shall be brought after the expiration of six years from the date on which the interest became due.

. . . . . .

Administration to date back to death

26.—For the purposes of the provisions of this Act relating to actions for the recovery of land and advowsons an administrator of the estate of a deceased person shall be treated as claiming as if there had been no interval of time between the death of the deceased person and the grant of the letters of administration.

Cure of defective disentailing assurance

27.—(1) This section applies where—

    (*a*) a person entitled in remainder to an entailed interest in any land makes an assurance of his interest which fails to bar the issue in tail or the estates and interests taking effect on the determination of the entailed interest, or fails to bar those estates and interests only; and

    (*b*) any person takes possession of the land by virtue of the assurance.

(2) If the person taking possession of the land by virtue of the assurance, or any other person whatsoever (other than a person entitled to possession

by virtue of the settlement) is in possession of the land for a period of twelve years from the commencement of the time when the assurance could have operated as an effective bar, the assurance shall thereupon operate, and be treated as having always operated, to bar the issue in tail and the estates and interests taking effect on the determination of the entailed interest.

(3) The reference in subsection (2) above to the time when the assurance could have operated as an effective bar is a reference to the time at which the assurance, if it had then been executed by the person entitled to the entailed interest, would have operated, without the consent of any other person, to bar the issue in tail and the estates and interests taking effect on the determination of the entailed interest.

Part II

Extension or Exclusion of Ordinary Time Limits

Disability

Extension of limitation period in case of disability

28.—(1) Subject to the following provisions of this section, if on the date when any right of action accrued for which a period of limitation is prescribed by this Act, the person to whom it accrued was under a disability, the action may be brought at any time before the expiration of six years from the date when he ceased to be under a disability or died (whichever first occurred) notwithstanding that the period of limitation has expired.

(2) This section shall not affect any case where the right of action first accrued to some person (not under a disability) through whom the person under a disability claims.

(3) When a right of action which has accrued to a person under a disability accrues, on the death of that person while still under a disability, to another person under a disability, no further extension of time shall be allowed by reason of the disability of the second person.

(4) No action to recover land or money charged on land shall be brought by virtue of this section by any person after the expiration of thirty years from the date on which the right of action accrued to that person or some person through whom he claims.

(5) If the action is one to which section 10 of this Act applies, subsection (1) above shall have effect as if for the words "six years" there were substituted the words "two years."

(6) If the action is one to which section 11 or 12 (2) of this Act applies, subsection (1) above shall have effect as if for the words "six years" there were substituted the words "three years."

Acknowledgment and part payment

Fresh accrual of action on acknowledgment or part payment

29.—(1) Subsections (2) and (3) below apply where any right of action (including a foreclosure action) to recover land or an advowson or any right of action (including a foreclosure action) to recover land or an advowson or any right of a mortgagee of personal property to bring a foreclosure action in respect of the property has accrued.

(2) If the person in possession of the land, benefice or personal property

in question acknowledges the title of the person to whom the right of action has accrued—

    (*a*) the right shall be treated as having accrued on and not before the date of the acknowledgment; and

    (*b*) in the case of a right of action to recover land which has accrued to a person entitled to an estate or interest taking effect on the determination of an entailed interest against whom time is running under section 27 of this Act, section 27 shall thereupon cease to apply to the land.

(3) In the case of a foreclosure or other action by a mortgagee, if the person in possession of the land, benefice or personal property in question or the person liable for the mortgage debt makes any payment in respect of the debt (whether of principal or interest) the right shall be treated as having accrued on and not before the date of the payment.

(4) Where a mortgagee is by virtue of the mortgage in possession of any mortgaged land and either—

    (*a*) receives any sum in respect of the principal or interest of the mortgage debt; or

    (*b*) acknowledges the title of the mortgagor, or his equity of redemption;

an action to redeem the land in his possession may be brought at any time before the expiration of twelve years from the date of the payment or acknowledgment.

(5) Subject to subsection (6) below, where any right of action has accrued to recover—

    (*a*) any debt or other liquidated pecuniary claim; or

    (*b*) any claim to the personal estate of a deceased person or to any share or interest in any such estate;

and the person liable or accountable for the claim acknowledges the claim or makes any payment in respect of it the right shall be treated as having accrued on and not before the date of the acknowledgment or payment.

(6) A payment of a part of the rent or interest due at any time shall not extend the period for claiming the remainder then due, but any payment of interest shall be treated as a payment in respect of the principal debt.

(7) Subject to subsection (6) above, a current period of limitation may be repeatedly extended under this section by further acknowledgments or payments, but a right of action, once barred by this Act, shall not be revived by any subsequent acknowledgment or payment.

Formal provisions as to acknowledgments and part payments

30.—(1) To be effective for the purposes of section 29 of this Act, an acknowledgment must be in writing and signed by the person making it.

(2) For the purposes of section 29, any acknowledgment or payment—

    (*a*) may be made by the agent of the person by whom it is required to be made under that section; and

    (*b*) shall be made to the person, or to an agent of the person, whose title or claim is being acknowledged or, as the case may be, in respect of whose claim the payment is being made.

Effect of acknowledgment or part payment on persons other than the maker or recipient

31.—(1) An acknowledgment of the title to any land, benefice, or mortgaged personalty by any person in possession of it shall bind all other persons in possession during the ensuing period of limitation.

(2) A payment in respect of a mortgage debt by the mortgagor or any other person liable for the debt, or by any person in possession of the mortgaged property, shall, so far as any right of the mortgagee to foreclose

or otherwise to recover the property is concerned, bind all other persons in possession of the mortgaged property during the ensuing period of limitation.

(3) Where two or more mortgagees are by virtue of the mortgage in possession of the mortgaged land, an acknowledgment of the mortgagor's title or of his equity of redemption by one of the mortgagees shall only bind him and his successors and shall not bind any other mortgagee or his successors.

(4) Where in a case within subsection (3) above the mortgagee by whom the acknowledgment is given is entitled to a part of the mortgaged land and not to any ascertained part of the mortgage debt the mortgagor shall be entitled to redeem that part of the land on payment, with interest, of the part of the mortgage debt which bears the same proportion to the whole of the debt as the value of the part of the land bears to the whole of the mortgaged land.

(5) Where there are two or more mortgagors, and the title or equity of redemption of one of the mortgagors is acknowledged as mentioned above in this section, the acknowledgment shall be treated as having been made to all the mortgagors.

(6) An acknowledgment of any debt or other liquidated pecuniary claim shall bind the acknowledgor and his successors but not any other person.

(7) A payment made in respect of any debt or other liquidated pecuniary claim shall bind all persons liable in respect of the debt or claim.

(8) An acknowledgment by one of several personal representatives of any claim to the personal estate of a deceased person or to any share or interest in any such estate, or a payment by one of several representatives in respect of any such claim shall bind the estate of the deceased person.

(9) In this section "successor," in relation to any mortgagee or person liable in respect of any debt or claim, means his personal representatives and any other person on whom the rights under the mortgage or, as the case may be, the liability in respect of the debt or claim devolve (whether on death or bankruptcy or the disposition of property or the determination of a limited estate or interest in settled property or otherwise).

Fraud, concealment and mistake

Postponement of limitation period in case of fraud, concealment or mistake

32.—(1) Subject to subsection (3) below, where in the case of any action for which a period of limitation is prescribed by this Act, either—

    (*a*) the action is based upon the fraud of the defendant; or

    (*b*) any fact relevant to the plaintiff's right of action has been deliberately concealed from him by the defendant; or

    (*c*) the action is for relief from the consequences of a mistake;

the period of limitation shall not begin to run until the plaintiff has discovered the fraud, concealment or mistake (as the case may be) or could with reasonable diligence have discovered it.

References in this subsection to the defendant include references to the defendant's agent and to any person through whom the defendant claims and his agent.

(2) For the purposes of subsection (1) above, deliberate commission of a breach of duty in circumstances in which it is unlikely to be discovered for some time amounts to deliberate concealment of the facts involved in that breach of duty.

(3) Nothing in this section shall enable any action—

    (*a*) to recover, or recover the value of, any property; or

    (*b*) to enforce any charge against, or set aside any transaction affecting, any property;

to be brought against the purchaser of the property or any person claiming through him in any case where the property has been purchased for valuable consideration by an innocent third party since the fraud or concealment or (as the case may be) the transaction in which the mistake was made took place.

(4) A purchaser is an innocent third party for the purposes of this section—

(a) in the case of fraud or concealment of any fact relevant to the plaintiff's right of action, if he was not a party to the fraud or (as the case may be) to the concealment of that fact and did not at the time of the purchase know or have reason to believe that the fraud or concealment had taken place; and

(b) in the case of mistake, if he did not at the time of the purchase know or have reason to believe that the mistake had been made.

. . . . . .

Interpretation

38.—(1) In this Act, unless the context otherwise requires—

"action" includes any proceedings in a court of law, including an ecclesiastical court;

"land" includes corporeal hereditaments, tithes and rentcharges and any legal or equitable estate or interest therein, including an interest in the proceeds of the sale of land held upon trust for sale, but except as provided above in this definition does not include any incorporeal hereditament;

"personal estate" and "personal property" do not include chattels real;

"personal injuries" includes any disease and any impairment of a person's physical or mental condition, and "injury" and cognate expressions shall be construed accordingly;

"rent" includes a rentcharge and a rentservice;

"rentcharge" means any annuity or periodical sum of money charged upon or payable out of land, except a rent service or interest on a mortgage on land;

"settled land," "statutory owner" and "tenant for life" have the same meanings respectively as in the Settled Land Act 1925;

"trust" and "trustee" have the same meanings respectively as in the Trustee Act 1925; and

"trust for sale" has the same meaning as in the Law of Property Act 1925.

(2) For the purposes of this Act a person shall be treated as under a disability while he is an infant, or of unsound mind.

(3) For the purposes of subsection (2) above a person is of unsound mind if he is a person who, by reason of mental disorder within the meaning of the Mental Health Act 1959, is incapable of managing and administering his property and affairs.

(4) Without prejudice to the generality of subsection (3) above, a person shall be conclusively presumed for the purposes of subsection (2) above to be of unsound mind—

(a) while he is liable to be detained or subject to guardianship under the Mental Health Act 1959; and

(b) while he is receiving treatment as an in-patient in any hospital or mental nursing home within the meaning of that Act, without being liable to be detained under that Act, being treatment which follows without any interval a period during which he was liable to be detained or subject to guardianship under that Act or by virtue of any enactment repealed or excluded by that Act.

(5) Subject to subsection (6) below, a person shall be treated as claiming through another person if he became entitled by, through, under, or by the act of that other person to the right claimed, and any person whose estate or interest might have been barred by a person entitled to an entailed interest in possession shall be treated as claiming through the person so entitled.

(6) A person becoming entitled to any estate or interest by virtue of a special power of appointment shall not be treated as claiming through the appointor.

(7) References in this Act to a right of action to recover land shall include references to a right to enter into possession of the land or, in the case of rentcharges and tithes, to distrain for arrears of rent or tithe, and references to the bringing of such an action shall include references to the making of such an entry or distress.

(8) References in this Act to the possession of land shall, in the case of tithes and rentcharges, be construed as references to the receipt of the tithe or rent, and references to the date of dispossession or discontinuance of possession of land shall, in the case of rent charges, be construed as references to the date of the last receipt of rent.

(9) References in Part II of this Act to a right of action shall include references to—

(*a*) a cause of action;

(*b*) a right to receive money secured by a mortgage or charge on any property;

(*c*) a right to recover proceeds of the sale of land; and

(*d*) a right to receive a share or interest in the personal estate of a deceased person.

(10) References in Part II to the date of the accrual of a right of action shall be construed—

(*a*) in the case of an action upon a judgment, as references to the date on which the judgment became enforceable; and

(*b*) in the case of an action to recover arrears of rent or interest, or damages in respect of arrears of rent or interest, as references to the date on which the rent or interest became due.

. . . . . .

Short title, commencement and extent

41.—(1) This Act may be cited as the Limitation Act 1980.

(2) This Act, except section 35, shall come into force on 1st May 1981.

. . . . . .

SCHEDULES

Section 15 (6), (7)   SCHEDULE 1

PROVISIONS WITH RESPECT TO ACTIONS TO RECOVER LAND

PART I

ACCRUAL OF RIGHTS OF ACTION TO RECOVER LAND

Accrual of right of action in case of present interests in land

1. Where the person bringing an action to recover land, or some person through whom he claims, has been in possession of the land, and has while entitled to the land been dispossessed

or discontinued his possession, the right of action shall be treated as having accrued on the date of the dispossession or discontinuance.

2. Where any person brings an action to recover any land of a deceased person (whether under a will or on intestacy) and the deceased person—

(*a*) was on the date of his death in possession of the land or, in the case of a rentcharge created by will or taking effect upon his death, in possession of the land charged; and

(*b*) was the last person entitled to the land to be in possession of it;

the right of action shall be treated as having accrued on the date of his death.

3. Where any person brings an action to recover land, being an estate or interest in possession assured otherwise than by will to him, or to some person through whom he claims, and—

(*a*) the person making the assurance was on the date when the assurance took effect in possession of the land or, in the case of a rentcharge created by the assurance, in possession of the land charged; and

(*b*) no person has been in possession of the land by virtue of the assurance;

the right of action shall be treated as having accrued on the date when the assurance took effect.

Accrual of right of action in case of future interests

4. The right of action to recover any land shall, in a case where—

(*a*) the estate or interest claimed was an estate or interest in reversion or remainder or any other future estate or interest; and

(*b*) no person has taken possession of the land by virtue of the estate or interest claimed;

be treated as having accrued on the date on which the estate or interest fell into possession by the determination of the preceding estate or interest.

5.—(1) Subject to sub-paragraph (2) below, a tenancy from year to year or other period, without a lease in writing, shall for the purposes of this Act be treated as being determined at the expiration of the first year or other period; and accordingly the right of action of the person entitled to the land subject to the tenancy shall be treated as having accrued at the date on which in accordance with this sub-paragraph the tenancy is determined.

(2) Where any rent has subsequently been received in respect of the tenancy, the right of action shall be treated as having accrued on the date of the last receipt of rent.

6.—(1) Where—

(*a*) any person is in possession of land by virtue of a lease in writing by which a rent of not less than ten pounds a year is reserved; and

(*b*) the rent is received by some person wrongfully claiming to be entitled to the land in reversion immediately expectant on the determination of the lease; and

(*c*) no rent is subsequently received by the person rightfully so entitled;

the right of action to recover the land of the person rightfully so entitled shall be treated as having accrued on the date when the rent was first received by the person wrongfully claiming to be so entitled and not on the date of the determination of the lease.

(2) Sub-paragraph (1) above shall not apply to any lease granted by the Crown.

Accrual of right of action in case of forfeiture or breach of condition

7.—(1) Subject to sub-paragraph (2) below, a right of action to recover land by virtue of a forfeiture or breach of condition shall be treated as having accrued on the date on which the forfeiture was incurred or the condition broken.

(2) If any such right has accrued to a person entitled to an estate or interest in reversion or remainder and the land was not recovered by virtue of that right, the right of action to recover the land shall not be treated as having accrued to that person until his estate or interest fell into possession, as if no such forfeiture or breach of condition had occurred.

Right of action not to accrue or continue unless there is adverse possession

8.—(1) No right of action to recover land shall be treated as accruing unless the land is in the possession of some person in whose favour the period of limitation can run (referred to below in this paragraph as "adverse possession"); and where under the preceding provisions of this Schedule any such right of action is treated as accruing on a certain date and no person is in adverse possession on that date, the right of action shall not be treated as accruing unless and until adverse possession is taken of the land.

(2) Where a right of action to recover land has accrued and after its accrual, before the right is barred, the land ceases to be in adverse possession, the right of action shall no longer be treated as having accrued and no fresh right of action shall be treated as accruing unless and until the land is again taken into adverse possession.

(3) For the purposes of this paragraph—

(*a*) possession of any land subject to a rentcharge by a person (other than the person entitled to the rentcharge) who does not pay the rent shall be treated as adverse possession of the rentcharge; and (*b*) receipt of rent under a lease by a person wrongfully claiming to be entitled to the land in reversion immediately expectant on the determination of the lease shall be treated as adverse possession of the land.

(4) For the purpose of determining whether a person occupying any land is in adverse possession of the land it shall not be assumed by implication of law that his occupation is by permission of the person entitled to the land merely by virtue of the fact that his occupation is not inconsistent with the latter's present or future enjoyment of the land.

This provision shall not be taken as prejudicing a finding to the effect that a person's occupation of any land is by implied permission of the person entitled to the land in any case where such a finding is justified on the actual facts of the case.

Possession of beneficiary not adverse to others interested in settled land or land held on trust for sale

9. Where any settled land or any land held on trust for sale is in the possession of a person entitled to a beneficial interest in the land or in the proceeds of sale (not being a person solely or absolutely entitled to the land or the proceeds), no right of action to recover the land shall be treated for the purposes of this Act as accruing during that possession to any person in whom the land is vested as tenant for life, statutory owner or trustee, or to any other person entitled to a beneficial interest in the land or the proceeds of sale.

(1981 c. 54)

An Act to consolidate with amendments the Supreme Court of Judicature (Consolidation) Act 1925 and other enactments relating to the Supreme Court in England and Wales and the administration of justice therein; to repeal certain obsolete or unnecessary enactments so relating; to amend Part VIII of the Mental Health Act 1959, the Courts-Martial (Appeals) Act 1968, the Arbitration Act 1979 and the law relating to county courts; and for connected purposes.

[28th July 1981]

Number of personal representatives

114.—(1) Probate or administration shall not be granted by the High Court to more than four persons in respect of the same part of the estate of a deceased person.

(2) Where under a will or intestacy any beneficiary is a minor or a life interest arises, any grant of administration by the High Court shall be made either to a trust corporation (with or without an individual) or to not less than two individuals, unless it appears to the court to be expedient in all the circumstances to appoint an individual as sole administrator.

(3) For the purpose of determining whether a minority or life interest arises in a particular case, the court may act on such evidence as may be prescribed.

(4) If at any time during the minority of a beneficiary or the subsistence of a life interest under a will or intestacy there is only one personal representative (not being a trust corporation), the High Court may, on the application of any person interested or the guardian or receiver of any such person, and in accordance with probate rules, appoint one or more additional personal representatives to act while the minority or life interest subsists and until the estate is fully administered.

(5) An appointment of an additional personal representative under subsection (4) to act with an executor shall not have the effect of including him in any chain of representation.

Grants to trust corporations

115.—(1) The High Court may—

    (*a*) where a trust corporation is named in a will as executor, grant probate to the corporation either solely or jointly with any other person named in the will as executor, as the case may require; or

    (*b*) grant administration to a trust corporation, either solely or jointly with another person;

and the corporation may act accordingly as executor or administrator, as the case may be.

(2) Probate or administration shall not be granted to any person as nominee of a trust corporation.

(3) Any officer authorised for the purpose by a trust corporation or its directors or governing body may, on behalf of the corporation, swear affidavits, give security and do any other act which the court may require with a view to the grant to the corporation of probate or administration; and the acts of an officer so authorised shall be binding on the corporation.

Power of court to pass over prior claims to grant

116.—(1) If by reason of any special circumstances it appears to the High Court to be necessary or expedient to appoint as administrator some person other than the person who, but for this section, would in accordance with probate rules have been entitled to the grant, the court may in its discretion appoint as administrator such person as it thinks expedient.

(2) Any grant of administration under this section may be limited in any way the court thinks fit.

Administration pending suit

117.—(1) Where any legal proceedings concerning the validity of the will of a deceased person, or for obtaining, recalling or revoking any grant, are pending, the High Court may grant administration of the estate of the deceased person in question to an administrator pending suit, who shall, subject to subsection (2), have all the rights, duties and powers of a general administrator.

(2) An administrator pending suit shall be subject to the immediate control of the court and act under its direction; and, except in such circumstances as may be prescribed, no distribution of the estate, or any part of the estate, of the deceased person in question shall be made by such an administrator without the leave of the court.

(3) The court may, out of the estate of the deceased, assign an administrator pending suit such reasonable remuneration as it thinks fit.

Effect of appointment of minor as executor

118. Where a testator by his will appoints a minor to be an executor, the appointment shall not operate to vest in the minor the estate, or any part of the estate, of the testator, or to constitute him a personal representative for any purpose, unless and until probate is granted to him in accordance with probate rules.

Administration with will annexed

119.—(1) Administration with the will annexed shall be granted, subject to and in accordance with probate rules, in every class of case in which the High Court had power to make such a grant immediately before the commencement of this Act.

(2) Where administration with the will annexed is granted, the will of the deceased shall be performed and observed in the same manner as if probate of it had been granted to an executor.

Power to require administrators to produce sureties

120.—(1) As a condition of granting administration to any person the High Court may, subject to the following provisions of this section and subject to and in accordance with probate rules, require one or more sureties to guarantee that they will make good, within any limit imposed by the court on the total liability of the surety or sureties, any loss which any person interested in the administration of the estate of the deceased may suffer in consequence of a breach by the administrator of his duties as such.

(2) A guarantee given in pursuance of any such requirement shall enure for the benefit of every person interested in the administration of the estate of the deceased as if contained in a contract under seal made by the surety or sureties with every such person and, where there are two or more sureties, as if they had bound themselves jointly and severally.

(3) No action shall be brought on any such guarantee without the leave of the High Court.

(4) Stamp duty shall not be chargeable on any such guarantee.

(5) This section does not apply where administration is granted to the Treasury Solicitor, the Official Solicitor, the Public Trustee, the Solicitor for the affairs of the Duchy of Lancaster or the Duchy of Cornwall or the Crown Solicitor for Northern Ireland, or to the consular officer of a foreign state to which section 1 of the Consular Conventions Act 1949 applies, or in such other cases as may be prescribed.

Part B

LAND REGISTRATION

Land Registration Act 1925
(as amended)

(15 & 16 Geo. 5, c. 21)

Arrangement of Sections

Part I

Preliminary

Part II

Registration of Land

Freehold Land

Leasehold Land

Preliminaries to Registration

Part III

Registered Dealings with Registered Land

Dispositions of Freehold Land

Dispositions of Leasehold Land

An Act to consolidate the Land Transfer Acts and the statute law relating to registered land.   [9th April, 1925]

PART I

PRELIMINARY

Registers to be continued

1. There shall continue to be kept at His Majesty's Land Registry, a register of title to freehold land and leasehold land.

What estates may be registered

2.—(1) After the commencement of this Act, estates capable of subsisting as legal estates shall be the only interests in land in respect of which a proprietor can be registered and all other interests in registered land (except overriding interests and interests entered on the register at or before such commencement) shall take effect in equity as minor interests, but all interests (except undivided shares in land) entered on the register at such commencement which are not legal estates shall be capable of being dealt with under this Act:

Provided that, on the occasion of the first dealing with any such interest, the register shall be rectified in such manner as may be provided by rules made to secure that the entries therein shall be similar to those which would have been made if the title to the land had been registered after the commencement of this Act.

(2) Subject as aforesaid, and save as otherwise expressly provided by this Act, this Act applies to land registered under any enactment replaced by this Act in like manner as it applies to land registered under this Act.

Interpretation

3. In this Act unless the context otherwise requires, the following expressions have the meanings hereby assigned to them respectively, that is to say:—

   (i) "Charge by way of legal mortgage" means a mortgage created by charge under which, by virtue of the Law of Property Act 1925, the mortgagee is to be treated as an estate owner in like manner as if a mortgage term by demise or subdemise were vested in him, and "legal mortgage" has the same meaning as in that Act;

   (ii) "the Court" means the High Court of Justice, [*and also the Court of Chancery of the County Palatine of Lancaster or Durham,*][1] or the county court, where those courts respectively have jurisdiction;

  (iii) [*Repealed by the Finance Act 1975 (c. 7), Sched. 13.*]

  (iv) "Estate owner" means the owner of a legal estate, but an infant is not capable of being an estate owner;

   (v) "Gazette" means the London Gazette;

  (vi) "Income" includes rents and profits;

 (vii) "Instrument" does not include a statute, unless the statute creates a settlement;

(viii) "Land" includes land of any tenure (including land, subject or not to manorial incidents, enfranchised under Part V of the Law of Property Act 1922), and mines and minerals, whether or not held with the surface, buildings or parts of buildings (whether the division is horizontal, vertical or made in any other way) and other corporeal hereditaments; also a manor, an advowson, and a rent and other incorporeal hereditaments, and an easement, right, privilege, or benefit in, over, or derived from land; but not an undivided share in land; and "hereditaments" mean real property

---

[1] Words in square brackets repealed by the Courts Act 1971 (c. 23), s.56, 11th Sched., Pt. 11.

which on an intestacy might, before the commencement of this Act, have devolved on an heir;

(ix) ["Land charge" means a land charge of any class described in section 2 of the Land Charges Act 1972 or a local land charge;[2]

(x) "Lease" includes an under-lease and any tenancy or agreement for a lease, under-lease or tenancy;

(xi) "Legal estates" mean the estates interests and charges in or over land subsisting or created at law which are by the Law of Property Act 1925 authorised to subsist or to be created at law; and "Equitable interests" mean all the other interests and charges in or over and or in the proceeds of sale thereof; an equitable interest "capable of subsisting at law" means such as could validly subsist at law if clothed with the legal estate;

(xii) "Limitation Acts" mean the Real Property Limitation Acts 1833, 1837 and 1874 and any Acts amending those Acts;

(xiii) "Manorial incidents" have the same meaning as in Part V of the Law of Property Act 1922;

(xiv) "Mines and minerals" include any strata or seam of minerals or substances in or under any land, and powers of working and getting the same, but not a undivided share thereof;

(xv) "Minor interests" mean the interests not capable of being disposed of or created by registered dispositions and capable of being overriden (whether or not a purchaser has notice thereof) by the proprietors unless protected as provided by this Act, and all rights and interests which are not registered or protected on the register and are not overriding interests, and include—

(*a*) in the case of land held on trust for sale, all interests and powers which are under the Law of Property Act 1925 capable of being overridden by the trustees for sale, whether or not such interests and powers are so protected; and

(*b*) in the case of settled land, all interests and powers which are under the Settled Land Act 1925 and the Law of Property Act 1925, or either of them, capable of being overridden by the tenant for life or statutory owner, whether or not such interests and powers are so protected as aforesaid;

(xvi) "Overriding interests" mean all the incumbrances, interests, rights, and powers not entered on the register but subject to which registered dispositions are by this Act to take effect, and in regard to land registered at the commencement of this Act include the matters which are by any enactment repealed by this Act declared not to be incumbrances;

(xvii) "Personal representative" means the executor, original or by representation, or administrator for the time being of a deceased person, and as regards any liability for the payment of death duties includes any person who takes possession of or intermeddles with the property of a deceased person without the authority of the personal representatives or the court; and where there are special personal representatives for the purposes of any settled land, it means, in relation to that land, those representatives;

(xviii) "Possession" includes receipt of rents and profits or the right to receive the same, if any;

(xix) "Prescribed" means prescribed by general rules made in pursuance of this Act;

(xx) "Proprietor" means the registered proprietor for the time being of an estate in land or of a charge;

[2] Words in square brackets substituted by the Local Land Charges Act 1975 (c. 76), Sched. 1.

(xxi) "Purchaser" means a purchaser in good faith for valuable consideration and includes a lessee, mortgagee, or other person who for valuable consideration acquires any interest in land or in any charge on land;

(xxii) "Registered dispositions" means dispositions which take effect under the powers conferred on the proprietor by way of transfer, charge, lease or otherwise and to which (when required to be registered) special effect or priority is given by this Act on registration;

(xxiii) "Registered estate," in reference to land, means the legal estate, or other registered interest, if any, as respects which a person is for the time being registered as proprietor, but does not include a registered charge and a "registered charge" includes a mortgage or incumbrance registered as a charge under this Act;

(xxiv) "Registered land" means land or any estate or interest in land the title to which is registered under this Act or any enactment replaced by this Act, and includes any easement, right, privilege, or benefit which is appurtenant or appendant thereto, and any mines and minerals within or under the same and held therewith;

(xxv) "Rent" includes a rent service or a rent-charge, or other rent, toll, duty, royalty, or annual or periodical payment, in money or money's worth, issuing out of or charged upon land, but does not include mortgage interest;

(xxvi) "Settled land" "settlement" "tenant for life" "statutory owner" "trustees of the settlement" "capital money" . . . [3] "trust corporation" "trust instrument" "vesting deed" "vesting order" "vesting assent" and "vesting instrument" have the same meanings as in the Settled Land Act 1925;

(xxvii) A "term of years absolute" means a term of years, whether at a rent or not, taking effect either in possession or in reversion, with or without impeachment for waste, subject or not to another legal estate and either certain or liable to determination by notice, re-entry, operation of law, or by a provision for cesser on redemption, or in any other event (other than the dropping of a life, or the determination of a determinable life interest), but does not include any term of years determinable with life or lives or with the cesser of a determinable life interest, nor, if created after the commencement of this Act, a term of years which is not expressed to take effect in possession within twenty-one years after the creation thereof where required by the Law of Property Act 1925 to take effect within that period; and in this definition the expression "term of years" includes a term of less than a year, or for a year or years and a fraction of a year or from year to year;

(xxviii) "Trust for sale," in relation to land, means an immediate binding trust for sale, whether or not exercisable at the request or with the consent of any person, and with or without a power at discretion to postpone the sale;

(xxix) "Trustees for sale" mean the persons (including a personal representative) holding land on trust for sale;

(xxx) "United Kingdom" means Great Britain and Northern Ireland;

(xxxi) "Valuable consideration" includes marriage, but does not include a nominal consideration in money;

(xxxii) "Will" includes codicil.

---

[3] Omitted words repealed by the Mental Health Act 1959 (7 & 8 Eliz. 2, c. 72), s.149 (2) and 8th Sched.

PART II

REGISTRATION OF LAND

Freehold Land

Application for registration of freehold land[4]

4. Where the title to be registered is a title to a freehold estate in land—

   (*a*) any estate owner holding an estate in fee simple (including a tenant for life, statutory owner, personal representative, or trustee for sale) whether subject or not to incumbrances; or

   (*b*) any other person (not being a mortgagee where there is a subsisting right of redemption or a person who has merely contracted to buy land) who is entitled to require a legal estate in fee simple whether subject or not to incumbrances, to be vested in him;

may apply to the registrar to be registered in respect of such estate, or, in the case of a person not in a fiduciary position, to have registered in his stead any nominee, as proprietor with an absolute title or with a possessory title:

Provided that—

   (i) Where an absolute title is required the applicant or his nominee shall not be registered as proprietor until and unless the title is approved by the registrar;

   (ii) Where a possessory title is required the applicant or his nominee may be registered as proprietor on giving such evidence of title and serving such notices, if any, as may for the time being be prescribed;

   (iii) If, on an application for registration with possessory title, the registrar is satisfied as to the title to the freehold estate, he may register it as absolute, whether the applicant consents to such registration or not, but in that case no higher fee shall be charged than would have been charged for registration with possessory title.

Effect of first registration with absolute title

5. Where the registered land is a freehold estate, the registration of any person as first proprietor thereof with an absolute title shall vest in the person so registered an estate in fee simple in possession in the land, together with all rights, privileges and appurtenances belonging or appurtenant thereto, subject to the following rights and interests, that is to say,—

   (*a*) Subject to the incumbrances, and other entries, if any, appearing on the register; and

   (*b*) Unless the contrary is expressed on the register, subject to such overriding interests, if any, as affect the registered land; and

   (*c*) Where the first proprietor is not entitled for his own benefit to the registered land subject, as between himself and the persons entitled to minor interests, to any minor interests of such persons of which he has notice,

but free from all other estates and interests whatsoever, including estates and interests of His Majesty.

---

[4] As to souvenir land, see the Land Registration and Land Charges Act 1971 (c. 54), s.4, *post*, p. 458 and the Land Registration (Souvenir Land) Rules 1972 (No. 985). The operation of this section was modified by the Land Registration Act 1966 (c. 39), s. 1 (2) *post*, p. 455.

Effect of first registration with possessory title

6. Where the registered land is a freehold estate, the registration of any person as first proprietor thereof with a possessory title only shall not affect or prejudice the enforcement of any estate, right or interest adverse to or in derogation of the title of the first proprietor, and subsisting or capable of arising at the time of registration of that proprietor, but, save as aforesaid, shall have the same effect as registration of a person with an absolute title.

Qualified title

7.—(1) Where an absolute title is required, and on the examination of the title it appears to the registrar that the title can be established only for a limited period, or only subject to certain reservations, the registrar may, on the application of the party applying to be registered by an entry made in the register, except from the effect of registration any estate, right or interest—

(*a*) arising before a specified date, or

(*b*) arising under a specified instrument or otherwise particularly described in the register,

and a title registered subject to such excepted estate, right, or interest shall be called a qualified title.

(2) Where the registered land is a freehold estate, the registration of a person as first proprietor thereof with a qualified title shall have the same effect as the registration of such person with an absolute title, save that registration with a qualified title shall not affect or prejudice the enforcement of any estate, right or interest appearing by the register to be excepted.

Leasehold Land

Application for registration of leasehold land[5]

8.—(1) Where the title to be registered is a title to a leasehold interest in land—

(*a*) any estate owner (including a tenant for life, statutory owner, personal representative, or trustee for sale, but not including a mortgagee where there is a subsisting right of redemption), holding under a lease for a term of years absolute of which more than twenty-one are unexpired, whether subject or not to incumbrances, or

(*b*) any other person (not being a mortgagee as aforesaid and not being a person who has merely contracted to buy the leasehold interest) who is entitled to require a legal leasehold estate held under such a lease as aforesaid (whether subject or not to incumbrances) to be vested in him,

may apply to the registrar to be registered in respect of such estate, or in the case of a person not being in a fiduciary position to have registered in his stead any nominee, as proprietor with an absolute title, with a good leasehold title or with a possessory title:

Provided that—

(i) Where an absolute title is required, the applicant or his nominee shall not be registered as proprietor until and unless

[5] As to souvenir land, see the Land Registration and Land Charges Act 1971 (c. 54), s.4, *post*, p. 458 and the Land Registration (Souvenir Land) Rules 1972 (No. 985). The operation of this section was modified by the Land Registration Act 1966 (c. 39), s. 1 (2), *post*, p. 455.

the title both to the leasehold and to the freehold, and to any intermediate leasehold that may exist, is approved by the registrar;

   (ii) Where a good leasehold title is required, the applicant or his nominee shall not be registered as proprietor until and unless the title to the leasehold interest is approved by the registrar;

  (iii) Where a possessory title is required, the applicant or his nominee may be registered as proprietor on giving such evidence of title and serving such notices, if any, as may for the time being be prescribed;

  (iv) If on an application for registration with a possessory title the registrar is satisfied as to the title to the leasehold interest, he may register it as good leasehold, whether the applicant consents to such registration or not; but in that case no higher fee shall be charged than would have been charged for registration with possessory title.

(2) Leasehold land held under a lease containing an absolute prohibition against all dealings therewith inter vivos shall not be registered in pursuance of this Act; and leasehold land held under a lease containing a restriction on any such dealings, shall not be registered under this Act unless and until provision is made in the prescribed manner for preventing any dealing therewith in contravention of the restriction by an entry on the register to that effect, or otherwise.

(3) Where on an application to register a mortgage term, wherein no right of redemption is subsisting, it appears that the applicant is entitled in equity to the superior term, if any, out of which it was created, the registrar shall register him as proprietor of the superior term without any entry to the effect that the legal interest in that term is outstanding, and on such registration the superior term shall vest in the proprietor and the mortgage term shall merge therein:

Provided that this subsection shall not apply where the mortgage term does not comprise the whole of the land included in the superior term, unless in that case the rent, if any, payable in respect of the superior term has been apportioned, or the rent is of no money value or no rent is reserved, and unless the covenants, if any, entered into for the benefit of the reversion have been apportioned (either expressly or by implication) as respects the land comprised in the mortgage term.

Effect of first registration with absolute title

9. Where the registered land is a leasehold interest, the registration under this Act of any person as first proprietor thereof with an absolute title shall be deemed to vest in such person the possession of the leasehold interest described, with all implied or expressed rights, privileges, and appurtenances attached to such interest, subject to the following obligations, rights and interests, that is to say,—

   (a) Subject to all implied and express covenants, obligations, and liabilities incident to the registered land; and

   (b) Subject to the incumbrances and other entries (if any) appearing on the register; and

   (c) Unless the contrary is expressed on the register, subject to such overrriding interests, if any, as affect the registered land; and

   (d) Where such first proprietor is not entitled for his own benefit to the registered land subject, as between himself and the persons entitled to minor interests, to any minor interests of such persons of which he has notice;

but free from all other estates and interests whatsoever, including estates and interests of His Majesty.

Effect of first registration with good leasehold title

10. Where the registered land is a leasehold interest, the registration of a person as first proprietor thereof with a good leasehold title shall not affect or prejudice the enforcement of any estate, right or interest affecting or in derogation of the title of the lessor to grant the lease, but, save as aforesaid, shall have the same effect as registration with an absolute title.

Effect of first registration with possessory title

11. Where the registered land is a leasehold interest, the registration of a person as first proprietor thereof with a possessory title shall not affect or prejudice the enforcement of any estate, right, or interest (whether in respect of the lessor's title or otherwise) adverse to or in derogation of the title of such first registered proprietor, and subsisting or capable of arising at the time of the registration of such proprietor; but, save as aforesaid, shall have the same effect as registration with an absolute title.

Qualified title

12.—(1) Where on examination it appears to the registrar that the title, either of the lessor to the reversion or of the lessee to the leasehold interest, can be established only for a limited period, or subject to certain reservations, the registrar may, upon the request in writing of the person applying to be registered, by an entry made in the register, except from the effect of registration any estate, right or interest—

(*a*) arising before a specified date, or

(*b*) arising under a specified instrument, or otherwise particularly described in the register,

and a title registered subject to any such exception shall be called a qualified title.

(2) Where the registered land is a leasehold interest, the registration of a person as first proprietor thereof with a qualified title shall not affect or prejudice the enforcement of any estate, right, or interest appearing by the register to be excepted, but, save as aforesaid, shall have the same effect as registration with a good leasehold title or an absolute title, as the case may be.

Preliminaries to Registration

Regulations as to examination of title by registrar

13. The examination by the registrar of any title under this Act shall be conducted in the prescribed manner:

Provided that—

(*a*) Due notice shall be given, where the giving of such notice is prescribed, and sufficient opportunity shall be afforded to any persons desirous of objecting to come in and state their objections to the registrar; and

(*b*) The registrar shall have jurisdiction to hear and determine any such objections, subject to an appeal to the court in the prescribed manner and on the prescribed conditions; and

(*c*) If the registrar, upon the examination of any title, is of the opinion that the title is open to objection, but is nevertheless a title the holding under which will not be disturbed, he may approve of such title, or may require the applicant to apply to the court, upon a statement signed by the registrar, for its sanction to the registration.

Evidence required before registration

14.—(1) Before the completion of the registration of any estate in land in respect of which an examination of title is required, the applicant for registration and his solicitor, shall each, if required by the registrar, make an affidavit or declaration that to the best of his knowledge and belief all deeds, wills, and instruments of title, and all charges and incumbrances affecting the title which is the subject of the application, and all facts material to such title, have been disclosed in the course of the investigation of title made by the registrar.

(2) The registrar may require any person making an affidavit or declaration in pursuance of this section to state in his affidavit or declaration what means he has had of becoming acquainted with the several matters referred to in this section; and if the registrar is of opinion that any further or other evidence is necessary or desirable, he may refuse to complete the registration until such further or other evidence is produced.

(3) Before the registration of any person who has not previously acquired the estate intended to be registered, the registrar shall be satisfied that all *ad valorem* stamp duty, if any, which, if the estate had been acquired by him, would have been payable in respect of the instrument vesting that estate in him, has been discharged.

Production of deeds

15.—(1) When an application has been made to the registrar for the registration of any title to land, then if any person has in his possession or custody any deeds, instruments or evidences of title relating to or affecting such title, to the production of which the applicant or any trustee for him is entitled, the registrar may require such person to show cause, within a time limited, why he should not produce such deeds, instruments, or evidences of title to the registrar, or otherwise, as the registrar may deem fit; and, unless cause is shown to the satisfaction of the registrar within the time limited, such deeds, instruments, and evidences of title may be ordered by the registrar to be produced at the expense of the applicant, at such time and place, and in such manner, and on such terms, as the registrar thinks fit.

(2) Any person aggrieved by an order of the registrar under this section may appeal in the prescribed manner to the court, which may annul or confirm the order of the registrar with or without modification.

(3) If any person disobeys any order of the registrar made in pursuance of this section, the registrar may certify such disobedience to the court, and thereupon such person, subject to such right of appeal as aforesaid, may be punished by the court in the same manner in all respects as if the order made by the registrar were the order of the court.

Deeds to be marked with notice of registration

16. A person shall not be registered as proprietor until, if required by the registrar, he has produced to him such documents of title, if any, as will, in the opinion of the registrar, when stamped or otherwise marked, give notice to any purchaser or other person dealing with the land of the fact of the registration, and the registrar shall stamp or otherwise mark the same accordingly, unless the registrar is satisfied that without such stamping or marking the fact of such registration cannot be concealed from a purchaser or other person dealing with the land.

Provided that, in the case of registration with a possessory title, the registrar may act on such reasonable evidence as may be prescribed as to the sufficiency of the documents produced, and as to dispensing with their production in special circumstances.

Costs of application for registration

17.—(1) All costs, charges and expenses that are incurred by any parties in or about any proceedings for registration shall, unless the parties otherwise agree, be taxed by the taxing officer of the court as between solicitor and client, but the persons by whom and the proportions in which such costs, charges, and expenses are to be paid shall be in the discretion of the registrar, and shall be determined according to orders of the registrar, regard being had to the following provision, namely, that any applicant under this Act is liable prima facie to pay all costs, charges, and expenses incurred by or in consequence of his application, except—

(*a*) in a case where parties object whose rights are sufficiently secured without their appearance;
and

(*b*) where any costs, charges, or expenses are incurred unnecessarily or improperly.

Provided that any party aggrieved by any order of the registrar under this section may appeal in the prescribed manner to the court, which may annul or confirm the order of the registrar, with or without modification.

(2) If any person disobeys any order of the registrar made in pursuance of this section, the registrar may certify such disobedience to the court, and thereupon such person, subject to such right of appeal as aforesaid, may be punished by the court in the same manner in all respects as if the order made by the registrar were the order of the court.

PART III

REGISTERED DEALINGS WITH REGISTERED LAND

Dispositions of Freehold Land

Powers of disposition of registered freeholds

18.—(1) Where the registered land is a freehold estate the proprietor may, in the prescribed manner, transfer the registered estate in the land or any part thereof, and, subject to any entry in the register to the contrary, may in the prescribed manner—

(*a*) transfer the fee simple in possession of all or any mines or minerals apart from the surface; or of the surface without all or any of the mines and minerals;

(*b*) grant an annuity or a rentcharge in possession (either perpetual or for a term of years absolute) in any form which sufficiently refers in the prescribed manner to the registered land charged;

(c) grant in fee simple in possession any easement, right, or privilege in, over, or derived from the registered land or any part thereof, in any form which sufficiently refers, in the prescribed manner, to the registered servient tenement and to the dominant tenement, whether being registered land or not;

(*d*) transfer the fee simple in possession of the registered land or any part thereof, subject to the creation thereout, by way of reservation, in favour of any person of an annuity or a rentcharge in possession (either perpetual or for a term of years absolute), or of any easement, right, or privilege in possession (either in fee simple or for a term of years absolute);

(*e*) grant (subject or not to the reservation of an easement, right, or privilege) a lease of the registered land or any part thereof, or of all or any mines and minerals apart from the surface, or of the surface without all or any of the mines and minerals, or of an easement, right, or privilege in or over the land, or any part thereof, for any term of years absolute for any purpose (but where by way of mortgage subject to the provisions of this Act and the Law of Property Act 1925 relating thereto), and in any form which sufficiently refers, in the prescribed manner, to the registered land.

(2) A perpetual annuity or rentcharge in possession may be granted or reserved to any person with or without a power of re-entry, exercisable at any time, on default of payment thereof, or on breach of covenant, and shall have incidental thereto all the powers and remedies (as varied if at all by the disposition creating the rentcharge) for recovery thereof conferred by the Law of Property Act 1925; and where an easement, right, or privilege is reserved in a registered disposition for a legal estate, the reservation shall operate to create the same for the benefit of the land for the benefit of which the right is reserved.

(3) A lease for a term, not exceeding twenty-one years, to take effect in possession or within one year from the date thereof at a rent without taking a fine may be granted and shall take effect under this section notwithstanding that a caution, notice of deposit of a certificate, restriction, or inhibition (other than a bankruptcy inhibition) may be subsisting, but subject to the interests intended to be protected by any such caution, notice, restriction, or inhibition.

(4) The foregoing powers of disposition shall (subject to the express provisions of this Act and of the Law of Property Act 1925 relating to mortgages) apply to dispositions by the registered proprietor by way of charge or mortgage; but no estate, other than a legal estate, shall be capable of being disposed of, or created under, this section.

(5) In this Act "transfer" or "disposition" when referring to registered freehold land includes any disposition authorised as aforesaid; and "transferee" has a corresponding meaning.

Registration of disposition of freeholds

19.—(1) The transfer of the registered estate in the land or part thereof shall be completed by the registrar entering on the register the transferee as the proprietor of the estate transferred, but until such entry is made the transferor shall be deemed to remain proprietor of the registered estate; and, where part only of the land is transferred, notice thereof shall also be noted on the register.

(2) All interests transferred or created by dispositions by the proprietor, other than a transfer of the registered estate in the land, or part thereof, shall, subject to the provisions relating to mortgages, be completed by registration in the same manner and with the same effect as provided by this Act with respect to transfers of registered estates and notice thereof shall also be noted on the register:

Provided that nothing in this subsection—

(*a*) shall authorise the registration of a lease granted for a term not exceeeding twenty-one years, or require the entry of a notice of such a lease if it is granted at a rent without taking a fine; or

(*b*) shall authorise the registration of a mortgage term where there is a subsisting right of redemption; or

(*c*) shall render necessary the registration of any easement, right, or privilege except as appurtenant to registered land, or the entry of notice thereof except as against the registered title of the servient land.

Every such disposition shall, when registered, take effect as a registered disposition, and a lease made by the registered proprietor under the last foregoing section which is not required to be registered or noted on the register shall nevertheless take effect as if it were a registered disposition immediately on being granted.

(3) The general words implied in conveyances under the Law of Property Act 1925 shall apply, so far as applicable thereto, to dispositions of a registered estate.

Effect of registration of dispositions of freeholds

20.—(1) In the case of a freehold estate registered with an absolute title, a disposition of the registered land or of a legal estate therein, including a lease thereof, for valuable consideration shall, when registered, confer on the transferee or grantee an estate in fee simple or the term of years absolute or other legal estate expressed to be created in the land dealt with, together with all rights, privileges, and appurtenances belonging or appurtenant thereto, including (subject to any entry to the contrary in the register) the appropriate rights and interests which would, under the Law of Property Act 1925, have been transferred if the land had not been registered, subject—

   (*a*) to the incumbrances and other entries, if any, appearing on the register [*and any charge for capital transfer tax subject to which the disposition takes effect under section 73 of this Act*][6]; and

   (*b*) unless the contrary is expressed on the register, to the overriding interests, if any, affecting the estate transferred or created,

but free from all other estates and interests whatsoever, including estates and interests of His Majesty, and the disposition shall operate in like manner as if the registered transferor or grantor were (subject to any entry to the contrary in the register) entitled to the registered land in fee simple in possession for his own benefit.

(2) In the case of a freehold estate registered with a qualified title a disposition of the registered land or of a legal estate therein, including a lease thereof, for valuable consideration shall, when registered, have the same effect as it would have had if the land had been registered with an absolute title, save that such disposition shall not affect or prejudice the enforcement of any right or interest appearing by the register to be excepted.

(3) In the case of a freehold estate registered with a possessory title, a disposition of the registered land or of a legal estate therein, including a lease thereof, for valuable consideration shall not affect or prejudice the enforcement of any right or interest adverse to or in derogation of the title of the first registered proprietor, and subsisting or capable of arising at the time of the registration of such proprietor; but, save as aforesaid, shall when registered have the same effect as it would have had if the land had been registered with an absolute title.

(4) Where any such disposition is made without valuable consideration, it shall, so far as the transferee or grantee is concerned, be subject to any minor interests subject to which the transferor or grantor held the same, but, save as aforesaid, shall, when registered, in all respects, and in particular as respects any registered dealings on the part of the transferee or grantee, have the same effect as if the disposition had been made for valuable consideration.

Dispositions of Leasehold Land

Powers of disposition of registered leaseholds

21.—(1) Where the registered land is a leasehold interest the proprietor may, in the prescribed manner, transfer the registered estate in the land or any part thereof, and, subject to any entry in the register to the contrary may in the prescribed manner—

   (*a*) transfer all or any of the leasehold mines and minerals apart from

[6] The words in square brackets were added by the Finance Act 1975 (c. 7), Sched 12.

the surface; or the surface without all or any of the leasehold mines and minerals;

(*b*) grant (to the extent of the registered estate) any annuity or rentcharge in possession, easement, right or privilege in, or derived from the registered land or any part thereof, in any form which sufficiently refers, in the prescribed manner, to the registered lease, and to the dominant tenement, whether being registered land or not;

(*c*) transfer the registered land or any part thereof subject to a reservation to any person of any such annuity, rentcharge, easement, right, or privilege;

(*d*) grant (subject or not to the reservation of an easement, right, or privilege) an underlease of the registered land, or any part thereof, or of all or any mines and minerals apart from the surface, or of the surface without all or any of the mines and minerals, or of an easement, right or privilege, in or over the registered land or any part thereof, for any term of years absolute of less duration than the registered estate and for any purpose (but where by way of mortgage, subject to the provisions of this Act and of the Law of Property Act 1925 relating thereto), and in any form which sufficiently refers in the prescribed manner to the registered land, and in the case of an easement, right, or privilege, to the dominant tenement, whether being registered land or not.

(2) A disposition of registered leasehold land may be made subject to a rent legally apportioned in the prescribed manner, or to a rent not so apportioned.

(3) An underlease for a term, not exceeding twenty-one years, to take effect in possession or within one year from the date thereof, at a rent without taking a fine, may be granted and shall take effect under this section, notwithstanding that a caution, notice of deposit of a certificate, restriction, or inhibition (other than a bankruptcy inhibition) may be subsisting, but subject to the interests intended to be protected by any such caution, notice, restriction or inhibition.

(4) The foregoing powers of disposition shall (subject to the express provisions of this Act and of the Law of Property Act 1925 relating to mortgages) apply to dispositions by the registered proprietor by way of charge or mortgage, but no estate, other than a legal estate, shall be capable of being disposed of or created under this section.

(5) In this Act "transfer" or "disposition" when referring to registered leasehold land includes any disposition authorised as aforesaid, and "transferee" has a corresponding meaning.

Registration of dispositions of leaseholds

22.—(1) A transfer of the registered estate in the land or part thereof shall be completed by the registrar entering on the register the transferee as proprietor of the estate transferred, but until such entry is made the transferor shall be deemed to remain the proprietor of the registered estate; and where part only of the land is transferred, notice thereof shall also be noted on the register.

(2) All interests transferred or created by dispositions by the registered proprietor other than the transfer of his registered estate in the land or in part thereof shall (subject to the provisions relating to mortgages) be completed by registration in the same manner and with the same effect as provided by this Act with respect to transfers of the registered estate, and notice thereof shall also be noted on the register in accordance with this Act:

Provided that nothing in this subsection—
  (*a*) shall authorise the registration of an underlease originally granted for a term not exceeding twenty-one years, or require the entry of a notice of such an underlease if it is granted at a rent without taking a fine; or
  (*b*) shall authorise the registration of a mortgage term where there is a susbsisting right of redemption, or
  (*c*) shall render necessary the registration of any easement, right, or privilege except as appurtenant to registered land, or the entry of notice thereof except as against the registered title of the servient land.
Every such disposition shall, when registered, take effect as a registered disposition, and an underlease made by the registered proprietor which is not required to be registered or noted on the register shall nevertheless take effect as if it were a registered disposition immediately on being granted.
(3) The general words implied in conveyances under the Law of Property Act 1925 shall apply, so far as applicable thereto, to transfers of a registered leasehold estate.

Effect of registration of dispositions of leaseholds

23.—(1) In the case of a leasehold estate registered with an absolute title, a disposition (including a subdemise thereof) for valuable consideration shall, when registered, be deemed to vest in the transferee or underlessee the estate transferred or created to the extent of the registered estate, or for the term created by the subdemise, as the case may require, with all implied or expressed rights, privileges, and appurtenances attached to the estate transferred or created, including (subject to any entry to the contrary on the register) the appropriate rights and interests which would under the Law of Property Act 1925 have been transferred if the land had not been registered, but subject as follows:
  (*a*) To all implied and express covenants, obligations, and liabilities incident to the estate transferred or created; and
  (*b*) To the incumbrances and other entries (if any) appearing on the register [*and any charge for capital transfer tax subject to which the disposition takes effect under section 73 of this Act*][7]; and
  (*c*) Unless the contrary is expressed on the register, to the overriding interests, if any, affecting the estate transferred or created,
but free from all other estates and interests whatsoever, including estates and interests of His Majesty; and the transfer or subdemise shall operate in like manner as if the registered transferor or sublessor were (subject to any entry to the contrary on the register) absolutely entitled to the registered lease for his own benefit.
(2) In the case of a leasehold estate registered with a good leasehold title, a disposition (including a subdemise thereof) for valuable consideration shall, when registered, have the same effect as it would have had if the land had been registered with an absolute title, save that it shall not affect or prejudice the enforcement of any right or interest affecting or in derogation of the title of the lessor to grant the lease.
(3) In the case of a leasehold estate registered with a qualified title, a disposition (including a subdemise thereof) for valuable consideration shall, when registered, have the same effect as it would have had if the land had been registered with an absolute title, save that such disposition shall not affect or prejudice the enforcement of any right or interest (whether in respect of the lessor's title or otherwise) appearing by the register to be excepted.

[7] The words in square brackets were added by the Finance Act 1975 (c. 7), Sched. 12.

(4) In the case of a leasehold estate registered with a possessory title, a disposition (including a subdemise thereof) for valuable consideration shall not affect or prejudice the enforcement of any right or interest (whether in respect of the lessor's title or otherwise) adverse to or in derogation of the title of the first registered proprietor, and subsisting or capable of arising at the time of the registration of such proprietor, but save as aforesaid shall, when registered, have the same effect as it would have had if the land had been registered with an absolute title.

(5) Where any such disposition is made without valuable consideration it shall, so far as the transferee or underlessee is concerned, be subject to any minor interests subject to which the transferor or sublessor held the same; but, save as aforesaid, shall, when registered, in all respects, and in particular as respects any registered dealings on the part of the transferee or underlessee, have the same effect as if the disposition had been made for valuable consideration.

Implied covenants on transfers of leaseholds

24.—(1) On the transfer, otherwise than by way of underlease, of any leasehold interest in land under this Act, unless there be an entry on the register negativing such implication, there shall be implied—

(*a*) on the part of the transferor, a covenant with the transferee that, notwithstanding anything by such transferor done, omitted, or knowingly suffered, the rent, covenants, and conditions reserved and contained by and in the registered lease, and on the part of the lessee to be paid, performed, and observed, have been so paid, performed, and observed up to the date of the transfer; and

(*b*) on the part of the transferee, a covenant with the transferor, that during the residue of the term the transferee and the persons deriving title under him will pay, perform, and observe the rent, covenants, and conditions by and in the registered lease reserved and contained, and on the part of the lessee to be paid, performed, and observed, and will keep the transferor and the persons deriving title under him indemnified against all actions, expenses, and claims on account of the non-payment of the said rent or any part thereof, or the breach of the said covenants or conditions, or any of them.

(2) On a transfer of part of the land held under a lease, the covenant implied on the part of the transferee by this section shall be limited to the payment of the apportioned rent, if any, and the performance and observance of the covenants by the lessee and conditions in the registered lease so far only as they affect the part transferred. Where the transferor remains owner of part of the land comprised in the lease, there shall also be implied on his part, as respects the part retained, a covenant with the transferee similar to that implied on the part of the transferee under this subsection.

Charges on Freehold and Leasehold Land

Proprietor's power to create charges

25.—(1) The proprietor of any registered land may by deed—

(*a*) charge the registered land with the payment at an appointed time of any principal sum of money either with or without interest;

(*b*) charge the registered land in favour of a building society under the Building Societies Acts 1874 to 1894[8] in accordance with the rules of that society.

---

[8] See now the Building Societies Act 1962 (10 & 11 Eliz. 2, c. 37).

(2) A charge may be in any form provided that—

    (*a*) the registered land comprised in the charge is described by reference to the register or in any other manner sufficient to enable the registrar to identify the same without reference to any other document;

    (*b*) the charge does not refer to any other interest or charge affecting the land which—

        (i) would have priority over the same and is not registered or protected on the register,

        (ii) is not an overriding interest.

(3) Any provision contained in a charge which purports to—

    (i) take away from the proprietor thereof the power of transferring it by registered disposition or of requiring the cessation thereof to be noted on the register; or

    (ii) affect any registered land or charge other than that in respect of which the charge is to be expressly registered,

shall be void.

Registration of charges

26.—(1) The charge shall be completed by the registrar entering on the register the person in whose favour the charge is made as the proprietor of such charge, and the particulars of the charge.

(2) A charge may be registered notwithstanding that it contains any trust, power to appoint new trustees, or other provisions for giving effect to the security.

(3) Where the land, in respect of which a charge is registered, is registered with a good leasehold, qualified or possessory title, the charge shall take effect subject to the provisions of this Act with respect to land registered with such a title.

Terms of years implied in or granted by charges

27.—(1) A registered charge shall, unless made or taking effect by demise or subdemise, and subject to any provision to the contrary contained in the charge, take effect as a charge by way of legal mortgage.

(2) Subject to the provisions of the Law of Property Act 1925, a registered charge may contain in the case of freehold land, an express demise, and in the case of leasehold land an express subdemise of the land to the creditor for a term of years absolute, subject to a proviso for cesser on redemption.

(3) Any such demise or subdemise or charge by way of legal mortgage shall take effect from the date of the delivery of the deed containing the same, but subject to the estate or interest of any person (other than the proprietor of the land) whose estate or interest (whenever created) is registered or noted on the register before the date of registration of the charge.

(4) Any charge registered before the commencement of this Act shall take effect as a demise or subdemise of the land in accordance with the provisions of the Law of Property Act 1925, and the registered estate shall (without prejudice to any registered charge or any term or subterm created by a charge or by this Act) vest in the person appearing by the register to be entitled to the ultimate equity of redemption.

Implied covenants in charges

28.—(1) Where a registered charge is created on any land there shall be implied on the part of the person being proprietor of such land at the time of the creation of the charge, unless there be an entry on the register negativing such implication—

   (*a*) a covenant with the proprietor for the time being of the charge to pay the principal sum charged, and interest, if any, thereon, at the appointed time and rate; and

   (*b*) a covenant, if the principal sum or any part thereof is unpaid at the appointed time, to pay interest half yearly at the appointed rate as well after as before any judgment is obtained in respect of the charge on so much of the principal sum as for the time being remains unpaid.

(2) Where a registered charge is created on any leasehold land there shall (in addition to the covenants aforesaid) be implied on the part of the person being proprietor of such land at the time of the creation of the charge, unless there be an entry on the register negativing such implication, a covenant with the proprietor for the time being of the charge, that the person being proprietor of such land at the time of the creation of the charge, or the persons deriving title under him, will pay, perform, and observe the rent, covenants, and conditions, by and in the registered lease reserved and contained, and on the part of the lessee to be paid, performed, and observed, and will keep the proprietor of the charge, and the persons deriving title under him, indemnified against all proceedings, expenses, and claims, on account of the non-payment of the said rent, or any part thereof, or the breach of the said covenants or conditions, or any of them.

Priorities of registered charges

29.—Subject to any entry to the contrary on the register, registered charges on the same land shall as between themselves rank according to the order in which they are entered on the register, and not according to the order in which they are created.

Protection of charges for securing further advances

30.—(1) When a registered charge is made for securing further advances, the registrar shall, before making any entry on the register which would prejudicially affect the priority of any further advance thereunder, give to the proprietor of the charge at his registered address, notice by registered post[9] of the intended entry, and the proprietor of the charge shall not, in respect of any further advance, be affected by such entry, unless the advance is made after the date when the notice ought to have been received in due course of post.

(2) If, by reason of any failure on the part of the registrar or the post office in reference to the notice, the proprietor of the charge suffers loss in relation to a further advance, he shall be entitled to be indemnified under this Act in like manner as if a mistake had occurred in the register; but if the loss arises by reason of an omission to register or amend the address for service, no indemnity shall be payable under this Act.

[(3) Where the proprietor of a charge is under an obligation, noted on the register, to make a further advance, a subsequent registered charge shall take effect subject to any further advance made pursuant to the obligation.][10]

---

[9] The recorded delivery service is an alternative to registered post: Recorded Delivery Service Act 1962 (10 & 11 Eliz. 2, c. 27), s.1 (1).

[10] Subs. (3) inserted by the Law of Property (Amendment) Act 1926 (16 & 17 Geo. 5, c. 11), s.5.

Alteration of charges

31.—(1) The proprietor of a charge may by deed, in the prescribed manner, alter the terms of the charge, with the consent of the proprietor of the registered land and of the proprietors of all registered charges (if any) of equal or inferior priority, affected by the alteration.

(2) A deed of alteration of a charge may contain an express demise or subdemise in like manner as an original deed of charge, and the provisions of this Act relating to a demise or subdemise contained in a deed of charge shall apply accordingly.

(3) The alteration shall be completed by the registrar entering it on the register.

Provisions when charge registered in names of several proprietors

32. Where a charge is registered in the names of two or more proprietors (whether jointly or in undivided shares) the mortgage term implied or comprised in the charge shall (but without prejudice to the beneficial interests in the mortgage money) vest in them as joint tenants, and the proprietors or the survivors or survivor of them or the personal representatives of the last survivor, shall have power to give valid receipts, notwithstanding that the mortgage money may be held in undivided shares, in like manner as if the money had been held on a joint account.

Transfer of charges

33.—(1) The proprietor of any registered charge may, in the prescribed manner, transfer the charge to another person as proprietor.

(2) The transfer shall be completed by the registrar entering on the register the transferee as proprietor of the charge transferred, but the transferor shall be deemed to remain proprietor of the charge until the name of the transferee is entered on the register in respect thereof.

(3) A registered transferee for valuable consideration of a charge and his successors in title shall not be affected by any irregularity or invalidity in the original charge itself of which the transferee did not have notice when it was transferred to him.

(4) On registration of any transfer of a charge, the term or subterm (if any) granted expressly or by implication by the charge or any deed of alteration shall, without any conveyance or assignment and notwithstanding anything to the contrary in the transfer or any other instrument, vest in the proprietor for the time being of the charge.

(5) Subject to any entry to the contrary on the register, the vesting of any term or subterm in accordance with this section in the proprietor of a charge shall, subject to the right of redemption, have the same effect as if such proprietor had been registered as the transferee for valuable consideration of the term or subterm.

Powers of proprietor of charge

34.—(1) Subject to any entry on the register to the contrary, the proprietor of a charge shall have and may exercise all the powers conferred by law on the owner of a legal mortgage.

(2) Subject to any entry to the contrary on the register and subject to the right of any persons appearing on the register to be prior incumbrancers, the proprietor of a charge may, after entry into possession and after having acquired a title under the Limitations Acts, execute a declaration, in the prescribed form, that the right of redemption is barred, and thereupon he shall be entitled, subject to furnishing any evidence which may be prescribed in support thereof, to be registered as proprietor of the land,

with the same consequences as if he had been a purchaser for valuable consideration of the land under the power of sale.

(3) An order for foreclosure shall be completed by the registration of the proprietor of the charge (or such other person as may be named in the foreclosure order absolute for that purpose) as the proprietor of the land, and by the cancellation of the charge and of all incumbrances and entries inferior thereto; and such registration shall operate in like manner and with the same consequences as if the proprietor of the charge or other person aforesaid had been a purchaser for valuable consideration of the land under a subsisting power of sale.

(4) A sale by the court or under the power of sale shall operate and be completed by registration in the same manner, as nearly as may be (but subject to any alterations on the register affecting the priority of the charge), as a transfer for valuable consideration by the proprietor of the land at the time of the registration of the charge would have operated or been completed, and, as respects the land transferred, the charge and all incumbrances and entries inferior thereto shall be cancelled.

(5) Notwithstanding the creation of a term or subterm, expressly or by implication, under this Act, such transfer shall (subject to any prior incumbrances or other entries on the register) operate to transfer the registered estate, and the mortgage term or subterm shall become merged, and any purported disposition of or dealing with the mortgage term or subterm apart from the charge, and any process or act purporting to keep alive that term or subterm after the cessation of the charge shall be void.

(6) For the purposes of this section an incumbrance or entry on the register shall not be deemed to be inferior to the charge in right of which title is made if the incumbrance or other interest is given the requisite priority by statute or otherwise.

Discharge of charges

35.—(1) The registrar shall, on the requisition of the proprietor of any charge, or on due proof of the satisfaction (whole or partial) thereof, notify on the register in the prescribed manner, by cancelling or varying the original entry or otherwise, the cessation (whole or partial) of the charge, and thereupon the charge shall be deemed to have ceased (in whole or in part) accordingly.

(2) On the notification on the register of the entire cessation of a registered charge, whether as to the whole or part only of the land affected thereby, the term or subterm implied in or granted by the charge or by any deed of alteration, so far as it affects the land to which the discharge extends, shall merge and be extinguished in the registered estate in reversion without any surrender.

Rules as to subcharges

36.—Rules shall be made for applying the provisions of the Law of Property Act 1925 and of this Act to the case of charges by way of sub-mortgage, whether registered before or after the commencement of this Act.

As to Dealings generally

Powers of persons entitled to be registered

37.—(1) Where a person on whom the right to be registered as proprietor of registered land or of a registered charge has devolved by reason of the death of the proprietor, or has been conferred by a disposition or charge, in accordance with this Act, desires to dispose of or charge the land or to deal with the charge before he is himself registered as proprietor, he may do so in the prescribed manner, and subject to the prescribed conditions.

(2) Subject to the provisions of this Act with regard to registered dealings for valuable consideration, a disposition or charge so made shall have the same effect as if the person making it were registered as proprietor.

(3) Rules may be made for extending the provisions of this section to the case of any person entitled to be registered as first proprietor, and to any other case for which it may be deemed expedient to prescribe.

Certain provisions of the Law of Property Act to apply

38.—(1) The provisions as to execution of a conveyance on sale contained in the Law of Property Act 1925 shall apply, so far as applicable thereto, to transfers on sale of registered land.

(2) Rules may be made for prescribing the effect of covenants implied by virtue of the Law of Property Act 1925 in dispositions of registered land.

Deeds off register, how far to be void

39.—(1) Where any transaction relating exclusively to registered land or to a registered charge is capable of being effected and is effected by a registered disposition, then, subject to any prescribed exceptions, any deed or instrument, other than the registered disposition, which is executed by the proprietor for the purpose of giving effect to the transaction shall be void, but only so far as the transaction is carried out by the registered disposition.

(2) Rules may be made for providing for cases in which any additional deed or instrument may be properly executed and for enabling the registrar to certify that in any special cases an additional deed or instrument will be proper and valid.

Creation and discharge of restrictive covenants

40.—(1) Subject to any entry to the contrary on the register, and without prejudice to the rights of persons entitled to overriding interests (if any) and to any incumbrances entered on the register, who may not concur therein, the proprietor may in any registered disposition or other instrument by covenant, condition, or otherwise, impose or make binding, so far as the law permits, any obligation or reservation with respect to the building on or other user of the registered land or any part thereof, or with respect to mines and minerals (whether registered separately or as part of the registered land), or with respect to any other thing in like manner as if the proprietor were entitled to the registered land for his own benefit.

(2) The proprietor may (subject as aforesaid) release or waive any rights arising or which may arise by reason of any covenant or condition, or release any obligation or reservation the benefit of which is annexed or belongs to the registered land, to the same extent and in the same manner as if the rights in respect of the breach or the benefit of the covenant, condition, obligation, or reservation had been vested in him absolutely for his own benefit.

This subsection shall authorise the proprietor in reference to the registered land to give any licence, consent or approval which a tenant for life is by the Settled Land Act 1925 authorised to give in reference to settled land.

(3) Entries shall be made on the register in the prescribed manner of all obligations and reservations imposed by the proprietor, of the release or

waiver of any obligation or reservation, and of all obligations and reservations acquired by him for the benefit of the registered estate.

Transmissions of Land and Charges on Death and Bankruptcy

Transmissions of land and charges on death of proprietor

41.—(1) On the death of the sole proprietor, or of the survivor of two or more joint proprietors, of any registered land or charge, the personal representative of such sole deceased proprietor, or of the survivor of such joint proprietors, shall be entitled to be registered as proprietor in his place:

Provided that, where a special or additional personal representative is appointed by the court in reference to a registered estate, then on production of the order he shall be registered as proprietor either solely or jointly with any of the other personal representatives, as the case may require, and a copy of the order shall be filed at the registry.

(2) Pending an application for the appointment of a special or additional personal representative, a caution against dealings may be lodged under this Act by any person intending to apply to the court for the appointment.

(3) Subject as aforesaid, provision shall be made by rules for the manner in which effect is to be given on the register to transmissions on death.

(4) An assent by a personal representative shall, in the case of registered land, be in the prescribed form and the production of the assent in that form shall authorise the registrar to register the person named in the assent as the proprietor of the registered land.

Transmissions on bankruptcy of proprietor

42.—(1) Upon the bankruptcy of the proprietor of any registered land or charge his trustee shall (on production of the prescribed evidence to be furnished by the official receiver or trustee in bankruptcy that the land or charge is part of the property of the bankrupt divisible amongst his creditors) be entitled to be registered as proprietor in his place.

The official receiver shall be entitled to be registered pending the appointment of a trustee.

(2) Where a trustee in bankruptcy disclaims a registered lease under section fifty-four of the Bankruptcy Act 1914, and an order is made by the court vesting the lease in any person, the order shall direct the alteration of the register in favour of the person in whom the lease is so vested, and in such case the registrar shall, on being served with such order, forthwith (without notice to the bankrupt or any other person and without requiring production of the land certificate) alter the register accordingly, and no right to indemnity under this Act shall arise by reason of such alteration.

Effect of transmissions

43. Any person registered in the place of a deceased or bankrupt proprietor shall hold the land or charge in respect of which he is registered upon the trusts and for the purposes upon and subject to which the same is applicable by law, and subject to any minor interests subject to which the deceased or bankrupt proprietor held the same; but, save as aforesaid, he shall in all respects and in particular as respects any registered dealings with such land or charge, be in the same position as if he had taken such land or charge under a transfer for valuable consideration.

Vesting of term or subterm on transmission of charge

44.—(1) On the registration of any transmission of a charge the term or subterm granted (expressly or by implication) by the charge or any deed of alteration shall without any conveyance or assignment vest in the proprietor for the time being of the charge.

(2) Subject to any entry to the contrary on the register, the vesting of a term or subterm in accordance with this section in the proprietor of a charge, shall, subject to the right of redemption, have the same effect as if such proprietor had been registered as the transferee for valuable consideration of the term or subterm.

Proof of transmission of registered proprietorship

45. The fact of any person having become entitled to any registered land or charge in consequence of the death or bankruptcy of any proprietor shall be proved in the prescribed manner.

Subsidiary Provisions

Determination of leases, incumbrances, etc

46. The registrar shall, on proof to his satisfaction of—

> (*a*) the determination of any lease, rentcharge, or other estate or interest the title to which is registered under this Act; or
>
> (*b*) the discharge or determination (whole or partial) or variation of any lease, incumbrance, rentcharge, easement, right or other interest in land which is noted on the register as an incumbrance,

notify in the prescribed manner on the register the determination (whole or partial) or variation of such lease or other interest.

Vesting instruments and dispositions in name of proprietor

47.—(1) The registrar shall give effect on the register to any vesting order or vesting declaration (express or implied) made on the appointment or discharge of a trustee or otherwise, and to dispositions made in the name and on behalf of a proprietor by a person authorised to make the disposition; and the provisions of the Trustee Act 1925 relating to the appointment and discharge of trustees and the vesting of trust property, shall apply to registered land subject to the proper entry being made on the register.

(2) The registrar shall also give effect on the register in the prescribed manner to any vesting instrument which may be made pursuant to any statutory power.

PART IV

NOTICES, CAUTIONS, INHIBITIONS AND RESTRICTIONS

Notices

Registration of notice of lease

48.—(1) Any lessee or other person entitled to or interested in a lease of registered land, where the term granted is not an overriding interest, may apply to the registrar to register notice of such lease in the prescribed manner, and when so registered, every proprietor and the persons deriving title under him shall be deemed to be affected with notice of such lease, as being an incumbrance on the registered land in respect of which the notice is entered:

Provided that a proprietor of a charge or incumbrance registered or protected on the register prior to the registration of such notice shall not be deemed to be so affected by the notice unless such proprietor is, by reason of the lease having been made under a statutory or other power or by reason of his concurrence or otherwise, bound by the terms of the lease.

(2) In order to register notice of a lease, if the proprietor of the registered land affected does not concur in the registration thereof, the applicant shall obtain an order of the court authorising the registration of notice of the lease, and shall deliver the order to the registrar, accompanied with the original lease or a copy thereof, and thereupon the registrar shall make a note in the register identifying the lease or copy so deposited, and the lease or copy so deposited shall be deemed to be the instrument of which notice is given; but if the proprietor concurs in the notice being registered, notice may be entered in such manner as may be agreed upon:

Provided that, where the lease is binding on the proprietor of the land, neither the concurrence of such proprietor nor an order of the court shall be required.

Rules to provide for notice of other rights, interests and claims

49.—(1) The provisions of the last foregoing section shall be extended by the rules so as to apply to the registration of notices of or of claims in respect of—

(*a*) The grant or reservation of any annuity or rentcharge in possession, either perpetual or for a term of years absolute:

(*b*) The severance of any mines or minerals from the surface, except where the mines and minerals severed are expressly included in the registration:

(*c*) Land charges until the land charge is registered as a registered charge:

(*d*) The right of any person interested in the proceeds of sale of land held on trust for sale or in land subject to a settlement to require that (unless a trust corporation is acting as trustee) there shall be at least two trustees of the disposition on trust for sale or of the settlement:

(*e*) The rights of any widow in respect of dower or under the Intestates' Estates Act 1890 and any right to free bench or other like right saved by any statute coming into force concurrently with this Act (which rights shall take effect in equity as minor interests):

(*f*) Creditors' notices and any other right, interest, or claim which it may be deemed expedient to protect by notice instead of by caution, inhibition, or restriction.

[(*g*) Charging orders (within the meaning of the Charging Orders Act 1979) which in the case of unregistered land may be protected by registration under the Land Charges Act 1972 and which, notwithstanding section 59 of this Act, it may be deemed expedient to protect by notice instead of by caution.][11]

(2) A notice shall not be registered in respect of any estate, right, or interest which (independently of this Act) is capable of being overridden by the proprietor under a trust for sale or the powers of the Settled Land Act 1925, or any other statute, or of a settlement, and of being protected by a restriction in the prescribed manner:

Provided that notice of such an estate right or interest may be lodged pending the appointment of trustees of a disposition on trust for sale or a settlement, and if so lodged, shall be cancelled if and when the appointment is made and the proper restriction (if any) is entered.

(3) A notice when registered in respect of a right, interest, or claim shall not affect prejudicially—

(*a*) The powers of disposition of the personal representative of the

[11] Added by the Charging Orders Act 1979 (c. 53), s.3 (3).

deceased under whose will or by the operation of whose intestacy the right, interest, or claim arose; or

(*b*) The powers of disposition (independently of this Act) of a proprietor holding the registered land on trust for sale.

Notices of restrictive covenants

50.—(1) Any person entitled to the benefit of a restrictive covenant or agreement (not being a covenant or agreement made between a lessor and lessee) with respect to the building on or other user of registered land may apply to the registrar to enter notice thereof on the register, and where practicable the notice shall be by reference to the instrument, if any, which contains the covenant or agreement, and a copy or abstract of such instrument shall be filed at the registry; and where any such covenant or agreement appears to exist at the time of first registration, notice thereof shall be entered on the register. In the case of registered land the notice aforesaid shall take the place of registration as a land charge.

(2) When such a notice is entered the proprietor of the land and the persons deriving title under him (except incumbrancers or other persons who at the time when the notice is entered may not be bound by the covenant or agreement) shall be deemed to be affected with notice of the covenant or agreement as being an incumbrance on the land.

(3) Where the covenant or agreement is discharged [*modified or dealt with*][12] by an order under the Law of Property Act 1925, or otherwise, or the court refuses to grant an injunction for enforcing the same, the entry shall either be cancelled or reference made to the order or other instrument and a copy of the order, judgment, or instrument shall be filed at the registry.

(4) The notice shall, when practicable, refer to the land, whether registered or not, for the benefit of which the restriction was made.

Notice of manorial incidents

51. Where land is affected by manorial incidents, the registrar may enter a note of that fact on the register, and may cancel such note when extinguishment of the manorial incidents has been proved to his satisfaction.

Effect of notices

52.—(1) A disposition by the proprietor shall take effect subject to all estates, rights, and claims which are protected by way of notice on the register at the date of the registration or entry of notice of the disposition, but only if and so far as such estates, rights, and claims may be valid and are not (independently of this Act) overridden by the disposition.

(2) Where notice of a claim is entered on the register, such entry shall operate by way of notice only, and shall not operate to render the claim valid whether made adversely to or for the benefit of the registered land or charge.

Cautions

Cautions against first registration

53.—(1) Any person having or claiming such an interest in land not already registered as entitles him to object to any disposition thereof being made without his consent, may lodge a caution with the registrar to the effect that the cautioner is entitled to notice in the prescribed form, and to

[12] Words in square brackets substituted by the Law of Property Act 1969 (c. 59), s.28 (7).

be served in the prescribed manner, of any application that may be made for the registration of an interest in the land affecting the right of the cautioner.

(2) The caution shall be supported by an affidavit or declaration in the prescribed form, stating the nature of the interest of the cautioner, the land and estate therein to be affected by such caution, and such other matters as may be prescribed.

(3) After a caution has been lodged in respect of any estate, which has not already been registered, registration shall not be made of such estate until notice has been served on the cautioner to appear and oppose, if he thinks fit, such registration, and the prescribed time has elapsed since the date of the service of such notice, or the cautioner has entered an appearance, whichever may first happen.

Cautions against dealings

54.—(1) Any person interested under any unregistered instrument, or interested as a judgment creditor, or otherwise howsoever, in any land or charge registered in the name of any other person, may lodge a caution with the registrar to the effect that no dealing with such land or charge on the part of the proprietor is to be registered until notice has been served upon the cautioner:

Provided that a person whose estate, right, interest, or claim has been registered or protected by a notice or restriction shall not be entitled (except with the consent of the registrar) to lodge a caution in respect of such estate, right, interest, or claim, but this provision shall not operate to prevent an incumbrancer or assignee of a life interest, remainder, reversion or executory interest, from lodging a priority caution in a specially prescribed form.

(2) A caution lodged under this section shall be supported by such evidence as may be prescribed.

Effect of cautions against dealings

55.—(1) After any such caution against dealings has been lodged in respect of any registered land or charge, the registrar shall not, without the consent of the cautioner, register any dealing or make any entry on the register for protecting the rights acquired under a deposit of land or charge certificate or other dealing by the proprietor with such land or charge until he has served notice on the cautioner, warning him that his caution will cease to have any effect after the expiration of the prescribed number of days next following the date at which such notice is served; and after the expiration of such time as aforesaid the caution shall cease unless an order to the contrary is made by the registrar, and upon the caution so ceasing the registered land or charge may be dealt with in the same manner as if no caution had been lodged.

(2) If before the expiration of the said period the cautioner, or some person on his behalf, appears before the registrar, and where so required by the registrar gives sufficient security to indemnify every party against any damage that may be sustained by reason of any dealing with the registered land or charge, or the making of any such entry as aforesaid, being delayed, the registrar may thereupon, if he thinks fit to do so, delay registering any dealing with the land or charge or making any such entry for such period as he thinks just.

General provisions as to cautions

56.—(1) Any person aggrieved by any act done by the registrar in relation to a caution under this Act may appeal to the court in the prescribed manner.

(2) A caution lodged in pursuance of this Act shall not prejudice the claim or title of any person and shall have no effect whatever except as in this Act mentioned.

(3) If any person lodges a caution with the registrar without reasonable cause, he shall be liable to make to any person who may have sustained damage by the lodging of the caution such compensation as may be just, and such compensation shall be recoverable as a debt by the person who has sustained damage from the person who lodged the caution.

(4) The personal representative of a deceased cautioner may consent or object to registration or a dealing in the same manner as a cautioner.

Inhibitions

Power for court or registrar to inhibit registered dealings

57.—(1) The court, or, subject to an appeal to the court, the registrar, upon the application of any person interested, made in the prescribed manner, in relation to any registered land or charge, may, after directing such inquiries (if any) to be made and notices to be given and hearing such persons as the court or registrar thinks expedient, issue an order or make an entry inhibiting for a time, or until the occurrence of an event to be named in such order or entry, or generally until further order or entry, the registration or entry of any dealing with any registered land or registered charge.

(2) The court or registrar may make or refuse to make any such order or entry, and annex thereto any terms or conditions the court or registrar may think fit, and discharge such order or cancel such entry when granted, with or without costs, and generally act in the premises in such manner as the justice of the case requires.

(3) Any person aggrieved by any act done by the registrar in pursuance of this section may appeal to the court in the prescribed manner.

(4) The court or the registrar may, in lieu of an inhibition, order a notice or restriction to be placed on the register.

Restrictions

Power to place restrictions on register

58.—(1) Where the proprietor of any registered land or charge desires to place restrictions on transferring or charging the land or on disposing of or dealing with the land or charge in any manner in which he is by this Act authorised to dispose of or deal with it, or on the deposit by way of security of any certificate, the proprietor may apply to the registrar to make an entry in the register that no transaction to which the application relates shall be effected, unless the following things, or such of them as the proprietor may determine, are done—

(*a*) unless notice of any application for the transaction is transmitted by post to such address as he may specify to the registrar;

(*b*) unless the consent of some person or persons, to be named by the proprietor, is given to the transaction;

(*c*) unless some such other matter or thing is done as may be required by the applicant and approved by the registrar:

Provided that no restriction under this section shall extend or apply to dispositions of or dealings with minor interests.

(2) The registrar shall thereupon, if satisfied of the right of the applicant to give the directions, enter the requisite restriction on the register, and no transaction to which the restriction relates shall be effected except in conformity therewith; but it shall not be the duty of the registrar to enter any such restriction, except upon such terms as to payment of fees and

otherwise as may be prescribed, or to enter any restriction that the registrar may deem unreasonable or calculated to cause inconvenience.

(3) In the case of joint proprietors the restriction may be to the effect that when the number of proprietors is reduced below a certain specified number no disposition shall be registered except under an order of the court, or of the registrar after inquiry into title, subject to appeal to the court, and, subject to general rules, such an entry under this subsection as may be prescribed shall be obligatory unless it is shown to the registrar's satisfaction that the joint proprietors are entitled for their own benefit, or can give valid receipts for capital money, or that one of them is a trust corporation.

(4) Any such restrictions, except such as are in this section declared to be obligatory, may at any time be withdrawn or modified at the instance of all the persons for the time being appearing by the register to be interested in such directions, and shall also be liable to be set aside by an order of the court.

(5) Rules may be made to enable applications to be made for the entry of restrictions by persons other than the proprietor.

Protection of various Interests

Writs, orders, deeds of arrangement, pending actions, etc.

59.—(1) A writ, order, deed of arrangement, pending action, or other interest which in the case of unregistered land may be protected by registration under the Land Charges Act 1925[13] shall, where the land affected or the charge securing the debt affected is registered, be protected only by lodging a creditor's notice, a bankruptcy inhibition or a caution against dealings with the land or the charge.

(2) Registration of a land charge (other than a local land charge) shall, where the land affected is registered, be effected only by registering under this Act a notice caution or other prescribed entry:

Provided that before a land charge including a local land charge affecting registered land (being a charge to secure money) is realised, it shall be registered and take effect as a registered charge under this Act in the prescribed manner, without prejudice to the priority conferred by the land charge.

(3) A person interested under a writ or order for enforcing a judgment against registered land or a registered charge, may inspect and make copies of and extracts from the register and documents referred to therein which are in the custody of the registrar, so far as the same relate to the registered land or charge, and may, in accordance with this Act, lodge a caution against dealings therewith.

(4) When a land charge protected by notice has been discharged as to all or any part of the land comprised therein, the notices relating thereto and to all devolutions of and dealings therewith shall be vacated as to the registered land affecting by the discharge.

(5) The foregoing provisions of this section shall apply only to writs and orders, deeds of arrangement, pending actions and land charges which if the land were unregistered would for purposes of protection be required to be registered or re-registered after the commencement of this Act under the Land Charges Act 1925; and for the purposes of this section a land charge does not include a puisne mortgage or an Inland Revenue charge.

(6) Subject to the provisions of this Act relating to fraud and to the title of a trustee in bankruptcy, a purchaser acquiring title under a registered disposition, shall not be concerned with any pending action, writ, order, deed of arrangement, or other document, matter, or claim (not being an

[13] Now the Land Charges Act 1972 (c. 61) *ante.,* p. 320.

overriding interest [*or a charge for capital transfer tax subject to which the disposition takes effect under section 73 of this Act*][4]) which is not protected by a caution or other entry on the register, whether he has or has not notice thereof, express, implied, or constructive.

(7) In this section references to registration under the Land Charges Act 1925[13] apply to any registration made under any other statute which, in the case of unregistered land, is by the Land Charges Act 1925 to have effect as if the registration had been made under that Act.

Notice of incumbrances registered under the Companies Act

60.—(1) Where a company, registered under the Companies (Consolidation) Act 1908,[15] is registered as proprietor of any estate or charge already registered, the registrar shall not be concerned with any mortgage, charge, debenture, debenture stock, trust deed for securing the same, or other incumbrance created or issued by the company, whether or not registered under that Act, unless the same is registered or protected by caution or otherwise under this Act.

(2) No indemnity shall be payable under this Act by reason of a purchaser acquiring any interest under a registered disposition from the company free from any such incumbrance.

Protection of creditors prior to registration of trustee in bankruptcy

61.—(1) The registrar shall as soon as practicable after registration of a petition in bankruptcy as a pending action under the Land Charges Act 1925,[16] register a notice (in this Act called a creditor's notice) against the title of any proprietor of any registered land or charge which appears to be affected, and such notice shall protect the rights of all creditors, and unless cancelled by the registrar in the prescribed manner such notice shall remain in force until a bankruptcy inhibition is registered or the trustee in bankruptcy is registered as proprietor.

No fee shall be charged for the registration of the notice.

(2) Until a creditor's notice is registered, a petition in bankruptcy filed after the commencement of this Act shall not, as respects any registered disposition for money or money's worth of any registered land or charge, be notice or evidence of any act of bankruptcy therein alleged.

(3) The registrar shall, as soon as practicable after registration of a receiving order in bankruptcy under the Land Charges Act 1925,[16] enter an inhibition (in this Act called a bankruptcy inhibition) against the title of any proprietor of any registered land or charge which appears to be affected.

No fee shall be charged for the registration of the inhibition.

(4) From and after the entry of a bankruptcy inhibition (but without prejudice to dealings with or in right of interests or charges having priority over the estate or charge of the bankrupt proprietor), no dealing affecting the registered land or charge of the proprietor, other than the registration of the trustee in bankruptcy, shall be entered on the register until the inhibition is vacated as to the whole or part of the land or charge dealt with.

(5) If and when a proprietor of any registered land or charge is adjudged bankrupt, his registered estate or interest, if belonging to him beneficially, and whether acquired before or after the date of adjudication, shall vest in the trustee in bankruptcy in accordance with the statutory provisions relating to bankruptcy for the time being in force.

---

[14] The words in square brackets were added by the Finance Act 1975 (c. 7), Sched. 12.
[15] See now the Companies Acts 1948 to 1967.
[16] Now the Land Charges Act 1972 (c. 61), *ante.*, p. 320.

(6) Where under a disposition to a purchaser in good faith for money or money's worth such purchaser is registered as proprietor of an estate or a charge, then, notwithstanding that an available act of bankruptcy has been committed by the person making the disposition, the title of his trustee in bankruptcy acquired after the commencement of this Act shall, as from the date of such disposition, be void as against such purchaser unless at the date of such disposition, either a creditor's notice or a bankruptcy inhibition has been registered, but a purchaser who, at the date of the execution of the registered disposition, has notice of an available act of bankruptcy, or of the receiving order, or adjudication, shall not be deemed to take in good faith.

Nothing in this section shall impose on a purchaser a liability to make any search under the Land Charges Act 1925.[16]

(7) Where the estate or assets of a bankrupt proprietor suffer loss by reason of the omission of the registrar to register a creditor's notice or bankruptcy inhibition, as required by this section, or on account of the execution or registration of a disposition after a petition is registered as a pending action or after a receiving order is registered and before the registration of a creditor's notice or bankruptcy inhibition, the trustee in bankruptcy shall be entitled to indemnity as a person suffering loss by reason of an error or omission in the register.

(8) If neither a creditor's notice nor a bankruptcy inhibition is registered against a bankrupt proprietor, nothing in this section shall prejudicially affect a registered disposition of any registered land or charge acquired by the bankrupt after adjudication which would have been valid by virtue of section forty-seven of the Bankruptcy Act 1914, if the land or charge had not been registered.

(9) If and when a bankruptcy inhibition is wholly or partially vacated, for any cause other than by reason of the registration of the trustee in bankruptcy, any registered estate or interest vested in the trustee in bankruptcy shall, as respects the registered land or charge to which the vacation extends, be divested and the same shall vest in the proprietor in whom it would have been vested if there had been no adjudication in bankruptcy.

(10) The official receiver or trustee in bankruptcy may inspect the register so far as it relates to any proprietor against whom a receiving order has been made, and any creditor, on behalf of himself and all other creditors, or the official receiver or trustee in bankruptcy, may lodge a caution against any such proprietor in respect of any minor interest affecting the registered land.

Rules to be made as to certain details

62. Rules shall be made under this Act—

    (*a*) For postponing the registration of a creditor's notice or bankruptcy inhibition, where the name, address and description of the debtor appearing in the application for the registration of the pending action or receiving order are not identical with those stated in the register, until the registrar is satisfied as to the identity of the debtor;

    (*b*) For requiring the official receiver to notify the registrar any mistake occurring in the receiving order or any other fact relevant to any proposed amendment in the register; and for enabling the registrar to make any consequential amendment;

    (*c*) For providing for the whole or partial vacation (subject to notice to the official receiver or trustee in bankruptcy and to his right to appeal to the court) of a bankruptcy inhibition, where the receiving order is rescinded or the bankruptcy is annulled, or the registrar is satisfied that the bankruptcy proceedings do not affect or have ceased to affect the statutory powers of the bankrupt to deal with the registered land or charge.

Part V

Land and Charge Certificates

Issue of land and charge certificates

63.—(1) On the first registration of a freehold or leasehold interest in land, and on the registration of a charge, a land certificate, or charge certificate, as the case may be, shall be prepared in the prescribed form: it shall state whether the title is absolute, good leasehold, qualified or possessory, and it shall be either delivered to the proprietor or deposited in the registry as the proprietor may prefer.

(2) If so deposited in the registry it shall be officially endorsed from time to time, as in this Act provided, with notes of all subsequent entries in the register affecting the registered land or charge to which it relates.

(3) The proprietor may at any time apply for the delivery of the certificate to himself or to such person as he may direct, and may at any time again deposit it in the land registry.

(4) The preparation, issue, endorsement, and deposit in the registry of the certificate shall be effected without cost to the proprietor.

Certificates to be produced and noted on dealings

64.—(1) So long as a land certificate or charge certificate is outstanding, it shall be produced to the registrar—
  (*a*) on every entry in the register of a disposition by the proprietor of the registered land or charge to which it relates; and
  (*b*) on every registered transmission; and
  (*c*) in every case (except as hereinafter mentioned) where under this Act or otherwise notice of any estate right or claim or a restriction is entered or placed on the register, adversely affecting the title of the proprietor of the registered land or charge, but not in the case of the lodgement of a caution or of an inhibition or of a creditor's notice, or of the entry of a notice of a lease at a rent without taking a fine [*or a notice of a charge for capital transfer tax.*][17]

(2) A note of every such entry or transmission shall be officially entered on the certificate and the registrar shall have the same powers of compelling the production of certificates as are conferred on him by this Act as to the production of maps, surveys, books and other documents.

(3) On the completion of the registration of a transferee or grantee of any registered land or charge, the registrar shall deliver to him a land certificate or charge certificate, and where part only of the land is dealt with shall also deliver to the transferor or grantor of a land certificate containing a description of the land retained by him.

(4) Where a transfer of land is made by the proprietor of a registered charge in exercise of any power vested in him, it may be registered, and a new land certificate may be issued to the purchaser, without production of the former land certificate (when not deposited at the registry), but the charge certificate, if any, must be produced or accounted for in accordance with this section.

The provisions of this subsection shall be extended in the prescribed manner to the cases of—
  (*a*) an order for foreclosure absolute;

---

[17] The words in square brackets were substituted by the Finance Act 1975 (c. 7), Sched. 12.

(*b*) a proprietor of a charge or a mortgage obtaining a title to the land under the Limitation Acts;

(*c*) title being acquired under a title paramount to the registered estate, including a title acquired pursuant to a vesting or other order of the court or other competent authority.

Deposit at registry of certificate of mortgaged land

65. Where a charge or mortgage (otherwise than by deposit) is registered, or is protected by a caution in a specially prescribed form, the land certificate shall be deposited at the registry until the charge or mortgage is cancelled.

Creation of liens by deposit of certificates

66. The proprietor of any registered land or charge may, subject to the overriding interests, if any, to any entry to the contrary on the register, and to any estates, interests, charges, or rights registered or protected on the register at the date of the deposit, create a lien on the registered land or charge by deposit of the land certificate or charge certificate; and such lien shall, subject as aforesaid, be equivalent to a lien created in the case of unregistered land by the deposit of documents of title or of the mortgage deed by an owner entitled for his own benefit to the registered estate, or a mortgagee beneficially entitled to the mortgage, as the case may be.

Issue of new certificates

67.—(1) The registrar may when a land certificate or charge certificate is produced to him grant a new land certificate or charge certificate in the place of the one produced.

(2) A new land certificate or charge certificate may be issued in place of one lost or destroyed, or in the possession of a person out of the jurisdiction of the High Court, on such terms as to advertisement notice or delay as may be prescribed.

Certificates to be evidence

68. Any land certificate or charge certificate shall be admissible as evidence of the several matters therein contained.

Part VI

General Provision as to Registration and the Effect thereof

Effect of registration on the legal estate

69.—(1) The proprietor of land (whether he was registered before or after the commencement of this Act) shall be deemed to have vested in him without any conveyance, where the registered land is freehold, the legal estate in fee simple in possession, and where the registered land is leasehold the legal term created by the registered lease, but subject to the overriding interests, if any, including any mortgage term or charge by way of legal mortgage created by or under the Law of Property Act 1925, or this Act or otherwise which has priority to the registered estate.

(2) Where any legal estate or term left outstanding at the date of first registration (whether before or after the commencement of this Act), or disposed of or created under section forty-nine of the Land Transfer Act 1875, before the commencement of this Act, becomes satisfied, or the proprietor of the land becomes entitled to require the same to be vested in or surrendered to him, and the entry, if any, for protecting the same on the

register has been cancelled, the same shall thereupon, without any conveyance, vest in the proprietor of the land, as if the same had been conveyed or surrendered to him as the case may be.

(3) If and when any person is registered as first proprietor of land in a compulsory area after the commencement of this Act the provisions of the Law of Property Act 1925, for getting in legal estates shall apply to any legal estate in the land which was expressed to be conveyed or created in favour of a purchaser or lessee before the commencement of this Act but which failed to pass or to be created by reason of the omission of such purchaser or lessee to be registered as proprietor of the land under the Land Transfer Act 1875 and 1897, and shall operate to vest that legal estate in the person so registered as proprietor on his registration, but subject to any mortgage term or charge by way of legal mortgage having priority thereto.

(4) The estate for the time being vested in the proprietor shall only be capable of being disposed of or dealt with by him in manner authorised by this Act.

(5) Nothing in this section operates to render valid a lease registered with possessory or good leasehold title.

Liability of registered land to overriding interests

70.—(1) All registered land shall, unless under the provisions of this Act the contrary is expressed on the register, be deemed to be subject to such of the following overriding interests as may be for the time being subsisting in reference thereto, and such interests shall not be treated as incumbrances within the meaning of this Act (that is to say):—

(*a*) Rights of common, drainage rights, customary rights (until extinguished), public rights, profits à prendre, rights of sheepwalk, rights of way, watercourses, rights of water, and other easements not being equitable easements required to be protected by notice on the register;

(*b*) Liability to repair highways by reason of tenure, quit-rents, crown rents, heriots, and other rents and charges (until extinguished) having their origin in tenure;

(*c*) Liability to repair the chancel of any church;

(*d*) Liability in respect of embankments, and sea and river walls;

(*e*) Land tax [*tithe rentcharge*],[18] payments in lieu of tithe, and charges or annuities payable for the redemption of tithe rentcharges;

(*f*) Subject to the provisions of this Act, rights acquired or in course of being acquired under the Limitation Acts;

(*g*) The rights of every person in actual occupation of the land or in receipt of the rents and profits thereof, save where enquiry is made of such person and the rights are not disclosed;

(*h*) In the case of a possessory, qualified, or good leasehold title, all estates, rights, interests, and powers excepted from the effect of registration;

(*i*) Rights under local land charges unless and until registered or protected on the register in the prescribed manner;

(*j*) Rights of fishing and sporting, seignorial and manorial rights of all descriptions (until extinguished), and franchises;

(*k*) Leases for any term or interest not exceeding twenty-one years, granted at a rent without taking a fine;

(*l*) In respect of land registered before the commencement of this Act, rights to mines and minerals, and rights of entry, search, and user, and other rights and reservations incidental to or required for the

---

[18] Words in square brackets repealed by the Tithe Act 1936 (26 Geo. 5 & 1 Edw. 8, c. 43), ss. 1, 48, 9th Sched. Land tax abolished by the Finance Act 1963 (c. 25).

purpose of giving full effect to the enjoyment of rights to mines and minerals or of property in mines or minerals, being rights which, where the title was first registered before the first day of January, eighteen hundred and ninety-eight, were created before that date, and where the title was first registered after the thirty-first day of December, eighteen hundred and ninety-seven, were created before the date of first registration:

Provided that, where it is proved to the satisfaction of the registrar that any land registered or about to be registered is exempt from land tax, or tithe rentcharge or payments in lieu of tithe, or from charges or annuities payable for the redemption of tithe rentcharge, the registrar may notify the fact on the register in the prescribed manner.

(2) Where at the time of first registration any easement, right, privilege, or benefit created by an instrument and appearing on the title adversely affects the land, the registrar shall enter a note thereof on the register.

(3) Where the existence of any overriding interest mentioned in this section is proved to the satisfaction of the registrar or admitted, he may (subject to any prescribed exceptions) enter notice of the same or of a claim thereto on the register, but no claim to an easement, right, or privilege not created by an instrument shall be noted against the title to the servient land if the proprietor of such land (after the prescribed notice is given to him) shows sufficient cause to the contrary.

Dispositions by virtue of overriding interests

71. Where by virtue of any interest or power which is an overriding interest a mortgagee or other person disposes of any estate, charge, or right in or upon a registered estate, and the disposition is capable of being registered, the registrar shall, if so required, give effect to the disposition on the register.

Appurtenances

72. If before the registration of any freehold or leasehold interest in land with an absolute or good leasehold title any easement, right, or privilege has been acquired for the benefit thereof, then, on such registration, the easement, right, or privilege shall, subject to any entry to the contrary on the register, become appurtenant to the registered land in like manner as if it had been granted to the proprietor who is registered aforesaid.

. . . . . .

Notice of trust not to affect registered dealing

74. Subject to the provisions of this Act as to settled land, neither the registrar nor any person dealing with a registered estate or charge shall be affected with notice of a trust express implied or constructive, and references to trusts shall, so far as possible, be excluded from the register.

Acquisition of title by possession

75.—(1) The Limitation Acts shall apply to registered land in the same manner and to the same extent as those Acts apply to land not registered, except that where, if the land were not registered, the estate of the person registered as proprietor would be extinguished, such estate shall not be extinguished but shall be deemed to be held by the proprietor for the time being in trust for the person who, by virtue of the said Acts, has acquired title against any proprietor, but without prejudice to the estates and interests of any other person interested in the land whose estate or interest is not extinguished by those Acts.

(2) Any person claiming to have acquired a title under the Limitation

Acts to a registered estate in the land may apply to be registered as proprietor thereof.

(3) The register shall, on being satisfied as to the applicant's title, enter the applicant as proprietor either with absolute, good leasehold, qualified, or possessory title, as the case may require, but without prejudice to any estate or interest protected by any entry on the register which may not have been extinguished under the Limitation Acts, and such registration shall, subject as aforesaid, have the same effect as the registration of a first proprietor; but the proprietor or the applicant or any other person interested may apply to the court for the determination of any question arising under this section.

(4) [*Repealed by the Land Registration and Land Charges Act* 1971, *s.* 14(1), (2)(*a*); 2*nd Sched.*, *Pt.* I.]

(5) Rules may be made for applying (subject to any necessary modifications) the provisions of this section to cases where an easement, right or privilege has been acquired by prescription.

Description of registered land

76. Registered land may be described—

- (*a*) by means of a verbal description and a filed plan or general map, based on the ordnance map; or
- (*b*) by reference to a deed or other document, a copy or extract whereof is filed at the registry, containing a sufficient description, and a plan or map thereof; or
- (*c*) otherwise as the applicant for registration may desire, and the registrar, or, if the applicant prefers, the court, may approve,

regard being had to ready identification of parcels, correct descriptions of boundaries, and, so far as may be, uniformity of practice; but the boundaries of all freehold land and all requisite details in relation to the same, shall whenever practicable, be entered on the register or filed plan, or general map, and the filed plan, if any, or general map shall be used for assisting the identification of the land.

Conversion of possessory into absolute or good leasehold title

77.—(1) Where land has been registered with a possessory title before the commencement of this Act, and the registrar is satisfied as to the title, he may register it at any time as absolute or good leasehold, whether the proprietor consents to such registration or not, but, unless the registration is made at the request of the proprietor, without charging any fee therefor.

(2) Where the registrar is satisfied as to the title he may, on a transfer for valuable consideration of land registered with a qualified, good leasehold or possessory title, enter the title of a transferee or grantee as absolute or good leasehold, as the case may require or admit, whether the transferee or grantee consents or not, but in that case no additional fee shall be charged.

(3) The following provisions shall apply with respect to land registered with a qualified or possessory title:—

- (*a*) Where the title registered is possessory, the application for the registration of a transfer for valuable consideration shall, subject to any provisions to the contrary which may be prescribed, be accompanied by all the documents of or relating to the title (including contracts, abstracts, counsel's opinions, requisitions and replies, and other like documents), in the applicant's possession or under his control; and where the title registered is qualified, such application shall be accompanied by such documents, if any, as may relate to the matters excepted from the effect of registration;
- (*b*) Where the land has been registered, if freehold land, for fifteen

years, or if leasehold land, for ten years, with a possessory title, the registrar shall, if satisfied that the proprietor is in possession, and after giving such notices, if any, as may be prescribed, enter the title of the proprietor of the freehold land as absolute, and the title of the proprietor of the leasehold land as good leasehold, save that if the date of first registration occurred before the first day of January, nineteen hundred and nine, the registrar shall have power to postpone the registration of an absolute or good leasehold title until, after investigation, he is satisfied in regard to the title.

(4) Where the land has been registered with a good leasehold title for at least ten years, the registrar may, subject to the payment of any additional insurance fee and to any advertisements or inquiries which may be prescribed, and if he is satisfied that the proprietor or successive proprietors has or have been in possession during the said period, at the request of the proprietor enter his title as absolute.

(5) If any claim adverse to the title of the proprietor has been made, an entry shall not be made on the register under this section unless and until the claim has been disposed of.

(6) Any person, other than the proprietor, who suffers loss by reason of any entry on the register made by virtue of this section shall be entitled to be indemnified under this Act as if a mistake had been made in the register.

Provisions as to undivided shares in land

78.—(1) Where in the case of land belonging to persons in undivided shares the entirety of the land is registered at the commencement of this Act, and the persons entitled to the several undivided shares are registered as proprietors, the registrar shall, on the occasion of the first dealing affecting the title after the commencement of this Act, rectify the register by entering as the proprietors of the entirety of the land the persons in whom the legal estate therein has become vested by virtue of the Law of Property Act, 1925, and it shall be the duty of the persons registered as the proprietors of the undivided shares in the land to furnish to the registrar such evidence as he may require to enable him to ascertain the persons in whom such legal estate has become so vested as aforesaid.

(2) Where at the commencement of this Act the title to an undivided share in land is registered but the entirety of the land is not registered, the registrar may, at any time, after giving notice to the proprietor and to the other persons, if any, who appear by the register to be interested therein, remove from the register the title to the undivided share, and such removal shall have the like effect as if it had been effected by the proprietor with the assent of such other persons as aforesaid in pursuance of the power in that behalf contained in this Act:

Provided that, if within one year from the commencement of this Act or such extended time as the registrar may allow, and before the removal of the undivided share from the register in manner aforesaid, the persons in whom the legal estate of the entirety of the land is vested by virtue of the Law of Property Act, 1925, or any persons interested in more than an undivided half of the land or the income thereof, make an application in the prescribed manner for the purpose and furnish the prescribed evidence, the registrar shall, without charging any fee, register the persons in whom such legal estate is so vested as proprietors of that estate, subject to any incumbrance capable of registration affecting the entirety of the land, but free from any charge or incumbrance (whether formerly registered or not) affecting an undivided share, and when the title to the entirety of the land is so registered, the title to the undivided share shall be closed.

(3) If the person in whom the legal estate in the entirety of the land is so

vested in the Public Trustee, he shall not be registered as proprietor pursuant to this section unless and until he has been duly requested to act in accordance with the Law of Property Act, 1925, and has accepted the trust.

(4) After the commencement of this Act, no entry other than a caution against dealings with the entirety shall be made in the register as respects the title to an undivided share in land.

Addresses for service and notices

79.—(1) Every person whose name is entered on the register as proprietor of any registered land or charge, or as cautioner, or as entitled to receive any notice, or in any other character shall furnish to the registrar a place of address in the United Kingdom.

(2) Every notice by this Act required to be given to any person shall be served personally, or sent through the post in a registered letter[19] marked outside "His Majesty's Land Registry," and directed to such person at the address furnished to the registrar, and, unless returned, shall be deemed to have been received by the person addressed within such period, not less than seven days, exclusive of the day of posting, as may be prescribed.

(3) The Postmaster-General[20] shall give directions for the immediate return to the registrar of all letters marked as aforesaid, and addressed to any person who cannot be found, and on the return of any letter containing any notice, the registrar shall act in the matter requiring such notice to be given in such manner as may be prescribed.

(4) A purchaser shall not be affected by the omission to send any notice by this Act directed to be given or by the non-receipt thereof.

Bona vacantia and forfeiture

80. Subject to the express provisions of this Act relating to the effect of first registration of title and the effect of registration of a disposition for valuable consideration, nothing in this Act affects any right of His Majesty to any bona vacantia or forfeiture.

Power to remove land from the register

81.—(1) The proprietor of registered land not situated in an area where the registration of title is compulsory, and, in every case where the entirety of the land is not registered, the proprietor of an undivided share in land, may, with the consent of the other persons (if any) for the time being appearing by the register to be interested therein, and on delivering up the land certificate and, if the land is subject to any registered charges, the charge certificates, remove the land (including an undivided share) from the register.

(2) After land is removed from the register no further entries shall be made respecting it, and inspection of the register may be made and office copies of the entries therein may be issued, subject to such regulations as may be prescribed.

(3) If the land so removed from the register is situated within the jurisdiction of the Middlesex or Yorkshire registries, it shall again be subject to such jurisdiction as from the date of the removal.[21]

---

[19] The recorded delivery service is an alternative to registered post: Recorded Delivery Service Act 1962 (10 & 11 Eliz. 2, c. 27), s. 1(1).

[20] Now the Post Office.

[21] The Middlesex Deeds Registry has been finally closed for all purposes (Land Registration Act 1936 (26 Geo. 5 & 1 Edw. 8, c. 26), s. 2; Middlesex Deeds Act 1940 (3 & 4 Geo. 6, c. 34), s. 1). As to the closure of the Deeds Registries in the Ridings of Yorkshire, see the Law of Property Act 1969 (c. 59), ss. 16–22. As to the actual closing of the Registries in the North and West Ridings, see *ibid.* ss. 16, 17(1) and The Registration of Title (Teesside, Leeds and Sheffield) Order 1970.

Part VII

Rectification of Register and Indemnity

Rectification of the register

82.—(1) The register may be rectified pursuant to an order of the court or by the registrar, subject to an appeal to the court, in any of the following cases, but subject to the provisions of this section:—

(*a*) Subject to any express provisions of this Act to the contrary, where a court of competent jurisdiction has decided that any person is entitled to any estate right or interest in or to any registered land or charge, and as a consequence of such decision such court is of opinion that a rectification of the register is required, and makes an order to that effect;

(*b*) Subject to any express provision of this Act to the contrary, where the court, on the application in the prescribed manner of any person who is aggrieved by any entry made in, or by the omission of any entry from, the register, or by any default being made, or unnecessary delay taking place, in the making of any entry in the register, makes an order for the rectification of the register;

(*c*) In any case and at any time with the consent of all persons interested;

(*d*) Where the court or the registrar is satisfied that any entry in the register has been obtained by fraud;

(*e*) Where two or more persons are, by mistake, registered as proprietors of the same registered estate or of the same charge;

(*f*) Where a mortgagee has been registered as proprietor of the land instead of as proprietor of a charge and a right of redemption is subsisting;

(*g*) Where a legal estate has been registered in the name of a person who if the land had not been registered would not have been the estate owner; and

(*h*) In any other case where, by reason of any error or omission in the register, or by reason of any entry made under a mistake, it may be deemed just to rectify the register.

(2) The register may be rectified under this section, notwithstanding that the rectification may affect any estates, rights, charges, or interests acquired or protected by registration, or by any entry on the register, or otherwise.

(3) The register shall not be rectified, except for the purpose of giving effect to an overriding interest, [or an order of the court]²² so as to affect the title of the proprietor who is in possession—

(*a*) [unless the proprietor has caused or substantially contributed to the error or omission by fraud or lack of proper care; or]²³

(*b*) [. . .]²⁴

(*c*) unless for any other reason, in any particular case, it is considered that it would be unjust not to rectify the register against him.

(4) Where a person is in possession of registered land in right of a minor interest, he shall, for the purposes of this section, be deemed to be in possession as agent for the proprietor.

(5) The registrar shall obey the order of any competent court in relation to any registered land on being served with the order or an official copy thereof.

(6) On every rectification of the register the land certificate and any

---

²² Words inserted by the Administration of Justice Act 1977 (c. 38), s. 24.
²³ Substituted by the Administration of Justice Act 1977 (c. 38), s. 24.
²⁴ Repealed by the Administration of Justice Act 1977 (c. 38), s. 24.

charge certificate which may be affected shall be produced to the registrar unless an order to the contrary is made by him.

Right to indemnity in certain cases

83.—(1) Subject to the provisions of this Act to the contrary, any person suffering loss by reason of any rectification of the register under this Act shall be entitled to be indemnified.

(2) Where an error or omission has occurred in the register, but the register is not rectified, any person suffering loss by reason of such error or omission, shall, subject to the provisions of this Act, be entitled to be indemnified.

(3) Where any person suffers loss by reason of the loss or destruction of any document lodged at the registry for inspection or safe custody or by reason of an error in any official search, he shall be entitled to be indemnified under this Act.

(4) Subject as hereinafter provided, a proprietor of any registered land or charge claiming in good faith under a forged disposition shall, where the register is rectified, be deemed to have suffered loss by reason of such rectification and shall be entitled to be indemnified under this Act.

(5) No indemnity shall be payable under this Act in any of the following cases:—

    (*a*) [*The following was substituted by the Land Registration and Land Charges Act* 1971, *s.* 3(1)]. Where the applicant or a person from whom he derives title (otherwise than under a disposition for valuable consideration which is registered or protected on the register) has caused or substantially contributed to the loss by fraud or lack of proper care;

    (*b*) On account of any mines or minerals or of the existence of any rights to work or get mines or minerals, unless a note is entered on the register that the mines or minerals are included in the registered title;

    (*c*) On account of costs incurred in taking or defending any legal proceedings without the consent of the registrar.[25]

(6) Where an indemnity is paid in respect of the loss of an estate or interest in or charge on land the amount so paid shall not exceed—

    (*a*) Where the register is not rectified, the value of the estate, interest or charge at the time when the error or omission which caused the loss was made;

    (*b*) Where the register is rectified, the value (if there had been no rectification) of the estate, interest or charge, immediately before the time of rectification.

(7) [*Repealed: Land Registration and Land Charges Act* 1971, *s.* 14(2) (*b*); *2nd Sched., Pt.* II.]

[*The following was substituted by the Land Registration and Land Charges Act* 1971, *s.* 2(4).

(8) Subject to subsection (5)(*c*) of this section, as amended by section 2(2) of the Land Registration and Land Charges Act 1971—

    (*a*) an indemnity under any provision of this Act shall include such amount, if any, as may be reasonable in respect of any costs or expenses properly incurred by the applicant in relation to the matter; and

    (*b*) an applicant for an indemnity under any such provision shall be entitled to an indemnity thereunder of such amount, if any, as may be reasonable in respect of any such costs or expenses, notwithstanding that no other indemnity money is payable thereunder.]

---

[25] See now the Land Registration and Land Charges Act 1971 (c. 54), s. 2(2), *post*, p. 457.

(9) Where indemnity is paid for a loss, the registrar, on behalf of the Crown, shall be entitled to recover the amount paid from any person who has caused or substantially contributed to the loss by his fraud.

(10) The registrar shall be entitled to enforce, on behalf of the Crown, any express or implied covenant or other right which the person who is indemnified would have been entitled to enforce in relation to the matter in respect of which indemnity has been paid.

(11) A liability to pay indemnity under this Act shall be deemed a simple contract debt; and for the purposes of the Limitation Act [1980][26] the cause of action shall be deemed to arise at the time when the claimant knows, or but for his own default might have known, of the existence of his claim:

Provided that, when a claim to indemnity arises in consequence of the registration of an estate in land with an absolute or good leasehold title, the claim shall be enforceable only if made within six years from the date of such registration, except in the following cases:

(*a*) Where at the date of registration the person interested is an infant, the claim by him may be made within six years from the time he attains full age[27];

(*b*) In the case of settled land, or land held on trust for sale, a claim by a person interested in remainder or reversion, may be made within six years from the time when his interest falls into possession;

(*c*) Where a claim arises in respect of a restrictive covenant or agreement affecting freehold land which by reason of notice or the registration of a land charge or otherwise was binding on the first proprietor at the time of first registration, the claim shall only be enforceable within six years from the breach of the covenant or agreement;

(*d*) Where any person interested is entitled as a proprietor of a charge or as a mortgagee protected by a caution in the specially prescribed form, the claim by him may be made within six years from the last payment in respect of principal or interest.

(12) This section applies to the Crown in like manner as it applies to a private person.

Application of indemnity in case of settled land

84. Where any indemnity is paid in respect of settled land, and not in respect of any particular estate, remainder, or reversion therein, the money shall be paid to the trustees of the settlement and held by them as capital money for the purposes of the Settled Land Act 1925, arising from the settled land.

Insurance fund for providing indemnity

85. [*Repealed* (as to subs. (5) as from October 2, 1972): *Land Registration and Land Charges Act* 1971, *s.* 14(2)(*b*); *Sched.* 2, *Pt.* II.]

PART VIII

APPLICATION TO PARTICULAR CLASSES OF LAND

Registration of settled land

86.—(1) Settled land shall be registered in the name of the tenant for life or statutory owner.

---

[26] Substituted by the Limitation Act 1980 (c. 58), Sched. 3, para. 1.
[27] See now the Family Law Reform Act 1969 (c. 46), ss. 1, 12.

(2) The successive or other interests created by or arising under a settlement shall (save as regards any legal estate which cannot be overridden under the powers of the Settled Land Act 1925, or any other statute) take effect as minor interests and not otherwise; and effect shall be given thereto by the proprietor of the settled land as provided by statute with respect to the estate owner, with such adaptations, if any, as may be prescribed in the case of registered land by rules made under this Act.

(3) There shall also be entered on the register such restrictions as may be prescribed, or may be expedient, for the protection of the rights of the person beneficially interested in the land, and such restrictions shall (subject to the provisions of this Act relating to releases by the trustees of a settlement and to transfers by a tenant for life whose estate has ceased in his lifetime) be binding on the proprietor during his life, but shall not restrain or otherwise affect a disposition by his personal representative.

(4) Where land already registered is acquired with capital money, the same shall be transferred by a transfer in a specially prescribed form to the tenant for life or statutory owner, and such transfer shall state the names of the persons who are trustees of the settlement for the purposes of the Settled Land Act 1925, and contain an application to register the prescribed restrictions applicable to the case; a transfer made in the specially prescribed form shall be deemed to comply with the requirements of that Act, respecting vesting deeds; and where no capital money is paid but land already registered is to be made subject to a settlement, it shall not be necessary for the trustees of the settlement to concur in the transfer.

(5) References in this Act to the "tenant for life" shall, where the context admits, be read as referring to the tenant for life, statutory owner, or personal representative who is entitled to be registered.

Changes of ownership of settled land

87.—(1) On the death of a proprietor, or of the survivor of two or more joint proprietors of settled land (whether the land is settled by his will or by an instrument taking effect on or previously to his death), his personal representative shall hold the settled land subject to payment or to making provision for payment of all death duties and other liabilities affecting the land, and having priority to the settlement, upon trust to transfer the same by an assent in the prescribed manner to the tenant for life or statutory owner, and in the meantime upon trust to give effect to the minor interests under the settlement; but a transfer shall not be made to an infant.

(2) Rules may be made—

    (*a*) for enabling a personal representative or proprietor in proper cases to create legal estates by registered dispositions for giving effect to or creating interests in priority to the settlements;

    (*b*) to provide for the cases in which application shall be made by the personal representative or proprietor for the registration of restrictions or notices; and

    (*c*) for discharging a personal representative or former proprietor who has complied with the requirements of this Act and rules from all liability in respect of minor interests under a settlement.

(3) Where a tenant for life or statutory owner who, if the land were not registered, would be entitled to have the settled land vested in him, is not the proprietor, the proprietor shall (notwithstanding any stipulation or provision to the contrary) be bound at the cost of the trust estate to execute such transfers as may be required for giving effect on the register to the rights of such tenant for life or statutory owner.

(4) Where the trustees of a settlement have in the prescribed manner released the land from the minor interests under such settlement, the

registrar shall be entitled to assume that the settlement has determined, and the restrictions for protecting the minor interests thereunder shall be cancelled.

(5) Where an order is made under the Settled Land Act 1925, authorising the trustees of the settlement to exercise the powers on behalf of a tenant for life who is registered as proprietor, they may in his name and on his behalf do all such acts and things under this Act as may be requisite for giving effect on the register to the powers authorised to be exercised in like manner as if they were registered as proprietors of the land, but a copy of the order shall be filed at the registry before any such powers are exercised.

(6) Where a proprietor ceases in his lifetime to be a tenant for life, he shall transfer the land to his successor in title, or, if such successor is an infant, to the statutory owner, and on the registration of such successor in title or statutory owner it shall be the duty of the trustees of the settlement, if the same be still subsisting, to apply for such alteration, if any, in the restrictions as may be required for the protection of the minor interests under the settlement.

Settlement may be filed in registry

88.—(1) The settlement, or an abstract or copy thereof, may be filed in the registry for reference in the prescribed manner, but such filing shall not affect a purchaser from the proprietor with notice of its provisions, or entitle him to call for production of the settlement, or for any information or evidence as to its contents.

(2) In this section "settlement" includes any deed stating who are the trustees of the settlement, and the vesting instrument, and any transfer or assent in the prescribed form taking the place, in the case of registered land, of a vesting instrument, as well as the trust instrument and any other instruments creating the settlement.

Registrar's certificate authorising proposed dealing with settled land

89. The registrar may, notwithstanding any restriction entered on the register, grant a certificate that an intended registered disposition is authorised by a settlement or otherwise, and will be registered, and a purchaser who obtains such a certificate shall not be concerned to see that the disposition is authorised, but where capital money is paid to the persons to whom the same is required to be paid by a restriction or into court no such certificate shall be required.

Charges for money actually raised

90. The proprietor of settled land which is registered and all other necessary parties, if any, shall, on the request, and at the expense of any person entitled to an estate, interest, or charge conveyed or created for securing money actually raised at the date of such request, charge the land in the prescribed manner with the payment of the money so raised, but so long as the estate, interest or charge is capable of being overridden under the Settled Land Act 1925, or the Law of Property Act 1925, no charge shall be created or registered under this section.

Minorities[28]

91. The following provisions shall have effect as respects settled land (being registered land) during a minority:

(1) The personal representatives under the will or intestacy under which the settlement is created or arises shall, during the minority,

---

[28] See now the Family Law Reform Act 1969 (c. 46), s. 1.

be registered as proprietors, and in reference to the settled land shall have all the powers conferred by the Settled Land Act 1925, on a tenant for life and on the trustees of the settlement; but if and when the personal representatives would, if the infant had been of full age, have been bound to transfer the registered land to him, the personal representatives shall (unless themselves the statutory owners) thenceforth during the minority give effect on the register to the directions of the statutory owner, and shall apply for the registration of any restriction which may be prescribed, but shall not be concerned with the propriety of any registered disposition so directed to be made if the same appears to be a proper disposition under the powers of the statutory owner and the capital money, if any, arising under the disposition is paid to the trustees of the settlement or into court; but a purchaser dealing with the personal representatives, who complies with the restrictions, if any, which any be entered on the register, shall not be concerned to see or inquire whether any such directions have been given:

(2) If an infant becomes entitled in possession (or will become entitled in possession on attaining full age) to registered land otherwise than on a death, the statutory owners during the minority shall be entitled to require the settled land to be transferred to them and shall be registered as proprietors accordingly:

(3) If and when the registered land would (if not registered) have become vested in the trustees of the settlement pursuant to the Law of Property Act 1925, such trustees shall (unless they are already registered) be entitled to be registered as proprietors thereof, and shall in the prescribed manner apply for registration accordingly, and no fee shall be charged in respect of such registration or consequential alteration in the register.

Rights of tenants for life and statutory owners to be registered as proprietors

92. The foregoing provisions of this Part of this Act relating to settled land apply in every case where pursuant to the Settled Land Act 1925, settled land is to be vested in a tenant for life or statutory owner whether the estate was registered before or after the commencement of this Act, and the proprietor of settled land (not being the tenant for life or statutory owner entitled to the same) shall be bound to make such dispositions as may be required for giving effect to the rights of the tenant for life or statutory owner:

Provided that, where the registered land is not, at the commencement of this Act, registered in the name of a tenant for life or statutory owner, or personal representative who, if the land were not registered, would by virtue of the Settled Land Act 1925, or of the Law of Property Act 1925, be entitled to have the settled land vested in him, any such person shall (without any transfer) be entitled to be registered as proprietor thereof, and shall in the prescribed manner apply for registration accordingly, and no fee shall be charged in respect of such registration or consequential alteration in the register.

As to persons in a fiduciary position

93. A person in a fiduciary position may apply for, or concur in, or assent to, any registration authorised by the provisions of this Act, and, if he is a proprietor, may execute a charge or other disposition in favour of any person whose registration is so authorised.

Land held on trust for sale

94.—(1) Where registered land is subject to a trust for sale, express or implied, whether or not there is power to postpone the sale, the land shall be registered in the names of the trustees for sale.

(2) Where an order, obtained under section seven of the Settled Land Act 1884 is in force at the commencement of this Act, the person authorised by the order to exercise any of the powers conferred by the Settled Land Act 1925 may, in the names and on behalf of the proprietors, do all such acts and things under this Act as may be requisite for giving effect on the register to the powers authorised to be exercised in like manner as if such person were registered as proprietor of the land, and a copy of the order shall be filed at the registry.

(3) Where, by virtue of any statute, registered land is made subject to a trust for sale, the trustees for sale (unless already registered) shall be registered as proprietors thereof, and shall in the prescribed manner apply for registration accordingly, and no fee shall be charged in respect of such registration or consequential alteration of the register, but this subsection has effect subject to the provisions of this Act relating to the registration of the Public Trustee and the removal of an undivided share from the register before the title to the entirety of the land is registered.

Restriction on number of trustees

95. The statutory restrictions affecting the number of persons entitled to hold land on trust for sale and the number of trustees of a settlement apply to registered land.

Crown and Duchy land

96.—(1) With respect to land or any estate, right, or interest in land vested in His Majesty, either in right of the Crown or of the Duchy of Lancaster, or otherwise, or vested in any public officer or body in trust for the public service, the public officer or body having the management thereof, if any, or, if none, then such person as His Majesty may by writing under his sign manual appoint, may represent the owner of such land, estate, right, or interest for all the purposes of this Act, and shall be entitled to such notices, and may make and enter any such application or cautions, and do all such other acts as any owner of land, or of any estate, right or interest therein, as the case may be, is entitled to receive, make, enter, or do under this Act.

(2) With respect to land or any estate, right, or interest in land belonging to the Duchy of Cornwall, such person as the Duke of Cornwall for the time being, or as the person for the time being entitled to the revenues and possessions of the Duchy of Cornwall, may in writing appoint, may act as and represent the owner of such land, estate, right, or interest for all the purposes of this Act, and shall be entitled to receive such notices, and may make and enter any such application or cautions, and do all such other acts as any owner of land or of any estate, right, or interest in land (as the case may be) is entitled to make, enter, or do under this Act.

Foreshore

97.—(1) If it appears to the registrar that any land, application for registration whereof is made to him, comprises foreshore, he shall not register an estate in the land unless and until he is satisfied that at least one month's notice in writing of the application has been given to the Board of Trade, and—

> (*a*) in case of land in the county palatine of Lancaster, also to the proper officer of the Duchy of Lancaster; and

(*b*) in case of land in the counties of Cornwall or Devon, also to the proper officer of the Duke of Cornwall; and

(*c*) in the case of land within the jurisdiction of the Port of London Authority, also to that authority; and

(*d*) in all other cases, also to the Commissioners of Woods.

(2) This section does not apply to the registration of an estate with a possessory title or with a good leasehold title.

Land subject to charitable trusts

98.—Where an application is made to register a legal estate in land subject to charitable trusts and that estate is vested in the official trustee of charity lands, he shall, notwithstanding that the powers of disposition are vested in the managing trustees or committee, be registered as proprietor thereof.

Land belonging to benefices

99.—(1) Where the incumbent of a benefice and his successors are the registered proprietors of land—

(i) No disposition thereof shall be registered unless a certificate in the prescribed form has been obtained—

(*a*) in case of sales under the Parsonages Acts, 1838, or the Church Building Act, 1839, or any Acts amending or extending the same respectively, from Queen Anne's Bounty; or

(*b*) in case of sales under the Glebe Lands Act, 1888, or any Acts amending or extending the same, from the Minister of Agriculture and Fisheries; or

(*c*) in any other case from the Ecclesiastical Commissioners;

(ii) No lien shall be created by deposit of the land certificate, and an inhibition shall be placed on the register and on the land certificate accordingly.

The production of a certificate from any of the above-mentioned bodies shall be a sufficient authority to the registrar to register the disposition in question, and it shall be the duty of the proper body to grant such certificate in all cases in which the facts admit thereof.

(2) On the registration of the incumbent of a benefice and his successors as the proprietors of a legal estate in land, if it is certified by Queen Anne's Bounty, or otherwise appears, that the land was originally purchased by Queen Anne's Bounty or was otherwise appropriated or annexed by or with the consent or the concurrence of Queen Anne's Bounty to the benefice for the augmentation thereof, the registrar shall enter a note to that effect on the register.

(3) Where the incumbent of a benefice is entitled to indemnity under the provisions of this Act, the money shall be paid to Queen Anne's Bounty and appropriated by them to the benefice.

(4) "Benefice" in this section includes all rectories with cure of souls, vicarages, perpetual curacies, donatives, endowed public chapels and parochial chapelries, and chapelries or districts belonging, or reputed to belong, or annexed, or reputed to be annexed, to any church or chapel.

Small holdings

100.—(1) Where a county council apply in pursuance of the Small Holdings and Allotments Act, 1908, for registration as proprietors, they may be registered as proprietors with any such title as is authorised by this Act.

(2) Where a county council, after having been so registered, dispose of any interest in the land for the purposes of a small holding to a purchaser or

lessee, he shall be registered as proprietor of the interest transferred or created (being an interest capable of registration) with an absolute title, subject only to such incumbrances as may be created under the Small Holdings and Allotments Act, 1908, but freed from all other liabilities not being overriding interests, and in any such case the remedy of any person claiming by title paramount to the county council in respect either of title or incumbrances shall be in damages only, and such damages shall be recoverable against the county council.

(3) Where under the powers conferred by subsection (4) of section twelve of the said Act, a county council by notice require registered land to be sold to themselves, the council shall, after such date as may be specified by the notice mentioned in that subsection and on production to the registrar of evidence—

(*a*) of service of such notice; and

(*b*) of the payment of the sum agreed or determined in manner provided by that subsection or of the tender of such payment be registered as the proprietors of the land in place of the proprietor, and such registration shall operate as a registration on a transfer for valuable consideration under this Act.

(4) Rules under this Act may—

(*a*) adapt this Act to the registration of small holdings with such modifications as appear to be required; and

(*b*) on the application and at the expense of a county council provide by the appointment of local agents or otherwise for the carrying into effect of the objects of this section; and

(*c*) enable the registrar to obtain production of the land certificate.

(5) For the purposes of this section "county council" includes [the Greater London Council.][29]

Part IX

Unregistered Dealings with Registered Land

Powers of dealing with Registered Land off the Register

Dispositions off register creating "minor interests"

101.—(1) Any person, whether being the proprietor or not, having a sufficient interest or power in or over registered land, may dispose of or deal with the same, and create any interests or rights therein which are permissible in like manner and by the like modes of assurance in all respects as if the land were not registered, but subject as provided by this section.

(2) All interests and rights disposed of or created under subsection (1) of this section (whether by the proprietor or any other person) shall, subject to the provisions of this section, take effect as minor interests, and be capable of being overridden by registered dispositions for valuable consideration.

(3) Minor interests shall, subject to the express exceptions contained in this section, take effect only in equity, but may be protected by entry on the register of such notices, cautions, inhibitions and restrictions as are provided for by this Act or rules.

[29] The words in square brackets were substituted by the Local Government Act 1972 (c. 70), Sched. 29.

(4) A minor interest in registered land subsisting or capable of taking effect at the commencement of this Act, shall not fail or become invalid by reason of the same being converted into an equitable interest; but after such commencement a minor interest in registered land shall only be capable of being validly created in any case in which an equivalent equitable interest could have been validly created if the land had not been registered.

(5) Where after the commencement of this Act, the proprietor of the registered estate which is settled, disposes of or deals with his beneficial interest in possession in favour of a purchaser, and accordingly the minor interest disposed of or created would, but for the restrictions imposed by the Law of Property Act 1925, and this section, on the creation of legal estates, have been a legal estate, the purchaser (subject as provided by the next following section in regard to priorities) may exercise all such rights and remedies as he might have exercised had the minor interest been a legal estate, and the reversion (if any) on any leases or tenancies derived out of the registered estate had been vested in him.

(6) A minor interest created under this section does not operate to prevent a registered estate passing to the personal representative of a deceased proprietor, or to the survivor or survivors of two or more joint proprietors, nor does this section effect the right of any person entitled to an overriding interest, or having any power to dispose of or create an overriding interest, to dispose of or create the same.

Priorities as between minor interests

102.—(1) If a minor interest subsisting or capable of taking effect at the commencement of this Act, would, if the Law of Property Acts 1922 and 1925 and this Act had not been passed have taken effect as a legal estate, then (subject and without prejudice to the estate and powers of the proprietor whose estate is affected) the conversion thereof into an equitable interest shall not affect its priority over other minor interests.

(2) Priorities as regards dealings effected after the commencement of this Act between assignees and incumbrancers of life interests, remainders, reversions and executory interests shall be regulated by the order of the priority cautions or inhibitions lodged (in a specially prescribed form) against the proprietor of the registered estate affected, but, save as aforesaid, priorities as between persons interested in minor interests shall not be affected by the lodgment of cautions or inhibitions.

(3) The lodgment of a priority caution or inhibition shall not affect the powers of the proprietor whose estate is affected by the minor interest.

Obligation to give effect on the register to certain minor interests

103.—(1) Where by the operation of any statute or statutory or other power, or by virtue of any vesting order of any court or other competent authority, or an order appointing a person to convey, or of a vesting declaration (express or implied) or of an appointment or other assurance, a minor interest in the registered land is disposed of or created which would, if registered, be capable of taking effect as a legal estate or charge by way of legal mortgage, then—

    (i) if the estate owner would, had the land not been registered, have been bound to give effect thereto by conveying or creating a legal estate or charge by way of legal mortgage, the proprietor shall, subject to proper provision being made for payment of costs, be bound to give legal effect to the transaction by a registered disposition:

    (ii) if the proprietor is unable or refuses to make the requisite disposition or cannot be found, or if for any other reason a disposition by him cannot be obtained within a reasonable time, or if, had the land not been registered, no conveyance by the estate owner would have been required to give legal effect to the transaction, the registrar shall give effect thereto in the prescribed manner in like manner and with the like consequences as if the transaction had been carried out by a registered disposition:

Provided that—

(a) So long as the proprietor has power under the Settled Land Act 1925, or any other statute conferring special powers on a tenant for life or statutory owner, or under the settlement, to override the minor interest so disposed of or created, no estate or charge shall be registered which would prejudicially affect any such powers:

(b) So long as the proprietor holds the land on trust for sale, no estate or charge shall be registered in respect of an interest which, under the Law of Property Act 1925, or otherwise, ought to remain liable to be overridden on the execution of the trust for sale:

(c) Nothing in this subsection shall impose on a proprietor an obligation to make a disposition unless the person requiring the disposition to be made has a right in equity to call for the same:

(d) Nothing in this subsection shall prejudicially affect the rights of a personal representative in relation to the administration of the estate of the deceased.

(2) On every alteration in the register made pursuant to this section the land certificate and any charge certificate which may be affected shall be produced to the registrar unless an order to the contrary is made by him.

Protection of leases granted under statutory powers by persons other than registered proprietor and restriction on power

104. All leases at a rent for a term of years absolute authorised by the powers conferred by the Law of Property Act 1925, or the Settled Land Act 1925, or any other statute (whether or not as extended by any instrument) may be granted in the name and on behalf of the proprietor by any other person empowered to grant the same, and shall be valid at law or in equity (as the case may require) and shall be protected by notice on the register and registered in the same cases, in like manner and with the same effect as if the lease had been granted by the proprietor of the land, and without prejudice to any priority acquired by the exercise of the power; but nothing in this section shall authorise any person granting any lease in the name of the proprietor to impose (save in regard to the usual qualified covenant for quiet enjoyment) any personal liability on such proprietor.

As to minor interests in mortgage debts

105. Rules may be made for applying the provisions of this Part of this Act as to minor interests to the case of minor interests in a debt secured by a registered charge.

[Creation and protection of mortgages of registered land

106.—(1) The proprietor of any registered land may, subject to any entry to the contrary on the register, mortgage, by deed or otherwise, the land or any part of it in any manner which would have been permissible if the land had not been registered and, subject to this section, with the like effect.

(2) Unless and until the mortgage becomes a registered charge,—

(*a*) it shall take effect only in equity, and

(*b*) it shall be capable of being overridden as a minor interest unless it is protected as provided by subsection (3) below.

(3) A mortgage which is not a registered charge may be protected on the register by—

(*a*) a notice under section 49 of this Act,

(*b*) any such other notice as may be prescribed, or

(*c*) a caution under section 54 of this Act.

(4) A mortgage which is not a registered charge shall devolve and may be transferred, discharged, surrendered or otherwise dealt with by the same instruments and in the same manner as if the land had not been registered.][30]

Power for proprietors to bind successors and to enforce contracts

107.—(1) Subject to any entry to the contrary on the register, the proprietor of any registered land or charge may enter into any contract in reference thereto in like manner as if the land or charge had not been registered, and, subject to any disposition for valuable consideration which may be registered or protected on the register before the contract is completed or protected on the register, the contract may be enforced as a minor interest against any succeeding proprietor in like manner and to the same extent as if the land or charge had not been registered.

(2) A contract entered into for the benefit of any registered land or charge may (if the same would have been enforceable by the owner for the time being of the land or charge, if not registered, or by a person deriving title under the party contracting for the benefit) be enforced by the proprietor for the time being of the land or charge.

Acquisition of easements and other benefits

108. The proprietor of registered land may accept for the benefit thereof the grant of any easement, right, or privilege or the benefit of any restrictive covenant or provision (affecting other land, whether registered or not) in like manner and to the same extent as if he were legally and beneficially entitled to the fee simple in possession, or to the term created by the registered lease, for his own benefit free from incumbrances.

Restriction on exercise of powers off the register

109. Subject to the express provisions relating to leases and mortgages, nothing in this Part of this Act shall be construed as authorising any disposition of any estate, interest, or right or other dealing with land to be effected under this Part of this Act if the disposition or dealing is one which could be effected under another Part of this Act, and any such disposition or dealing shall be effected under and in the manner required by such other Part of this Act, and when so required shall be registered or protected as provided by this Act or the rules.

---

[30] This section was substituted by the Administration of Justice Act 1977 (c. 38), s. 26(1). S. 26(2) provides that the Chief Land Registrar may arrange for the conversion into a registered charge, in such circumstances and subject to such conditions as he may direct, of any mortgage protected by a caution in a specially prescribed form entered on the register before the coming into force of this section.

Part X

Miscellaneous Provisions

Provisions as between vendor and purchaser

110. On a sale or other disposition of registered land to a purchaser other than a lessee or chargee—

(1) The vendor shall, notwithstanding any stipulation to the contrary, at his own expense furnish the purchaser with an authority to inspect the register, and, if required, with a copy of the subsisting entries in the register and of any filed plans and copies or abstracts of any documents or any part thereof noted on the register so far as they respectively affect the land to be dealt with (except charges or incumbrances registered or protected on the register which are to be discharged or overridden at or prior to completion):

Provided that—

> (*a*) unless the purchase money exceeds one thousand pounds the costs of the copies and abstracts of the said entries plans and documents shall, in the absence of any stipulation to the contrary, be borne by the purchaser requiring the same;

> (*b*) nothing in this section shall give a purchaser a right to a copy or abstract of a settlement filed at the registry:

(2) The vendor shall, subject to any stipulation to the contrary, at his own expense furnish the purchaser with such copies, abstracts and evidence (if any) in respect of any subsisting rights and interests appurtenant to the registered land as to which the register is not conclusive, and of any matters excepted from the effect of registration as the purchaser would have been entitled to if the land had not been registered:

(3) Except as aforesaid, and notwithstanding any stipulation to the contrary, it shall not be necessary for the vendor to furnish the purchaser with any abstract or other written evidence of title, or any copy or abstract of the land certificate, or of any charge certificate:

(4) Where the register refers to a filed abstract or copy of or extract from a deed or other document such abstract or extract shall as between vendor and purchaser be assumed to be correct, and to contain all material portions of the original, and no person dealing with any registered land or charge shall have a right to require production of the original, or be affected in any way by any provisions of the said document other than those appearing in such abstract, copy or extract, and any person suffering loss by reason of any error or omission in such abstract, copy or extract shall be entitled to be indemnified under this Act:

(5) Where the vendor is not himself registered as proprietor of the land or the charge giving a power of sale over the land, he shall, at the request of the purchaser and at his own expense, and notwithstanding any stipulation to the contrary, either procure the registration of himself as proprietor of the land or of the charge, as the case may be, or procure a disposition from the proprietor to the purchaser:

(6) Unless the certificate is deposited at the registry the vendor shall deliver the land certificate, or the charge certificate, as the case may be, to the purchaser on completion of the purchase, or, if only a part of the land comprised in the certificate is dealt with, or only a derivative estate is created, he shall, at his own expense, produce, or procure the production of, the certificate in accordance with this Act for the completion of the purchaser's registration. Where the certificate has been lost or destroyed, the vendor shall, notwith-

standing any stipulation to the contrary, pay the costs of the proceedings required to enable the registrar to proceed without it:

(7) The purchaser shall not, by reason of the registration, be affected with notice of any pending action, writ, order, deed of arrangement or land charge (other than a local land charge) to which this subsection applies which can be protected under this Act by lodging or registering a creditor's notice, restriction, inhibition, caution or other notice, or be concerned to make any search therefor if and so far as they affect registered land.

This subsection applies only to pending actions, writs, orders, deeds of arrangement and land charges (not including local land charges) required to be registered or re-registered after the commencement of this Act, either under the Land Charges Act 1925[31] or any other statute registration whereunder has effect as if made under that Act.

Infants,[32] defectives and [persons of unsound mind][33]

111.—(1) A purported disposition of any registered land or charge to an infant made after the commencement of this Act, or by the will of a proprietor dying after such commencement, shall not entitle the infant to be registered as proprietor of the registered land or charge until he attains full age, but in the meantime shall operate only as a declaration binding on the proprietor or personal representative that the registered land or charge is to be held on trust to give effect to minor interests in favour of the infant corresponding, as nearly as may be, with the interests which the disposition purports to transfer or create; and the disposition or a copy thereof or extract therefrom shall be deposited at the registry, and shall, unless and until the tenants for life, statutory owners, personal representatives or trustees for sale are registered as proprietors, be protected by means of a restriction or otherwise on the register:

Provided that—

(*a*) If the disposition is made to the infant jointly with another person of full age, that person shall, during the minority, be entitled to be registered as proprietor, and the infant shall not be registered until he attains full age;

(*b*) Where the registered land or charge is subject to any trusts or rights of redemption in favour of any person other than the infant, nothing in this section shall affect such trusts or rights of redemption;

(*c*) Where by reason of the minority or otherwise the land is settled land, the provisions of this Act relating to settled land shall apply thereto.

(2) Where an infant becomes entitled under a will or on an intestacy to any registered land or charge, the same shall not be transferred by the personal representative to the infant until he attains full age.

(3) Where an infant becomes entitled to the benefit of a registered charge, the charge shall during the minority be registered in the names of the personal representatives, trustees, or other persons who if the charge had affected unregistered land would have been able to dispose of the same, and they shall for the purposes of this Act have the same powers in reference thereto as the infant would have had if of full age.

(4) A caution may be lodged in the name or on behalf of an infant by his parent, trustee or guardian.

---

[31] Now the Land Charges Act 1972 (c. 61), *ante*, p. 320.

[32] See now the Family Law Reform Act 1969 (c. 46), ss. 1, 12.

[33] These words were substituted for the word "lunatic" by the Mental Treatment Act 1930 (20 & 21 Geo. 5, c. 23), s. 20(5), but no change was made by the Mental Health Act 1959 (7 & 8 Eliz. 2, c. 72).

(5) Where a proprietor of any registered land or charge is incapable, by reason of mental disorder within the meaning of the Mental Health Act 1959, of managing and administering his property and affairs, his receiver or (if no receiver is acting for him) any person authorised in that behalf shall, under an order of the authority having jurisdiction under Part VIII of the Mental Health Act 1959, or of the court, or under any statutory power have and may exercise in the name and behalf of the proprietor all the powers which under this Act the proprietor could have exercised if free from disability, and a copy of every such order shall be filed with the registrar and may be referred to on the register.[34]

(6) All the provisions of the Trustee Act 1925, and Part VIII of the Mental Health Act 1959, and of any Act amending the same, shall apply to estates and charges registered under this Act, subject to the express provisions of this Act and to the rules made thereunder.[34]

Inspection of register and other documents at land registry

112. Subject [to Section 112A below and][35] to the provisions of this Act as to furnishing information to Government departments and local authorities and to such regulations and exceptions and to the payment of such sums as may be made or fixed by general rules, any person registered as proprietor of any land or charge, and any person authorised by any such proprietor, or by an order of the court, or by general rule, but no other person, may inspect and make copies of and extracts from any register or document in the custody of the registrar relating to such land or charge.

[Inspection in connection with criminal proceedings, etc.

112A.—(1) If—
    (*a*) the Director of Public Prosecutions, a chief officer of police or an official receiver applies to the registrar for permission to make an inspection under this section in relation to a person specified in the application or to property so specified, and
    (*b*) gives the registrar an appropriate certificate,
the registrar shall permit him to inspect and make copies of and extracts from any register or document kept in the custody of the registrar so far as it relates to the person or property so specified.

(2) In subsection (1) above "appropriate certificate" means a certificate—
    (*a*) that—
        (i) a criminal offence specified in the certificate has been or is reasonably suspected to have been committed, and
        (ii) there is reason to believe that the register may contain information relevant to the investigation of the offence or to the institution of proceedings for it, or
    (*b*) that—
        (i) a person specified in the certificate has been convicted of a criminal offence so specified, and
        (ii) there is reason to believe that the register may contain information relevant to the institution of proceedings for making available for distribution or otherwise for recovering the proceeds of the commission of that offence or any other offence taken into consideration by the court dealing with him for it.

---

[34] These subsections are printed with wording substituted by the Mental Health Act 1959 (7 & 8 Eliz. 2, c. 72), s. 149(1) and 7th Sched.
[35] Added by the Administration of Justice Act 1977 (c. 38), s. 25.

(3) The powers conferred on a chief officer of police by this section may be exercised on behalf of a chief officer of police by any police officer not below the rank of superintendent.

(4) In this section "official receiver" means an official receiver appointed under section 70 of the Bankruptcy Act 1914 or section 233 of the Companies Act 1948.][36]

Office copies to be evidence

113. Office copies of and extracts from the register and of and from documents and plans filed in the registry shall be admissible in evidence in all actions and matters, and between all persons or parties, to the same extent as the originals would be admissible, but any person suffering loss by reason of the inaccuracy of any such copy or extract shall be entitled to be indemnified under this Act, and no solicitor, trustee, personal representative, or other person in a fiduciary position shall be answerable in respect of any loss occasioned by relying on any such copy or extract.

Fraudulent dispositions, how far to be void

114. Subject to the provisions in this Act contained with respect to indemnity and to registered dispositions for valuable consideration, any disposition of land or of a charge, which if unregistered would be fraudulent and void, shall, notwithstanding registration, be fraudulent and void in like manner.

. . . . . .

PART XI

COMPULSORY REGISTRATION

Power to make orders rendering registration compulsory in certain areas

120.—(1) His Majesty may, by Order in Council, declare, as respects any county or part of a county mentioned or defined in the Order, that, on and after a day specified in the Order, registration of title to land is to be compulsory on sale:

Provided that nothing in this Act or in any such Order shall render compulsory the registration of the title to an incorporeal hereditament or to mines and minerals apart from the surface, or to corporeal hereditaments parcel of a manor and included in the sale of a manor as such.[37]

(2) Any such Order may be made—
    (*a*) at any time at the instance of the county council concerned; and
    (*b*) at any time after the expiration of ten years from the commencement of this Act otherwise than at the instance of a county council;

subject in either case to compliance with the provisions hereinafter contained relating to such Orders respectively:

Provided that any proceedings preliminary to the making of the first Order to be made otherwise than at the instance of a county council may be taken before the expiration of the said period.

(3) Any Order made under this section shall be made with due regard to the utilisation, if practicable, of any land registry existing in the county to which the order relates or conveniently near thereto.

---

[36] Added by the Administration of Justice Act 1977 (c. 38), s. 25.
[37] See Orders 1973 (No. 1764), 1974 (No. 250), 1974 (No. 559), 1975 (No. 160), 1976 (No. 1782) and 1977 (No. 828).

(4) [*Repealed by the Local Government Act* 1972 (*c.* 70), *Sched.* 30.]

(5) [*Repealed by the Local Government Act* 1972 (*c.* 70), *Sched.* 30.]

(6) Any Order made under this Part of this Act or under any corresponding provision in any enactment replaced by this Act may be revoked or varied by a subsequent Order.

(7) For the purposes of this Part of this Act, "county" means the administrative county, [. . .][38]

. . . . . .

Effect of Act in areas where registration is compulsory

123.[39]—(1) In any area in which an Order in Council declaring that registration of title to land within that area is to be compulsory on sale is for the time being in force, every conveyance on sale of freehold land and every grant of a term of years absolute not being less than forty years from the date of the delivery of the grant, and every assignment on sale of leasehold land held for a term of years absolute having not less than forty years to run from the date of delivery of the assignment, shall (save as hereinafter provided), on the expiration of two months from the date thereof or of any authorised extension of that period, become void so far as regards the grant or conveyance of the legal estate in the freehold or leasehold land comprised in the conveyance, grant, or assignment, or so much of such land as is situated within the area affected, unless the grantee (that is to say, the person who is entitled to be registered as proprietor of the freehold or leasehold land) or his successor in title or assign has in the meantime applied to be registered as proprietor of such land:

Provided that the registrar, or the court on appeal from the registrar, may, on the application of any persons interested in any particular case in which the registrar or the court is satisfied that the application for first registration cannot be made within the said period, or can only be made within that period by incurring unreasonable expense, or that the application has not been made within the said period by reason of some accident or other sufficient cause, make an order extending the said period; and if such order be made, then, upon the registration of the grantee or his successor or assign, a note of the order shall be endorsed on the conveyance, grant or assignment:

In the case of land in an area where, at the date of the commencement of this Act, registration of title is already compulsory on sale, this subsection shall apply to every such conveyance, grant, or assignment, executed on or after that date.

(2) Rules under this Act may provide for applying the provisions thereof to dealings with the land which may take place between the date of such conveyance, grant, or assignment and the date of application to register as if such dealings had taken place after the date of first registration, and for registration to be effected as of the date of the application to register.

(3) In this section the expressions "conveyance on sale" and "assignment on sale" mean an instrument made on sale by virtue whereof there is conferred or completed a title under which an application for registration as first proprietor of land may be made under this Act, and include a conveyance or assignment by way of exchange where money is paid for equality of exchange, but do not include an enfranchisement or extinguishment of manorial incidents, whether under the Law of Property Act, 1922, or otherwise, or an assignment or surrender of a lease to the owner of the immediate reversion containing a declaration that the term is to merge in such reversion.

[38] The words omitted were repealed by the Local Government Act 1972 (c. 70), Sched. 30.

[39] This section does not apply to souvenir land: Land Registration (Souvenir Land) Rules 1972 (No. 985).

Compulsory provisions bind the Crown

124.—This Part of this Act, as respects transactions completed after the commencement of this Act, binds the Crown.

.   .   .   .   .   .

PART XII

ADMINISTRATIVE AND JUDICIAL PROVISIONS

His Majesty's Land Registry

His Majesty's Land Registry

126.—(1) There shall continue to be an office in London to be called His Majesty's Land Registry, the business of which shall be conducted by a registrar to be appointed by the Lord Chancellor and known as the Chief Land Registrar, with such officers (namely, registrars, assistant registrars, clerks, messengers, and servants), as the Lord Chancellor, with the concurrence of the Treasury as to number, may appoint.

(2) A person shall not be qualified to be appointed Chief Land Registrar unless he is a barrister of not less than ten years' standing, and a person shall not be qualified to be appointed a registrar or an assistant registrar unless he is either a barrister or solicitor of not less than five years' standing.

(3) The Chief Land Registrar, registrars, assistant registrars, clerks, messengers, and servants shall receive such salaries or remuneration as the Treasury may from time to time direct.

(4) The salaries of the Chief Land Registrar, registrars, assistant registrars, clerks, messengers, and servants, and such incidental expenses of carrying this Act into effect may be sanctioned by the Treasury, shall continue to be paid out of money provided by Parliament.

(5) The Lord Chancellor may make regulations for the land registry, and for assigning the duties to the respective officers, and determining the acts of the registrar which may be done by a registrar or assistant registrar, and for altering or adding to the official styles of the Chief Land Registrar and other officers of the land registry. Subject to such regulations, anything authorised or required by this Act to be done to or by the registrar shall be done to or by the Chief Land Registrar. All such regulations for the time being in force shall have effect as if they were enacted in this Act.

(6) The Lord Chancellor may also make regulations as to the conduct of business at the land registry during any vacancy in the office of Chief Land Registrar, and for distributing the duties amongst the respective officers, and for assigning to a registrar or assistant registrar all or any of the functions and authorities by this Act or any other Act assigned to or conferred on the registrar, and all acts done by a registrar or assistant registrar under any such regulations shall have the same effect in all respects as if they had been done by the Chief Land Registrar.

(7) There shall continue to be a seal of the land registry and any document purporting to be sealed with that seal shall be admissible in evidence.

Conduct of business by registrar

127. Subject to the provisions of this Act, the Chief Land Registrar shall conduct the whole business of registration under this Act, and shall frame and cause to be printed and circulated or otherwise promulgated such forms and directions as he may deem requisite or expedient for facilitating proceedings under this Act.

Power for registrar to summon witnesses

128.—(1) The Chief Land Registrar, or any officer of the land registry authorised by him in writing, may administer an oath or take a statutory declaration in pursuance of this Act in that behalf for any of the purposes of this Act, and the Chief Land Registrar may, by summons under the seal of the land registry, require the attendance of all such persons as he may think fit in relation to the registration of any title; he may also, by a like summons, require any person having the custody of any map, survey, or book made or kept in pursuance of any Act of Parliament to produce such map, survey, or book for his inspection; he may examine upon oath any person appearing before him and administer an oath accordingly; and he may allow to every person summoned by him the reasonable charges of his attendance:

Provided that no person shall be required to attend in obedience to any summons or to produce such documents as aforesaid unless the reasonable charges of his attendance and of the production of such documents be paid or tendered to him.

(2) Any charges allowed by the registrar in pursuance of this section shall be deemed to be charges incurred in or about proceedings for registration and may be dealt with accordingly.

(3) If any person, after the delivery to him of such summons as aforesaid, or of a copy thereof, and payment or tender of his reasonable charges for attendance, wilfully neglects or refuses to attend in pursuance of such summons, or to produce such maps, surveys, books, or other documents as he may be required to produce under the provisions of this Act, or to answer upon oath or otherwise such questions as may be lawfully put to him by the registrar under the powers of this Act, he shall be liable on summary conviction to a fine not exceeding twenty pounds.

Interchange of information between Land Registry and other Departments

129. The Commissioners of Inland Revenue and other Government Departments, and local authorities, may furnish to the registrar on his request such particulars and information in regard to land and charges, and the registrar may in like manner furnish to the Commissioners of Inland Revenue, other Government Departments, and local authorities on their request such particulars and information as they are respectively by law entitled to require owners of property to furnish to them direct.

Statutory acknowledgments on return of documents

130. When any document is delivered or returned by the registrar to any person he may, at the cost of the registry, require such person to give a statutory acknowledgment of the right of the registrar and his successors in office to production of such document and to delivery of copies thereof, and may endorse notice of such right on the document, and the acknowledgment shall not be liable to stamp duty.

Indemnity to officers of registry

131. The Chief Land Registrar shall not, nor shall a registrar or assistant registrar nor any person acting under the authority of the Chief Land Registrar or a registrar or assistant registrar, or under any order or general rule made in pursuance of this Act, be liable to any action or proceeding for or in respect of any act or matter done or omitted to be done in good faith in the exercise or supposed exercise of the powers of this Act, or any order or general rule made in pursuance of this Act.[40]

District Registries

Power to form district registries by general orders

132.—(1) The Lord Chancellor, with the concurrence of the Treasury, shall have power by general orders from time to time to do all or any of the following things:—

(a) To create district registries for the purposes of registration of titles to land within the defined districts respectively, and to alter any districts which may have been so created:

(b) To fix, by notice to be published in the Gazette, the time for the commencement of registration at a district registry so created of titles to land within a district so defined:

(c) To direct registration of land to be commenced in any one or more district or districts pursuant to any such notice:

(d) To appoint district registrars, assistant district registrars, clerks, messengers, and servants to perform the business of registration in any district which may from time to time be created a district for registration under this Act:

(e) To provide for the mode in which district registrars are to be remunerated:

(f) To modify the provisions of this Act with respect to the formation and constitution of district registries, except the provision relating to the qualifications of district registrars, and assistant district registrars.

(2) A person shall not be qualified to be appointed district registrar under this Act unless he is a barrister or solicitor [or certificated conveyancer[41]] of not less than ten years' standing, and a person shall not be qualified to be appointed an assistant district registrar under this Act unless he is either a barrister or solicitor or certificated conveyancer of not less than five years' standing.[42]

(3) A district registrar or assistant district registrar may, with the assent of the Lord Chancellor, follow another calling.

(4) A seal shall be prepared for each district registry and any instrument purporting to be sealed with such seal shall be admissible in evidence.

Powers of district registrar, and appeals from him

133. Subject to general rules each district registrar, and assistant district registrar shall, as regards the land within his jurisdiction, have the same powers and indemnity as are herein given to the registrars and assistant registrars in the land registry, and there shall be the same right to appeal as in the case of the registrar; an order of a district registrar may be enforced and any breach thereof punished in like manner as if the order had been made by the Chief Land Registrar:

Provided that the Lord Chancellor may, by general rules, make provision—

(a) for the duties of a district registrar as regards all or any of the proceedings preliminary to first registration, or as regards any

---

[40] See now the Land Registration and Land Charges Act 1971 (c. 54), ss. 2(2) 4(4), *post*, pp. 457, 459.

[41] This term was rendered obsolete by the Solicitors, Public Notaries, etc. Act 1949 (12, 13 & 14 Geo. 6, c. 21). The 1949 Act was repealed by the Solicitors Act 1974 (c. 47), s. 89(2), Sched. 4.

[42] See the Land Registration (District Registries) Order 1979 (No. 1019) and S.I. 1980 (No. 1499).

matters which the district registrar has to determine, or any other matters being performed by the Chief Land Registrar or a registrar or assistant registrar in the land registry; and

(*b*) for any district registrar obtaining directions from or acting with the sanction of the Chief Land Registrar or a registrar or assistant registrar.

Application of general orders, etc., to districts

134. The general orders, rules, forms, directions, and fees for the time being applying to and payable in the land registry shall also apply to and be payable in all the district registries, subject to any alteration or addition for the time being made for any district by the Lord Chancellor with the advice and assistance of the Rule Committee, and, so far as they relate to fees, with the concurrence of the Treasury.

. . . . . .

Description and Powers of the Court

Jurisdiction of High Court and county courts

138.—(1) For the purposes of this Act, "the court" means the High Court [*and also the Court of Chancery of the County Palatine of Lancaster or the Court of Chancery of the County Palatine of Durham*][43] or the county court, where those courts respectively have jurisdiction, according as the one or other of such courts may be prescribed by the general rules[44] made for carrying this Act into effect.

(2) All matters within the jurisdiction of the High Court under this Act shall, subject to the enactments for the time being in force, relating to the Supreme Court of Judicature, be assigned to the Chancery Division of the court; and every application to the court under this Act shall, except where it is otherwise expressed and subject to any rules of court to the contrary, be by summons at chambers.

(3) The county court shall, in cases where it has jurisdiction under this Act, have, for all the purposes of such jurisdiction, all the powers of the High Court.

(4) The court shall have full power and discretion to make such order as it thinks fit respecting the costs, charges and expenses of all or any of the parties to any application.

(5) The Lord Chancellor may from time to time assign the duties vested in the High Court in relation to all or any matters under this Act, including appeals from the county court, to any particular judge or judges of that court.

Powers of court in action for specific performance

139.—(1) Where an action is instituted for the specific performance of a contract relating to registered land, or a registered charge, the court having cognizance of the action may, by summons, or by such other mode as it deems expedient, cause all or any parties who have registered interests or rights in the registered land or charge, or have entered up notices, cautions, restrictions, or inhibitions against the same to appear in such action, and show cause why such contract should not be specifically performed, and the court may direct that any order made by the court in the action shall be binding on such parties or any of them.

---

[43] Words in square brackets repealed by the Courts Act 1971 (c. 23), s. 56 and 11th Sched., Pt. II.
[44] See the Land Registration Rules 1967, r. 3.

(2) All costs incurred by any parties so appearing in an action to enforce against a vendor specific performance of his contract to sell any registered land or charge shall be taxed as between solicitor and client,[45] and, unless the court otherwise orders, be paid by the vendor.

Power of registrar to state case for the court

140.—(1) Whenever, upon the examination of the title to any interest in land, the registrar entertains a doubt as to any matter of law or fact arising upon such title, he may (whether or not the matter has been referred to a conveyancing counsel in the prescribed manner), upon the application of any party interested in such land—

  (*a*) refer a case for the opinion of the High Court and the court may direct an issue to be tried before a jury for the purpose of determining any fact;
  (*b*) name the parties to such case;
  (*c*) give directions as to the manner in which proceedings in relation thereto are to be brought before the court.

(2) The opinion of any court to whom any case is referred by the registrar shall be conclusive on all the parties to the case, unless the court permits an appeal.

Intervention of court in case of persons under disability

141. Where a person under disability, or person outside the jurisdiction of the High Court, or person yet unborn, is interested in the land in respect of the title to which any question arises as aforesaid, any other person interested in such land may apply to the court for a direction that the opinion of the court shall be conclusively binding on the person under disability, person outside the jurisdiction, or unborn person.

Power for court to bind interests of persons under disability

142.—(1) The court shall hear the allegations of all parties appearing.

(2) The court may disapprove altogether or may approve, either with or without modification, of the directions of the registrar respecting any case referred to the court.

(3) The court may, if necessary, appoint a guardian, next friend or other person to appear on behalf of any person under disability, person outside the jurisdiction, or unborn person.

(4) If the court is satisfied that the interest of any person under disability, outside the jurisdiction, or unborn, will be sufficiently represented in any case, it shall make an order declaring that all persons, with the exceptions, if any, named in the order, are to be conclusively bound, and thereupon all persons, with such exceptions, if any, as aforesaid, shall be conclusively bound by any decision of the court in which any such person is concerned.

Appeals

143.—(1) Any person aggrieved by any order of a judge of a county court may, within the prescribed time and in the prescribed manner, appeal to the High Court.

(2) The court on hearing such appeal may give judgment affirming, reversing, or modifying the order appealed from, and may finally decide thereon, and make such order as to costs in the court below and of the appeal as may be agreeable to justice; and if the court alter or modify the order, the order so altered or modified shall be of the like effect as if it were the order of the county court.

---

[45] Now taxed on the common fund basis: R.S.C., Ord. 62, r. 28.

The High Court may also, in cases where the court thinks it expedient so to do, instead of making a final order, remit the case, with such directions as the court may think fit, to the court below.

(3) Any person aggrieved by an order made under this Act by the High Court otherwise than on appeal from a county court, [*or by the Court of Chancery of Lancaster or Durham,*]⁴⁶ may appeal within the prescribed time in the same manner and with the same incidents in and with which orders made by the High Court [*or such Court of Chancery respectively*]⁴⁶ in cases within the ordinary jurisdiction of such court may be appealed from.

PART XIII

RULES, FEE ORDERS, REGULATIONS, SHORT TITLE, COMMENCEMENT AND EXTENT

. . . . . .

Repeals, savings and construction

147.—(1) [*The Acts mentioned in the Schedule to this Act are hereby repealed to the extent specified in the third column of that Schedule*: *Provided that,*]⁴⁷ without prejudice to the provisions of section thirty-eight of the Interpretation Act 1889:—

(*a*) Nothing in this repeal shall, save as otherwise expressly provided in this Act, affect any transfer of any interest in land or entry in the register made before the commencement of this Act, or any title or right acquired or appointment made before the commencement of this Act:

(*b*) Nothing in this repeal shall affect any rules, regulations, orders, or other instruments made under any enactment so repealed, but all such rules, regulations, orders, and instruments shall, until superseded, continue in force as if made under the corresponding provision of this Act:

(*c*) Nothing in this repeal shall affect the tenure of office or salary or right to pension or superannuation allowance of any officer appointed before the commencement of this Act:

(*d*) References in any document to any enactment repealed by this Act shall be construed as references to the corresponding provisions of this Act.

(2) References to registration under the Land Charges Act 1925⁴⁸ apply to any registration made under any other statute which is by the Land Charges Act 1925⁴⁸ to have effect as if the registration had been made under that Act.

Short title, commencement and extent

148.—(1) This Act may be cited as the Land Registration Act 1925.

(2) This Act shall come into operation on the first day of January nineteen hundred and twenty-six, but shall be deemed to come into operation immediately after the Law of Property Act 1925, the Settled Land Act 1925, the Land Charges Act 1925, the Trustees Act 1925 and the Administration of Estates Act 1925 come into operation.

(3) This Act extends to England and Wales only.

---

⁴⁶ Words in square brackets repealed by the Courts Act 1971 (c. 22), s. 56 and 11th Sched., Pt. II.

⁴⁷ Repealed S.L.R. 1950.

⁴⁸ Now the Land Charges Act 1972 (c. 61), *ante*, p. 320.

Land Registration Rules 1925

(as amended)

(S.R. & O. 1925 No. 1093)

Dated November 3, 1925

I, George Viscount Cave, Lord High Chancellor of Great Britain with the advice and assistance of the Rule Committee appointed in pursuance of section 144 of the Land Registration Act 1925 do, in exercise of the powers vested in me by that section and all other powers enabling me in this behalf, hereby make the following Rules.

Interpretation

1.—(1) In these rules "the Act" means the Land Registration Act, 1925, and words or expressions defined in the Act have the same meanings in these rules.

(2) The Interpretation Act, 1889 is to apply for the purpose of the interpretation of these rules as it applies for the purpose of the interpretation of an Act of Parliament, except so far as it may be inconsistent with the Act or these rules.

(3) "Statutory declaration" includes affidavit.

(4) "Forms" in these rules, means the Forms in the Schedule hereto.

(5) The "Companies Acts" mean the Companies Acts, 1908 to 1917 and any Acts replaced thereby.

[(5A) "Proper office" means the district land registry designated as the proper office by the Land Registration (District Registries) Order 1978.

(5B) In rules 24, 83 and 85 "day" means a day on which the Land Registry is open to the public and in rules 83, 84 and 85 "application" means an application for making, rectifying or cancelling any entry in the register of a registered title.][1]

(6) The marginal notes to these rules shall not affect the construction thereof.

PART I

THE REGISTER

Parts of register and title number

2. The register shall consist of three parts, called the Property Register, the Proprietorship Register, and the Charges Register. The title to each registered property shall bear a distinguishing number.

Property Register

3. The Property Register shall contain—
> (1) The description of the land and estate comprised in the title, with a reference to the General Map or to the filed plan of the land referred to in Part V of these rules.
> (2) Such notes as have to be entered relating—
>> (*a*) to the ownership of the mines and minerals;
>> (*b*) to exemption from any of the overriding interests mentioned in Section 70 of the Act;
>> (*c*) to easements, rights, privileges, conditions and covenants for the benefit of the land, and other like matters.

Addition to and removals from register

4. Where land is removed from, or, with the consent of the Registrar, added to a title, the register shall be cleared and a new edition thereof made showing the land comprised in the title after the addition or removal and the subsisting entries relating thereto, or, where for reasons for expense or otherwise this is not practicable, the register shall be amended to show the land which has been added or removed.

Leasehold land, rentcharges and land subject thereto

5.—(1) In the case of leasehold land there shall be entered in the Property Register a reference to the registered lease, and such particulars

[1] Words added by Land Registration Rules 1978 (No. 1601).

of the lease, and of the exceptions or reservations therefrom (if any) as the applicant may desire, and the Registrar approve; and a reference to the lessor's title, if registered.

(2) In the case of rentcharges created by an instrument, that instrument shall be referred to in the Property Register.

(3) Where land is acquired in consideration of the reservation of a rent-charge and the grant of the land contains any exceptions or reservations, that grant shall be referred to in the Property Register.

Proprietorship Register

6. The Proprietorship Register shall state the nature of the title, and shall contain the name, address, and description of the proprietor of the land, and cautions, inhibitions, and restrictions affecting his right of disposing thereof.

Charges Register

7. The Charges Register shall contain—
- (*a*) incumbrances subsisting at the date of first registration;
- (*b*) subsequent charges, and other incumbrances (including notices of leases and other notices of adverse interests or claims permitted by the Act);
- (*c*) such notes as have to be entered relating to covenants, conditions, and other rights adversely affecting the land;
- (*d*) all such dealings with registered charges and incumbrances as are capable of registration.

[Entry in the day list

7A.—(1) There shall be kept, in relation to the relevant title numbers, a record (known as the "day list") of the date of delivery of every pending application for first registration and every pending application for making, rectifying or cancelling any entry in the register of a registered title.

(2) The day list may be kept by means of a computer.][2]

Index Map and Parcels Index

8.—(1) Index Maps shall be kept in the Registry which shall show the position and extent of every registered estate, provided that, where practicable, the General Map shall be used for this purpose.

(2) Where the General Map is used as the Index Map the current number under which each estate is registered shall be shown in the Parcels Index.

(3) Where there is a separate Index Map, the number under which each estate was first registered shall be shown thereon, or, where practicable, the current title number.

[Index of proprietors' names

9.—(1) There shall also be kept an index of proprietors' names showing in respect of the register of each title the name of the proprietor of the land and of the proprietor of any registered charge, together in each case with the title number:

Provided that it shall not be necessary for there to be entered in the index either—
(*a*) the name of any building society, local authority or government department as proprietor of a charge, or

---

[2] Words added by Land Registration Rules 1978 (No. 1601).

(*b*) until such time as the Lord Chancellor shall direct, the name of any corporate or joint proprietor of land or of a charge registered as proprietor prior to 1st May 1972.

(2) Any person may apply in Form 104 for a search to be made in the index in respect of either his own name or the name of some other person in whose property he is able to satisfy the Registrar that he is interested generally (for instance, as his trustee in bankruptcy or his personal representative).

(3) On receiving any such application the Registrar shall make the search and shall supply the applicant with details of every entry in the index relating to the particulars stated in the application, together with a short description of the property comprised in each title concerned and in the case of the proprietor of a charge, the date of the charge.

(4) In this rule "index" includes any device or combination of devices serving the purpose of an index.][3]

[List of pending applications for first registration

10. Until the estate in land comprised in a pending application for first registration is shown on the Index Map, the title number and a short description of the land shall be entered in a list known as the list of pending applications for first registration.][4]

Minor Interests Index

11.—(1) There shall also be kept an Index to be called the Minor Interests Index in which all priority cautions and inhibitions relating to dealings with minor interests, which do not affect the powers of disposition of the proprietor, shall be entered.

(2) This Index shall be in such form and contain such particulars as the Registrar may from time to time determine. The entries therein shall not form part of the register, nor shall any purchaser be concerned with that Index.

Documents open to Inspection

12.—(1) The Index Maps, the General Map and the Parcels Index, and the list of pending applications [for first registration][5] but no other book map plan or document, shall be open to general public inspection, at any time during office hours.

(2) [*Repealed by the Land Registration Rules 1976 (No. 1332), Sched.*]

Correction of register

13. Where any clerical error or error of a like nature is discovered in the register, or in any plan or document referred to therein, which can be corrected without detriment to any registered interest, the registrar may (if he thinks fit, and after giving any notices, and calling for any evidence or obtaining any assent he may deem proper) cause the necessary correction to be made.

Registrations in error

14. Where it is proved to the satisfaction of the Registrar that the whole of the land comprised in a title, or too large a part to be properly dealt with

---

[3] This rule was substituted by the Land Registration Rules 1976 (No. 1332), r. 2(1).
[4] This rule was substituted by the Land Registration Rules 1978 (No. 1601).
[5] Words added by *ibid.*

under the last preceding rule, has been registered in error, the Registrar may enter notice of the fact in the register, and he may either—

  (*a*) with the consent of the proprietor and of all other persons appearing by the register to be interested in the land, or
  (*b*) after notice to the persons aforesaid and such inquiry, if any, as he may consider proper, and upon the production of such evidence as he may deem necessary; cancel the registration wholly or to the extent required.

Production of certificates

15. For the purpose of these rules the Registrar may make such order as to the production of the land and charge certificates (if any) as may be deemed necessary.

Cancellation of determined entries

16. The Registrar may, at any time after such inquiry and notices, if any, as he may consider proper, and upon the production of such evidence as is required by these rules or as he may deem necessary, withdraw from the register by cancellation or otherwise any lease, incumbrance, charge, note, notice, or other entry, which he is satisfied has determined, or ceased, or been discharged, or for any other reason no longer affects or relates to registered land.

New editions of the register

17.—(1) The Registrar may, on the application of, or after notice to the persons appearing by the register to be interested, when he considers it practicable and desirable, clear the register by closing the same and making a new edition thereof containing the subsisting entries only, and may, in doing so, make any rearrangement that may appear to him conducive to clearness, including the division of the title into two or more titles and the altering of the number of the title.

(2) Such arrangements shall be made as to the recalling of the land and charge certificates and for the issue of new certificates as may be necessary.

(3) No fee shall be charged for clearing the register under this rule, unless it is done on the application of the parties at a time when there is no dealing with the land in respect of which a fee is payable.

.   .   .   .   .   .

PART II

FIRST REGISTRATION AND CONVERSION

General Provisions

.   .   .   .   .   .

Documents to be delivered with application for first registration

20. The application shall (unless the Registrar shall otherwise direct) be accompanied by—

  (i) all such original deeds and documents relating to the title as the applicant has in his possession or under his control, including opinions of counsel, abstracts of title, contracts for or conditions of sale, requisitions, replies and other like documents, in regard to the title,

(ii) a copy or sufficient abstract of the latest document of title, not being a document of record,

(iii) sufficient particulars, by plan or otherwise, to enable the land to be fully identified on the Ordnance Map or Land Registry General Map,

(iv) a list in triplicate of all documents delivered.

Lease and certified copy to accompany application

21.—(1) In the case of leasehold land, a certified copy of the lease, or if approved by the Registrar, an abstract or other sufficient evidence of its contents, shall be deposited with the application if the original lessee is the applicant, and in other cases likewise if required by the Registrar.

(2) In all cases the lease itself shall accompany the application if in the possession or control of the applicant.

. . . . . .

[Delivery of applications for first registration

24.—(1) Every application for first registration shall be delivered at the proper office and, when so delivered, shall be allotted a title number and shall be dated as of the day on which it is deemed by this rule to have been delivered.

(2) Every application for first registration delivered at the proper office after 11.00 hours on one day and before or at 11.00 hours on the next day shall be deemed to have been delivered at the same time, namely, immediately after 11.00 hours on the second day.

(3) For the purpose of this rule an application for first registration includes the lodging of a priority notice under rule 71 of these rules and a caution against first registration under section 53 of the Act.][6]

Examination of title by Registrar

25. Where land is proposed to be registered with absolute or good leasehold title, the title shown by the documents accompanying the application shall be examined by or under the superintendence of the Registrar; and he may make such searches and enquiries and give such notices to tenants and occupiers and other persons as he may deem expedient.

Reference to special conveyancing or other counsel

26. The whole or any portion of the examination of the title may be referred by the Registrar, if he thinks fit, for the opinion of one of the special conveyancing counsel for the purposes of these rules, and the Registrar may act on such opinion:

Provided that where the title has already been examined on a sale by counsel of not less than 7 years' standing the Registrar may act on his opinion, or he may refer the application to him for further consideration and act on his further opinion.

Searches and enquiries by the Registrar

27. All searches, official certificates of search and enquiries which the Registrar may consider necessary in the examination of, or in relation to, the title shall be made or obtained by such person and in such manner as the Registrar shall direct.

---

[6] This rule was substituted by Land Registration Rules 1978 (No. 1601).

Modifications of examinations of title by Registrar

28. Where either—
    (*a*) the land has been sold or purchased under an order of the Court, or
    (*b*) it shall appear to the Registrar that the title has been sufficiently investigated on a transaction for value,
the examination of the title may be modified in such manner as the Registrar may think fit.

Certificate by a solicitor as to title on first registration

29. In cases of sale in a district where registration of title is compulsory on sale and—
    (*a*) the value of the land does not exceed £700, or
    (*b*) where there has been a sale by or after public auction within two years previous to the application, and the value of the land does not exceed £1,000,
the Registrar may, if he thinks fit, register a title as absolute or good leasehold, on production of a certificate by a solicitor, at the expense of the applicant, to the effect that—
    (*a*) he acted for the applicant on the purchase, which induced the registration,
    (*b*) he investigated, or caused to be investigated, the title in the usual way on the applicant's behalf, and made, or caused to be made, all such searches or official certificates of search, as he considered necessary,
    (*c*) the whole of the purchase money was paid to the person mentioned in that behalf in the conveyance or assignment,
    (*d*) he believes, as the result of his investigation, that the conveyance or assignment validly conveyed or assigned to the applicant the estate and interest thereby purported to be conveyed or assigned, free from any adverse rights or incumbrances (including restrictive covenants affecting the land by way of notice actual or constructive or by reason of the registration of a land charge), which were not shown by the conveyance or assignment.

Certificate by a solicitor as to title on conversion

30. On an application for conversion to an absolute or good leasehold title on the occasion of a sale where the value of the land does not exceed £2,000, the Registrar may act on a certificate by a solicitor at the expense of the applicant to the effect that—
    (*a*) he investigated the title prior to first registration in the usual way on the applicant's behalf,
    (*b*) he believes, as the result of his investigation, that the conveyance or assignment to the first registered proprietor validly conveyed or assigned to him the estate and interest thereby purported to be conveyed or assigned, free from any adverse rights or incumbrances (including restrictive covenants affecting the land by way of notice actual or constructive or by reason of the registration of a land charge), which were not shown by the conveyance or assignment.

Advertisements

31. Save as hereinafter expressly provided, before any registration is completed with absolute or good leasehold title, an advertisement shall be inserted in the Gazette and in such local or other newspaper or newspapers, if any, and in such manner as shall be decided by the Registrar in each case.

Contents of advertisements

32. The advertisement shall give the name and address of the person to be registered, a short description of the land, and the situation thereof, and shall require objections (if any) to be made before the expiration of a stated period, not less than fourteen days from the appearance of the advertisement in the Gazette.

Advertisements when dispensed with

33. Where the original lessee is registered as first proprietor, or if the land be situated in a district in which registration of title is compulsory on sale, and the applicant is a purchaser on a sale completed within the year preceding the application, an advertisement shall not, unless the Registrar thinks it necessary or advisable, be issued.

Objections to registration

34.—(1) Any person may, by notice in writing, signed by himself or his solicitor and delivered at the Registry before the completion of the registration, object to the registration.

(2) Such notice shall state concisely the grounds of the objection and give an address in the United Kingdom of the person objecting, to which all notices and other communications for him may be sent through the post.

Hearing of objections

35.—(1) The Registrar shall thereupon give notice to the applicant of the objection, and the title shall not be registered until the objection has been withdrawn or otherwise disposed of.

(2) The applicant may obtain an appointment before the Registrar for the hearing of any objection, as prescribed by these rules, and the objector shall be given at least seven clear days' notice of such appointment.

. . . . . .

Entry of incumbrances in the register

40. Incumbrances, conditions, and other burdens (including fee farm grants, or other grants reserving rents or services) to which the land may be subject, shall be entered in the register and may be entered either directly, or by reference to the instruments by which they are created or by setting out extracts therefrom.

Adverse easements

41.—(1) Notice of an easement, right, or privilege created by an instrument and operating at law which appears to the Registrar to affect adversely the land shall, if the Registrar thinks fit, be entered in the register.

(2) Such entry shall, so far as practicable and convenient, be by reference to the instrument by which the easement, right or privilege is created or by setting out an extract therefrom.

Completion of registration

42. When—

    (*a*) all objections (if any) have been disposed of,
    (*b*) the time fixed by the advertisements and notices (if any) has expired,

(*c*) it has been determined with what title the registration is to be made, and the requirements of Sections 14 and 16 of the Act have been complied with,

the registration shall be completed as of the day on which, and of the priority in which, the application was delivered,[7] and the documents of title, other than such as have under the Act or rules to be retained in the Registry, shall be delivered to the applicant.

·   ·   ·   ·   ·   ·

Leasehold Land

Registration of and dealing with underleases

44. Where any intermediate leasehold interest subsists between the freehold reversion and the leasehold estate which is the subject of registration, the words "lessor" and "lease," in these rules and in Sections 10 and 23 of the Act, shall be read as applying to a sub-lessor and a sub-lease.

Lease containing prohibition against alienation without licence

45. On the registration of any leasehold land held under a lease containing a prohibition against alienation without licence, all estates, rights, interests, powers, and remedies under such lease, arising upon, or by reason of, any alienation without licence, shall be expressly excepted from the effect of registration.

Notice of lease

46.—(1) Where a lease, affecting land already registered, is registered in pursuance of these rules, notice of the registration thereof shall be given to the proprietor of the freehold land or of the superior lease out of which the lease is derived, as the case may be.

(2) If no valid objection be made within seven days after service of the notice, or if the proprietor of the freehold or of the superior lease consents in writing (by himself or his solicitor) to the application, the lease shall be noted against the title to the freehold or to the superior lease in the same manner as notices of leases have to be entered under Section 48 of the Act and these rules.

·   ·   ·   ·   ·   ·

Conversion of Possessory into Absolute or Good Leasehold Title

Application for conversion under subsections (3) (b) and (4) of Section 77 of the Act

48.—(1) An application by the proprietor of the land for conversion under subsection (3) (*b*) or subsection (4) of Section 77 of the Act, need not be accompanied by all the documents of or relating to the title as required by subsection (3) (*a*), but shall be in Form 6 or Form 7 as the case may require.

·   ·   ·   ·   ·   ·

[7] See the Land Registration (District Registries) (No. 2) Order 1974, para. 3.

Manors, Advowsons, Rents, Tithe Rentcharges, and other Incorporeal Hereditaments, Mines and Minerals severed from the Land, Cellars, Flats and similar Hereditaments

Registration of incorporeal hereditaments

50. Application for registration of manors, advowsons, rents, tithe rentcharges, or other incorporeal hereditaments, mines and minerals severed from the land, cellars, flats, and other similar hereditaments, not including an undivided share, shall be made according to the rules above prescribed, and shall be proceeded with in the same manner, subject only to such modifications as the nature of the case may require and the Registrar may approve: provided that where a rentcharge is created by an instrument, that instrument shall be referred to in the register.

. . . . . .

Settled Land

Settled land; restriction required

56. Where application is made for registration of settled land, a statement in writing of the proper restriction shall be left with the application, or the Registrar shall be furnished with the information necessary to enable him to frame the proper restriction.

Principle governing restrictions

57. In framing restrictions for the protection of persons interested in settled land, it shall not be the duty of the trustees of the settlement or of the Registrar to protect the interests of any person who would not have been a necessary party to a disposition thereof under the powers of the Settled Land Act 1925, as extended by the settlement, if the land had been unregistered; but it shall be the duty of the trustees, or, if there are no trustees, of the Registrar, to give notice of the restrictions to such of the beneficiaries (if any) as the Registrar shall direct, and any such person can, if he desires (but at his own risk), lodge a caution or apply for an inhibition.

Forms of restrictions applicable to settled land

58.—(1) The restrictions given in Forms 9 to 11 shall apply respectively to the various cases set forth in those forms, and may be modified according to circumstances as the parties may require and the Registrar may deem fit.

(2) For the purposes of those restrictions, references to the powers conferred by the Settled Land Act 1925 shall include any powers conferred by the settlement in extension of those statutory powers.

Settlement may be filed

59.—(1) The settlement, whether consisting of one or two or more documents, or a copy or abstract thereof, may be filed in the Registry for safe custody and future reference.

(2) It shall not be referred to in the register, but shall be filed separately under the number of the title to which it relates.

. . . . . .

Cautions against Entry of Land on the Register

Form of cautions against first registration

64. A caution against entry of land on the register, lodged under Section 53 of the Act, shall be in Form 13, and shall be signed by the cautioner or his solicitor, and shall contain an address for service in the United Kingdom, and shall refer to, and be accompanied by, sufficient particulars, by plan or otherwise, to identify on the Ordnance Map or the Land Registry General Map, the land to which the caution relates.

. . . . . .

Form of statutory declaration

66. The statutory declaration in support of the caution shall be in Form 14, and shall be delivered with the caution.

Period for objections

67. The period to be limited by the notice to be served on the cautioner under subsection (3) of Section 53 of the Act shall be fourteen days, or such other period (not being less than seven days) as the Registrar may under special circumstances direct. The notice shall be in Form 15.

68.—(1) The caution may at any time be withdrawn in respect of the whole or any part of the land to which it relates upon an application for that purpose in Form 16, signed by the cautioner or his solicitor, or the person entitled to the benefit of the caution or his solicitor.

(2) Where the withdrawal is in respect of a part only of the land the application shall refer to, and be accompanied by, sufficient particulars, by plan or otherwise, to identify on the Ordnance Map or on the General Map the part to which the withdrawal relates.

Consent by cautioner

69. At any time after the notice required by subsection (3) of Section 53 of the Act has been served, the cautioner may, by writing signed by himself or his solicitor, consent to the registration, and the consent may be either absolute, or conditional on some special entry being made on the register.

Inspection of cautions

70. The Registrar may, if he thinks fit, allow any person interested in the land to inspect the caution and the statutory declaration lodged in support of it.

Priority Notices against First Registration

Form and effect of Priority Notices against first registration

71.—(1) A person entitled to apply for registration as first proprietor of land (whether his application requires the consent of any other person or not) or his solicitor, or, with his consent in writing, any other person or his solicitor, may lodge at the Registry a notice (to be called a Priority Notice) in Form 17, reserving priority for a specified application intended to be subsequently made, and a written acknowledgment of the receipt of the notice shall be given him.

(2) If within fourteen days from the lodgment of the notice or within such further time as the Registrar shall think fit, application is made in accordance with the notice and is accompanied by the acknowledgment, it

shall be dealt with in priority to any other application affecting the same land which may have been made in the meantime.

(3) On the expiration of the period fixed as aforesaid for the operation of the notice it may be cancelled.

Dealings prior to Registration

Dealings by persons having right to apply for first registration

72.—(1) Where a person having the right to apply for registration as first proprietor desires to deal with the land in any way permitted by the Act before he is himself registered as proprietor he may do so in the manner, and subject to the conditions, which would be applicable if he were in fact the registered proprietor. In the case of a transfer, the transferee shall be deemed to be the applicant for first registration and shall be entered on the register accordingly.

(2) Subject to any prior rights obtained by registration under the Act and rules, a dealing so made shall, when completed by registration, have the same effect as if the person making it were registered as proprietor.

(3) Provided that a dealing, other than a lease, shall not be accepted for registration until an application has been made for the registration of the estate to which it relates, and if the application for registration of the estate is subsequently refused, or withdrawn, or abandoned, the registration of such dealing shall be annulled.

Effect of dealings prior to first registration

73.—(1) Pursuant to subsection (2) of Section 123 of the Act, it is hereby provided that any dealing with land which takes place between the date of a conveyance, grant, or assignment necessitating compulsory registration of land and the date of application to register, shall (subject to the provisions of subsection (1) of the said Section) take effect as if it had taken place after the date of first registration, which shall be effected as of the date of the application to register.

(2) Where a dealing is a charge or other incumbrance, capable of registration in the Charges Register of the title affected, the person for the time being entitled to it shall have power to lodge an application on behalf of the proper applicant for the first registration of the estate on which such charge or incumbrance has been created.

PART III

REGISTERED DEALINGS WITH REGISTERED LAND

As to Registered Dispositions generally

i. *Form*

Forms to be used

74. The forms in the Schedule hereto shall be used in all matters to which they refer, or are capable of being applied or adapted, with such alterations and additions, if any, as are necessary or desired and the Registrar allows.

Instruments where no form is prescribed

75. Instruments for which no form is provided or to which the scheduled forms cannot conveniently be adapted, shall be in such form as the Registrar shall direct or allow, the scheduled forms being followed as nearly as circumstances will permit.

Implied covenants

76. For the purpose of introducing the covenants implied under Sections 76 and 77 of the Law of Property Act 1925 a person may, in a registered disposition, be expressed to execute, transfer, or charge as beneficial owner, as settlor, as trustee, as mortgagee, as personal representative of a deceased person, as committee of a lunatic, or as receiver of a defective, or under an order of the court: and an instrument of transfer or charge, and any instrument affecting registered land, or a registered charge, may be expressed accordingly, but no reference to covenants implied under Section 76 aforesaid shall be entered in the register.

Special provisions as to implied covenants

77. Pursuant to subsection (2) of Section 38 of the Act, it is hereby provided that—

(1) Any covenant implied by virtue of Section 76 of the Law of Property Act 1925 in a disposition of registered land shall take effect as though the disposition was expressly made subject to—
   (*a*) all charges and other interests appearing or protected on the register at the time of the execution of the disposition and affecting the title of the covenantor;
   (*b*) any overriding interests of which the purchaser has notice and subject to which it would have taken effect, had the land been unregistered; and

(2) The benefit of any covenant implied under Sections 76 and 77 aforesaid, or either of them shall, on and after the registration of the disposition in which it is implied, be annexed and incident to and shall go with the registered proprietorship of the interest for the benefit of which it is given and shall be capable of being enforced by the proprietor for the time being thereof.

(3) The provisions of this rule are in addition to and not in substitution for the other provisions relating to covenants contained in the said Act.

(4) Provided that where covenants are to be implied under Section 77 aforesaid, with or without modification, express reference shall be made in the disposition to that section or to the Parts of the 2nd Schedule to that Act in which the covenants are set out.

Power for Registrar to decline to enter improper forms

78. If it appears to the Registrar that any instrument or entry proposed to be entered or made in the register is improper in form or in substance, or is not clearly expressed, or does not indicate with sufficient precision the particular interest of land which it is intended to affect, or refers only to matters which are not the subject of registration under the Act, or, being a condition, does not run with the land, or is not capable of being legally annexed thereto, or of affecting assigns by registration of a notice or other entry, or being a restriction, is unreasonable or calculated to cause inconvenience, or is otherwise expressed in a manner inconsistent with the principles upon which the register is to be kept, he may decline to enter the same in the register, either absolutely or subject only to such modifications therein as he shall approve; or he may himself, with the applicant's consent, settle the form of the entry to be made.

. . . . . .

Instruments by persons entitled to be registered as proprietor

81. An instrument executed under Section 37 of the Act, or under the rules relating to dealings prior to first registration, by a person entitled to be registered as proprietor of any interest in land, or of a charge, before he has been registered as such, shall be in the same form as is required for a disposition by the proprietor with such modification, if any, as may be necessary to define clearly the land affected. But no registration of such instrument shall be made until the person executing the same has been registered as proprietor, or his right to be so registered has been shown to the satisfaction of the Registrar.

. . . . . .

iii. *Registration*

[Delivery of applications

83.—(1) Every application shall be delivered at the proper office and, when so delivered, shall be allocated an official reference number and shall be dated as of the day on which it is deemed under rule 85 of these rules to have been delivered.

(2) The application shall be completed by registration as of the day on which and, subject to the effect of any provision of the Act or of any rules made thereunder, of the priority in which it is deemed to have been delivered.

Priority of applications

84.—(1) Where two or more applications relating to a particular title are deemed to have been delivered at the same time, the order in which, as between each other, they shall rank in priority shall, subject to the effect of any provision of the Act or of any rules made thereunder, be determined in the manner prescribed by this rule.

(2) Where the applications are made by the same applicant, they shall rank in such order as he shall specify.

(3) Where the applications are not made by the same applicant, they shall rank in such order as may be agreed between the applicants or, failing agreement, as may be determined under rule 298 of these rules.

(4) Where one transaction is dependent upon another the registrar may assume (unless or until the contrary appears) that the applicant or applicants have specified or agreed that the applications shall have priority so as to give effect to the sequence of the instruments effecting the transactions.

Date of delivery of applications

85. Every application delivered at the proper office after 11.00 hours on one day and before or at 11.00 hours on the next day shall be deemed to have been delivered at the same time, namely, immediately after 11.00 hours on the second day.][8]

. . . . . .

Retention of documents in Registry

90. Except where otherwise provided by the Act or these rules, all deeds, applications, and other documents on which any entry in the register is founded shall be retained, and shall not be taken away from the Registry, except under a written order of the Registrar or an order of the court.

Endorsement of registration with lessor

91.—(1) Where registered leasehold land is held under a lease which requires a disposition to be produced to the lessor or his agent, or to be

[8] Rules 83 to 85 substituted by Land Registration Rules 1978 (No. 1601).

produced to and endorsed by him, such a stipulation shall, as regards any transfer or charge, be sufficiently complied with by production of the instrument or a copy thereof to him and by endorsement, if required, of the instrument of transfer or charge or of a copy thereof, or, after the registration thereof, by production, if required, of the land certificate or charge certificate, as the case may be, and by endorsement on the lease.

(2) Such endorsement shall not be made on the land or charge certificate, and if so made, after the commencement of the Act, shall be void.

Return of Building Society charges after registration

92.—(1) Upon the registration of a charge in favour of a Building Society, Friendly Society (including a branch society), or Industrial and Provident Society, the instrument of charge may (if it is so desired) be delivered to them, after registration, upon their delivering at the Registry a copy thereof, verified by the signature of the secretary or solicitor as being a correct copy.

(2) Such copy—
    (*a*) shall be admissible for all purposes as sufficient evidence of the contents and execution thereof, without the production of the original charge;
    (*b*) need not be stamped;
    (*c*) must be filed in the Registry.

Endorsement of Certificate of Registration on Building Society charges

93.—(1) Where an instrument of charge in favour of a Building Society, Friendly Society (including a branch society), or Industrial and Provident Society is delivered to the society under the preceding rule, it shall be endorsed with a Certificate of Registration, and the instrument so endorsed shall be treated for all purposes as the charge certificate.

(2) It shall be endorsed with notes of transfers, part discharges, and other dealings, and when the charge is wholly discharged shall be delivered up, cancelled, and retained in the Registry.

. . . . . .

v. *Deeds and Instruments off the Register*

Certificate as to the necessity of deeds off the register

96. Pursuant to Section 39 of the Act it is hereby provided that, where a transaction (though relating exclusively to registered land or to a registered charge) is of such a character (by reason, for instance, of its being accompanied by lengthy recitals or personal covenants not affecting the substance of the transaction in relation to the registered land or charge or of its being closely involved with other transactions or of its being necessary that duplicates should be held by different persons) as to render it necessary or useful that the registered disposition should be accompanied by an additional deed or instrument, the Registrar may issue a certificate to that effect in such form as he shall think fit, and in that case the additional deed or instrument shall, if in accordance with such certificate, be an exception within the meaning of the said Section and shall not be rendered void by that Section.

Minor interests in mortgage debts

97. Section 101 of the Act shall, so far as applicable, apply to a minor interest in a debt secured by a registered charge, as if that debt had been referred to in place of registered land.

Transfers of Land

. . . . . .

Transfer of land into settlement

99. A transfer of land into settlement shall be made by a vesting transfer in one of the Forms 21 or 22, with the addition of the proper restrictions to be entered in the register, according to the principles prescribed by these rules, and the Registrar shall, on receipt thereof, register the transferee (being the tenant for life of full age, statutory owner or personal representative, as the case may require) named therein as the proprietor of the land, and shall enter in the register the restrictions contained in the transfer.

Registered land brought into settlement

100. Where registered land has been settled and the existing registered proprietor is the tenant for life under the settlement, the proprietor shall make a declaration in Form 23 and shall apply for the registration of a restriction in Form 9, or such other restriction as may be required, having regard to the terms of the settlement and the Settled Land Act 1925.

. . . . . .

Transfer to statutory owners

102. A transfer to the statutory owners under subsection (2) of Section 91 of the Act shall not refer to the settlement and shall be in the ordinary form, with the addition of a restriction against any disposition not authorised by the Settled Land Act 1925 or the settlement.

Creation of interests affecting settled land in priority to the settlement

103. Pursuant to subsection (2) of Section 87 of the Act it is hereby provided as follows:—
 (i) Where a proprietor or the personal representative of a deceased proprietor has power under a settlement to create a legal estate in priority to the settlement, he may do so by any document sufficient at law to create it.
 (ii) The document shall be completed by registration and shall be a registered disposition and shall vest a legal estate in the grantee.
 (iii) On production of such a document purporting to be in exercise of such a power executed by such proprietor or personal representative the Registrar shall, without inquiry as to the existence or terms of the power, register notice of the estate created as an incumbrance on the land, and shall inform all persons, appearing by the register to be interested, that he has done so.
 (iv) The registration of such a notice shall not confer on the grantee any greater estate or interest, as against the other persons interested under the settlement, than it would have conferred if the land had not been on the register.

Duty to apply for restrictions when land is settled

104.—(1) On the creation of a settlement it shall be the duty of the proprietor, or (if there is no proprietor) the personal representatives of a deceased proprietor, to apply to the Registrar for the entry of such restrictions or inhibitions or notices as may be appropriate to the case.

The application shall state that they are required for the protection of the minor interests under the settlement.

(2) The Registrar shall enter such restrictions, inhibitions or notices without inquiry as to the terms of the settlement provided they are not in his opinion unreasonable or calculated to cause inconvenience, and shall inform all persons, appearing by the register to be affected thereby, that he has done so.

(3) Nothing in this rule shall affect the rights and powers of a personal representative for purposes of administration.

Discharge from liability in respect of minor interests under a settlement

105. Where a proprietor or personal representative of a deceased proprietor has, in good faith, complied with the requirements of the Act in executing a vesting deed, assent or transfer of land or discharge of trustees and in applying for the necessary and proper restrictions or other entries (if any) that may be required for the protection of minor interests under a settlement, he shall be absolutely discharged from all liability in respect of the equitable interests and powers taking effect under the settlement, and shall be entitled to be kept indemnified at the cost of the trust estate from all liabilities affecting the settled land, but the proprietor for the time being (not being a purchaser for value or his successor in title) shall hold the land upon the trusts (if any) affecting the same.

Release of land from minor interests under a settlement

106. Where the trustees of a settlement desire to release registered land from the minor interests under such settlement they may do so by any document sufficient at law to release it, and, on an application made for that purpose, effect shall be given to the transaction by making the consequential alterations in the register.

Transfer of land in consideration of a rent

107.—(1) A transfer of land in consideration or partly in consideration of a rent may be made by the proprietor of the land by an instrument in any form legally sufficient for the purpose of which the Registrar may approve.

(2) The transferee shall be registered as the proprietor of the land, and the rent shall be entered in the Charges Register as an incumbrance.

Separate title for proprietor of a rent

108. The transferor shall be registered as the proprietor of the rent under a separate title, and a reference to that title shall be made in the title of the transferee.

Implied covenants on a transfer of freehold land subject to a rent

109. On a transfer of freehold land subject to an existing rent, covenants (similar to those implied by Section 24 of the Act on a transfer of leasehold land) shall be implied under Section 77 of the Law of Property Act 1925, but such implication may be negatived by adding suitable words to the instrument of transfer as in Form 33, and in that case a note thereof shall be entered in the register.

If it is desired to substitute modified covenants for the covenants implied by this rule, the necessary variations may be made in the transfer.

Covenants for indemnity

110. On a transfer of land subject to a charge or other incumbrance appearing on the register, or, in the case of a possessory or qualified title, an incumbrance not affected by the registration, covenants by either party to pay the money owing and to indemnify the other party may be added to the instrument of transfer and may be noted on the register.

. . . . . .

Transfer of leasehold land

115.—(1) A transfer of leasehold land shall be made by an instrument in Form 32, and all or any of the covenants implied by Section 24 of the Act on a transfer of leasehold land may, if it is desired, be negatived by adding suitable words to the instrument of transfer, and in that case an entry negativing the implied covenants shall be entered in the register.

(2) If it is desired to substitute modified covenants, by reference to Section 77 of the Law of Property Act 1925, or otherwise, for the covenants implied by Section 24, the necessary variations may be made in the transfer.

. . . . . .

Variation of implied covenants

117. On a transfer of part of the land held under a lease, the covenants implied by Section 24 of the Act, or Section 77 of the Law of Property Act 1925, may, if it is desired, be modified or negatived by adding suitable words to the instrument of transfer, and a note shall be made in the register.

. . . . . .

Where power of disposing of registered land has become vested in some person other than the proprietor

131. Where the power of disposing of registered land has, by the operation of any statute or statutory power or by Order of Court or by paramount title, become vested in some person other than the proprietor (as, for instance, in the case of a deed poll executed under Section 77 of the Lands Clauses Consolidation Act 1845, or of a vesting in a co-tenant for life of full age, or the trustees of a settlement in the case of an infant under the First Schedule to the Law of Property Act 1925, or the Second Schedule to the Settled Land Act 1925, or of a declaration express or implied vesting an estate made under any statute, or of a sale by a mortgagee with a title paramount to the title registered) and the proprietor refuses to execute a transfer, or his execution of a transfer cannot be obtained, or can only be obtained after undue delay or expense, the Registrar may—

(*a*) after due notice under these rules to such proprietor,
(*b*) on production of the land certificate, unless an order to the contrary is made by the Registrar,
(*c*) on such other evidence as he may deem sufficient,

make such entry in or correction of the register as under the circumstances he shall deem fit, for the purpose of vesting the registered land in the same person in whom the legal estate would have been vested if the land had not been registered.

. . . . . .

Charges

. . . . . .

Charge negativing or modifying implied covenants

140. The registration of an instrument of charge negativing or modifying the provisions of Sections 28, 29 and 34 of the Act, or any of them, shall for the purposes of those Sections be deemed a sufficient negative or contrary entry on the register.

Effect of powers, of the registration of a charge

141.—(1) The proprietor of the land, while in possession, shall have all the powers of leasing and of accepting surrenders of leases conferred by Sections 99 and 100 of the Law of Property Act 1925, as extended by the instrument of charge or any instrument varying the terms thereof, but subject to any contrary intention expressed in any such instrument, a note of which intention shall, under an application to be made for that purpose, be entered in the register.

(2) The proprietor of a charge, while in possession, or after a receiver has been appointed, or such receiver on his behalf, shall have all the powers conferred by the said two Sections (as extended as aforesaid), but subject to any contrary intention expressed as aforesaid, a note of which intention shall, under an application to be made for that purpose, be entered in the register.

(3) The proprietor of an annual sum, within the meaning of Section 121 of the Law of Property Act 1925, charged on registered land or the income thereof, shall have power to create a term in accordance with that Section; and if that term would have been legal, or clothed with a legal estate (had the land not been registered), it may, on an application made for that purpose, be registered.

(4) Subject as aforesaid all dispositions, by the proprietor of the land, authorised by Sections 18 and 21 of the Act, shall, unless the proprietor of the charge concurs in the disposition, take effect subject to any charge registered at the time of the disposition.

(5) This rule has effect without prejudice to Section 104 of the Act.

. . . . . .

Charge under s.90 of the Act (settled land)

144.—(1) A charge under Section 90 of the Act shall be in Form 45.

(2) It shall not refer to the settlement, but shall be accompanied by the land certificate and by such evidence or other particulars as may be necessary to satisfy the Registrar that it is created for securing money actually raised and that it is not capable of being overridden under the Settled Land Act 1925 or the Law of Property Act 1925.

(3) When registered it shall take effect and be dealt with in the same manner, by the same instruments, and with the same results in all respects as in the Act and these rules provided with regard to charges generally.

(4) Provided that, in cases in which under these rules, a charge does not take priority, according to date of registration, the requisite note shall be added and shall have effect accordingly.

. . . . . .

Mortgage debt held in shares

146. Where it appears from a charge that the money secured is advanced by two or more persons, but not on joint account, they shall be entered as joint proprietors of the charge as a whole, but the register may show the shares in which the money is held.

Entry to be made in register on foreclosure

147. Where the proprietor of a charge obtains an order for foreclosure absolute, the order, or an office copy thereof, shall be delivered to the Registrar, who shall thereupon enter the proprietor of the charge as proprietor (subject to prior charges) of the land the equity of redemption in which is foreclosed. The charge certificate shall accompany the application.

Effect of dispositions by proprietor of a charge

148. Subject to any entry to the contrary on the register, any disposition by the proprietor of a charge (other than a lease within Section 104 of the Act) shall have the same effect as dispositions under Sections 20, 23 and 40 of the Act, as the case may be, save that such dispositions shall be subject only to the overriding interests (if any) and to the incumbrances and other entries (if any) appearing on the register which have priority over the charge under which the disposition is made.

Declaration by the proprietor of a charge who has acquired a title by possession

149.—(1) The declaration to be made pursuant to subsection (2) of Section 34 of the Act by the proprietor of a charge who has acquired a title by possession shall be by a deed poll in Form 52, with such modifications (if any) as the circumstances may require.

(2) The evidence in support shall consist of a statutory declaration by an independent and trustworthy person as to the fact of the entry upon the land or into receipt of the rents and profits and as to the possession having been continuous and undisputed.

(3) The beneficial title to the equity of redemption must also, if required, be proved to the satisfaction of the Registrar so as to show that there is no person entitled to redeem.

Alteration of terms of a registered charge

150. An application to alter the terms of a registered charge under Section 31 of the Act shall be in Form 51, and shall be executed by the proprietors of the charge and of the land and of every charge of equal or inferior priority prejudicially affected by the alteration.

Discharge of a registered charge

151. A discharge wholly or in part of a registered charge shall be made by an instrument in Form 53 and shall be signed by the proprietor of the charge, but the Registrar shall be at liberty to accept and act upon any other proof of satisfaction of a charge which he may deem sufficient.

Discharge of a Building, Friendly or Industrial and Provident Society mortgage

152.—(1) When all money intended to be secured by any mortgage or charge to or in favour of any Building Society, Friendly Society (including a branch society), or Industrial and Provident Society has been fully paid or satisfied, an instrument of discharge in Form 53 may be used.

(2) The instrument shall be under the seal of such Society, if incorporated, or under the hands and seals of the trustees for the time being of, or acting in that matter for, such Building or Friendly Society, or other the proper officers thereof, if such society is not incorporated, and countersigned by the secretary; or under the hands and seals of two

members of the committee of an Industrial and Provident Society, if unincorporated and countersigned by the secretary.

(3) The instrument shall have the same effect and operation in vacating the mortgage or charge, and in determining the mortgage term (if any) and otherwise, as a receipt indorsed on such mortgage or charge, duly made, signed, and attested in such form and manner and by such persons as is prescribed by, and otherwise in conformity with, the provisions of Section 5 of 6 & 7 Will. IV., cap. 32; Section 42 of the Building Societies Act, 1874; (*a*) Section 43 of the Industrial and Provident Societies Act, 1893; (*b*) and Section 53 of the Friendly Societies Act, 1896, (*c*) respectively, as varied, in the case of unregistered land, by Section 115 of the Law of Property Act, 1925.

.   .   .   .   .   .

Consolidation of charges

154.—(1) Where a charge, whether affecting the whole or a part of the land comprised in a title, reserves the right to consolidate, it shall not on that account only be registered against any other land than that expressly described in it.

(2) But where the right reserved is to consolidate with a specified charge, or an application in writing is made to register the right in respect of a specified charge, the Registrar shall require the production of the land certificates[9] of all the titles affected, and, on the production thereof, shall enter in the register a notice that the specified charges are consolidated.

Land charges when registered as charges

155.—(1) Land charges for securing money, within the proviso to subsection (2) of Section 59 of the Act, required to be registered before realisation (being Classes A and B and local land charges as defined in the Land Charges Act 1925[10]), shall be deemed to be created by the person registered as proprietor of the land at the date of the charge, and shall be capable of registration accordingly.

(2) Where such a charge is registered, the term and covenants specified in Sections 27 and 28 of the Act shall not be implied, and the proprietor of the charge shall not by virtue of such registration be entitled to any rights under Section 34 of the Act to which he would not have been entitled if the charge had not been so registered.

Notice of priority for any subsequent charge made for giving effect to a minor interest

156.—(1) Where the proprietor would, if the land were not registered, be bound under subsection (1) of Section 16 of the Settled Land Act 1925 to state in a mortgage of settled land that it shall take effect subject to any equitable charges or powers of charging which have priority, as in that section mentioned, he shall be bound to—

(*a*) refer to the minor interest having such priority in the instrument of charge,

(*b*) furnish such evidence respecting the minor interest for filing or otherwise as the Registrar may reasonably require.

(2) The entry of the charge in the register, containing such a reference, shall be deemed a sufficient entry of notice on the register to secure the

---

[9] In view of the provisions of s. 65 of the Land Registration Act 1925 (15 & 16 Geo. 5, c. 21) (p. 381, *ante*), it is clearly necessary to read "charge certificates" for "land certificates."

[10] Now the Land Charges Act 1972 (c. 61), *ante*, p. 320, and the Local Land Charges Act 1975 (c. 76).

priority of any charge subsequently made for giving effect to the minor interest on the register.

. . . . . .

Adaptation to Incumbrances prior to Registration and to Sub-mortgages of the provisions of the Act with regard to Charges

Registration of proprietor of incumbrances prior to first registration of land

160.—(1) Where it appears that any person is entitled to an incumbrance created prior to the first registration of land, the Registrar shall, on the application or with the consent of the person so entitled and on due proof of his title and after notice to the proprietor of the land, register such person as the proprietor of such incumbrance.

(2) Where there are two or more such incumbrances, their relative priorities shall not be affected by the registration of some or one of them only, or by the order in which such of them as are registered are entered in the register.

Dispositions of incumbrances

161. From and after the registration of the proprietor of an incumbrance, all transfers and other dispositions thereof or thereunder shall be entered in the register and shall (subject to any entry to the contrary in the register) rank, as between themselves, for purposes of priority in the order in which they are registered; and the incumbrance shall cease to be subject to the jurisdiction of any local Deed Registry.

. . . . . .

Sub-charge

163.—(1) The proprietor of a charge or incumbrance may at any time charge the mortgage debt with the payment of money in the same manner as the proprietor of land can charge the land; and such charges are in these rules referred to as sub-charges.

(2) The proprietor of a sub-charge shall, subject to any entry to the contrary in the register, have the same powers of disposition, in relation to the land, as if he had been registered as proprietor of the principal charge.

Dispositions of sub-charges

164.—(1) A sub-charge shall be completed, transferred, and discharged in the same form and manner as a charge.

(2) Subject to any entry in the register to the contrary—

    (*a*) a sub-charge shall, as against the person creating it, imply the same covenants and, as against that person and all persons over whose interests the charge confers power, confer the same powers and have the same effect as a charge,

    (*b*) registered sub-charges on the same charge or incumbrance shall, as between themselves, rank according to the order in which they are entered on the register and not according to the order in which they are created.

Production of certificate on registration

165. On the registration of a sub-charge, the charge certificate or incumbrance shall be produced and a note of the sub-charge shall be entered therein.

Form of certificates of incumbrance and sub-charge

166.—(1) Certificates of incumbrance and of sub-charge shall be prepared in like forms and be issued and dealt with and may be used to create a lien by deposit in the same manner as charge certificates.

(2) They shall be produced on the same occasions and their production may be dispensed with on the same terms as charge certificates.

. . . . . .

Transmissions of Land and Charges

i. *On death*

Registration of a personal representative

168.—(1) On production of the probate or letters of administration of a sole (or sole surviving) proprietor of land or of a charge, dying after 1897, the personal representative named in such probate or letters shall be registered as proprietor in the place of the deceased proprietor with the addition of the words "executor *or* executrix (*or* administrator *or* administratrix) of [*name*] deceased."

(2) Provided that in the case of land settled previously to the death of the proprietor, the special personal representatives in whom the land vests under the Administration of Estates Act 1925 shall be registered as proprietors.

. . . . . .

Transfer, etc., by personal representative

170. Pursuant to subsection (3) of Section 41 of the Act it is hereby provided that—

(1) The personal representative of a deceased proprietor may, without being himself registered, transfer any registered land or charge of which the deceased was registered as proprietor, or may dispose of it by way of assent or appropriation or vesting assent.

(2) If he transfers the transfer shall be in the usual form.

(3) If he assents or appropriates or executes a vesting assent the instrument shall be in Forms 56 or 57, as the case may be.

(4) On delivery of the transfer, assent, appropriation or vesting assent at the Registry, accompanied, if the personal representative is not already registered as proprietor, by the probate or letters of administration, the Registrar shall register the person named in the instrument for that purpose as proprietor, together with the restrictions (if any) contained therein.

(5) It shall not be the duty of the Registrar nor shall he be entitled to consider or to call for any information concerning the reason why any transfer is made, or as to terms of the will, and, whether he has notice or not of its contents, he shall be entitled to assume that the personal representative is acting (whether by transfer, assent or appropriation or vesting assent) correctly and within his powers.

Minorities

171.—(1) Where a settlement is created or arises under a will or intestacy and an infant becomes beneficially entitled to an estate in fee simple or a term of years absolute in the registered land, or would if he were of full age be or have the powers of a tenant for life, the statutory owners shall, after administration is completed as respects the registered land, direct the personal representatives to apply for the proper restrictions (if any) according to the principles prescribed by these rules.

(2) The application shall be in Form 76, and on receipt of an application from the personal representatives in that form, accompanied by the land certificate, it shall not be the duty of the Registrar, nor shall he be entitled to consider or call for any information concerning the reason why the application is made or as to the terms of the will or the devolution under the intestacy, or as to whether the direction by the statutory owners was actually given or not, or as to its terms, and whether he has notice of those matters or not, he shall be entitled to assume that the personal representatives are acting according to the directions given and that the directions were given by the statutory owners and were correct.

(3) Where under subsection (3) of Section 19 of the Settled Land Act 1925 there is a tenant for life of full age, he shall be entitled to be registered as proprietor during any minority therein referred to, but subject to the prescribed restrictions.

(4) Nothing in this rule shall affect the right of statutory owners to be registered as proprietors.

Death of a joint proprietor

172. If one of two or more joint proprietors of land or of a charge dies, his name shall be withdrawn from the register on proof of death, or on production of probate or letters of administration, together with such other evidence (if any) as the Registrar may require.

. . . . . .

ii. *On Bankruptcy or Liquidation*

Registration of Official Receiver

174.—(1) On production to the Registrar of an office copy of an order of a Court having jurisdiction in bankruptcy adjudging a proprietor bankrupt, or directing the estate of a deceased proprietor to be administered under Section 130 of the Bankruptcy Act 1914, together with a certificate signed by the Official Receiver that any registered land or charge is part of the property of the bankrupt or deceased proprietor divisible amongst his creditors, the Official Receiver may be registered as proprietor in place of the bankrupt or deceased proprietor.

(2) Nothing in these rules shall affect the provisions of Section 103 of the Settled Land Act 1925.

. . . . . .

Creditor's notice

179. A creditor's notice shall be entered in the Proprietorship Register in the following form, "Creditor's Notice in respect of a petition in bankruptcy protecting the rights of all creditors," and notice of the entry shall be given to the proprietor.

Bankruptcy inhibition

180. A bankruptcy inhibition shall be entered in the Proprietorship Register in the following form,"Bankruptcy Inhibition. No disposition or transmission is to be registered until a trustee in bankruptcy is registered," and notice of the entry shall be given to the proprietor.

. . . . . .

Part IV

Minor Entries in the Register

Notices of leases or agreements

186.—(1) An application to register notice of a lease or agreement for a lease, under Section 48 of the Act, may be made either by the lessee or by any person entitled to or interested in the lease or agreement or by the proprietor of the land against which the notice is to be entered.

(2) The application shall be accompanied by the lease or counterpart, or by the agreement or duplicate, as the case may be, also by a copy or full abstract thereof, and a copy or tracing of the plan (if any) thereon.

(3) Except where the application is made by the proprietor, it shall be accompanied also by either the consent of the proprietor in writing signed by himself or his solicitor, or by an order of the Court authorising the registration of the notice.

(4) Consent to the registration of a notice of a lease or agreement may be given either before or after its execution.

When notice of a lease affects incumbrances

187. Where, after the creation of an incumbrance, a lease is executed which would, apart from the Act, be binding on the incumbrancer, and notice of such lease is registered under Section 48 of the Act, that notice shall be effectual against the incumbrancer, notwithstanding that his incumbrance was registered before the registration of the notice.

Form of entry of notice of lease

188. The notice in the register shall give the term, and may include such other short particulars as can be conveniently entered. The lease or agreement shall be marked with a note of the entry and shall be returned to the applicant.

Statutory declaration where lease is not produced

189. If the lease or counterpart or the agreement or duplicate is not produced, a statutory declaration by the applicant or his solicitor, stating the reason of the non-production and verifying the copy or abstract, shall be furnished.

Notices under s. 49 of the Act (rights and claims)

190.—(1) Application for the registration of notices of or claims in respect of any of the matters set out in Section 49 of the Act shall be in Form 59, and shall state concisely the facts or documents on which the claim depends.

(2) The evidence in support of the application shall be delivered therewith and the matter shall be proceeded with, and such entry made on the register as the Registrar shall direct.

. . . . . .

Miscellaneous Entries

Notice of freedom from or the existence of overriding interests

197.—(1) Where any person desires to have an entry made in the register of the freedom from or the existence of an overriding interest mentioned in Section 70 of the Act, the application shall be made in writing and shall state the particulars of the entry required to be made.

(2) If the applicant is the proprietor of the land or the liability, right, or interest has been created by the proprietor of the land, and if, in either case, there is no caution, restriction, or inhibition on the register, an entry of the existence of the liability, right, or interest may be made accordingly.

(3) In other cases evidence satisfactory to the Registrar shall be produced of the existence or discharge of the liability, right, or interest, as the case may require.

(4) The proprietor of the land, if not the applicant, shall have notice of the application, and the matter shall be proceeded with as the Registrar shall direct.

(5) Any entry of the existence of the liability, right, or interest, if made, shall be against the title in the Charges Register, and such entry shall be made so far as practicable and convenient by reference to the instrument creating the right or by setting out an extract therefrom.

(6) Any entry, showing that the registered land is free from any one or more of the liabilities, rights, or interest, mentioned in Section 70 of the Act, shall be made in the Property Register.

Notice to proprietor of servient tenement as to easement, etc.

198. The notice required to be served on the proprietor of the servient tenement, before an entry can be made against it, of the existence of an easement, right, or privilege, not created by an instrument, shall be fourteen days or such longer period as the Registrar may deem advisable.

Entry as to trivial rights not required

199. The Registrar shall not be required to enter notice of any liability, right, or interest which shall appear to him to be of a trivial or obvious character, or the entry of which on the register is likely to cause confusion or inconvenience.

Determination of registered estates

200. Where the title to a lease, rentcharge or other estate or interest has been registered under the Act, the determination thereof may be notified on the register, upon the production of a surrender or other sufficient release or discharge, executed by the proprietor thereof and every person appearing by the register to be interested therein.

Determination of leases, etc., noted, where there has been no dealing

201. Where the title is not so registered, but a lease, incumbrance, rentcharge, easement, right or other interest is noted on the register as an incumbrance, and there has been no dealing therewith or transmission thereof, the determination may be notified on the register on production of the document (if any) creating it, with a sufficient release or discharge thereof executed by the incumbrancer named therein.

Determination of leases, etc., noted, where there has been a dealing

202. If, in the like case, there has been a dealing with or transmission of the incumbrance the application shall also be accompanied by sufficient evidence of the applicant's title (with an abstract if required by the Registrar) as in cases of examination of title on first registration.

Method of entry of determination of leases, etc.

203.—(1) The determination may be notified on the register either by cancelling the original entry, or by noting the fact, as the Registrar may think fit.

(2) Where the title to the lease or other incumbrance has been registered such title shall be closed.

Note of variation of lease, etc., on register

204. The variation of a lease or other estate, right, or interest registered or noted on the register shall be notified in such manner and on such evidence as the Registrar shall deem appropriate and sufficient.

Restrictive covenants under a building scheme

205. On the determination, otherwise than by effluxion of time, of a lease, containing restrictive covenants which the Registrar has reason to believe may be enforceable by persons other than the lessor, the Registrar may, if he thinks fit, make an entry on the register to the effect that the land is subject to such liability (if any) as may be subsisting by reason of those covenants.

Where lease may be treated as merged

206. Where—
   (*a*) the proprietor of any land, comprised in a leasehold title, becomes, by any means, the proprietor of the land comprised in the title against which the lease is noted as an incumbrance, or
   (*b*) a lease or agreement for a lease, noted as an incumbrance only, is vested in such proprietor,
the Registrar may, unless the contrary appears, treat the lease as merged, in which case the title shall be closed, or the note shall be cancelled, as the case may require.

Entries as to merged interests

207. Where any interest in land, situated in a compulsory area, would, on registration under a separate title, be immediately merged in a superior registered estate, or otherwise determined, it shall not be necessary to register such interest, but the Registrar shall have power to make such entries (if any) in the register of any superior registered estate as may be necessary, as if a separate title had been opened and closed on merger, or otherwise.

Production of determined leases

208. Where, under these rules, an entry is to be made of the determination of a lease, or agreement for a lease, or a note is to be cancelled, the lease or agreement shall be produced and marked with notice of the entry, and the land certificate of the title closed and the charge certificates (if any) thereon shall be delivered up and cancelled.

. . . . . .

Entry and discharge of restrictive covenants

212. Restrictive covenants created under Section 40, or noted against a title under Section 50 of the Act, shall be entered in the Charges Register, in the method directed by Section 50, and any release, waiver, discharge, or modification shall be noted on the register in such manner as the Registrar may direct.

Entry restraining a disposition by a sole surviving proprietor

213.—(1) An entry under subsection (3) of Section 58 of the Act shall be in Form 62, and need only be made where, by law, the survivor of the joint proprietors will not have power to give a valid receipt for capital on a disposition of the land or charge, or where the Registrar, for any special reason, considers that such an entry would be desirable.

(2) Such an entry may at any time be made with the consent of joint proprietors entitled in their own right.

(3) No entry shall be made under this rule where the prescribed restrictions, applicable to settled land, are entered on the register.

Production of the equitable title required before entry of a disposition

214. When such an entry has been made and the joint proprietors have been reduced to the number specified therein, the Registrar shall, before entering on the register any disposition by the proprietor, require the production of the equitable title; and may give such notices to the persons, or some or one of the persons, equitably entitled, as he may deem expedient.

Cautions (except Cautions against entry of Land on the Register)

Caution against dealings

215.—(1) A caution against dealings with registered land or a registered charge, lodged under Section 54 of the Act, shall be in Form 63.

(2) A caution against the registration of a possessory or good leasehold or qualified title as good leasehold or qualified or absolute shall be in Form 69.

(3) The caution shall be signed by the cautioner or his solicitor and shall contain an address for service in the United Kingdom.

(4) The declaration in support of the caution shall be in Form 14, or to the like effect, and shall contain a reference to the land or charge to which it relates, and to the registered number of the title, and shall also state the nature of the interest of the cautioner in such land or charge.

. . . . . .

Service of notice on cautioner

218.[11]—(1) On the application at any time in writing of the proprietor of the land or of a charge to which a caution relates, or when a dealing affecting such land or charge is brought in for registration without the consent of the cautioner, the notice under Section 55 of the Act shall be served on the cautioner.

(2) The period to be limited by such notice shall be fourteen days or such other period (not being less than seven days) as the Registrar may, under special circumstances, direct.

(3) The notice shall be in Form 70.

Objection by cautioner to registration of a dealing

219. At any time before the expiration of the period limited by the notice, or such extension thereof as may be granted by the Registrar, the cautioner or his personal representative may show cause why the caution should continue to have effect, or why the dealing should not be registered—as, for instance, that it has been obtained by fraud or mistake, or that it is inconsistent with a prior dealing or with some adverse right or

[11] See also the Land Registration (Matrimonial Homes) Rules 1967, r. 6 (No. 1792).

minor interest which would not be overridden if the land were not registered.

Hearing of cautioner by Registrar

220.—(1) Cause may be shown either by the cautioner appearing before the Registrar or by his delivering a statement in writing, signed by him or his solicitor, setting forth the grounds on which cause is shown.

(2) The Registrar may thereupon either order that the caution shall thenceforth cease to have effect and that the entry thereof on the register be cancelled, or he may appoint a time for the proprietor or the applicant for registration, as the case may be, and the cautioner or his personal representative and such other persons (if any) as he may deem expedient, to appear before him.

(3) After hearing all such persons, and serving such notices (if any) as he shall think necessary, the Registrar shall make such order in the matter as he shall think just, as, for instance, that the caution shall continue to have effect, or that it shall cease to have effect and that the entry thereof on the register be cancelled, or that the registration be refused either with or without an inhibition against registration at any future time, or that it be completed forthwith, or after an interval, or that it be completed conditionally or with some modification, or subject to the prior registration of a dealing in favour of the cautioner, or subject to some notice, condition, restriction, or inhibition under the Act.

(4) The Registrar may refer the matter, at any stage, or any question arising thereon, for the decision of the Court.

Cancellation of a caution on expiry of notice

221. When the notice required by a caution has been given in respect of the whole of the land or charge affected thereby and the period named in the notice has expired, the caution shall, unless the Registrar shall otherwise direct, be deemed to be exhausted, and shall be cancelled on the register.

Cancellation of a caution on an application therefor

222. A caution may at any time be cancelled upon an application for that purpose in Form 71, signed by the cautioner or his personal representative, or his solicitor, and thereupon the entry thereof on the register shall be cancelled; but any liability previously incurred under the Act of a cautioner to indemnify or make compensation shall not be affected by such withdrawal.

Caution in specially prescribed form to protect mortgages

223.—(1) A caution under subsection (2) of Section 106 of the Act to protect a mortgage by deed or devolutions or dealings therewith shall be called a mortgage caution and shall be in Forms 64, 65 or 66, as the case may require.

(2) The mortgage caution shall be accompanied by the land certificate, the mortgage or other document on which it is founded and a certified copy thereof.

(3) The Registrar shall, on being satisfied that the mortgage produced is in accordance with the terms of the caution, enter the mortgage caution in the Proprietorship Register and shall give notice to the proprietor of the land that he has done so.

The entry in the register shall be in Form 67.

(4) If the person applying for the caution is not the mortgagee named in the mortgage, he shall prove his title to the mortgage in the usual way to

the satisfaction of the Registrar, and the documents in support thereof, with certified copies for filing, must be produced.

(5) In the case of a mortgage caution to protect a devolution or dealing with a mortgage, the Registrar shall on being satisfied that the document is in accordance with the terms of the caution, make an entry thereof in the register in Form 68.

(6) In all cases the Registrar shall retain the certified copy of the mortgage or other document in the Registry, and shall mark the original with a note of the registration and shall return it to the applicant.

Withdrawal of mortgage caution

224.—(1) A mortgage caution may be withdrawn at any time in the same manner and on the same conditions as an ordinary caution.

(2) A mortgage caution may be vacated, subject to the requisite evidence being furnished to the Registrar of the discharge of the mortgage.

Dealing with land affected by a mortgage caution

225. On the lodgment for registration of any dealing with the land to which it relates, a mortgage caution shall be dealt with in the same manner as a caution under Section 54 of the Act, save that it cannot be warned off the register by service of notice on the cautioner; and the dealing, if registered, shall take effect subject to the rights, if any, protected by the mortgage caution.

Registration of mortgage as a charge

226.—(1) If and when application is made to register the mortgage as a charge, the registration of the charge and of all dealings and devolutions affecting the mortgage shall have the same priority as the mortgage cautions by which they were respectively protected on the register, or such of them as are then subsisting and capable of taking effect.

(2) If the applicant is the person appearing by the register to be entitled to the benefit of the mortgage caution, the registration shall be made forthwith, and the applicant or his nominee shall be entered as proprietor of the charge.

(3) In other cases the application must be accompanied by proof of the applicant's title and shall be proceeded with as the Registrar shall direct.

Effect of registration

227. On the registration of the mortgage as a charge, all mortgage cautions relating to it shall be cancelled.

Sub-mortgage cautions to protect sub-mortgages

228.—(1) The provisions of Section 106 of the Act and of the Rules and Forms relating thereto, shall apply to sub-mortgages, by deed, of mortgages protected under the same section with the necessary modifications.

(2) Where a mortgage protected by a mortgage caution on the register is the subject of a sub-mortgage, the sub-mortgagee may apply for the registration of a sub-mortgage caution in his favour to protect the sub-mortgage.

(3) If the person creating the sub-mortgage is not the person entered on the register as entitled to the benefit of the mortgage caution protecting the original mortgage, proof of devolution of the title from that person must be produced to the satisfaction of the Registrar, together with such certified copies of any documents as the Registrar may require for filing.

(4) A sub-mortgage caution shall be entered in the Charges Register, and notice of any dealing with or cancellation of the mortgage caution shall be served on the sub-mortgage cautioner.

(5) The sub-mortgage shall not be registered as a sub-charge unless and until the original mortgage is so registered.

Minor Interests Index

Cautions and inhibitions to secure priority between persons entitled to minor interest, on a dealing therewith

229.—(1) A priority caution, lodged under subsection (2), of Section 102 of the Act, shall be entered in the Minor Interests Index, and notice of the entry shall be given to the proprietor, and, in the case of settled land, to the trustees of the settlement.

But a person who lodges a priority caution is not entitled to notice of any intended registered disposition or entry in the register.

(2) An application for the entry of a priority caution shall be in Form 72 or such other form as the Registrar may approve.

(3) The provisions of the Act and rules with respect to the warning off of a caution, by the service of a notice, do not apply to priority cautions; but, subject to the requisite evidence being furnished, of the determination or discharge of the minor interest to which the caution relates, the Registrar may vacate a priority caution.

(4) As respects registered land and registered charges, the registration of a priority caution shall take the place of any notice or endorsed memorandum which, in the case of unregistered land, would, under Section 137 of the Law of Property Act 1925, be given or made.

(5) As respects registered land and registered charges, the provisions of Section 138 of the Law of Property Act 1925 shall apply as if the Registrar were the trust corporation nominated for the purposes of that section, and the Minor Interests Index were the register therein referred to.

(6) The foregoing provisions of this rule apply to priority inhibitions in like manner as they apply to priority cautions, save that, where the applicant claims to have acquired an absolute interest, free from any right of redemption, the entry shall be referred to as a priority inhibition.

Inhibitions

Application for an inhibition

230.—(1) An application for an inhibition under Section 57 of the Act shall either be accompanied by the consent in writing of the proprietor of the land, or shall be supported by the statutory declaration of the applicant and such other evidence (if any) as the Registrar may deem necessary.

(2) Pending the result of any hearing before the Registrar as prescribed by these rules, the Registrar may, if for any reason he thinks it desirable, enter an inhibition preventing any dealing with the land or any charge thereon.

Cancellation of inhibition entered under order of Court

231.—(1) Except as to inhibitions originally entered pursuant to an order of the Court, any application to discharge or cancel the same shall be made to the Registrar.

(2) The applications may be made by any person aggrieved by the inhibition.

Restrictions

. . . . . .

Application for a restriction by persons other than the proprietor

236.—(1) An application for a restriction by persons other than the proprietor shall be in Form 75 modified as required to meet the circumstances of the case.

(2) It shall set out the grounds on which the application is made, and shall be accompanied by such evidence as the Registrar may direct.

Orders under inhibitions and restrictions

Order of Registrar in anticipation of a dealing

237.—(1) Application may be made to the Registrar for an order under an inhibition or restriction, or a certificate under Section 89 of the Act, in anticipation of an intended dealing, and the Registrar may, on any such application, make an order or grant a certificate that the dealing be registered either unconditionally or subject to such limitations or conditions as he may think fit.

(2) The order need not be entered on the register, but shall be filed, and, so long as it is in force, shall be shown to any person searching the register.

. . . . . .

Notice of Deposit of Certificate

Notice of deposit of certificate

239.—(1) Any person with whom a land certificate or charge certificate is deposited as security for money may, by registered letter or otherwise, in writing give notice to the Registrar of such deposit, and of his name and address.

(2) The notice shall describe (by reference to the district and parish or place and number of the title) the land to which the certificate relates.

(3) On receipt of such notice the Registrar shall enter notice of the deposit in the Charges Register, and shall give a written acknowledgment of its receipt.

(4) Such notice shall operate as a caution under Section 54 of the Act.

(5) The provisions of Section 66 of the Act, and of these rules, as respects the deposit of a charge certificate, shall apply to the deposit of a certificate of sub-charge or of an incumbrance in like manner.

Notice of intended deposit of certificate

240. A person applying for registration as proprietor of land or of a charge may, whether the land or charge is already registered or not, create a lien on the land or charge equivalent to that created by a deposit of a certificate by giving notice in writing, signed by himself, to the Registrar, that he intends to deposit the land certificate or charge certificate, when issued, with another person as security for money.

Particulars to be given on notice of intended deposit

241.—(1) The notice of such intended deposit shall state the name and address of the person with whom the certificate is to be deposited, and shall describe the land or charge to which the certificate relates by reference to the district or parish or place and number of the title or (in the case of unregistered land) by reference to the deed or document by which the land was last dealt with, or otherwise to the satisfaction of the Registrar.

(2) The Registrar shall enter notice of the intended deposit in the register and give a written acknowledgment of its receipt.

Effect of notice of intended deposit

242.—(1) A notice of intended deposit shall operate as a caution under Section 54 of the Act.

(2) The certificate shall, when issued or re-issued, be delivered by the Registrar to the person named in that behalf in the notice.

When notice of deposit may not be entered

243. Notice of deposit or intended deposit of a certificate shall not be entered while another such notice is on the register, nor as to part only of the land or charge to which the certificate relates.

Certificate left while notice of deposit on register

244. If, while a notice of deposit or intended deposit is on the register, the certificate is left in the Registry for any purpose, it shall be dealt with, notwithstanding the notice, and shall be returned to the person leaving it or as he may in writing direct.

When new certificate may not be issued

245. So long as a notice of such deposit is on the register no new certificate shall be issued—

    (*a*) under Section 67 of the Act,

    (*b*) under Section 64 on a sale under a charge subsequent in priority to the notice of deposit, without notice similar to that given under a caution,

    (*c*) in the other cases mentioned in paragraphs (*a*) to (*c*) of subsection (4) of Section 64, without a notice similar to that given under a caution.

Withdrawal of notice of deposit

246. The notice of deposit or notice of intended deposit may be withdrawn from the register on a written request or consent signed by the person entitled to the lien created by the deposit, or notice of intended deposit, or his successor in title; accompanied in either case by the land certificate, or charge certificate.

Entry of Value of Land on the Register

Value entered on register

247.—(1) On the first registration of land, and on subsequent changes of proprietorship, the Registrar shall, [if the proprietor so requests],[12] enter in the register and on the land certificate the price paid or value declared.

(2) [*Revoked by the Land Registration Rules 1976 (No. 1332), Sched.*]

. . . . . .

---

[12] The words in square brackets were substituted by the Land Registration Rules 197.' 1332), r. 2 (2).

PART V

MISCELLANEOUS

Acquisition of Rights by Prescription

Acquisition of adverse easements by prescription

250.—(1) Pursuant to subsection (5) of Section 75 of the Act, it is hereby provided that easements, rights, and privileges adversely affecting registered land may be acquired in equity by prescription in the same manner and to the same extent as if the land were not registered.

(2) If any easement, right, or privilege so acquired is of such estate and nature as is capable of taking effect at law it shall take effect at law also, and in that case—

(*a*) if it is an overriding interest, notice of it may be entered on the register if the Registrar thinks fit under subsection (3) of Section 70 of the Act.

(*b*) if it has been acquired for the benefit of registered land, it may, if the Registrar thinks fit, be registered as part of the description of the land.

Appurtenances and Easements

Registration vests appurtenances

251. The registration of a person as proprietor of land shall vest in him, together with the land, all rights, privileges, and appurtenances appertaining or reputed to appertain to the land or any part thereof, or, at the time of registration, demised, occupied, or enjoyed therewith, or reputed or known as part or parcel of or appurtenant to the land or any part thereof, including the appropriate rights and interests which, had there been a conveyance of the land or manor, would under Section 62 of the Law of Property Act 1925 have passed therewith.

Application for entry of appurtenant right on register

252.—(1) Where the proprietor wishes (whether on first registration or at any other time) to have a specific entry on the register of any appurtenant right, capable of subsisting as a legal estate, to which he may be entitled, he may apply to the Registrar in writing, signed by himself or his solicitor, for such an entry to be made.

(2) The application shall state the nature of the right and shall furnish evidence of its existence.

Notice to be served regarding adverse rights

253.—(1) The Registrar shall thereupon give such notice (if any) to the person in possession of the land affected as he may deem advisable.

(2) If the land affected is registered he shall give notice to the proprietor and to every person appearing by the register to be interested, and shall, if he thinks fit, enter notice of it against such land.

Entry of appurtenant right and its effect

254.—(1) If the Registrar is satisfied that the right is capable of subsisting as a legal estate and appurtenant to the land, he may enter it as part of the description of the land in the Property Register, and the effect of such entry shall be to confer an absolute, good leasehold, qualified or possessory title to the right, according to the nature of the title to the land.

(2) If the Registrar is not satisfied that the right is appurtenant, he shall enter it with such qualification as he may deem advisable, or he may merely enter notice of the fact that the proprietor claims it.

Entries by reference

255. The entry shall be made as far as practicable by reference to the instrument (if any) creating the right, or by setting out an extract therefrom.

Transfer of benefit

256. On any registered disposition of the land or of a charge thereon, the benefit of the entry shall, on registration, but without prejudice to any express exception or reservation, accrue to the grantee as part of the registered estate.

Positive registration

257. The benefit of an easement, right, or privilege shall not be entered on the register except as appurtenant to a registered estate, and then only if capable of subsisting as a legal estate.

Adverse easements treated as overriding interests

258. Rights, privileges, and appurtenances appertaining or reputed to appertain to land or demised, occupied, or enjoyed therewith or reputed or known as part or parcel of or appurtenant thereto, which adversely affect registered land, are overriding interests within Section 70 of the Act, and shall not be deemed incumbrances for the purposes of the Act.

. . . . . .

Certificates

. . . . . .

Form of charge certificate

262.—(1) A charge certificate shall certify the registration of the charge and shall contain—
    (*a*) an office copy of the charge,
    (*b*) a description (if no description is contained in the charge) of the land affected,
    (*c*) the name and address of the proprietor of the charge,
    (*d*) a list of the prior incumbrances (if any) appearing on the register.
    (2) There shall also be added such further particulars, if any, as the Registrar shall think fit, and the Land Registry seal shall be affixed to it.
    (3) Notes of subsequent dealings affecting the charge shall from time to time be entered on the certificate, or a new certificate shall be issued in place thereof, as may be more convenient.

. . . . . .

When production of land certificate may be required or new one issued

266. On any application for registration made by or with the consent of the proprietor of the land or of a charge or incumbrance, the Registrar may require the production of the land certificate or charge certificate or incumbrance, and may refuse to proceed with the application until the certificate is produced:
    Provided that a new certificate may be issued, without the production of

the original certificate, in any of the cases mentioned in subsection (4) of Section 64 of the Act, but subject to such notices or inquiries (if any) being given or made as the Registrar may, in any case, deem necessary.

Cancellation of certificate

267. When a certificate is produced on the closing of a title, the clearing of the register, or the discharge of a charge or incumbrance, the land or charge certificate (as the case may be) shall be retained in the Registry and cancelled.

Purposes for which certificates may be retained

268.—(1) The Registrar shall have power to retain a certificate produced under Section 64 of the Act for the purpose of making an entry thereon.

(2) On the registration of any transaction for which the production of a land certificate or charge certificate is required, the certificate shall, before it is re-issued, be made to correspond with the register.

Certificate deposited for specified purpose only

269.—(1) A certificate may be deposited in the Registry with written directions that it is to be held for a specified purpose only.

(2) Save for the purposes of the last preceding rule, a certificate so deposited shall not be used, or be deemed to be in the Registry for any other purpose, without the written consent of the person by whom such directions were given, or his successor in title or his solicitor.

Receipt for land certificate produced instead of land certificate

270. [*Revoked by the Land Registration Rules* 1930, *r.* 5. *A new provision was substituted for sub-paragraphs* (1) *and* (2) (*see Land Registration Rules* 1930, *r.* 5(2)) *which has now also been revoked* (*see Land Registration (Official Searches) Rules* 1969, *r.* 13, *3rd Sched.*).]

(3) When deposited pursuant to Section 65 of the Act, the land certificate need not be made to correspond with the register from time to time and a new certificate may be issued in place thereof on the cancellation of the charge or mortgage.

Lost certificates

271.—(1) Where it is proved to the satisfaction of the Registrar that a certificate has been lost or destroyed, or that it is in the possession of a person out of the jurisdiction of the Court or its production cannot be obtained without undue delay or expense, he may issue a new one, after taking such indemnities as he may consider necessary, and after giving such public notice in the Gazette and in such local or other newspapers (if any) and in such manner as shall appear to him sufficient in each case.

(2) The notice shall give the name and address of the proprietor and the registered description of the land, and shall state that it is proposed to issue a new certificate and shall request any person in whose possession the certificate may be, or who has any objection in such issue, to inform the Registrar of the fact.

Maps and Verbal Descriptions of Land

Ordnance Map

272. The Ordnance Map shall be the basis of all registered descriptions of land.

. . . . . .

Parcels Index

274.—(1) A Parcels Index shall be kept in the Registry containing any reference numbers on the parcels of registered land shown on the General Map, and showing, with regard to each of such parcels, the numbers of the titles, and, as respects land which has not been registered, of the cautions and priority notices against first registration (if any) relating to it.

. . . . . .

Fixed boundaries

276. If it is desired to indicate on the filed plan or General Map, or otherwise to define in the register, the precise position of the boundaries of the land or any parts thereof, notice shall be given to the owners and occupiers of the adjoining lands, in each instance, of the intention to ascertain and fix the boundary, with such plan, or tracing, or extract from the proposed verbal description of the land as may be necessary, to show clearly the fixed boundary proposed to be registered; and any question of doubt or dispute arising therefrom shall be dealt with as provided by these rules.

Note as to fixed boundaries in register

277. When the position and description of the boundaries of the land have been thus ascertained and determined, the necessary particulars shall be added to the filed plan or General Map, and a note shall be made in the Property Register to the effect that the boundaries have been fixed. The plan or General Map shall then be deemed to define accurately the fixed boundaries.

General boundaries

278.—(1) Except in cases in which it is noted in the Property Register that the boundaries have been fixed, the filed plan or General Map shall be deemed to indicate the general boundaries only.

(2) In such cases the exact line of the boundary will be left undetermined—as, for instance, whether it includes a hedge or wall and ditch, or runs along the centre of a wall or fence, or its inner or outer face, or how far it runs within or beyond it; or whether or not the land registered includes the whole or any portion of an adjoining road or stream.

(3) When a general boundary only is desired to be entered in the register, notice to the owners of the adjoining lands need not be given.

(4) This rule shall apply notwithstanding that a part or the whole of a ditch, wall, fence, road, stream, or other boundary is expressly included in or excluded from the title or that it forms the whole of the land comprised in the title.

Where physical boundaries do not exist

279. Where, and so far as, physical boundaries or boundary marks do not exist, the fullest available particulars of the boundaries shall be added to the filed plan or General Map.

. . . . . .

Official Search of the Index Map, etc.

Official certificate of search of Index Map

286.—(1) Any person may apply to the Registrar in writing to make an official search in the Index Map and Parcels Index and to issue a certificate of the result.

(2) The application shall describe the land to which it relates by means of a copy of or extract from the Ordnance Map on the largest scale published.

(3) The Registrar shall on receipt of such application make the search and issue a certificate accordingly.

(4) The certificate shall state whether the land is registered or not, and, if registered, whether as freehold or leasehold land, or otherwise as the case may be, and in the case of leasehold land shall also state the date of and parties to the lease.

(5) If the land is not registered the certificate shall show any cautions against first registration and priority notices affecting the land.

Inspection, Searches, and Copies of the Register

Authority to inspect the register

287. Subject to the provisions of Sections 59, 61 and 112 of the Act, any entry in the register, and any document in the custody of the Registrar and referred to in the register, may be inspected by or under the authority of the proprietor of the land or of any charge or incumbrance thereon.[13]

Inspection of Property Register only and of other entries after notice to proprietor

288.—(1) The Property Register and the filed plan of any title may be inspected by any person interested in the land or in any adjoining land or in a charge or incumbrance thereon.

(2) Other entries in the register and documents referred to therein, and the statutory declaration in support of a caution, may be inspected by any person interested, on giving three days' notice to the proprietor or on satisfying the Registrar that, by reason of the death of a sole proprietor, or for any other sufficient reason, he cannot obtain the requisite authority for or consent to such inspection, and that such inspection is reasonable and proper.

Information as to the entries in the register at a specified date; also regarding closed registers and cancelled entries

289.—(1) The proprietor of the land, or of a charge or incumbrance, may by an instrument in Form 80, or to the like effect, authorise an application to be made to the Registrar for information as to the entries in the register at or prior to the date of such authority.

(2) A copy of the authority may be filed in the Registry.

(3) The Registrar shall at any time furnish, to any person producing the authority, such information as to the state of the register at the date mentioned in the authority as may be reasonably required.

(4) This rule shall apply to the inspection of a register which has been closed, and may be extended to any person who may satisfy the Registrar that he is interested in the land or charge or incumbrance in question, and that the application is reasonable.

. . . . . .

Official search exonerates from responsibility for error

295.[14]—(1) When a solicitor or other person obtains an official certificate of the result of a search he shall not be answerable in respect of loss that may arise from any error therein.

---

[13] See also the Land Registration Rules 1967, r. 3 (3), *post*, p. 456.
[14] But see Land Registration (Official Searches) Rules 1981, rr. 8 (4) and 10 (3), *post*, p. 462.

(2) When the certificate is obtained by a solicitor acting for trustees, personal representatives, or other persons in a fiduciary position, those persons also shall not be so answerable.

. . . . . .

Hearings before the Registrar

Hearing before the Registrar

298.—(1) If any question, doubt, dispute, difficulty or complaint arises before the Registrar upon any application or during any investigation of title—

    (*a*) as to the registration of a title, incumbrance, or charge,

    (*b*) as to any dealing with any registered title, incumbrance, or charge, or any matter entered or noted in or omitted from the register, or

    (*c*) as to the amendment or withdrawal from the register or production to the Registrar of any certificate or other document, or

    (*d*) in any registration or other proceeding in the Registry, or

    (*e*) as to any claim for indemnity,[15]

(whether such questions relate to the construction, validity, or effect of any instrument, or the persons interested, or the nature or extent of their respective interests or powers, or as to order of priority, or the mode in which any entry should be made or dealt with in the register or otherwise), the Registrar shall hear and determine the matter and, subject to appeal to the Court, make such order in the matter as he shall think just.

(2) But the Registrar may, if he thinks fit, instead of deciding the question himself, refer the matter at any stage, or any question thereon, for the decision of the Court.

Appeal to the Court

299. Any person aggrieved by an order or decision of the Registrar may appeal to the Court.

Notice as to hearing to be served

300. Notice that the Registrar will hear and determine the matter at the Registry shall be served by him on all persons appearing to be interested, stating the time of such hearing and that such persons may attend before him at that time in person, or by his solicitor or counsel.

Notice of appeal to be entered in the register

301. No appeal from a decision or order of the Registrar, or (unless otherwise ordered) of the Court, shall affect any dealing for valuable consideration which has been duly registered before a notice in writing of the intention to appeal has been delivered at the Registry on the part of the appellant. Such notice shall be entered in the register.

Preparation and Service of Notices and Summonses

. . . . . .

Notices to be deemed to be received within seven days

313.—(1) Every notice sent through the post shall, unless returned by the Post Office, and in the absence of evidence of its actual delivery, be deemed to have been received by the person addressed within seven days

---

[15] But see now the Land Registration and Land Charges Act 1971 (c. 54), s. 2 (4).

of its issue, exclusive of the day of posting, and the time fixed by the notice for taking any step thereunder is to be calculated accordingly.

(2) A copy of this rule shall be set out at the foot of or endorsed on each such notice.

. . . . . .

Discretionary Power of Registrar

Power to relax regulations, etc.

322.—(1) The Registrar, if he so thinks fit, may, in any particular case, extend the time limited, or relax the regulations made by general rules, for any purpose; and may at any time adjourn any proceeding, and make any new appointment.

(2) If at any time he is of opinion that the production of any further documents, or evidence, or the giving of any further notices is necessary or desirable, he may refuse to complete or proceed with a registration, or to do any act, or make any entry until such further documents, or evidence, or notices have been supplied or given.

Holidays

Holidays

323. The Registry shall be open to the public daily, except on Sundays, Good Friday, Easter Eve, Monday and Tuesday in Easter week, Monday in Whitsun week, Christmas Day, and the next following working day, and all days duly appointed by proclamation to be observed as days of general fast, humiliation, or thanksgiving, and any other days appointed by the Lord Chancellor in that behalf.

. . . . . .

THE SCHEDULE

. . . . . .

FORM 9.—*Restriction where Tenant for Life is registered as proprietor.* (*Rule* 58)

No disposition under which capital money arises is to be registered unless the money is paid to A.B., of &c., and C.D., of &c. (the trustees of the settlement, of which there must be two and not more than four individuals, or a trust corporation), or into Court.

Except under an order of the Registrar, no disposition is to be registered unless authorised by the Settled Land Act 1925.

Note.—In cases where the Settlement so provides a further provision may be added to the Restriction that no transfer of the mansion house (shown on an attached plan or otherwise adequately described to enable it to be fully identified on the General Map, Ordnance Map, or Filed Plan) is to be registered without the consent of the said A.B. and C.D., or an Order of the Court.

FORM 10.—*Restriction where Statutory owners or trustees holding on trust for sale are entered as proprietors.*[16] (*Rule* 58)

Except under an Order of the Registrar, no disposition is to be registered unless authorised by the Settled Land Act 1925, and except where the sole proprietor is a trust corporation, no disposition under which capital money arises is to be registered unless the money is paid to at least two proprietors.

Note.—This restriction does not apply where the statutory owners are not the trustees of the settlement.

. . . . . .

[16] Despite the heading, this restriction does not relate to a trust for sale.

FORM 14.—*Statutory Declaration in support of a Caution*
(*Rules* 66 *and* 215)

(Heading as in Form 1)

I, A.B., of &c., solemnly and sincerely declare that I am interested in the land (*or* charge), referred to in the caution now produced and shown to me marked A [*here state the nature of the declarant's interest* "as beneficial owner in fee simple," "beneficially entitled to the lease referred to therein," "tenant for life within the meaning of the Settled Land Act, 1925," "purchaser under a contract for sale, dated, &c.," "plaintiff in an action in the Chancery Division of the High Court of Justice, B. *v.* C., 1897, B. 145," "equitable mortgagee under a memorandum of charge dated   under the hand of   ," *or as the case may be*].
And I make, &c.

(To be declared by the cautioner, or, with the necessary alterations, by his solicitor.)

. . . . . .

FORM 19.—*Transfer of Freehold Land* (*Whole*). (*Rule* 98)

H.M. LAND REGISTRY

LAND REGISTRATION ACT, 1925

District..
Title No...
Property ....
(*Date.*) In consideration of   pounds (£   ) I, A.B., of &c., hereby transfer to C.D., of &c., the land comprised in the title above referred to.

Signed, sealed and delivered ⎫
   by the said A.B., in the ⎬   (*Signature of A.B.*)   (Seal.)
   presence of E.F., of &c. ⎭

. . . . . .

FORM 59.—*Application to enter Notice of Right under Section* 49 *of the Act.* (*Rule* 190)

(Heading as in Form 19)

I, A.B., of &c., being entitled to (*give particulars of the Estate or Right*) in the land comprised in the title above referred to, by reason of [*state concisely the facts or documents on which the claim depends*], hereby apply for registration of notice thereof.
(To be signed by the applicant or his (*or* her) solicitor)
Note.—The application should be accompanied by evidence of the facts on which the claim depends.

. . . . . .

FORM 63.—*Caution* (*under Section* 54 *of the Act*) *against Dealings with Registered Land or a Charge.* (*Rule* 215)

(Heading as in Form 58)

(*Date.*) A.B. [*the cautioner*], of &c., requires that no dealing with the land (*or* charge) above referred to (*or* with the land shown and edged with red on the plan hereto) shall be registered until notice has been served upon him or his personal representative.
(To be signed by the cautioner or his solicitor)
(*Note*).—If the cautioner's address is not within the United Kingdom, an address for service within that area must also be given.

. . . . . .

FORM 75.—*Application to register a Restriction under Section* 58 *of the Act.* (*Rule* 235)

(Heading as in Form 19)

(*Date.*) A.B. (*the proprietor*), of &c., hereby applies to the Registrar to enter the following restriction against the title (*or* charge) above referred to.
Restriction.—Except under an order of the Registrar, no disposition shall be registered without the consent of C.D., of &c. (or otherwise—*see* examples in Forms 9 to 11 or 12).

Land Registration Act 1966

(1966 c. 39)

An Act to alter the provisions of Part XI of the Land Registration Act 1925 relating to the making of orders creating areas of compulsory registration, to restrict the rights under that Act to register unregistered land in other areas, to amend its provisions relating to losses indemnifiable under that Act and to repeal section 11 of the Small Holdings and Allotments Act 1926.　　　　[13th December 1966]

Amendments of Land Registration Act 1925

1.—(2) Applications under sections 4 and 8 of the said Act (first registration of title) as respects land outside an area of compulsory registration shall not be entertained except in such classes of cases as the registrar may, by notice published in such way as appears to him appropriate, from time to time specify and in those cases the registrar may require the applicant under either of those sections to show that there are special considerations which make it expedient to grant the application.

In this subsection "area of compulsory registration" means an area as respects which an Order in Council made or having effect under the said section 120 is in force.

．　．　．　．　．　．

The Land Registration Rules 1967
(amended)

(S.I. 1967 No. 761 (L. 5))

Dated May 15, 1967

I, Gerald, Baron Gardiner, Lord High Chancellor of Great Britain, with the advice and assistance of the Rule Committee appointed in pursuance of section 144 of the Land Registration Act 1925, do, in exercise of the powers vested in me by that section and by sections 112 and 138 of that Act, hereby make the following Rules:—

．　．　．　．　．　．

3.—(1) In this Rule, unless the context otherwise requires—

"court" means the High Court [*the Court of Chancery of the County Palatine of Lancaster, and the Court of Chancery of the County Palatine of Durham*[1]] or a county court;

"judgment creditor" in relation to a court means a person who has obtained a judgment or order of that court for the payment of money and "judgment debtor" means any person against whom the judgment or order has been obtained.

(2) On the application of a judgment creditor, supported by *prima facie* evidence that the judgment debtor is the proprietor (either solely or jointly with some other person or persons) of land or a charge the title to which is

---

[1] Spent.

registered under the Land Registration Acts 1925 to 1966, the court may order that the register of that title be produced to the judgment creditor without the authority of the judgment debtor.

(3) Any order made by virtue of this Rule shall have the same effect as an authority given by the judgment debtor pursuant to Rule 287 of the Land Registration Rules 1925, as amended,[2] to inspect the register of the title to which the order relates.

(4) For the purposes of this Rule a judgment, order, decree or award (however called) of any court or arbitrator (including any foreign court or foreign arbitrator) which is or has become enforceable (whether wholly or to a limited extent) as if it were a judgment or order of the High Court or a county court shall be deemed to be a judgment or order of the High Court or the county court, as the case may be.

[2] There are no relevant amendments.

Land Registration and Land Charges Act 1971

(1971 c. 54)

An Act to amend the Land Registration Acts 1925 to 1966; . . . and for connected purposes. [27th July 1971]

PART I

AMENDMENT OF LAND REGISTRATION ACTS 1925 TO 1966

Payment of indemnity

1.—(1) Any indemnity payable after the commencement of this section under any provision of the Land Registration Act 1925, including so much of any indemnity which has become so payable at any time before then as has not then been paid, shall, instead of being paid out of the insurance fund, be paid by the registrar out of moneys provided by Parliament; and no other person shall thereafter be under any liability to pay any such indemnity.

(2) Any money which at the commencement of this section stands to the credit of the insurance fund shall be paid into the Consolidated Fund, and any other assets then comprised in the insurance fund shall be realised forthwith, and the proceeds thereof shall be paid into the Consolidated Fund; and as soon as its assets have been so dealt with, the insurance fund shall cease to exist.

(3) In this section "the insurance fund" means the insurance fund established under the Land Transfer Act 1897.

Determination of questions as to right to or amount of indemnity

2.—(1) If any question arises as to whether a person is entitled to an indemnity under any provision of the Land Registration Act 1925 or as to the amount of any such indemnity, he may apply to the court to have that question determined.

(2) Section 83 (5)(c) of the Land Registration Act 1925 (by virtue of which no indemnity is payable under that Act on account of costs incurred in taking or defending any legal proceedings without the consent of the registrar) shall not apply to the costs of an application to the court under subsection (1) above or of any legal proceedings arising out of such an

application; and as regards any such application or proceedings section 131 of that Act (which provides that the registrar, among others, shall not be liable to any action or proceeding for or in respect of anything done or omitted as there mentioned) shall not apply to the registrar.

(3) On an application under subsection (1) above the court shall not order the applicant, even if unsuccessful, to pay any costs except his own unless it considers that the application was unreasonable.

(4) [*Repeals Land Registration Act* 1925 (15 & 16 *Geo.* 5, *c.* 21), *s.* 83 (7), *supra, and amends ibid. s.* 83 (8), *supra, p.* 388.]

(5) Nothing in this section shall be taken to preclude the registrar from settling by agreement claims for indemnity under the Land Registration Act 1925.

(6) Where any such question as is mentioned in subsection (1) above has arisen (whether before or after the passing of this Act) before the time of the commencement of this section and has not before that time been referred to the court in pursuance of rules under the Land Registration Act 1925, that subsection shall apply to it notwithstanding that it arose before that time; but where any such question has been so referred before that time, it shall be determined as if this section and, so far as it relates to the repeal of section 83 (7) of the Land Registration Act 1925 and section 1 (3) of the Land Registration Act 1966, section 14 (2)(*b*) of this Act had not come into force.

Right to indemnity not to be excluded by reason of act etc. not amounting to fraud or lack of proper care

3.—(1) [*Amends the Land Registration Act* 1925 (15 & 16 *Geo.* 5, *c.* 21), *s.* 83 (5), *supra, p.* 388, *and repeals the Land Registration Act* 1966 (*c.* 39), *s.* 1 (4).]

(2) Subsection (1) above shall have effect in relation to any claim for indemnity made before the time of the commencement of this section and not settled by agreement or finally determined before that time, as well as to all such claims made after that time.

Souvenir land

4.[1]—(1) The Lord Chancellor may by rules made with the advice and assistance of the Rule Committee make provision—

(*a*) for enabling the registrar, in such circumstances and subject to such conditions as may be specified in the rules, to declare any area of land to be subject to a souvenir land scheme if the registrar is satisfied that the land comprised in that area consists wholly or mainly of land which has been or is proposed to be disposed of (by way of sale or otherwise) in souvenir plots or of which part has been, and the remainder is proposed to be, so disposed of;

(*b*) with respect to the cancellation of declarations and the extension or reduction of the area to which any declaration relates;

(*c*) for authorising or requiring the registrar not to accept applications under the Land Registration Act 1925 relating to souvenir land or cautions or other documents relating to such land;

(*d*) for excepting souvenir land from the operation of section 123 of that Act (effect of that Act in areas where registration is compulsory);

(*e*) for securing that transactions relating to souvenir land which is registered land take effect as if the souvenir land in question were not registered land; and

---

[1] See the Land Registration (Souvenir Land) Rules 1972 (No. 985).

(*f*) generally for modifying or excluding in relation to souvenir land the operation of any provision contained in the Land Registration Acts 1925 to 1966 or any general rules thereunder.

(2) Rules under this section may include such supplemental, consequential or incidental provision as may appear to the Lord Chancellor to be necessary or expedient for the purposes of the rules, and may make different provision for souvenir land in general and souvenir land so far as it consists or does not consist of souvenir plots, and for other different circumstances.

(3) The power to make rules under this section shall be exercisable by statutory instrument, and a statutory instrument containing any such rules shall be laid before Parliament after being made.

(4) Section 131 of the Land Registration Act 1925 (indemnity to officers of registry) shall apply in relation to rules made under this section as it applies in relation to general rules made in pursuance of that Act.

(5) For the purposes of this section—

"declaration" means a declaration by the registrar, made in pursuance of rules under this section made by virtue of subsection (1)(*a*) above, that an area of land is subject to a souvenir land scheme;

"souvenir land" means land situated within an area in respect of which a declaration is for the time being in force;

"souvenir plot" means any piece of land which, being of inconsiderable size and little or no practical utility, is unlikely to be wanted in isolation except for the sake of pure ownership or for sentimental reasons or commemorative purposes.

· · · · · ·

PART III

MISCELLANEOUS AND GENERAL

Meaning of "Her Majesty's Land Registry"

12. Section 126 (1) of the Land Registration Act 1925 (which provides that there shall continue to be an office in London to be called Her Majesty's Land Registry) shall not be construed as requiring the whole of the business of Her Majesty's Land Registry to be conducted in London; [. . .]²

Expenses

13. There shall be paid out of moneys provided by Parliament any increase in the expenses of the Chief Land Registrar which is attributable to any provision of this Act.

Repeals

14. [*Repeals, inter alia, the Land Registration Act* 1925 (15 & 16 *Geo.* 5, *c.* 21), *s.* 75 (4) *and, subject to s.* 2 (6), *ibid. ss.* 83 (7) *and* 85, *supra; the Land Registration Act* 1936 (26 *Geo.* 5 & 1 *Edw.* 8, *c.* 26), *ss.* 2 *to* 6 *and* 8; *the Land Registration Act* 1966 (*c.* 39), *s.* 1 (3) *and* (4).]

· · · · · ·

² The words omitted were repealed by the Land Charges Act 1972 (c. 61), Sched. 5.

(S.I. 1981 No. 1135)

Dated 1st October 1981

The Lord Chancellor, with the advice and assistance of the Rule Committee appointed in pursuance of section 144 of the Land Registration Act 1925, in exercise of the powers conferred on him by that section, hereby makes the following rules:—

Citation, commencement and interpretation

1. These rules may be cited as the Land Registration (Official Searches) Rules 1981 and shall come into operation on 1st October 1981.

2.—(1) In these rules, unless the context otherwise requires:—

"the Act" means the Land Registration Act 1925;

"the principal rules" means the Land Registration Rules 1925;

"purchaser" means any person (including a lessee or chargee) who in good faith and for valuable consideration acquires or intends to acquire a legal estate in land and "purchase" has a corresponding meaning;

"official search" means a search of the register made by officers of the Land Registry pursuant to an application on one of the forms prescribed by these rules and "official certificate of search" means a certificate given in the prescribed form of the result of an official search;

"priority period" means the period beginning at the time when an application for an official search is deemed by virtue of paragraph (3) below to have been delivered and ending immediately after 11.00 hours on the thirtieth day thereafter;

"day list" means the record kept pursuant to rule 7A of the principal rules;

"proper office" means the district land registry designated as the proper office by the Land Registration (District Registries) Order 1980;

"day" means a day when the Land Registry is open to the public.

(2) A form referred to by number means the form so numbered in Schedule 1 to these rules.

(3) An application for an official search made by a purchaser in accordance with rule 3 of these rules which is delivered after 11.00 hours on one day and before or at 11.00 hours on the next day shall be deemed to have been delivered immediately before 11.00 hours on the second day.

Official search by purchaser

3.—(1) A purchaser may apply on form 94A or form 94B for an official search of a register which he has authority to inspect.

(2) The application shall be delivered in duplicate at the proper office and, if in order, shall be entered on the day list and an official certificate of search shall be issued in form 94D or form 94E giving the result of the search as at the time and date it is deemed to have been delivered.

4. During the priority period a duplicate of the application for official search and of the official certificate of search shall be open to inspection by any person entitled to inspect the register of the title concerned.

5. Where a purchaser has applied in accordance with these rules for an official search, any entry which is made in the register during the priority period relating to that search shall be postponed to a subsequent application to register the instrument effecting the purchase and, if the purchase is dependent on a prior dealing, to a subsequent application to register the instrument effecting that dealing provided each such subsequent application:

    (i) is deemed to have been delivered at the proper office within the priority period;

    (ii) affects the same land or charge as the postponed entry; and

    (iii) is in due course completed by registration.

6.—(1) Where two or more official certificates of search relating to the same land or the same charge have been issued and are in operation pursuant to these rules, such certificates shall, as far as relates to the priority thereby conferred, take effect, unless the applicants otherwise agree, in the order in which the applications for official search were deemed to have been delivered.

(2) Where two or more applications for official search relating to the same land or the same charge are deemed to have been delivered at the same time, the official certificates of search shall, as far as relates to the priority thereby conferred, take effect in such order as may be agreed by the applicants or failing agreement, as may be determined under rule 298 of the principal rules.

(3) Where one transaction is dependent upon another the registrar may for the purpose of this rule assume (unless or until the contrary appears) that applicants for search have agreed that their applications shall have priority as between each other so as to give effect to the sequence of the instruments effecting their transactions.

(4) Where an official search has been made in respect of a particular title and, by virtue of rule 85 of the principal rules, an application relating to that title is deemed to have been delivered at the same time as the expiry of the priority period relating to that search, the time of delivery of the application shall be deemed to be within that priority period.

Search by telephone or teleprinter

7.—(1) A person having authority to inspect the entries in the register may apply by his solicitor to the proper office by telephone or by teleprinter for a search to ascertain whether any adverse entry has been made in the register since a given date being either the date of the issue of an office copy of the subsisting entries thereon or the date on which the land or charge certificate was last made to correspond with the register.

(2) Where an application is made by telephone:

    (i) an undertaking shall be given that an application for an official search on form 94A, form 94B or form 94C will be sent forthwith to the proper office accompanied by the appropriate Land Registry fee for the search made under this rule or by a request for payment thereof through a credit account.

    (ii) the following particulars shall be supplied:

        (*a*) the title number and a short description of the property;

        (*b*) the full name of the proprietor who has authorised the inspection of the register;

        (*c*) the name, address and telephone number of the solicitor making the application together with the name of the person for whom he is acting; and

        (*d*) the date from which the search is to be made.

(3) An application by teleprinter shall be made in the form set out in Schedule 2.

8.—(1) Upon receipt of an application by telephone or by teleprinter, the search shall be made as soon as practicable and without regard to any pending applications not yet entered on the day list.

(2) When the result of a search is given by telephone it shall include:
  (i) the number of the title;
  (ii) a statement as to whether the search has extended to the whole or been limited to a part of the land comprised in the title;
  (iii) a short description of the property; and
  (iv) the date from which the search has been made.

(3) The result of a search sent by teleprinter shall be in the form set out in Schedule 2.

(4) A search made pursuant to this rule shall not be regarded as an official search for the purpose of section 83(3) of the Act or of rule 295 of the principal rules and shall not in itself confer upon the applicant priority for the registration of any dealing.

(5) The registrar may, in his discretion, suspend or limit the facilities provided by this rule for searches to be made by telephone or teleprinter.

Official search without priority

9.—(1) A person (not being a purchaser requiring an official search under rule 3 of these rules) who has authority to inspect a register may apply on form 94C for an official search of that register.

(2) Form 94C shall be delivered in duplicate to the proper office and on completion of the search an official certificate of search shall be issued in form 94D or form 94E but this certificate shall not confer upon the applicant priority for the registration of any dealing.

Certificate of official inspection of filed plan

10.—(1) A person may apply on form 101 for a certificate of official inspection of a filed plan which he has authority to inspect.

(2) Form 101 shall be delivered in duplicate to the proper office and on completion of the inspection an official certificate of inspection shall be issued in form 102 but this shall not confer upon the applicant priority for the registration of any dealing.

(3) An official inspection of the filed plan made pursuant to an application under this rule shall be regarded as an official search for the purpose of section 83(3) of the Act and rule 295 of the principal rules.

Revocation

11. The Land Registration (Official Searches) Rules 1978 are hererby revoked.

INDEX